Solaris™

Operating Environment Boot Camp

David Rhodes
Dominic Butler

Sun Microsystems Press • *A Prentice Hall Title*

Printed in the United States of America

10 9 8 7 6 5

ISBN 0-13-034287-4

Sun Microsystems Press
A Prentice Hall Title

To Diane, Alex, and Rob
— David

To Alison, Megan, and Finlay
— Dominic

17 Adding SCSI Devices   395

Introduction

Objectives

The aim of this book is not to be just another "Guide for System Administrators," but rather a workshop manual that describes the tasks that need to be performed to build a complex network using the standard components delivered with the system.

We present the chapters in the same chronological order that the system administrator follows to build systems in real life. For example, we start by adding users onto a single system, add the system to the network, move on to configuring services such as NFS and NTP (which rely on the newly configured network), and so forth until we have built a complex of networked machines using NIS, NTP, and a multitude of other services.

We describe an environment consisting of a number of networked machines, including connections to the outside world. These systems will be used as the basis for all the examples, although the chapters can be isolated and will remain general enough to be adapted to any system.

So, what will you see in the book? We've covered all the tasks you'll need to get the environment up and running, including some of the following:

- We'll describe the boot process and talk about details such as the PROM, starting the system, the initialization process, and the shutdown process.

- We'll discuss users, create them with `useradd` and RBAC, and work through assigning quotas to them. When we move on to permissions, we'll look at "general" details, along with *setuid*, *setgid*, and Access Control Lists (ACLs).

- We'll add SCSI devices and look at how things like the device tree, instances, and *path_to_inst* work. We'll also add a custom tape device and create an *st.conf* entry for it. We'll learn about the different types of file systems and how things like superblocks and inodes are used. Then we'll partition, add, and use the devices within our system.

- We'll discuss class-based and classless IP addressing schemes. Then we'll split our environment into two subnets and configure them both. We'll include routing and external gateways to the Internet. We'll also use PPP to provide connectivity into remote networks, which also means configuring the associated UUCP databases.

- We'll configure services on the system to aid administration. We'll create an NTP server, after looking at how "time" works, and add some NIS masters/slaves to provide centralized administration. Within NIS we'll also create a custom map and tighten password security.

- We'll look at DNS and configure our domain for the public-facing machines. We'll also add a small mail server to the system, configure *sendmail.cf* using the m4 macroprocessor, and update the DNS entries to suit.

- We'll take an in-depth look at packages—building our own in the process. We'll also work through the patching mechanism.

- Lastly, we'll look at some of the tools that are available to back up and restore all this data that we've created.

We firmly believe that showing lots of code examples is a very good way of explaining how the operating system works. As anyone who has worked with UNIX knows, there are many different ways of performing nearly every task. All users have their favorite commands they use to do this; some people will only use awk, while others know sed inside out. For this reason, we have tried to use different commands to perform the same task throughout the book. We hope this will be a useful way of showing some of the various options.

All the tasks we carry out are command-line based, which means they will all work regardless of whether you are using a graphics console or working remotely via a telnet connection. We've adopted this approach because we think it's a better way of seeing what's happening, rather than simply clicking on a button in a GUI.

The major system configuration details are described in Appendix A to allow you to see which machine we are talking about at a glance, which we hope will let you become familiar with the system we are describing.

Chapter Format

Each chapter begins with a list of all the relevant online manual pages (along with their section numbers). We have taken the view that it is better to use code examples, wherever possible, to illustrate how commands may be used rather than provide a series of reference pages, which the user must determine how to use. Everyone has access to the manual pages, either online or at sites such as Sun's documentation site (*http://docs.sun.com*), these can be referred to for further information about any of the commands that have been run.

After that, we list the files that may be affected when carrying out any actions shown within the chapter. This allows the reader to follow the changes to these files as the reader progresses.

Next, we describe the task in depth: explaining what is taking place, showing the commands that need to be run, and showing the output that will be seen during execution.

We also have a section that shows ways of checking the parts of the system that relate to the chapter. For example, in the chapter that talks about adding users, we show how to check the password, shadow, and group files for invalid entries or corruption. These may be built into a suite of utility programs that are useful to the administrator for both general use and checking the health of the system.

In short, the aim is to provide the user with enough information to determine how commands are working while providing the information to allow them to determine how to take things further.

Conventions Used

We've used a number of style conventions throughout the book; these are shown in following table, along with an example of each.

Text Conventions

Object	Style	Example Display
Host names	Normal style, no quotes	hydrogen
User names	Shown in italics	*root*
Filenames	Shown in italics	*/etc/passwd*
Programs to run	Shown in Courier font	`useradd`
Environmental variables	Uppercase and underscores	MANPATH
Variables "internal" to scripts	lowerThenUpperCase	thisIsAnIntVariable
Domain name	Set to solarisbootcamp.com	—

Code Examples

The code examples used have all been built and tested on the systems used to describe the setup. We have tried to achieve a balance between including lots of comments in the code and making it readable.

We create a number of tools, which can be used to monitor and manage the system, and define a hierarchy that we will use to configure both the servers and the clients. The examples try to use this defined hierarchy, but again it can be easily altered should you not wish to use our definition.

Public Domain Tools

There is no denying that many public domain tools are very useful, and that some are even considered irreplaceable! Even so, we are aware that several companies do not allow these to be loaded on to their systems. For this reason, we have tried to limit the commands we use to those supplied with the operating system.

Acknowledgments

A big thanks go to Greg Doench, Jim Markham, Kathleen Caren, Eileen Clark, and everyone else we worked with at Prentice Hall.

Thanks also to Geoff Carrier at Sun Microsystems for all his efforts reviewing the work and providing valuable feedback, which made a big difference to the final text.

1

THE SYSTEM ADMINISTRATOR'S ROLE

Manual Pages

su (1M)
sulog (4)

Files Affected

/etc/default/login
/etc/default/su
/var/adm/sulog

An important part of running a UNIX system is allocating someone to look after it and ensure that it is working correctly. In this chapter, we'll look at what a system administrator is, along with what tasks he or she must perform.

The Importance of a System Administrator

"Just put it in the corner and we will switch it on when we need it."

"Yes, we know what to do; we have used a PC before."

"Leave it there, I'll sort it out later."

These are some of the misconceptions that users have when installing their first UNIX system. They assume the machines can sit happily in the corner and be switched on and off whenever they require to use them, and that they will function correctly throughout their lifetime. Unfortunately, this isn't the case—the machines are much more complex than that.

The reason for this is mainly because they provide the user with a level of services that is not available on many non-UNIX machines. These services include facilities such as:

- The ability to allow many users to log on to the system at any one time (termed *multi-user*)
- A mechanism to allow users to work on more than one "job" at a time (termed *multitasking*)
- A printing service that schedules jobs sent by any number of users to the same printer
- The ability to communicate with users both local and remote to the system
- The ability to schedule tasks for "out-of-work" time hours

As you would expect, although many services are provided with the system, they will not configure, run, and monitor themselves—all those tasks are the job of the system administrator. Some common tasks that would need performing are as follows:

- Starting the system in the correct sequence
- Shutting the system down correctly
- Adding users to the system (and removing them)
- Backing up and restoring the data on the system
- Adding software packages to the system
- Connecting hardware to the system
- Administering the system disks and filesystems
- Managing network connectivity
- Knowing what to do when something goes wrong

To enable the system administrator to actively monitor all those tasks, the system provides us with a number of log files. These are files that record such things as who has been connected to the system. The potential problem with these is that, if left unattended, they will grow and grow until they fill up all the available disk space on the system. Managing these is also a task for the administrator.

We stated earlier that UNIX is a multi-user, multitasking operating system, and as such there can be many different users logging on to the system at any one time. There needs to be a mechanism for providing users with some degree of security for their files, and for specifying to the system which users are allowed to actually log on to it. This is another role of the system administrator.

If anyone and everyone were allowed to manipulate the system files and perform the tasks listed earlier, it would be a recipe for disaster, especially on large systems where hundreds of users can be connected at once. By assigning a system administrator, we can control the number of people that are able to make changes to the system, and, from there, maintain a smooth running system.

Who Is the System Administrator?

Now that we've looked at the role of the system administrator, we need to know how someone assumes it. To do this, we need to understand a little more about what it means to be a "user," although we'll look at this in more detail in Chapter 3, "User Administration."

Anyone wishing to use the system is allocated a login name, a password, and an identification number, known as a UID (User Identification). Any user that is assigned a UID of 0 possesses special privileges, commonly known as "super-user" privileges. This means they have the power to do anything they wish! The user commonly associated with this is known as the system administrator and has a login name of *root*, although it's worth remembering that any user with a UID of 0 has this power. In fact, a number of other administrative users with a UID of 0 are predefined on the system.

There are two ways to become the system administrator: the first is to login to the system directly as *root* (although this may not be allowed, as we'll see later). The second is by logging on as a "normal" user and "switching" to the *root* user from there, which is the recommended way of doing things. This helps to protect the system by ensuring a user only has *root* privileges when needed, which means the user shouldn't accidentally remove any files (although everyone has done this at some time!).

The system administrator will normally use a personal account on a day-to-day basis, only switching to *root* when it is actually needed. A command named su is provided to save them from logging out of the system, and thus avoid having to save the current session they are working on. This actually allows any user to "switch" to any other user (assuming they have the correct password), although it is most commonly used to temporarily switch to the *root* account. Once the required tasks have been carried out, users can simply exit back to their normal account.

In practice, more that one person will normally have access to the *root* password—even if this is just to prevent it from being forgotten, as the recovery method from a forgotten *root* password can take some time and leaves the system inaccessible while it is being performed.

Role Based Access Control

Allowing one account, *root*, to have "super-user" privileges has been the common way of working in UNIX for a long time. Unfortunately, it also brings along some potential problems. For example:

- Once users have the *root* password, they can perform any task they wish.

- It is awkward to track which users have carried out certain tasks—they will all show up as root in the accounting files.

Available from Solaris 8 is a mechanism named Role Based Access Control (RBAC), which enables us to fix these problems. It allows us to delegate the "super-user" privileges to "normal" users, and, at the same time, tightly control the tasks they are allowed to perform.

To do this a set of "roles" are defined, such as "Password Manager," "Printer Manager," "Operator," and so forth. The granularity of the role can be altered to suit the company—some may define a basic set, such as "Administrator" and "User," while others may create as many as possible.

For our purposes, we can think of these as being similar to a user account—in fact, we even access them using the su command we described earlier.

Each role has a series of permissions, or authorizations, associated with it. These are described in a hierarchical fashion, each level providing more control over the task. For example, the authorization *solaris.admin.usermgr.pswd* allows a role to only make password changes, whereas *solaris.** allows any system administration task to be carried out.

Once the roles have been generated and authorized, they can be assigned to one or more users as required. This means that rather than have one global system administrator, we may have many "mini" system administrators instead—each one working within a predefined boundary.

Who's Been Logging In?

There are two ways of checking who has been accessing the system: The first is to use the command last, which records all logins and logouts. The second is by looking at the contents of the */var/adm/sulog* file. This file records all the information about users that have switched to another user, including those that have failed to switch. An example of each is shown here:

```
hydrogen# last | more
root      pts/3    helium   Wed Nov  3 13:58   still logged in
msmith    ftp      hydrogen Wed Nov  3 13:34 - 13:34  (00:00)
testuser  pts/3    hydrogen Wed Nov  3 13:31 - 13:33  (00:02)
sysadmin  ftp      tin      Wed Nov  3 12:17 - 12:19  (00:01)
sysadmin  ftp      helium   Wed Nov  3 10:52 - 10:52  (00:00)
hydrogen#
```

```
hydrogen# cat /var/adm/sulog
SU 06/26 16:25 + syscon root-root
SU 06/26 17:39 + syscon root-root
SU 07/02 11:11 + console root-sysadmin
SU 07/02 11:19 + console root-mgreen
SU 07/07 09:11 + pts/1 sysadmin-root
SU 07/08 10:45 + pts/4 testuser-root
hydrogen#
```

We can see that the *sulog* output is particularly useful for tracking any users that have switched to *root*. However, it doesn't really help if anyone has logged in directly as *root*, for example, through a `telnet` session. The good news is that a file named */etc/default/login* can be used to configure login sessions and control this.

For example, to stop users logging in directly as *root* anywhere other than the main system console, we need to set the CONSOLE variable as follows:

```
hydrogen# grep CONSOLE /etc/default/login
CONSOLE=/dev/console
hydrogen#
```

While to stop them logging in as *root* anywhere at all (including the system console) we would set the variable to NULL, as shown in the following example. This allows us to use the *sulog* to determine *all* users that have switched to *root*:

```
hydrogen# grep CONSOLE /etc/default/login
CONSOLE=
hydrogen#
```

Checking the Sulog

Now we'll create a script that will parse the entries logged in *sulog*, searching for any failures. These will indicate that a user has failed to `su` any other user, not only *root* (although we're primarily interested in the *root* ones at the moment).

Running this on a regular basis will highlight any attempts to break into the *root* account:

```
hydrogen# cat checkSuLog
#!/bin/ksh
# Script to check the su logfile looking
# for failed login's.
#
adminAccount=root     # who to send mail to
tmpSuOut=/tmp/checkSuLog.out$$
# determine the location of the sulog file
sulogLocation=$(cat /etc/default/su | awk -F= ' \
  $1 ~ /^SULOG/ { print $2 }')
```

```
# now look for failed su's
cat ${sulogLocation} | awk ' \
  $4 == "-" { printf ("\t%s\n", $0) }' > ${tmpSuOut}

# if we have any output - mail it
if [ -s ${tmpSuOut} ]; then
  cat ${tmpSuOut} | mail -s "Failed su's found"
${adminAccount}
  rm ${tmpSuOut}
fi
exit
hydrogen#
```

This will send mail to the system administrator (or whoever is specified as the admin account) if it detects any failed logins.

Automating the Check

As we progress through the book, we will see how to build up a number of "check" scripts. These scripts will be automated by running them via cron; in readiness for this, we will create a *crontab* entry that will be added to later. It doesn't matter whether the hierarchy we use makes sense or not yet, as it will all become clear later in the book:

```
hydrogen# crontab -l
<lines removed for clarity>
#
# check the su log for failed logins
#
15 02 * * 1-5 /usr/local/utils/bin/checkSuLog
<lines removed for clarity>
hydrogen#
```

2

BOOTING AND HALTING THE SYSTEM

Manual Pages

boot (1M)
eeprom (1M)
fastboot (1B)
fasthalt (1B)
halt (1M)
init (1M)
kill (1)
pgrep (1)
pkill (1)
preap(1)
ps (1)
reboot (1M)
shutdown (1)
signal (5)
sync (1M)
trap (1)
wall (1M)
who (1)

Files Affected

/etc/init.d
/etc/inittab
/etc/rc*.d

Objectives

In this chapter we will look at all aspects of the start-up (boot) and shut-down procedures for computers running the Solaris Operating System. As well as looking at stages of the boot operation through the start up of Solaris processes, we will also look at a number of the Solaris daemon processes, including how to start, stop, and manage them. The chapter will end with a description of the OpenBoot Programmable Read-Only Memory (PROM), which allows some control over the management of the system boot and can be used to help debug boot problems.

Switching On

When we first switch on a Solaris system, we are immediately presented with what is generally referred to as the OK prompt. This prompt belongs to the PROM or monitor program and has nothing to do with Solaris itself so you cannot type UNIX commands here. We will look at the PROM in more detail at the end of this chapter. For now we just need to know that when we get the OK prompt the system is ready to bootup and load Solaris.

The Boot Process

At the OK> prompt we type "boot" to cause the system to begin the process of loading Solaris, which ends with the display of the console login prompt. Here we will look at what actually happens during this process.

Once you have typed your boot command, the boot PROM performs a self-diagnostic test that verifies that the system hardware and memory are functioning correctly. The PROM then loads and runs the primary boot program called bootblk. The job of bootblk is to locate the secondary boot program (ufsboot) on the default (or specified) device, load this into memory, and then execute it. The boot process will then load the Solaris kernel. The kernel initializes itself and then begins to load the kernel modules. It will initially use ufsboot to read these modules, but once the modules needed to mount the *root* filesystem are loaded the kernel will unmap ufsboot and continue the boot process using its own resources. The kernel will now create the first Solaris process.

Once Solaris is up and running, new processes are created by an already running process being copied in memory and then the copy being overlaid with the new process. This cannot happen until at least one process is running, so the first process has to be created directly in memory (it is said to be "hand crafted"). This first process is the scheduler process. Since it is the first process, it is given a process ID of 0 (zero). The next process to be created is init and, not surprisingly, it gets a process ID of 1. Init is the first Solaris process to be created in the standard way; it can be thought of as the parent of all the other processes, apart from the scheduler. The scheduler process remains special and cannot be treated like other processes. One of its jobs is to swap processes between memory and disk (see Chapter 7 "Swap Space"). If it were a normal process, there would be nothing to prevent it from copying itself out to disk and then there would be nothing left in memory to swap it back in again.

Now that init is running, its first job is to read the configuration file (/etc/inittab) and start the processes defined in it. The boot process completes with init executing the run commands (rc) scripts that perform such tasks as mounting the remainder of the filesystems and starting applications. At this point Solaris is up and running and has full control of the computer. Table 2.1 summarizes the boot process.

Table 2.1 *Boot Process Summary*

The boot PROM phase:
The boot PROM runs self-diagnostic tests.
The boot PROM loads the bootblk program.

The boot programs phase:
The bootblk program loads the ufsboot program.
The ufsboot program loads the kernel.

The kernel initialization phase:
The kernel initializes itself and loads the modules needed to mount the root (/) filesystem.
The kernel starts the init process.

The init phase:
The init process reads the /etc/inittab file and runs the system's rc scripts.

Once the boot process has completed, the server is ready for use. At this point it will normally be in multi-user mode. This means that many people are able to use the computer at the same time, usually connecting across a network. The fact that Solaris has a multi-user mode implies that it also has a single-user mode, and this is the case. The mode that the server is in is usually referred to as the run level, and one of the jobs of the init process is to control the system run level. You can find out the current run level using the who command:

```
hydrogen# who -r
.         run-level 3  Aug 28 09:22     3      0  S
hydrogen#
```

In this case, we are in run-level 3, which means the system is in multi-user mode and all network services are available. The second field from the right tells us how many times we have been in this run level since the last reboot (in this case, zero times), and the field on the right tells us the last run level the system was in (in this case, single user).

Run Levels

A run level can be thought of as a predefined known state. Each run level has a set of processes that will be started or stopped when the run level is entered or left. A number of run levels have been predefined by Solaris (and are shown in Table 2.2) but others can be defined and used if required, although I have only worked on one site that has ever used a custom run level. You can change the run level at any time by typing init followed by the level to which you wish to change (e.g., init 2). Table 2.2 describes the predefined Solaris run levels.

Table 2.2 *Run Levels*

Run Level	Description
0	When the system is in run-level 0 it is shut down and in a state where it is safe to switch the power off.
1 (s or S)	Run-level 1 is single-user mode. Only the console port is available for logging in. Sometimes called "run-level s" (or "S").
2	This is multi-user mode. All network services are running apart from the Network File System (NFS).
3	Run-level 3 is multi-user mode with NFS activated.
4	This run level is defined in the Solaris manual as "not currently supported." It is, however, quite possible to use it to construct your own run level.
5	This run level is similar to 0 in that the operating system has shut down, but if the hardware supports it, the power will also be switched off.
6	This run level causes the server to reboot by first shutting down to run-level 0 then booting up to the default run level.

The init process controls the movement between run levels and will run processes (or kill processes) each time a run level change is made. It knows what to do when a run level changes by looking at instructions in the system file /etc/inittab.

Here we have a copy of the */etc/inittab* file from one of our servers:

```
ap::sysinit:/sbin/autopush -f /etc/iu.ap
ap::sysinit:/sbin/soconfig -f /etc/sock2path
fs::sysinit:/sbin/rcS sysinit  >/dev/msglog 2<>/dev/msglog </dev/console
is:3:initdefault:
p3:s1234:powerfail:/usr/sbin/shutdown -y -i5 -g0   >/dev/msglog 2<>/dev/
   msglog
sS:s:wait:/sbin/rcS            >/dev/msglog 2<>/dev/msglog </dev/console
s0:0:wait:/sbin/rc0            >/dev/msglog 2<>/dev/msglog </dev/console
s1:1:respawn:/sbin/rc1         >/dev/msglog 2<>/dev/msglog </dev/console
s2:23:wait:/sbin/rc2           >/dev/msglog 2<>/dev/msglog </dev/console
s3:3:wait:/sbin/rc3            >/dev/msglog 2<>/dev/msglog </dev/console
s5:5:wait:/sbin/rc5            >/dev/msglog 2<>/dev/msglog </dev/console
s6:6:wait:/sbin/rc6            >/dev/msglog 2<>/dev/msglog </dev/console
fw:0:wait:/sbin/uadmin 2 0     >/dev/msglog 2<>/dev/msglog </dev/console
of:5:wait:/sbin/uadmin 2 6     >/dev/msglog 2<>/dev/msglog </dev/console
rb:6:wait:/sbin/uadmin 2 1     >/dev/msglog 2<>/dev/msglog </dev/console
sc:234:respawn:/usr/lib/saf/sac -t 300
co:234:respawn:/usr/lib/saf/ttymon -g -h -p "`uname -n` console login:
   " -T sun -d /dev/console -l console -m ldterm,ttcompat
```

The file contains one record per line and each record contains colon-separated fields. The field contents are described in Table 2.3.

Table 2.3 */etc/inittab Fields*

Field	Description
tag	This field contains a name for each entry (it does not need to be unique).
rstate	This specifies the run level in which the process should be executed. You can specify more than one run level if required.
action	This describes how init should run the specified process when the run level is entered. **once**: Start this process (if it is not already running) and move straight on to the next *inittab* entry. If it terminates do not restart it. **respawn**: Start the process (if it isn't already running); if it ever terminates while in this run level, restart it. **wait**: Start the process and wait until it terminates before moving on to the next *inittab* entry. (If this process hangs, you can be in big trouble since init will not do anything else until it has completed.)

Table 2.3 /etc/inittab Fields (Continued)

Field	Description
action *(con't)*	**boot**: These entries will only be dealt with during init's initial boot time read of the *inittab* file. The process will be started then init will move on to the next entry without waiting. These entries are useful if you need to initialize something (e.g., a hardware device) each time the system reboots.
	bootwait: Any "bootwait" entry will be processed by init when the system first moves from single-user mode to multi-user mode. Each process listed will be started and init will wait for it to terminate before carrying on.
	sysinit: These entries will only be run during bootup and before the console login has appeared. Init will wait for these entries to complete before moving on.
	powerfail: Execute this process when the init command receives the power fail signal (SIGPWR).
	powerwait: Execute this process when the init command receives the power fail signal (SIGPWR), but wait until it has completed before continuing to process the *inittab* file.
	off: If the process is already running, init will kill it. If it is not running, init will do nothing.
	ondemand: Any on-demand entries in *inittab* are treated in exactly the same way as "respawn" entries, but they are not tied to a particular run level. See below for more information on these entries.
	initdefault: This entry is only read the first time init looks through the file. It tells init which run level we want it to take the system to.
process	This is the process to run based on the rules for that record.

There is one entry in /etc/inittab that does not conform to the above specification and that is the "initdefault" record. This simply tells the init process what run level to take the system to at system boot-time. It is not a good idea to set the default run level to 0 or 6. The former would cause Solaris to shut itself down every time it booted up, while the latter would cause the system to reboot itself continuously (which would make a very interesting problem to try and troubleshoot).

When we want to change to a new run level we simply type init followed by the new run level and init will read the *inittab* file to see what processes it needs to run when it moves to that level. When it has completed this task the run level is set to the one specified. This saves us, as administrators, from needing to know what processes should be running for specific situations. We know that every time we go to a specific run level the process defined to run at that run level, in *inittab*, will be run by init. We can also control processes from *inittab*, but without needing to change the run level to run them. These are the *on-demand* processes. If an entry in the *inittab* file has its action field set to "on-demand," it will be treated in a similar way to one that has "respawn" in that field. The difference is that an on-demand job will not have a run level in its rstate field. Instead it will have one of the letters a, b, or c. If you type "init" followed by the letter a, b, or c, then init will run any on-demand jobs with the same letter in their rstate field as though they were respawn jobs. Since a, b, and c are not valid run levels, the run level will not actually change, so no other entries in *inittab* will be acted upon.

If you make a change to the *inittab* file, init will not act upon the change until the next time it reads the file. It will normally only read the file at system startup or when the current run level is changed, but you can tell it to read the file with the command init q.

RC Scripts

You may have noticed that the example *inittab* file contains a number of entries to run programs with a name that matches /sbin/rcX, where the "X" represents a run level. These programs are actually shell scripts, and you will see that they are each defined as running only at that run level (apart from /sbin/rc2, which we will look at in a moment). The purpose of these scripts is to start and stop all the processes needed when a new run level is entered. Rather than doing this directly, which would lead to them needing updating whenever something new needed starting, they call a series of separate scripts. These scripts are located in the subdirectories of /etc named rcX.d, where the "X," again, refers to a run level. This means that if we wanted to add a new process that needed starting when a specific run level was entered, we do not need to change the rcX script. We can simply create a new script in the appropriate /etc/rc.X directory. We will look at how to add a new rc script later. The scripts located within these directories have names that follow the format Snnscriptname or Knnscriptname. The S scripts are for starting processes or applications and are executed when a run level is entered. The K scripts are for killing (or stopping) things and run when you leave a run level. The "nn" refers to a number, and this number controls the order that the scripts will run. The exact order that the scripts will run can be seen by running ls | more in the relevant *rc* directory. During a change of run level init will call the /sbin/rcX script, which will in turn run all the K scripts and S scripts in the equivalent /etc/rc.X directory. The scripts are always run in ascending order according to the number after the S or K. The K scripts are run first followed by the S scripts.

You may notice that certain script names exist in more that one *rc* directory and you will also notice that these files are actually linked. In fact, every script in a *rc* directory should be linked to a script in the directory */etc/init.d*. This directory is the master directory for scripts called when `init` changes run levels. The fact that they are linked means that if you need to change any script it only needs doing once. If you look even more closely at the links, you will see that the S scripts are also linked to the K scripts. When the appropriate `/bin/rcX` script calls an S script it will supply the single parameter "start" and when it calls a K script it uses "stop" as the parameter. This again enables a single file to be edited regardless of whether changes need to be made to the way something is started, stopped, or both.

You may find that the K script is often located in a different directory to the S script. The directory containing the S script tells you which run level you need to enter to start the applications or subsystem, and the directory containing the K script tells you which run level you need to enter in order for the application or subsystem to be shut down.

We saw that in the *inittab* file the entry for the `/sbin/rc2` script is set to run in both run-level 2 and run-level 3. This is because run-levels 2 and 3 are similar. Run-level 2 is referred to as multi-user mode without NFS running, and run level 3 is multi-user mode, with NFS running. The directory */etc/rc2.d* contains the scripts that will be run when the system goes to run-level 2, but the directory */etc/rc3.d* only contains the scripts to get NFS (and possibly one or two other subsystems) running. Therefore, if we enter run-level 2 we want all the S scripts in */etc/rc2.d* to run (as would be expected), but if we enter run-level 3 we want to run the run-level 2 scripts (if they haven't already been run) followed by the run-level 3 scripts. If you look in the `/sbin/rcX` scripts, you will see that as well as knowing the run level being moved to, they also know the run level being moved from (they are stored in shell variables). So if you move from run-level 2 to run-level 3, only the scripts in */etc/rc3.d* will run, but if you move from single-user mode straight to run-level 3, then the */etc/rc2.d* scripts will run (from `/sbin/rc2`) followed by the */etc/rc3.d* scripts (from `/sbin/rc3`).

Adding a New RC Script

If you install a piece of software on one of your Solaris systems that needs to be started automatically at boot-time, the usual method of starting it will be by its own rc script. Some software packages will set up the rc script themselves, but if it doesn't then it is a task that you will need to do yourself. This can be particularly important with some applications, for example databases, since if they are not stopped correctly when the system is shut down, they may need to perform some kind of recovery action when they are next started up.

Before you can start you need to know what the command to start the new piece of software is, what user the command should be run as, and whether any environment variables need to be defined before the command is run. You will also need to know in which run level(s) the software should run and shut down. Once you have all this information you can create the script and add it to the correct directory.

When writing the script you need to be aware that when it runs it will be called with one of two possible parameters: either "start" when it should start the new software, or "stop" when it should stop it.

For the purpose of this example, the command to start the new piece of software is:

```
/opt/app_dir/bin/start_app
```

And the command to stop it is:

```
/opt/app_dir/bin/stop_app
```

We will also assume that the command should be run as the user *app_owner* and an environment variable called APP_DATA needs to be set before the command can be run.

The rc script we write will look something like this:

```
#!/bin/sh
# script to start and stop the app software
# version 1.0
# August 12th 2001

APP_DATA=/opt/app_dir/data_area
export APP_DATA

case $1 in
  start)
    su - app_owner -c "/opt/app_dir/bin/start_app"
    echo "Started app"
    exit 0
    ;;
  stop)
    su - app_owner -c "/opt/app_dir/bin/stop_app"
    echo "Stopped app"
    exit 0
    ;;
  *)
    echo "usage: $0 start|stop"
    exit 1
    ;;
esac
```

We now have our script so we need to give it a name (app_control will do), and we should place it in the directory */etc/init.d*.

This directory is the master directory for rc scripts that will be called, indirectly, from init. None of the scripts are ever run from this directory, but, as mentioned, they will be linked to files in the actual *rc* directory where they will be run from.

Before we can create the links, we need to know what run level the software should start in and when it should be stopped. This is a multi-user application, so it will need to run in multi-user mode, but even though we normally run our systems in run-level 3, it is better to put the script in */etc/rc2.d* so it can still be used if we need to put the system in that run level for any reason. If the software needs to make use of NFS, then it would make sense to put the script in *etc/rc3.d* since we would not want it to run if NFS was not running.

We should start the software as we enter run-level 2, so we need to link the file from *etc/init.d* to *etc/rc2.d*. However, we need to know what to call the file in *etc.rc2.d*. Since the script will be starting the software, we need to start the name with "S," but we also need to assign it a number to determine at what stage it runs.

The current contents of *etc/rc2.d* are as follows:

```
hydrogen# ls -g
total 132
-rwxr--r--   6 sys       861 Sep  1 1998 K07dmi
-rwxr--r--   6 sys       404 Sep  1 1998 K07snmpdx
-rwxr--r--   6 sys      2307 Sep  1 1998 K28nfs.server
-rw-r--r--   1 sys      1369 Sep  1 1998 README
-rwxr--r--   3 sys      1886 Sep  9 1999 S01MOUNTFSYS
-rwxr--r--   2 sys      2004 Sep  1 1998 S05RMTMPFILES
-rwxr--r--   2 sys       624 Sep  1 1998 S20sysetup
-rwxr--r--   2 sys       989 Sep  1 1998 S21perf
-rwxr-xr-x   2 other    1644 Sep 11 1998 S30sysid.net
-rwxr--r--   5 sys       359 Jun 29 1999 S40llc2
-rwxr--r--   5 sys      7317 Sep  1 1998 S69inet
-rwxr--r--   5 sys      2750 Oct 14 1999 S71rpc
-rwxr-xr-x   2 other    1498 Sep 11 1998 S71sysid.sys
-rwxr-xr-x   2 other    1558 Sep 11 1998 S72autoinstall
-rwxr--r--   5 sys      7430 Sep  1 1998 S72inetsvc
-rwxr--r--   2 sys      1113 Sep  1 1998 S73cachefs.daemon
-rwxr--r--   3 sys      1223 Oct 14 1999 S73nfs.client
-rwxr--r--   5 sys       364 Oct 14 1999 S74autofs
-rwxr--r--   5 sys       867 Oct 14 1999 S74syslog
-rwxr--r--   5 sys       942 Sep  1 1998 S74xntpd
-rwxr--r--   5 sys       504 Sep  1 1998 S75cron
-rwxr--r--   2 sys      2519 Sep  1 1998 S75savecore
-rwxr--r--   5 sys       563 Sep  1 1998 S76nscd
-rwxr--r--   5 sys       460 Sep  1 1998 S80lp
-rwxr--r--   2 sys       256 Sep  1 1998 S80PRESERVE
-rwxr--r--   5 sys       610 Sep  1 1998 S80spc
-rwxr--r--   5 sys      1959 Sep  1 1998 S85power
-rwxr--r--   5 sys       868 Sep  1 1998 S88sendmail
-rwxr--r--   5 sys       597 Sep  1 1998 S88utmpd
-rwxr--r--   5 sys       391 Oct 14 1999 S92volmgt
-rwxr--r--   2 sys       364 Sep  1 1998 S93cacheos.finish
-rwxr--r--   5 sys       447 Sep  1 1998 S99audit
-rwxr--r--   5 sys      2804 Sep 12 1998 S99dtlogin
-rwxr--r--   2 sys       449 Oct 14 1999 S99tsquantum
hydrogen#
```

You will see that although most scripts in *rc2.d* are S scripts, there are three K scripts. These are the scripts that are linked to the S scripts in `rc3.d`, and they are needed because if we move from run-level 3 to run-level 2 we want these services to stop running. The scripts will also run if we move from single-user mode to run-level 2, but since the run-level 3 services would not have been running in that run level the scripts will have no effect.

We would ideally like our new software package to run after everything else has started. However, since there are already a few rc scripts with S99 as their prefix we will choose S95, as it doesn't matter if our script runs before the existing S99 rc scripts. To create the link we would use the following command:

```
hydrogen# ln /etc/init.d/app_control /etc/rc2.d/S95app_control
hydrogen# cd /etc/rc2.d
hydrogen# ls -l S95app_control
-rw-r--r--   2 root    other      373 Sep   5 13:33 S95app_control
hydrogen#
```

We can see that the script now has two links, but this only affects starting the software. We will also need to create a link to a name beginning with "K" so the software can be correctly stopped when we shut the server down. However, since we also want it to stop if the system is put into single-user mode, we will need to create several links. These will be in the directories */etc/ rc0.d*, */etc/rc1.d*, and */etc/rcS.d*.

```
hydrogen# cd /etc/init.d
hydrogen# ln app_control /etc/rc0.d/K95app_control
hydrogen# ln app_control /etc/rc1.d/K95app_control
hydrogen# ln app_control /etc/rcS.d/K95app_control
hydrogen#
```

This means that our new software will start automatically each time the system goes into multi-user mode (either run-level 2 or run-level 3). It will also be shut down when the system either goes into single-user mode or is shut down itself. Because all the files are linked, if we ever need to make a change we only need to edit the script once. We can double-check that all the links are set up correctly with the following find command:

```
hydrogen# find /etc -name "*app_control" -exec ls -ild {} \;
6415 -rw-r--r--   5 root   other   373 Sep  5 13:33 /etc/init.d/app_control
6415 -rw-r--r--   5 root   other   373 Sep  5 13:33 /etc/rc0.d/K95app_control
6415 -rw-r--r--   5 root   other   373 Sep  5 13:33 /etc/rc1.d/K95app_control
6415 -rw-r--r--   5 root   other   373 Sep  5 13:33 /etc/rc2.d/S95app_control
6415 -rw-r--r--   5 root   other   373 Sep  5 13:33 /etc/rcS.d/K95app_control
hydrogen#
```

Because we included the "-i" option with the ls command, we can confirm that they all have the same inode number (6415). Of course, we can also see that they have the correct number of links set.

Solaris Processes

So far, we have looked at the first two processes to be created when the system boots up. These are sched, which has process ID 0, and init, which has process ID 1. They are different because the sched process is actually part of the Solaris kernel, whereas init is a normal program that is stored in a filesystem (in the directory /etc) just like other Solaris commands we have looked at. The difference between init and commands such as ls or who is that init runs all the time, not just when its name is typed. Processes that run all the time are called "daemon" processes; at any time there will be many daemon processes running.

In this section we will look in more detail at how processes are handled by Solaris and how they can be managed by the system administrator. Before we look at Solaris processes in general, the most common Solaris daemon processes are listed and described in Table 2.4. Where a particular daemon is dealt with in more detail in another chapter, that chapter is listed.

Table 2.4 *Solaris Daemon Processes*

Process	RC Script (in */etc/init.d*)	Description
sched	n/a	This is the first Solaris process, created during the boot process. It is hand crafted, but most other processes are created from a copy of their parent process.
init	n/a	This is the parent of all standard Solaris processes. It runs the rc scripts that start and stop other daemons, and it clears up after all processes when they complete.
pageout	n/a	This is similar to the sched process, as it is not a regular daemon process but part of the Solaris kernel.
fsflush	n/a	This is part of the Solaris kernel and is responsible for writing file changes from memory back to the filesystem on the disk.
in.routed	inetinit	This daemon process manages the network routing tables. See Chapter 11, "Connecting to the Local Area Network."
sac	n/a	This is the Service Access Controller daemon. It controls the port monitor processes sacadm and pmadm. See Chapter 14, "Connecting Serial Devices."
devfseventd	devfsadm	The job of this process is to inform the devfsadmd daemon when devices are added or removed from the device tree.

Table 2.4 *Solaris Daemon Processes (Continued)*

Process	RC Script (in *etc/init.d*)	Description
devfsadmd	devfsadm	This daemon process manages the */dev* and */devices* namespaces. See Chapter 21, "Kernels and All About Them."
statd	nfs.client	This daemon is part of the NFS subsystem. It works with lockd to provide crash and recovery functions for networked filesystems. See Chapter 18, "NFS, DFS, and Autofs."
keyserv	rpc	This daemon stores users' private encryption keys for access to secure network services, such as secure NFS and NIS+.
rpcbind	rpc	This daemon acts as a server to convert Remote Procedure Call (RPC) program numbers to universal addresses. When a client wishes to make an RPC call to a program on this server it makes a call to rcpbind to find out what address to send its RPC request to. See Chapter 18, "NFS, DFS, and Autofs."
lockd	nfs.client	The lockd daemon handles locking within the NFS subsystem. It will send requests to lock files on a remote host and it will lock local files upon receiving a lock request. See Chapter 18, "NFS, DFS, and Autofs."
syslogd	syslog	The syslogd daemon forwards system messages to the log files or users specified in the file */etc/syslog.conf*.
automountd	autofs	This daemon is actually an RPC server. It answers mount and unmount requests and will undertake such tasks as automatically mounting a CD when inserted in the drive. See Chapter 18, "NFS, DFS, and Autofs."
powerd	power	This daemon is responsible for shutting down Solaris if the power is getting low or the system has been configured to shut down after a specific idle period.

Table 2.4 *Solaris Daemon Processes (Continued)*

Process	RC Script (in */etc/init.d*)	Description
inetd	inetsvc	The inet daemon (inetd) is the server process for Internet standard services, and it can also handle RPC services. It is inetd that spawns the in.telnetd processes when a telnet connection is received.
cron	cron	This daemon process is responsible for running commands at specific dates and times. It looks in configuration files held under */var/spool/cron/crontabs* when it first starts up to see what it needs to run and when.
lpsched	lp	This daemon manages the local printer services.
nscd	nscd	This is the Name Service Cache Daemon. It provides caching for various databases (e.g., *passwd*, *group*, and *hosts*) based on the settings in its configuration file */etc/nscd.conf*.
vold	volmgt	This daemon performs automatic mounting of CDs and floppy disks based on the configuration file */etc/vold.conf*.
in.telnetd	n/a	This daemon is not started by an rc script, but by the inetd daemon process when a connection is initiated via telnet. There will be one occurrence of this daemon running for each telnet session. Other Transmission Control Protocol/Internet Protocol (TCP/IP) programs work in a similar way (e.g., ftp and rlogin).
utmpd	utmpd	This daemon monitors the */var/adm/utmp* file and all currently running processes to ensure that when a process terminates, its entry in */var/adm/utmp* gets removed. The same applies for the file */var/adm/utmpx*. *Utmp* is being phased out in favor of *utmpx*.

Table 2.4 *Solaris Daemon Processes (Continued)*

Process	RC Script (in */etc/init.d*)	Description
snmpdx	init.snmpdx	This daemon process is the Sun Solstice Enterprise Master Agent. It handles Simple Network Management Protocol (SNMP) requests that enable you to do such things as provide alerts of critical events (such as a filesystem filling up) to a central node or alert monitoring tool.
dmispd	init.dmi	This daemon is also part of the Sun Solstice Enterprise System and is the Digital Multiplexed Interface (DMI) service provider.
snmpXdmid	init.dmi	This is also part of the Sun Solstice Enterprise System. This particular daemon maps SNMP requests from snmpdx into DMI requests and vice versa.
mibiisa	init.snmpdx	This daemon is the Sun SNMP agent. This passes SNMP traps to be dealt with by the snmpdx daemon.
ttymon	n/a	This daemon sets up and monitors ports (e.g., the console) and will spawn a program such as login, as configured by the sacadm command. See Chapter 14, "Connecting Serial Devices."
sendmail	sendmail	The sendmail daemon (as its name suggests) is responsible for sending mail. It will determine if the recipient is local or not and ensure the message is directed to the correct network or host. See Chapter 20, "Setting Up the Mail System."

Processes can be viewed using the ps command. The following ps listing shows all the processes that can be found running on a sample Solaris system. There are no third-party applications running so all the processes we can see are Solaris processes:

```
hydrogen# ps -ef
    UID   PID PPID  C    STIME TTY      TIME CMD
   root     0    0  0 15:46:55 ?       0:01 sched
   root     1    0  0 15:46:58 ?       0:01 /etc/init -
   root     2    0  0 15:46:58 ?       0:00 pageout
   root     3    0  0 15:46:58 ?       0:22 fsflush
   root   112    1  0 15:47:52 ?       0:00 /usr/sbin/in.routed -q
```

```
   root   251     1   0 15:48:33 ?         0:00 /usr/lib/saf/sac -t 300
   root    49     1   0 15:47:18 ?         0:00 /usr/lib/devfsadm/devfseventd
   root    51     1   0 15:47:20 ?         0:00 /usr/lib/devfsadm/devfsadmd
 daemon   149     1   0 15:47:58 ?         0:00 /usr/lib/nfs/statd
   root   118     1   0 15:47:54 ?         0:00 /usr/sbin/keyserv
   root   116     1   0 15:47:53 ?         0:00 /usr/sbin/rpcbind
   root   150     1   0 15:47:58 ?         0:00 /usr/lib/nfs/lockd
   root   172     1   0 15:48:06 ?         0:01 /usr/sbin/syslogd
   root   162     1   0 15:48:03 ?         0:00 /usr/lib/autofs/automountd
   root   208     1   0 15:48:15 ?         0:00 /usr/lib/power/powerd
   root   147     1   0 15:47:58 ?         0:01 /usr/sbin/inetd -s
   root   174     1   0 15:48:07 ?         0:00 /usr/sbin/cron
   root   195     1   0 15:48:11 ?         0:00 /usr/lib/lpsched
   root   190     1   0 15:48:10 ?         0:00 /usr/sbin/nscd
   root   217     1   0 15:48:16 ?         0:02 /usr/sbin/vold
   root   544   147   0 17:28:02 ?         0:00 in.telnetd
   root   221     1   0 15:48:17 ?         0:00 /usr/lib/utmpd
   root   546   544   0 17:28:02 pts/0    0:00 -sh
   root   252     1   0 15:48:33 console  0:00 /usr/lib/saf/ttymon -g -h
    -p hydrogen console login:   -T sun -d /dev/console -l
   root   236     1   0 15:48:26 ?         0:00 /usr/lib/snmp/snmpdx -y -c
    /etc/snmp/conf
   root   602   597   2 17:37:10 pts/1    0:00 ps -ef
   root   244     1   0 15:48:31 ?         0:02 /usr/lib/dmi/dmispd
   root   247     1   0 15:48:32 ?         0:01 /usr/lib/dmi/snmpXdmid
    -s hydrogen
   root   253   236   0 15:48:33 ?         0:12 mibiisa -r -p 32784
   root   255   251   0 15:48:36 ?         0:00 /usr/lib/saf/ttymon
   root   272     1   0 15:49:19 ?         0:00 /usr/lib/sendmail -bd -q15m
   root   595   147   1 17:37:02 ?         0:00 in.telnetd
   root   597   595   2 17:37:03 pts/1    0:00 -sh
hydrogen#
```

Table 2.5 describes the column headings that ps presents us with.

Table 2.5 *Column Headings from* `ps -ef`

Column Heading	Description
UID	The first column lists the UID of the user that initiated this process.
PID	This column lists the process ID of this process.
PPID	This column lists the process ID of the parent of this process. Daemon processes will usually have a PPID of 1 (init); processes initiated by a user will usually have a PPID equal to that of the user's shell.
C	This column is actually obsolete now, but used to contain the processor utilization of this process and was used for scheduling purposes.

Table 2.5 *Column Headings from* `ps -ef` *(Continued)*

Column Heading	Description
STIME	This is the time (or date) that the process started running. If the process has been running for less than 24 hours, you will see the time it started; otherwise you will see the date.
TTY	This is the teletype (TTY) device that the process was run from. If the process was not initiated by a logged-in user, this column will contain a question mark (?).
TIME	This is the total time the process has spent running. You will notice that this does not relate to the actual time that has passed since the process was started, but is literally the time it has spent running on a processor (which is generally not very long).
CMD	This is the full command that was run, including all its arguments (up to a limit of 80 characters).

The TTY column shows which terminal (or TTY device) that process is attached to (or was executed from). We can see that when the above ps command was run there were two users logged in (both as *root*): one on device pts/0 (which is the user that actually ran the ps -ef command) and the other on pts/1. There is a process attached to the console, but it does not mean someone has logged in on the console; it is actually the console login prompt.

All the processes that have a question mark in the TTY column are not associated with any terminal and are daemon processes. Daemon processes are named after the Daemons of Greek mythology who ran around the Underworld doing lots of jobs; this is pretty much what daemon processes do. They may run constantly, but they are not necessarily active the whole time. They may spend most of their time asleep and just wake up every now and again to perform an action, or they may spend their time waiting for a certain event or condition to be met and then spring into action.

Most Solaris daemons are started at boot-time when the rc scripts run, though some, such as the ttymon process that runs on the console, are started and managed directly by init and have their own entries in the */etc/inittab* file. If a problem arises that causes a daemon process to fall over and the process is defined in the *inittab* file, then init may automatically restart it, depending on the value in the action field (see above). If, however, the daemon process was started by an rc script, then it is usually up to the system administrator to get it going again. Usually the safest thing to do, after locating the correct rc script, is to first run the script with the parameter "stop" and then run it again with the parameter "start." This will ensure that you are performing a clean shutdown of that application or subsystem before starting it again.

Killing Processes

If you need to terminate a process for any reason, you can use the `kill` command. The name of this command is actually rather misleading. Although it is normally used to kill processes, that is not its only purpose. The actual purpose of the `kill` command is for it to ask the kernel to tell the process that a certain event has occurred by sending it a specific signal. The kernel will only send the signal if the user is either the owner of the process or *root*. A signal is basically a number that will mean something to that process (see Table 2.6). By default the `kill` command will request the kernel to send signal number 15 to the specified process. This indicates that we don't want it to run any longer and should cause the process to terminate. However, the program may have been written to ignore signal 15 and simply carry on running. Alternatively it may perform some action (such as removing a temporary file or tidying up after itself) before it terminates. The process will usually terminate at this point, but it might not, and we'll look at why in a moment. First we will look at how the `kill` command works:

```
hydrogen# sleep 500 &
339
hydrogen# ps
PID TTY        TIME CMD
   283 pts/1    0:01 sh
   340 pts/1    0:00 ps
   339 pts/1    0:00 sleep
hydrogen# kill 339
339 Terminated
hydrogen# ps
PID TTY        TIME CMD
   283 pts/1    0:01 sh
   341 pts/1    0:00 ps
hydrogen#
```

In the above example, the `kill` command requested the Solaris kernel to send signal number 15 to the `sleep` process. We could also have typed the following command to achieve the same effect:

```
hydrogen# kill -15 <pid>
hydrogen#
```

Table 2.6 describes the most useful of the many signals. The full list is described in the signal man page (`man -s 5 signal`).

Table 2.6 *Solaris Signals*

No.	Signal	Description
1	SIGHUP	This is the hangup signal. It will be sent to any background processes you have started but have not finished when you log out. If you run a background process with nohup, it will ignore the SIGHUP and carry on running. This signal will cause some daemon processes to reread their configuration files rather than terminate.
2	SIGINT	This is sent to your currently running program when you type the interrupt key (usually <control c>). The default action is to cause the program to terminate, but it won't if the process "traps" the signal (see below).
3	SIGQUIT	This signal will cause the process it is sent to to terminate and produce a core dump. It can usually be sent to the current process by typing <control \> (control backslash).
4	SIGILL	This signal is normally sent to a process by the kernel to signify that it has performed an illegal instruction.
6	SIGABRT	This signal will cause a program to abort and produce a core dump.
8	SIGFPE	The kernel will send this signal to a program if it tries to perform a divide by zero.
9	SIGKILL	This signal causes a process to terminate, but unlike some of the other signals, it cannot be trapped.
10	SIGBUS	This signal tells the process a bus error has occurred.
11	SIGSEGV	This signal is sent by the kernel to any process that tries to access any part of the system memory outside of the part that has been allocated to it. This will cause a program to end with the error "segmentation violation." This is invariably caused by an error in the program.
14	SIGALRM	This signal is used to wake up a sleeping process.

Table 2.ö *Solaris Signals (Continued)*

No.	Signal	Description
15	SIGTERM	This is the default signal sent by the `kill` command. It will cause a process to terminate unless it traps this signal.
19	SIGPWR	This is used to signal a loss of power or system restart. If the system has a soft power button, this signal will be sent to all processes when it is pressed. Most processes will probably ignore it, but `init` will respond by running the "power-fail" entry in */etc/inittab*.
23	SIGSTOP	This will cause a process to move into a suspend state. It will no longer run, but its state is preserved and it can be made to carry on from the point it was suspended by sending SIG-CONT.
25	SIGCONT	This will cause a suspended process to carry on running from the point at which it was suspended.

In practice, the signals that are usually sent using the `kill` command are 15 (the default) and 9. Signal 9 requests a process to terminate much as signal 15 does, but in this case, the process cannot ignore it (or perform any alternative action). This means that if the program needs to tidy up after itself, for example, a different signal should be sent, and signal 9 should only be used as a last resort.

The majority of the Solaris signals are only sent by the kernel if one of two situations arises:

- To let a process know that an external event has occurred that has some impact on it (for example, signal 1 is sent to a process if the processes TTY connection is closed)

- To let the process know that it has done something it shouldn't have, such as perform a divide by 0 (signal 8) or try to update a memory address that is outside of its allocated address space (signal 11)

If you wish to prove the effect any of the Solaris signals has on a process, you can check using the `kill` command:

```
hydrogen# sleep 500 &
335
hydrogen# ps
```

```
PID TTY        TIME CMD
   283 pts/1   0:01 sh
   336 pts/1   0:00 ps
   335 pts/1   0:00 sleep        .
hydrogen# kill -11 335
335 Segmentation Fault - core dumped
hydrogen# ps
PID TTY        TIME CMD
   283 pts/1   0:01 sh
   337 pts/1   0:00 ps
hydrogen#
```

Trapping Signals

It is possible to make any shell scripts you write handle signals by using the `trap` command. Using `trap` will enable your scripts to either ignore certain signals (there are some that cannot be ignored) or perform specific actions if a certain signal is received by the script. Two common uses of `trap` are to prevent users from being able to break out of a script by hitting <control c> (which will send signal 2 to the script) or to make sure that if a process is killed for any reason it clears out any temporary files it may have created.

We will look at the former first, as it is the simplest. We simply need to put the following line at the start of the script that we want to prevent users from breaking out of:

```
trap '' 2 3 15
```

The format of the `trap` command is to say what action we want to perform, inside quotes, followed by a list of the signals that will trigger that action when they are received. In the above example, there is no action, so if the script receives signals 2, 3, or 15 it will do nothing and then carry on with whatever it was doing when the signal was received. In other words, it will ignore signals 2, 3, and 15. We see the `trap` command used in this way in Chapter 5, "Shells," to prevent users from breaking out of the system profile (*/etc/profile)* while logging in.

The following code segment can be used in any script to tidy up after itself if it receives any of the common signals:

```
#!/bin/ksh
# generate a unique temporary filename
tempFile=/tmp/bigfile.$$
# delete the temp file before exiting upon receipt of
# signal 2, 3, or 15
trap "rm -f ${tempFile}; exit 1" 2 3 15
<put the rest of your code here>
```

In this example we make sure that the temporary file is deleted if the script is ever terminated by one of the signals at the end of the `trap` line. We have used the "-f" option with `rm` to ensure that we do not get an error if the temporary file has not yet been created, and we need to put the whole command in double quotes rather than single as it contains a shell variable. If we did not specifically put the exit command in the line, the script would actually carry on running after deleting the temporary file, which is not what we want.

Additional Process Management Tools

Traditionally, if we had wanted to include code to kill a specific process in a shell script, we would use a combination of grep and awk as follows:

```
pid=$(ps -ef | grep 'proc_name$' | grep -v grep | awk '{print $2}')
kill ${pid}
```

Here we use grep to find the line of the ps -ef output for process proc_name and awk to obtain the process ID of that process. If we forget to include "grep -v grep" we can have a problem because there are now two processes running that contain the string proc_name (the process itself and also the grep process) as the following example demonstrates:

```
hydrogen# ps -ef | grep "sleep"
    root   398   375  0 11:49:41 pts/4    0:00 sleep 500
    root   410   404  1 11:54:57 pts/5    0:00 grep sleep
hydrogen#
```

Solaris 8 provides us with two new utilities that save us from having to go to such lengths to either get the process ID of a process or kill a process. These are pgrep and pkill. The first of these (pgrep) will return the process ID of all processes that match the argument supplied (which is what we needed grep and awk to do before):

```
hydrogen# pgrep "sleep 500"
398
hydrogen#
```

The second utility is very similar, but instead of just listing the process ID (or IDs) that match it, will kill them:

```
hydrogen# pkill "sleep 500"
hydrogen# pgrep "sleep 500"
hydrogen#
```

The use of constructs such as "$()" and the pipe symbol are described in more detail in Chapter 5, "Shells."

Defunct Processes

Once init has started running, all processes are created by an existing process. The existing process will be the parent of the process it created (which will be called the child process). The parent should wait for the kernel to inform it that the child process has finished running (by means of signal 18, SIGCLD), and the child process can then be removed from the process table and cleaned up. However, if the parent process does not wait for the child and simply exits itself, when the child exits there is no parent to receive the signal. When this happens the exited child process becomes a defunct (or zombie) process. These tend to hang around and, although the odd one won't cause too much of a problem, if a number of processes become defunct they can use up system resources.

A defunct process will show up in a `ps` listing as follows:

```
hydrogen# ps -ef
<lines removed for clarity>
root    489    404   0                      0:00 <defunct>
hydrogen#
```

You will notice that we don't even get to see what the process was before it became defunct.

If you are running Solaris 8 or below, there is little you can do about these processes other than ignore them or reboot the system. However, Solaris 9 has introduced a new command, `preap`, that can be used to remove a zombie process. The usage is as follows:

```
hydrogen# preap PID
hydrogen#
```

It can only be used to clear defunct processes, so if you try it on a normal running process you will get the following error:

```
hydrogen# preap 422
preap: process not defunct: 422
hydrogen#
```

Switching Off

A Solaris system is normally shut down using the `shutdown` command. This can only be run by the *root* user, and it is recommended that it be run from the *root* directory. On older versions of Solaris, the command actually checked that you were in the *root* directory, but more recent versions don't bother—they simply change you to that directory. However, if you always run it from the *root* directory, you won't have problems unmounting a filesystem that you happened to be in when you ran the command.

You may find that the `shutdown` command is not in your PATH, since some companies prefer not to be in a position where it can be called accidentally. If this is the case it needs to be called using its full path name (either */etc/shutdown* or */usr/sbin/shutdown*; the two are linked). If run with no options, `shutdown` will ask if you are sure that you really want to do this before continuing. If you answer in the affirmative, a message will be broadcast (using the `wall` command) to warn all users that the system will be shut down in 60 seconds. The script will then wait 60 seconds before issuing a further warning and proceeding with the actual shutdown. If you want to shut down immediately, the following is the usual way to achieve this:

```
hydrogen#
hydrogen# /etc/shutdown -y -g0 -i0
Shutdown started. Mon Apr  8 15:34:40 CEST 2002

Changing to init state 0 - please wait
Broadcast Message from root (pts/5) on hydrogen Mon Apr  8
15:34:41...
THE SYSTEM hydrogen IS BEING SHUT DOWN NOW ! ! !
Log off now or risk your files being damaged
hydrogen#
```

The "-y" flag causes the `shutdown` program to not bother asking if you are sure you wish to do this. The "-g0" sets the grace period to 0 (so the users don't get any time to finish what they are doing). If the "-g" flag is not used the default grace period is 60 seconds. The "-i0" flag specifies that the run level should change to 0 (so if you used "-i6" instead, the system would reboot).

In the above example, the command was run from a terminal session other than the system console so we see the output shown and return to our shell prompt. Meanwhile, the shutdown continues with output directed to the system console.

An alternative version of the shutdown command is available for people more used to administering a Berkeley Software Distribution (BSD) UNIX system. This is located in the /usr/ucb directory and is simply used by running the command with a single parameter saying when you wish the shutdown to take place. For example, to shut the system down immediately we would run the command as follows:

```
hydrogen# /usr/ucb/shutdown now
Shutdown at 13:18 (in 0 minutes) [pid 450]
hydrogen#
 *** FINAL System shutdown message from root@hydrogen ***

System going down IMMEDIATELY

System shutdown time has arrived
```

Both of the above examples will end by calling `init`, which will handle the remainder of the shutdown process by calling the appropriate scripts under the *rc* directories using the parameter "stop."

Occasionally, there may be a situation where you do not want to perform a normal shutdown of the server. You may want to just get it down in the quickest possible time. There are a number of ways of doing this; the simplest is probably by using either the `halt` or `poweroff` command. Both of these will simply perform a `sync` (to save any data that was in the process of being written to disk) and then shut down the system. The only difference between the two commands is that `poweroff` will also attempt to power the server off, which will only work if the hardware supports it. Both of them support a "-n" option, which will prevent them from even doing the `sync` before shutting down.

The OpenBoot PROM

We've mentioned that when a Solaris server is switched on, we are presented with the OK prompt of the PROM, or monitor program, as it is also known. Its purpose is to enable us to:

- Identify basic system information
- Set the boot device
- Boot the system from local disk
- Boot the system across the network
- Perform hardware checks
- Modify Electrically Erasable/Programmable ROM (EEPROM) parameters
- Recover from a hung system

Since revision 2, the Solaris PROM has been called the OpenBoot PROM (OBP). The aim of this was to end up with a firmware that could probe hardware devices installed within the system and automatically download the required device driver from the device into the PROM.

The PROM actually consists of a chip on the system board that contains the following four sections:

- Power on self-test (POST) diagnostics code
- Basic device drivers
- User interface (or monitor program)
- Default parameter values

On older systems the PROM chip had to be replaced to upgrade it to a newer revision, but in newer systems (PROM revision 3 and above) the chip is permanently fixed and is, instead, flash upgradeable. Apart from the ability to flash-upgrade the entire PROM code, no changes can be made to any of the code or parameters in it. The PROM has an associated chip called the Non-Volatile RAM (NVRAM). This works in conjunction with the PROM and holds any changes you make to any of its parameters.

The NVRAM has its own battery, so it can retain data while the system is powered off. It holds the following information:

- System host ID
- Current date and time
- System Ethernet address (for the onboard Ethernet card)
- EEPROM values

The system host ID is a unique code assigned to each Sun server and is often used for licensing software. If you ever need to replace a system board, you should ensure that you move the NVRAM chip from the old board to the new one.

If any of the default parameters of the PROM are changed, the changes are stored in the EEPROM section of the NVRAM chip.

Table 2.7 summarizes the most common of the PROM commands.

Table 2.7 *PROM Commands*

Command	Description
banner	This will display system information including PROM revision, memory installed, Ethernet address, and host ID.
boot	Start loading the operating system from the default device, or the device specified as an argument.
printenv	This command will display all the PROM environment variables along with their current settings, if no parameter is supplied; otherwise, it will display the value of the parameter supplied (e.g., printenv boot-device).
setenv *variable value*	This will assign the value specified to the PROM environment variable specified.
set-defaults	Typing this will revert the PROM to the original factory configuration settings.
reset	This command will store any changed PROM variables in the NVRAM and reboot the system.
probe-scsi	This will probe for Small Computer System Interface (SCSI) devices on the onboard SCSI controller and report all devices that can be seen.
probe-scsi-all	This command also probes for SCSI devices, but will look on the Sbus SCSI controllers as well as the onboard controller. This will also highlight most SCSI-related problems (such as duplicate SCSI IDs). See Chapter 17, "Adding SCSI Devices."
probe-ide	This can be used instead of probe-scsi on IDE-based Sun servers.
help	This will display a list of all available PROM commands and display help on individual commands.
see	This command will display a breakdown of the actions performed by the OBP command supplied as an argument.

Displaying System Information

The output from the `banner` command is displayed automatically during bootup, but it can be useful to run it manually if you are not quick enough to make a note of the information you require before it moves off the screen. It is often used to find how much memory is installed in a Sun server or to check the PROM revision level:

```
ok banner
SPARCstation LX, keyboard present
ROM Rev. 2.10 96 MB memory installed, Serial #7345324
Ethernet address 8:0:20:18:c9:6c, Host ID 807014ac.
ok
```

The PROM revision level in this example shows a major version of 2 so it is not flash upgradeable.

The `Boot` Command

At the start of this chapter, we saw that we can simply type "boot" at the OK prompt to bring the system up to the run level specified as the default in the */etc/inittab* file.

Typing "boot" on its own will cause the PROM to start loading Solaris from the default boot device, which is stored in the boot-device variable. If you wish to boot from an alternative device, you can type that instead. If you wanted to boot from a CD, you could enter "boot cdrom." You could even choose to boot across the network from another Solaris server by typing "boot net." The latter example will only work if at least one other server on the network has been set up to perform a remote boot of this server. You might also have a spare disk in your system with a Solaris image on it, so if your main disk fails you can boot the system by specifying that device as the parameter to boot.

The `boot` command can also take a number of options to alter the way in which it loads Solaris. These are summarized in Table 2.8.

Table 2.8 *Boot Summary*

Command	Description
`boot`	Load Solaris from the default boot-device.
`boot` alternate-device	Load Solaris from the device alternate-device. If booting across the network (`boot net`) the local ethernet address must have been registered with the host from which we want to boot.

Table 2.8 *Boot Summary (Continued)*

Command	Description
boot -r	The "-r" option tells Solaris to perform a reconfigure boot, which will cause all devices to be reprobed and the */devices* and */dev* entries are recreated.
boot -a	This option will perform an interactive boot procedure. You will be prompted to enter the root and swap devices and the path names of various system files. Default responses are provided to each question.
boot -s	This will bring the system up to single-user mode, rather than the run level defined as the default in */etc/inittab*.
boot -v	This option to boot will cause the system to boot in verbose mode. You will be given a lot more information about what is happening as the machine comes up.

Displaying and Changing PROM Parameters

The current value of all PROM parameters can be displayed using the Open-Boot PROM printenv command:

```
ok printenv
Variable Name                 Value             Default Value
tpe-link-test?                true              true
output-device                 screen            screen
input-device                  keyboard          keyboard
sbus-probe-list   40123                 40123
keyboard-click?   false                 false
keymap
ttyb-rts-dtr-off  false                 false
ttyb-ignore-cd                true              true
ttya-rts-dtr-off  false                 false
ttya-ignore-cd                false             false
ttyb-mode         9600,8,n,1,-          9600,8,n,1,-ttya-
ttya-mode         9600,8,n,1,-          9600,8,n,1,-ttya-
fcode-debug?                  false             false
diag-file
diag-device       net                   net
boot-file
boot-device       disk                  disk
auto-boot                     true              true
scsi-initiator-id             7                 7
<lines removed for clarity>
More [<space>,<cr>,q] ? q
```

In this output segment, the first column shows the parameter name, the second column shows the current parameter value, and the third column shows the default value. This allows you to see which parameters have been changed and what the values will go to should you set them all back to their factory defaults using the set-defaults command.

To find out the current boot-device we would use the printenv command as follows:

```
ok printenv boot-device
boot-device disk
ok
```

If we wanted to change the boot-device (for example, to boot over the network) we would use the setenv command to set the new boot-device and the reset command to store the new setting:

```
ok setenv boot-device net
ok printenv boot-device
boot-device net
ok reset
ok
```

You can also display and change the value of PROM parameters from the shell by using the eeprom command:

```
hydrogen# eeprom 'auto-boot?'
auto-boot?=true
hydrogen# eeprom 'auto-boot?=false'
hydrogen# eeprom | grep auto
auto-boot?=false
hydrogen#
```

When you change parameters using eeprom, you don't need to issue any further commands to save the value. The new value you have assigned will remain, even across reboots, until you next change it.

The "auto-boot?" parameter is an example of a Boolean PROM parameter; it can only be set to true or false. Boolean parameters are identifiable by the fact that they all end in a question mark character (?). The effect of setting the "auto-boot?" parameter to false is that when the server is next switched on or rebooted it will remain at the OpenBoot PROM OK prompt rather than automatically starting to boot from the default boot-device. It can be useful to do this if your server is having a problem causing it to crash and you want the system to remain at the OpenBoot PROM following a crash to attempt to gather some diagnostic information. By default a server will attempt to reload the operating system following a system crash. You may have noted that we quoted the above example. This was to hide the question mark character from the shell.

Getting to the OpenBoot PROM

It is also possible to get to the PROM while Solaris is running by pressing the <STOP> and letter <A> keys together on the system console (on older console keyboards the <STOP> key is marked as <L1>). If you arrive at the PROM this way, then you can return immediately to the state Solaris was in by typing the command "go." If you wish to reboot the system at this point, it is recommended that you first flush the disk buffers by typing "sync." If you wish to enter any diagnostic commands after pressing <STOP-A> while Solaris was running, you should first enter the reset command, which will clear any values left in the registers and buffers.

The <STOP> key can also be used in conjunction with a couple of other keys to help if the system appears to hang or get into difficulty. It should be noted that these can help resolve certain system problems, but are definitely not for everyday use. Table 2.9 summarizes the effect of the three available key combinations.

Table 2.9 *<STOP> Key Sequences*

Command	Description
<STOP-A>	If this key sequence is pressed during bootup or at any time while Solaris is running, you will be taken to the PROM OK prompt. Typing "go" will cause the system to resume from the point it was at when you pressed <STOP-A>.
<STOP-D>	This sequence will cause the NVRAM to switch to diagnostics mode and run a more extensive version of the power on a start-up test than is normally performed.
<STOP-N>	It is possible for a Solaris system to fail to boot due to incorrect NVRAM settings. If you suspect one of your systems is failing to boot for this reason, pressing STOP-N> while the power is turned on will set all the NVRAM parameters back to their default values.

In summary, the OpenBoot PROM provides a number of useful features that enable you to alter the configuration of many system attributes and also perform some useful diagnostics.

3

USER ADMINISTRATION

Manual Pages

auth_attr (4)
exec_attr (4)
group (4)
groupadd (1M)
groupdel (1M)
groupmod (1M)
grpck (1M)
login (1)
newgrp (1)
passmgmt (1M)
passwd (4)
pfexec (1)
policy.conf (4)
prof_attr (4)
pwck (1M)
pwconv (1M)
roleadd (1M)
roledel (1M)
rolemod (1M)
shadow (4)
useradd (1M)

Manual Pages *(Continued)*

user_attr (4)
userdel (1M)
usermod (1M)
vipw (1B)

Files Affected

User's home directory location
/etc/datemsk
/etc/default/passwd
/etc/exec_attr
~/.cshrc
~/.login
~/.logout
/etc/group
/etc/opasswd
/etc/oshadow
/etc/passwd
/etc/prof_attr
/etc/ptmp
/etc/security/auth_attr
/etc/security/exec_attr
/etc/security/prof_attr
/etc/shadow
/etc/user_attr
/usr/sadm/defadduser

Objectives

We briefly looked at users in Chapter 1, "The System Administrator's Role." Here, we'll expand on that to examine why they are required, and look at some of the ways in which they can be created—we'll also point out some commonly used shortcuts along the way!

As we work through the chapter, we'll decide upon a set of standards for user creation and then move on to create various users. After that, we'll examine RBAC and create a custom script for adding users.

What Are Users?

Anyone trying to access a UNIX system requires the correct login information, which is allocated by a system administrator. At login time, you are prompted to enter your login name, followed by your password; if this is correct, you will be allowed on the system. This process is carried out for a number of reasons, including the following:

- It ensures that the system remains secure by only allowing users that know a login name and corresponding password to access the system.
- It allows the administrator to determine who is logged on at any particular time and also how much time and/or space they are using.
- It allows users to be gathered together into groups and assigned permissions as required.

While we often think of a user as being an actual person, this doesn't have to be the case. For example, users are often defined to enable a task to be easily carried out, such as the *shutdown* user that can be used to power down the machine.

What Are Groups?

The system uses a number of mechanisms to make sure that users' files are protected from everyone else. Gathering related users together into "groups" is one of these mechanisms. This allows users to easily share any common resources, and it also provides an opportunity to control file access on a group basis. We'll look at user and group permissions in more detail in Chapter 4, "Permissions and All That."

To ensure this mechanism works, each user *must* be a member of at least one group, which is known as the user's primary group. In addition, users can also be members of a number of other groups, known as their secondary groups.

Using secondary groups provides a degree of flexibility for the user. For example, assume your primary group is set to *engineering* and you require access to files owned by the *sales* and *marketing* groups. Setting your secondary group membership to *sales* and *marketing* would quickly solve this problem. We'll look at this in more detail in "Primary and Secondary Groups" on page 46.

UIDs and GIDs

User names and group names are ideal for us to work with, but are less useful to the system—it prefers to deal in numbers. For this reason, when users are created they are allocated an identity number, known as a UID (User Identifier). The system uses this to manage users, only displaying their names for our convenience. Similarly, each group is allocated a GID (Group Identifier), which is used in the same manner by the system.

Each user should have a unique UID. However, it's possible to share one and there are valid reasons for doing so, as we explained for UID 0 in Chapter 1.

All the information used to identify a user is stored within a series of files: the password file, the shadow file, and the group file. Let's look at these now before we start to add any users.

Password File

The user's password information is located in a file named *letc/passwd*. This is an ASCII file and is readable by everyone, which isn't a problem because all the security information is located elsewhere (as we will see later). For the moment, we'll ignore the default entries that are in the file—suffice it to say that they are required by the system and their use will be explained as we come across them.

Let's have a look at what the password file contains:

```
hydrogen# cat /etc/passwd
root:x:0:1:Super-User:/:/sbin/sh
daemon:x:1:1::/:
bin:x:2:2::/usr/bin:
sys:x:3:3::/:/bin/ksh
adm:x:4:4:Admin:/var/adm:
lp:x:71:8:Line Printer Admin:/usr/spool/lp:
smtp:x:0:0:Mail Daemon User:/:
uucp:x:5:5:uucp Admin:/usr/lib/uucp:
nuucp:x:9:9:uucp Admin:/var/spool/uucppublic:/usr/lib/uucp/uucico
listen:x:37:4:Network Admin:/usr/net/nls:
nobody:x:60001:60001:Nobody:/:
noaccess:x:60002:60002:No Access User:/:
nobody4:x:65534:65534:SunOS 4.x Nobody:/:
hydrogen#
```

We can see from this example that each entry consists of the following seven fields, each separated by a colon (:), some of which may be blank.

Field 1: Login Name

A user must have a name that he or she will use to access the system. This name is chosen and added to the system files by the system administrator. The restrictions on this name are that:

- It must be unique.

- It should contain between two and eight characters, the first being a letter. It can actually be longer, but programs such as pwck (see "Checking the Files" on page 66) will report more than eight as an error. It is often an abbreviation of the user's full name; for example, given name and surname or first initial and surname.

- This field cannot be empty.

Field 2: Password

This originally contained the encrypted password on earlier versions of the operating system. Nowadays, however, it may also contain information that is used in conjunction with the shadow file, which now means the following types of entries are valid:

- Nothing; it may be an empty field.
- An "x" to indicate to other programs that the password is located elsewhere (see "Shadow File" on page 43).
- An encrypted password. This is the "original" format, and may be there for a number of reasons, such as the password has been manually inserted, or the file is from an old machine. The section on `pwconf` shows how this can be altered to the current format.

Field 3: User ID Number

This field contains the UID, which we've already mentioned should be unique. However, multiple login names assigned to a common UID can be used as a way of tracking specific users, as we'll show later with the *powerdown* user. In summary, this field's restrictions are as follows:

- The assigned UID should be between 0 and 60,000 for compatibility, but note that some UID numbers are special. For example, in Chapter 1 we showed that a UID number of 0 provides super-user privileges.
- UIDs between 0 and 99 are reserved for future use, so a good base to start would be 100.
- This field must have a value.

Field 4: Group ID Number

This contains the GID number of the user's primary group; we'll discuss these in more detail a little later. Some default groups are predefined on the system, such as *staff*, *operator*, and *other*. The field restrictions are as follows:

- Any number of users can be part of a specific group.
- This field should correspond to an entry in the group file.
- It must have a value—we stated earlier that a user must be a member of at least one group.
- It doesn't have to be unique.

Field 5: Comment Field

This field is commonly termed the "gecos" field (it used to contain information used by the system that ran the "General Electric Comprehensive Operating System") and can contain a comment string of some sort. It usually contains the user's full name or some similar relevant piece of information. This is because a number of other programs will read and use the contents of this field; for example, `mail` in its "From:" line and `finger` in its "In Real Life" line. This field can also contain an "&," which means "use the login name." For example, if an entry looked like the one shown below:

```
demo::100:100:The users name is &:/home/demo:/bin/ksh
```

—then the `finger` command would contain "The users name is demo" in its output.

This field can be empty, in which case any program that tries to use this field will simply output null values.

Field 6: The Home Directory

Every time the user logs on to the system, various start-up files are read from the home directory (see Chapter 5, "Shells"), after which the user is placed within the filesystem at this location. It is here that users are usually free to create files and directories and store any work. The usual method of creating home directories is to place all the users under a general location, such as */export/home* or */home*.

- The field must not be empty.
- The user should have permission to access the directory specified (see Chapter 4, "Permissions and All That").

Field 7: The Program to Run on Login

When users log on to the system, the program that is specified in this field is started on their behalf and continues to run until they logout or exit the program. Normally the program will be a shell (see Chapter 5, "Shells"), but can be any system program. For example, someone who is shutting down the system might run a `shutdown` program.

- This field can be empty, in which case the system will run the Bourne Shell (`/bin/sh`).

Shadow File

Like the password file, the shadow file is an ASCII file with the fields separated by a colon (:). It is named /etc/shadow and is used to store security-related details, such as encrypted passwords and password aging information. For this reason, it is designed not to be readable by the general public.

The shadow file, as distributed, will look similar to that shown here:

```
hydrogen# cat /etc/shadow
root:<encrypted root password>:6445::::::
daemon:NP:6445::::::
bin:NP:6445::::::
sys:NP:6445::::::
adm:NP:6445::::::
lp:NP:6445::::::
smtp:NP:6445::::::
uucp:NP:6445::::::
nuucp:NP:6445::::::
listen:*LK*:::::::
nobody:NP:6445::::::
noaccess:NP:6445::::::
nobody4:NP:6445::::::
hydrogen#
```

This example shows that for every entry in the password file, there should be a corresponding entry in the shadow file. See the "Checking the Files" section on page 66 for examples of commands that can be used to keep the files up-to-date. The field entries are as follows.

Field 1: Login Name

This field is for the user's login name; it matches the corresponding name in the password file. Matching on the name, rather than the UID, is required for any super-user type accounts. This is because they all share the same UID of 0 and therefore need some mechanism to allow them all to login as individual accounts. For example, we could create a user named *powerdown* by adding something similar to the following entry to /etc/passwd:

```
powerdown:x:0:1:/export/home/powerdown:/usr/sbin/halt
```

This user has a UID of 0, but will use a different password to the main *root* account, thereby providing the user with the ability to shut the machine down only.

Field 2: Encrypted Password

It is recommended that every user have a password to ensure that only authorized users can access the system. Note that giving users passwords does not deny anyone else from accessing their files; the system permissions can be easily altered so that access can be either granted or denied to any other user or group of users. If this field is empty, the user will not need a password to login, although passwords can be enforced by configuring a file named */etc/default/login*.

The encrypted password will either be a 13-character string, "NP" to indicate no password, or "*LK*" to indicate the account is locked—in fact, any number of characters less than 13 will lock the account.

Field 3: Password Change Date

This field contains the date when the password was last changed. It is shown as the number of days from January 1, 1970, or "0" if the user has been forced to change it at the next login.

Field 4: Minimum Change Days

This field contains the minimum number of days that must pass before the user is allowed to change his or her password again.

Field 5: Maximum Valid Days

This field contains the maximum number of days users can use the password before they are forced to change it.

Field 6: Number of Warning Days

This field contains the number of days before the password expires that the system will start to warn the user.

Field 7: Number of Inactive Days

This field contains the number of days of inactivity the user is allowed.

Field 8: Expiry Date

This field contains the date the account will expire. It is shown as the number of days from January 1, 1970.

Field 9: Not Used

This field is reserved for future use, so for now it should be empty.

Group File

This file is named */etc/group* and is similar to the password and shadow files; in other words, it is an ASCII file consisting of colon-separated strings. It contains definitions for all the groups that are used on the system and, by default, looks like the one shown here:

```
hydrogen# cat /etc/group
root::0:root
other::1:
bin::2:root,bin,daemon
sys::3:root,bin,sys,adm
adm::4:root,adm,daemon
uucp::5:root,uucp
mail::6:root
tty::7:root,tty,adm
lp::8:root,lp,adm
nuucp::9:root,nuucp
staff::10:
daemon::12:root,daemon
sysadmin::14:
nobody::60001:
noaccess::60002:
nogroup::65534:
hydrogen#
```

The field entries are as follows.

Field 1: Group Name

This is the actual group name.

Field 2: Group Password

This field is largely historical and now rarely used.

- It can be empty.
- It can contain an invalid encrypted password, such as an "*."
- It can contain a valid encrypted password (13 characters).

Unfortunately, there isn't any way to get a password in here other than manually inserting an already encrypted password. The effects of this field vary depending upon whether you are a member of the group or not. Let's leave group passwords for now and revisit them in the following section, "Primary and Secondary Groups."

Field 3: Group Identity Number

Similar to the UID, the GID is used to store the numerical ID of a group. The value should be less than 60,000 for compatibility with other systems.

Field 4: Group User List

This contains a comma-separated list of users who are allowed to be in this group. It is used in conjunction with newgrp, which we'll look at in the following section.

Primary and Secondary Groups

Now, let's try and clear up some of the confusion about how the password file relates to the group file, and see where primary and secondary groups come into the picture. We'll do this using the example users and groups listed in Table 3.1. This shows that *prim_user* and *sec_user* only have a primary group definition, while the user named *both_user* is also a member of a secondary group as well.

Table 3.1 *User Details*

User Name (UID)	Primary Group (GID)	Secondary Group (GID)
prim_user (200)	*prim* (500)	—
sec_user (201)	*sec* (501)	—
both_user (202)	*prim* (500)	*sec* (501)

We've already seen that a user's primary group is defined by that user's entry in */etc/passwd*, and that any secondary groups the user is also a member of are defined in */etc/group*. For the example users, we'll create the following password and group entries:

```
hydrogen# more /etc/passwd
<lines removed for clarity>
prim_user::200:500::/export/home/prim_user:/bin/ksh
sec_user::201:501::/export/home/sec_user:/bin/ksh
both_user::202:500::/export/home/both_user:/bin/ksh
hydrogen#

hydrogen# more /etc/group
<lines removed for clarity>
prim::500:
sec:MzQvs7gYIUVVQ:501:both_user
hydrogen#
```

We can see from the group file that the one named *prim* isn't used by anyone as a secondary group. However, the group named *sec* is the secondary group for the user named *both_user*; it also has a password set. Now let's su to *prim_user*, create a file, and check what the ownerships are on it:

```
hydrogen# su - prim_user
hydrogen$ touch file1
hydrogen$ ls -l
total 6
-rw-r--r--   1 prim_user prim          0 Feb 26 10:44 file1
hydrogen$ exit
hydrogen#
```

As expected, *file1* is owned by the user *prim_user,* and its group ownership is set to its primary group, *prim.* Now let's do the same for *sec_user*:

```
hydrogen# su - sec_user
hydrogen$ touch file1
hydrogen$ ls -l
total 6
-rw-r--r--   1 sec_user  sec           0 Feb 26 10:46 file2
hydrogen$ exit
hydrogen#
```

Again, the file has the correct ownerships, as expected. Now, let's try this with *both_user*. First we'll create a file that will take the user's primary group details. This is the user's default group so it will be set correctly when we log in as *both_user*.

```
hydrogen# su - both_user
hydrogen$ touch file3
hydrogen$ ls -l
total 6
-rw-r--r--   1 both_user  prim         0 Feb 26 10:46 file3
hydrogen$
```

Good. This also works exactly as expected; the file has the correct ownerships. However, we also know that *both_user* is a member of a secondary group. If we wish to create files owned by members of that group, we can use the newgrp command to switch to it before creating the file—just as we would su to a user if we wanted to carry out any tasks as someone else. Let's do that now:

```
hydrogen$ newgrp sec
hydrogen$ touch file4
hydrogen$ ls -l
total 6
-rw-r--r--   1 both_user  prim         0 Feb 26 10:46 file3
-rw-r--r--   1 both_user  sec          0 Feb 26 10:47 file4
hydrogen$ exit
hydrogen#
```

This shows that a different group owns each file, depending on which group we had set as the primary at the time. Notice that *both_user* wasn't prompted for a password when it ran `newgrp`. The reason for this is that *both_user* is a member of the *sec* group.

Now let's see what happens when a user who isn't a member of that group tries to run the same command:

```
hydrogen# su - prim_user
$ ls -l
total 6
-rw-r--r--    1 prim_user prim         0 Feb 26 10:44 file1
hydrogen$ newgrp sec
newgrp: Password
<enter group password>
hydrogen$ touch file2
hydrogen$ ls -l
total 6
-rw-r--r--    1 prim_user prim         0 Feb 26 10:44 file1
-rw-r--r--    1 prim_user sec          0 Feb 26 10:47 file2
hydrogen$ exit
hydrogen#
```

This time *prim_user* was prompted for the group password. Assuming we give the correct password, our primary group will be set to the new one (*sec*) and any files we create will have that group ownership.

The Implementation

Now we're ready to move on and add some users to our system. We've chosen to add the four listed in Table 3.2.

Table 3.2 *User Details*

Real Name	Login Name	UID	Group	GID
Test User	*testuser*	500	*test*	100
System Administrator	*sysadmin*	1000	*sysadmin*	14
Mike Smith	*msmith*	1001	*staff*	10
John Green	*jgreen*	1002	*staff*	10

The reasons for selecting these users are as follows:

- **Test User**: Creating this user allows us to test a variety of things, such as login scripts and checking initialization files, safe in the knowledge that we won't damage the running system. For this reason, test users will also be maintained along with all the standard users, although they will be placed in their own group.

- **System Administrator**: One of our important users. These users will be allowed to carry out some system administration tasks. We'll use RBAC later in the chapter to create and control them. This means that instead of logging in as *root* and having access to any command, we'll just let them have access to the commands we want them to run. This will (hopefully!) ensure that users are less likely to accidentally run some command with disastrous affects.

- **Mike Smith/John Green**: Two of our genuine users—we'll use these to show examples of `useradd` and our custom script later.

Our "Company Standards"

One of the first steps we need to take is to produce a set of standards that will be used throughout the company/department whenever we wish to add users. For example, should the login names be their first names only (not a good idea as we would soon run out of logins), or should we have the first initial followed by the next three characters of the surname? In a similar way, every other parameter is best decided upon before any users are added; otherwise, the system can become awkward to administer very quickly.

The following is a list of standards that we have decided to use for all the users we add:

- The login names will be based on a combination of the user's surname and first initial. We will limit them to eight characters, leaving up to seven characters for the surname.

- UIDs will be allocated sequentially. Having a certain number of UIDs available for each department, say 1,000 for sales, 2,000 for engineering, and so on, could be used to allocate UIDs, but this is really why the group file is there. Using that mechanism can also make it awkward to administer the UIDs as users are added and deleted later.

- We will split users into groups by department or function; for example, some groups we will implement are *sales*, *software*, and *marketing*. Doing this will allow us to restrict access to documents within each specific batch of users as required.

- All users will use the Korn Shell (see Chapter 5, "Shells"). We will set up some global start-up files to easily maintain them by linking users to this global file where possible.

- All users' home directories will be located in */export/home*.

- All users will be created with a default password of "changeme" and will be forced to change it at first login.
- Password aging will be used to force users to change their password at predefined intervals, this being 60 days.
- The system will warn users five days before the password expires that it requires changing.

Now let's start to create the users. There are various ways that this can be done—some easier than others. The first, and recommended way is by using a command named useradd or one of its variants (groupadd, roleadd, and so forth). These are the command line equivalents of the GUI admintool and are the methods we'll look at for the majority of users. They will perform all the tasks necessary to create the user, including things like making sure that duplicate UIDs aren't used.

A second method is to update all the relevant system files manually. This is a common task carried out by many system administrators, but the responsibility of getting things correct also rests with them—the system cannot check that everything has been carried out correctly.

A third method is to create a custom script that will enable us to "automate" the tasks that we need to perform to add the users and apply company-specific settings at the same time. Again, this is a common way to add users, often written as shell scripts, Perl scripts, or C programs. We'll actually create a simple example, based on useradd, at the end of this chapter.

Adding a Test User
with Groupadd and Useradd

To demonstrate the use of useradd, we'll create the test user and associated group first. First let's create the group as follows:

```
hydrogen# groupadd -g 100 test
hydrogen#
```

Now check that the group has been successfully added to the *etc/group* file:

```
hydrogen# grep test /etc/group
test::100:
hydrogen#
```

Good. We've defined the new group, so we can go ahead and create the test user:

```
hydrogen# useradd -c "Test User" -d /export/home/testuser -g
test -m -k /etc/skel -u 500 -s /bin/ksh testuser
6 blocks
hydrogen#
```

If we look at the entry that has been created in *letc/passwd*, we can see there is an "x" in the password field. This indicates there is a corresponding shadow entry, as we mentioned earlier:

```
hydrogen# grep testuser /etc/passwd
testuser:x:500:100:Test User:/export/home/testuser:/bin/ksh
hydrogen#
```

Looking at the *letc/shadow* entry, we can see the password is set to the locked string "*LK*" to show the account is locked. The account is automatically locked after it has been created with useradd:

```
hydrogen# grep testuser /etc/shadow
testuser:*LK*:::::::
hydrogen#
```

We could also have checked the password state by running the passwd command. This will display the status of the account and any aging details if they've been set. In this case it again confirms the password is locked:

```
hydrogen# passwd -s testuser
testuser  LK
hydrogen#
```

Setting the Password

We need to unlock the account before the user can login, so we will do that by allocating a password to the user using the passwd command.

```
hydrogen# passwd testuser
New password: <enter user's password>
Re-enter new password: <enter user's password>
passwd (SYSTEM): passwd successfully changed for testuser
hydrogen#
```

If we again check the *shadow* file, we can see that the user now has a valid password entry and can log in to the account correctly. Notice the password is encrypted and field 3 displays when this was altered. This is shown as the number of days since January 1, 1970.

```
hydrogen# grep testuser /etc/shadow
testuser:ba7btwLghQU86:10912::::::
hydrogen#
```

As seen here, passwd will show us that the account has a valid password assigned:

```
hydrogen# passwd -s testuser
testuser  PS
hydrogen#
```

Now, let's reset it to our standards for the company, which are five days warning and 60 days valid:

```
hydrogen# passwd -f -w 5 -x 60 testuser
hydrogen#
```

Looking at the *shadow* file, we can see the settings have been applied. Fields 3 and 4 are both set to "0" to force users to change their passwords at the next login.

```
hydrogen# grep testuser /etc/shadow
testuser:ba7btwLghQU86:0:0:60:5:::
hydrogen#
```

Once more, if we check this via passwd, it will also show the following aging details:

```
hydrogen# passwd -s testuser
testuser  PS    00/00/00    0   60   5
hydrogen#
```

Testing the Account

At this point, we can confirm that the user has been set up correctly by switching to that person's account. To do this, we'll run the following command and should see that the system offer us the user's default prompt:

```
hydrogen# su - testuser
hydrogen$
```

The "-" option will force su to reset the new environment to that of *testuser*. Once we have logged in and proven the account is OK, we can exit back to the *root* shell:

```
hydrogen$ exit
hydrogen#
```

Modifying with Usermod

Usermod allows us to modify the user's definition. As an example, we'll modify *testuser* so that it is included in additional groups such as *sys* and *adm*. First, let's confirm that *testuser* is only in the one group at present. We can do this by using grep to search the */etc/group* file as we have shown previously, or by running a command named groups, as shown below:

```
hydrogen# groups testuser
test
hydrogen#
```

Now that we know that *testuser* is only in the *test* group, let's modify its settings:

```
hydrogen# usermod -G sys,adm testuser
6 blocks
hydrogen#
```

Checking the *group* file shows the details have been added correctly:

```
hydrogen# grep testuser /etc/group
sys::3:root,bin,sys,adm,testuser
adm::4:root,bin,sys,adm,testuser
hydrogen#
```

Similarly, if we run `groups`, it provides us with a similar confirmation:

```
hydrogen# groups testuser
test adm sys
hydrogen#
```

Removing the User

The account has now been created and we have finished with it for the moment, so we want to ensure the system is secure by making sure no one is allowed access to it. We could achieve this by either deleting or locking the account. Deleting it would remove it from the system and mean that we cannot use it again for testing and so forth, while locking the account allows us to simply lock or unlock it at will. If we wished to delete it, we could run the `userdel` command as shown below:

```
hydrogen# userdel -r testuser
hydrogen#
```

Rather than remove the account, let's retain it for the moment, as this will allow us to use it to test similar user tasks. Therefore, we'll lock the account to ensure that it is secure:

```
hydrogen# passwd -l testuser
hydrogen#
```

Now we can check that the account has been locked; `passwd` will provide this information for us and also show the date the password was altered:

```
hydrogen# passwd -s testuser
testuser  LK    12/25/99    0  60   5
hydrogen#
```

Useradd Defaults

When adding users with `useradd`, it's possible to configure some settings that can be used as defaults. Let's take a look at these to see what they are currently set to:

```
hydrogen# useradd -D
group=other,1  basedir=/home  skel=/etc/skel
shell=/bin/sh  inactive=0  expire=
hydrogen#
```

This shows that we need to alter a couple of the values to fall in line with our standards—these being the basedir, group, and shell values. The first problem we can see is that `useradd` will not allow us to change the default shell. We'll look at this problem in a minute. First, let's set the default group to be *staff,* and the basedir directory to be */export/home*:

```
hydrogen# useradd -D -g 10 -b /export/home
group=staff,10  basedir=/export/home  skel=/etc/skel
shell=/bin/sh  inactive=0  expire=
hydrogen#
```

Good. The details have been altered correctly. Once the default values are changed, they are written away to a file named */usr/sadm/defadduser*. This doesn't exist by default; it's created the first time this command is run. If we look at the file we'll find it now contains the following details:

```
hydrogen# cat /usr/sadm/defadduser
#  Default values for useradd. Changed Wed Nov 17 12:13:00 1999
defgroup=10
defgname=staff
defparent=/export/home
defskel=/etc/skel
defshell=/bin/sh
definact=0
defexpire=
hydrogen#
```

This shows the new settings, along with the current default shell value. *Defadduser* is simply a text file, read by `useradd`, so let's manually alter the defshell variable and set it's value to */bin/ksh*:

```
hydrogen#
<edit /usr/sadm/defadduser and alter defshell=/bin/sh
   to defshell=/bin/ksh>
hydrogen# grep defshell /usr/sadm/defadduser
defshell=/bin/sh
hydrogen#
```

If we again run `useradd` to display the current default settings, we can see that the shell has been altered correctly:

```
hydrogen# useradd -D
group=staff,10  basedir=/export/home  skel=/etc/skel
shell=/bin/ksh  inactive=0  expire=
hydrogen#
```

Now that we've got the correct default values set, we can easily create users by specifying the minimum amount of information, such as that shown below:

```
hydrogen# useradd -c "Test User" -m -u 500 testuser
6 blocks
hydrogen#
```

Manually Updating the System Files

We mentioned at the beginning of this chapter that we would also show some shortcuts for adding users. We'll do that here, but before we do, we need to be aware that using these methods can be unsafe. The reason for this is that using them removes the safety checks built into programs such as useradd. For example, these programs maintain a backup copy of the major files and also perform some error checking, such as making sure the user doesn't already exist and that a unique UID is used.

However, for performing quick changes and things such as *root* password recovery, the manual method is ideal, and sometimes a necessity.

Let's run through the steps here by creating one of our "standard" users, *msmith*, a member of the *staff* group. We'll begin by checking the group file to ensure the *staff* group is there (it should be as it's a default group):

```
hydrogen# grep staff /etc/group
staff::10:
hydrogen#
```

Next, we'll create an entry for the user in */etc/passwd* by editing it with our favorite editor. After the changes have been made it will look like the following:

```
hydrogen# grep msmith /etc/passwd
msmith:x:1001:10:Mike Smith:/export/home/msmith:/bin/ksh
hydrogen#
```

Now, we'll create the corresponding entry in */etc/shadow*. This should contain the entry shown below after it has been altered:

```
hydrogen# grep msmith /etc/shadow
msmith:*LK*:0:0:60:5:::
hydrogen#
```

Here we have added the correct line, locked the account, and set the values for the expiration and warning days. Now let's create the user's home directory:

```
hydrogen# mkdir -p /export/home/msmith
hydrogen#
```

Solaris supplies a series of set-up files that are available for users. These are located in */etc/skel* and named *local.profile*, *local.cshrc*, and *local.login*— these being for the Korn, Bourne, and C Shells. Useradd will copy the correct file into the user's home directory when it is created (renaming it in the process), but we need to do that manually here. We'll do that now for the particular shell that is being used, which in this case is the *local.profile* for the Korn Shell (see Chapter 5, "Shells"):

```
hydrogen# cp /etc/skel/local.profile /export/home/msmith/.profile
hydrogen#
```

Now that we have all the basic files in place, we need to ensure that *msmith* can work with them and that he has permission to create files within his home directory. Let's change the ownership of it now, along with any files beneath it:

```
hydrogen# chown -R msmith:staff /export/home/msmith
hydrogen#
```

If we now list the newly created directory, we should see something similar to that shown below:

```
hydrogen# ls -ld /export/home/msmith
drwxr-xr-x  2 msmith  staff 512 Oct 22 1999 /export/home/msmith
hydrogen#
```

Now that the user has a valid home directory, we can set the password, which we'll do as follows. This will allow him to log in, but because we've also forced him to change his password at login time (fields 3 and 4 are set to "0"), he will be prompted to enter a new one:

```
hydrogen# passwd msmith
New password: <enter user's password>
Re-enter new password: <enter user's password>
passwd (SYSTEM): passwd successfully changed for msmith
hydrogen#
```

Good. Everything is in place; so let's test the account by trying to login as the user:

```
hydrogen# su - msmith
hydrogen$ pwd
hydrogen$ /export/home/msmith
hydrogen$ exit
hydrogen#
```

Good. *Msmith* has now been added to the system. This example shows that manually adding users is not a difficult task to perform—we just need to be careful and apply a few checks along the way.

Real and Effective IDs

We've come across the su command in a number of places now. In Chapter 1, it was to switch from a "normal" user to *root*, and in this chapter to switch from *root* to a "normal" user. Before we move on, let's take a brief look at some of the changes that occur when we run this command.

We already know that all users have a UID and GID associated with them—we've set these in the password file and can confirm what these are by running the id command, as shown below:

```
hydrogen# id
uid=0(root) gid=1(other)
hydrogen#
```

When you switch to another user, you need to inherit the UID and GID of the new user; otherwise, you won't be able to access the same files as that user. However, the system still needs to retain your original UID and GID so that it can reset correctly when you exit back to yourself. It accomplishes this by assigning you an "effective" UID and GID, known as your EUID and EGID, respectively.

To show this, let's run the id command again, but this time we'll switch to *testuser* first:

```
hydrogen# su - testuser
hydrogen$ id
uid=500(testuser) gid=100(test)
hydrogen$
```

Just as we expected—the system now believes that we are *testuser*. However, we can still determine our original values using a number of commands, including who, as shown below:

```
hydrogen$ id
uid=500(testuser) gid=100(test)
hydrogen$ who am i
root      console    Feb 16 13:34
hydrogen$
```

Using RBAC

Up to this point, we've managed to create some "normal" users, in addition to our existing super-user (*root*). The problem we now find is that the normal users have little power, while *root* has absolute power—we don't have anything in between! Unfortunately, this is the way UNIX has worked for quite some time.

Now, however, we can use a package known as RBAC (Role Based Access Control), which we briefly described in Chapter 1, to provide the functionality we want. Using RBAC allows us to accurately control which tasks users can perform and, therefore, reduce the risk of anyone accidentally destroying the system.

Therefore, in this section, we'll try to balance the power a little by creating a user that possesses some of *root*'s capabilities. The user we've chosen for this is the system administrator, which was listed earlier in Table 3.2.

How It Works

The steps we'll follow to configure RBAC are very similar to the ones we've already carried out for adding users, but in this case we're simply adding a role that a user will later assume. The commands used to do this are named roleadd, rolemod, and roledel and are almost identical to those used to administer the normal users—useradd, usermod, and userdel; in fact, the newer role* commands are linked to the older user* ones.

RBAC uses a set of components known as authorizations, profiles, and roles for its implementation. Each of these has an associated database, which is actually a flat ASCII text file.

Authorizations

First, let's look at authorizations. These are allocated to users (or roles) to give them the right to carry out a specific task, such as changing user passwords. Each authorization has a name associated with it, which is used as its reference and is written in a dotted notation that represents a hierarchy of privileges.

For example, if you have an authorization of *solaris.admin.usermgr.**, you will be allowed to carry out most tasks associated with administering users, whereas if you have *solaris.admin.usermgr.read*, you will only be allowed to view user details.

The authorizations that can be assigned are defined in a file named */etc/security/auth_attr*. If we look at this we'll see that it contains the following type of information:

```
hydrogen# more /etc/security/auth_attr
<lines removed for clarity>
solaris.admin.usermgr.:::User Accounts::
solaris.admin.usermgr.write:::Manage Users::
   help=AuthUsermgrWrite.html
solaris.admin.usermgr.read:::View Users and
Roles::help=AuthUsermgrRead.html
solaris.admin.usermgr.pswd:::Change Password::
   help=AuthUserMgrPswd.html
solaris.admin.logsvc.:::Log Viewer::
<lines removed for clarity>
```

Here we can see that like many administrative files, *auth_attr* is split into fields using colon-separated strings. The field we are really interested in here is the first one, which is the name of the authorization itself and is the information we'll use later.

Table 3.3 provides a guide to the database fields, using one of the entries from the file extract above as an example. Be aware that presently these authorizations are fixed and cannot be extended or altered in any way.

Table 3.3 *Authorization Database Details*

Field	Description
solaris.admin.usermgr.write	The authorization name
(empty)	Reserved for future use
(empty)	Reserved for future use
Manage Users	Short descriptive text
(empty)	Long descriptive text
help= AuthUsermgrWrite.html	The attributes for this authorization

Profiles

Once we have a list of authorizations, we can create a profile. Essentially, profiles allow us to group together a number of authorizations by assigning them a name. This information is split over two locations: the profile database and the exec database.

Profile Database

The available profiles are located in */etc/security/prof_attr*. Again, this is a colon-separated file, an example of which is shown below:

```
hydrogen# more /etc/security/prof_attr
<lines removed for clarity>
Primary Administrator:::Can perform all administrative
    tasks:auths=solaris.*,solaris.grant;help=RtPriAdmin.html
System Administrator:::Can perform most non-security adminis-
    trative tasks:profiles=Audit Review,Printer Management,Cron
    Management,Device Management,File System Management,Mail
    Management,Maintenance and Repair,Media Backup,Media
    Restore,Name Service Management,Network Management,Object
    Access Management,Process Management,Software Installa-
    tion,User Management,All;help=RtSysAdmin.html
Operator:::Can perform simple administrative tasks:pro-
    files=Printer Management,Media Backup,All;help=RtOpera-
    tor.html
<lines removed for clarity>
```

Let's take a look at one of the entries to see what information the fields contain. Table 3.4 uses the "Operator" entry above to show this information.

Table 3.4 *Profile Database Details*

Field	Description
Operator	The profile name
(empty)	Reserved for future use
(empty)	Reserved for future use
Can perform simple administrative tasks	Long descriptive text
profiles=Printer Management,Media Backup,All; help=RtOperator.html	The security attributes of the profile

This shows that single authorizations, a hierarchy of authorizations, or another profile can be included in the security attributes of a profile. For example, let's assume we have the following profile:

```
Dummy Profile:::This is a dummy profile:\
auths=solaris.admin.usermgr.read,\
        solaris.admin.usermgr.write
```

This only allows the user to read and manage user accounts, but not to change any passwords, as this requires the *solaris.admin.usermgr.pwsd* authorization. However, if we wanted to let this role carry out any *usermgr* tasks, we could simply assign the higher-level authorization, as shown below:

```
Dummy Profile:::This is a dummy profile:\
auths=solaris.admin.usermgr.*
```

Exec Database

This file, named */etc/security/exec_attr*, is used to control the security attributes for commands used within a profile. It defines an "object identifier," which is the path name of the command to be run. This may include the "*" metacharacter, to specify more than one file, such as */usr/sbin/*. Each entry also includes the account details that may be set when the command is run, such as the UID, GID, EUID, and EGID.

Let's have a look at an example of this file now:

```
hydrogen# cat /etc/security/exec_attr
Primary Administrator:suser:cmd:::*:uid=0;gid=0
Name Service Security:suser:cmd:::/usr/sadm/bin/
    smattrpop:uid=0;gid=sys
Software Installation:suser:cmd:::/usr/bin/pkgparam:uid=0
Network Management:suser:cmd:::/usr/sbin/in.named:uid=0
File System Management:suser:cmd:::/usr/sbin/mount:uid=0
Software Installation:suser:cmd:::/usr/bin/pkgtrans:uid=0
```

If we take one of the entries as an example, we can see that each entry is once more split into colon-separated fields. Table 3.5 uses the "Software Installation" entry above to show this information.

Table 3.5 *Exec Database Details*

Field	Description
Software Installation	The profile name
suser	The policy associated with the profile—"suser" is the only valid policy
cmd	The object type—"cmd" is the only valid object
(empty)	Reserved for future use
(empty)	Reserved for future use
/usr/bin/pkgparam	The object identifier
uid=0	The security attribute list

Roles

Now that we've created a profile (which contains some authorizations), we can generate a role, assign it the new profile, and, lastly, assign the role to a user. Once we have done this, the user can assume the role at any time by simply switching to it using su, as we've done before between users.

The role information is stored in a file named */etc/user_attr*. Let's look at the default file for a moment to see what it contains—ours is shown here:

```
hydrogen# cat /etc/user_attr
root:::::type=normal;auths=solaris.*,solaris.grant;profiles=All
```

Again, we can see that this file is formatted in a similar fashion to the previous ones. The "root" entry fields are described in Table 3.6.

Table 3.6 *User Database Details*

Field	Description
root	The user name
(empty)	Reserved for future use
(empty)	Reserved for future use
(empty)	Reserved for future use
type=normal; auths=solaris.*,solaris.grant;profiles=All	The security attributes of the role

In this example, we can see that *root* has been assigned all the available profiles and authorizations, as expected.

Create the System Administrator Role

Now that we've seen the format of the files, let's go ahead and create the *sysadmin* role. This is the one that users will be forced to switch to in order to be able to perform any system administration tasks:

```
hydrogen# roleadd -c "System Administrator" -d /export/home/
    sysadmin -g sysadmin -m -k /etc/skel -u 1000 -s /bin/ksh -P
    "System Administrator" sysadmin
6 blocks
hydrogen#
```

Next we'll assign a password to the role—just as we would if it were a normal user:

```
hydrogen# passwd sysadmin
New password:
Re-enter new password:
passwd (SYSTEM): passwd successfully changed for sysadmin
hydrogen#
```

Good. The role has been added, so now let's have a look at the database files to see what changes have been carried out:

```
hydrogen# grep sysadmin /etc/passwd
sysadmin:x:1000:14::/export/home/sysadmin:/bin/ksh
hydrogen#
```

```
hydrogen# grep sysadmin /etc/shadow
sysadmin:tJfxIIKL03KSA:11787::::::
hydrogen#
```

```
hydrogen# cat /etc/user_attr
<lines removed for clarity>
root:::::type=normal;auths=solaris.*,solaris.grant;profiles=All
sysadmin:::::type=role;profiles=System Administrator
hydrogen#
```

This shows that the */etc/passwd* and */etc/shadow* entries appear to be as normal; the one that is different is the entry in */etc/user_attr*. In here we've defined a role named *sysadmin* that is based on the System Administrator profile. If we do a quick check on this profile in */etc/security/prof_attr*, we'll see that it provides *sysadmin* with the following authorizations:

```
hydrogen# more /etc/security/prof_attr
<lines removed for clarity>
System Administrator:::\
  Can perform most non-security administrative tasks:\
  profiles=Audit Review,\
```

```
        Printer Management,\
        Cron Management,\
        Device Management,\
        File System Management,\
        Mail Management,\
        Maintenance and Repair,\
        Media Backup,\
        Media Restore,\
        Name Service Management,\
        Network Management,\
        Object Access Management,\
        Process Management,\
        Software Installation,\
        User Management,\
        All;\
    help=RtSysAdmin.html
<lines removed for clarity>
hydrogen#
```

We haven't actually assigned the profile to anyone yet, so we shouldn't be able to use it—let's confirm this using our *testuser* login. First, we'll need to su to *testuser*:

```
hydrogen# su - testuser
hydrogen$ su - sysadmin
Password:
Roles can only be assumed by authorized users
su: Sorry
hydrogen$
```

OK, so now we'll allocate the profile to *testuser*, which we can do using usermod. After that we'll try to switch to the role again:

```
hydrogen# usermod -R sysadmin testuser
hydrogen# su - testuser
hydrogen$ su - sysadmin
Password:
hydrogen$
```

Good. This time *testuser* was able to access the account. If we take a look in */etc/user_attr*, we'll see the reason why we're allowed to do so:

```
hydrogen# cat /etc/user_attr
<lines removed for clarity>
root:::::type=normal;auths=solaris.*,solaris.grant;profiles=All
sysadmin:::::type=role;profiles=System Administrator
testuser:::::type=normal;roles=sysadmin
hydrogen#
```

An entry for *testuser* has been added to *user_attr*, stating that *testuser* can assume the *sysadmin* role. This means we now have a *sysadmin* user that is allowed to run some super-user related commands.

An interesting point to note is that if we compare the entries for *root* and *sysadmin* in */etc/auth_attr*, we can see that the "type" fields are different.

This defines whether the account is a role (type=role) or whether a user can login directly to the account (type=normal). In other words, we can login as *root* or *testuser*, but not as *sysadmin*. Instead someone must assume its role—and that can only be done by *testuser*.

Creating a Custom Script

Now that we've looked at some of the different tools that are available for administering the user base, let's create a script that will take us a step further by automating some of the creation steps. This is a common requirement for many companies, because not only does it ease the task of user creation, it also allows us to enforce a set of standards, such as setting a default password, forcing a specific environment or login name, and so forth. The one shown here, for example, performs the following functions:

- Sets the user's initial password to the company default
- Sets the password time-out values
- Forces users to change their passwords at first login
- Implements quotas for the user

It's worthwhile making a few points before we look at the script. Firstly, we've tried to use the supplied tools whenever possible, rather than rely on manually editing the files. This provides us with the "safety buffer" we talked about earlier (backup copies of files, UID checking, etc.). That said, the only way we can enter a password using a shell script is to manually edit the files, which we've done using sed to insert an already encrypted password. If you need to perform something different, such as generate a different password for each user, then you'll need to use programs such as C or Perl to do this.

Lastly, near the end of the script, there is room for adding any company-specific settings that you need to apply, such as updating user profiles and so forth. We've used this section to initialize the user's quotas by copying them from an existing user:

```
hydrogen# cat createUser
#!/bin/ksh
#
# A script to create users in a "company format."
# This uses a default, encrypted passwd that has been
# obtained by pulling a known password from the shadow
# file. The users are forced to alter it as first login.
# It assumes the group already exists and is valid.
#

#
# set our company defaults
#
home=/export/home
shell=/bin/ksh
skel=/etc/skel
```

```
password=hViVZtexneY8Y  # default encrypted password (changeme)
warnDays=5
validDays=60
tmpPasswd=/tmp/passwd.$$
quotaAccount=testuser
#
# check we have the correct number of params
#
if [ $# -ne 3 ]; then
  echo "Usage: ${0} <login name> <gid> <comment>"
  exit 1
fi
#
# grab the user info
#
user=$1
gid=$2
comment=$3
#
# check the group is valid
#
egrep -s "${gid}" /etc/group
if [ $? -ne 0 ]; then
  echo "Please enter a valid gid and re-run"
  exit 1
fi
#
# add the user to the passwd file
#
useradd -c "${comment}" -d ${home}/${user} -g ${gid} -m -k
${skel} -s ${shell} ${user}
#
# insert the password to the password file
# (see below why the passwd and not the shadow file)
#
sed -e "s/^${user}:x:/${user}:${password}:/" /etc/passwd >
${tmpPasswd}
if [ -s ${tmpPasswd} ]; then
  mv ${tmpPasswd} /etc/passwd
  if [ $? -ne 0 ]; then
    echo "Error: Cannot copy new password file"
    exit 1
  fi
fi
#
# we are setting warning and expiration dates, so
# shadow needs to know when the password was updated -
# let pwconv handle this for us
#
pwconv
#
# set the password timeouts
#
passwd -f -w ${warnDays} -x ${validDays} ${user}
#
# update the account with any "standard" settings
#
```

```
edquota -p ${quotaAccount} ${user}
exit 0
hydrogen#
```

So now that we've got the script, how do we run it? This is actually very simple: The script checks for three arguments being passed in—the login name, the GID, and a comment for the "gecos" field. To run it for one of our example users, say John Green, we would enter the following command:

```
hydrogen# createUser jgreen 10 "John Green"
6 blocks
hydrogen#
```

Checking the Files

As users are added, updated, and deleted it's quite easy for the administrative files to get out of sync with each other—especially if any manual file edits have been performed. Therefore, in this last section we'll look at a few of the utilities that can be used to check and maintain the related files (*/etc/ passwd*, */etc/shadow*, and */etc/group*).

Pwconv

We've already come across pwconv—it was used in our custom script earlier. It is used to create or update the shadow file, which it does by synchronizing it with the password file.

It uses the second field of */etc/passwd* (the encrypted password field) to indicate that the password for this user can be found in */etc/shadow*. It does this by moving the encrypted password into */etc/shadow* and replacing the original password field in */etc/passwd* with an "x."

This means that if the field is empty, pwconv will create an entry in the shadow file and insert the required "x" into the password file. Similarly, if there is an entry in the shadow file and nothing in the password file, it will remove the shadow entry. It is intelligent enough to know that if a password exists in */etc/passwd*, but there isn't an entry for the user in the */etc/ shadow* file, it may be an old-style password file that is being used. In this case, it will create the correct entry in the shadow file and also move the password there too.

Let's look at the following example, which uses the old-style password entry. In other words, the encrypted password is stored in */etc/passwd* and the user doesn't have a */etc/shadow* entry:

```
hydrogen# grep testuser /etc/passwd
testuser:ba7btwLghQU86:500:100:Test User:/home/testuser:/bin/ksh
hydrogen#
```

Running `pwconv` and looking at the two files again will give the following result:

```
hydrogen# grep testuser /etc/passwd
testuser:x:500:100:Test User:/home/testuser:/bin/ksh
hydrogen#

hydrogen# grep testuser /etc/shadow
testuser:ba7btwLghQU86:::::::
hydrogen#
```

Pwck and Grpck

Two programs, named `pwck` and `grpck` are supplied to check the contents of */etc/passwd* and */etc/group*, respectively. They will look for missing passwords, incorrect fields, and so on.

To illustrate this, let's alter the *testuser*'s shell to be something that is non-existent, say `/bin/nosuchshell`. The output from `pwck` will report an error as shown below:

```
hydrogen# passmgmt -m -s /bin/nosuchshell testuser
hydrogen# pwck
testuser:x:500:100::/export/home/testuser:/bin/nosuchshell
        Optional shell file not found
hydrogen#
```

Using `grpck` to check the group file may display something similar to that shown below:

```
hydrogen# grpck
bin::2:root,bin,daemon
        bin - Duplicate logname entry (gid first occurs in
passwd entry)

sys::3:root,bin,sys,adm
        sys - Duplicate logname entry (gid first occurs in
passwd entry)
hydrogen#
```

Passwd

We saw earlier that the `passwd` command can be used to display a user's details. As a further note, by running it as shown here we can display all the entries in the */etc/passwd* file. From there, we can carry out tasks such as searching to locate all locked accounts (LKs) or all accounts without a valid password (NP).

```
hydrogen# passwd -sa
root   PS
daemon LK
bin    LK
```

```
sys  LK
adm  LK
lp  LK
smtp  LK
uucp  LK
nuucp  LK
listen  LK
nobody  LK
noaccess  LK
nobody4  LK
testuser  LK     12/07/99     0  60  5
hydrogen#
```

Conclusion

In this chapter, we've worked through the various methods that can be used to add users to the system and created our users in the process. We've also managed to create a system administrator account, using RBAC, which can perform some of the general system administration tasks.

Lastly, we've produced a script and looked at some associated programs that can be used to ease and maintain general user administration tasks.

4

PERMISSIONS AND ALL THAT

Manual Pages

bc (1)
chgrp (1)
chmod (1)
chown (1)
find (1)
getfacl (1)
ls (4)
newgrp (1)
rm (4)
sed (1)
setfacl(1)
umask (1)

Files Affected

All files

Objectives

This chapter is all about Solaris file permissions and explains how to interpret file permissions and how to alter them. It also explains how (and why) files get an owner and a group and how these may be changed. In most cases this will probably be enough information to effectively manage the permissions on a Solaris server, but for those instances where a more complex set of permissions is required, the chapter will also cover Access Control Lists (ACLs).

Why Do We Need Permissions?

If a computer is used only by a single user or is used only for something trivial, such as playing games, then there would probably be no real need to have permissions associated with files. However, computers in the workplace tend to be shared by many users, often simultaneously as in the case of Solaris, and also store sensitive information. Also, they are very likely to be attached to a network of some kind.

This means that if we don't do something to stop prying eyes from looking into our files, sooner or later the wrong people will see something they shouldn't or, possibly worse, delete something they shouldn't (but of course, we all make regular backups—don't we!).

Files are protected under Solaris by being given an owner, a group, and a set of permissions. The permissions say what the owner may do to the file, what users in the same group as the files may do, and what all other users may do.

How Permissions Are Represented

When users log in to a Solaris system, they enter a user name and a password. This mechanism establishes the user's identity and results in the user being awarded a specific user ID (UID) and a group ID (GID) as part of his or her credentials.

When we run the `ls -l` command in a directory containing files, we see that each file (or directory) also has a UID (the third column) and a GID (the fourth column):

```
hydrogen# ls -l
total 476
drwxrwxr-x   5 adm      adm          512 Jul  7 17:47 acct
-rw-------   1 uucp     bin            0 Jul  7 15:39 aculog
-r--r--r--   1 root     root          28 Aug 22 21:52 lastlog
drwxr-xr-x   2 adm      adm          512 Jul  7 15:38 log
-rw-r--r--   1 root     root      101744 Aug 22 21:52 messages
drwxr-xrwx   2 adm      adm          512 Jul  7 15:38 passwd
drwxrwxr-x   2 adm      sys          512 Jul  7 17:47 sa
drwxr-xr-x   2 root     sys          512 Jul  7 16:35 sm.bin
drwxr-xr-x   2 root     sys          512 Jul  7 15:38 streams
-rw-------   1 root     root         139 Aug 14 23:15 sulog
-rw-r--r--   1 root     bin         3348 Aug 22 22:56 utmpx
-rw-r--r--   1 adm      adm       103788 Aug 22 21:52 wtmpx
hydrogen#
```

The left-most column of the above output shows the file's permissions. These permissions, along with both the file and user's credentials, specify what the user may do with that file.

The permissions themselves consist of a 10-digit string of characters; the first digit actually represents the file type, so only the remaining nine are used to protect the file. This split is shown in the Table 4.1.

Table 4.1 *Permission Grouping*

File Type	Owner	Group	Other
d	rwx	rwx	r-x
—	rw-	---	---
—	rwx	r-x	r--

The different file types are described in Chapter 6, "The Filesystem and Its Contents." The remaining nine characters are split into three columns of three characters each. Each column represents a class of user, and three characters dictate what users belonging to that class may do with or to the file (or directory). The three classes are owner, group, and other. Within each class the three digits will normally consist of any of the characters "r," "w," "x," or "-." The first position is for reading the file, the second for writing to it, and the third for executing the file. If any position contains a dash, it means that class of user may not perform that action.

The owner class, obviously, can only contain one user, the group class contains any user who belongs to the same group as the file, and the other class contains all users who do not belong to either of the first two classes.

If the file is a directory, it may also have the "x" permission set, but in this case it means that the users belonging to that class are able to change into that directory (using the cd command). It also means they may run other programs that could try to change into the directory (e.g., find).

The user *root* has permission to do anything to any file regardless of the actual permissions, apart from being able to execute files that do not have execute permissions. This is to prevent a text file that happens to contain the names of Solaris commands accidentally being interpreted by the shell as if it were a shell script.

Setting Permissions

The permissions of all the files in the system would normally be set by the system administrator to fit in with the site security policy (which all sites should have). We will be looking at how to define default permissions to new files that are created, but first we will look at how to alter the permissions of an existing file.

The first thing we need to know is that only the owner of a file (or *root*) can change the permissions of a file, and the command we use is chmod (which is short for "change mode" as a file's permissions can also be referred to as its mode). There are two ways that the permissions of a file may be changed with chmod. The first uses absolute syntax and the second symbolic syntax.

Consider the following example:

```
hydrogen$ ls -l info
-rw-------   1 dbutler slackers     47 Jul  12 11:31 info
hydrogen$
```

The file called *info* is owned by user *dbutler* and belongs to the group *slackers*. The permissions show that *dbutler* can read the file and make changes to it, but no one else may do anything with it:

```
hydrogen$ chmod 664 info
hydrogen$ ls -l info
-rw-rw-r--   1 dbutler slackers     47 Jul  12 11:31 info
hydrogen$
```

After running the chmod command with a parameter of 664, the permissions now show that not only can *dbutler* read and alter the file, but so can the other users belonging to the group *slackers*. All other users on the system can now read the file, but cannot alter it. No one is able to execute the file.

So, how does the number 664 translate into a set of permissions?

To do this, we give each of the characters "r," "w," "x," and "-" a numeric value and add these values within each user class. The value assigned to each letter is as follows:

- r = 4
- w = 2
- x = 1
- - = 0

So rwxrwxrwx would equal 4+2+1, 4+2+1, and 4+2+1 or 777 (but NOT 21). Likewise rw-r--r-- would be represented by 644 (4+2+0, 4+0+0, and 4+0+0).

These numbers are actually an octal representation of the permissions. The following segment of shell script code can be used to demonstrate this:

```
echo "Enter permissions (e.g. rwxrw-r--):\c"
read perms
bin_perms=$(echo $perms | sed 's/[rwx]/1/g
s/-/0/g')
octal_perms=$(echo "obase=8\nibase=2\n${bin_perms}" | bc)
echo "Your permissions translate to $octal_perms"
```

The sed command converts the permissions into a binary number; this is then converted to octal using bc.

Using the absolute syntax, as we have here, is useful if you want to set the permissions of a file to a specific value and are not concerned with what they were originally. Sometimes, however, you may want to change a specific part of the permissions without altering the other parts. For example, if you wanted to add read and write permission to the group part of all the files in the current directory, you could not do it using the above method without first making a note of each file's existing permissions.

The way we would do this is by using chmod with symbolic syntax:

```
hydrogen# ls -l
total 476
drwxrwxr-x   5 adm      adm          512 Jul  7 17:47 acct
-rw-------   1 uucp     bin            0 Jul  7 15:39 aculog
-r--r--r--   1 root     root          28 Aug 22 21:52 lastlog
drwxr-xr-x   2 adm      adm          512 Jul  7 15:38 log
-rw-r-r--    1 root     root      101744 Aug 22 21:52 messages
drwxr-xrwx   2 adm      adm          512 Jul  7 15:38 passwd
drwxrwxr-x   2 adm      sys          512 Jul  7 17:47 sa
drwxr-xr-x   2 root     sys          512 Jul  7 16:35 sm.bin
drwxr-xr-x   2 root     sys          512 Jul  7 15:38 streams
-rw-------   1 root     root         139 Aug 14 23:15 sulog
-rw-r--r--   1 root     bin         3348 Aug 22 22:56 utmpx
-rw-r--r--   1 adm      adm       103788 Aug 22 21:52 wtmpx
hydrogen#
```

The following command uses the symbolic syntax to change only the group class of the permissions:

```
hydrogen# chmod g+rw *
hydrogen# ls -l
total 476
drwxrwxr-x   5 adm      adm          512 Jul  7 17:47 acct
-rw-rw----   1 uucp     bin            0 Jul  7 15:39 aculog
-r--rw-r--   1 root     root          28 Aug 22 21:52 lastlog
drwxrwxr-x   2 adm      adm          512 Jul  7 15:38 log
-rw-rw-r--   1 root     root      101744 Aug 22 21:52 messages
drwxrwxrwx   2 adm      adm          512 Jul  7 15:38 passwd
drwxrwxr-x   2 adm      sys          512 Jul  7 17:47 sa
drwxrwxr-x   2 root     sys          512 Jul  7 16:35 sm.bin
drwxrwxr-x   2 root     sys          512 Jul  7 15:38 streams
-rw-rw----   1 root     root         139 Aug 14 23:15 sulog
-rw-rw-r--   1 root     bin         3348 Aug 22 22:56 utmpx
-rw-rw-r--   1 adm      adm       103788 Aug 22 21:52 wtmpx
hydrogen#
```

When we use this method to change a file's permissions we can use the letters "u" (for user class), "g" (for group class), "o" (for other class), and "a" (for all classes), followed by a "+" (to add a permission), "-" to remove a permission, and "=" to set a permission. Full details of this syntax can be found in the chmod man page.

Default Permissions

When a file is first created, it will be given a default set of permissions. The default permissions are controlled using the umask command and are stored in the environment of each shell process (see Chapter 5, "Shells"). This means they are usually set in */etc/profile* to provide a system-wide setting or within each user's profile to allow users to have different default permissions. Seasoned administrators tend to refer to this process as setting the user's umask, rather than setting the user's default permissions.

The umask command can either be run with a single parameter or with no parameter. If run with no parameter, it will return the umask setting for that shell session. If run with a parameter, it will set the current shell's umask to be the value of the parameter.

The parameter supplied should be an octal number, which will be used as a mask to set the default permissions when a file or directory is created. The umask value is masked against the octal numbers 666 when creating a file and 777 when creating a directory.

If we were to set the umask to 22, it would be masked against 666 to give 644 when a file was created. This would have the following effect:

```
hydrogen# umask 22
hydrogen# echo "Hello world" >fred
hydrogen# ls -l fred
-rw-r--r--   1 root       other        12 Jun 30 12:11 fred
hydrogen# mkdir bill
hydrogen# ls -ld bill
drwxr-xr-x   2 root       other        69 Jun 30 12:12 bill
hydrogen#
```

Hopefully, the reason for handling default permission using a mask is apparent from the example above. It means that files will always be created with no execute permission, and directories will always be created with execute permissions (otherwise you would have to do a chmod on each newly created directory before you could change into it). This also means that newly created files cannot be accidentally executed if their name is typed at the shell prompt.

File Ownership

When a file is created on a Solaris server, it will take on the ownership and group of the user that created it.

```
hydrogen$ id
uid=1001(msmith) gid=10(staff)
hydrogen$ echo "Hello world" >file1
hydrogen$ ls -l file1
-rw-r--r--   1 msmith     staff        12 Aug  8 14:58 file1
hydrogen$
```

In the above example, the user *msmith* has created a file, so it is owned by *msmith* and in the group *staff*, as this was the primary group of *msmith* when the file was created. If *msmith* is moved into a different group after creating the file, it will not affect the group that the file belongs to. Both the owner of the file and the group to which it belongs are stored in the file's inode (see Chapter 6, "The Filesystem and Its Contents").

After creating the file, the user *msmith* is free to change the ownership of the file and the group to which it belongs because *msmith* owns it (only *root* or a file's owner may do this). The command for doing this is chown, which takes as arguments the user to change the ownership to and the file (or a list of the files) to change. It also has a "-R" flag which is very useful for changing ownership of all files (and directories) below a specific directory. The command chgrp works in the same way, but changes the group of the file rather than the owner:

```
hydrogen$ ls -l file1
-rw-r--r--   1 msmith    staff           12 Aug   8 14:58 file1
hydrogen$ chown jgreen file1
hydrogen$ ls -l file1
-rw-r--r--   1 jgreen    staff           12 Aug   8 14:58 file1
hydrogen$
```

The trouble is that once the ownership has been given away to another user, the original user is no longer the owner and cannot change the group or the ownership back to him or herself:

```
hydrogen$ ls -l file1
-rw-r--r--   1 jgreen    staff           12 Aug   8 14:58 file1
hydrogen$ chgrp other file1
chgrp: file1: Not owner
hydrogen$ chown msmith file1
chown: file1: Not owner
hydrogen$
```

In practice, if non-*root* users want to change the owner and group of one of their files, they should change the group first or do both at the same time with a command similar to this:

```
hydrogen$ ls -l file1
-rw-r--r--   1 jgreen    staff           12 Aug   8 14:58 file1
hydrogen$ chown jgreen:other file1
hydrogen$ ls -l file1
-rw-r--r--   1 jgreen    other           12 Aug   8 14:58 file1
hydrogen$
```

Because users can only change the ownership of files they own, and once they have given away ownership they cannot do it again, it is more likely that file ownership and group changes are performed by the system administrator. The more recent versions of Solaris will, by default, only allow file ownerships to be changed by *root* and will only allow a file's group to be changed by the owner to another group to which the user already belongs. If you tried the above examples and were unable to change the file ownership, then this is the likely cause. If you want to allow users to be able to change the ownership of their files, then add the following line to the */etc/system* file and reboot:

```
set rstchown = 0
```

To stop users from being able to change ownership of their files, set rstchown to "1" instead of "0" (or comment out the whole line—the comment character is an asterisk). The */etc/system* file is covered in more detail in Chapter 21, "Kernels and All About Them."

Sticky Bits

Occasionally, you may have come across a file or directory whose permissions contained something other than the "r," "w," "x," or "-" that we looked at earlier. These additional characters tend to be called "sticky bits." In fact, some of them are sticky bits, but others are *setuid* (set user ID) or *setgid* (set group ID) bits. Sticky bits and *setuid/setgid* bits can only appear in the part of the permissions that would normally hold an "x," and they will be either of the letters "s" or "t." The letter "s" can occur in either the user or group part of the permissions, while the "t" can only appear in the other part.

The meaning of these letters is different depending on whether they are applied to a file or a directory. We will look at the effect of the letter "t" (which is the only one that should be called the "sticky bit").

The Sticky Bit

If a directory has the sticky bit set, this affects the rules for removing or renaming files within that directory. If it is set, a file within such a directory can only be removed or renamed if at least one of the following conditions is met:

- The user is the owner of the file.
- The user is the owner of the directory.
- The user has permission to write to the file.
- The user is the super-user (*root*).

One directory that would normally have the sticky bit set is */tmp*:

```
hydrogen# ls -ld /tmp
drwxrwxrwt    6 sys        sys         313 Jul  1 16:45 /tmp
hydrogen#
```

This is to prevent users from removing files created by other users. It is recommended that all directories used by many users have the sticky bit set. You will notice that because the underlying directory permissions are 777, anybody is allowed to create files in */tmp*, but this also means that anybody is allowed to remove files from the directory. Thus, by setting the sticky bit we ensure that files created in that directory are safe from other users despite the directory's underlying permissions.

The fact that the sticky bit shown above has a lowercase "t" tells us that the execute permission is also set in this location. If the execute bit were not set, the permissions would contain a capital "T" instead; but this would not make sense, as it would prevent those users that fit into the other category from changing into that directory.

If you create a public directory and you wish to set the sticky bit, the simplest way is to use chmod +t, which will add the sticky bit, while leaving the remaining permissions as they were:

```
hydrogen# mkdir public_dir
hydrogen# ls -l
total 8
drwxr-xr-x   2 root      other         69 Jul  1 17:32 public_dir
hydrogen# chmod +t public_dir
hydrogen# ls -l
total 8
drwxr-xr-t   2 root      other         69 Jul  1 17:32 public_dir
hydrogen#
```

You can also set the sticky bit using the absolute method by placing a "1" in front of the three-digit octal number:

```
hydrogen# mkdir public_dir
hydrogen# ls -l
total 8
drwxr-xr-x   2 root      other         69 Jul  1 17:40 public_dir
hydrogen# chmod 1777 public_dir
hydrogen# ls -l
total 8
drwxrwxrwt   2 root      other         69 Jul  1 17:40 public_dir
hydrogen# chmod 1770 public_dir
hydrogen# ls -l
total 8
drwxrwx--T   2 root      other         69 Jul  1 17:40
hydrogen#
```

This example of chmod shows us changing the permissions so that the sticky bit is set, but we only want certain users to be able to use the directory. To achieve this, we have removed the permissions for *others* (not the group *other*, but everybody who is not *root* and not in the group *other*) to do anything with the directory.

You may have noticed that the last update time of the directory did not change each time we changed its permissions. This is because the permissions of a file or directory are not stored inside the file itself but in its inode, as we mentioned earlier.

We have seen why we might set the sticky bit on a directory, but not why we might want to set it on a file. You may also be wondering why on earth it is called a sticky bit, since nothing we have seen so far can be associated with the word "sticky." In fact, the term "sticky" arose many years ago when computers did not have much memory. Each time a program was run (either a compiled program or a shell script) it needed to be loaded into memory. It would run for its allotted time slice and then another program would run for its time slice. This process occurs for all programs, whether they are system processes or user-initiated programs. If there is enough memory on the system to hold all the currently running processes, things are fine; if not, then the system will copy a process out of memory to a special area of disk called *swap* (see Chapter 7, "Swap Space"). This is fine, since next time that process needs to run it will be copied back into memory from swap. This means that every process will still get its chance to run, but the performance of the server may not seem very good to the users, as swapping processes between memory and disk takes time. If the system is fairly heavily used, you could get a situation where lots of users are running the same application but are getting poor responses, since other processes cause this application to keep getting swapped out to disk all the time. This could be fixed by setting the sticky bit of the program, which would cause it to stick in memory (hence the name). Setting the sticky bit would not guarantee that the process would never be swapped out, but when the system did need to swap a process out it would always try and find one without the sticky bit set.

Hopefully this has given you a bit of background into why this is called the sticky bit, but because modern Solaris systems do not have the same memory constraints (or the same method of managing memory) you will find that setting the sticky bit on programs is no longer required. If you wish to search your filesystems to see if any of your files or directories have it set, you can use the following `find` command:

```
hydrogen# find / -perm -1000 -exec ls -ld {} \;
drwxrwxrwt   3 root    mail       512 May 19 11:11  /var/mail
drwxrwxrwt   3 bin     bin        512 Apr 22 10:10  /var/preserve
drwxrwxrwt   3 bin     bin        512 Apr 29 18:13  /var/spool/pkg
drwxrwxrwt  50 sys     sys       1536 Aug  6 10:02  /var/tmp
drwxrwxrwt   2 root    root       512 Dec 19  2000  /var/dt/tmp
drwxrwxrwt   6 sys     sys        275 Aug  6 17:15  /tmp
drwxrwxrwt   2 root    root       207 Aug  6 10:01  /tmp/.rpc_door
hydrogen#
```

You should find that the sticky bit is only set for directories, unless you have a very old Solaris system, in which case you may find some programs with it set.

Setuid and *Setgid*

We have seen what happens when a file or directory has a "t" in the permissions. Now we will look at why we might want to use the letter "s." The "s" may be placed in either the owner or the group part of the permissions. Like the "t," it can only go in the execute position.

Before we go into detail about what the *setuid* and *setgid* bits are for, we will look at a program that has the *setuid* bit set and see what the program does. The program in question is the `passwd` command, which is used by users to change their own passwords and by the *root* user to change anybody's password (see Chapter 3, "User Administration"). The permissions of this program are as follows:

```
hydrogen# ls -l /bin/passwd
-r-sr-sr-x   3 root      sys       99824 Sep  9  1999 /bin/passwd
hydrogen#
```

We can see that the permissions include a letter "s" in the user and group parts. This means that this file has both the *setuid* and the *setgid* bits set. Because the letter is lowercase, we know that the execute permission is also set, because it would be a capital letter if it wasn't. Because the file is owned by the *root* user, we also know that if the execute bit was not set, *root* would not be able to run the passwd command, which wouldn't make much sense at all.

As discussed in Chapter 3, Solaris stores all user passwords in a file called */etc/shadow*. Even though the passwords are encrypted, this file is crucial to the security of the systems, so it has very restrictive permissions.

```
hydrogen# ls -l /etc/shadow
-r--------   1 root      sys         277 Jan 14  2001 /etc/shadow
hydrogen#
```

This means that only the *root* user is able to read the contents of this file, and no one is allowed to do anything else to it. In fact, the *root* user may also write to the file because *root* is able to read or write from any file regardless of its permissions.

Let's now go back to the passwd command and see what happens when a normal user tries to change a password:

```
$ id
uid=1001(msmith) gid=10(staff)
$ passwd
passwd:  Changing password for msmith
Enter login password: (current password typed here)
New password: (new password typed here)
Re-enter new password: (new password typed again)
passwd (SYSTEM): passwd successfully changed for msmith
$ ls -l /etc/shadow
-r--------   1 root      sys         277 Aug  6 17:34 /etc/shadow
$
```

We can see that the command prompted the user for a new password and that the *shadow* file has been updated, but this should not have happened because the user *msmith* does not have permission to write to it (and nor does any other user).

The reason this command worked is that the passwd command has the *setuid* bit set. The *setuid* bit makes Solaris run the command with the same privileges as the person who owns the command, which in this case is *root* (although it may not always be). Each process that runs will have a user ID (UID) and a group ID (GID) associated with it which will always be equal to the UID of the user running the process and the GID of the group they are in. A process may also have an effective user ID (EUID) and an effective group ID (EGID). The EUID and EGID are set when the *setuid* or *setgid* bits are used, and these will override the process UID and GID.

Note: The passwd program also has its *setgid* bit set, which means that the program will also run with the group privileges of the group that it belongs to. However, the *setuid* bit along with *root* ownership is enough to be able to update the *shadow* file.

This is clearly a neat way of enabling users to perform tasks that update system files, but it is also something that the system administrator needs to be very wary of, as it could be used by unscrupulous individuals to do things they shouldn't. This is because it is also possible to use the *setuid* and *setgid* bits on some shell scripts, so if users were able to modify a *setuid* shell script that was owned by *root*, they would be able to put any command they liked into it, and it would run with *root* privileges.

Solaris will only allow you to use *setuid* and *setgid* on Korn Shell (ksh) scripts, as this feature was disabled from the Bourne shell some time ago. The following simple script demonstrates the effect of using *setuid* and *setgid* on a shell script. First, we will run it with no *setuid* or *setgid* and then look at the difference *setuid* and *setgid* make:

```
hydrogen$ id
uid=1001(msmith) gid=10(staff)
hydrogen$ ls -l showid
-r-xr-xr-x   1 root      other        31 Aug 23 12:06 showid
hydrogen$ cat showid
#! /bin/ksh
id
touch test_file
hydrogen$ ./showid
uid=1001(msmith) gid=10(staff)
hydrogen$ ls -l test_file
-rw-r--r--   1 msmith    staff         0 Aug 23 12:09 test_file
hydrogen$
```

Now we will add *setuid* and *setgid* to the permissions (which can only be done as *root*, of course) and let *msmith* run the script again:

```
hydrogen# rm test_file
hydrogen# chmod ug+s showid
hydrogen# ls -l showid
-r-sr-sr-x   1 root      other        31 Aug 23 12:06 showid
hydrogen#
```

Back to *msmith*'s login session:

```
hydrogen$ ./showid
uid=1001(msmith) gid=10(staff) euid=0(root) egid=1(other)
hydrogen$ ls -l test_file
-rw-r--r--   1 root      other         0 Aug 23 13:17 test_file
hydrogen$
```

We now see that although the process still has the UID and GID of *msmith*, because the *setuid* and *setgid* bits were set the process also has an EUID and an EGID equal to the owner and group of the script. Because the EUID and EGID override the UID and GID, the file created gets the owner and group it would have received if *root* was actually running the script.

If you ever need to implement any *setuid* or *setgid* scripts, make sure that nobody has permission to write to them, as this used to be a potential security loophole. Now, however, you will find that if a user does edit a *setuid* to *root* script, the *setuid* will disappear when the user saves the file. It is, however, advisable for system administrators to keep an eye on which files on their systems have the *setuid* or *setgid* bits set. If you have programs other than those provided as part of Solaris with these bits set, be sure that you trust what they do. Likewise, if you do need to write your own *setuid* program, ensure that you consider all the security implications when you write it and, if possible, try to achieve what you need to by using *setgid* rather than *setuid*. At the end of this section, we will look at how you can find all the *setuid* and *setgid* files on your systems. If you are using Solaris 8 or higher, there is less need to make use of *setuid* shell scripts thanks to the introduction of RBAC (which is covered in Chapter 3, "User Administration").

Setting the *setuid* and *setgid* bits is similar to setting the sticky bit. We can set the *setuid* bit using chmod u+s and set the *setgid* using chmod g+s. However, for security reasons, in addition to the fact that the *setuid* and *setgid* bits will disappear if the file is edited, as mentioned above, they will also disappear if the owner or group of the file is changed (unless it is *root* running the command).

It does not make sense for a file to have its *setuid* or *setgid* bit set without also having the equivalent execute bit set. If you try to do this using the symbolic method of changing permissions, you will get the following error message:

```
hydrogen# ls -l test_file
-rw-r--r--   1 root     other          0 Aug 10 14:22 prog
hydrogen# chmod g+s test_file
chmod: WARNING: Execute permission required for set-ID on
execution for test_file
hydrogen#
```

All the special permissions (*setuid*, *setgid*, and sticky bit) can also be set using the absolute method by placing an additional octal number in front of the three-digit octal permission you wish to set. In the section on setting the sticky bit, you can see that placing a "1" in front of the three-digit octal permission will set the sticky bit. The values that need to be used are shown below:

- t=1 (sticky bit)
- s=2 (*setgid* bit)
- s=4 (*setuid* bit)

So if we wanted to change the permission of a file to have the *setuid* bit set, we would put a "4" in front of the permissions. If we wanted to set both the *setuid* and *setgid* bits, we would put a "6" in front.

```
hydrogen# chmod 6555 prog
hydrogen# ls -l prog
-r-sr-sr-x   1 root      other        861 Aug  9 16:38 prog
hydrogen#
```

It is highly unlikely that you would find a directory with the *setuid* bit set, but you may find one with the *setgid* bit set. If a directory has the *setgid* bit set, it means that all files created under that directory will be owned by the group which owns the directory, rather than the group of the user creating the file.

Finding *Setuid* and *Setgid* programs

It is very important for the system administrator to know which files have the *setuid* and/or *setgid* bits set. The following find commands will produce a list of *setuid/setgid* files shown in ls -l output format so you can see who owns them and which group they belong to. You may prefer to redirect the output into a file, as there could be quite a lot of it.

To find files that have the *setuid* bit set use:

```
find / -perm -4000 -exec ls -ld {} \;
```

To find files that have the *setgid* bit set use:

```
find / -perm -2000 -exec ls -ld {} \;
```

To find files that have both the *setuid* and *setgid* bits set use:

```
find / -perm -6000 -exec ls -ld {} \;
```

In each of the above find commands, we have put a minus sign before the permissions to ensure that we are finding files that include the octal permissions shown. This means when we search for files with the *setuid* bit set it will also find files with the *setgid* bit set, but only if the *setuid* bit is also set. If we did not put a minus sign in front of the permissions, we would be searching for files with those permissions exactly, which would not be very helpful as there are likely to be no files on the system with permissions set to 4,000 (i.e., ---S------).

We are using the "-exec" option of find, which will cause find to execute the command following it for each file that matches the search pattern. Therefore, find will execute the command ls -ld each time it finds a file, supplying the file as the argument to ls. We need to use the "-d" option because if the file found by find is actually a directory, ls will list the files inside the directory rather than the directory itself.

The following example shows an abbreviated list of what you may expect to see:

```
hydrogen# find / -perm -4000 -exec ls -ld {} \;
-r-sr-xr-x   1 root   bin     650720 May   6  1999 /usr/lib/sendmail
-rwsr-xr-x   1 root   adm       5304 Sep   1  1998 /usr/lib/acct/accton
-r-sr-xr-x   1 root   sys      27628 Oct   6  1998 /usr/bin/sparcv7/ps
-r-sr-xr-x   2 root   bin      11528 Oct   6  1998 /usr/bin/sparcv7/uptime
-r-sr-xr-x   2 root   bin      11528 Oct   6  1998 /usr/bin/sparcv7/w
-rwsr-xr-x   1 root   sys      35916 Oct   6  1998 /usr/bin/at
-r-sr-xr-x   1 root   bin      17044 Oct   6  1998 /usr/bin/crontab
-r-sr-xr-x   1 root   bin      14352 Oct   6  1998 /usr/bin/eject
-r-sr-xr-x   1 root   bin      29292 Oct   6  1998 /usr/bin/login
-rwsr-xr-x   1 root   sys       7736 Oct   6  1998 /usr/bin/newgrp
-r-sr-sr-x   3 root   sys      99824 Sep   9  1999 /usr/bin/passwd
-r-sr-sr-x   3 root   sys      99824 Sep   9  1999 /usr/bin/yppasswd
<lines removed for clarity>
hydrogen#
```

You will notice that some files found also have the *setgid* bit set, but the output will not contain all the files with this bit set as we have told find to search for files with the *setuid* bit set. If you wish to be able to find all files with the *setuid* or *setgid* bit set, you can use the following find command:

```
hydrogen# find / \( -perm -4000 -o -perm -2000 \) -exec ls -ld {} \; |
    pg
-r-sr-xr-x   1 root   bin       6264 Sep   1  1998 /usr/bin/volcheck
-r-sr-sr-x   1 root   sys      24392 Sep   9  1999 /usr/dt/bin/dtaction
-r-sr-xr-x   1 root   bin      11176 Sep   1  1998 /usr/bin/volrmmount
-r-xr-sr-x   1 bin    mail   1552660 Aug   2  1999 /usr/dt/bin/dtmail
-r-xr-sr-x   1 bin    mail    555992 Aug  12  1999 /usr/dt/bin/dtmailpr
-r-sr-xr-x   1 root   bin     383552 Aug  12  1999 /usr/dt/bin/dtprintinfo
-r-sr-xr-x   1 root   bin     147908 May   6  1999 /usr/dt/bin/dtsession
drwxr-sr-x   5 root   bin        512 Oct  18  2000 /usr/dt/lib/fdl
drwxr-sr-x   3 root   bin        512 Oct  18  2000 /usr/dt/lib/fdl/adobe
<lines removed for clarity>
hydrogen#
```

Now we can see all the files that have either the *setuid*, *setgid*, or both bits set, but we also get the directories that have their *setgid* bit set. We can remove these by adding the option "-type f" to the above find command:

```
find / \( -perm -4000 -o -perm -2000 \) -type f -exec
    ls -ld {} \; >/tmp/permrep.out
```

The above command will find all files (but not directories) that have their *setuid* and/or *setgid* bit set and will produce an ls -ld listing of these files in the output file */tmp/permrep.out*. If you find anything suspicious in the output file, be sure to copy it out of */tmp* to ensure that you don't lose it should the system reboot.

File Locking

One special permissions bit we have not yet looked at enables files to be locked by Solaris when they are accessed by certain applications. The permission is represented by the letter "l" and is located in the group execute position of a file's permissions:

```
hydrogen# touch test_file
hydrogen# ls -l test_file
-rw-r--r--   1 root      other       0 Aug 10 14:35 test_file
hydrogen# chmod g+l test_file
hydrogen# ls -l test_file
-rw-r-lr--   1 root      other       0 Aug 10 14:35 test_file
hydrogen#
```

The file-locking bit can be set using absolute permissions in the same way you would set *setgid*, but with no execute bit set:

```
hydrogen# chmod 2666 test_file
hydrogen# ls -l test_file
-rw-rwlrw-  1 root      other       0 Aug 10 14:35 test_file
hydrogen#
```

This means it is not possible to have the *setgid* bit set as well as file locking. It also means that if you search for files with the *setgid* bit set using the "-perm" option of find, the output will also include any files that have file locking set.

Access Control Lists

Most of the time you should be able to achieve the file security you require using a combination of the standard Solaris permissions and Solaris groups. However, if you cannot easily achieve the desired result you can also make use of Access Control Lists (ACLs).

ACLs allow you to go beyond being able to set permissions for a file's owner, group, and others, and let you add specific permissions for specific users. They also allow the owner of the file to manage the ACL for that file so they do not have to rely on the system administrator for certain tasks (such as making changes to the */etc/group* file).

To make use of ACLs, you need to become familiar with two Solaris commands. These are getfacl, which will display a file's ACL; and setfacl, which will set a file's ACL. Even if you have not set any ACLs on a file, getfacl will still produce some output based on the existing standard permissions.

```
hydrogen# ls -l test_file
-rw-r-----  1 root      other       0 Aug 13 16:39 test_file
hydrogen# getfacl test_file

# file: test_file
# owner: root
# group: other
user::rw-
group::r--              #effective:r--
mask:r--
other:---
hydrogen#
```

From the `ls -l` output above we can see that the file is owned by *root* and belongs to the group *other*. The owner can read and write to the file, members of the group *other* can only read the file, and everybody else cannot do anything at all to the file.

The output from the `getfacl` command shows us the same information, but as an ACL. We can see who the owner and group are, and we can see that the owner (user) can read and write to the file, the group can read the file, and others cannot access the file at all. The file has a mask, which is set to "r--" and means "read only."

This specifies the maximum permissions that anybody who is not the owner can have, regardless of what that person's individual permission is set to. This is why the group entry also has an effective permissions entry next to it. Even though `getfacl` has returned the above information, there is actually no ACL for the file. The information presented is just inferred from the standard permissions. A file will not have an ACL unless one is set using the `setfacl` command.

As we have just seen, the above file (*test_file*) can be written to and read from by the owner and can only be read by members of its group. What if we had one more user that also needed to be able to write to the file? It would be no good putting that user in the group *other*, because then the user would only have read permission. If we were to create a new group with read and write permission and put the file and the user in that group, everybody in the group *other* would suddenly no longer be able to access the file. The only way we could achieve this specific requirement is by the use of ACLs. We can simply set an ACL for the new user, who will then be able to do what he or she needs to without any impact on anyone else.

The following example shows how the user *jgreen* can be given read and write permissions to the file *test_file*:

```
hydrogen# ls -l test_file
-rw-r-----  1 root      other        0 Aug 13 16:39 test_file
hydrogen# setfacl -m user:jgreen:rw- test_file
hydrogen# ls -l test_file
-rw-r-----+ 1 root      other        0 Aug 13 17:05 test_file
hydrogen# getfacl test_file

# file: test_file
# owner: root
# group: other
user::rw-
user:jgreen:rw-         #effective:r--
group::r--              #effective:r--
mask:r--
other:---
hydrogen#
```

The `setfacl` command above says that we want to modify the ACL for the file *test_file* to enable the user *jgreen* to have read and write access. Because we have used the `setfacl` command, the file does have an ACL now, and we can see this by the character "+" shown after the standard permissions on the output from `ls -l`.

We can see the effect of the command in the new output from `getfacl`. There is now an entry for the user *jgreen* stating that he has read and write permission. However, even though we have specifically said we want *jgreen* to have read and write access, he will only be able to read the file because the mask is set to "r--" (or read only).

We can issue a new `setfacl` command to change the mask and so let *jgreen* have the access we originally intended:

```
hydrogen# setfacl -m mask:rw- test_file
hydrogen# getfacl test_file

# file: test_file
# owner: root
# group: other
user::rw-
user:jgreen:rw-          #effective:rw-
group::r--               #effective:r--
mask:rw-
other:---
hydrogen#
```

Because the ACL mask is now set to "rw-," the effective permissions for *jgreen* can become the same as the value set. The ACL mask provides a way of temporarily restricting the permissions on a file without having to first note down what each of the ACL entries was. The mask can later be opened, and everyone will get the permissions they were originally allocated. The mask has only worked in this way since Solaris 7; prior to that, the mask was always the same as the file's group permission, so if the group permission was changed using `chmod`, it would also change to mask of the ACL.

ACL entries can be added to or changed using `setfacl` with the "-m" flag, as we have seen, but we can also use a "-s" flag, which will cause any existing ACL to be replaced by the one specified. The following example will set the owner's permissions to read and write, the group's permissions to read only, other's permissions to nothing, and the ACL mask to read and write. It also sets up ACL entries for the users *jgreen* (who gets read and write permission) and *msmsith* (who just gets read permission). Any previous ACLs for that file would be removed.

```
setfacl -s user::rw-,group::r--,other:---,mask:rw-
    ,user:jgreen:rw-,user:msmith:r-- new_file
```

Setting ACLs in this manner can become cumbersome, so it is also possible to set ACLs using a file containing the required ACL. The file should be in the same format as the output from `getfacl`. One way of speeding up the process of creating a large ACL is to store the output from a `getfacl` command into a file, edit the file so it reflects the actual ACL you require, and then use `setfacl` with the "-f" option:

```
hydrogen# getfacl test_file >/tmp/acl_file
<edit /tmp/acl_file>
hydrogen# setfacl -f /tmp/acl_file another_file
hydrogen#
```

When you edit the file containing the output from `getfacl` you do not need to bother about the effective permissions because the hash character (#) is treated as a comment by `setfacl`.

There is also a useful shortcut to give a file the same ACL as another:

```
hydrogen# touch test_file2
-rw-r-----+  1 root      other         0 Aug 13 17:05 test_file
-rw-r--r--   1 root      other         0 Aug 14 12:42 test_file2
hydrogen# getfacl test_file | setfacl -f - test_file2
hydrogen# ls -l test_file*
-rw-r-----+  1 root      other         0 Aug 13 17:05 test_file
-rw-r-----+  1 root      other         0 Aug 14 12:42 test_file2
hydrogen# getfacl test_file2

# file: test_file2
# owner: root
# group: other
user::rw-
user:jgreen:rw-          #effective:rw-
group::r--               #effective:r--
mask:rw-
other:---
hydrogen#
```

The minus sign following the "-f" tells `setfacl` that the file containing the ACL is actually its own standard input. You will see that, as well as setting the ACL of *test_file2* to be the same as *test_file*, the standard permissions have also changed.

ACLs will stay attached to a file even if it is copied or renamed, but they can be completely removed from a file using `setfacl` with the "-d" flag. Unfortunately, you have to remove each member of the ACL by name, but at least you only have to specify the named users and groups (i.e., not the owner, group, other, or mask). When the last member is removed, the ACL will be cleared and the plus sign will no longer appear in the output from the `ls -l` command. To completely remove the ACL for *test_file2*, we would only need to remove the entry for the user *jgreen*:

```
hydrogen# setfacl -d user:jgreen test_file2
hydrogen# ls -l test_file2
-rw-r-----   1 root      other         0 Aug 14 12:42 test_file2
hydrogen#
```

If you have tried any of the above examples and found that you were getting errors similar to the one below, now is the time to put you out of your misery.

```
hydrogen# touch test_file
hydrogen# ls -l test_file
-rw-r--r--   1 root      other         0 Aug 15 15:38 test_file
hydrogen# setfacl -s user::rw-,group::r--,other:---,mask:rw-
   ,user:jgreen:rw-,user:msmith:r-- test_file
```

```
test_file: failed to set acl entries
setacl error: Operation not applicable
hydrogen#
```

ACLs can only be used on certain types of filesystems, so if you received the above error it means you probably tried to set ACLs on a filesystem whose type does not support them. Chances are you tried the command out on a file in */tmp* (whose type, TMPFS, does not support ACLs). This also means that if you copy or move a file into */tmp* for any reason its ACL will be lost. ACLs can be used on UFS filesystems and over NFS, provided both client and server are running at least Solaris 2.5.

You should also note that if you use chmod to change the group permissions of a file with ACLs set, you might inadvertently also change the group ACL permission and the ACL mask. Therefore, it is best to either use set-facl to change the permissions or to ensure that you check the ACL first using getfacl.

ACLs can be set on directories as well as files. They are set in exactly the same way we have seen, but in addition directories can be given default ACLs. The default ACL setting for a directory will be used for any files or directories that are created under it. The following command will set an ACL for a directory (unfortunately, setting ACLs for directories involves a fairly long command):

```
hydrogen# ls -ld dir
drwxr-x---   2 jgreen    staff          512 Aug 15 16:47 dir
hydrogen# setfacl -s user::rwx,group::r-x,other:
   ---,mask:rwx,default:user::r-x,default:group::
   r-x,default:other:---,default mask:rwx dir
hydrogen# ls -ld dir
drwxr-x---+  2 jgreen    staff          512 Aug 15 16:47 dir
hydrogen# getfacl dir

# file: dir
# owner: jgreen
# group: staff
user::rwx
group::r-x                 #effective:r-x
mask:r-x
other:---
default:user::r-x
default:group::r-x
default:mask:rwx
default:other:---
hydrogen#
```

This means that when a directory is created under the directory *dir*, it will automatically get an ACL equal to the default values set within *dir*. Although files created under *dir* will not get an ACL set specifically, the default ACL of the directory will determine the permissions of the files rather than the umask.

```
hydrogen# umask
0022
hydrogen# touch new_file
hydrogen# ls -l new_file
-rw-r--r--   1 root      other          0 Aug 15 17:14 new_file
hydrogen# cd dir
hydrogen# touch new_file2
hydrogen# ls -l new_file2
-r--r-----   1 root      other          0 Aug 15 17:17 new_file2
hydrogen# mkdir new_dir
hydrogen# ls -ld new_dir
dr-xr-x---+  2 root      other        512 Aug 15 17:22 new_dir
hydrogen# getfacl new_dir

# file: new_dir
# owner: root
# group: other
user::r-x
group::r-x                 #effective:r-x
mask:rwx
other:---
default:user::r-x
default:group::r-x
default:mask:rwx
default:other:---
hydrogen#
```

You will see above that the directory created under *dir* does not receive the same permissions as *dir*, but permissions based on the default ACLs of *dir*. It is also possible to add default ACLs for specific users and groups to directory ACLs:

```
hydrogen# setfacl -m default:user:msmith:rwx dir
hydrogen# getfacl dir

# file: dir
# owner: jgreen
# group: staff
user::rwx
group::r-x                 #effective:r-x
mask:r-x
other:---
default:user::r-x
default:user:msmith:rwx
default:group::r-x
default:mask:rwx
default:other:---
hydrogen#
```

This will now cause all files and directories created under *dir* to have an ACL that also includes the above entry for user *msmith*:

```
hydrogen# cd dir
hydrogen# touch new_file3
hydrogen# getfacl new_file3
```

```
# file: new_file3
# owner: root
# group: other
user::r--
user:msmith:rwx              #effective:rw-
group::r--                   #effective:r--
mask:rw-
other:---
hydrogen#
```

One of the downsides of ACLs is that they are not easy to find, as there is no specific option to tell the `find` command to report them. The only real way is to examine the output from `ls -l`, which is not that practical and you cannot actually see what the ACL permissions are without using the `getfacl` command. This means that ACLs are a good way for hackers to add back-doors to your system without an easy way of finding them.

If a file has an ACL set, it will not be stored in the file's inode; instead, it is stored in a shadow inode. This means that if you use a large number of ACLs, you could find the filesystem running short of inodes.

The Implementation

To help us administer our systems, we have written a few short scripts (which can go in our standard toolset). The first will search for *root*-owned files with ACLs and report the filename along with the actual ACL to a log file. If we run this script from `cron` regularly and examine the log file, we can be sure that no one will hide anything in a file's ACL. The script is cumbersome in the way it finds the ACLs, so it is advisable to run it during a quiet time. The script is as follows:

```
#!/bin/ksh
# shell script called from the root crontab to
# search for files owned by root, but with ACLs set
# and report them to a log
#
date=$(date +%d%m%y)
aclLog=/usr/local/utils/logs/acl_${date}.log
prog=$(basename $0)
# for each file with ACLs set write the filename and the
# ACL to the log file


for file in $(find / -user root -exec ls -ld {} \; | grep
'^..........+' | sed 's/^.* //')
do
  echo "$file has the following ACL set:"
  getfacl $file
  echo "===================================="
done > $aclLog
```

The above script will only report ACLs on files and directories that belong to *root*. The sort of thing we would need to look out for is a file whose standard permissions only allow *root* to update it, but has an ACL set that allows some other user to update it also. The script could be improved by making it report only the files that were a potential threat (to save us from having to search through the log for them).

The second script is based on the examples we saw earlier of using find to report *setuid* files, but this time we have taken the work away from the administrator. The script looks for *setuid* files owned by *root* that are writeable by group or others. If any are found, an email is sent to the *root* user so the administrator does not need to examine any logs:

```
#!/bin/ksh
# shell script called from the root crontab to
# search for setuid files owned by root that are writeable
# by group or other
# Alert the system administrator of any found by email
grpw=$(find / -user root -perm -4000 -type f -exec ls -ld
    {} \; | grep '^.....w' | sed 's/.* //')
othw=$(find / -user root -perm -4000 -type f -exec ls -ld
    {} \; | grep '^........w' | sed 's/.* //')
if [[ ! -z ${grpw} ]]
then
    echo "WARNING - The following files are setuid root and
        writable by group\n$grpw" | mail root
fi
if [[ ! -z ${othw} ]]
then
    echo "WARNING - The following files are setuid root and
        writable by anyone\n$grpw" | mail root
fi
```

Octal Permissions Lookup Table

Table 4.2 shows a selection of octal permissions along with their actual permissions (as shown by the ls -l command). It may help you if haven't yet been able to get your head around using octal numbers to represent absolute permissions (don't worry—you'll get used to it!). Note: the initial character representing the file type is not included.

Table 4.2 *Octal Permissions Table*

Octal Permissions	Actual Permissions
400	r--------
440	r--r-----
444	r--r--r--
500	r-x------
550	r-xr-x---
555	r-xr-xr-x
600	rw-------
640	rw-r-----
660	rw-rw----
664	rw-rw-r--
666	rw-rw-rw-
700	rwx------
755	rwxr-xr-x
775	rwxrwxr-x
777	rwxrwxrwx
1777	rwxrwxrwt
2444	r--r-lr--
2555	r-xr-sr-x
4555	r-sr-xr-x
6555	r-sr-sr-x

5

SHELLS

Manual Pages

bash (1)
csh (1)
environ (5)
fc (1)
hash (1)
ksh (1)
sh (1)

Files Affected

/etc/default/login
/etc/passwd
/etc/profile
~/.cshrc
~/.profile

Objectives

The shell is a vast topic that is often, deservedly, the sole subject of a book. Since we want to cover other topics in this book, we must be somewhat restrictive about what we include here. This chapter is geared toward the novice system administrator, but we have tried to include more advanced concepts so that people at most levels will find at least something of interest. After a quick discussion on the different shells available, we will concentrate on the Korn Shell and cover such topics as shell and environment variables, simple shell scripting, positional parameters, wildcards and other shell metacharacters, redirection, piping, and command line parsing. We also include some example shell scripts at the end of the chapter.

What Is a Shell?

On a UNIX system, anyone wishing to log in and make use of anything other than an installed application will have to become familiar with using a shell. A shell is a program that sits between you (the user) and the UNIX kernel. You can tell the computer what to do by typing commands into the shell and it will run them for you. You can even write your own programs that can be run (interpreted) by the shell. These are generally called "shell scripts."

To make things difficult (or to make things easy—depending on how you look at it), there are a number of shells to choose from. Some have similar features to others, some are very different, and some also have rather strange names.

Whichever shell you use, they all have some things in common:

- You can type UNIX commands into them.

- You can write your own shell scripts (although the syntax will be different in some shells).

- You can define your own environment (again, this is done slightly differently in some shells).

When you first log in, a shell is started for you as part of the login procedure (see Chapter 3, "User Administration"). While you are logged in, the shell will continue running; when you log out, it stops. (For the pedants among us, it is actually the other way around—while the shell is running, we are logged in; when we stop the shell, we are no longer logged in.)

The shell reads a line of input from your keyboard, executes the command(s) on that line, and then waits for the next line. It will keep doing this until it receives the end-of-file character (<ctrl-d>) or a logout command such as `exit`.

Most commands typed in will be operating system commands that live in various locations on the hard disk (see Chapter 6, "The Filesystem and Its Contents"), but some are actually part of the shell. An example of a command that is built into the shell is `exit`. No file is associated with this command; the shell knows that when you type it in, it should stop running. Each different shell has different built-in commands, which only adds to the confusion. The next section will attempt to give some guidance on which shell is the best one to use.

What Shells? C Shells?

A number of shells are available and, in general, users will just get used to using the one they are assigned by their system administrator. They may not know which one they are using, or even be aware that alternatives exist.

Around 15 years ago when we began using UNIX, the choice was really between two shells: the Bourne Shell (/bin/sh) or the C Shell (/bin/csh). The general consensus at the time was that the Bourne Shell was the easier of the two to use. It had a simple interface and was less cryptic than the C Shell for writing shell scripts in. The scripts were also more portable across different flavors of UNIX. The C Shell had a syntax very similar to the C language so C programmers tended to favor it, but everyone else tended to use the Bourne Shell.

The C Shell, however, did have one big advantage over the Bourne Shell and that was its command line history and editing facilities. The C Shell could be told to keep a list of the commands you had typed in and allow you to rerun them without all the effort of retyping them. More useful, though, was the ability to alter lines so if you had typed in a long command but mistyped something you could correct and rerun the line with a few keystrokes. Though this was not a particularly intuitive interface, once learned most people found it very useful.

At the time, most of my colleagues and I preferred to use both shells. We would use the C Shell as our login shell, but write shell scripts using Bourne Shell syntax.

There are two ways of running a shell script. The first is to provide it as an argument to the shell command itself (i.e., `sh script_name` would cause the Bourne Shell to run the script and `csh script_name` would cause the C Shell to run it). This way allows you to run a Bourne Shell script from within a C Shell, but it is rather a pain and it would be better if you could run your script in the same way as other UNIX commands—by just typing their name. It is possible to do this if you first set execute permission on the shell script. The problem now is that if you type the script name from a C Shell prompt, the C Shell will try and run it itself (which will result in a serious number of syntax errors if it is a Bourne Shell script). What was needed was a way of specifying which shell should run a script without you needing to type it in each time you wanted to run it; fortunately a method existed. You could simply type "#!" followed by the full path of the shell you wished to use at the very start of your script.

The following at the start of a script identifies it as a Bourne Shell script; any shell would know how to run it:

```
#! /bin/sh
```

This may lead you to conclude that you should also use the C Shell for interactive work and the Bourne Shell for scripting, but this was some time ago and things have changed since then.

The Bourne Shell and C Shell still exist and are still widely used. However, a number of other shells have been added to their ranks. Most started off in the public domain and some were picked up by UNIX vendors and incorporated within their UNIX offering.

Solaris offers a choice of the following shells:

- Bourne Shell (`/bin/sh`)
- C Shell (`/bin/csh`)
- Trusted C Shell (`/bin/tcsh`)
- Korn Shell (`/bin/ksh`)
- Job Shell (`/bin/jsh`)
- Z Shell (`/bin/zsh`)
- Bash Shell (`/bin/bash`)

The Bourne Shell offers a simple interface with a standard and noncomplex scripting language. The C Shell offers a powerful user interface and complex scripting language. The TCSH Shell is based on the C Shell but with additional features such as spelling correction. The Korn Shell offers a powerful and simple user interface, is fully compatible with the Bourne Shell for scripting, and offers useful extensions. The Job Shell is the Bourne Shell with added job control commands that enable you to manipulate jobs (commands or programs) while they are running. The Z Shell closely resembles the Korn Shell and provides some enhancements. The Bash Shell (Bourne Again Shell) began life in the public domain and is similar to the Korn Shell, but with some extensions.

The shell you choose depends upon many factors and to some extent it is not too important. Many organizations tend to standardize on the Korn Shell since it is widely available, is fully compatible with the Bourne Shell, and tends to be the most widely used.

We will use the Korn Shell for all scripts and examples within this book. This chapter will contain a few references to other shells when appropriate.

Whatever shell you choose to provide for your users, it is important that you don't change the shell used by the *root* user. This is because most shells available in Solaris are dynamically linked. This means that when they are compiled, instead of all the libraries used in the code being included within the final executable file they are loaded as they are needed while the executable program runs. The advantage of this includes the fact that the executable will be smaller and will therefore take up less memory when it runs. Also, if any dynamic libraries are updated the executable will not need recompiling to include them.

The downside of using dynamically linked libraries is that if they are missing for any reason, programs that need to use them will not be able to run. These libraries are located in the */usr* filesystem so if this became corrupt or inaccessible, *root* would not be able to fix the problem if it had a dynamically linked shell. To avoid this problem, the shell `/sbin/sh` is statically linked so *root* should always have this one set in the */etc/passwd* file (see Chapter 3,

"User Administration"). It is also a good idea not to use a shell with a history facility for the *root* user, as it is easy to accidentally select the wrong command from the history list. This could cause all sorts of problems, as UNIX assumes you know what you are doing and tends not to ask if you really want to do something. And remember, *root* has permission to do anything.

Shell Variables

Programming languages allow the creation of variables as a mechanism to store data for later manipulation, and UNIX shells are no different. The way shell variables are assigned is different depending on the shell being used. Bourne Shell variables are assigned by simply entering the name of the variable followed by an equal sign and the value you wish to assign to it. They do not need to be defined first and therefore there is no need to say what type of data the variable will hold before it is assigned a value. If a variable holds a string of characters, you may manipulate it as you would the string of characters that was assigned to it, but you may not perform arithmetical operations on it. If the same variable were then to have a number assigned to it, you would be able to perform arithmetic on it.

The following example shows the assignment of a number of shell variables:

```
$ greeting=hello
$ age=21
$ formalGreeting="Good Morning"
$
```

Here we have created three variables. The variable name is the word to the left of the equal sign and the value assigned is to the right. In each case, if the variable had already existed its original value would be replaced with the value we assigned above. If it didn't previously exist, the shell would create it for us. In the final example we wanted to include a space in the variable value so we put quotes around the whole string. We can use any combination of letters and numbers for shell variable names, but we cannot use a number as the first character.

Using Shell Variables

We have seen that setting shell variables is a straightforward procedure. We just need to remember not to put any spaces around the equal sign, and if we want to include spaces in what we are assigning we should use quotes.

Using a variable is also straightforward. We simply put a dollar sign before the variable name and the shell will replace it with the value assigned to it:

```
$ firstname=dominic
$ lastname=butler
$ echo $firstname
dominic
$ echo $lastname
butler
$ echo $firstname $lastname
dominic butler
$
```

We can mix variables with straight text in a similar way:

```
$ echo My surname is $surname and my first is $firstname
My surname is butler and my first is dominic
$
```

The shell can tell which are the variable names since they begin with a dollar symbol and the last character of the name is followed by a space. However, if we didn't want to display a space between the contents of a variable and the following text, the shell would have a bit of a job knowing where the variable name ended and the text began:

```
$ name=fred
echo $name
fred
$ echo $namedy

$
```

Here we wanted to display the contents of the variable name followed by the text "dy" with no space between. The trouble is—how does the shell know that? It thinks we want to display the contents of a variable called "namedy," which it sees does not exist so it replaces it with an empty string. To do this, we need a way of telling the shell where the variable name ends; fortunately we can do this by using curly braces:

```
$ name=fred
$ echo ${name}dy
freddy
$
```

Now there is no confusion at all. The shell knows exactly what we want as we have specifically told it that the variable is called "name."

Using Variables in Shell Scripts

Shell variables tend to be used within shell scripts rather than at the shell prompt. Consequently, we will look at a few basic examples of shell scripts that make use of shell variables.

A shell script is simply a file that contains a number of UNIX commands. The shell executes the commands in order. Once we have created a shell script, if we give it execute permissions (see Chapter 4, "Permissions and All That") we can run it in the same way we run UNIX commands:

```
$ cat script1.sh
day=Monday
date="15/04/2002"
echo The date is $day the $date
$ ./script1.sh
The date is Monday the 15/04/2002
$
```

We put "./" in front of the script so that the shell knows that it is in our current directory. The shell can only run a command if it knows where it is (we will look at how this is dealt with later in the chapter).

This is very simple and only useful on Monday, April 15, 2002. It would be better if the user could supply the day and date to the script each time it ran. There are two ways of doing this: Either the script asks the user for the information or the user supplies the information on the command line when the script is executed.

We will look at how to do the former first:

```
$ cat script2.sh
echo what day of the week is it?
read day
echo what is the date?
read date
echo The date is $day the $date
$ ./script2.sh
what day of the week is it?
Tuesday
what is the date?
16/04/2002
The date is Tuesday the 16/04/2002
$
```

The read command is used to read input from the keyboard and store it in the variable that follows it.

The second way of writing this script makes use of positional parameters.

Positional Parameters

Positional parameters are used in most UNIX commands and consist of everything you type on the command line following the program name:

```
$ cat script3.sh
echo The date is $1 the $2
$ ./scripts3.sh Wednesday 17/04/2002
The date is Wednesday the 17/04/2002
$
```

This example is much shorter and makes use of some special shell variables that are used to handle positional parameters. Whenever a shell script is called, any parameters supplied on the command line are placed in these special variables (this also explains why we are not allowed to create our own variables beginning with a number). If there were more than nine parameters we would have a problem. For example, $10 would be treated by the shell as the variable $1 followed by a zero; we would need to use curly braces so the shell is sure what we mean. In fact, it is good practice to use curly braces with all shell variables.

As well as creating the variables to hold the positional parameters (${1}, etc.), the shell will also put the name of the shell script in the variable ${0}, the number of parameters in the variable ${#}, and the complete list of parameters in the variable ${*}.

```
$ cat script4.sh
echo this script is called ${0}
echo it was called with ${#} parameters
echo the parameters are ${*}
$ ./script4.sh one two three four five
this script is called ./script4.sh
it was called with 4 parameters
the parameters are one two three four
$
```

We can see if our current shell was called with any parameters by looking at these variables at the shell prompt:

```
$ echo ${0}
-ksh
$ echo ${#}
0
$ echo ${*}

$
```

We can see that it wasn't, but we can assign positional parameters using the set command:

```
$ set one two three
$ echo ${#}
3
$ echo ${*}
one two three
$
```

The shell was not supplied with these parameters when it was executed, but we have assigned them ourselves. This can be done within shell scripts, also.

Scope of Shell Variables

When a shell variable is created it can only be used within that shell. If you run a subshell the variable will effectively disappear, but when you return to your parent shell it will be available for use again. This means that if you create a variable in a subshell with the same name as one in the parent shell, you will not affect the contents of the variable in the parent shell at all:

```
$ name=fred
$ echo ${name}
fred
$ sh
$ echo ${name}

$ exit
$ echo ${name}
fred
$
```

If we want to see a variable created in a parent shell in its subshell, we can do so by exporting the variable:

```
$ name=fred
$ export name
$ sh
$ echo ${name}
fred
$ name=bill
$ echo ${name}
bill
$ exit
$ echo ${name}
fred
$
```

Now that we have exported the variable it can be seen and used in the subshell, but if we alter the value within the subshell we still cannot affect the value it had in the parent shell.

Exported variables have a special function within the shell; they are used to define the user's environment.

The Environment

A user's environment can be thought of as providing a similar function to user preference settings found within many PC Windows applications. Instead of these preference settings being entered using a nice graphical tool, they are set by assigning environment variables (this is UNIX, remember). An environment variable is simply a shell variable that has been exported. To help differentiate between shell variables and environment variables, the convention is to use lowercase letters for shell variables and uppercase for environment variables (though this is not enforced in any way). The system administrator will set up some of these environment variables for all users, but users may also set their own. In general, if you have access to a shell prompt you can change any aspect of the environment; however, the system administrator can set any of them to read-only to prevent you from doing so.

A number of environment variables are predefined when a user logs in, but the system administrator may define others.

Table 5.1 describes the major environment variables used within the Korn Shell.

Table 5.1 *Environment Variables*

Variable Name	Description
LOGNAME	This variable holds your login name.
TERM	This variable is used to tell applications and programs what kind of terminal or terminal emulator you are using. If you don't set this to the right value, programs such as vi will not function correctly.
TERMINAL_EMULATOR	An alternative to $TERM. Used by some applications instead of $TERM.
HOME	This holds the full path of the user's home directory and is set at login time.
MAIL	This variable holds the full path of the user's mail file.
MAILCHECK	This variable holds the number of seconds used as the interval between the shell checking the mail file for new mail (usually set to 600).
MAILMSG	This holds the message you would like displayed when you have new mail.
SHELL	This holds the full path to the shell you are using.
PATH	This is set to a colon-separated list of directories that the shell will search to run the commands you type in. If you don't have a PATH set, the only commands you can run are those that are built into the shell!
CDPATH	This is similar to the PATH variable in that it is set to a colon-separated list of directories, but it is used by the cd command to decide what directory to change to. It is not normally set by default.

Table 5.1 *Environment Variables (Continued)*

Variable Name	Description
MANPATH	This can also hold a colon-separated list of directories that the man command will look in for man pages.
LIBPATH	If this variable is set it will be used by C compilers to search for libraries with which to link your code.
TZ	This holds the time zone to use (e.g., GB).
LANG	This holds the language you are using (e.g., en_GB.ISO8859-15).
PS1	This variable holds your primary prompt. The default value is "$ " (a dollar sign followed by a space) for ordinary users and "# " for the *root* user. This can be changed, and often is.
PS2	The secondary prompt. The shell displays this if it decides that you haven't completed the previous command. The default value is "> ".
PS3	The default value is "#? ". This prompt is displayed when using the ksh select statement interactively.
PS4	The default value is "+ ". This is displayed when using the "-x" option to trace/debug a ksh shell script. This prompt is displayed at the beginning of each expanded line.
ENV	This can hold the name of a file that will be executed within the shell each time it is invoked (unlike *.profile* which is only invoked at login time).
TMOUT	If this is set to a value greater than zero, the shell will exit (thus logging you off) if a command is not entered within that number of seconds following the issuing of the PS1 prompt.
PWD	The shell sets this variable to hold your current directory. It is updated every time you use the cd command.
IFS	This variable (Internal Field Separator) is set, by default, to a space, a tab, and a newline character. The shell will treat all IFS characters as separators.

Shells

Table 5.1 *Environment Variables (Continued)*

Variable Name	Description
FCEDIT	This should be set to the name of the editor you wish to use when running the `fc` command (which allows you to edit your command history).
DISPLAY	If you are using X Windows to access a server running Solaris, this variable will hold the IP address of your PC or X Station. The address will end in ":0" or ":0.0" to signify that you are using the first screen at that address.
$?	Read-only. Holds the exit status of the last command executed by the shell.
$$	Read-only. Holds the process ID of the current process.
$0	Read-only. Holds the name of the currently executing program.
$@	Read-only. Holds a space-separated list of all the parameters supplied to the current program.
$*	Read-only. Holds all the parameters (as per $@), but when quoted they are separated by the first character of $IFS.
$#	Read-only. Holds the number of parameters supplied to the current program.
$1, $2, $3 etc.	Read-only. Each variable holds the corresponding parameter supplied to the current program. The Korn Shell can handle a large number of positional parameters, but to handle more than nine you must use curly braces (e.g., ${256}).

(Note: The shell will supply default values to PATH, PS1, PS2, PS3, PS4, MAILCHECK, FCEDIT, TMOUT, and IFS. The value of HOME is also set, but by the login program, not the shell.)

To view your current environment variables you can use the `env` command:

```
# env
HOME=/
HZ=100
LOGNAME=root
MAIL=/var/mail/root
PATH=/usr/sbin:/usr/bin
```

```
SHELL=/sbin/sh
TERM=vt100
TZ=Europe/Stockholm
#
```

This displays only the shell variables that have been exported. If you want to see the value of all your shell variables regardless of whether they have been exported or not, you can use set instead of env:

```
# set
HOME=/
HZ=100
IFS=

LOGNAME=root
MAIL=/var/mail/root
MAILCHECK=600
OPTIND=1
PATH=/usr/sbin:/usr/bin
PS1=#
PS2=>
SHELL=/sbin/sh
TERM=vt100
TZ=Europe/Stockholm
#
```

Assigning Shells to Users

A shell is assigned to a user when the user is first created by the system administrator (see Chapter 3, "User Administration") and the full path of the user's shell is stored in the rightmost field of the password file.

When users log in to the system, the program defined in the shell field of their password file entry is executed. If the field contained /bin/ksh then that is the command that would run. Likewise, if the field contained /bin/who then that would run instead. In this case, it would display a list of who is currently logged in (which would include the users in question) and then exit back to the login prompt. This kind of entry is often used to enable specific functions to be performed by users who do not have their own login on that server, for example a shutdown user (on no account create a shutdown user called *shutdown* with a password of shutdown!).

Assuming you have /bin/ksh in your password file entry, you will be presented with the usual $ prompt following a successful login. If you want to run the C Shell instead, you can type "csh" and you will now be presented with a % prompt (due to the default value of PS1 in the C Shell). You have not, however, replaced the Korn Shell with the C Shell; the C Shell is running as a subshell, as the ps command will show you:

```
% ps -f
  UID    PID    PPIP    C       STIME      TTY      TIME    CMD
  djb    421    419     0       22:19:58   pts/4    0:00    -ksh
  djb    428    421     0       22:34:13   pts/4    0:00    csh
  djb    430    428     2       22:35:15   pts/4    0:00    ps
%
```

The minus sign before the "ksh" shows that it is a login shell.

If you wanted to run a C Shell instead of the Korn Shell, rather than as a subprocess to your Korn Shell you could type:

```
$ exec csh
$
```

—and then ps would show:

```
% ps -f
  UID    PID    PPIP    C       STIME      TTY      TIME    CMD
  djb    421    419     1       22:19:58   pts/4    0:00    csh
  djb    455    421     1       22:43:38   pts/4    0:00    ps
%
```

Of course, if users want the C Shell instead of the Korn Shell on a permanent basis, the best course of action is for them to ask the system administrator to change their entry in the password file.

The UNIX command exec tells the shell to overlay (replace) itself with the command supplied as an argument to exec. If you supply another command (i.e., not a shell), the current shell will overlay that command, which will run; however, you will be logged out when that command completes (just as you would be when the new shell completes).

This function demonstrates how the login process actually operates.

The login prompt you see on your terminal is produced by the UNIX command /usr/bin/login. When you type a user name and password, the login program will first validate these against the password and shadow files, and then (if they are valid) will use exec to overlay the program specified in the rightmost field of the password file. This program would normally be a shell, but could be any program you wished. If, for example, a user was added that had /usr/bin/date as the shell field in the password file, then logging in as that user would cause the date and time to be displayed followed by your immediate logoff. You would see no prompt and you would not get any chance to type any commands in.

This method has been used on some sites to provide a *shutdown* user that will enable the server to be shut down by somebody who does not have enough authority to actually log in to perform this manually. The password entry for such a user might look like this:

```
shutdown:x:0:1:Shutdown User:/:/usr/sbin/shutdown
```

When the user logs in, the shutdown program runs instead of the shell and shuts down the server. The UID field must be set to 0 as only *root* can perform a shutdown. Also, if you decide to create a *shutdown* user, make sure the password is secure (and definitely NOT the same as the user name).

The shell is not a special program. It works just like any other UNIX program; it just happens that its purpose is to execute the commands that it reads on its standard input. A shell actually does a lot more than execute programs, and the next section offers a brief diversion for those interested.

Running Commands

The main purpose of the shell is to run commands and programs. UNIX commands and programs generally take the following syntax:

```
command options parameters
```

The *command* is the name of the file as it appears in the directory. The *options* generally change the way the command will function and will usually consist of single letters preceded by a minus sign. The *parameters* could be anything, such as filenames or user names.

All commands have a name (otherwise they would not exist), but they don't all take options and they don't all take parameters. Even those that do take options and/or parameters (which is most) don't always have to be supplied with them. (The Solaris man pages give the usage of all Solaris commands. It is recommended that you install them on at least one of your systems.)

To execute a command, the shell must know in which directory the command is stored on the hard disk. One way to tell the shell this is to provide the full path of the command when you use it. For example, the command ls can be found in the directory */bin*. So, if you type *"/bin/ls"* at the shell prompt, the shell knows exactly where to find the command and will run it for you.

This is not very practical because users don't like typing more than they have to. Also, there are many directories containing commands on a system and people cannot be expected to remember exactly which directory contains which command.

The way we get around this is mentioned in Table 5.1, "Environment Variables," on page 102, and makes use of the $PATH variable.

On our systems we have set the PATH variable for normal users as follows:

```
export PATH="/bin:/usr/sbin:/usr/local/bin:"
```

This means that each time you type in a command the shell will look for it in */bin* and if it is found there it will be run. If it isn't, the shell will look in the next directory in the list (*/usr/sbin*) and so on.

In the example above, the PATH ends with a colon. A colon at the beginning or the end (or two colons together in the middle) of the PATH represent the current directory. (You could also use a dot to represent your current directory.) In the example above, if the shell has not found your command in the named directories, it will look in the current directory. The shell does not look in your current directory by default so if you don't include it in your PATH you will not be able to run commands located there if you don't provide their path names.

It is often useful to have a different PATH for the *root* user as there are certain commands that are normal for *root* to run, but should not be accessible to ordinary users. For example:

```
export PATH="/etc:/bin:/usr/sbin:/usr/local/bin:/usr/local/
    utilities/bin"
```

We have added the directory */etc* to the start of the *root* PATH as it is traditionally the directory that contains administrative commands. We have also added */usr/local/utilities/bin* as it is the directory we have chosen to store the administrative scripts we have developed to help manage our servers. The other difference (which you have noticed, hopefully) is that we do not include the current directory. This is because *root* has the power to do anything on the server so it is important that when *root* runs a command the expected command runs. Having the current directory included in the *root* PATH could mean that the wrong command could be run by mistake due to a file with the same name existing in the current directory. This is not just preventing mistakes, since a malicious user could write a script, give it the same name as an administrative command, and then leave it in various directories in the hope that one day *root* may accidentally run it. This may seem far-fetched, but this sort of thing has happened. In general, malicious users (or hackers) will want to try and execute something as *root* (whatever their ends); this is one way that should not be left open.

Hopefully, this is fairly straightforward, but as with most areas of UNIX there is more to it than that.

In this case, the "more to it" is that there are a number of commands that exist in more than one directory. In most cases, these commands will perform the same function and produce the same output, but this is not always so. The main reason for this is compatibility with earlier UNIX variants. Solaris has been made as compatible as possible with older versions and has specific *bin* directories to hold commands that are compatible with specific versions. For example, the directory */usr/ucb* contains commands that are compatible with those found in the Berkeley version of UNIX (known as BSD), while */usr/sbin* contains those that are compatible with UNIX System 5 Release 4 (UNIX SVR4). Both these directories contain a `df` command; although both display the current filesystem usage, the output is different and they take different options.

With a PATH set to the value above, typing `df` would always cause the SVR5 version to run since */usr/ucb* is not included in the PATH. If we included */usr/ucb* into the PATH, its position in the PATH will decide which version of `df` actually gets run.

If you want to find out which version of a command your shell is going to run, you can use the `which` command:

```
$ which df
/bin/df
$
```

If you try this with a number of different commands, you will begin to get an idea of where different commands reside.

A similar command to which is called whereis. This command comes from BSD so if your PATH does not include *usr/ucb* you will not be able to run it unless you type the full path name. You can add *usr/ucb* to your PATH by typing:

```
$ export PATH="$PATH:/usr/ucb"
$ echo $PATH
/bin:/usr/sbin:/usr/local/bin::/usr/ucb
$
```

The order for the shell to search the PATH is now:

1. *bin*
2. *usr/sbin*
3. *usr/local/bin*
4. current directory
5. *usr/ucb*

The command whereis is similar to which, but instead of just displaying the first occurrence of the command you are looking for, it displays all of them:

```
$ whereis df
df: /usr/bin/df /usr/sbin/df /usr/ucb/df
$
```

There are three df commands listed, but the first two are identical. (Note: The reason the output displays *usr/bin/df* instead of *bin/df* is because *bin* is linked to *usr/bin*. Links are discussed in Chapter 6, "The Filesystem and Its Contents.")

Some commands don't exist in directories, but are actually built into the shell. Some of the most commonly used commands are built in, such as cd and echo. The which command won't tell us if a command is built in, but the command type will:

```
$ type cd
cd is a shell builtin
$ type type
type is a shell builtin
$
```

On your Solaris system you may find that if you use which with a command that is built into the shell you get an unexpected result:

```
$ which type
/bin/type
$
```

This is because the built-in commands each have a version in */bin*. But in all cases the version in */bin* is simply a shell script that calls the built-in version (as shown below):

```
#!/bin/ksh
#
# Copyright © 1995 by Sun Microsystems, Inc.
#
cmd=`basename $0`
$cmd "$@"
```

(Note: $0 represents the name of the script (in this case type); $@ represents all the parameters which have been supplied to the script.)

You will see that the directory */bin* contains a number of scripts with the same name as a command built in to the Korn Shell. If you look in any of them you will see that they are all identical. The reason they exist is to enable you to run the Korn Shell built-ins even if you are not actually using the Korn Shell (thanks to the first line of the script).

Wildcards

UNIX gives you various ways to be lazy, and one of the most useful is in the use of wildcards. If you are familiar with wildcards you may have thought that UNIX commands must be written to a standard so that they treat the wildcard characters in the same way. UNIX commands do have many standards, but this is not one of them. UNIX commands in general wouldn't know a wildcard character if it had "I AM A WILDCARD" tattooed across its chest.

Wildcards are, instead, dealt with by the shell. They are used as a way of matching filenames; the man pages refer to this as File Name Generation.

The wildcard characters are:

- *

- ?

- []

The asterisk (*) matches zero or more occurrences of any character. The question mark (?) matches a single character. The square brackets ([ ]) will match any of the characters included within the brackets.

For example, [A-L] would match any single character in the range A-L inclusive. This is case-specific; if you wanted to match all characters in the range A to L, you would specify [A-La-l]. If the first character after the "[" is "!" then it means "NOT." If you want to match a minus sign, put it just after the "[" or just before the "]" and it will not be treated as meaning a range of characters.

The following examples show how the wildcard characters can be used. They all use the `ls` command, but wildcard characters can be used with any command that can take filenames as parameters:

```
$ ls
abc
def
frank
fred
freddie
freddy
test
test1
test11
test12
test2
test21
$
```

The first example is nice and simple; it will match all files that begin with the letter "f."

```
$ ls f*
frank
fred
freddie
freddy
$
```

The next example uses "?," which will match any single character. So here we get the files with a name beginning with "test" followed by any single character:

```
$ ls test?
test1
test2
$
```

The pattern used in this example (???) matches all files with a name exactly three characters long:

```
$ls ???
abc
def
$
```

The final two examples make use of the square brackets, which match one of a range of characters:

```
$ ls test1[1-5]
test11
test12
$
```

In the previous example, we have said we want to match all files whose names begin "test1" followed by a single character that can be any in the range "1" to "5." If there had been a file called *test123*, it would not have matched since it has an extra character in its name and the square brackets only match a single character.

In this last example, we match all files with a first letter in the range "a" to "m":

```
$ ls [a-m]*
abc
def
frank
fred
freddie
freddy
$
```

These show a fair selection of wildcard examples. However, the best way of getting to grips with them is by practice (rm is probably not a good command to use for practicing wildcard usage).

Wildcard patterns can be grouped together into a pattern list. This is formed by putting the pipe symbol "|" between each pattern. The pattern list can then be placed within the constructs listed in Table 5.2 to offer more advanced filename matching.

Table 5.2 *Advanced Wildcard Usage*

Construct	Meaning
?(pattern list)	Will optionally match any one of the included patterns.
*(pattern list)	Will match zero or more occurrences of the included patterns.
+(pattern list)	Matches one or more occurrences of the included patterns.
@(pattern list)	Matches exactly one of the supplied patterns.
!(pattern list)	Will match anything except one of the supplied patterns.

For example:

```
$ ls ?(a*|*2)
abc
test12
test2
$
```

Here, a file matched if it either began with an "a" or ended with a "2."

Additional Notes on Wildcards

Most UNIX commands do not know what a wildcard is, but what about those that do? If the shell sees the wildcard, then the shell will replace it with the files that it matches. Even if the command does know about wildcards, it won't see it.

An example of a command that does know about wildcards is find. The find command is used to find files on your system that match certain criteria. This includes finding:

- Files with a certain name
- Files whose name matches a certain pattern of wildcards
- Files that haven't been accessed for a certain amount of time
- Files that are bigger than a certain size
- Files that are owned by a certain user
- Files that are a certain type (e.g., named pipes or directories)

Find doesn't just look for the first file that matches the search criteria. It will keep searching and report all the files that match, so it is great when you need to provide a list of files that can be passed to another command (such as a backup utility—see Chapter 22, "Backing Up and Restoring the System").

Full details of using find are described in the Solaris man pages. Here, however, we have a basic example so we can demonstrate how to use wildcards without the shell getting its hands on them first.

If you wanted to find all the files (including directories) called fred on the system, searching from the current directory downward you would use find as follows:

```
# cd /
# find . -name fred -print
./fred
./export/home/fred
./var/mail/fred
#
```

This command means "search for all files called fred starting in the current directory and print the results to the screen." The default action is to print to the screen, so the "-print" can be left off, though people tend to use it anyway. Because we used "." to specify "current directory," all the paths returned begin with a "." (they are relative to the starting directory). If we have put a slash ("/") to mean "start" at the *root* directory, the paths returned would have begun with a "/" and would be absolute path names. If you ever search for a file from the *root* directory as any user other than *root*, expect to get lots of errors back for all the directories that you do not have permission to access. This would be a good time to redirect all error messages to */dev/null*. An example of doing this is shown later in the chapter in the section "File Redirection" on page 119.

Now we get to the wildcards.

If we wanted to find all files from the current directory that began with an "f" then we would use the "*" wildcard after the "f" as follows:

```
# cd /
# find . -name f* -print
```

Now we can't show the next bit as there are three possible outcomes and the actual one is dependent on what other files exist in the directory from which the command was run.

- Outcome 1: Because the shell deals with wildcards, it will look for files in the current directory that match the wildcard pattern specified. If there are no files that match, the pattern will be left as you typed it and the above command would find all the files under the current directory that begin with an "f."

- Outcome 2: Because the shell deals with wildcards, it will look for files in the current directory that match the wildcard pattern specified. If there were one file in the current directory that began with an "f" the shell would replace the "f*" with that filename. Thus, in this case, the command you typed would find all files with that name, NOT all files that begin with "f."

- Outcome 3: Because the shell deals with wildcards, it will look for files in the current directory that match the wildcard pattern specified. If there were several files in the current directory that began with "f" the shell would replace the "f*" with all the names that match separated by a space. The outcome this time would be that, rather than the find command going off and doing the wrong thing, it will actually fail with a syntax error as only one filename can be supplied with the "-name" option.

To guarantee that the find command runs as expected, any filename containing a wildcard should have quotes around it (single or double). The shell cannot see wildcards when they are in quotes so the find command sees it and deals with it itself. We will look at hiding things from the shell in more detail in the next section.

If you are used to using wildcards on PCs you will use "*.*" to match all files. In UNIX, "*.*" will match all files that contain a dot, but not those that don't. To match all files in a directory use "*" (with no dot).

If a filename begins with a dot, it will not be matched by a single asterisk; you will need to specify the dot (i.e, ".*").

Hiding Things from the Shell

We have just looked at an example where we needed to hide a wildcard from the shell so that the find command could see it and deal with it instead. In that example we used quotes to hide the wildcard from the shell, but as we shall see there are a number of other ways of hiding things from the shell and a number of other reason we may wish to do so.

When we looked at shell variables earlier in the chapter we saw that if the shell sees any word beginning with a dollar sign it will assume it is a variable and will replace it with the contents of that variable. If there is no such variable defined then the shell will simply remove it. So if we had written a shell script that was a simple betting game and we wanted to print a message telling the user he had just won $1,000 you might try the following:

```
echo You have just won $1000
```

The shell will see the "$" and think "Ah! We have an environment variable here; let's replace it with its value."

The shell will actually recognize the $1 of the $1,000 and will think we want to print the contents of $1 followed by "000." If $1 has no value (because the shell was invoked with no parameters) then it will remove the $1 and print:

```
You have just won 000
```

If $1 contained the word "fred" then we would get:

```
You have just won fred000
```

Neither of these is what we wanted but if we could hide the "$" from the shell then we would be OK.

We saw that we could hide a wildcard using single (') or double (") quotes, but variables are different. If we use double quotes the shell will still see the "$," but if we use single quotes the shell won't. In this respect single quotes can be thought of as being stronger than double quotes.

So, to get the line we want we could type:

```
echo You have just won '$1000'
```

But it probably looks neater to type:

```
echo 'You have just won $1000'
```

Both of them will cause the correct result to be printed to the screen.

After getting this bit of your betting script working, you may decide you don't always want the message to print out that the user has won $1,000; you might want to hold the value in a variable and print that out. If the variable was called "value" we could set it as follows:

```
value=500
```

But we have a problem when we try to print the contents of $value with a "$" in front of it. If we try the following:

```
echo You have won $$value
```

We will get:

```
You have won 1421value
```

—or something similar because the environment variable $$ holds the process ID of the current shell. The problem we have is that we want the shell to see the "$" of $value, but not the other one.

There are two solutions. The first is to put single quotes around the first dollar sign:

```
echo You have won '$'$value
```

The second looks a bit neater and that is to put a backslash character (\) before the first dollar sign:

```
echo You have won \$$value
```

The backslash will hide the next character from the shell regardless of what it is.

In summary, we can use single quotes, double quotes, or the backslash to hide things from the shell, but double quotes are not as strong as the others are, since they do not hide variables from the shell. The reason that double quotes do not hide variables is deliberate and helps us get around a potential problem with the way the shell handles unassigned variables.

We saw above that if a variable has no value, the shell simply removes it from the command line. So if the variable $firstname has no value but $lastname is set to Butler, the following would happen:

```
$ echo My name is $firstname $lastname
My name is Butler
$
```

This is not such a problem when we are just printing something to the screen, but if we wanted to pass parameters to a command that expects a certain number we could have a problem.

If a program called name expected to be called with two parameters we could call it as follows:

```
$ name $firstname $lastname
$
```

But if $firstname was not set the shell would remove it from the command line and the program called name would complain that it had only been called with one parameter rather than the expected two. The way to fix this is to put double quotes around each of the variable names.

```
$ name "$firstname" "$lastname"
$
```

Even though the empty variable is removed from the line, the now empty first set of double quotes remains and is treated as an empty parameter by the program.

There are in fact a whole selection of characters that have a special meaning to the shell (the correct term for them is "shell metacharacters") and all can be hidden from the shell if required. Single quotes will hide everything they enclose, double quotes will hide everything apart from the dollar symbol, and a backslash will hide the next single character, whatever it is.

Command Substitution

We have looked at the use of the single quote (') and the use of the double quote ("), but the back quote (`) is also a shell metacharacter and it is used to enable command substitution.

If the shell sees a pair of back quotes in a command line it will execute the entire command contained inside the back quotes first and then replace it with the output from that command. Then it will run the original command.

So if we wanted to edit a script called `script1.sh` that existed in a directory included in our path we could use the `which` command (we've already described this earlier) to locate the script and then type in the full path name:

```
$ which script1.sh
/usr/local/bin/script1.sh
$ vi /usr/local/bin/script1.sh
<output removed for clarity>
$
```

Alternatively we could make use of command substitution to do the whole thing in one command:

```
$ vi `which script1.sh`
<output removed for clarity>
$
```

The shell will first run the command enclosed in the back quotes and then replace the back quotes and their contents with the output from that command, which then becomes the parameter to the `vi` command.

The back quote is actually a construct from the Bourne Shell, but it also works with the Korn Shell as the Korn Shell is fully compatible with the Bourne Shell. In the future this compatibility cannot be guaranteed so it is better to use the actual Korn Shell syntax, which is to use "$(" in place of the opening back quote and ")" in place of the closing back quote. So the above example would be written as follows:

```
$ vi $(which script1.sh)
<output removed for clarity>
$
```

Shortcuts

This section looks at some more useful shortcuts that are available to users of the Korn Shell.

Home Directory

Instead of having to type in the full path of a user's home directory, you can just type a tilde (~) character followed by the user's login name:

```
$ cd ~jgreen
$ pwd
/export/home/jgreen
$
```

Previous Directory

The Korn Shell remembers which directory you where last in so you can move to it without needing to type it in. Just type "cd -":

```
$ pwd
/really/long/pathname/that/I/can/never/remember
$ cd /tmp
$ pwd
/tmp
$ cd -
$ pwd
/really/long/pathname/that/I/can/never/remember
$
```

Aliases

The Korn Shell allows you to create shortcuts to commands. For example, the following will create an alias called ll which will run an ls -l.

```
$ alias ll="ls -l"
$
```

So now whenever you want to run ls -l you can type "ll" instead. If you type "alias" on its own, you will get a list of all the aliases you have set up within your shell. Creating an alias will only affect you and you can use the unalias command to remove an alias.

```
$ unalias ll
$
```

When you run alias by itself, you will notice that there are aliases in addition to the ones you set up. You may even notice that the number of aliases can change during a login session. This is because the Korn Shell creates its own aliases, which are called "tracked aliases."

The first time you run a command after logging in, the shell will search for it using your path. Once it has found the location of this command it will create a tracked alias. This means that the next time you run that command, because the tracked alias exists, the shell doesn't need to waste time finding it again using your path. If you change the value of $PATH during the session, all tracked aliases are unaliased to ensure your changes are acted upon. The `hash` command will display the tracked aliases and you can clear them yourself by running `hash -r`:

```
$ hash
ls=/usr/bin/ls
$ cat /etc/passwd
<lines removed for clarity>
$ hash
cat=/usr/bin/cat
ls=/usr/bin/ls
$ hash -r
$ hash
$
```

What Else Does the Shell Do?

When you type a command in at the shell prompt, the shell will analyze the line you have typed and make changes to it before it actually executes it. In actual fact, the shell will read each line a number of times before deciding it is happy with it.

Before we go through the main actions undertaken by the shell, it would make sense to ensure that you are familiar with how UNIX handles reading from and writing to files. This is one of the strong features of UNIX and has contributed to its success and longevity.

File Redirection

For a process to read from a file or write to a file, it must first be opened. This is an action performed by the operating system so you won't actually need to do it yourself, but you do need to be aware of it. When the file is opened, Solaris gives it a file descriptor, which is a number. The numbers start at 0, and the lowest unused number will always be assigned. Once a file is open, it is accessed by the file descriptor rather than the name. The sequence of events is that the program will say to the operating system (or the Solaris kernel to be more precise): "Please will you open this file for me and when you've done it give me the file descriptor that you have assigned to it." From that moment on, every time the program wants to either read from or write to the file it will do so via the file descriptor. When the program has finished using the file it should ask the operating system to close it, which will in turn free up the file descriptor allocated to it so it can be used if another file is opened. If the program forgets to tidy up after itself by closing the files it had open, they will all be closed automatically when the program stops running. File descriptors are allocated per process rather than across all the running processes, so even though many processes will be using the same file descriptor number that does not mean they have the same file open.

When a user first logs in and the shell starts up, one of the first things the shell does is open three files. These special files are called *standard input* or *stdin* (which is actually attached to your keyboard), *standard out* or *stdout* (attached to your screen), and *standard error* or *stderr* (also attached to your screen). Because they are always opened in this order, *stdin* gets file descriptor 0, *stdout* gets 1, and *stderr* gets 2. This is the same with all shells so all UNIX commands that expect to read from the keyboard have, in fact, been written so they read from file descriptor 0. Likewise, if they write output to the screen they use file descriptor 1 or 2, depending on whether it is normal output or an error message.

In general, each UNIX command is written to perform one specific task. In doing so, it will generally read some data from somewhere, process this data in some way, and output the result to somewhere. The place where the data comes from is usually a file, as is the place the data is sent.

A simple example of this is the cat command, which is commonly used to display the contents of a file:

```
$ cat testfile
This is the first line of the test file
This is the second line of the test file
This is the third line of the test file
$
```

Here the command reads its input from the file *testfile*, does absolutely nothing to change it, and then writes the unchanged data to a file. It just happens that the file it writes the output to is the one with file descriptor 1 (your screen).

Because our screen and keyboard can be treated like files, it is a fairly simple task for the shell to enable us to redirect output that was intended to go to our screen into a file and in the same way redirect input that would normally come from our keyboard to come from a file (and vice versa). The general rule is that if a command reads its input from the keyboard, you can also make it read that input from a file. Likewise, if it sends output to the screen you can make this output go to a file instead. Like wildcards, this is something you may think is handled by the commands themselves, but it is actually handled by the shell. It is achieved by manipulating the file descriptors mentioned above.

Output Redirection

UNIX commands that send their output to the screen have all been written to write this output to file descriptor 1 (*stdout*); as we saw above, when the shell starts up, file descriptor 1 is always attached to your screen so everything works as expected. If we would like the output of a command to appear in a file instead, all we need to do is assign file descriptor 1 to that file and the output from the command will appear there instead of the screen. Because Solaris always gives a file the lowest available file descriptor when it is opened, all we need to do is close the screen (which will free up file descriptor 1) and then open any other file we choose. That file will be guaranteed to get file descriptor 1; as the command writes its output to file descriptor 1, it will end up in that file. We saw earlier that the lowest file descriptor is 0, but that cannot be assigned when we redirect the standard output because it is already assigned to the standard input.

To tell the shell that we want to redirect the output from a command, we use the file descriptor we wish to redirect followed by the "greater than" symbol (>).

```
$ who 1>fred
$ cat fred
sysadmin    pts/0        Feb 18 14:12    (helium)
jgreen      pts/1        Feb 18 14:15    (carbon)
$
```

In the above example, we ran the who command and redirected the output to a file called *fred*. The result is that we don't see any output at all on the screen, and when we look inside *fred* we see output that the who command would normally have displayed on the screen.

The way this works is that the shell sees that we want to redirect standard output (because it sees the "1>" characters), so it closes the file that did have file descriptor 1 and then opens the file *fred*. *Fred* is assigned the lowest available file descriptor (which is 1); this construct tells the shell to close file descriptor 1 and open *fred* before executing the who command. When the command finishes running, *fred* is closed and file descriptor 1 is once more associated with the screen.

If the file *fred* did not exist when the above command was typed, it would be created. If it already existed, then it would be emptied before the command ran. If you wish a command's output to be appended to a file, then you should use ">>" rather than ">":

```
$ date 1>>fred
$ cat fred
sysadmin    pts/0        Feb 18 14:12    (birka)
jgreen      pts/1        Feb 18 14:15    (junibacken)
Sunday February 18 17:11:47 GMT 2001
$
```

If any of the above commands had produced an error message it would not have appeared in the file we were redirecting to, but would have gone to the screen as usual. This is because all UNIX commands write their error messages to file descriptor 2, not file descriptor 1. (Remember, both these are normally attached to your screen, so you would normally see both standard output and error output on your screen.)

If you want to redirect the error messages to a file, I'm sure you've already worked out that you follow the same procedure as above but replace the "1" with a "2":

```
$ find / -name passwd -print 2>find.errors
/usr/bin/passwd
/var/adm/passwd
/etc/default/passwd
/etc/passwd
$
```

The find command has found four files named *passwd* and no error messages have gone to the screen. To see if any have gone to our file we can simply view its contents with cat:

```
$ cat find.errors
find: cannot read dir /lost+found: Permission denied
find: cannot read dir /usr/lost+found: Permission denied
find: cannot read dir /var/lost+found: Permission denied
find: cannot read dir /var/spool/lp/tmp: Permission denied
find: cannot read dir /var/spool/mqueue: Permission denied
find: cannot read dir /var/crash/skansen: Permission denied
find: cannot read dir /var/dt/sdtlogin: Permission denied
find: cannot read dir /opt/lost+found: Permission denied
<lines removed for clarity>
$
```

The error file contains many lines telling us all the places we do not have permission to look in. If we hadn't redirected these messages, then it would have been very hard to see the output we wanted since it would have been mixed up with all the errors. In fact, whenever a non-*root* user performs a find from the *root* directory, there will always be several pages of error messages. We now know how to stop them from appearing on our screen, but we don't really want them sitting in files on the hard disk. Consequently, it is common practice to redirect unwanted output to a special file called */dev/null*:

```
$ find / -name passwd -print 2>/dev/null
$
```

This file is special, as it always remains empty regardless of how much data is written to it.

If you do want to keep the error messages and you wish them to be redirected to the same file as the standard output, then the common method of doing this is as follows:

```
$ find / -name passwd -print 1>find.ouput 2>&1
$
```

In term of redirection, the ampersand can be thought of as meaning "the same as." So, in the above we are saying "send file descriptor 1 output to the file *find.output* and send the file descriptor 2 output to the same file as file descriptor 1."

If you have used redirection before, you may be slightly puzzled since you are unlikely to have ever used 1>. This is because the default output stream to redirect is standard output, so if you don't specify the number it defaults to 1. Thus, all the above examples would be valid with all the 1s removed; this is how it normally is in the real world (why type something you don't need to?).

Input Redirection

Input redirection is often a harder concept to grasp than output redirection, but it is basically the same principle.

We have seen that any UNIX command that sends its output to the screen can have it redirected to a file, but it is also true that any command that reads its input from the keyboard can be told to read that input from a file instead. A command that is suitable for input redirection is the `mail` command:

```
$ mail jgreen <memo.text
```

This will send a mail message to the user *jgreen*, but instead of `mail` expecting you to type the mail message at the keyboard it reads the full contents of the file *memo.text* instead.

The command could have been written `mail jgreen 0<memo.text` to show that it is file descriptor 0 that is being redirected, but this is the default so is not required. The procedure is much the same as with output redirection. The shell closes the standard input file, thus freeing up file descriptor 0, and then opens the file following the "less than" symbol (<). This file is then given the lowest free file descriptor (0), and since the `mail` command reads its input from file descriptor 0, it is none-the-wiser that anything different has even happened. Commands such as who, `date`, and `ls` do not read their input from standard input so are not suitable for input redirection. The following is a partial list of commands that do read standard input. In some cases, the command will read from a file if it is supplied as an argument and standard input if not (e.g., `cat`):

- `mail`
- `cat`
- `more`
- `pg`
- `cpio`
- `lp`

Pipelines

We have seen that you can send the output of a command to a file and you can also make a command read its input from a file. Sometimes you may want these files to be the same one file:

```
$ find / -name "a*" -print >a-files 2>/dev/null
$
```

The output file is likely to be very large so we may choose to view it with the pg command:

```
$ pg a-files
<output not shown for clarity>
$
```

We could actually achieve the same result in a single line and cut out the middle man:

```
$ find / -name "a*" -print 2>/dev/null | pg
<output not shown for clarity>
$
```

Here we have used a pipe symbol (|) to show that we want the standard output from one command to become the standard input to the next command following the pipe. We still don't want to see the error messages so we still redirect standard error (*stderr*) to */dev/null*.

This is again handled by the shell so the commands themselves do not need to know what a pipe is. The command on the left of the pipe sends its output into one end of the pipe and the command to the right of the pipe reads the data going down the pipe as its own input.

The rules for using pipes are that any command on the left of a pipe must be one that writes its output to standard output, and any command to the right of a pipe must read its input from standard input. As long as you follow this rule, you can have as many commands connected this way as you like.

And the Rest

We have seen how the shell enables redirection. Now we'll see a few more things that the shell does with your command lines.

Each time you hit <return> while typing into the shell, the shell will scan the line you typed several times before it actually goes ahead and executes what you typed. In fact, the shell is reading data from the file with descriptor 0, processing it, and producing output to the screen.

The scans include the following checks and actions:

- First the shell will check if the first word is contained on its list of aliases. If so, it is replaced with the value it is aliased to.

- Next the shell will look for any unquoted words that begin with a "~." If any are found, the word following the "~" is expected to be a user name and it will be replaced by the full path of that user's home directory.

- The shell will now look to see if the string "$(" exists. If it does, and there is a matching ")", then a subshell is spawned and the contents of the $() construct are executed within it. The output of this command will replace the original line in place of the entire $() contruct.

- After dealing with $() the shell looks to see if you have used $(()) in your line. If it is found, the contents are expected to be an arithmetic expression. The expression will be evaluated and the result put in place of the $(()) construct.

- Then it looks for an equal sign within the first word. If it finds one, a variable is created and the word is removed.

- Now it looks for words that begin with a dollar sign. These are assumed to be variables and are replaced by the value assigned to that variable (or null if the variable does not exist).

- At this stage the shell will look for any wildcards on the line (*?[]). If any are found, they will be replaced by the files they match.

- Next the shell looks for redirection symbols (<, >, and 2>). For each one found, the appropriate file is closed (*stdin*, *stdout*, or *stderr*) and the filename to the right of the symbol is opened, thus producing the input or receiving the output.

- One of the final steps the shell performs is checking for completeness. If you have failed to close any quotes or have used any built-in shell constructs (such as while) the shell will assume you want to carry on and will display the secondary prompt ($PS2) and expect you to carry on typing the rest of your command. This will, of course, also be parsed in the same way from the first step above. When the shell feels the command is complete it will be executed.

During the above process any special characters preceded by a backslash (\) will be left untouched, as will any within single quotes (' '). If the shell finds double quotes it will ignore some special characters (such as wildcards) but will still process shell variables.

Once the shell has completed messing around with your command line, it will often bear little resemblance to what you actually typed in. This way of operating does, however, mean that when you write a UNIX command (or shell script) you do not need to worry about how redirection or wildcards work as the shell handles it all for you. The shell will now execute your command and, when complete, respond with the shell prompt ($PS1) ready for you to type in the next command.

The above list shows the main steps taken when the Korn Shell parses your commands. If you want to know the complete list of steps, this is documented in great detail in the ksh man page, which is a light read at only 62 pages long!

If you run a Korn Shell with the "-x" option, the shell will display each line you have typed (or each line of a shell script) after the shell has finished parsing it. This is very useful for debugging shell scripts.

Shell Start-Up Files

We have seen that the shell automatically defines some environment variables at login time. The values assigned to these variables are obtained from fields within the password file, but how do the others get set up?

These need to be assigned at login time, but to save this being done manually every time you log in, each shell provides a method of automating this process using files called "profiles." If the system administrator wants to set specific environment variables that will apply to all users on the system, the variables would be set up in the system-wide profile, which is */etc/profile.*

The shell executes this file every time a user logs in. It will generally contain assignments for such variables as $PATH (so users have access to all the standard places programs will be stored) and $PS1 (so users can have a prompt that is slightly more useful that a dollar sign).

If the administrator wants to set up specific variables for specific users or groups of users, this would be done in the user's personal profile. This is located in the user's home directory and is called *.profile.* Since the filename begins with a dot, it is referred to as a "hidden file." This means that the ls command will not display it unless the "-a" option is used and wildcards will not match it unless the leading dot is specified.

Some companies have a policy that users are not allowed to make changes to their personal profiles, in which case the permissions (see Chapter 4, "Permissions and All That") will be set to prevent them from doing so. The system administrator may even create each users *.profile* as a link (see Chapter 6, "The Filesystem and Its Contents") to a master profile to ease the process of making changes to users' profiles. Other companies will have no such policy so that users can update this file and customize their environment as they see fit. Because the personal profile is executed after the system-wide profile, anything set in the system profile can be unset or overridden (unless it has been made read-only by the system administrator).

The files */etc/profile* and *~/.profile* are login shell start-up files. They are executed every time a login shell is started, but once you have logged in they will not be re-executed even if you run another shell process. The ability to execute a file every time a shell starts regardless of whether it is a login shell is available within the Korn Shell if the environment variable $ENV is set. For example, if you set ENV=~/.login then each time a new subshell was spawned, the file called *.login* in your home directory would be executed.

The login profiles are executed in the following order: */etc/profile*, then *~/.profile*, and finally *~/.login* (provided that is what you set $ENV to contain). It is not compulsory for any of these files to exist. Once you are logged in, every time you spawn a subshell the *~/.login* file will be re-executed. You will probably find that, in practice, $ENV is rarely used, but you could use it, for example, to warn users that they have entered a subshell.

If you are using a different shell the above will not necessarily apply, but for most shells */etc/profile* will be run first followed by a profile for the user. The C Shell (csh) will first source */etc/.login* (rather than */etc/.profile*) and then will look for a file called *.login* in your home directory. This is the equivalent to the Korn Shell *.profile* in that it will only run at login and not if you execute the C Shell from within another shell. In addition, in the ~ /.login file the C Shell will look for a ~ /.cshrc (C Shell run commands) file. If this exists, it will be run each time you spawn a new C Shell (similar to the $ENV of the Korn Shell). The order for the C Shell is /etc /.login, followed by ~ /.cshrc, and finally ~ /.login.

The Implementation

This section contains the shell start-up files that we will be using on each of our systems. They are designed so that they will be identical on every system on our networks so that we don't have to manage them individually—we can make a change on one server and then copy the file to all the others. This also means that when we build new servers in the future, we can have a standard set of profiles to install, rather than having to perform a piece of customization for each new server.

/Etc/profile

This file is executed for all users at login time. We have used it to set environment variables that all users will share. If users require anything different or additional to this file it can be specified in their own profile, which is located in their home directory.

In this system-wide profile we start off by using the `trap` command to prevent users from breaking out of the profile before it has set their environment. This could be a potential security loophole if we didn't include it.

We also have a stab at setting the user's terminal type correctly. In this case, we have assumed that if you logged in on the system console you are using a Sun color terminal, or if you have logged in from any other source you are using a vt220 emulator. Users that prefer to use a different emulator or terminal (e.g., an X station) can set the variable TERM in their own profile.

The next section of code ensures that if users are using a POSIX-compliant shell, then we will display the current message of the day (stored in /etc/ *motd*) and display whether they have mail or not. If a file called *.hushlogin* exists, then we skip these.

The final section sets up environment variables. We ensure that the user has a PATH so the user can run Solaris commands. We set the prompt to include the host name to help make sure the user doesn't run the wrong command on the wrong host (which we've all done at some point!). Then we set the `umask` so that users can create files with sensible permissions.

We now unset the `trap` so users can break out of the login process if they like:

```
# The profile that all logins get before using
# their own .profile

# The next line will prevent users from breaking out
# of the profile before it has finished.
trap "" 2 3

if [ "$TERM" = "" ]
then
  TTY=`tty`
  if [ "$TTY" = "/dev/console" ]
  then
    TERM=sun-cmd
  else
    TERM=vt220
  fi
  export TERM
fi

# Login and -su shells get /etc/profile services
# -rsh is given its environment in its .profile

case $0 in
  -sh | -ksh | -jsh)
    if [ ! -f .hushlogin ]
    then
      /bin/cat /etc/motd
      /bin/mail -E
      case $? In
        0)
          echo "You have new mail."
          ;;
        2)
          echo "You have mail."
          ;;
      esac
    fi
esac

# Set a variable to hold the location of our own system
# utilities, though we won't add it to the path here as
# that would make it available to all users.
LOCAL_UTILS=/usr/local/utilities
export LOCAL_UTILS

PATH="/bin:/usr/sbin:/usr/local/bin:"

PS1="${HOSTNAME}$ "

Export PATH PS1
# Set the umask to give write permissions to owner
# and read to group and others
umask 022

# Allow users to break out now
trap 2 3
```

Root *User's* .profile

This profile is just used for the *root* user. It sets the prompt to include a hash mark rather than a dollar sign to remind you that you are logged in as *root* and it also adds directories containing administrative commands to the PATH. You will see that we have also added the *bin* directory that contains our own scripts. These would not be added to the PATH of an ordinary user, who would not have permission to perform administrative tasks.

```
# This is the profile for the root user.

# Set the shell prompt to remind us we are root:
PS1="${HOSTNAME}# "

# Ensure we can run our local system utilities:
PATH=${PATH}:$LOCAL_UTILS/bin:/etc

export PATH PS1
```

Other Users' .profile

This is the profile that is assigned to all standard users. It is placed in the home directory of each user.

```
# .profile for standard users

# If users have their own bin directory, add it to their PATH:
if [ -d "$HOME/bin" ]
then
    PATH="$PATH:$HOME/bin"
fi

# Set the backspace key for erase:
stty erase ^h

# Create any local aliases:
alias ll="ls -l"
alias li="ls -li"
alias lr="ls -lrt"
alias cx="chmod +x"
```

Example Shell Scripts

This script does the same thing as the which command. It will search the user's PATH for the first occurrence of the command supplied as a parameter:

```
#!/bin/ksh
if [[ -z ${1} ]]
then
  echo "usage: ${0} command" >&2
  exit 1
```

```
else
  cmd=${1}
fi
dirs=$(echo ${PATH} | sed 's/^:/. /
                            s/::/ . /
                            s/:$/ ./
                            s/:/ /g')
for dir in ${dirs}
do
  if [[ -f ${dir}/${cmd} ]]
  then
    echo ${dir}/${cmd}
    exit
  fi
done
echo "no ${cmd} in ${dirs}"
```

(Note: Some implementations of which do not display anything if the command supplied is not found. If you want to emulate this behavior, simply remove the final echo statement.)

This second example is a script that will allow you to change permission of a file (or files) using the full text representation of the permissions rather than the octal version. For example, if the script were called chmode (so as not to clash with chmod), it could be used as follows:

```
chmode rwxrwxr-x t*
```

This will change the permissions of all files in the current directory beginning with the letter "t" to 775 without you needing to work out the 755 bit.

This script was included here as it demonstrates a number of common and useful constructs, namely:

- Handling wildcards (although the shell does the hard part)
- Dealing with a variable number of filename parameters
- The use of command substitution
- Creating a wrapper around an existing UNIX command
- Redirecting error messages (in this case, throwing them away)
- Writing your own error message to standard error

```
#!/bin/ksh
if [[ ${#} -lt 2 ]]
then
  echo "usage: ${0} permissions file??"
  exit 1
fi
perms=${1}
shift
binPerms=$(echo ${perms} | sed 's/[rwx]/1/g
                                 s/-/0/g')
octPerms=$(echo "obase=8\nibase=2\n${binPerms}" | bc)
for i in ${*}
```

```
do
  chmod ${octPerms} ${i} 2>/dev/null
  if [[ ${?} -ne 0 ]]
  then
    echo "${0}: could not change permissions of ${i}" >&2
  fi
done
```

(Note: This script does not handle special cases of permissions such as the *setuid* or *setgid* bits. You may wish to incorporate these into this script.)

6

THE FILESYSTEM AND ITS CONTENTS

Manual Pages

df (4)
du (4)
ff (1)
fmthard (1M)
format (1M)
fs (1M)
fsck (1M)
fstyp
fuser
mkfs (1)
mount (1M)
newfs (1)
prtvtoc (1M)
umount (1M)

Files Affected

/etc/default/fs
/etc/mntab
/etc/vfstab

Objectives

Most computers these days have hard disks for data storage. On a Windows PC or Macintosh, this data is stored in the form of files and folders. Folders can contain both files and other folders, which provides a good way to organize the huge quantity of data that hard disks are now capable of holding. Solaris provides the same method of file management but folders are called "directories" and, unless you are using an X Windows front-end, you won't be seeing them as colorful icons.

In this chapter, we will be looking at how Solaris organizes the files and directories on the hard disk and how we can create and effectively manage filesystems.

Note that a Solaris server will contain at least one hard disk (depending on the model) and the number of disks will determine how you choose to make use of them. For simplicity we have assumed all our example systems have just a single hard disk (we will look at how to add a second disk to one of them in Chapter 17, "Adding SCSI Devices"). This ensures that everything we do to configure the disks on our systems can also be done on yours.

What Is a Filesystem?

A filesystem is an area of storage medium (e.g., disk or tape) that has been made ready for holding data in file and directory format. A filesystem is given a name when it is created, and it can only be used once it has been made available. The process of making a filesystem available for use is called "mounting." When a filesystem is mounted, it has the effect of it becoming attached to one of the directories that exists on a different filesystem. When used in this way, the directory is called a "mount point." Normally, the mount point a filesystem uses will exist within a previously mounted filesystem. The *root* filesystem, mounted on "/," is the most fundamental because it is mounted first, when the system boots, using a low-level process. The *root* filesystem contains the system *root* directory and key system files.

A filesystem can be mounted on any existing directory and the name of the directory does not need to match the name of the filesystem. This does mean, however, that there must always be at least one filesystem mounted or there would be no directories available to mount any additional filesystems on. The directory that a filesystem is mounted on does not need to be empty, though if it isn't any files or directories contained in it will not be visible or accessible while the filesystem is mounted over it.

Solaris supports three types of filesystems: disk-based, network-based, and virtual filesystems. A disk-based filesystem is a set of structures held in disk blocks capable of supporting the UNIX tree structure and being included in it. Most of this chapter is concerned with disk-based filesystems, though we will also take a brief look at virtual filesystems. (Network-based filesystems are covered in Chapter 18, "NFS, DFS, and Autofs").

Before a filesystem can be created on a disk, the disk must be formatted and partitioned. These days, disks will normally be formatted before they are shipped so this is not a common task and a system administrator is not likely to need to perform this action very often. However, you are likely to need to partition a disk and you will definitely need to understand the process of creating partitions and how to create a filesystem on a partition.

On a Solaris system each disk always contains eight partitions, which are often called "slices." It is entirely up to you how you make use of them, and you do not have to use them all. The information about the partitions is stored on the disk in an area called the "disk label." The label is also known as the "VTOC" (volume table of contents) and is located in the first block of the disk. A label contains information about the disk's controller, geometry, and partitions. The part of the label that holds the information about the partitions is called the "partition table."

Each partition can hold one or zero filesystems, which means a disk can hold up to eight filesystems, though it is unusual to actually create eight. The practical maximum is seven filesystems since partition number two is usually reserved for a special purpose, which will become clear later on in this chapter.

The relationship between a filesystem and a partition is that a partition can hold one or zero filesystems and a filesystem may not span across more than one partition. A filesystem does not have to be as large as the partition, but space will be wasted if it is smaller.

Before going ahead and creating filesystems all over the place, a fair bit of planning should be undertaken. The number of disks you have and the size of them will play a large part in this.

Table 6.1 shows an example of how a disk could be partitioned (based on a 1.7 GB disk).

Table 6.1 *Example Partitions*

Part	Tag	Flag	Cylinders	Size	Blocks	
0	root	wm	0–62	50.30 MB	(63/0/0)	103005
1	swap	wu	144–243	79.83 MB	(100/0/0)	163500
2	backup	wm	0–2104	1.64 GB	(2105/0/0)	3441675
3	unassigned	wm	0	0	(0/0/0)	0
4	var	wm	63–143	64.67 MB	(81/0/0)	132435
5	unassigned	wm	244–294	40.72 MB	(51/0/0)	83385
6	usr	wm	295–1297	800.73 MB	(1003/0/0)	1639905
7	home	wm	1298–2099	640.27 MB	(802/0/0)	1311270

In this example all but two of the partitions contain filesystems. You might assume that these are the partitions numbered 3 and 5, as these both have a tag of *unassigned*. This, however, is not the case. Although the tag names do tie in with the filesystem name in some cases, the tag *unassigned* does not mean the partition has no filesystem. In fact, from the table above we can infer which partitions do not have filesystems, but we cannot tell whether the others have them or not, though we can make assumptions. The more obvious of the two partitions without filesystems is partition 3. It has a size of 0 so it cannot have a filesystem on it, and one could not be created on it unless another partition is made smaller to free up some space. The other partition with no filesystem is partition 2, which actually encompasses the whole disk. This is set up automatically by Solaris and the size of partition 2 should not be changed, since this slice is used as a way of backing up or copying the whole disk.

Table 6.2 describes the attributes that are associated with a disk partition.

Table 6.2 *Partition Attributes*

Partition Attribute	Description
Partition Number	Each disk has eight available partitions (or slices) numbered 0 to 7.
Tag	The tag describes what type of filesystem has been placed on each partition. Tags are represented by a hex number in the range (0-a). The available tags are: 0x00 *unassigned* 0x01 *boot* 0x02 *root* 0x03 *swap* 0x04 *usr* 0x05 *backup* 0x06 *stand* 0x07 *var* 0x08 *home* 0x09 *altsctr* 0x0a *cache*
Flag	The flag shows how the partition should be mounted. Flags are represented by a hex value, but are sometimes shown as two letters: 0x00 mw mountable, read and write 0x01 uw unmountable, read and write 0x10 mr mountable, read-only

Table 6.2 *Partition Attributes (Continued)*

Partition Attribute	Description
Cylinders	A disk is divided into a number of cylinders. This shows the range of cylinders that have been allocated to this partition.
Size	This shows the actual space taken up by the partition in an appropriate unit (e.g., megabytes or gigabytes).
Blocks	The left column shows the total number of cylinders per partition. The rightmost column shows the number of sectors per partition.

To recap: A disk is split into partitions (or slices) upon which filesystems can be created—one filesystem per partition. The terms "partition" and "slice" have exactly the same meaning in Solaris and we deliberately use both in this book. This is because some system administrators will always use one, some the other, and some will use both.

To create a filesystem on a partition, we need to have a way of referring to it. Solaris allows us to do this by providing a series of special files under the */dev* directory. There is one file for each partition (or slice) on the disk. The UNIX command df is generally used to show how full a filesystem is, but it also shows the name of the special device file that goes with each partition/filesystem:

```
hydrogen# df -k
Filesystem           kbytes   used   avail capacity  Mounted on
/proc                     0      0       0     0%    /proc
/dev/dsk/c0t2d0s0     48349  16889   26626    39%    /
/dev/dsk/c0t2d0s6    770543 522712  193893    73%    /usr
fd                        0      0       0     0%    /dev/fd
/dev/dsk/c0t2d0s1     61463   5592   49725    11%    /var
/dev/dsk/c0t2d0s7    519718  82791  384956    18%    /export/home
/dev/dsk/c0t2d0s5     38539   5928   28758    18%    /opt
swap                 130064     28  130036     1%    /tmp
hydrogen#
```

The name of the file tells us some information about the part of the physical disk that it refers to. If we look at the *device* file for the *root* filesystem (shown in the first column), we see that the *root* filesystem is located on disk controller 0, target 2, drive 0, and slice 0. If your system only has one disk controller, then all disks will start "c0." The "t" represents the physical bus target number; this can usually be set on the disk itself using jumpers. The "d" represents the drive number, which is the disk's Logical Unit Number (LUN). If the disk has an embedded controller, then the drive value will usually be 0. Most disks have embedded controllers these days.

We have already seen that each disk can hold up to eight slices (or partitions) numbered 0 to 7 and partition 2 is usually used to represent the whole disk. The disk in our system has a target of 2, so if we were to add any more disks onto controller 0 we would need to make sure the target was set to a different number. Consequently, if the system had a second disk, it might be referred to as c0t3d0s2, depending on what we set the target to.

The df command will only show the slices that contain filesystems and have been mounted. If we want to see all the partitions on a disk, we can use the prtvtoc command:

```
hydrogen# prtvtoc /dev/rdsk/c0t2d0s2
* /dev/rdsk/c0t2d0s2 partition map
*
* Dimensions:
*      512 bytes/sector
*      109 sectors/track
*       15 tracks/cylinder
*     1635 sectors/cylinder
*     2372 cylinders
*     2105 accessible cylinders
*
*     1635 sectors/cylinder
*     2372 cylinders
*     2105 accessible cylinders
*
* Flags:
*    1: unmountable
*   10: read-only
*
* Unallocated space:
*         First      Sector      Last
*         Sector     Count       Sector
*        3435135     6540       3441674
*
*
*                        First Sector   Last
* Partition Tag Flags   Sector Count Sector Mount Directory
       0      2   00        0   103005   103004   /
       1      7   00   103005   132435   235439   /var
       2      5   00        0  3441675  3441674
       3      3   01   235440   163500   398939
       4      9   00  3229125   206010  3435134
       5      0   00   398940    83385   482324   /opt
       6      4   00   482325  1639905  2122229   /usr
       7      8   00  2122230  1106895  3229124   /export/home
hydrogen#
```

The tag and flag columns are displayed in hex notation, but these can be translated to their text equivalent using Table 6.2 shown earlier. The right-most column, headed Mount Directory, will show the directory on which the partition's filesystem is currently mounted. If a directory is not shown, it does not mean that the partition has no filesystem on it, but just that it is not currently mounted.

Why Do We Use Filesystems?

We know that we must have at least one filesystem (the *root* filesystem), but why do we bother with any others? There are a number of reasons for splitting a disk into filesystems and some of them are historical. For example, the System V filesystem type did not scale well, so as the size increased the performance fell. Consequently, it was advantageous to have many smaller filesystems rather than a few bigger ones. Also, a filesystem has a maximum size and a maximum number of files that it can hold (dependent on the filesystem type), and the limits increased as new filesystem types were developed. As long as our disk was small enough, we could choose to have just one large filesystem, or if we had many disks we could choose one filesystem per disk. This would greatly simplify the set up of the system and it should reduce the problems of filesystems filling up. This may be a sensible way of configuring a system, but it also may not be. It all depends on the way the system will be used.

If the system has many applications installed, then it is sensible to keep these in separate filesystems so they don't interfere with each other. If one application goes berserk and starts filling up the disk, it will stop when its own filesystem is full and won't cause any problems to other applications. Also, if an application is to be taken offline for any reason, the filesystem could be physically unmounted—which would prevent anybody from playing with it. It is also often desirable to keep the application code and data on separate disks (and even separate disk controllers) to prevent performance bottlenecks; this can only be achieved by using a combination of separate filesystems on separate disks.

Preparing the Disk
to Receive Filesystems

Solaris provides a menu-based utility (format) that allows you to format, label, and define the slices on a disk. When you run format you are provided with a list of all the disks Solaris can see, numbered from zero upwards, and you are prompted to select the one you wish to work with. As with most commands involving disk and filesystem management, format can only be run by the *root* user:

```
hydrogen# format
Searching for disks...done

AVAILABLE DISK SELECTIONS:
0. c0t2d0 <Micropolis 2217-15 cyl 2105 alt 3 hd 15 sec 109>
/iommu@0,10000000/sbus@0,10001000/espdma@4,8400000/
esp@4,8800000/sd@2,0
Specify disk (enter its number):
```

Obviously, we don't have much choice here as our system only has a single hard disk. We can see that its address is c0t2d0 (controller 0, target 2, device 0). If your system only has one disk, then the actions you can perform on it within `format` are somewhat limited since your operating system will be running from that disk and filesystems will be mounted from it. Once you have entered the number of the disk you wish to work with (in our case 0), `format` presents the following menu:

```
FORMAT MENU:
        disk        - select a disk
        type        - select (define) a disk type
        partition   - select (define) a partition table
        current     - describe the current disk
        format      - format and analyze the disk
        repair      - repair a defective sector
        label       - write label to the disk
        analyze     - surface analysis
        defect      - defect list management
        backup      - search for backup labels
        verify      - read and display labels
        save        - save new disk/partition definitions
        inquiry     - show vendor, product and revision
        volname     - set 8-character volume name
        !<cmd>      - execute <cmd>, then return
        quit
format>
```

Table 6.3 provides a brief overview of each of the commands available at the "format>" prompt.

Table 6.3 *Format Menu Options*

Format Command	Description
disk	This option allows you to select another disk in the same way you did when you first ran format.
type	This allows you to select a disk type from a list of types that your system knows about. The list of available disk types is held in the file /etc/format.dat.
partition	Typing this brings up the Partition Menu. Any changes you wish to make to the layout or partitions on the disk will be done here, so we will look at this in more detail later.
current	This reminds you which disk is currently selected.

Table 6.3 *Format Menu Options (Continued)*

Format Command	Description
format	This option will cause the current disk to be completely reformatted, so this should be selected with caution. Formatting a disk can take well over an hour and it is not a procedure that can safely be aborted once it has begun.
repair	This option will attempt to repair defects on the disk. If selected, you are prompted to enter the absolute block number of the defect you wish to repair. The block numbers of the defects can be obtained from the defect command menu. This can often fix problems that would normally require a disk to be returned to the manufacturer.
label	This command writes the current disk label back to the disk. If you change any partitions on the disk, you need to use the label command to save them.
analyze	This command takes you to the analyze submenu. This provides a number of options for checking the disk for errors. Some options are safe to run on a disk that is in use and others will corrupt the data, so they can only be used on spare disks. These are clearly marked so you don't accidentally destroy all the data on your system disk.
defect	This command takes you to a submenu that allows you to find out any defects that exist on the disk. It can find out what defects were there when the disk was made and what defects have occurred since.
backup	This command will cause format to search for any backup disk labels. If one is found, it will be used to overwrite (or recreate) the primary disk label. It is, therefore, useful if you mess up the primary disk label and want to revert to the previous one.
verify	This will display the contents of the current primary label. This command is there so you can double-check that you are happy with it before storing it back to the disk.
save	This will save your new partition definitions.
inquiry	This will display the disk manufacturer, product code, and revision level of the currently selected disk.

Table 6.3 *Format Menu Options (Continued)*

Format Command	Description
volname	This allows you to set a volume name for the disk. It can be up to eight characters in length and is stored within the disk label.
!<cmd>	You may run operating system commands without leaving format by entering an exclamation point (!) followed by the command you wish to run.
quit	Self-explanatory, really! Don't type this if you want to stay in the format utility.

The format utility works in the same way as the shell in that it displays a prompt and waits for commands (which match the menu options) to be entered. You do not need to type the whole command; you just need to type enough of it to let format know which one you wish to run. If the menu has disappeared off the screen, you can get format to redisplay it by entering a question mark (?).

Although format can perform a large number of low-level disk activities, it is likely to be most often used to change the disk partition map. When you enter the partition command into the format main menu you are presented with the Partition Menu:

```
PARTITION MENU:
        0      - change `0' partition
        1      - change `1' partition
        2      - change `2' partition
        3      - change `3' partition
        4      - change `4' partition
        5      - change `5' partition
        6      - change `6' partition
        7      - change `7' partition
        select - select a predefined table
        modify - modify a predefined partition table
        name   - name the current table
        print  - display the current table
        label  - write partition map and label to the disk
        !<cmd> - execute <cmd>, then return
        quit
partition>
```

If we want to make any changes to the partition table, we can enter the number of the partition we wish to change and we will be prompted for the new attributes. However, before doing this it is probably best to use the print command to see the attributes of the current partition table:

```
partition> print
Current partition table (original):
Total disk cylinders available: 2105 + 3 (reserved cylinders)

Part       Tag   Flag   Cylinders       Size           Blocks
0         root   wm       0 -   62    50.30MB   (63/0/0)      103005
1          var   wm      63 -  143    64.67MB   (81/0/0)      132435
2       backup   wm       0 - 2104     1.64GB   (2105/0/0)   3441675
3         swap   wu     144 -  243    79.83MB   (100/0/0)     163500
4   alternates   wm    1975 - 2100   100.59MB   (126/0/0)     206010
5   unassigned   wm     244 -  294    40.72MB   (51/0/0)       83385
6          usr   wm     295 - 1297   800.73MB   (1003/0/0)   1639905
7         home   wm    1298 - 1974   540.48MB   (677/0/0)    1106895

partition>
```

If we wanted to change the attributes of a partition, we would simply enter the partition number and we would then be prompted to enter each of the new values for that partition. If we entered "4" at the partition prompt we would get the following dialogue:

```
partition> 4
Part        Tag   Flag   Cylinders     Size          Blocks
4 alternates   wm   1975 - 2100   100.59MB   (126/0/0)     206010

Enter partition id tag[alternates]:
Enter partition permission flags[wm]:
Enter new starting cyl[1975]:
Enter partition size[206010b, 126c, 100.59mb, 0.10gb]:
partition>
```

The process is made fairly easy because for each value we are prompted for, the previous value is shown in square brackets. When it comes to entering the partition size we can choose how we want to specify it. We can enter it in blocks, cylinders, megabytes, or gigabytes. With each question we are asked, if we hit <return> the value will not be changed. If you do make any changes to the partition table, the change will not be written back to the disk unless you use the label command.

Hopefully, you will agree that setting up and changing partition values is made simple through the format utility. A number of things can make this process a bit more difficult, though. For instance, if the partition you want to change has a filesystem containing data on it, you will not be able to make the change while the filesystem is available to users (mounted) so you will first need to take it offline (unmount it). You will now be able to make the change, but once that partition has been changed you will need to recreate the filesystem before you can use it again. This also has the consequence that all the data on the filesystem will have been lost, so you will need to restore it from the backup you made before changing the partition. Oh, and that's another thing. Always back up a filesystem before trying to make changes to the partition it was created on.

You can find that it may cause a few headaches trying to increase the size of a partition when there is no unallocated space on the disk, or when the unallocated space is not adjacent to the partition you wish to increase. This can mean manipulation of other partitions, which in turn means we might need to back up, recreate, and restore more filesystems than just the one we actually want to change.

What Type of Filesystem Should We Use?

A number of different filesystem types are available, but there isn't usually much choice over which type you are going to use once you know what the filesystem is going to be used for. We will look mainly at disk-based filesystems in this section, but will also have a brief overview of virtual filesystems. (We cover network-based filesystems in Chapter 18, "NFS, DFS, and Autofs.") Virtual filesystems are generally memory-based filesystems, but the CacheFS and TMPFS types do make use of the disk. Table 6.4 lists the filesystem types, showing which class they belong to.

Table 6.4 *Filesystem Types*

Filesystem Group	Filesystem Type	Description
Disk-Based	s5	This is quite a dated filesystem type and not used too often. It is mentioned here since it is simple and was the standard until UFS took over.
	UFS	This is currently the standard filesystem type for user-created hard disk-based filesystems. It has taken over from s5 as the default filesystem type on Solaris systems and has many improvements.
	HSFS	HSFS is the High Sierra and ISO 9660 filesystem. This is a read-only filesystem and is mainly used on CD-ROMs. Solaris HSFS supports extensions to ISO 9660, which, if present, provide UFS filesystem semantics and file types (but obviously read-only).
	PCFS	This filesystem type is generally only used on floppy disks. It allows the transfer of data between Solaris and DOS/Windows-based PCs.

Table 6.4 *Filesystem Types (Continued)*

Filesystem Group	Filesystem Type	Description
Network-Based	NFS	NFS is the only network filesystem type available on Solaris. It is used to enable a filesystem created on one server to be mounted onto another server (or client) over the network. See Chapter 18, "NFS, DFS, and Autofs."
Virtual	CACHEFS	The Cache filesystem can be used to improve performance of remote filesystems or some slow devices such as CD-ROM drives.
	TMPFS	The temporary filesystem type is the default filesystem type for the */tmp* filesystem on Solaris systems. It uses the area of disk allocated to swap, but disk reads and writes are performed directly to and from memory so any process that uses temporary files will be sped up.
	LOFS	This is the loop-back filesystem. It is used to allow an existing filesystem or directory tree to be mounted in a different part of the filesystem. Thus any file contained on it can be referred to by its real path and its virtual path.
	PROCFS	The process filesystem type is specific to the */proc* directory. It is memory-resident and contains an entry for each running process.

Since they are used rarely and in rather specific circumstances, we will not be looking any further at the virtual filesystem types CACHEFS and LOFS. Creating HSFS filesystems is also beyond the scope of this book.

The early filesystem types were fairly basic and had various drawbacks, so over time new filesystem types were designed to get around these drawbacks and provide additional features. These tended to grow in complexity, but this doesn't need to worry us too much because at the end of the day they all perform the same basic function, which is to provide a way of storing files and directories on disk with a consistent user interface.

The current Solaris default filesystem type is the UNIX filesystem (UFS), and this is the recommended one to use. However, we will look at the older System V (s5) filesystem type in detail first. This is because it is more basic and therefore the concepts should be easier to understand. The UFS type was developed as an improvement over the s5 type, but has the same fundamental principles.

System V Filesystem Type

The s5 filesystem is created on a disk partition and is split into four parts. The smallest two are one block in size each and are the boot block and the superblock. The boot block contains information about which blocks in the other two parts are free to use. Of the remaining two parts, the largest contains the actual data being stored in the files and directories and the other contains some things we will look at in more detail later called "inodes."

The map of a typical s5 filesystem is as follows:

Boot Block
Superblock
Inodes
Data Storage

The data area is split into data blocks, the size of which are defined when the filesystem is created, but s5-type filesystems tend to have a block size of 512 bytes. The size of the data area will then govern how many data blocks can fit onto it, and since each nonempty file will use up at least one data block, this also determines how many files will fit. All inodes are the same size so the number of inodes, which is also specified when creating the filesystem, determines the space taken up by the inode area. Each file, or directory, has a single inode associated with it and takes up at least one data block (apart from empty files). If you have some idea of the likely number of files and their sizes, some optimization of the filesystem, at creation time, is possible. For example, if you know the filesystem will have very few files, then creating the filesystem with a small number of inodes will allow more space for file data. On the other hand, if you run out of inodes it will not be possible to create any more files in that filesystem, no matter how much space is free in the data area.

The term "inode" stands for "information node." Each inode holds information about a single file. We will be looking at inodes in more detail later in this chapter.

The superblock contains a list of free inodes and free data blocks, so if it becomes corrupt this type of filesystem can become unusable. This was one of the reasons that more robust and complex filesystem types were developed. The most popular filesystem type to supercede s5 was called the UFS type. This was based on the BSD Fast Filesystem that was provided with BSD 4.3.

Recent versions of Solaris do not provide support for the s5 filesystem type by default; there should be no normal circumstance where you would need to create a filesystem of this type. It has been included here since it is simple and therefore useful in demonstrating how a filesystem works.

The s5 filesystem type was successfully used for many years, but it did have a number of drawbacks. These include the following:

- As the filesystem increases in size, performance decreases.
- The directory format is fixed (14 bytes for each filename and 2 bytes for the inode number, which resulted in a maximum filename size of 14 characters).
- There can be a maximum of 65,536 inodes, which limits both the number of files the filesystem can have and its maximum size.
- There is only one superblock, so if it becomes corrupt the filesystem is unusable.

UFS Type

The UFS type provides many advantages over the s5 type, but it is also more complex. It is the default filesystem type on Solaris, so you will need to become familiar with it.

UFS types have the following features:

- State flag settings that reduce the need to check the filesystem on startup, leading to a quicker boot-time.
- Extended Fundamental Types (EFTs). Basically, this allows more users, groups, and devices to exist as 32-bit numbers are used to represent them.
- Large filesystems. A UFS can be as large as 1 terabyte, though this may not be achievable as a UFS cannot span multiple disks, unless an underlying volume management tool is used, and hard disks may not reach 1 terabyte in size for a while yet.
- Larger files. By default, an individual file can be created in excess of 2 GB. However, if you specify the "nolargefiles" flag when the filesystem is created, a limit of 2 GB will be enforced.
- Backup superblocks. When a UFS is created, a number of backup superblocks are created so if the primary superblock becomes corrupt it can be recovered from one of the backups.

The UFS type is similar to the s5 type in that it contains the same four types of blocks. However, the internals are more complex (see Table 6.5).

Table 6.5 *Four Types of Blocks in a UFS*

Block Type	Description
Boot	This area contains information that is used when the system boots.
Superblock	The superblock holds information about the filesystem itself. This includes: • Filesystem state flag • Filesystem name • Filesystem size • Number of inodes • Date and time of last update • Cylinder group size • Number of data blocks in each cylinder group • Directory that the filesystem was last mounted on • Free block count • Free inode count
Inode	This section holds all the inodes. An inode holds all the information about a file apart from its name.
Data	This section holds all the data contained in the files in this filesystem.

An s5-type filesystem has a fixed block size for the data storage area that is defined at filesystem creation. A UFS filesystem also has its data storage area block size defined when it is created, but to allow more flexibility there is a logical block size and a fragmentation size. The defaults are for an 8 KB logical block size and a 1 KB fragmentation size. The reason for this is to reduce disk fragmentation (holes caused by partially allocated blocks). As a file is written, it will be allocated logical blocks at first, then it will be allocated fragments. Very small files will just have fragments allocated. Both the logical block size and fragment size can be set when the filesystem is created, but they cannot be changed at a later time without recreating the filesystem. In general, the default 8 KB logical block size is a good compromise for most situations; however, if you have a large filesystem that you know will contain large files you could improve efficiency by choosing a larger logical block size. Likewise, if you know the filesystem will mostly contain small files you could choose a smaller logical block size. When it comes to choosing a fragment size, the general rule is that a large fragment size will increase the speed of file access but reduce the space optimization, and a smaller fragment size will reduce fragmentation but cause file access to be slightly slower. The default size of 1 KB should be suitable for most general-purpose filesystems, but the rule of thumb is the same as for logical blocks. Increase the fragment size for filesystems containing mostly large files and decrease it for filesystems containing mostly small files. You can use the command `quot -c` to obtain information about the distribution of files by block size.

The logical disk size has nothing to do with the physical block size. The physical block size is the smallest chunk of data that can be transferred by the disk controller; this is usually 512 bytes. The logical block size is the chunk size that the UNIX kernel will use.

The UFS filesystem type improved on all the major weaknesses of the s5 type:

- UFS has multiple superblocks, so the filesytem can still be mounted if the main superblock is corrupt.
- Filenames can now be up to 255 characters and the inode number is now 4 bytes.
- UFS has a larger block size (8 KB).

Although the UFS type contains multiple superblocks, they are not all updated together. Only the first superblock is updated online; the backups simply contain static data such as fragment size, block size, filesystem size, etc. If the main superblock becomes corrupt the filesystem checker (`fsck`) will update the copy to be used by performing an audit of the filesystem.

Prior to Solaris 8, the maximum filesystem block size was equal to the memory page size, but from Solaris 8 onwards this restriction was lifted. The block size represents the unit of transfer between disk and memory.

The UFS type is split into cylinder groups and each cylinder group contains a backup superblock. The backup superblock is positioned at a different offset from the beginning of each cylinder group.

The map of a typical UFS-type filesystem is as follows:

Cylinder Group 0

Boot Block
Superblock
Cylinder Group Map
Inodes
Data Storage

Cylinder Group 1

Data Storage
Superblock Copy
Cylinder Group Map
Inodes
Data Storage

Cylinder Group 2 (etc.)

Data Storage
Superblock Copy
Cylinder Group Map
Inodes
File Data

In addition to the superblock copy, each cylinder group contains a cylinder group map. This contains information about which data blocks are free along with information about the fragments that will help prevent fragmentation from affecting disk performance.

When data is written to a UFS filesystem, it will normally be done with the filesystem in time optimization mode. This means the filesystem is trying to be as quick as possible and doesn't care too much if it wastes a bit of space here or there. However, once the filesystem becomes near to filling up, the optimization changes to space. Now the filesystem is trying to write data so as little space as possible is wasted, resulting in possible performance degradation. Once the filesystem size falls below the threshold, optimization will move back to time-based.

TMPFS Type

The TMPFS type was devised as a means of speeding up the performance of programs that create temporary files. On a Solaris system, the TMPFS type is the default for the /tmp filesystem. Once mounted, it looks like any other filesystem and can be used in exactly the same way; however, when it is unmounted all files stored in it are lost. The speed improvements are due to the fact that this filesystem type is memory-based. This means that when a file is created under /tmp it exists in memory only, so there is no overhead associated with creating the file on a hard disk. If many temporary files are created and memory begins to fill up, then the temporary files will be transferred to disk. This is enabled because the TMPFS types also make use of the swap area of the disk. When a file is created in /tmp it will never be created on the swap area of the disk, but will always be created in memory. It is only when memory resources become constrained that the temporary file(s) will be moved to swap. Since swap is there for the purpose of storing memory pages (see Chapter 7, "Swap Space"), nothing very different is happening here. In normal circumstances this arrangement works very well; however, there are times when problems can be noticed. The problems are likely to be that /tmp has become full or there is not enough swap space available. If either of these events occurs, it is likely to have been caused by one of the following reasons. Either memory and swap are being overused, causing there to be no room for temporary files; or, there are some very large files in /tmp, which have been moved to the swap area and are not leaving enough free swap for the system. The solution would be to either remove the large files from /*tmp* or to increase swap. Increasing or adding more swap space is covered in Chapter 7, "Swap Space."

PROCFS Type

Each Solaris system has one filesystem of the virtual filesystem type PROCFS called /*proc*. The filesystem is created automatically by Solaris and, as it is virtual, is memory-based rather than being stored on disk. It contains a file for each process running with a name equal to the process ID. It is not recommended that processes are killed by removing their /*proc* entries and there should never be any need to perform housekeeping on this filesystem.

File Descriptor Filesystem (FDFS) Type

A common misconception is that the FDFS type is for floppy disks and that FDFS stands for "Floppy Disk File System." This, however, is not the case. FDFS stands for "File Descriptor File System" and it is actually used by Solaris to allocate file descriptors to *setuid* and *setgid* shell scripts. It is a common mistake for administrators to comment the /*dev*/*fd* filesystem out of the *vfstab* file, thinking they do not need it since they do not use floppy disks with their system. If they don't have any *setuid* or *setgid* shell scripts they will not see any problems; but if they ever do create any, they will find they won't work and get an error message along the lines of "/dev/fd/3: cannot open."

Creating and Removing Filesystems

The standard UNIX command for creating a filesystem is `mkfs`, but Solaris also provides a simple wrapper to this called `newfs` that can be used to create UFS type filesystems. Before you can create a filesystem you need to create a label for the disk that includes the partition table. The new filesystem can then be created on one of these partitions. This process will normally be carried out using the Solaris `format` utility (discussed earlier).

If we wanted to create a UFS filesystem on the partition c0t2d0s4, assuming we had defined the partition and written the label to disk we could issue the following `newfs` command:

```
hydrogen# newfs /dev/dsk/c0t2d0s4
newfs: /dev/rdsk/c0t2d0s4 last mounted as /usr/local/utils
newfs: construct a new file system /dev/rdsk/c0t2d0s4: (y/n)?
```

If the partition previously had a filesystem on it, `newfs` will let us know where it was last mounted, just in case we have accidentally typed in the wrong device name. As an additional safeguard, if you enter "y" to proceed with the filesystem creation, newfs will respond with "/dev/dsk/c0t2d0s4 is mounted, can't mkfs" if that filesystem is currently mounted.

Assuming that this is the correct partition to use and it is not currently mounted, newfs will proceed as follows:

```
/dev/rdsk/c0t2d0s4:      206010 sectors in 126 cylinders of
15 tracks, 109 sectors
        100.6MB in 8 cyl groups (16 c/g, 12.77MB/g, 6144 i/g)
super-block backups (for fsck -F ufs -o b=#) at:
 32, 26304, 52576, 78848, 105120, 131392, 157664, 183936,
hydrogen#
```

The newfs command actually uses the UNIX mkfs command to create the filesystem. As mkfs requires a minimum selection of options and arguments, these are obtained from the partition table by newfs. You will see that the example above provides the locations of the backup superblocks. It is a good idea to make a note of these so if the main superblock becomes corrupt you know the location of an alternative one to use.

Once we have created a filesystem we cannot use it straight away; it needs to be mounted first. As we saw earlier, a filesystem is mounted onto a directory that belongs to an already mounted filesystem. The directory chosen is called a "mount point" and it is sensible for this to be an empty directory, because if it contained any files or directories, they would become hidden as soon as the new filesystem was mounted. They wouldn't actually be deleted—they would still be there when the filesystem was next unmounted—but it makes more sense to use an empty directory for a mount point.

So, we have just made a filesystem on the disk slice c0t2d0s4. Now we'll create a mount point and mount it so we can use it. We have decided that this filesystem is to be used to hold some scripts and utilities that will help us to look after the system. We want it under the *usr/local* directory since it is customary to store locally produced files and programs here. We will create the mount point in the *usr/local* directory and call it "utils":

```
hydrogen# cd /usr/local
hydrogen# mkdir utils
hydrogen# mount /dev/dsk/c0t2d0s4 /usr/local/utils
hydrogen# df -k
Filesystem              kbytes     used    avail capacity  Mounted on
/proc                        0        0        0       0%  /proc
/dev/dsk/c0t2d0s0        48349    25654    17861      59%  /
/dev/dsk/c0t2d0s6       770543   557662   158943      78%  /usr
fd                           0        0        0       0%  /dev/fd
/dev/dsk/c0t2d0s1        61463     5783    49534      11%  /var
/dev/dsk/c0t2d0s7       519718   112161   355586      24%  /export/home
/dev/dsk/c0t2d0s5        38539     6089    28597      18%  /opt
swap                    133460        8   133452       1%  /tmp
/dev/dsk/c0t2d0s4        96716        9    87036       1%  /usr/local/
utils
hydrogen#
```

The df command confirms that our filesystem is now mounted on the mount point */usr/local/utils* (you could also just type the mount command on its own—there is always more than one way of doing something on a UNIX system). The mount command we used had two parameters: The first was the name of the slice of the disk that contained the filesystem; the second was the name of the directory on which we wanted to mount it. If the filesystem is of the UFS type, then mount should have no problems mounting it. But if mount could not work out what type the filesystem was, it would complain that it was not able to mount it. In this case, you can specifically tell mount what the filesystem type is by using the "-F" flag. The default filesystem type is defined in the file */etc/default/fs*.

```
hydrogen# mount -F ufs /dev/dsk/c0t2d0s4 /usr/local/utils
hydrogen#
```

If you have been trying out these commands, or examining them with a fine-tooth comb, you may have noticed that when we created the filesystem the path name of the partition (or slice) was */dev/rdsk/c0t2d0s4*, but when we mounted it we used */dev/dsk/c0t2d0s4*. Both paths refer to the same slice on the disk (and therefore the same filesystem); the difference is that the paths specify how that part of the disk will be accessed. If we have a look at the files with the following ls commands we see that the output line for the *dsk* slice begins with a "b" and the line for the *rdsk* slice a "c."

```
hydrogen# ls -lL /dev/dsk/c0t2d0s4
brw-r-----   1 root    sys      32, 20 Oct 19 00:47 /dev/dsk/c0t2d0s4
hydrogen# ls -lL /dev/rdsk/c0t2d0s4
crw-r-----   1 root    sys      32, 20 Apr  1 18:48 /dev/rdsk/c0t2d0s4
hydrogen#
```

The "b" stands for block and the "c" for character. If we access the disk slice using the *dsk* path, this means that we will be transferring data to and from the disk in block units (or multiples of blocks). If, on the other hand, we use the *rdsk* path, we will be communicating with the slice a character at a time (which equates to a byte at a time). This latter method tends to be called "raw input and output" (or raw I/O) and is what the "r" in *rdsk* stands for. When we create a filesystem the newfs (or mkfs) command creates the filesystem byte by byte so the raw device is the most appropriate. When the filesystem is mounted, accessing the data byte by byte would not be good for performance, so in this situation the block device is the correct one to use.

If you create a new filesystem and you want Solaris to mount it automatically when the system boots up, or you wish to use an abbreviated form of the mount command, you should achieve this by adding an entry for it in the */etc/vfstab* file (see Table 6.6). This file is scanned every time Solaris boots or the mount command is used. At boot-time all the filesystems in this file that are marked for automatic mount will be mounted. An entry in */etc/vfstab* allows a filesystem to be mounted or unmounted without needing to remember the device that holds the filesystem's partition.

The contents of *letc/vfstab* is as follows:

```
#device         device          mount           FS      fsck    mount   mount
#to mount       to fsck         point           type    pass    at boot options
#
fd      -       /dev/fd fd      -       no      -
/proc   -       /proc   proc    -       no      -
/dev/dsk/c0t2d0s3       -       -       swap    -       no      -
/dev/dsk/c0t2d0s0       /dev/rdsk/c0t2d0s0      /       ufs     1       no
-
/dev/dsk/c0t2d0s6       /dev/rdsk/c0t2d0s6      /usr    ufs     1       no
-
/dev/dsk/c0t2d0s1       /dev/rdsk/c0t2d0s1      /var    ufs     1       no
-
/dev/dsk/c0t2d0s7       /dev/rdsk/c0t2d0s7      /export/home    ufs     2
yes     -
/dev/dsk/c0t2d0s5       /dev/rdsk/c0t2d0s5      /opt    ufs     2       yes
-
/dev/dsk/c0t2d0s4       /dev/rdsk/c0t2d0s4      /usr/local/utils        ufs
2       yes     -
swap    -       /tmp    tmpfs   -       yes     -
```

Table 6.6 *The* Vfstab *File*

Field	Description
device to mount	This holds the full path of the device file that should be used by the `mount` command to mount the filesystem. This will generally be a block device under */dev*, but may be a special tag for certain filesystem types (e.g., */tmp*).
device to fsck	This holds the full path of the device to be used by `fsck` if the filesystem needs checking at boot-time. This is expected to be a block device, or a "-" if it is not appropriate to run `fsck` against the filesystem (e.g., */proc*).
mount point	This should hold the full path of the directory upon which the filesystem is to be mounted.
FS type	This is the type of the filesystem that exists on the partition specified in the first column of the file.
fsck pass	This field is used to determine if the filesystem should be checked by `fsck` on boot. The field could contain any of the following: • - (do not check the filesystem) • 0 (check the filesystem for all types other than UFS) • 1 (all UFS filesystems are checked sequentially) • >1 (all UFS filesystems will be checked in parallel)

Table 6.6 *The* Vfstab *File (Continued)*

Field	Description
mount at boot	If this is set to "yes," the filesystem will be mounted automatically when the system boots.
mount options	If this is set, it will contain a comma-separated list of options to be supplied to the mount command when mounting this filesystem.

Each record in */etc/vfstab* must have the correct number of fields. If it is not appropriate to put in a value, then a "-" should be used. The field separator is any white space character.

Solaris does not provide a command to remove a filesystem, because there is no need to have one. If you no longer need a filesystem you can just unmount it and remove its entry from */etc/vfstsb* (or comment it out if you prefer). If you wish to create a new filesystem over the top of an existing one, then just use newfs or mkfs and the new one will be created over the top of the old one. If you wish to remove a filesystem so you can alter the size of its partition before recreating it in a different size, then again there is no need to remove the filesystem. Just change the size using the format utility and create the new filesystem on the partition.

Checking and Repairing Filesystems

Solaris provides a program for checking and repairing filesystems called fsck. It runs every time the system boots and will check any filesystem that does not have its state flag set to "clean," "stable," or "logging." The */etc/vfstab* file specifies which filesystems should be checked by fsck if required. If you want to run fsck manually against a filesystem it must first be unmounted, although if you ever need to run fsck the chances are you won't be able to mount the filesystem until after you have run fsck. You should always run fsck against the raw device containing the filesystem rather than the block device (which is used for mounting the filesystem). The following example shows the checks that are performed when fsck is run on a filesystem:

```
hydrogen# umount /usr/local/utils
hydrogen# # fsck /dev/rdsk/c0t2d0s4
** /dev/rdsk/c0t2d0s4
** Last Mounted on /usr/local/utils
** Phase 1 - Check Blocks and Sizes
** Phase 2 - Check Pathnames
** Phase 3 - Check Connectivity
** Phase 4 - Check Reference Counts
** Phase 5 - Check Cyl groups
12 files, 13 used, 96703 free (39 frags, 12083 blocks,
0.0% fragmentation)
hydrogen# mount /usr/local/utils
hydrogen#
```

In this instance, as expected, there were no problems, but if `fsck` does find anything wrong it will propose an action to fix the problem and will prompt you to confirm that you wish the action to be taken. If you want `fsck` to run noninteractively and not prompt before fixing, you can run it with the "-y" flag, but you must be aware of what the consequences are!

Phase 1—Check Blocks and Sizes

In this phase `fsck` checks for bad and duplicate blocks and verifies that the size and format of each inode is correct. It also checks that the filesystem size is correct.

Phase 2—Check Path Names

Here, `fsck` checks the path name of each file to make sure all the directories contained in it exist. If any bad inodes were found in phase 1, they will be removed during this phase.

Phase 3—Check Connectivity

This phase checks the connectivity of all directories to their parents using dot and dot dot. Any unconnected directories will be placed in the *lost+found* directory.

Phase 4—Check Reference Counts

Here, the number of links assigned to each file and directory is checked.

Phase 5—Check Cyl Groups

In this phase, `fsck` checks the blocks in the free block list and makes sure none of them are referenced by any file. When this is complete, the number of free blocks is added to the number of allocated blocks to make sure this is equal to the number of blocks the filesystem should have.

Lost+found *Directories*

All UFS- and s5-type filesystems should also have a directory called *lost+found* in their root. The exception to this is that a UFS-type filesystem mounted with the "logging" option set will not need this directory. The purpose of this directory is to receive files and directories that become disconnected. When `fsck` checks a filesystem, it may find inodes that are valid but no directory in the filesystem makes any reference to them. There is no way that `fsck` can work out which directory the inode belongs to, so it will be put in *lost+found*. Since a directory simply holds filenames and their inode numbers, and this is the only place the filename is stored, `fsck` has no way of knowing what the name of the file originally was. Because of this, you will notice that if you ever do find files or directories inside a *lost+found* directory, they all have a number for their name. This number is actually the file's inode number.

As the system administrator, it is your job to determine where files and directories in *lost+found* belong. If the entry is a directory with contents, then the contents should still have their original names, so this may tell you where it came from. If the entry in *lost+found* is a text file, then you can look at its contents, but if it is a binary file, it may be difficult to know exactly where it came from. As you become more experienced as a system administrator, you should be better able to judge where anything in *lost+found* originally came from. If a *lost+found* directory contains a large number of entries following a crash or other system event, you may find the best way to recover from the situation is to restore the whole filesystem from the most recent backup. If a UFS filesystem is mounted with the "logging" option set, then a power outage or system crash is unlikely to cause a problem that would result in files being placed in *lost+found*. However, it is still possible for corruption to creep into a filesystem by other methods (for example, by restoring data from a slightly corrupt backup).

If the `fsck` program finds that you have no *lost+found* directory, it will create it. If it does exist, but does not have enough space allocated to it, `fsck` will increase its size. So you should not worry too much about your *lost+found* directories. Just perform regular checks for entries in them, which would be a good thing to do in a script.

You could choose to regularly run the `ff` command as a cron job. This provides a mapping of inode number to a filename. If the output is stored, then you greatly increase the chances of reconnecting any files found in *lost+found*.

Files and Directories

When files are created on a filesystem they are stored inside a directory. A directory is simply a file that has a particular format. It is stored on the disk in the same way as ordinary files. The only reason you can't edit them like an ordinary file is because the editor programs (such as `vi`) specifically stop you from doing so. We will use the directory */var/adm* as an example to demonstrate the structure of a directory.

As you know, the `ls` command is provided to list the contents of a directory:

```
hydrogen# cd /var/adm
hydrogen# ls
aculog     log        passwd     sulog      utmpx      wtmp
lastlog    messages   spellhist  utmp       vold.log   wtmpx
hydrogen#
```

This has shown us the names of the files and directories that are in the directory */var/adm*, but we cannot tell which are files and which are directories. If we use the "-l" option with `ls` we can see quite a bit more information about the contents of */var/adm*:

```
hydrogen# ls -l
total 1036
-rw-------   1 uucp     bin           0 Oct 23 22:21 aculog
-r--r--r--   1 root     other        28 Apr 16 18:19 lastlog
drwxrwxr-x   2 adm      adm         512 Oct 23 22:20 log
-rw-r--r--   1 root     root     212878 Apr 16 15:15 messages
drwxrwxr-x   2 adm      adm         512 Oct 23 22:20 passwd
-rw-rw-rw-   1 bin      bin           0 Oct 23 22:21 spellhist
-rw-------   1 root     root          0 Jan 20 16:19 sulog
-rw-r--r--   1 root     bin         396 Apr 16 18:19 utmp
-rw-r--r--   1 root     bin        4092 Apr 16 18:19 utmpx
-rw-rw-rw-   1 root     root       4756 Apr 16 15:14 vold.log
-rw-rw-r--   1 adm      adm       25200 Apr 16 18:19 wtmp
-rw-rw-r--   1 adm      adm      260400 Apr 16 18:19 wtmpx
hydrogen#
```

You may be tempted to think all this information is stored within the directory, but the actual directory contents are closer to the first ls listing we saw. On our server, the directory */var/adm* actually contains the information listed in Table 6.7 and nothing more.

Table 6.7 *The Real Contents of /Var/adm*

Column 1	Column 2
18	.
2	..
11344	*log*
15122	*passwd*
24	*aculog*
25	*spellhist*
26	*utmp*
27	*utmpx*
28	*wtmp*
29	*wtmpx*
14	*messages*
252	*vold.log*
254	*lastlog*
270	*sulog*

The column headings are just for reference and are not actually held in the directory, but everything else is.

The second column contains the names of the files and directories (as shown by the ls command), but the directory does not hold any more information about the file other than the file's inode number. This (you will have worked it out by a process of elimination) is in the first column.

There are two entries within the directory that did not show up in the ls output. These are "." (dot) and ".." (dot dot). The reason that ls did not display these entries (which are actually directories) is because UNIX convention has it that files beginning with a dot are classed as hidden files and ls does not show hidden files unless the "-a" option is supplied. In fact, every single directory contains two entries called dot and dot dot. We will see that these entries are crucial to the way that directories and subdirectories are linked together.

So, at the moment we know that a directory is actually a file that simply contains the names of the files and directories that belong in it. Along with each name is a number called the inode number.

When we looked at the format of a filesystem we saw that the largest areas are the inode area and the data area. The data area holds the actual data contained within the files; since a directory is a special type of file we know that the data we saw in Table 6.7 (inode numbers and filenames) is stored somewhere in this part of the filesystem. The inode area of the filesystem contains the actual inodes. As each inode is 128 bytes in size, this section of the filesystem will be a multiple of 128 bytes in length. This 128 bytes contain all the information about a file apart from its name.

Each inode contains the information provided in Table 6.8.

Table 6.8 *The Contents of an Inode*

Field	Description
file type	This is a single byte and will be one of the following characters: • - (for a regular file) • d (for a directory) • b (for a block special file) • c (for a character special file) • L (for a symbolic link) • p (for a named pipe or FIFO file) File types are also mentioned in Chapter 4, "Permissions and All That."
file mode	The access permissions that belong to the file. See Chapter 4, "Permissions and All That," for more information.

Table 6.8 *The Contents of an Inode (Continued)*

Field	Description
number of hard links	This is equal to the number of references there are inside directories to this inode. When a file is deleted, this number is reduced by one. When it goes to zero the inode becomes "free."
user ID	This is equal to the user ID of the file owner.
group ID	This is equal to the group ID that the file belongs to.
number of bytes	This shows how many bytes in the filesystem data area belong to this file.
15 disk block addresses	These addresses are numbered 0 to 14 and each one contains the address of a data block in the filesystem data area. These addresses are described in more detail later.
last access date and time	This is the date and time the file was last opened.
last modification date and time	This is the date and time that the contents of the file last changed. (This is not the same as the contents of the inode getting changed.)
file creation date and time	This is not the date and time that the file was created, but is actually the date and time that the inode last changed.

Most information in the inode can be displayed using the ls command with various options. For example, the "-i" option will display the inode number of each file:

```
hydrogen# ls -ia
       18 .
        2 ..
       24 aculog
      254 lastlog
    11344 log
       14 messages
    15122 passwd
       25 spellhist
      270 sulog
       26 utmp
       27 utmpx
      252 vold.log
       28 wtmp
       29 wtmpx
hydrogen#
```

The inode number is shown before each filename. Since we also included the "-a" flag, we can see the entries for dot and dot dot. The above example shows the true contents of the directory *var/adm* as all the other information about the files is stored in the individual inodes. If you try to look at a directory using the `cat` command, you will not see the output in a very readable format as the terminal emulator is likely to be confused by the inode numbers since they are not stored in text format. You can, however, use the `od` command to verify that a directory really is just a file containing inode numbers and filenames. The best way to do this is to run `od -bc dir_name`.

Each file that exists on a Solaris UFS filesystem has an entry in a directory that contains the file's name and the number of the inode that contains information about that file. Part of the information is the address (or addresses) of the blocks that actually hold the data that form the contents of the file. As mentioned earlier, the inodes are stored in a separate part of the filesystem from the data blocks. Every file has one inode allocated to it as soon as it is created. If the file has any contents, these will be stored in blocks within the data area. If the file is empty, it will not have any space in the data area allocated to it.

If the file is not empty, the address of each data block allocated to that file is stored within the inode. The inode contains 15 slots for addresses (numbered 0 to 14). A quick calculation may lead you to believe that a file can only have a maximum size of 15 times the filesystem's block size. This certainly doesn't add up to anywhere near the maximum supported file size; that is because the 15 slots don't work quite as simply as the last sentence suggests.

In fact, the first 12 address slots in the inode each hold the address of a single block that contains part of the file's data. Slot 12 also holds the address of a block in the data area, but this is called an "indirect block." Instead of it containing data that belong to the file, it contains more addresses of allocated blocks. If the file is so big that the indirect block can't accommodate it, then slot 13 will hold the address of a double indirect block. This block contains addresses of other indirect blocks. In the rare chance that the file is still too big to be accommodated, the final address slot is reserved for the address of a triple indirect block.

The inode number associated with each file is unique within each filesystem. The inode number of the filesystem's top-level directory is always 2 (inode numbers 0 and 1 exist, but are reserved).

When a directory is created, the entries dot and dot dot are placed inside it. The file called "." has the same inode number as the directory in which it resides and the file called ".." has the same inode number as the directory in which its directory resides (or the parent directory). It is not possible for two inodes to have the same inode number (within the same filesystem), so if two files have the same inode number they must be the same file but with two different names. A file that refers to an existing file's inode number is called a "link." There is no concept of one being the master and the other being linked to that file. They can be thought of literally as alternative names for the same file.

This means that a directory will always start with two links (or two references), the first being its name in the parent directory and the second being "." (dot), which appears as an entry within itself. If a subdirectory is created within this directory then the number of links goes up to three as the entry called ".." (dot dot) in the subdirectory is another link to this directory.

The directory tree is managed by the use of links. The dot dot entry in every directory is linked to the dot entry in the directory above, and that in turn is linked to its name in its parent directory.

Files can also be linked using the `ln` command. When a file is created it will have one link, but you can effectively create another name that refers to the same file by creating another link:

```
hydrogen# ln sulog link_to_sulog
hydrogen# ls -l sulog link_to_sulog
-rw-------    2 root     root          157 Jan 20 16:19 sulog
-rw-------    2 root     root          157 Jan 20 16:19 link_to_sulog
hydrogen#
```

The file now has two names by which it can be referred, but both names have the same inode number so they share the inode and they share the data. If one of the files is deleted, the link count of the other will drop to one. If that file is deleted, the inode count drops to zero and the inode is added to the free inode list.

Files can be linked in this way anywhere within the same filesystem. If you wish to create a link across filesystems you need to use a symbolic link (`ln -s`). A symbolic link is simply a file that contains the path to the file to which it is symbolically linked. You can tell it is a symbolic link since its file type will be "L" and the path it points to is also shown in the output from an `ls -l` command.

If you wish to view the contents of an inode, it is possible using the `fsdb` utility (filesystem debugger). This is a very powerful tool that can be used to perform a number of low-level operations on a filesystem, so do not try anything other than the command listed here as it could cause damage if used incorrectly:

```
hydrogen# umount /usr/local/utils
hydrogen# fsdb /dev/rdsk/c0t2d0s4
fsdb of /dev/rdsk/c0t2d0s4 (Read only) -- last mounted on /usr/
local/utils
fs_clean is currently set to FSCLEAN
fs_state consistent (fs_clean CAN be trusted)
/dev/rdsk/c0t2d0s4 >:inode 2
i#: 2              md: d---rwxr-xr-x  uid: 0              gid: 0
ln: 5              bs: 2             sz : 200
db#0: 330
        accessed: Sun Apr 22 18:16:50 2001
        modified: Mon Apr 16 18:06:37 2001
        created : Mon Apr 16 18:06:37 2001
/dev/rdsk/c0t2d0s4 > :quit
hydrogen#
```

The `fsdb` prompt is the device containing the filesystem followed by a "greater than" symbol. Each `fsdb` command should be preceded by a colon.

In the above example we have asked `fsdb` to display the contents of inode 2 (which is the root directory of the filesystem). We can see that the name of the file does not appear anywhere and we know the file is less than one block in size since only one data block address is shown. So we know that the contents of this directory are stored in block number 330 in the data storage area of the filesystem. One of the three times displayed is marked as "created"; this is not the time the file was created since this is not stored. This time is actually the time the inode was last updated, and is a well-known bug in `fsdb`.

Devices

Solaris provides a directory called */dev* that contains a series of special files. Each file is linked to a device of some sort. We have already seen that each disk partition has two entries under */dev*: a raw (or character) device and a block device. There are also entries for tape devices, floppy disks, and even the system's memory. The reason these exist is to provide a standard interface to all devices that acts in the same way as a normal Solaris file. Therefore, these entries have permissions, owners, and groups just like a normal file does. The Solaris kernel contains a device driver for each device that basically converts the file type operation performed on the file under */dev* into instructions that the actual device understands. This is one of the strengths of the UNIX operating environment.

Solaris Directories

When Solaris is first installed, literally hundreds of directories are created. Until you have been using Solaris for some time, you will not remember all the important locations. Table 6.9 lists the directories you most likely need to know about from the *root*, *usr*, and *var* filesystems.

Table 6.9 *Standard Directory Locations*

Directory	Description
/	The very top-level directory.
/dev	Where all the special device files live. They are grouped into subdirectories.
/dev/rdsk	Location of raw special files for disk slices.
/dev/dsk	Location of block special files for disk slices.

Table 6.9 *Standard Directory Locations (Continued)*

Directory	Description
/dev/rmt	Location of raw tape device special files.
/dev/mt	Location of block tape device special files.
/dev/term	Location of terminal special device files (for async connections).
/dev/pts	Location of pseudo TTY slave devices (for telnet sessions, etc.).
/etc	Houses the host-specific administrative configuration files.
/etc/default	Contains a number of files containing various default settings.
/etc/inet	Contains configuration files for Internet services.
/etc/init.d	Contains scripts that run when run levels change. The files located here are linked to files under */etc/rcX.d*.
/etc/net	Location of configuration files for network services.
/etc/skel	Default location of master user profiles.
/export	Default root for exported filesystems.
/home	Default location of user home directories.
/kernel	Location of loadable kernel modules.
/mnt	Empty directory normally used as a temporary mount point.
/opt	Usual location of additional Solaris packages.
/sbin	Bin directory that contains the essential system programs required during bootup and manual system recovery procedures.
/stand	Default location of standalone programs.
/tmp	Temporary directory usually located on system swap area and cleared out during a reboot.
/usr	Mount point for the */usr* filesystem.
/var	Mount point for the */var* filesystem. (Var is short for "varying," since it contains files likely to change.)
/var/adm	Location of system logs and accounting files.
/var/mail	Location of user mail files.
/var/preserve	Contains backups of interrupted editor sessions.

Table 6.9 *Standard Directory Locations (Continued)*

Directory	Description
/var/spool/cron	Location of *cron* and at control files.
/var/tmp	Temporary directory that does not get cleared at boot-time.
/usr/bin	Standard location of operating system commands.
/usr/include	Header files for C programs.
/usr/lib	Location of libraries.
/usr/local	Directory for in-house programs, etc.
/usr/sbin	Location of system administration programs.
/usr/ucb	Location of BSD variants of operating system commands.

In earlier versions of UNIX the */var* filesystem did not exist and these files were contained in the */usr* filesystem. With the introduction of UNIX System V Release 4 (SVR4), upon which Solaris is based, the old */usr* was split into two separate filesystems (*/usr* and */var*). */usr* housed the files that tended to remain static (such as programs and library files) and */var* took all the volatile files (such as log files, configuration files, and temporary files). Links exist in */usr* to provide backward compatibility. This can lead to a common problem when */usr* fills up because of the system administrator thinking (s)he is clearing files from */usr*, but df continues to report it is 100 percent full. This is because it is actually */var* that is being cleared out.

Log Files

Log files are used to hold information intended for the system administrator to look at when required. They need to be looked at depending on the type of information they contain, but if they are never likely to be looked at there is probably little point wasting disk space by storing the data. The major log files you need to be aware of are shown in Table 6.10, with guidance on how to keep them from growing too large.

Table 6.10 *Common Solaris Log Files*

Log	Description	Housekeeping Method
/var/adm/utmp	Contains information about who is currently logged in and is read by the who command. Do not trim or remove this file unless it becomes corrupt. Replaced by */var/adm/utmpx* in Solaris 9.	Do not touch this file unless the who command gives corrupt output, in which case you can empty it (all users should be logged off first). *cp /dev/null /var/adm/utmp*
/var/adm/wtmp	This contains an accumulative log of all users who have logged in. It is not a text file, but can be viewed using the who command (who */var/adm/wtmp*). When users log in, they are added to both the *utmp* file and *wtmp* file. When they log out, they are removed from the *utmp* file but not *wtmp*. This file can grow very large if left unchecked. This file is being phased out to be replaced by *wtmpx*.	Empty the file when required. *cp /dev/null /var/adm/wtmp*
/var/adm/wtmpx	This log file is similar to the *wtmp* file (and Solaris 9 has completely replaced it) in that it holds accumulated login information and is not a text file. It is read by the last command.	Empty the file when required. *cp /dev/null /var/adm/wtmpx*
/var/adm/sulog	This is a text file containing a record of all attempts made by users to switch to another user's ID. The entry will contain a "+" if the attempt succeeded or a "-" if it failed. This should be looked through on a regular basis for anything suspicious, such as a user gaining access to *root* that shouldn't (see Chapter 1, "The System Administrator's Role").	This file can either be emptied or you could remove all but the last "X" number of lines. If you wish to keep a long history of login attempts, this file can be rotated as shown in the housekeeping script at the end of this chapter.
/var/adm/messages	This text file is very important to the system administrator. It contains information on a variety of system events.	Solaris automatically rotates this file, so it should not need any special treatment.

The Implementation

For the example servers within this book, we will be sticking to a standard design for filesystems on all our servers. This greatly simplifies the management of the servers and also simplifies the process of documenting them. In a large company with many Solaris servers, it is of great benefit to design a standard set of filesystems and use this design every time a new server is built. It means the build process is simpler and backups from one system can more easily be used to help recover from an emergency situation on another server. It also means that the support staff know what to expect and where to look when they get problems on any of their servers. A good idea is to define and document naming standards and stick to these on all servers.

For our servers we will use the information in Table 6.11 as our standard.

Table 6.11 *Standard Disk Layout*

Filesystem Name	Mountpoint	Device
root	*/*	c0t2d0s0
usr	*/usr*	c0t2d0s6
var	*/var*	c0t2d0s1
opt	*/opt*	c0t2d0s5
home	*/export/home*	c0t2d0s7
tmp	*/tmp*	swap (c0t2d0s3)
system_tools	*/usr/local/utils*	c0t2d0s4

The filesystem mounted on */usr/local/utils* is used to hold our own scripts that help us manage and support the servers. Among the scripts included are one that will housekeep log files to prevent them from filling up filesystems and another that can check how full each filesystem is and send a mail message to a specified user if any are getting too full. As long as the mail gets checked regularly, we should have time to do something before the filesystem actually fills up.

Housekeeping the Log Files

We could have written a script to clear out log files with the names of the logs hard coded in the script. But this is not a good practice, since it means that if one system has different log files on it you need to edit the script itself. This can lead to problems in the future since when you roll out a new version of the script to all your systems you will lose the changes you made and you

then have to spend time managing the scripts rather than the systems. To get
around this problem, we use a separate file to hold the names of each log file
to be housekept along with the rule for housekeeping it. The script reads the
information from this file so we can have the same version of the script on all
servers; if we improve it later, we can deliver it to all the servers knowing we
will not overwrite any local change.

From examining the log files in the previous section, we can see that there
are at least three different ways we might want to housekeep a log file. We
might want to empty it, remove some old lines in it, or actually delete it. We
have designed the file that holds the log file names so that we can specify
what we want to do to each file to housekeep it. Instead of creating an action
that simply deletes a log file, we have decided to call the action "move." It will
cause the specified log file to be backed up before emptying it, so that we can
still access the information in the backup copy. Next time the script runs, the
backup copy will be overwritten with the log file's current contents. Here is
an example of the housekeeping configuration file:

```
# This file is used by the script tidyLogs.
# It holds the name of each log to tidy and rules
# on how to tidy it.
# The format is:
# name_of_file:action(zero,move,reduce):lines_to_keep
# (only applies to reduce)
/var/adm/wtmpx:zero:
/var/adm/wtmp:move:
/var/adm/sulog:reduce:100
```

The file contains one log file per line and the fields are colon-separated, as
many other Solaris system and configuration files are (e.g., *etc/passwd*).

This example contains one line for each type of housekeeping we perform.
The first entry is for the *wtmpx* file. We aren't interested in using the information stored in here so we have chosen to empty the file each time the
tidyLogs housekeeping script runs. For the *wtmp* file, we will opt to back up
the file before emptying it, and for the *sulog* file we will keep the 100 most
recent entries.

The script that reads this file and actually keeps the log files in check is
shown here in its entirety:

```
#!/bin/ksh
# shell script to be called from the root crontab that will tidy
# log files using the file /usr/local/utils/logsToTidy
# to provide the log filename and the action to take.
#
logCfg=/usr/local/utils/logsToTidy
tidyLog=/usr/local/utils/logs/tidyLog.log
prog=$(basename $0)
if [[ ! -f "$logCfg" ]]
then
  echo "$0: cannot find $logCfg"
  exit 1
else
  for file in $(grep -v '^#' $logCfg | awk -F: '{print $1}')
```

```
do
   action=$(grep "^$file:" $logCfg | awk -F: '{print $2}')
   case $action in
      zero)  cp /dev/null $file
             echo "$prog:$(date):$file emptied" >>$tidyLog
             ;;
      move)  cp $file ${file}.old
             cp /dev/null $file
             echo "$prog:$(date):$file backed up and emptied" >>$tidyLog
             ;;
      reduce) keep=$(grep "^$file:" $logCfg | awk -F: '{print $3}')
             lines=$(cat $file | wc -l)
             if [[ "$lines" -gt "$keep" ]]
             then
                cp $file /tmp/tidy.$$
                tail -$keep /tmp/tidy.$$ >$file
                rm -f /tmp/tidy.$$
                echo "$prog:$(date):$file reduced to $keep lines"
                     >>$tidyLog
             fi
             ;;
   esac
done
fi
```

This script is fairly basic, but you could use it as a starting point to build a script capable of more complex housekeeping tasks. For example, you could amend it to cycle a log file, so the current log gets moved to *logname*.1, *logname*.1 gets moved to *logname*.2, and so forth. Of course, you would need to move the current one last to avoid overwriting the older logs before you have moved them. You could then define an extra action for this in the *logsTo-Tidy* configuration file.

Another improvement to the script would be to make it handle wildcards in the *logsToTidy* file. With a bit more judicial coding, you could end up with a script that can perform actions as complicated as deleting all log files in a directory that are older than 30 days, for example.

We have chosen to run this script once a month. If we ran it more often, the log files might not always have enough information in them to help us do our job; if we ran it less frequently, there is a chance that they might fill up a file-system in between runs. The following cron entry will run the script on the first day of each month at 07:15 in the morning:

```
15 7 1 * * /usr/local/utils/bin/tidyLogs >/dev/null 2>&1
```

The part of the entry from the "greater than" symbol to the end of the line ensures that any output from the script is redirected to a special file called */dev/null*. This is usually added to all cron entries because cron always mails the output of any jobs it runs to the owner of the cron file, and this tends to just fill the user's mail file with unwanted mail. The process of redirection is covered in Chapter 5, "Shells."

Checking Filesystem Usage

The script shown below is intended to be executed from the *root crontab* file at a regular interval. It checks each filesystem's percentage of fullness and alerts if one is greater than 90 percent full.

```ksh
#!/bin/ksh
# simple shell script to be called from the root crontab that will
# check the usage of each filesystem and mail an alert if any are
# more than 90% full
#
mailWarn=/usr/local/utils/mailWarnings
fswarnLog=/usr/local/utils/logs/fswarn.log
mailProg=mailx
alarm=90
prog=$(basename $0)
# alerts will be mailed to the mail list/user specified in $mailWarn if
# it exists, otherwise mail to root
if [[ -f "$mailWarn" ]]
then
   mailTo=$(cat ${mailWarn} | grep -v "^#")
else
   mailTo=root
fi
df -k | while read line
do
   if echo $line | grep '^Filesystem' >/dev/null
   then
     continue
   fi
   set $line
   pcntFull=$(echo $5 | sed 's/%//')
   fs=$6
   if [[ "$pcntFull" -gt "$alarm" ]]
   then
     # send warning to logfile and mail to the administrator
     echo "WARNING: $fs is $pcntfull percent full at $(date)" \
          >> $fswarnLog
     echo "WARNING: $fs is $pcntfull percent full at $(date)" \
          | $mailProg $mailTo
   fi
done
```

There are two ways you could improve upon this script. Some filesystems (such as */usr*) are fairly static, so you may not care if they are more than 90 percent full since there is little chance of them filling up quickly. Also, if it is a very large filesystem, even if it is 95 percent full there could still be over 100 MB free. So one improvement you could make would be to create a configuration file that contained the name of the filesystem and the percentage it needs to be full before it alerts. The entry for */usr* might read:

```
/usr:98
```

The other improvement you could make would be to check how many inodes are free. Remember, if you run out of inodes you cannot create any more files in that filesystem no matter how much free space there is. Running the df command with the "-e" option will display the number of free inodes for each filesystem.

The script is run by the following cron entry in the *root crontab* file:

```
0,15,30,45 * * * * /usr/local/utils/bin/fswarn >/dev/null 2>&1
```

This will cause the script to run every 15 minutes to ensure that when a filesystem reaches the 90 percent threshold we have a chance of doing something before it actually reaches 100 percent. If your system is heavily loaded and you do not wish this script to interfere as much, it could be run every half-hour or even every hour.

7

SWAP SPACE

Objectives

Swap has existed since the first days of UNIX, although its implementation has changed greatly over the years and across the different UNIX flavors. In this chapter, we will be looking at the Solaris implementation of swap. This will include a description of what swap is and how it fits into the memory management scheme of a Solaris server. We will also look at the kernel parameters that define how swap is used, how we can monitor our swap space, and what signs can tell us that we may have problems with it.

Swapping and Paging

To understand swap, we'll look at it in relation to the rest of the memory management mechanism system (i.e., virtual memory and paging). The reason for this is that they are all tied to each other quite tightly.

Solaris uses a virtual memory model that is made up from the total amount of physical memory installed on the system and the amount of swap space that has been defined. For example, if we had 4 GB of physical memory and created a swap area of 10 GB, this would provide us with 14 GB of virtual memory.

Paging

Whenever a program runs it is first allocated an amount of memory. The program code is split into chunks by the kernel; each of these is known as a "page." The kernel also loads a few of these pages into the memory space that has been allocated for the program; here, it will start to run the pages it has in memory. Additional pages will also be loaded when the first ones have been used. If a required page isn't found, a page fault occurs indicating that the kernel should load more pages into memory. This is known as "demand paging."

Once the amount of available free memory falls below a certain limit (lotsfree—see Table 7.1), paging will occur. The page scanner runs and, using a Least Recently Used (LRU) algorithm, determines any pages that have not been accessed for a while. These will be marked as unused; if they are still unused after a period of time, the page will be reclaimed and put back on the free list.

A number of variables can be set to tweak the way paging works. Although we should point out now that you must be aware of what you are doing if you change any of this—the default values have been tried and tested and should be the best overall solution. The variables can be set by adding the required setting to */etc/system*. Some of the more common paging variables are shown in Table 7.1.

Table 7.1 *Common Paging Tuneable Variables*

Variable	Value	Description
lotsfree	The greater of $1/64$ of physical memory, or 512 KB	When paging occurs.
desfree	lotsfree/2	Amount of desired free memory.
minfree	desfree/2	Minimum acceptable memory level.

Table 7.1 *Common Paging Tuneable Variables (Continued)*

Variable	Value	Description
throttlefree	minfree	Level at which blocking memory allocation requests are put to sleep.
pageout_reserve	throttlefree/2	Number of pages reserved for the pageout or scheduler threads.
cachefree	2 × lotsfree	Not used in Solaris 8—was used in priority paging to free file system data pages.
priority_paging	—	Not used in Solaris 8—was used to enable priority paging.
fastscan	The minimum of 64 MB or ½ physical memory	Maximum number of pages per second that the system will look at.
slowscan	The smaller of $1/20$ of physical memory or 100 pages	Minimum number of pages per second that the system will look at.

Swapping

Let's assume that the system has been working happily and paging has been occurring at normal levels. Suddenly, the system doesn't have enough memory to allocate to any new processes, which means an existing process, in its entirety, must be moved out of the way to let the new one run.

This is swapping. The process that is being swapped out is moved to a temporary area reserved for the kernel (i.e., swap space). In other words, swap is an area that can be used by the kernel to store running programs when there is not enough space in memory.

Which Is Best?

Paging is the mechanism of choice—it is much smoother than swapping and doesn't affect system performance anywhere near as much. It relies on the fact that "20 percent of a process's memory pages do 80 percent of the work!"

Swapping, on the other hand, is a harsh process that takes its toll on system resources and can cause problems such as disk thrashing as it moves whole processes in and out of swap. It is really used as a last resort, such as when the system must swap to avoid crashing.

Is Swap Really Needed?

In short, the answer is—maybe! Depending on the version of the operating system you are running, and possibly even the patch levels that have been applied, the amount of swap required may range from zero up to the same amount as physical memory.

The swapping and paging mechanisms are often changed between releases to make them more efficient. This quickly becomes a very complex subject, which is beyond the scope of this chapter, so let's just make a few points:

- Early versions of Solaris used to implement an early allocation mechanism. When a process was started, space for it was reserved in swap in the event it would be swapped out. This meant that swap space needed to be at least as large as the physical memory.

- Priority paging was introduced in Solaris 7 and made available to Solaris 2.5.1 and 2.6 through kernel patches. It was enabled by setting "priority_paging" in */etc/system*. This is no longer supported in Solaris 8, as the memory allocation mechanism used is now more efficient that priority paging.

Nowadays it is possible to create swapless systems by adding enough physical memory to the machine to satisfy its requirements. The main problem here is how to determine exactly how much "enough" is, other than by carrying out tests on the system.

The Scheduler

The task of choosing which process gets swapped out is undertaken by process 0 (the sched process, which is part of the Solaris kernel). If possible, the process swapped out will be in a sleeping state so as not to interrupt one that is actually running on a CPU at the time. Once the new process is running in memory, it too could be swapped out to the swap partition to make room for another new process.

Of course, when a process has been swapped out, it is not simply left there, as it would never get a chance to run again. So the sched process also manages the swapping back in of swapped-out processes. If there is not enough room in memory to swap a process back in, then another will have to be swapped out first. This juggling of processes between memory and disk uses up system resources and can have quite an impact on the overall performance of the system. In general, the more memory you have installed, the less often a process will need to be swapped out. Of course, this is heavily dependent on what the system is actually used for.

The amount of memory is important to the performance of the system, but the size of swap space is also important. If the swap space is not big enough, you could get a situation where sched needs to swap a process out of memory, but the swap space is already full so there is no room for it. A situation like this would cause the failure of many running processes and could lead to a system crash.

In times of yore when memory was expensive and disks were not that big, the sizing of the swap space could be a rather delicate balancing act. Thankfully, nowadays systems can support larger amounts of cheap memory, and available disk sizes still seem to be growing exponentially. This makes the planning of swap space less of an issue, though it is still important and something you need to be aware of.

How Big Should It Be?

The exact amount of swap space required is dependent on many factors, one of the most important being the requirements of the application(s) you are running on the server.

Many applications and databases have specific swap requirements and will describe in great detail how you should calculate the size based on the number of users, size of database, likely rate of transactions, and so forth. If you will be running an application or database on one of your servers, you should follow the guidance of the application installation guide rather than anything recommended in this chapter.

When Solaris is installed, it will create a swap partition based on the amount of memory installed in the computer. The rules it uses are shown in Table 7.2.

Table 7.2 *Default Swap Space Sizes (Solaris 7)*

Installed Memory (MB)	Swap Space Size (MB)
16–64	32
64–128	64
128–512	128
Greater than 512	512

This means that the maximum swap size that Solaris 7 will create during an automated install is 512 MB. (For Solaris 8, the maximum size created will be 256 MB rather than 512 MB, but all other values are as per the Solaris 7 table). This may be enough for the system, but it may not. It is much better to spend some time checking this out, rather than just accepting the default and leaving things to chance.

As already mentioned, the most important factor in sizing swap correctly is likely to be the applications that will be run on the server. On top of this, the following points may also prove useful in determining if you have enough swap space or not:

- When the system crashes, a crash dump will be written to the swap device. The size of the crash is not fixed, but in the worst case it could be as large as the entire installed memory. Therefore, if you want to guarantee that you will always have enough swap to hold a system crash dump, you should make swap at least as large as the system memory.

- We saw in Chapter 6, "The Filesystem and Its Contents," that /tmp is actually memory-resident, but it also makes use of the swap partition. If you know that the system will make heavy use of /tmp, then you may want to increase the size of swap to compensate for the space that may be lost to /tmp.

The 2 GB Swap Limit

If you are running the 32-bit version of Solaris, only the first 2 GB of a swap partition can be used. Therefore, if you need to have a swap space larger than this you will need to create multiple swap partitions. The 64-bit version of Solaris can support a single swap space up to 2**63-1 (which, when converted into English, means quite a lot more than 2 GB). It's also worth noting that swap space is crudely "striped." This means that if multiple swap locations are defined, they will be used in rotation. This effectively distributes the load evenly across the swap sites. Because of this, it's not a good idea to place separate swap locations on the same disk, as it will be detrimental to performance.

You can tell if your system is running the 32-bit or the 64-bit version of Solaris by running the isainfo command:

```
hydrogen# isainfo -v
64-bit sparcv9 applications
32-bit sparc applications
hydrogen#
```

The above output shows that the system is running 64-bit Solaris (what it is actually saying is that the operating system can support both 32-bit and 64-bit applications). If you get the output shown below, then you have a system running 32-bit Solaris:

```
hydrogen# isainfo -v
32-bit sparc applications
hydrogen#
```

In addition to there being a maximum size for swap, there is also a minimum size (though you are unlikely to ever want to create a swap partition as small as this). The minimum size exists because the first page of swap is never used. The reason for this is to allow the swap partition to be placed at the start of a disk while ensuring that the disk's VTOC does not get overwritten. This means that to actually have something that can be used, each swap partition should be at least two pages in size. The size of a memory page is not fixed but can be determined on any Solaris server by using the `pagesize` command, as follows (the output is shown in bytes).

```
hydrogen# pagesize
8192
hydrogen#
```

Swap Locations

Swap space can be built up from raw disk partitions and/or swap files. In this section we'll have a look at both of these. We'll start with the most commonly used type—disk partitions.

Raw Disk Partitions

When you first install Solaris, a default swap partition will normally be created for you, so it is unlikely that you would need to create the main swap partition. You are much more likely to need to create an additional swap partition or alter the size of the one that Solaris created for you.

Using raw disk areas for swap size is a very simple procedure—we simply need to define the partition boundaries, just as we would for a normal file system (see Chapter 6, "The Filesystem and Its Contents"). In fact, the only difference between creating a swap partition and one that will be used with a filesystem is that you don't actually create anything on the partition used for swap. All we need to do is inform the system about the new area, after which the kernel will start to use it (if it needs to!).

For example, if we have a look at the following label from a boot disk, the only difference we can see between the partitions is that partition 3 has its flags set to "unmountable" and it doesn't have a mount point, although this does not prove we are looking at a swap partition:

```
hydrogen# prtvtoc /dev/rdsk/c0t2d0s2
<lines removed for clarity>
* Flags:
*    1: unmountable
*   10: read-only
<lines removed for clarity>
*                      First   Sector    Last
* Partition Tag Flags  Sector  Count   Sector  Mount Directory
      0       2   00        0  103005   103004  /
      1       7   00   103005  132435   235439  /var
      2       5   00        0 3441675  3441674
      3       3   01   235440  163500   398939
      4       9   00  3229125  206010  3435134
      5       0   00   398940   83385   482324  /opt
      6       4   00   482325 1639905  2122229  /usr
      7       8   00  2122230 1106895  3229124  /export/home
hydrogen#
```

Now, we have a valid swap space. We'll look at some of the options we can use to access it in a moment. For now, we'll move on and look at the second type of swap location—swap files.

Swap Files

As well as defining a swap partition, we can also create a swap file. This is a file that resides within a standard filesystem for the sole use of the kernel. Swap files have many of the same attributes as a standard file, in that they appear in ls output. Their sizes can be seen with programs such as du and df.

Swap files have a number of advantages over raw partitions. For example, they can be quickly added or removed, and it's very easy to alter their size.

Interestingly, there is no difference in performance between a swap partition and a swap file. This is because the swap file is not accessed through the normal filesystem mechanism. Instead, it is accessed directly by the kernel, in exactly the same way as a swap partition.

Let's work through the creation of a 100 MB swap file now—the first step is to create the actual file itself. For this, we need to choose a filesystem that has enough space to hold the file. We also need to make sure that it's not one of the most heavily used. We'll use the *export/home* filesystem for this, as it meets both of the above criteria; we'll call the file *extra_swap*:

```
hydrogen# mkfile 100m /export/home/extra_swap
hydrogen# ls -l /export/home/extra_swap
-rw------T   1 root      other       104857600 Nov  4 15:35
   /export/home/extra_swap
hydrogen#
```

When mkfile is run by *root*, it automatically sets the sticky bit on the newly created file, but without the execute bit; hence the "T" instead of "t." It is still possible for non-*root* users to use mkfile, but they need to manually set the sticky bit.

This is a specific state that only applies to files being used as swap space—the reason being that it turns an inode's access time update (atime) into an asynchronous (nonblocking) update, rather than the normal, synchronous update.

The mkfile command creates a file of the size specified and fills it with nulls (a null is represented by the key sequence backslash zero—"\0"). The file is created in this way so that the space allocated to it is contiguous on the disk.

It is important that the permissions are set to prevent the file from being accidentally overwritten.

Adding the Swap Devices

Now we've got two swap devices: a raw disk and a swap file. The next job is to let the system know they are available. We can do this in two ways:

- At boot-time, using */etc/vfstab*
- Dynamically, using the `swap` command

Statically with */etc/vfstab*

The first point to be aware of is that the system isn't really concerned about whether it's using a disk or a file. They can both be mounted at boot-time by defining entries in */etc/vfstab*. Similarly, they can both be manipulated using the `swap` command. We will create the *vfstab* entry for the raw disk here and add the swap file entry later.

We can see from the following entry that we don't provide any information about the swap size, just the name of the device that should be used. Also, no checking is done for the devices specified. The kernel will simply use the area. This means that if, for example, a filesystem already exists on the partition specified, it would be destroyed—provided it was not already mounted.

Our file will be as follows:

```
hydrogen# cat /etc/vfstab
#device      device     mount    FS     fsck   mount     mount
#to mount    to fsck    point    type   pass   at boot   options
#
<lines removed for clarity>
/dev/dsk/c0t2d0s3 -     -        swap   -      no        -
swap                    /tmp     tmpfs  -      yes       -
hydrogen#
```

This example shows that the swap partition is located on the disk partition */dev/dsk/c0t2d0s3*. You will also notice that the device for */tmp* is defined as being the swap partition. This does not mean that */tmp* has been created on the swap partition; it is actually created in memory, but it may make use of the swap partition, since most things in memory are fair game for the `sched` process to swap out (see Chapter 6, "The Filesystem and Its Contents").

So, how does swap get mounted? The simple answer is "It doesn't." As we mentioned earlier, the swap area is not a filesystem—it's just a partition on a disk. The data that is stored there is under the control of the kernel rather than the user. It is not the user who requests that a specific part of memory should be copied to swap in order for a different process to make use of it. The swap is only used while the system is actually running, so there should be no need to keep the data between reboots (as there would be with most filesystems).

Therefore, all the system really needs to know is which device is allocated for use as swap, each time it reboots. It does this by running the script */etc/init.d/standardmounts* (linked to */etc/rcS.d/S40standardmounts.sh*), which in turn calls `swapadd`. This searches */etc/vfstab* for any swap partitions and adds them. (There is no man page for the `swapadd` script, since a system administrator should never have to run it directly.)

Dynamically with Swap

We said that one advantage of using swap files is that it's a quick and easy method. For this reason, they are often added dynamically (as a temporary measure to get around a problem, for example). Now let's add a file device to our existing swap space:

```
hydrogen# swap -a /export/home/extra_swap
hydrogen#
```

The swap file is now available for use. However, if the machine were to be shut down or the */export/home* filesystem were unmounted, it would no longer be available. To make the setting permanent, we need to add the following entry to */etc/vfstab*:

```
/export/home/extra_swap  -  -  swap  -  no  -
```

Now we just need to check that the new swap space is available:

```
hydrogen swap -l
swapfile dev swaplo blocks free
/dev/dsk/c0t2d0s3           32,27      8 163288 163288
/export/home/extra_swap    -          8 204792 204792
hydrogen#
```

A swap partition can also be removed using the `swap` command. If any blocks within the swap area are in use, they will be moved into an alternative active swap partition:

```
hydrogen# swap -d /export/home/extra_swap
hydrogen# swap -l
swapfile                 dev  swaplo blocks    free
/dev/dsk/c0t2d0s3    32,27      8 163288 163288
hydrogen#
```

This command will not actually delete the file, but will de-allocate it from use as swap. Consequently, you will need to manually remove the file and also remove the entry from */etc/vfstab*.

```
hydrogen# rm /export/home/extra_swap
hydrogen#
```

Good. Now we know how to manipulate the swap devices as we please.

Monitoring Swap Space

Somehow we need to check how our swap space is being used. We can't check it in the same way we would check a filesystem. The reason for this is that when a swap area is created, whether it's a raw partition or a file, we simply create the "full thing" and pass it onto the system to use as it sees fit. For example, earlier we defined a disk partition that was around 80 MB in size. At this time, we have no idea how full it is. Similarly, we created a 100 MB swap file. Utilities such as df and du will report its size correctly, but again will be unable to tell us how much of it is actually used at present.

So, now let's look at some ways of determining what's happening with swap. First, we can see the current swap allocation on a system as follows:

```
hydrogen# swap -l
swapfile              dev  swaplo blocks    free
/dev/dsk/c0t2d0s3  226,7      16 16774704 16774640
hydrogen#
```

The columns shown are described in Table 7.3.

Table 7.3 *Column Details*

Column Heading	Description
swapfile	This is the path name of the disk partition or file on which the swap space is located.
dev	This is the major and minor number of the partition. It will contain a dash (-) if the swap space is located on a file.
swaplo	This is the starting location of the swap space shown as an offset from the beginning of the partition or file.
blocks	This is the size of the swap file in 512-byte blocks.
free	This is the number of 512-byte blocks of swap that are not currently allocated.

We can get some additional information on swap usage by running swap -s:

```
hydrogen# swap -s
total: 311704k bytes allocated + 55592k reserved = 367296k used,
   14658824k available
hydrogen#
```

The "bytes allocated" refers to the amount of swap that has been allocated and is in use, while the term "reserved" refers to the amount of swap that has been claimed for possible future use but is not actually being used at the moment. These values are added up to give the total in use, the remainder being the swap still available. Note that the size of swap displayed by the "-s" option is shown in kilobytes and includes the system RAM, whereas the "-l" displays sizes in 512-byte blocks and does not include the size of RAM in its calculations.

If your system is suffering from problems caused by a lack of swap space, you may see any of the following error messages:

- *program* out of memory
- malloc error 0
- WARNING: Sorry, no swap space to grow stack for *pid*
- */tmp*: File system full, swap space limit exceeded
- */tmp*: File system full, memory allocation failed

The latter two examples may at first seem to point to the fact that */tmp* has filled, possibly because somebody has been creating something very large in it. This could cause the problem, but because */tmp* has a filesystem type of TMPFS it will be affected by lack of memory or swap space. These problems all indicate that you probably need to increase the amount of swap space you have.

If you are worried that abusers of */tmp* will cause you to run out of swap space, you can actually set a limit on the maximum size it can become by setting a mount option in the */etc/vfstab* file. Altering the entry to be the same as the following example will set an effective limit of 100 MB on it:

```
swap    -      /tmp        tmpfs    -      yes      size=100m
```

Using **sar**

If you suspect that you may not have sufficient swap space, you can run the sar command with the "-r" option at regular intervals:

```
hydrogen# sar -r 5 5
14:23:29 freemem  freeswap
14:23:34   846214 29678904
14:23:39   847907 29738202
14:23:44   849603 29797696
14:23:49   846218 29678980
14:23:54   849603 29797696
hydrogen#
```

The above example takes five samples with a five-second interval between each sample and shows the amount of free memory (in pages) and free swap space (in disk blocks) at each sample. If you wish to monitor this over a period of time, an entry would usually be added to the *sys crontab* file:

```
0,10,20,30,40,50 * * * * /usr/lib/sa/sa1
```

If the above *crontab* entry was used, then sar statistics would be collected every 10 minutes and stored in a file for each day of the month in the directory */var/adm/sa*. We could look at the memory and swap statistics using the sar command as follows:

```
hydrogen# sar -r -f sa30
<lines removed for clarity>
17:00:00   775787 27679278
17:10:00   774895 27664929
17:20:00   769536 27653001
17:30:00   681201 27630680
17:40:01   681820 27664144
17:50:01   682670 27602540
18:00:00   704518 27673268
18:10:00   697904 27616876
18:20:00   683044 27655721
18:30:01   695920 27704512
18:40:00   700563 27649453
18:50:00   700633 27649167
19:00:00   700626 27648279
<lines removed for clarity>
hydrogen#
```

This shows us all the sar -r statistics that were gathered at 10-minute intervals for the 30th day of the month. The files get overwritten each month, so if you wish to keep more than a month's worth of statistics you need to save each file before it is overwritten.

Using Vmstat

The sar command is fine for what it does, but the information it gives us is fairly limited. If we want to monitor our memory and swap usage in much more detail, then we can use the vmstat command. This command, like sar, will take samples at regular intervals over a period of time. For example, the following will check memory usage every 10 seconds and report the results to the screen:

```
hydrogen# vmstat 10
procs     memory            page            disk          faults      cpu
 r b w   swap  free  re  mf pi po fr de  sr s0 s1 s6 s1   in   sy  cs us sy id
 0 0 0 12582944 4575224 40 95  160 31 31 0 0 2  0  0  2 2657  792 390  1  3 97
 0 0 0 12222880 3971448 0 1   0  0   0  0 0 0  0  0  0 2609  518 217  0  0 100
 0 0 0 12222880 3971448 14 157 0 0   0  0 0 2  0  0  2 2621  800 363  0  1 99
 0 0 0 12222880 3971448 0 19  0  0   0  0 0 0  0  0  0 2615  965 249  0  0 100
hydrogen#
```

This is a lot of output to digest. Table 7.4 shows details of the data each column refers to.

Table 7.4 *Vmstat Output*

Column Heading		Description
procs	r	Number of processes in the run queue.
	b	Number of processes blocked for resource I/O or paging and so forth.
	w	Number of processes currently swapped.
memory	swap	Current free swap (KB).
	free	Current free memory (KB).
page	re	Page reclaims per second.
	mf	Minor faults per second.
	pi	KB paged in per second.
	po	KB paged out per second.
	fr	KB freed per second.
	de	Anticipated short-term memory shortfall (KB) per second.
	sr	Pages scanned by clock algorithm per second.
disk	s0	Number of disk operations per second on SCSI disk target 0 (there can be up to four columns of information under the disk heading, depending on how many disks you have installed).
faults	in	Device interrupts per second.
	sy	System calls per second.
	cs	CPU context switches per second.
cpu	us	Percentage CPU time in user mode.
	sy	Percentage CPU time in system mode.
	id	Percentage CPU time idle.

If we see very low values in the pages scanned column (page/sr), this is a sure sign that we are not experiencing any memory shortage problems. If, on the other hand, we see very high values (around 200 or higher) we may have a problem, but not definitely. We would need to monitor the situation for a while before making a judgment. If the value falls again, it may have been that a process was reading a large quantity of uncached data, so we can ignore it. However, if it remains high, then it is likely that we are short of memory.

8

ADMINISTERING
PACKAGES

Manual Pages

admin (4)
pkgadd (1m)
pkgask(1m)
pkgchk (1m)
pkginfo (1)
pkginfo (4)
pkgmap (4)
pkgmk (1)
pkgparam (1)
pkgproto (1)
pkgrm (1m)
pkgtrans (1)
removef (1m)

Files Affected

/var/sadm

Objectives

In this chapter, we start by looking at what a package is and how to see what packages are installed on our Solaris servers. We then look at how to add, remove, and manipulate packages before moving on to the more advanced topics of the internal format of a package and how we can create packages of our own (including why we might want to do this).

What Is a Package?

Most people who have some contact with computers will know that you can go to your local branch of PC World and buy a software package. This could be a spreadsheet, a word processor, or maybe a game. Packages also exist for Solaris, but they are not necessarily shrink-wrapped and almost certainly aren't available from a mainstream store.

A package can be defined as a collection of programs and/or files that provide certain functionality along with a method of managing their installation and removal. Software does not have to be commercial to be classed as a package, nor is there a minimum size or minimum number of files needed. If you have a collection of scripts that you would like to have on all your servers, it would make a lot of sense to create a package from them and install it on each server. You may feel there's not much point going to the trouble, especially if there are only a few scripts involved, but if you do this you can be sure you have a consistent set of scripts on each server. You can then also keep track of the version of the package on each server and as the scripts change you can easily manage their updating across all the servers.

Using Packages

A Solaris package is a collection of programs and files that will, usually, also contain all the scripts necessary to install and remove that package. When you install a package, Solaris keeps a note of it along with information about it, such as its version number.

What Packages Have I Got Loaded?

To see what packages are currently installed on a server, you should use the `pkginfo` command. If you run `pkginfo` without any options you will get output similar to this:

```
hydrogen# pkginfo
system     SUNWab2m      Solaris Documentation Server Lookup
system     SUNWadmap     System administration applications
system     SUNWadmc      System administration core libraries
```

```
system    SUNWadmr     System & Network Administration Root
system    SUNWarc      Archive Libraries
system    SUNWatfsr    AutoFS, (Root)
system    SUNWatfsu    AutoFS, (Usr)
system    SUNWaudio    Audio applications
system    SUNWbcp      SunOS 4.x Binary Compatibility
system    SUNWbtool    CCS tools bundled with SunOS
system    SUNWcar      Core Architecture, (Root)
system    SUNWcg6      GX (cg6) Device Driver
system    SUNWcg6h     GX (cg6) Header Files
system    SUNWcpr      Suspend, Resume package
system    SUNWdoc      Documentation Tools
system    SUNWdpl      Developer Profiled Libraries
system    SUNWdtab     CDE DTBUILDER
system    SUNWdtct     UTF-8 Code Conversion Tool
system    SUNWdtdmn    CDE daemons
system    SUNWdtdst    CDE Desktop Applications
system    SUNWdtdte    Solaris Desktop Login Environment
system    SUNWdthe     CDE HELP RUNTIME
system    SUNWdthed    CDE HELP DEVELOPER ENVIRONMENT
system    SUNWxcu4     XCU4 Utilities
system    SUNWxcu4t    XCU4 make and sccs utilities
application SUNWxgldg   XGL Generic Loadable Libraries
application SUNWxgler   XGL English Localization
application SUNWxglft   XGL Stroke Fonts
application SUNWxglh    XGL Include Files
application SUNWxglrt   XGL Runtime Environment
application SUNWxildh   XIL Loadable Pipeline Libraries
application SUNWxilh    XIL API Header Files
<lines removed for clarity>
hydrogen#
```

You should find that you have well over 100 packages installed. The reason for this is that Solaris itself is split into many different packages. This enables Solaris to be very flexible by allowing the system administrator control over which parts are installed on each server. For example, a server used for development may require software development tools and the online manuals to be installed, but it would be a waste of disk space to install these on a server that was just being used as a mail gateway.

When you install Solaris itself onto a server, you are prompted to select one of five package clusters that are available to install. Each cluster is simply a predefined collection from the individual packages that Solaris is made up of. They are there to enable you to build a system suitable for your needs without your needing to go through a huge amount of trouble or know too much about Solaris at a package level (though you can choose to perform a custom install, if you wish). Table 8.1 contains the cluster names along with a brief description of the type of install they perform.

Table 8.1 *Solaris Package Clusters*

Cluster Name	Description
SUNWCreq	This contains the absolute minimum packages required to run Solaris. This would be chosen if you have a severe shortage of disk space or very limited requirements of the server to be built.
SUNWCuser	This contains the packages recommended for a basic end-user system. It contains all you are likely to need to run an application without extras such as man pages, development tools, and so forth.
SUNWCprog	This should be suitable for a system used by developers. It includes the man pages and various development tools, but not a C compiler (which needs to be purchased separately).
SUNWCall	This cluster contains the complete Solaris installation. It takes longer to install and needs plenty of disk space.
SUNWCXALL	This is the largest cluster. It contains the entire distribution plus Original Equipment Manufacturer (OEM) packages.

In the output from `pkginfo` we see a list of the installed packages along with some basic information. The first column shows the class of package, the second the actual package name, and the remainder of the line the package description. The package name is often called the "package tag."

If you wish to go into more detail about an individual package, you can use the "-l" option with `pkginfo`:

```
hydrogen# pkginfo -l SUNWaudio
   PKGINST:  SUNWaudio
      NAME:  Audio applications
  CATEGORY:  system
      ARCH:  sparc
   VERSION:  3.6.4,REV=1.98.08.13
   BASEDIR:  /
    VENDOR:  Sun Microsystems, Inc.
      DESC:  Audio binaries
    PSTAMP:  dtbuild37s19980813171753
  INSTDATE:  Oct 18 2000 23:12
   HOTLINE:  Please contact your local service provider
    STATUS:  completely installed
     FILES:      5 installed pathnames
                 2 shared pathnames
                 2 directories
                 3 executables
               700 blocks used (approx)
hydrogen#
```

The "-l" option tells `pkginfo` to display all the available information about the package. For most packages, this will provide similar information to the above example, but it depends on how much information was actually provided with the package.

Most of this information is fairly self-explanatory, but it is described in more detail when we look at how a package is put together.

The information about installed packages is held under the directory */var/ sadm/pkg*. This location contains a subdirectory for each installed package, and this is where the `pkginfo` command gets its information. We will have a poke around in here later and see what is actually kept here and why.

Adding, Removing, and Checking Packages

Adding Packages

Packages are installed using the `pkgadd` command. This is usually an interactive procedure, but we will also look at how packages can be installed without requiring any operator input. This can be useful if you need to install the same package on many servers. Once you are happy with the installation process for that package on a test server, you can automate the process for your remaining systems.

Packages can be stored in either of two possible formats. They can be held within a single package file or they can be in an exploded (or directory) format. If a package is being installed from tape it will be in single-file format; if it is being installed from CD it could be in either. Packages can be freely transferred between these two formats (using the `pkgtrans` command). The `pkgadd` command can install exploded packages in much the same way as the single-file versions.

The most common method of installing a package manually is to use `pkgadd` with the "-d" option. The "-d" should be followed by the name of the device containing the package. If the package is on tape, the device specified would be the tape device (e.g., */dev/rmt/0*); if it is a single file on disk, then the filename would follow the "-d." If the package is in exploded format, then the directory containing the package directory is supplied as the argument following the "-d."

Examples of using `pkgadd` are as follows:

```
hydrogen# pkgadd -d /dev/rmt/0
hydrogen# pkgadd -d package.pkg
hydrogen# pkgadd -d /export/package_dir
```

Each of the above examples will result in `pkgadd` listing all the available packages on that device, so you can select which you actually want to install. This is because each of them may contain more than one package. If you know the package name(s) you wish to install, you can supply it/them at the end of any of the above commands. Alternatively, if you know you wish to install all the packages, you can use the keyword "all" instead.

We will now look at the full process of installing an actual package. Rather than using a third-party package that you may not be able to get hold of easily, we will use one that is on the Solaris CD that wasn't installed because we didn't choose the SUNCall cluster (which installs everything) at install time. The package we will install contains the System Activity Reporting (sar) tool, which can be useful for helping diagnose performance problems on the system. We will use this as a way of getting used to adding and removing packages, and then we will examine it in detail so we understand how a package is made up.

The sar program is contained in the System Accounting package, which has two parts: a root package and a user package. These two packages can be found on your Solaris CD in the directory */cdrom/cdrom0/s0/Solaris_2.7/ Product* (assuming you have the Solaris 7 CD). The packages are called SUNWaccr (the root part) and SUNWaccu (the user part). Since they live in a directory with several hundred other packages, we will copy them onto the hard disk and install them from there to make things simpler. We could have installed them directly from their directory on the CD if we wished. All the Solaris packages that live on the CD are in exploded format but we will be converting them into a single file when we transfer them. This can be achieved with the pkgtrans command (which is used specifically for converting packages between file and directory formats). The following commands will do this for us:

```
hydrogen# mkdir /export/packages
hydrogen# cd /cdrom/cdrom0/s0/Solaris_2.7/Product
hydrogen# pkgtrans . /export/packages/sar.pkg SUNWaccr SUNWaccu
hydrogen# cd /export/packages
hydrogen# ls -l
hydrogen# -rw-r--r--  1 root     other      150016 Mar 14 18:15 sar.pkg
hydrogen# pkginfo -d sar.pkg
system      SUNWaccr      System Accounting, (Root)
system      SUNWaccu      System Accounting, (Usr)
hydrogen#
```

The pkginfo command allows us to double-check that the file created does in fact contain the two packages we expect, so that we can go ahead and install them with the following pkgadd command:

```
hydrogen# pkgadd -d sar.pkg
The following packages are available:
  1  SUNWaccr      System Accounting, (Root)
                   (sparc) 11.7.0,REV=1998.09.01.04.16
  2  SUNWaccu      System Accounting, (Usr)
                   (sparc) 11.7.0,REV=1998.09.01.04.16

Select package(s) you wish to process (or 'all' to process
all packages). (default: all) [?,??,q]:
```

This is informing us that the file (or device) *sar.pkg* contains two packages and is asking us what we want to do with them. Hitting <return> will select the default action and cause all packages to be installed, so we'll do that. The pkgadd command now installs each of the packages in turn. We are presented with some information about the first package (SUNWaccr) before being asked one of a number of questions we need to respond to. We will look at how we can skip the interactive bits later.

```
Processing package instance <SUNWaccr> from </export/sar.pkg>

System Accounting, (Root)
(sparc) 11.7.0,REV=1998.09.01.04.16
Copyright 1998 Sun Microsystems, Inc. All rights reserved.
Using </> as the package base directory.
## Processing package information.
## Processing system information.
   10 package pathnames are already properly installed.
## Verifying package dependencies.
## Verifying disk space requirements.
## Checking for conflicts with packages already installed.
## Checking for setuid/setgid programs.

This package contains scripts which will be executed with super-user
permission during the process of installing this package.

Do you want to continue with the installation of <SUNWaccr> [y,n,?]
```

The first question is warning us that the package contains scripts that need to perform an action that only *root* is able to do. These scripts are not being installed by the package, but will actually be executed during the installation procedure and will perform a specific task, such as creating a user. As we know that this package came straight from the Solaris CD, we can trust that it is not going to do anything untoward. Consequently, we can say, "Yes, we do want to continue." However, we need to be aware that, although unlikely, this is a way that unscrupulous individuals could get to run anything they wanted as *root*!

```
Installing System Accounting, (Root) as <SUNWaccr>

## Installing part 1 of 1.
[ verifying class <preserve> ]
[ verifying class <initd> ]
/etc/rc2.d/S21perf <linked pathname>

Installation of <SUNWaccr> was successful.

Processing package instance <SUNWaccu> from </export/sar.pkg>

System Accounting, (Usr)
(sparc) 11.7.0,REV=1998.09.01.04.16
Copyright 1998 Sun Microsystems, Inc. All rights reserved.
Using </> as the package base directory.
## Processing package information.
```

```
## Processing system information.
   4 package pathnames are already properly installed.
## Verifying package dependencies.
## Verifying disk space requirements.
## Checking for conflicts with packages already installed.
## Checking for setuid/setgid programs.

The following files are being installed with setuid and/or setgid
permissions:
   /usr/lib/acct/accton <setuid root>

Do you want to install these as setuid/setgid files [y,n,?,q]
```

The package installation has completed the root part of the package and moved onto the user part. The next pause is to warn us that the SUNWaccu package contains a program that has its *setuid* bit set to run as *root*. This message is different from the warning we saw earlier. This doesn't mean that the installation procedure will do something with *root* privileges; it means that it will actually install a program on the system that will have *root* privileges whenever it is run. This type of program is usually referred to as *setuid* or *setgid* (see Chapter 4, "Permissions and All That"). Again, since this is an official Sun package, we can safely continue.

```
This package contains scripts which will be executed with
super-user permission during the process of installing this package.

Do you want to continue with the installation of <SUNWaccu> [y,n,?]
```

We now have the same warning about scripts running as *root*, but this time for the second of the two packages. Answer "y" to this question and the installation will complete:

```
Installing System Accounting, (Usr) as <SUNWaccu>

## Installing part 1 of 1.

Installation of <SUNWaccu> was successful.
```

We can now check that the new package is installed correctly using the pkginfo command:

```
hydrogen# pkginfo -l SUNWaccr SUNWaccu
    PKGINST:  SUNWaccr
       NAME:  System Accounting, (Root)
   CATEGORY:  system
       ARCH:  sparc
    VERSION:  11.7.0,REV=1998.09.01.04.16
    BASEDIR:  /
     VENDOR:  Sun Microsystems, Inc.
       DESC:  utilities for accounting and reporting of system activity
     PSTAMP:  on99819980901043848
   INSTDATE:  Mar 17 2001 18:49
    HOTLINE:  Please contact your local service provider
     STATUS:  completely installed
```

```
     FILES:     22 installed pathnames
                10 shared pathnames
                 1 linked files
                16 directories
                 2 executables
                 7 blocks used (approx)

   PKGINST:  SUNWaccu
      NAME:  System Accounting, (Usr)
  CATEGORY:  system
      ARCH:  sparc
   VERSION:  11.7.0,REV=1998.09.01.04.16
   BASEDIR:  /
    VENDOR:  Sun Microsystems, Inc.
      DESC:  utilities for accounting and reporting of system activity
    PSTAMP:  on99819980901043848
  INSTDATE:  Mar 17 2001 19:12
   HOTLINE:  Please contact your local service provider
    STATUS:  completely installed
     FILES:      47 installed pathnames
                  4 shared pathnames
                  6 directories
                 39 executables
                  1 setuid/setgid executables
                507 blocks used (approx)
hydrogen#
```

The status of both packages is "completely installed." We now have the sar tool installed should we need to use it later.

```
hydrogen# which sar
/bin/sar
hydrogen#
```

Not all packages are split into two parts as this one was; some will contain only one part and others may contain many more. Those that have root and user parts tend to be SUNW packages that form part of Solaris itself. They are split in this way to give you an idea of where the files in each package will be installed. The files in the root package will be installed in the *root* filesystem and the files from the user package will be installed in the */usr* filesystem. Third-party packages vary depending on the size and structure of the package. You may find that some third-party packages are split into separate packages so you can easily choose which features of the package you actually want to install.

Removing Packages

Package removal is achieved by using the pkgrm command. If you type pkgrm on its own, it will display a list which includes every package installed on the system and allow you to choose which package you wish to remove. A far easier way to remove packages is to specify them by name as arguments to pkgrm. If you are not sure of the correct package name you can use pkginfo to display it for you:

```
hydrogen# pkginfo | grep acc
system        SUNWaccr        System Accounting, (Root)
system        SUNWaccu        System Accounting, (Usr)
hydrogen#
```

Once you have the names, you can remove the package or packages as follows:

```
hydrogen# pkgrm SUNWaccr SUNWaccu

The following package is currently installed:
   SUNWaccr        System Accounting, (Root)
                   (sparc) 11.7.0,REV=1998.09.01.04.16

Do you want to remove this package?
```

pkgrm will deal with each package supplied in turn, so we will answer "y" here to remove the SUNWaccr package:

```
## Removing installed package instance <SUNWaccr>
## Verifying package dependencies.
## Processing package information.
## Removing pathnames in class <initd>
/etc/rc2.d/S21perf
/etc/init.d/perf
/etc/init.d/acct
## Removing pathnames in class <preserve>
/var/spool/cron/crontabs/sys
/etc/acct/holidays
## Removing pathnames in class <none>
/var/spool/cron/crontabs <shared pathname not removed>
/var/spool/cron <shared pathname not removed>
/var/spool <shared pathname not removed>
/var/adm/sa
/var/adm/acct/sum
/var/adm/acct/nite
/var/adm/acct/fiscal
/var/adm/acct
/var/adm <shared pathname not removed>
/var <shared pathname not removed>
/etc/rc2.d <shared pathname not removed>
/etc/rc1.d <shared pathname not removed>
/etc/rc0.d <shared pathname not removed>
/etc/init.d <shared pathname not removed>
/etc/datemsk
/etc/acct
/etc <shared pathname not removed>
## Updating system information.

Removal of <SUNWaccr> was successful.

The following package is currently installed:
   SUNWaccu        System Accounting, (Usr)
                   (sparc) 11.7.0,REV=1998.09.01.04.16
```

```
Do you want to remove this package?
<remainder of output removed for clarity>
hydrogen#
```

Removing a package is not simply a matter of deleting all the files that were installed in that package. Some packages have dependencies on other packages being installed. When you install a package with dependencies, pkgadd performs a check that the packages it is dependent upon exist during the installation process. If they are not already installed, pkgadd will not install the new package. This means that after the package has been installed we know all its prerequisites have been met. But if someone were to remove one of the packages it was dependent on, then it may no longer function correctly. This is clearly not a good situation to get into. Consequently, package dependencies are not simply checked when a new package is installed—they also need to be checked every time a package is removed.

When pkgrm is happy that the removal of the package will not cause dependency issues, it will begin to remove the files and directories that were installed with the package. It does this by class. In the above output extract, we can see that the SUNWaccr package has three classes—initd, preserve, and none. For each path that belongs to the package, pkgrm will first check that it is not also used by another package before actually removing it.

When a package is being installed, all the information that pkgadd needs is held as part of the package (whether on tape, CD, or another medium). However, it is not practical to expect the original package media to be available when removing packages. This problem is resolved by storing all the information about the package in a central location at install time. This means that pkgrm can make use of this information when a package is removed, but the information can also be used to check that the packages you have installed are still in a consistent state.

Checking Packages

The command pkgchk has been provided to check that packages are in a consistent state. You might think there is not much reason for having a command to check packages, since once they are installed they are unlikely to change and should just keep on working. Unfortunately, because packages can place files in any part of the filesystem and the system administrator has full access to all directories, it is possible that over time items that are part of a package could change. This could be the outcome of housekeeping a filesystem, changing the permissions of a file, or removing a file you think is no longer needed. It is therefore a good idea to run pkgchk on a regular basis so you can become aware of any inconsistencies that may have crept into the system. You can also use pkgchk to fix some of the problems it may find.

By default, pkgchk will check each file contained in the package specified and report if any of the file's attributes and contents are different from when it was installed. In situations where a configuration file has been delivered by a package, it may not be a problem if the contents are reported as incorrect because you may have updated it. If you just want to check the attributes, you can use a "-a" flag; if you just want to check file contents, you can use a "-c" flag. If you do not supply a package name to check, pkgchk will check all packages for attributes and contents.

The following example will check the files contained in the SUNWpsr and SUNWpsu packages. These are the root and user parts of the SunSoft Print Server package:

```
hydrogen# pkgchk SUNWpsr SUNWpsu
ERROR: /var/spool/lp
    permissions <0755> expected <0775> actual
    group name <tty> expected <lp> actual
hydrogen#
```

This tells us that the directory */var/spool/lp* has incorrect permissions and an incorrect group. This is probably not something to get too worried about, but we can attempt to fix things by using the "-f" flag:

```
hydrogen# pkgchk -f SUNWpsr SUNWpsu
hydrogen# pkgchk SUNWpsr SUNWpsu
hydrogen#
```

Neither command produced any output so we know the problem is now resolved. The "-f" will only attempt to fix problems associated with the file's attributes; it will never alter the contents of a file.

You can also use pkgchk to find out which package a file belongs to:

```
hydrogen# pkgchk -l -p /usr/bin/ls
Pathname: /usr/bin/ls
Type: regular file
Expected mode: 0555
Expected owner: bin
Expected group: bin
Expected file size (bytes): 18120
Expected sum(1) of contents: 53113
Expected last modification: Oct 06 08:43:05 AM 1998
Referenced by the following packages:
        SUNWcsu
Current status: installed
hydrogen#
```

This tells us that the ls program belongs to the SUNWcsu package; we can find out the full package name using pkginfo:

```
hydrogen# pkginfo SUNWcsu
system          SUNWcsu          Core Solaris, (Usr)
hydrogen#
```

As well as telling us which package ls belongs to, pkgchk will also tell us what the attributes and check sum of the file should be. However, pkgchk can only tell us this information if it was held within the package control files (which we will look at in detail when we dissect a package).

Dissecting a Package

As discussed previously, packages can be in either of two possible formats. The package we installed earlier was stored on the Solaris CD in exploded (or directory) format, but we converted it into a single file on the hard disk before installing it. To examine the files and installation scripts within a package, it needs to be in the exploded form. Packages can be freely transferred between these two formats (using `pkgtrans`). The `pkgadd` command can install exploded packages in much the same way as we have seen it install the single-file versions.

To create an exploded package from a single file, we use the `pkgtrans` as follows:

```
hydrogen# cd /export/packages
hydrogen# pkgtrans sar.pkg /export/pkgdir

The following packages are available:
  1  SUNWaccr      System Accounting, (Root)
                   (sparc) 11.7.0,REV=1998.09.01.04.16
  2  SUNWaccu      System Accounting, (Usr)
                   (sparc) 11.7.0,REV=1998.09.01.04.16

Select package(s) you wish to process (or 'all' to process
all packages). (default: all) [?,??,q]:all
Transferring <SUNWaccr> package instance
Transferring <SUNWaccu> package instance
hydrogen#
```

Here, we were presented with the same initial dialogue as when we installed the packages. If we had specified the package names on the command line (or the keyword "all"), this would not have been displayed (this is also true when installing packages).

```
hydrogen# pkgtrans sar.pkg /export/pkgdir all
Transferring <SUNWaccr> package instance
Transferring <SUNWaccu> package instance
hydrogen#
```

This will create a directory in */export/pkgdir* for each of the packages transferred. Not surprisingly, each directory is named after the package. Each of these package directories will contain some standard files and directories that are used to manage the installation and removal of the package along with the files and directories that the package delivers.

To understand how a package fits together, we will now look at the SUNWaccr package in detail. It is rare to find a package that makes use of all the available features of the Solaris package management system, so reference will be made here to scripts and features even though they are not specifically used within this package:

```
hydrogen# cd /export/pkgdir/SUNWaccr
hydrogen# ls -l
# ls -l
total 12
drwxr-xr-x  2 root    staff       512 Mar 18 13:37 archive
drwxr-xr-x  2 root    staff       512 Mar 18 13:37 install
-rw-r--r--  1 root    other       516 Oct 15  1999 pkginfo
-rw-r--r--  1 root    other      1084 Oct 15  1999 pkgmap
drwxr-xr-x  4 root    staff       512 Mar 18 13:37 reloc
hydrogen#
```

All packages must have a *pkginfo* and *pkgmap* file, and most will also have the *install* and *reloc* directories. The *archive* directory is used within most packages on the Solaris CD, but it is not compulsory and, in fact, it is not usually considered part of the standard package format.

Pkginfo

The *pkginfo* file, as you may guess, contains information about the package. You may see a similarity between the contents of this file and the output from the *pkginfo* -l command, because this is where *pkginfo* gets its information.

```
PKG=SUNWaccr
NAME=System Accounting, (Root)
ARCH=sparc
VERSION=11.7.0,REV=1998.09.01.04.16
SUNW_PRODNAME=SunOS
SUNW_PRODVERS=5.7/Generic
SUNW_PKGTYPE=root
MAXINST=1000
CATEGORY=system
DESC=utilities for accounting and reporting of system activity
VENDOR=Sun Microsystems, Inc.
HOTLINE=Please contact your local service provider
EMAIL=
CLASSES=none preserve initd
BASEDIR=/
SUNW_PKGVERS=1.0
PSTAMP=on99819980901043848
PKG_SRC_NOVERIFY= none
PKG_DST_QKVERIFY= none
PKG_CAS_PASSRELATIVE= none
#FASPACD= none
PATCHLIST=
```

You will notice that the file contains a collection of variable assignments. Some of the variables contain information about the package and the company that produced it, but the file may also contain variables that are used by the scripts that manage the package installation and removal. The *pkginfo* file is created by the package developer and does not need to contain all the variables described here, though certain of them must exist. Table 8.2 describes the ones you are most likely to see. (If you are interested in seeing a full list, run man -s 4 pkginfo, though of course they don't have to be on this list to be used here.)

Table 8.2 *Pkginfo Contents*

Variable Name	Description
PKG	This is the name of the package that is used with the package manipulation commands (e.g., pkgadd and pkgrm). It is customary to make the first four letters represent your company name, so all Sun package names begin "SUNW."
NAME	This is the more human-friendly version of the package name.
CATEGORY	This holds the category (or categories) to which the package belongs. Every package must belong to at least the *system* or *application* category.
ARCH	This is the architecture the package is designed for. Solaris is available for SPARC and INTEL architectures.
VERSION	This one speaks for itself. Solaris practice for version numbers is <major revision>.<minor revision[.<micro revision>], where each revision is an integer.
BASEDIR	This is the default directory under which the package files will be installed. This exists because some packages can be installed in a location of your choice, rather than a location forced upon you. If this is not set, then the package is not relocatable.
VENDOR	This should be set to the name of the company that holds the copyright to the package.
DESC	This is a long description of the package (up to 256 characters).
CLASSES	If this exists, it will contain a space-separated list of classes that have been defined for this package.
ISTATES	If this exists, it will be set to a list of init states (or run levels) that the system must be in to install the package.
RSTATES	This is the same as ISTATES, but it is for removing rather than installing packages.
HOTLINE	This should contain an address or phone number that can be used for support, bug reports, and so forth.
INTONLY	If this is set, it means the package may only be installed interactively.
MAXINST	This tells you the maximum number of instances of a package you may install on one server. If it is not set, you may only install the package once.

Note: Variables that are compulsory are underlined.

Pkgmap

The other file in this directory, *pkgmap*, is likely to be much larger than *pkginfo* as it usually contains an entry for every file contained in the package. The entries hold information about file ownership and permissions along with some checksum information, which is used at install time to verify that the package is complete and not corrupt in any way.

Here we have the *pkgmap* file for the SUNWaccr package:

```
: 1 58
1 i copyright 59 5234 904648577
1 i depend 875 7018 904648578
1 d none etc 0755 root sys
1 d none etc/acct 0775 adm adm
1 e preserve etc/acct/holidays 0664 bin bin 289 22090 904647603
1 f none etc/datemsk 0444 root sys 446 24974 904647726
1 d none etc/init.d 0775 root sys
1 e initd etc/init.d/acct 0744 root sys 833 62528 904647604
1 e initd etc/init.d/perf 0744 root sys 989 10168 904647868
1 d none etc/rc0.d 0775 root sys
1 d none etc/rc1.d 0775 root sys
1 d none etc/rc2.d 0775 root sys
1 l initd etc/rc2.d/S21perf=../../etc/init.d/perf
1 i i.initd 6368 3209 904648578
1 i i.preserve 186 13489 904648578
1 i pkginfo 516 41176 904649950
1 d none var 0755 root sys
1 d none var/adm 0775 root sys
1 d none var/adm/acct 0775 adm adm
1 d none var/adm/acct/fiscal 0775 adm adm
1 d none var/adm/acct/nite 0775 adm adm
1 d none var/adm/acct/sum 0775 adm adm
1 d none var/adm/sa 0775 adm sys
1 d none var/spool 0755 root bin
1 d none var/spool/cron 0755 root sys
1 d none var/spool/cron/crontabs 0755 root sys
1 e preserve var/spool/cron/crontabs/sys 0644 root sys 308
22063 28800
```

The first line of the file is required and contains two pieces of information. The first is the number of parts to the package and the second is the maximum part size (which is shown in 512-byte blocks).

The remaining lines describe each file that the package contains, including those that are only used during the installation or removal processes. The fields are described in Table 8.3.

Table 8.3 *Pkgmap Contents*

Field Name	Description
part	This optional field holds the part of the package that the file belongs to. If no part is specified, part 1 is implied.
file type	This field contains a single character to represent the type of the specified file. This could be any of the following: b: block special device c: character special device d: directory e: file that will be edited upon installation or removal f: standard executable or data file i: installation script or information file l: linked file (the path of the link is also shown) p: named pipe s: symbolic link v: file whose contents will change (e.g., a logfile) x: directory that will only be accessed by the package
class	This is the class to which the file belongs. This package has defined three classes: none, preserve, and initd. Files of type "i" do not belong to a class—just the files that are actually being delivered.
pathname	This contains the path name of the file. It will usually be a relative path name, which means the package is installable in a location of the operator's choosing.
major	This will only be included for device files and represents the device's major number.
minor	This field is also for devices only and represents the minor device number.
mode	This value represents the permissions of the file in octal format.
owner	The owner of the file is specified in this field. If there is a question mark here, it means the file ownership will not get changed when the file is installed.
group	This is the group to which the file belongs. Again, if it contains a question mark, the group will be left alone.
size	This is the size of the file in bytes. This will not be specified for certain file types (e.g., devices and directories).
checksum	This is the checksum for the file. It will not be specified for devices, directories, or other special files (as with the size field).
modification time	The number here represents the time the file was last modified. As with the previous two fields, it will only exist for ordinary files.

Reloc

The fact that a directory called *reloc* exists means that this package is relocatable. Therefore, the system administrator is able to install the package in a directory other than its default if required. Most application packages are relocatable and so can be installed in a location of your choosing. Relocatable packages have a default location; this is set in the BASEDIR variable in the *pkginfo* file.

The following extract shows the files and directories stored under the *reloc* directory for the SUNWaccr package. Each file or directory must also have an entry in the *pkgmap* file:

```
hydrogen# cd reloc
hydrogen# ls -lR
.:
total 4
drwxr-xr-x 4 root    staff       512 Mar 18 13:37 etc
drwxr-xr-x 3 root    staff       512 Mar 18 13:37 var
./etc:
total 4
drwxr-xr-x 2 root    staff       512 Mar 18 13:37 acct
drwxr-xr-x 2 root    staff       512 Mar 18 13:37 init.d
./etc/acct:
total 2
-rw-r--r-- 1 root    staff       289 Sep  1  1998 holidays
./etc/init.d:
total 4
-rwxr--r-- 1 root    staff       833 Sep  1  1998 acct
-rwxr--r-- 1 root    staff       989 Sep  1  1998 perf
./var:
total 2
drwxr-xr-x 3 root    staff       512 Mar 18 13:37 spool
./var/spool:
total 2
drwxr-xr-x 3 root    staff       512 Mar 18 13:37 cron
./var/spool/cron:
total 2
drwxr-xr-x 2 root    staff       512 Mar 18 13:37 crontabs
./var/spool/cron/crontabs:
total 2
-rw-r--r-- 1 root    staff       308 Jan  1  1970 sys
hydrogen#
```

The *reloc* directory contains two subdirectories: *etc* and *var*. Because the package BASEDIR is set to the *root* directory, all files and directories contained here will be created under */etc* or */var*. If the BASEDIR was changed, then the files would be installed relative to the new BASEDIR. Each file under *reloc* must have an entry in the *pkgmap* file with matching attributes, otherwise the pkgadd command will refuse to install the package as it will assume it is corrupt.

Install

The *install* directory contains files and scripts that are used during the installation process.

A package may contain any, all, or none of these files within its install directory:

```
hydrogen# ls -l
total 24
-rw-r--r-- 1 root     staff        59 Sep  1 1998 copyright
-rw-r--r-- 1 root     staff       875 Sep  1 1998 depend
-rw-r--r-- 1 root     staff      6368 Sep  1 1998 i.initd
-rw-r--r-- 1 root     staff      1935 Jul 28 1999 i.none
-rw-r--r-- 1 root     staff       186 Sep  1 1998 i.preserve
hydrogen#
```

The *copyright* file is not compulsory. If is exists, it will be a text file containing a copyright message. Its contents are displayed by pkgadd during the installation process.

The *depend* file, if it has any contents, will contain a list of packages that this package is dependent on (i.e., they must be installed prior to this one). However, it could also contain packages that are incompatible with the one you are installing, or even ones with a reverse dependency. The *depend* file for SUNWsccr contains the following entries:

```
P SUNWcar        Core Architecture, (Root)
P SUNWkvm        Core Architecture, (Kvm)
P SUNWcsr        Core Solaris, (Root)
P SUNWcsu        Core Solaris, (Usr)
P SUNWcsd        Core Solaris Devices
P SUNWcsl        Core Solaris Libraries
```

The "P" in the first column indicates that the six packages listed are prerequisites of SUNWaccr, so it will not be installed unless those six are already fully installed. Instead of a "P" the first column could have an "I" to indicate an incompatible package or an "R" to indicate a reverse dependency. If an incompatible package had been specified in the *depend* file, its existence on the server would prevent this package from being installed. It is rare to see a package with a reverse dependency. This would only happen to identify that another package had a dependency on this package, and would only be used where the other package was an older one created before dependency files were introduced.

The remaining three files (i.initd, i.none, and i.preserve) are called "class action scripts." There is one for each of the classes defined in the *pkginfo* file, and these scripts are executed in the order that the classes are defined. The pkgadd program will pass each file listed in the *pkgmap* file, that is a member of that class, to its class action script. It is up to the class action script to install the file (or do whatever else it wants with it). This will be done for the none class first, and the process will then be repeated for the classes preserve and initd.

The `i.none` class action script runs first. This is the script that installs most of the files contained in the package. The files installed by this script are in a zip file called *none* in the *archive* directory (see below). The `i.none` script changes the directory to the package base directory and then simply unzips the files into this location.

Next, the `i.preserve` script runs. This simple script copies the System Accounting *holidays* file and the *sys crontab* file (which are supplied as arguments by `pkgadd`) into their appropriate destination directories.

Finally, the `i.initd` script runs. This script creates the correct links in the *rc* directories for the files *acct* and *perf* which, if you look in the *pkgmap* file above, you will see are delivered into */etc/init.d*.

The files mentioned below do not exist in this package but have standard names and do exist in many third-party packages. You are likely to use some of them if you create any packages of your own. They are all shell scripts whose names, hopefully, describe their functions. They are executed by the `pkgadd` command in the following order (assuming they exist):

The `checkinstall` script is executed first. It should contain code to verify that the system is in a position to have the package installed. These checks could include making sure that particular filesystems exist, that there is enough disk space, and that a suitable version of Solaris is installed.

The `preinstall` script should perform any actions that need to be run before the package's files are copied into place. This might include creating specific filesystems and users. It may also involve backing up some existing files that may get overwritten by the package, so they can be restored if the package is subsequently removed.

The `postinstall` script runs after the package contents are put in place. It is likely to perform such tasks as checking that the package is installed correctly and setting up any final configurations that may be required.

The `preremove` and `postremove` scripts will not be run during a package install. They are placed in the software product database (under */var/sadm/pkg/pkg_name*) for use by the `pkgrm` command when the package is removed.

Archive

This directory will not always exist within packages. In this case, it contains a single zip file called *none*. The file contains the vast majority of the files and scripts that make up this package, and they are installed from the `i.none` script in the *install* directory.

This way of delivering files is not the only way of doing so and might even be considered nonstandard. Normally the files that a package delivers will be stored under the *reloc* directory and will be listed in the *pkgmap* file. A number of packages on the Solaris CD are stored and delivered with the files zipped instead. The advantage of creating packages like this is that because the files are zipped they take up less space on the CD. The disadvantage is that you may not be able to find a file if you want to browse the CD to see which package it belongs to.

Advanced Concepts

We have seen that as well as the files that are installed by a package, a package also contains files that are executed during the installation process and files that provide information about the package, such as how it should be installed and removed, and also checksum information. When a package has been installed the files that provide information about the package are stored under the directory *Ivar/sadm/packages*. This directory is called the software package management database.

A subdirectory exists for each package that has been installed using the pkgadd command. Some packages do not conform to the Solaris package standards and are installed by a proprietary method. This is not the recommended way for packages to be delivered, as they cannot be managed effectively after they have been installed.

As well as *Ivar/sadm* holding the information about the packages installed, it also holds some files that control the way packages in general are installed. The most important file that manages this is the package administration file. This is located in the file *Ivar/sadm/install/admin/default*.

The contents of the default administration file are as follows:

```
#ident   "@(#)default    1.4     92/12/23 SMI"   /* SVr4.0
1.5.2.1     */
mail=
instance=unique
partial=ask
runlevel=ask
idepend=ask
rdepend=ask
space=ask
setuid=ask
conflict=ask
action=ask
basedir=default
```

Each option in the package administration file tells pkgadd how to behave in certain circumstances. In all cases, apart from the mail entry, the value may be set to "ask," which will cause pkgadd to ask the person installing the package what to do. Table 8.4 describes each variable and shows the additional values that may be assigned to them. Leaving a variable unassigned has the same effect as setting it to "ask."

Table 8.4 *Package Administration File Contents*

Variable Name	Description
mail	If this value is set, it should be set to a list of users who should receive an email message from pkgadd each time a package is installed. If the entry is left unassigned, no mail message will be sent.
instance	This tells pkgadd how to act if a previous version of the package is already installed. The valid values for this entry are: • quit (will cause pkgadd to quit) • overwrite (will cause the installed version to be overwritten) • unique (the new version of the package will be installed as a separate instance, thus preserving the original)
partial	This tells pkgadd what to do if the package being installed has been partially installed previously. The valid entries are: • quit (pkgadd will quit) • nocheck (pkgadd will not bother checking for this)
runlevel	This tells pkgadd what to do if the packages run-level requirements are not met. The following two options are valid: • quit (pkgadd will abort the installation if the system is not in the required run level) • nocheck (pkgadd will not bother checking)
idepend	This tells pkgadd whether to check for package dependencies. The valid options are: • quit (will cause pkgadd to quit if the dependencies are not met) • nocheck (tells pkgadd not to check for dependencies)
rdepend	This tells pkgrm whether to check for dependencies when a package is being removed. The available options are the same as for *idepend*.
space	This tells pkgadd what to do if the packages disk space requirements are not met. The valid options are: • quit (pkgadd will abort the installation) • nocheck (pkgadd will not bother checking, but the installation will fail if it runs out of space)

Table 8.4 *Package Administration File Contents (Continued)*

Variable Name	Description
setuid	This tells pkgadd what to do if it finds any *setuid* or *setgid* files in the package it is installing. Here are the valid alternatives: • quit (pkgadd will abort the installation if any are found) • nocheck (pkgadd will not bother to check) • nochange (will cause pkgadd to carry on with the installation, while removing any *setuid* or *setgid* bits from the permissions)
conflict	This tells pkgadd what to do if a package tries to install a file that already exists (i.e., if it was installed by a different package). The available options are: • quit (pkgadd will abort the installation) • nocheck (pkgadd will not bother checking and the file in question will be overwritten) • nochange (pkgadd will carry on with the installation without installing the conflicting file)
action	Pkgadd checks action scripts contained in packages to see if they do anything that could have a negative impact on system security. The following may be set to control this: • quit (pkgadd will abort the installation) • nocheck (pkgadd will not bother performing these checks)
basedir	This tells pkgadd how to determine the package base directory. It can be set to "ask" or "default." If set to "ask," the person installing the package will be asked to supply a base directory. If it is set to "default," the base directory supplied with the package (i.e., BASEDIR in the *pkginfo* file) will be used instead.

Earlier in the chapter, we mentioned that it is possible to install a package without any user interaction so that a package could be installed from within a script or unattended. You may have surmised that this is achieved by altering the administration file. It could be done this way, but as this file affects the way that all packages are installed a better way is to create a different administration file and tell pkgadd to look in that one instead of the default one. The following could be used as an administration file that will cause pkgadd to install a package without asking any questions:

```
hydrogen# cat local_admin
mail=
instance=unique
partial=nocheck
runlevel=quit
idepend=quit
```

```
rdepend=quit
space=quit
setuid=nocheck
conflict=nochange
action=nocheck
basedir=default
hydrogen#
```

The values we have chosen for the local administration file are not the only ones that will allow an unattended install. We have chosen the ones that we feel will not cause too big a problem in the event that some of the conditions checked for actually exist. For example, we have chosen "quit" as the option for space, because if we set it to "nocheck" and the filesystem filled during the install we would be left with the package in an unpredictable state. The basic rule is that if you want to perform an automated install you should set the variables to anything other than "ask."

This is how we could install the System Accounting package (sar) without pkgadd asking for any input from the user:

```
hydrogen# pkgadd -a local_admin -d sar.pkg all
Processing package instance <SUNWaccr> from </export/packages/sar.pkg>

System Accounting, (Root)
(sparc) 11.7.0,REV=1998.09.01.04.16
Copyright 1998 Sun Microsystems, Inc. All rights reserved.
Using </> as the package base directory.
## Processing package information.
## Processing system information.
   10 package pathnames are already properly installed.
## Verifying package dependencies.
## Verifying disk space requirements.

Installing System Accounting, (Root) as <SUNWaccr>

## Installing part 1 of 1.
[ verifying class <preserve> ]
[ verifying class <initd> ]
/etc/rc2.d/S21perf <linked pathname>

Installation of <SUNWaccr> was successful.

Processing package instance <SUNWaccu> from </export/packages/sar.pkg>
System Accounting, (Usr)
(sparc) 11.7.0,REV=1998.09.01.04.16
Copyright 1998 Sun Microsystems, Inc. All rights reserved.
Using </> as the package base directory.
## Processing package information.
## Processing system information.
   4 package pathnames are already properly installed.
## Verifying package dependencies.
## Verifying disk space requirements.

Installing System Accounting, (Usr) as <SUNWaccu>

## Installing part 1 of 1.

Installation of <SUNWaccu> was successful.
hydrogen#
```

The "-a" option tells pkgadd to use an alternative administration file and the package now installs without any input required from the installer.

When a package is installed, the information that was in the *pkgmap* file is added to the software product database contents file. This file is located in the directory */var/sadm/install* in a file called *contents*. This file can be very large since it could contain a very large percentage of the files on your system (depending how they were installed). This file is used by the pkgchk command to verify packages and tell you which package a file belongs to.

In addition to the *contents* file being updated, a directory is created under */var/sadm/pkg* for each package installed. The name of the directory is the same as the package name (i.e., the *pkg* entry of the *pkginfo* file), and pkgadd places the *pkginfo* file along with any of the files under the package *install* directory that may be needed later. This includes the *copyright* and *depend* files along with any postremove and preremove scripts.

This method of automating the installation of a package will work in most cases, but occasionally a package will ask the user a question that cannot be covered by use of the administration file alone. One such example is the sunforum package SUNWdat, which asks the user which directory it should be installed in (with a default of */opt*). In such cases, it is not possible to automate the installation using an administration file alone, but some input redirection is also required. The following command shows one way of getting around this issue. It is not particularly elegant, and if you want to install a package like this on many servers you may choose to write your own installation script that actually contains a pkgadd command similar to this one:

```
hydrogen# echo "/usr/local/opt" | pkgadd -a local_admin
   -d SUNWdat all
<lines removed for clarity>
hydrogen#
```

Creating Your Own Packages

If you wish to create packages of your own, you can manually create a structure that matches the exploded package format, ensuring you enter the correct checksums in the *pkgmap* file. Alternatively, Solaris provides a number of utilities that you can use to make things a little easier.

We will look at the latter method first, though it is not the most straightforward of procedures. In fact, writing a script to create a package would be a worthwhile project for anybody who will need to create a package.

Our package will comprise a number of scripts that have been developed to assist with the support and administration of a Solaris system. The package will be called DADWutils (Dom and Dave's utilities). It will be packaged as a relocatable package with a default location of */usr/local/utils*. We won't be storing the files in a zip file within an archive directory as the Sun packages do; instead all the files to be delivered will be held under the reloc directory and therefore described in the *pkgmap* file.

To create the package, we will need to know where the master copy of the scripts that make up the package are located and we will need to create a work directory to use while we actually create the package. In this case, the master scripts are located in *export/master/utils* with the same directory structure they will have when they are installed, and we will create the directory *export/pkgdir/work* as our temporary work directory. The final package will be created in the directory *export/pkgdir/DADWutils* (but we don't need to create it as it will be done for us later).

Once we have created the work directory, we need to create a *reloc* directory under it:

```
hydrogen# mkdir -p /export/pkgdir/work
hydrogen# cd /export/pkgdir/work
hydrogen# mkdir reloc
hydrogen# ls -l
total 2
drwxr-xr-x   2 root    other      512 Apr  1 18:56 reloc
hydrogen#
```

We should now create the *pkginfo* file in our work directory. Ours will be as follows:

```
PKG=DADWutils
NAME=Administration and Support utilities
ARCH=sparc
VERSION=1.0.0.0
MAXINST=1
CATEGORY=application
DESC=Dom and Dave's Support Utilities
VENDOR=Dom and Dave
HOTLINE=contact Dom and Dave
EMAIL=info@solarisbootcamp.com
CLASSES=none
BASEDIR=/usr/local/utils
```

The *pkgmap* file is not quite as simple to create, so it will be done in stages using a couple of Solaris utilities. (We have reduced the number of files that we will put in our DADWutils package so the outputs shown are not too cluttered.)

The next step is to copy the package files to the work *reloc* directory:

```
hydrogen# cd /export/master/utils
hydrogen# ls -R
.:
bin         lib         logs        logsToTidy

./bin:
fswarn      startPPP stopPPP  tidyLogs

./lib:

./logs:
hydrogen# find . |cpio -pvd /export/pkgdir/work/reloc
```

```
/export/pkgdir/work/reloc/.
/export/pkgdir/work/reloc/bin
/export/pkgdir/work/reloc/bin/startPPP
/export/pkgdir/work/reloc/bin/stopPPP
/export/pkgdir/work/reloc/bin/tidyLogs
/export/pkgdir/work/reloc/bin/fswarn
/export/pkgdir/work/reloc/lib
/export/pkgdir/work/reloc/logs
/export/pkgdir/work/reloc/logsToTidy
11 blocks
hydrogen#
```

Now we will create what is called a "prototype file" using the `pkgproto` command. This is an interim file used to help create the *pkgmap* file.

From the work directory (*/export/pkgdir/work*) we run the following `pkg-proto` command:

```
hydrogen# cd /export/pkgdir/work
hydrogen# pkgproto reloc=. >prototype
hydrogen#
```

We now have a file called *prototype*, which has the following contents:

```
d none bin 0755 root other
f none bin/startPPP=reloc/bin/startPPP 0744 root other
f none bin/stopPPP=reloc/bin/stopPPP 0744 root other
f none bin/tidyLogs=reloc/bin/tidyLogs 0744 root other
f none bin/fswarn=reloc/bin/fswarn 0744 root other
f none bin/fswarnLog=reloc/bin/fswarnLog 0644 root other
d none lib 0755 root other
d none logs 0755 root other
f none logsToTidy=reloc/logsToTidy 0644 root other
```

This file does not need to be called *prototype*, but this is the convention. The *prototype* file will not actually be delivered as part of the package, but we will use it to help create the *pkgmap* file.

Before we can do this, we need to add the following line to the end of the *prototype* file:

```
i pkginfo=./pkginfo
```

Now we run the Solaris command `pkgmk`, which will use the *prototype* file and the other files we put in our work directory to create the initial version of our package, complete with a *pkgmap* file:

```
hydrogen# pkgmk -d /export/pkgdir -f prototype
## Building pkgmap from package prototype file.
## Processing pkginfo file.
WARNING: parameter <PSTAMP> set to "hydrogen20010429200612"
## Attempting to volumize 8 entries in pkgmap.
part  1 -- 26 blocks, 10 entries
## Packaging one part.
/export/pkgdir/DADWutils/pkgmap
/export/pkgdir/DADWutils/pkginfo
```

```
/export/pkgdir/DADWutils/reloc/bin/fswarn
/export/pkgdir/DADWutils/reloc/bin/startPPP
/export/pkgdir/DADWutils/reloc/bin/stopPPP
/export/pkgdir/DADWutils/reloc/bin/tidyLogs
/export/pkgdir/DADWutils/reloc/logsToTidy
## Validating control scripts.
## Packaging complete.
hydrogen#
```

This created the basic package for us in the directory */export/pkgdir/ DADWutils*. We didn't specify this directory in the previous command; we just specified the parent directory. But pkgmk looked in the *pkgino* file and created the directory with the same name as our package (i.e., the value assigned to PKG). The warning message we got was because we did not create a PSTAMP entry in our *pkginfo* file so pkgmk created one for us:

```
hydrogen# cd /export/pkgdir
hydrogen# ls -l
total 4
drwxr-xr-x    3 root    other      512 Apr  1 17:49 DADWutils
drwxr-xr-x    4 root    other      512 Apr  1 17:24 work
hydrogen# rm -r work
hydrogne# cd DADWutils
hydrogen# ls -l
total 6
-rw-r--r--    1 root    other      302 Apr  1 17:49 pkginfo
-rw-r--r--    1 root    other      420 Apr  1 17:49 pkgmap
drwxr-xr-x    3 root    other      512 Apr  1 17:49 reloc
hydrogen# cat pkgmap
: 1 26
1 d none bin 0755 root other
1 f none bin/fswarn 0755 root other 1034 14901 1017671085
1 f none bin/startPPP 0755 root other 698 58124 1017670893
1 f none bin/stopPPP 0755 root other 358 27164 1017670893
1 f none bin/tidyLogs 0755 root other 1594 33412 1017671035
1 d none lib 0755 root other
1 d none logs 0755 root other
1 f none logsToTidy 0644 root other 364 32935 1017671147
1 i pkginfo 302 25229 1017676159
hydrogen#
```

We have now removed the work directory, as it is no longer needed. All our files are now under the *DADWutils* directory. Because the *pkgmap* file contains checksums for each of the files in the package, we need to be aware that if we change any of them our *pkgmap* file will no longer be valid.

The package is in directory format and is now ready to install, but we may want to add some files that live in the *install* directory. For this example, we will add a copyright file and a postinstall script. If we needed to add a depend file, or any others, we would follow exactly the same principle.

First we will make the *install* directory and create the *copyright* file in it:

```
hydrogen# cd /export/pkg/DADWutils
hydrogen# mkdir install
hydrogen# cd install
hydrogen# cat copyright
This software is the property of Dom and Dave Enterprises.
hydrogen#
```

Now we will create the postinstall script, which in this case will add a few entries to the *root crontab* file. We should also create a postremove script that will remove the entries when the package is removed; however, we won't bother for this example since it is exactly the same procedure as creating the postinstall script:

```
hydrogen# cat postinstall
#!/bin/ksh
# postinstall script for DADWutils
crontab -l | grep -v tidyLogs | grep -v fswarn >/tmp/crontab.$$
echo "15 7 1 * * /usr/local/utils/bin/tidyLogs >/dev/null 2>&1"
    >>/tmp/crontab.$$
echo "0,15,30,45 * * * * /usr/local/utils/bin/fswarn >/dev/null
    2>&1" >>/tmp/crontab.$$
crontab /tmp/crontab.$$
rm -f /tmp/crontab.$$
echo "DADWutil entries added to root crontab"
exit 0
hydrogen#
```

We have almost finished now, but before we can install the package we need to add an entry to the *pkgmap* file for each of these two files. To do this, we need to get the checksum information for the files. This can be obtained using the Solaris commands sum and cksum:

```
hydrogen# sum *
5433 1 copyright
31110 1 postinstall
hydrogen# cksum *
3976077735      59      copyright
2725132244      381     postinstall
hydrogen#
```

From the above output we can work out the checksums and add the following two lines to the *pkgmap* file:

```
1 i copyright 59 5433 3976077735
1 i postinstall 381 31110 2725132244
```

The package is now ready to install. It is currently in directory format, but we will convert it to a single file so it can be transferred easily to our other servers for installation.

```
hydrogen# cd /export/pkgdir
hydrogen# pkgtrans . /export/packages/dadutils.pkg DADWutils
Transferring <DADWutils> package instance
hydrogen#
```

We can now install *DADWutils* on all our other servers:

```
lithium# pkgadd -a local_admin -d dadutils.pkg all

Processing package instance <DADWutils> from </export/packages/
    dadutils.pkg>

Administration and Support utilities
(sparc) 1.0.0.0
This software is the property of Dom and Dave Enterprises.
Using </usr/local/utils> as the package base directory.
## Processing package information.
## Processing system information.
## Verifying disk space requirements.

Installing Administration and Support utilities as <DADWutils>

## Installing part 1 of 1.
/usr/local/utils/bin/fswarn
/usr/local/utils/bin/fswarnLog
/usr/local/utils/bin/startPPP
/usr/local/utils/bin/stopPPP
/usr/local/utils/bin/tidyLogs
/usr/local/utils/logsToTidy
[ verifying class <none> ]
## Executing postinstall script.
DADWutil entries added to root crontab

Installation of <DADWutils> was successful.
lithium#
```

You will see that our copyright message is displayed at the appropriate point and the postinstall script is executed after the package files have been extracted from under the *reloc* directory.

We can now install version 1.0.0.0 of *DADWutils* on all our servers and know they all have a consistent set of support tools installed.

9

PATCHING THE
SYSTEM

Manual Pages

patch (1)
patchadd (1M)
patchrm (1M)
pkgadd (1)
pkginfo (1)
pkginfo (4)
pkgparam (1)
pkgrm (1)
showrev (1M)

Files Affected

<patch id>/.diPatch
/tmp/log.<patch id>
/var/sadm/patch/*
/var/sadm/patch/.patchDB
/var/sadm/pkg/<package>/pkginfo
/var/sadm/pkg/<package>/save/<patch id>/*

Objectives

Patching the system is carried out to ensure that the system runs as efficiently as possible. Here, we'll look at some of the tasks that need to be performed to do this, including how the patching mechanism itself works, where and how patches can be obtained, and how patches are installed and generally managed.

What Are Patches?

Patching provides a means for software providers to fix their programs by updating some or all of their code. While this also includes third-party software, suppliers are likely to use their own mechanism for patching their software, so it is normally used to relate to the operating system components only. For this reason, in this chapter we'll just look at patching Solaris and the mechanism used by Sun to do this.

Patches are administered using the `patchadd` and `patchrm` commands, or the (older) `installpatch` and `backoutpatch` programs. `Patchadd` and `patchrm` are supplied with the operating system and are the recommended way to administer patches, while `installpatch` and `backoutpatch` are the original programs that were, and still are, supplied with the patch itself, although they will be removed at some point in the future.

Patches are actually based on the package format, which means that `patchadd` and `patchrm` use `pkgadd` and `pkgrm`, respectively, to install or remove patches as required.

They are numbered in a way that identifies both the patch itself and the particular revision of the patch. The naming convention used is <patch number>-<patch revision>. For example, 101580-09 would be revision 9 of patch 101580.

Each patch file is delivered with a *README* file that contains important information such as the bugs that are fixed (along with the bug numbers), a list of the packages that are affected, the files to be installed, which other patches are required for this one to work, and which patches this one obsoletes, if any.

Some patches may be aimed at fixing one particular problem and contain a very small number of files, while others(known as "jumbo patches") may fix a whole suite of programs or functionality. Common examples of these are the kernel and printing jumbo patches, both of which are frequently updated and tend to have high revision numbers.

Recommended Patches

Recommended patches are those that Sun suggests should be loaded onto the system, either at build time or as soon as possible after, even if you are not currently seeing any issues. These patches have been tested to work in conjunction with each other and will not cause any problems with the operating system. They are available from a number of locations, such as the Sunsolve CD-ROM, which is distributed to customers who have a maintenance contract, and Sun's Web site (*sunsolve.sun.com, sunsolve.sun.co.uk*, and other mirror sites).

Sun's recommended patches are grouped by Solaris version number and can be installed by using the `patchinstall` script supplied on the Sunsolve CD-ROM, or the `install_cluster` command provided with the downloadable cluster, as described later in this chapter.

Kernel Patches

These are patches that affect the main running kernel—UNIX itself. It is useful to note that we can also determine the version of the kernel jumbo patch that is installed by running `uname`. This will display the system type along with the kernel revision and will produce output similar to that shown below:

```
hydrogen# uname -a
SunOS hydrogen 5.6 Generic_105181-03 sun4u sparc SUNW,Ultra-5_10
hydrogen#
```

From this we know that the kernel jumbo patch on our system is patch number 105181, revision 3.

Security Patches

Sun investigates any issues that may allow users to gain unlawful access to the system. If any problems are seen, they are fixed and the patch is released as a "security patch." It will depend on the use of the system as to whether all or none of the security patches will be installed. This will have to be determined by the system administrator.

Public Patches

Public patches are provided by Sun to allow noncontract customers to gain access to the important recommended and security patches. They are located on the Sunsolve Web sites and can be downloaded as required.

Maintenance Updates

These are a group of patches designed to upgrade the whole of Solaris to a new defined patch level. They are easier and faster to install than individual patches.

Files and Their Locations

The patch locations may vary, depending on the version of the operating system you are using. Let's first take a brief look at the two mechanisms that you may see.

Progressive versus Direct Instance Patching

Prior to Solaris 2.5, a mechanism known as "Progressive Instance Patching" was used to apply patches. For this, a new instance of a package was created whenever any patches were being applied that affected the package.

For example, if 101580-09 patched the package SUNWcsr, then after it had been applied we would find that there were two instances of the package. The first (and original) would be found in */var/sadm/pkg/SUNWcsr*, while the second (patched) version would be found in */var/sadm/pkg/SUNWcsr.2*.

The ancillary patch files would be located in */var/sadm/patch/101580-09*. This would also contain all the patch backout information, which was stored as a cpio-formatted file under */var/sadm/patch/101580-09/save*.

Since Solaris 2.5, Direct Instance Patching has been the norm. In this case, the original installed package is modified. The ancillary patch files are still located under */var/sadm/patch/101580-09*, but now the backout information is stored with the package directory as a package stream. For our example patch, it would be found in */var/sadm/pkg/SUNWcsr/save/101580-09/undo.Z*.

All Direct Instance Patches include a file named *.diPatch* with their distribution, which is used to inform system utilities such as installpatch that they are dealing with a Direct Instance Patch. The file doesn't contain any important information; installpatch simply checks for its existence. In fact, if we look at the file we will normally see it contains something similar to the following:

```
hydrogen# cd /tmp/101580-09
hydrogen# cat .diPatch
This file tells installpatch that this is a direct instance patch
DO NOT DELETE
hydrogen#
```

Since Direct Instance Patching is now the norm, we will assume that this mechanism is being used for the remainder of this chapter, which means there are two main locations for patches and the packages that they affect.

/Var/sadm/patch

This is used to store information relating to the patch itself, and will generally include the following files:

- *backoutpatch*
- *log*
- *README.<patch id>*

The *backoutpatch* file is essentially a copy of the `patchrm` script and is used to remove the patch from the system. The *log* file is a copy of the patch installation, while the *README* file contains information about the patch itself.

Whenever a patch is added to the system a directory, named after the patch, is created for it in */var/sadm/patch*. For example, in the case of 101580-09, we would find a directory named */var/sadm/patch/101580-09* with the following contents:

```
hydrogen# ls /var/sadm/patch/101580-09
backoutpatch    log    README.101580-09
hydrogen#
```

/Var/sadm/pkg

This is the location where any package information will be found on the system. It is explained in depth in Chapter 8, "Administering Packages."

When patches are added, copies of the files that are being replaced are (optionally) stored in an area within the package itself. This is the backout information, and in our example, `patchadd` would create a "save" file named */var/sadm/pkg/SUNWcsr/save/101580-09/undo.Z*. (Note that the file is compressed in this case.)

We mentioned earlier that the backout files are stored as a package stream, which we can confirm by running the following commands:

```
hydrogen# cd /var/sadm/pkg/SUNWcsr/save/101580-09
hydrogen# ls -l undo*
-rw-r-r--  1  root  other 1345638  Dec 24 10:40 undo.Z
hydrogen#
```

If the file is compressed, first uncompress it:

```
hydrogen# uncompress undo.Z
hydrogen# pkginfo -l -d ./undo
   PKGINST:  SUNWcsr
      NAME:  Core Solaris, (Root)
  CATEGORY:  system
      ARCH:  sparc
   VERSION:  11.6.0,REV=1997.07.15.21.46
   BASEDIR:  /
    VENDOR:  Sun Microsystems, Inc.
      DESC:  core software for a specific instruction-set architecture
    PSTAMP:  on297-patchm06153920
   HOTLINE:  Please contact your local service provider
    STATUS:  spooled
     FILES:     14 spooled pathnames
                10 executables
                 4 package information files
              2979 blocks used (approx)
hydrogen#
```

The above output confirms the file is indeed using the package format. Now recompress the file if it was originally compressed:

```
hydrogen# compress undo
hydrogen#
```

Disk Space

One important thing we can see from the above descriptions is that */var/ sadm* contains the patch and package administration files. It is very important that there is always enough space in this area, otherwise numerous problems could be seen and patch installations may fail.

Determining What's Installed

There are various ways to determine which patches are installed on the system, using either the patchadd or showrev commands. Both these will produce output similar to that shown below:

```
hydrogen# patchadd -p
Patch: 105416-01 Obsoletes: Requires: Incompatibles: Packages:
SUNWaccu
Patch: 105800-01 Obsoletes: Requires: Incompatibles: Packages:
SUNWadmap
Patch: 105421-01 Obsoletes: Requires: Incompatibles: Packages:
SUNWapppr
Patch: 105621-02 Obsoletes: Requires: Incompatibles: Packages:
SUNWarc, SUNWcsu
Patch: 105405-01 Obsoletes: Requires: Incompatibles: Packages:
SUNWarc, SUNWcsu
Patch: 105210-01 Obsoletes: Requires: Incompatibles: Packages:
SUNWarc, SUNWcsu
Patch: 105472-01 Obsoletes: Requires: Incompatibles: Packages:
SUNWatfsu
Patch: 105377-03 Obsoletes: Requires: Incompatibles: Packages:
SUNWbcp
<lines removed for clarity>
hydrogen#
```

This displays a list of the patches installed, along with any patches that they make obsolete, any they require to work correctly, any they are incompatible with, and the packages that are affected by the patch.

Detecting Patches

We've already mentioned that each package installs into its own subdirectory within */var/sadm/pkg*. This package location also includes files containing information about the package.

For example, for the Core Solaris (Root) package, the package name is SUNWcsr, so the package information will be found in the package information file for it, named */var/sadm/pkg/SUNWcsr/pkginfo*, which should be something similar to that shown below:

```
hydrogen# cat /var/sadm/pkg/SUNWcsr/pkginfo
CLASSES=none
BASEDIR=/
TZ=GB
PATH=/sbin:/usr/sbin:/usr/bin:/usr/sadm/install/bin
OAMBASE=/usr/sadm/sysadm
PKG=SUNWcsr
NAME=Core Solaris, (Root)
ARCH=sparc
VERSION=11.6.0,REV=1997.07.15.21.46
PRODNAME=SunOS
PRODVERS=5.6/Generic
SUNW_PKGTYPE=root
SUNW_OBSOLETES=
MAXINST=1000
CATEGORY=system
DESC=core software for a specific instruction-set architecture
VENDOR=Sun Microsystems, Inc.
HOTLINE=Please contact your local service provider
EMAIL=
SUNW_REQUIRES=
SUNW_INCOMPAT=
SUNW_PATCHID=105181-03
PSTAMP=on297-patchm06153920
PKGINST=SUNWcsr
PKGSAV=/var/sadm/pkg/SUNWcsr/save
PATCHLIST=105181-03 105847-01 105845-01 105836-01 105797-01
PATCH_INFO_105181-03=Installed: Tue Feb  3 17:03:47 PST 1998
From: fern
    Obsoletes:  Requires: Incompatibles:
PATCH_INFO_105847-01=Installed: Tue Feb  3 17:06:46 PST 1998
From: fern
    Obsoletes:  Requires: Incompatibles:
PATCH_INFO_105845-01=Installed: Tue Feb  3 17:07:55 PST 1998
From: fern
    Obsoletes:  Requires: Incompatibles:
PATCH_INFO_105836-01=Installed: Tue Feb  3 17:09:43 PST 1998
From: fern
    Obsoletes:  Requires: Incompatibles:
PATCH_INFO_105797-01=Installed: Tue Feb  3 17:11:52 PST 1998
From: fern
    Obsoletes:  Requires: Incompatibles:
INSTDATE=Oct 07 1999 15:21
UPDATE=yes
PATCH_PROGRESSIVE=false
PATCH_UNCONDITIONAL=false
PATCH_NO_UNDO=true
PATCH_BUILD_DIR=none
PATCH_UNDO_ARCHIVE=none
INTERRUPTION=no
hydrogen#
```

To determine the patches installed, this file is parsed by the `patchadd` command. It pulls out all the patch-related information contained in the PATCH_INFO fields.

In fact, if we search for this field we'll see that the information we get is very similar to the output produced by `patchadd`:

```
hydrogen# grep PATCH_INFO /var/sadm/pkg/SUNWcsr/pkginfo
PATCH_INFO_105181-03=Installed: Tue Feb  3 17:03:47 PST 1998
From: fern
    Obsoletes:  Requires: Incompatibles:
PATCH_INFO_105847-01=Installed: Tue Feb  3 17:06:46 PST 1998
From: fern
    Obsoletes:  Requires: Incompatibles:
PATCH_INFO_105845-01=Installed: Tue Feb  3 17:07:55 PST 1998
From: fern
    Obsoletes:  Requires: Incompatibles:
PATCH_INFO_105836-01=Installed: Tue Feb  3 17:09:43 PST 1998
From: fern
    Obsoletes:  Requires: Incompatibles:
PATCH_INFO_105797-01=Installed: Tue Feb  3 17:11:52 PST 1998
From: fern
    Obsoletes:  Requires: Incompatibles:
hydrogen#
```

Pkgparam

We can also use a command named `pkgparam` to detect which packages will be affected by the patch installation. This again uses the *pkginfo* file to locate its information. We can see that every line in the *pkginfo* file consists of a variable and a value that is assigned to that variable. For example, the following line assigns the list of patch IDs to a variable named PATCHLIST:

```
PATCHLIST=105181-03 105847-01 105845-01 105836-01 105797-01
```

We could determine which patches affect the SUNWcsr package by using `pkgparam` to query the package as shown below:

```
hydrogen# pkgparam SUNWcsr PATCHLIST
105181-03 105847-01 105845-01 105836-01 105797-01
hydrogen#
```

Similarly, to display the full information about a particular patch, run the following on the patch ID:

```
hydrogen# pkgparam SUNWcsr PATCH_INFO_105181-03
Installed: Oct 22 17:00:01 GMT 1999 From: fern Obseletes:
   Requires: Incompatibles:
hydrogen#
```

We can see from the above examples that the *pkginfo* file is important for patches as well as packages. If this file should become corrupt or is removed, it will be very difficult to determine which patches are installed on the system. It will also become impossible for programs such as `patchadd` and patchrm to administer the system (since they cannot detect which patches have been installed) or update the system by adding or removing any patches.

PatchDB

Whenever patchadd -p runs, it will first check to see if a file named */var/ sadm/patch/.patchDB* exists and is up to date. To check this, a command (similar to the following one) first runs to calculate the checksum of all the *pkginfo* files on the system:

```
nawk '/PATCHID/ {print} /PATCHLIST/ {print}' /var/sadm/pkg/*/
    pkginfo | sum
```

Once this has been obtained, it is compared to the checksum value stored in the *.patchDB* file. If the two agree, the *.patchDB* file is assumed to be correct and its contents are read and displayed.

This file contains the list of patches installed on the system, formatted exactly as patchadd displays. It is used because determining the installed patches can be quite time-consuming, and it allows the utilities to display the list of patches as fast as possible. If, for any reason, *.patchDB* is removed, becomes corrupt, or produces checksum mismatches, it will simply be recreated the next time patchadd or patchrm is run.

The following extract from a *.patchDB* file shows the checksum information, which in this case is 35957:

```
hydrogen# more /var/sadm/patch/.patchDB
Version 1.0 35957
Patch: 105416-01 Obsoletes: Requires: Incompatibles: Packages:
SUNWaccu
Patch: 105800-01 Obsoletes: Requires: Incompatibles: Packages:
SUNWadmap
<lines removed for clarity>
hydrogen#
```

Adding Patches

Patches are added using either patchadd (the recommended way) or the installpatch script that is supplied with each patch. As installpatch will soon be unsupported, we will deal exclusively with patchadd here.

Parts of the patch installation are carried out using the *nobody* user and this needs to be able to create directories as required. To allow this to happen, Sun recommends that patch installs should always be carried out from */tmp* and the user *nobody* should always have an entry in the password file.

Patches can be installed with the "backout" option. This allows them to be removed should the system administrator wish, should a patch make a particular problem worse, for example, or not work with another one installed.

Apart from the recommended patches, normally it is advisable to install as few as possible. The reason for this is that it's virtually impossible to check every combination of patching that can be applied to the system to ensure they all operate together. Consequently, indiscriminate patch loading can lead to some patches being installed that will break others that were previously working.

Lots of patches, such as jumbo kernel patches, need to be installed in single-user mode (in fact, do this whenever possible) for a number of reasons: It allows the system to be as inactive as possible and it ensures that users cannot access any data while the change is occurring. Also, it may be that the patch replaces programs that would be running while in multi-user mode.

Removing Old Revisions

Should old patch revisions be removed before new ones are applied? This is a common question that unfortunately doesn't have an easy answer. However, a number of points can be taken into consideration to help with the decision.

First, and perhaps most importantly, is that it isn't a problem if old patches remain on the system, since all the standard utilities will still continue to work and will always use the highest patch revision. Leaving patches intact is the least time-consuming way of dealing with old revisions, although this method may take up valuable disk space

On the other hand, a big advantage with backing out the older patches is that all the files that were related to the patch will also be removed, which may free lots of disk space. For example, if we remove 105181-17, the following directories will disappear:

- */var/sadm/patch/105181-17*
- */var/sadm/pkg/<all the packages this patch affects>/save/105181-17*

Carrying out this task will make the system "neater," but it could also be very time-consuming for a large number of patches, which could be a major problem on a heavily used system.

If this process were followed, the old patch should be removed before the new revision is applied. This allows the original files to be backed out (assuming they were saved) before being backed up again by the new revision. Some system administrators actually remove the old patch directories manually, while retaining the information in the *pkginfo* files. This is not recommended since it is very easy to break the system, causing programs such as patchrm to fail because there are no backout files. (Although programs such as pkgparam and showrev will still work, allowing an "audit trail" of patch installs.) In short, the decision to remove old patches ultimately rests with each system administrator and may depend on things such as company policies and allowable machine downtime.

Installing Recommended Patches

The two ways to install recommended patches are from the Sunsolve maintenance CD-ROM or the Sunsolve Web site. Both ways will allow the whole set to be installed easily.

From the CD-ROM

Installation from the CD-ROM is an easy process and is automated using a script named `patchinstall`. This is a menu-driven terminal interface that allows the user to select the patches to install. It provides a way of installing either particular patches or the recommended set by entering "suggested" when the user is requested for the patch ID.

`Patchinstall` will first determine the version of the operating system and the architecture of the system, and from this information will build a filename formatted as follows:

- *.sunos.<OS Release><X86 ref>.suggestedpatches*

For example, a system running Solaris 5.6 on a SPARC will be referenced as *.sunos.5.6.suggestedpatches*, while an X86-based Solaris 2.5 system would be *.sunos.5.5_x86.suggestedpatches*.

The file contains the list of current recommended patches needed for the particular system, and is used by `patchinstall` to determine which ones need to be installed. `Patchinstall` will then try and locate this file on the CD-ROM, read it, and start the installation.

An example installation of recommended patches is shown below. It's also interesting to note that by default they won't have the backup option. If you want them to be backed up, then make sure you let `patchinstall` know when it asks!

```
hydrogen# cd /cdrom/cdrom0
hydrogen# ./patchinstall
============================================================

       patchinstall - install a patch

   Copyright (c) 1993 Sun Microsystems, Inc. All Rights Reserved.
          Printed in the United States of America.
2550 Garcia Avenue, Mountain View, California, 94043-1100 U.S.A.

Patches are distributed to SunService Contract Customers ONLY.
Redistribution to unauthorized parties is prohibited by the
SunService Contract.

Installation of all patches is not suggested as some patches may
conflict with one another. Please make sure that the patch you are
installing is necessary before actually installing the patch.


============================================================
```

During the installation, default answers will be provided inside
brackets '[]'
Pressing the <Return> key will select the default provided.

Press <Ctrl-C> at any time to stop the installation.

Continue with patch installation? [Y]y

<Next screen>
Installation of patches will use several temporary files, and may
need several megabytes of space. Please enter the name of a directory that can be used for these temporary files (the directory must
exist before running the installation!)

Where should I store temporary files? [/tmp]

<Next screen>
The installation for Solaris 2.x patches provides the option of
saving the original versions of the software being patched.
Unfortunately, this occasionally will cause your /var/sadm/patch
directory to grow too large. By default, this installation will NOT
save your original versions of software.

Would you like to save the original versions of the software? [no]

<Next screen>
Patches already installed:
<Display list of patches on the system>
Next you will be prompted for the patches you wish to install. If
you would like to install the suggested patches, enter "suggested".
Otherwise enter the patch id.

To see a list of the patches you have entered, type a '?' <Return>

To start the installation, press <Return> when prompted for a patch
id.

Patch to install (patchid, suggested, ?):suggested

<Next screen>
Patch installation setup:

        Temporary directory: /tmp
        Save old versions of files: FALSE
        Patches to install: suggested

Is this correct? [y]y
Installing suggested patches for release 5.6
Copying 106125-05 to /tmp
x 106125-05, 0 bytes, 0 tape blocks
<installation of patches continues>
hydrogen#

Once this has completed, the system can be rebooted for the patches to
take effect. Running patchadd should confirm the patches have been
installed correctly.

From the Web Site

First, we need to find the correct patch cluster and download it. We can do this at one of Sun's Sunsolve sites (*sunsolve.sun.com, Sunsolve.sun.co.uk*, and other mirror sites). Again, this will be related to both the Solaris version and the architecture of the machine. When it has been downloaded, you will have a file containing all the required patches. As explained earlier, it is recommended that the installation is carried out from within */tmp*, so that's where we'll download our cluster to:

```
hydrogen# cd /tmp
<download recommended patches from Sun site>
hydrogen# ls -l 2_6_Recommended_tar.Z
-rwxrwxr-x root other 1 36694000 2_6_Recommended_tar.Z
hydrogen#
```

The patch cluster is supplied as a compressed tar file, so we now need to decompress and un-tar the file.

```
hydrogen# zcat 2_6_Recommended_tar.Z | uncompress - | tar xf -
hydrogen#
```

This will leave us with a directory, in this case named *2.6_Recommended*, that contains a series of patch directories and all the ancillary files that are required for the install:

```
hydrogen# ls -l 2_6*
total 212
drwxr-xr-x  12 root      root          512 Dec 17 09:38 105181-17
drwxr-xr-x   4 root      root          512 Dec 17 09:38 105210-25
<lines removed for clarity>
hydrogen#
```

An install script named install_cluster is provided, so we'll run that now to start the installation:

```
hydrogen# ./install_cluster

Patch cluster install script for Solaris 2.6 Recommended

*WARNING* SYSTEMS WITH LIMITED DISK SPACE SHOULD *NOT* INSTALL
PATCHES:
With or without using the save option, the patch installation
process will still require some amount of disk space for instal-
lation and administrative tasks in the /, /usr, /var, or /opt
partitions where patches are typically installed. The exact
amount of space will depend on the machine's architecture, soft-
ware packages already installed, and the difference in the
patched objects size. To be safe, it is not recommended that a
patch cluster be installed on a system with less than 4 MBytes
of available space in each of these partitions. Running out of
disk space during installation may result in only partially
loaded patches. Check and be sure adequate disk space is avail-
able before continuing.
```

```
Are you ready to continue with install? [y/n]: y
Determining if sufficient save space exists...
Sufficient save space exists, continuing...
Installing patches located in /tmp/2.6_Recommended
Using patch_order file for patch installation sequence
Installing 106125-08...
<patch installation continues>
hydrogen#
```

Once this has completed, running `patchadd` will again confirm that all the required patches have been installed.

Adding Individual Patches

On occasions, it may be necessary to install a small number of patches. Usually this will be to fix a known problem that has occurred on the system. The first step is to get a copy of the patch itself. This may come from a number of sources; it may be downloaded from the Sunsolve Web site, loaded from a copy of the Sunsolve CD-ROM, or perhaps sent via email by a Sun support engineer.

We'll use patch 105181 from the Sunsolve CD-ROM for our example. Although we could use the `patchinstall` script (similar to the way we did for the recommended patch cluster), we'll do it manually to show the whole process.

Remember to do this in single-user mode if at all possible. First, we need to copy the file from the CD-ROM into our install directory, which will be */tmp*:

```
hydrogen# cd /cdrom/cdrom0/files
hydrogen# cp 105181* /tmp
hydrogen# cd /tmp
hydrogen#
```

In this case the patch is a gzip compressed tar file, so we need to decompress and un-tar it. Always remember to copy the compressed tar file to the install location before extracting it so as not to forget to copy the hidden *.diPatch* file, and to make sure the correct permissions on the extracted files are retained. We can use the gzip utilities supplied on the CD-ROM to uncompress the file:

```
hydrogen# /cdrom/cdrom0/gzip/bin/svr4/gzcat 105181-03.tar.gz|tar xf -
hydrogen# ls -ld 105181*
drwxr-xr-x  11 root      root         707 Sep 16  1998 105181-03
-r--r--r--   1 root      other    3674621 Jan  3 13:15 105181-03.tar.gz
hydrogen#
```

We'll follow the recommendation that all patches are installed with the backout option. Although this uses up more space, it ensures that the system can be recovered in the most efficient fashion should it be required. Let's start the patch install:

```
hydrogen# patchadd 105181-03

Checking installed patches...
Executing prepatch script...

If possible, perform patch installation in single user mode. If
this can not be done, we recommend having the system in as quiet
a state as possible: no users logged on, no user jobs running.

Do you wish to continue this installation {yes or no} [yes]?
(by default, installation will continue in 60 seconds)

Verifying sufficient filesystem capacity (dry run method)...
Installing patch packages...


Patch number 105181-03 has been successfully installed.
See /var/sadm/patch/105181-03/log for details

Patch packages installed:
  SUNWcsr
hydrogen#
```

There are times when we may not want to retain the backout data; for example, this machine may be one that has been fully tested with the patches we are installing. To install and not save backout data we would run `patchadd` with slightly different options, as shown below:

```
hydrogen# patchadd -d 105181-03
hydrogen#
```

Loading Multiple Patches

If we have a number of patches that are needed to fix a problem, it is often easier to load them all at the same time, rather than through numerous calls to `patchadd`. This can be accomplished by calling `patchadd` with the directory that contains the patches and either a list of patches or a file that contains the list of them.

For example, assuming we had 101580-02, 102300-05, and 104500-01 to install and they were located in *tmp/patches*, we could run the following command:

```
hydrogen# patchadd -M /tmp/patches 101580-02 102300-05 104500-01
hydrogen#
```

Alternatively we could create a file that contains the patches and install as shown below:

```
hydrogen# cat /tmp/listToInstall
101580-02
102300-05
104500-01
hydrogen# patchadd -M /tmp/patches /tmp/listToInstall
hydrogen#
```

Obsolete Patches

There are a number of reasons why a patch may become obsolete; for instance, a newer version of it may have been released, or a different patch that replaces the obsolete one may have been installed.

When this happens, the original patch files will remain on the system, but the *undo* file will be renamed "obsolete." A file named *obsoleted_by* will also be created that contains the ID of the new patch.

Let's take a look at how this works. The following steps show how the files are manipulated by installing the newer patch. For this example, we already have 105463-06 on the system and have just installed 105463-07:

```
hydrogen# patchadd -p | grep 105463
Patch: 105463-06 Obsoletes: Requires: Incompatibles: Packages:
SUNWvxvm
Patch: 105463-07 Obsoletes: Requires: Incompatibles: Packages:
SUNWvxvm
hydrogen#
```

Patchadd has determined that we have both versions of the patch installed. To clarify this, let's look at the patch directory:

```
hydrogen# ls -ld /var/sadm/patch/105463*
drwxr-xr-x   2 root       other        512 Dec 18 00:23 105463-06
drwxr-xr-x   2 root       other        512 Dec 18 00:23 105463-07
hydrogen#
```

The previous patch is indeed still installed on the system; the reason for this is that we have installed 105463-07 without first backing out 105463-06.

Let's have a look in the package area to see the hierarchy that's been created within the *save* area:

```
hydrogen# cd /var/sadm/pkg/SUNWvmman/save
hydrogen# ls -l
total 8
drwxr-xr-x   2 root       other        512 Dec 18 00:23 105463-06
drwxr-xr-x   2 root       other        512 Dec 18 00:23 105463-07
hydrogen#

hydrogen# ls -l 105463-06
total 7746
-rw-r--r--   1 root       other    3951033 Mar 31  1999 obsolete.Z
-rw-r--r--   1 root       other         10 Dec 18 00:23
obsoleted_by
hydrogen#

hydrogen# ls -l 105463-07
total 8496
-rw-r--r--   1 root       other    4336103 Dec 18 00:23 undo.Z
hydrogen#
```

Here we can see that `patchadd` has created the *undo* file as expected. It's also moved the original *undo* file to an *obsolete* file and created the *obsoleted_by* file to inform the system utilities of the change.

If we now check the *obsoleted_by* file in *105463-06*, it should confirm the newer revision of the patch:

```
hydrogen# cat 105463-06/obsoleted_by
105463-07
hydrogen#
```

Removing Patches

`Patchrm` is the recommended way of removing patches from the system, although the version of `backoutpatch` that is supplied with the patch itself can also be used if required. Don't forget that patches cannot be backed out if the "-d" option was used to install them, since this does not save copies of the replaced software.

For example, to backout patch 105181-03, we would run the following:

```
hydrogen# cd /var/sadm/patch
hydrogen# patchrm 105181-03

Checking installed patches...

Backing out patch 105181-03...

Patch 105181-03 has been backed out.
hydrogen#
```

The removal process is simply a reverse of the installation process: The patch directory itself (*/var/sadm/patch/<patch id>*) will be removed. The *save* file that was created for every package affected by the patch (*/var/ sadm/pkg/<package>/save/<patch id>*) will be extracted and the original binaries put back in place. Finally, the packages will be updated so that all traces of the patch are removed from the system.

A more complex issue is removing patches that have been made obsolete by a subsequent patch.

When `patchrm` runs, one of the checks it performs is to see if the patch has been made obsolete and whether it can be safely backed out or not. This means that to back out the obsoleted patch, we would need to backout the patch that has made it obsolete in the first place—the system would become very confused if it let you do otherwise!

The following example shows the type of errors you will see if you try to do this incorrectly:

```
hydrogen# patchrm 105463-06
Checking installed packages and patches...
This patch was obsoleted by patch 105463-07.
```

```
Patches must be backed out in the reverse order in
which they were installed.

Patchrm exiting.
hydrogen#
```

In this case, we would have to backout 105463-07 first, which would then allow us to backout 105463-06.

Checking the System

The patch levels of the system ought to be checked and repatched on a regular basis, especially some of the jumbo patches since these can change frequently. This can be a very time-consuming process and will obviously depend on the system—it may be a heavy production server that only has downtime available every few months, or it may be a desktop system that gets turned off every night.

Fortunately, a few tools are available from Sun to help automate this task. These are changed from time to time, but the process revolves around downloading a file that contains a listing of every patch and its revision, and checking your system against the list to produce a report detailing the list of patches required to bring the machine up-to-date.

The tools and related files listed below are all available for download from Sun's Sunsolve Web site.

- *patchdiag.xref.* This is the cross-reference file that the machine is checked against. It is updated on the Web site regularly.

- patchdiag. This is a script that runs and compares the patches on the machine against the cross-reference file and produces a report. From here, the patches can either be manually downloaded or automated using a public domain tool named wget (see Sun's Sunsolve Web site for details).

- patchcheck. This is similar to patchdiag but also allows you to download the required patches using a browser.

Patchdiag is only available to customers who have a support contract. Patchcheck is available to everyone, but you need to have a support contract to be able to use the automated patch download facility.

10

ADMINISTERING QUOTAS

Objectives

The aim of this chapter is to determine how to allocate and control both the disk space and the number of files that users are allowed to use.

What Are Quotas?

Quotas are a way of controlling the amount of space that a user, or a number of users, is allowed to utilize on the system. By setting limits for users, quotas force users to clean up and generally maintain their allocated directories.

Quotas are normally only used on systems where disk space is critical. They are set on a per-filesystem basis and control both disk space and the number of files. Users are allowed a soft limit and a hard limit for both the amount of disk space they can use and the number of files they can create. They may use up to their soft limit without any problems; in fact, they can even exceed it for a predefined time period—a soft limit is there to provide a buffer for the user. The hard limit is a finite limit—users cannot use more than this value.

Users are notified if their soft limit is exceeded. From here, they must tidy up their files. Otherwise, if the usage still exceeds the soft limit, when the time period expires it becomes a hard limit and is enforced as such.

Enabling Quotas

The first thing we need to do is ensure that the filesystem that contains the users is configured to run quotas. This is a simple task and is achieved by mounting the required filesystem with the "quota" option enabled. We also need to create a file, named *quotas*, in the top level (mount point) of each filesystem. This file provides a location for the system to store quota information for that particular filesystem.

All our users are located on one filesystem—*/export/home*—therefore, we only need to configure this for quotas. To do this, we modify the "mount" options in the */etc/vfstab* file. Ours is shown below after modification. Although we have used the "rq" option, we could just have easily used "rw,quota."

```
hydrogen# cat /etc/vfstab
#device           device       mount   FS    fsck  mount      mount
#to mount         to fsck      point   type  pass  at boot    options
#
fd                   -                        /dev/fd       fd - no -
/proc                -                        proc          proc - no -
/dev/dsk/c0t0d0s0 /dev/rdsk/c0t0d0s0 /        ufs 1 no -
/dev/dsk/c0t0d0s1 -                  -        swap - no -
/dev/dsk/c0t0d0s4 /dev/rdsk/c0t0d0s4 /var     ufs 1 no -
/dev/dsk/c0t0d0s5 /dev/rdsk/c0t0d0s5 /opt     ufs 1 no -
/dev/dsk/c0t0d0s6 /dev/rdsk/c0t0d0s6 /usr     ufs 1 no -
/dev/dsk/c0t0d0s7 /dev/rdsk/c0t0d0s7 /export/home ufs 1 no rq
swap              -                  /tmp     tmpfs - yes -
hydrogen#
```

Before we activate the *vfstab* changes, we'll create the *quotas* file and set the correct permissions on it to make sure users can't read it and determine everyone else's quotas. Again, since we have only enabled quotas on one file-system, we only need to create the one file as shown below:

```
hydrogen# touch /export/home/quotas
hydrogen# chmod 600 /export/home/quotas
hydrogen#
```

Quotas are enabled at boot time through the start-up script named MOUNTFSYS. The code extract below shows the lines that are used to carry this out:

```
hydrogen# more /etc/init.d/MOUNTFSYS
<lines removed for clarity>
if cut -f 4 /etc/mnttab | \
        egrep '^quota|,quota' >/dev/null 2>&1; then
    echo 'Checking UFS quotas: \c'
    /usr/sbin/quotacheck -a -p
    echo 'done.'
    /usr/sbin/quotaon -a
fi
<lines removed for clarity>
hydrogen#
```

We can see from this that MOUNTFSYS searches */etc/mnttab* for any entries that have mount options of quota set, which is why we need to update */etc/vfstab*. To do this, we can either reboot the system or remount the device. In our case, we will remount the device, which means we are bypassing the MOUNTFSYS script. So, we'll have to manually turn quotas on and run quotacheck to determine the current user quotas:

```
hydrogen# umount /export/home
hydrogen# mount /export/home
hydrogen# quotaon -a
hydrogen# quotacheck -av
*** Checking quotas for /dev/rdsk/c0t0d0s7 (/export/home)
hydrogen#
```

If we take a look at our *mnttab*, we can see that */export/home* has now been mounted with the correct quota options:

```
hydrogen# cat /etc/mnttab
/proc /proc proc rw,suid,dev=2940000 969653177 /dev/dsk/
c0t0d0s0 / ufs rw,suid,dev=1980000 969653177
/dev/dsk/c0t0d0s4 /var ufs rw,suid,dev=1980003 969653177
/dev/dsk/c0t0d0s5 /opt ufs rw,suid,dev=1980006 969653177
/dev/dsk/c0t0d0s6 /usr ufs rw,suid,dev=1980009 969653177
/dev/dsk/c0t0d0s7 /export/home ufs rw,suid,dev=1980012,quota
969653177
fd /dev/fd fd rw,suid,dev=2a00000 969653177
swap /tmp tmpfs rw,dev=1 969653178
hydrogen#
```

To verify that quotas are configured correctly, we could run `repquota`. Although it won't display any user information (as we haven't entered any yet), it will still output the header information, which indicates that everything is working correctly:

```
hydrogen# repquota -a
/dev/dsk/c0t0d0s7 (/export/home):
            Block limits                 File limits
User used  soft  hard  timeleft  used  soft  hard  timeleft
hydrogen#
```

Configuring the User's Quotas

The next step is to configure the limits for each user. We can manipulate the hard and soft limits individually for every user. The timeout period can also be altered, but only on a per-filesystem basis.

We will start by assigning the same values, listed below, to each user. We have provided quite a large buffer between the soft and hard limits. This should allow the user to easily perform tasks such as transferring large files and creating large tar files. It also means that should our first guess at the user's limits be incorrect, the user will have time to inform us before the hard limit is met:

- Soft limit for file size: 300 MB (300,000 1 kB blocks)
- Hard limit for file size: 500 MB (500,000 1 kB blocks)
- Soft limit for number of files: 400
- Hard limit for number of files: 500
- Soft limit timeout period: 10 days

As usual, we'll apply the settings to the test account to be certain we are happy with them before we apply them to the genuine user accounts. (We set up the test account earlier in Chapter 3, "User Administration," with a login name of *testuser*.)

Let's first alter the hard and soft limits using `edquota`. This will bring up the configuration data in our default editor (probably "`vi`"); we simply need to alter the values and save the file for the changes to take effect:

```
hydrogen# edquota testuser
fs /export/home blocks (soft = 300000, hard = 500000)
    inodes (soft = 400, hard = 500)
hydrogen#
```

Now, we'll alter the soft limit timeout period default to 10 days:

```
hydrogen# edquota -t
fs /export/home blocks time limit = 10 day, files time
    limit = 10 day
hydrogen#
```

Running `quota` will confirm that the user's soft and hard limits have been modified correctly:

```
hydrogen# quota -v testuser
Disk quotas for testuser (uid 500):
Filesystem  usage  quota  limit  timeleft  files  quota  limit     timeleft
/export/home    0 300000 500000                 0    400    500
hydrogen#
```

Checking the Limits

At this point, everything is configured. Now, let's run some tests to check that it all works as expected. At the moment, *testuser* only has a small number of files, such as profiles and so on. So, checking *testuser*'s quotas now will simply return without showing anything, unless we use the "verbose" option:

```
hydrogen# quota testuser
hydrogen# quota -v testuser
Disk quotas for testuser (uid 500):
Filesystem   usage  quota  limit  timeleft  files  quota  limit    timeleft
/export/home    6 300000 500000                 5    400    500
hydrogen#
```

Testuser should be allowed to create files below its limit without any problems. Let's use *testuser*'s account to create a file and check this:

```
hydrogen# su - testuser
hydrogen$ mkfile 100m file1
hydrogen$ ls -l file1
-rw------T  1 testuser test  104857600  Sep 16 15:56 file1
hydrogen$ quota
hydrogen$ quota -v
Disk quotas for test (uid 500):
Filesystem   usage  quota  limit  timeleft  files  quota  limit   timeleft
/export/home 102465 300000 400000                 7    400    500
hydrogen$
```

OK, that seems to work fine. Now let's create another file that will just push *testuser* over its soft limit:

```
hydrogen$ mkfile 250m file2
quota_ufs: Warning: over disk limit (pid 369, uid 500, inum 5012,
    fs /export/home)
hydrogen$ ls -l file*
-rw------T  1 testuser test   104857600 Sep 16 15:56 file1
-rw------T  1 testuser test   262144000 Sep 16 15:56 file2
hydrogen# quota
Over disk quota on /export/home, remove 58601K within 1.4 weeks
hydrogen$ quota -v
Disk quotas for test (uid 500):
Filesystem    usage  quota  limit  timeleft   files  quota  limit   timeleft
/export/home 358601 300000 500000  1.4 weeks      7    400    500
hydrogen$
```

Also, running a quota report on the filesystems will confirm that *testuser* has reached its soft limit:

```
hydrogen# repquota -a
/dev/dsk/c0t0d0s7 (/export/home):
                        Block limits              File limits
User          used    soft    hard   timeleft  used  soft   hard   timeleft
testuser  +- 358601 300000 500000   1.4 weeks    8   400    500
hydrogen#
```

Now, we'll create one more file to push *testuser* over its hard limit.
Although we will be able to create the file, we will be told that we are over
our hard limit. From there, any other file we try to create will fail:

```
hydrogen# su - testuser
hydrogen$ mkfile 250m file3
quota_ufs: over hard disk limit (pid 375, uid 500, inum 5017,
    fs /export/home)
file3: Disc quota exceeded
hydrogen$ ls -l file*
-rw------T   1 testuser test    104857600 Sep 16 15:56 file1
-rw------T   1 testuser test    262144000 Sep 16 16:15 file2
-rw------T   1 testuser test    262144000 Sep 16 16:56 file3
hydrogen$ quota
Over disk quota on /export/home, remove 199993K within 1.4 weeks
hydrogen$ rm file?
hydrogen$
```

We can see that *testuser* may carry on storing data on the filesystem so
long as the time period doesn't exceed the soft limit. After this time period
has expired or *testuser* has exceeded its hard limit, *testuser* cannot store any
more data on the system. In fact, if tried, *testuser* would see a similar error
message to that shown.

We would also see a similar effect if *testuser* were to create a number of
files that would take it over its file allocation limits. For example, running the
following test script below would show this:

```
hydrogen# su - testuser
hydrogen$ cat testFileQuotas
#!/bin/ksh
count=0
while [ count -lt 550 ]; do
  touch filenum$count
  if [ $? -ne 0 ]; then
    exit 1
  else
    count=$(($count + 1))
  fi
done
hydrogen$ ./testFileQuotas
quota_ufs: Warning: too many files (pid 3040, uid 500, fs /export/home)
quota_ufs: over file hard limit (pid 3045, uid 500, fs /export/home)
touch: filenum475 cannot create
hydrogen$ quota -v
Disk quotas for test (uid 500):
Filesystem    usage  quota  limit  timeleft  files  quota  limit  timeleft
/export/home    154 300000 500000              500    400    500  1.43 weeks
hydrogen$ rm filenum*
hydrogen$ exit
hydrogen$
```

Setting Default User Quotas

Rather than manually creating user quotas, the easiest way of setting them is to copy an existing user. For example, now that we have assigned *testuser*'s quotas, we could create another user, say *realuser*, and assign them the same quotas as *testuser* by running the following command:

```
hydrogen# edquota -p testuser realuser
hydrogen#
```

We will take this idea a step further and incorporate it into our standard user setup by modifying the createUser script that we built in Chapter 3, "User Administration." This ensures that any new user will be created with all the correct quotas. *Testuser*'s values will be used, and we'll modify the script by adding the lines shown in bold:

```
hydrogen# more createUser
<lines removed for clarity>
#
# set our company defaults
#
home=/export/home
shell=/bin/ksh
skel=/etc/skel
password=hViVZtexneY8Y  # default encrypted password
warnDays=5
validDays=60
quotaAccount=testuser
<lines removed for clarity>
#
# set the password timeouts
#
passwd -f -w ${warnDays} -x ${validDays} ${user}
#
# update the account with any "standard" settings
#
edquota -p ${quotaAccount} ${user}
exit 0
hydrogen#
```

Disabling User Quotas

If we ever wish to disable quotas for every user, the easiest way is to remove the *quota* file and alter the "mount" option in */etc/vfstab*, then either remount the device and run quotaoff, or simply reboot the system.

However, if we only want to disable quotas for one particular user, we would run edquota and set the relevant entry back to "0." This will be taken to mean "unlimited." For example, the values below would disable all quotas for *testuser*:

```
hydrogen# edquota testuser
fs /export/home blocks (soft = 0, hard = 0) inodes (soft = 0,
    hard = 0)
hydrogen#
```

Automatically Checking the Limits

As we saw earlier, another method of checking quotas is to use `repquota`. Using the options below will generate a report for all users that have quotas allocated on all filesystems:

```
hydrogen# repquota -av
/dev/dsk/c0t0d0s7 (/export/home):
                        Block limits                    File limits
User           used    soft   hard   timeleft   used   soft   hard   timeleft
testuser   +- 358601 300000 500000  1.4 weeks      8   400
hydrogen#
```

This output can be analyzed on a regular basis and used by the system administrator to inform users if they are approaching their limits. The script below shows an example of how this can be done. It parses the output and sends mail to the administrator and the users concerned when they reach a predetermined limit:

```
hydrogen# cat checkQuotas
#!/bin/ksh
#
# Script to check the quotas of all "registered" users.
# It will send mail back to the users when they have used
# a predetermined amount of their soft limit.
#
# The output from repquota is formatted as shown below:
#
#/dev/dsk/c0t3d0s0 (/):
#       Block limits                    File limits
#User      used  soft  hard timeleft used soft hard timeleft
#test1 +- 14995 10000 15000 6.9       6    100  200
#test2 -- 0     10000 15000           0    100  200
#
#User settable variables
softLimitHighMark=85                   # % value when we alert
adminAccount=root                      # who to send the mail
repquotaOutput=/tmp/rep.out$$
listOfUsers=/tmp/list_of_users$$
tmpOutput=/tmp/quotaMailTest.$$

# Set up the path—
PATH=/usr/ucb:/bin:/etc:/usr/sbin:./bin:/usr/etc:.
# generate the report...
repquota -va > ${repquotaOutput}
if [ $? -ne 0 ]; then
  echo "Error running repquota"
  exit 1
fi
```

```
# ...and create a list of users in the report.
awk '{ \
  if ($0 !~ /Block limits/ && \
      $1 != "User" && \
      $1 !~ /^\/dev.*\/dsk/) { \
    print $1 \
  } \
}' ${repquotaOutput} > ${listOfUsers}
# Now start to parse the file.
# Generate a piece of mail for each user.
for person in `cat ${listOfUsers}`; do
  awk '{ \
    # throw away the following lines that are normally
    # produced as part of the report;
    #      Block limits File limits
    #      User used soft hard..
    if ($0 !~ /Block limits/ && $1 != "User") { \
      # at this point we are left with
      #
      # test5 +- 14995 10000 15000 EXPIRED 6 100 200
      # test6 -- 1   10000   15000 120 100 200 EXPIRED
      #
      # Start with the "Block" calculations.
      # First see if we have exceeded the soft limit.
      # We will have a "timeleft" value when
      # this has occurred
      if ($1 == thisUser) { \
        # Split the "+-" quota flag into its two values.
        # From here, ignore if its a + as they will already
        # know they are over-quota.
        if (substr ($2, 1, 1) == "-"){ \
          # below block soft limit
          blockUsed = $3; \
          blockSoft = $4; \
          if (blockUsed > 0 && blockSoft > 0) { \
            SoftLimit = (blockUsed / blockSoft * 100); \
            if (SoftLimit > '${softLimitHighMark}') { \
            printf ("%s is using %d%% of their block soft limit
                    [%d]\n", \
                    $1, SoftLimit, blockSoft); \
            } \
          } \
        } \
        if (substr ($2, 2, 1) == "-"){ \
          # below file soft limit
          if (NF == 8){ \
            fileUsed = $6; \
            fileSoft = $7; \
          } \
          if (NF == 9){ \
            fileUsed = $7; \
            fileSoft = $8; \
          } \
          if (fileUsed > 0 && fileSoft > 0) { \
            SoftLimit = (fileUsed / fileSoft * 100); \
            if (SoftLimit > '${softLimitHighMark}') { \
```

```
            printf ("%s is using %d%% of their file soft limit
                [%d]\n", \
                $1, SoftLimit, fileSoft); \
          } \
        } \
      } \
      if (substr ($2, 1, 1) == "+"){ \
        print "Warning: Block soft limit has already expired
            for",$1 \
      } \
      if (substr ($2, 2, 1) == "+"){ \
        print "Warning: File soft limit has already expired
            for",$1 \
      } \
    } \
  } \
}' thisUser=${person} ${repquotaOutput} > ${tmpOutput}
# if we have any output - mail it
if [ -s ${tmpOutput} ]; then
  cat ${tmpOutput} | mail -s "Quota check - ${person}"
    ${person} ${adminAccount}
fi
rm ${tmpOutput}
done
# Clean up by removing the temp files
rm -f ${repquotaOutput} ${listOfUsers}
exit 0
hydrogen#
```

The Crontab *Entry*

We'll automate this by running it from `cron` once a day on every working day. The *crontab* entry to do this is shown below:

```
hydrogen# crontab -l
<lines removed for clarity>
#
# check user disk quotas
#
35 01 * * 1-5 /usr/local/utils/bin/checkQuotas
<lines removed for clarity>
hydrogen#
```

Should We Use Them?

There are pros and cons to running quotas. Implementing them usually has some performance issues. It takes slightly longer to boot the system and there are delays at login time as the user's quotas are being checked. These delays may be insignificant, depending on the number of filesystems and users that are using quotas. For these reasons, as we pointed out earlier, they are normally only run on critical areas.

On the other hand, users rarely tidy their areas up unless they are forced to—it is common knowledge that as soon as any disk space appears, someone will fill it up again almost as quickly. By allocating realistic quotas, this space becomes easier to manage. If the total hard limits are less than the total amount of disk space, the system is protected from failure due to a lack of disk space.

11

CONNECTING TO
THE LOCAL AREA
NETWORK

Manual Pages

arp (1M)
arp (7P)
ethers (4)
hme (7D)
hosts (4)
ifconfig (1M)
in.rarpd (1M)
in.rdisc (1M)
in.routed (1M)
ip (7P)
ip6 (7P)
le (7D)
ndd (1M)
netmasks (4)
netstat (1M)
ping (1M)
route (1M)
tcp (7P)

Files Affected

/etc/defaultrouter
/etc/ethers
/etc/inet/hosts
/etc/inet/netmasks
/etc/hostname.<interface>.<instance>
/etc/hostname6.<interface>.<instance>
/etc/nodename
/etc/notrouter

Objectives

Most systems need to communicate with each other. This may be to share data, transfer files, or send email, for example. In this chapter, we'll look at how we can achieve this by connecting them all to a common network. To do this, we'll see how to assign Internet Protocol (IP) addresses, configure networking-related files, and check that the system is correctly connected to the Local Area Network (LAN).

Description

Many decisions need to be made before we can begin to configure the network interfaces. These can be, and in fact normally are, both complex and highly dependent upon many "local" factors. Some of these are listed below:

- Are the systems located in separate buildings or connected to different physical networks, requiring hardware to bridge them?
- Will they be connecting to systems running protocols other than TCP/IP?
- Will one or more machines be connected to the outside world?
- Will there be any gateway systems to other locations (extranets)?
- How secure should the network be?
- How many systems will be connected in total?
- How will the network be split into subnetworks?

We have decided to implement our network in a number of stages. The first stage, covered by this chapter, is to connect all the systems to a private network, or LAN. We will split this into a number of subnetworks based on the tasks that each system carries out. For example, the main servers and the general clients will be known as the "internal" systems and will be in one subnet, while the systems that will later allow us to connect to the outside world will be known as the "external" facing systems and will be located in a second subnet.

This allows us to isolate the tasks that are described here to those that deal with local connections only, and will hopefully provide a better understanding of the processes involved. The downside of this is that we may be doing some portions of the work a number of times, as we rework some of these settings in later chapters. This isn't a problem for our network as we can simply alter the files as we wish, but it will probably be more difficult in a production environment. So please be aware of this if you decide to use some of our values!

IP Addressing Schemes

One of the biggest problems is to choose the correct IP address range to use. So before we can continue with the task of allocating an address for each machine we need to be aware of some of the addressing schemes that are used.

We'll briefly describe three main schemes below. Class-based and subnetting, although still widely used, have largely been overtaken by the classless scheme known as Classless Inter-Domain Routing (CIDR), pronounced "cider."

Class-Based

IP addresses have historically been based on the "class" system. For this, various classes were created: "A," "B," "C," and "extended addressing mode." "A," "B," and "C" were assigned a network portion and a host portion, which was a fixed value for each. An escape code was provided to access "extended addressing mode," which would later be split further into classes "D" and "E" (multicast and experimental, respectively).

There was no concept of subnetting within the classes; routers would simply examine the address and deduce its class based on the value of its high-order bits. The network information would be obtained based on the global rules for that class (i.e., what portion of the address relates to the network and which portion relates to the host). This information is summarized in Table 11.1.

Table 11.1 *Bit Information for Class-Based Schemes*

Class	High-Order Bits	Network Bits	Host Bits	Address Bits (b=high order n=network h=host)
A	0	7	24	bnnnnnnn.hhhhhhhh.hhhhhhhh.hhhhhhhh
B	10	14	16	bbnnnnnn.nnnnnnnn.hhhhhhhh.hhhhhhhh
C	110	21	8	bbbnnnnn.nnnnnnnn.nnnnnnnn.hhhhhhhh
Extended Addressing Mode	111	—	—	

Using the information shown here, we can calculate the number of hosts that are available in each network and also the number of networks that are available in each class. For example, class "A" has 7 bits available for network addresses and 24 bits for host addresses. Converting this to decimal provides us with 126 subnets and 16,777,216 hosts in each network. Table 11.2 shows these details for each class.

Table 11.2 *Host Information for Class-Based Schemes*

Class	Address Range	First Byte Binary/ Decimal	Number of Available Classes	Max Number of Addresses per Network
A	1.0.0.0–126.255.255.255	00000000/0	126	16,777,216
B	128.0.0.0–191.255.255.255	10000000/128	16,384	65,536
C	192.0.0.0–223.255.255.255	11000000/192	2,097,152	256
D (Multicast)	224.0.0.0–239.255.255.255	11100000/224	—	—
E (Reserved)	240.0.0.0–255.255.255.254	11110000/240	—	—

This method of addressing became regarded as inflexible for a number of reasons, the main one being that the number of addresses available for each class is fixed. This often led to address wastage, because, for example, if a company required 2,000 addresses, a class "C" address was too small, while a class "B" was too large. The result was usually to assign a class "B," which can contain over 65,000 addresses. The company would use just 2,000 of them, resulting in over 60,000 being wasted. It soon became obvious that some other method of address allocation was required.

Subnetting

The problems with address wastage led to subnetting being introduced. This allows the IP address to be split into subnets by applying a netmask to it. To accommodate this within the standard 32-bit address, the subnet details are contained in the host portion. The subnet mask is used to determine which portions of the host component are actually subnet information. The network portion of the address is never affected and so routing still works in a similar way as classful addressing.

Every "1" bit in the subnet mask is used to indicate the network portion of the address, while every "0" bit indicates the host portion. Because the original network portion of the class itself remains the same, each class will have a minimum subnet mask "value." Table 11.3 shows examples of various subnet masks across different classes.

Table 11.3 *Bit Information for Subnetting*

Class	Subnet Mask	Address Bits (b=high order n=network s=subnet h=host)
A	255.255.0.0	bnnnnnnn.ssssssss.hhhhhhhh.hhhhhhhh
A	255.255.255.240	bbnnnnnn.ssssssss.ssssssss.sssshhhh
B	255.255.252.0	bbbnnnnn.nnnnnnnn.ssssssnn.hhhhhhhh
C	255.255.255.248	bbbnnnnn.nnnnnnnn.nnnnnnnn.ssssshhh

We can also see from this that—because the subnet information "eats" into the host details—as the number of subnets increases, the number of hosts available will decrease, and vice versa. Using this information, let's look at an example of how to calculate the available hosts and subnets for an IP address:

- Class "C" IP address: 192.168.22.1
- Network address: 192.168.22.0
- Subnet mask: 255.255.255.192
- The subnet mask in binary will be: 11111.11111.11111.11000000
- The netmask will be applied as: bbbnnnnn.nnnnnnnn.nnnnnnnn.sshhhhhh

From this, we see that the last six zeros will form the host component and the preceding two bits will be the subnet. Converting the binary values to decimal leaves us with four subnets each comprising 64 host addresses. Table 11.4 shows the subnets and address ranges that would be generated using this netmask.

Table 11.4 *Address Ranges for a Subnetted Address*

Subnet Address	Address Range	Broadcast Address
192.168.22.0	192.168.22.1–192.168.22.62	192.168.22.63
192.168.22.64	192.168.22.65–192.168.22.126	192.168.22.127
192.168.22.128	192.168.22.129–192.168.22.190	192.168.22.191
192.168.22.192	192.168.22.193–192.168.22.254	192.168.22.255

Alternatively, we could have applied a netmask of 255.255.255.128 to get two subnets, each comprising 126 hosts, or a mask of 255.255.255.248 to get 32 subnets of six hosts each, and so forth.

CIDR

CIDR takes the concept of subnetting a step further. It was introduced to allow a more flexible approach to assigning addresses and is supported in Solaris 2.6 and above. Whereas subnetting can never alter the network portion of the address, CIDR removes these rules and allows users to assign a mask consisting of an arbitrary number of bits. This mask is known as either a "bit mask" or "supernet mask." CIDR addresses are displayed as "network address/bit mask," although the dotted notation is still used by many people.

For example, if we were using a class "C" address of 192.168.22.0 and we wanted to use a bit mask of 25 bits, we would indicate this by writing 192.168.22.0/25. This means that the network portion of the address comprises the first 25 bits, and the host component the last seven bits. Table 11.5 shows an example of calculating the network and host details for the previous syntax.

Table 11.5 *CIDR Address Range Calculation*

Description of Calculation	Value
Network number	192.168.22.0/25
Supernet mask (binary)	11111111.11111111.11111111.10000000
Supernet mask converted to "dot" notation	255.255.255.128
Network number converted to binary	11000000.10101000.00010110.00000000
First 25 bits of the network number	11000000.10101000.00010110.0
Last seven bits—the host component range (binary)	0000000 to 1111111
Last seven bits—the host component range (decimal)	0 to 127

This shows this subnet has an addresses range from 0 to 127—a total of 128. However, 0 refers to the network itself and 127 will be the broadcast address, so we have 126 addresses available for use: 1 through 126.

Table 11.6 shows the CIDR bitmask value for every possible address and the classful equivalent it would have.

Table 11.6 *CIDR Bitmask Values*

CIDR Bitmask Value	Dotted Notation	Max Number of Addresses	Equivalent Classful Value
/1	128.0.0.0	2,147,483,648	128 As
/2	192.0.0.0	1,073,741,824	64 As
/3	224.0.0.0	536,870,912	32 As
/4	240.0.0.0	268,435,456	16 As
/5	248.0.0.0	134,217,728	8 As
/6	252.0.0.0	67,108,864	4 As
/7	254.0.0.0	33,554,432	2 As
/8	255.0.0.0	16,777,216	Class A network
/9	255.128.0.0	8,388,608	128 Bs
/10	255.192.0.0	4,194,304	64 Bs
/11	255.224.0.0	2,097,152	32 Bs
/12	255.240.0.0	1,048,576	16 Bs
/13	255.248.0.0	525,288	8 Bs
/14	255.252.0.0	262,144	4 Bs
/15	255.254.0.0	131,072	2 Bs
/16	255.255.0.0	65,536	Class B network
/17	255.255.128.0	32,768	128 Cs
/18	255.255.192.0	16,384	64 Cs
/19	255.255.224.0	8,192	32 Cs
/20	255.255.240.0	4,096	16 Cs
/21	255.255.248.0	2,048	8 Cs
/22	255.255.252.0	1,024	4 Cs
/23	255.255.254.0	512	2 Cs
/24	255.255.255.0	256	Class C network
/25	255.255.255.128	128	$1/2$ C
/26	255.255.255.192	64	$1/4$ C

Table 11.6 *CIDR Bitmask Values (Continued)*

CIDR Bitmask Value	Dotted Notation	Max Number of Addresses	Equivalent Classful Value
/27	255.255.255.224	32	$1/8$ C
/28	255.255.255.240	16	$1/16$ C
/29	255.255.255.248	8	$1/32$ C
/30	255.255.255.252	4	$1/64$ C
/31	255.255.255.254	2	$1/128$ C
/32	255.255.255.255	1	—

Unicast, Multicast, and Broadcast Addresses

Normal TCP/IP communication is based on unicast addresses. This means data is sent from one host and directed to another host (i.e., single host-to-host traffic). For this type of communication, the assigned host address of the system would be used; for example, 192.168.22.10.

The broadcast address is derived from the host's network address, but with the host component set to all one's (for example, 192.168.22.255). Whenever data is sent to the broadcast address, all hosts on that network will receive the data.

Multicast addresses are designed to allow a group of hosts to register an interest in receiving a set of data. This means the hosts have a choice of whether to receive the data or not. It is normally controlled at the program level. For example, Network Time Protocol (NTP) has been allocated a multicast address of 224.0.1.1. This will be used by the client programs to perform time queries.

Illegal Addresses

A number of addresses cannot be assigned to a host, for various reasons. Table 11.7 shows these, along with an example of each.

Table 11.7 *Illegal Addresses*

Address Type	Examples	Reason
0.0.0.0	0.0.0.0	Used to indicate the default route
x.x.x.0	192.168.22.0	Used to signify the network address
x.x.x.255	192.168.22.255	Used for the broadcast address
255.255.255.255	255.255.255.255	Used to refer to all hosts on the local network
127.x.x.x	127.0.0.10	The loopback interface (described later)
128.0.x.x	128.0.1.1	Reserved by the Network Information Center
129.0.0.x	129.0.0.1	Reserved by the Network Information Center
191.255.x.x	191.255.1.1	Reserved by the Network Information Center
223.255.255.x	223.255.255.1	Reserved by the Network Information Center
Multicast Address	224.0.0.1	Reserved for multicast addresses
Experimental Address	240.0.0.1	Reserved for experimental use

Choosing an IP Address

Now that we know the range of addresses that are available, does it matter which one we use? Well, that depends upon how the systems are connected, as we hinted at earlier. The reason is that every system directly connected to a public network (such as the Internet) must have an individual IP address that doesn't conflict with any other. Some companies simply pick a range at random; others may use one they know belongs to someone else, safe in the knowledge that the two will never clash (always a dangerous practice!).

Both these methods are fine in theory, but problems can occur if, for example, someone connects the system and forgets to alter its address. Another method is to use a "reserved" address.

Reserved Addresses

A number of addresses have been reserved for use in private networks where the systems will not be directly connected to an external network. However, they do carry some restrictions; for example, any routers that receive packets from one should reject them without producing errors and shouldn't propagate the private address information around the network. This ensures that anyone can use these, safe in the knowledge that should a system be accidentally connected to a public network, it won't cause any problems to anyone else.

The reserved addresses are shown in Table 11.8 and are displayed in CIDR format. The recommended method for choosing an address range to use is to simply select one at random.

Table 11.8 *Reserved Addresses for Private Networks*

Address	Equivalent Class	Number of Subnets	Address Range	Max Number of Available Addresses
10.0.0.0/8	A	1	10.0.0.0–10.255.255.255	16,777,214
172.16.0.0/12	B	16	172.16.0.0–172.31.255.255	1,048,574
192.168.0.0/16	C	256	192.168.0.0–192.168.255.255	65,534

Our Values

We have already said that our system will not be connected to a public network (at least, not for the next few chapters!), so we'll use an address reserved for private networks. Figure 11.1 shows an overview of what we are trying to achieve.

We are using a small number of machines, less than 20, so we only require a minimal number of addresses and subnets. As we stated earlier, we have decided to split the system into two subnets; the internal systems on one, and the external facing systems on the other. To make it easy for us to identify them, we will allocate the internal systems a host address between 1 and 49, and the external systems one between 50 and 99.

If we apply a supernet mask of 255.255.255.128, which is a 25-bit mask in CIDR notation, we get a subnet of 126 usable addresses, which is ample for our needs. These are shown in Table 11.9.

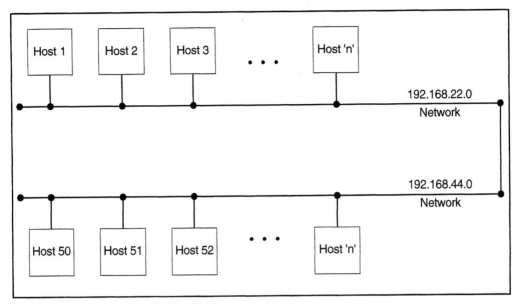

Figure 11.1 *The network design.*

Table 11.9 *Our Address Range*

Network Description	Network Address	Number of Usable Addresses	Address Range	Supernet Mask	Broadcast Address
Internal Systems	192.168.22.0/25	126	192.168.22.1–192.168.22.126	255.255.255.128	192.168.22.127
External Systems	192.168.44.0/25	126	192.168.44.1–192.168.44.126	255.255.255.128	192.168.44.127

From this table we can see we have defined two subnets. By applying the specified supernet mask to the correct network address, we have generated a list of systems with a range of 126 addresses. Our systems will use a sequential host address, the internal ones starting from 1 and the external ones starting from 50. By combining these with the correct network address we will generate the following set of usable addresses:

- 192.168.22.1 to 192.168.22.49 inclusive for the internal systems
- 192.168.44.50 to 192.168.44.99 inclusive for the external systems

Now we have a good indication of a system's role by knowing either its network address or its host address.

Naming Systems

Each system (or network interface, to be correct) is assigned a name and, if connected to the network, an IP address. The kernel uses the address for communication but allows us to use names, as they are generally much easier to remember than batches of numbers. It also carries out any tasks that are required to map between the hostname and the IP address using something known as a "Name Service."

Network Information Service (NIS), NIS+, Domain Name System (DNS), Lightweight Directory Access Protocol (LDAP), and "local files" are all well-known examples of naming services. We needn't be concerned with how they work or what the differences are at the moment, since we will cover this in later chapters. Suffice it to say that at present we are using "local files," which, as the name implies, are where the host information is stored in a local file—*/etc/inet/hosts* (*/etc/hosts* is a link to */etc/inet/hosts*, so use whichever you feel more familiar with). As the files are local to each machine, any changes made to one system need to be propagated onto the remaining ones.

Host Names

How do we decide on a name for each system? Again, this is site-specific and may depend on the numbers of machines in use. Often, administrators will try and use a "set" of something, be it a list of their favorite football teams or the names of Snow White's dwarfs (obviously not much use if you have, or are likely to have, more than seven machines!).

We have chosen to base our names on the periodic table of elements. This probably seems like an awkward thing to do (considering the names of some of the elements), but we hope it will help as we progress throughout the book for the following reasons:

- The host addresses will match the atomic number. For example, hydrogen will be 1, helium 2, lithium 3, and so on.

- Each system is allowed a number of names—its host name and a number of aliases. We will use the element name as the primary host name, and the chemical symbol as its first alias. For example, hydrogen will have an alias of "h" and helium will have an alias of "he." This will allow us to use the alias to easily indicate the particular host in the illustrations throughout the book where space is at a premium!

- This method will be fine for a network of systems of around 100 systems, and although the names can get quite complicated the aliases are very easy to use.

Using this information, we have generated the *hosts* file shown below and will use this as our current master copy:

```
hydrogen# cat /etc/inet/hosts
127.0.0.1          localhost     loghost
#
# Main servers and clients on subnet 192.168.22.0
# Supernet mask: 255.255.255.128
#
192.168.22.1        hydrogen      h
192.168.22.2        helium        he
192.168.22.3        lithium       li
192.168.22.4        beryllium     be
192.168.22.5        boron         b
192.168.22.6        carbon        c
192.168.22.7        nitrogen      n
192.168.22.8        oxygen        o
192.168.22.9        flourine      f
192.168.22.10       neon          ne
#
# Gateway machine with two interfaces
# Supernet mask: 255.255.255.128
#
192.168.22.49       indium        in
192.168.44.50       tin           sn
#
# External facing servers on subnet 192.168.44.0
# Supernet mask: 255.255.255.128
#
192.168.44.51       antimony      sb
192.168.44.52       tellurium     te
192.168.44.53       iodine        i
192.168.44.54       xenon         xe
hydrogen#
```

Loopback Interface

All systems have a "loopback" interface, regardless of whether they are connected to the network or not. This is not a true network interface, but acts as one to allow some network-aware programs (such as RPC) to be able to connect to both the remote and local host in the same way.

We don't need to be concerned with configuring it, as this is performed by the operating system, but we do need to make certain that the local host address remains in the host file. We can display the current loopback settings using `ifconfig`:

```
hydrogen# ifconfig lo0
lo0: flags=849<UP,LOOPBACK,RUNNING,MULTICAST> mtu 8232
        inet 127.0.0.1 netmask ff000000
hydrogen#
```

We can see that this has a netmask of 255.0.0.0 (FF000000 in hex), as we would expect from a class "A" address. The address should be defined as 127.0.0.1 on every host.

Initial Network Testing

Because the loopback interface responds to all network commands in the same way as a remote host, it can be used to provide limited network testing, such as checking that the correct commands are installed and that all the required drivers are loaded. Because of this, it also provides a useful way of fault-finding network problems by providing another interface to test.

For example, the interface will respond to ping, and its statistics can be displayed using netstat:

```
hydrogen# ping localhost
localhost is alive
hydrogen#
```

The network is "alive," so let's see how fast it appears to be or whether we are seeing any problems, such as packet loss:

```
hydrogen# ping -s localhost 64 5
PING localhost: 64 data bytes
72 bytes from localhost (127.0.0.1): icmp_seq=0. time=0. ms
72 bytes from localhost (127.0.0.1): icmp_seq=1. time=0. ms
72 bytes from localhost (127.0.0.1): icmp_seq=2. time=0. ms
72 bytes from localhost (127.0.0.1): icmp_seq=3. time=0. ms
72 bytes from localhost (127.0.0.1): icmp_seq=4. time=0. ms

----localhost PING Statistics----
5 packets transmitted, 5 packets received, 0% packet loss
round-trip (ms)  min/avg/max = 0/0/0
hydrogen#
```

We see zero packet loss. The time taken to send and receive the packet is also reported as zero, which is exactly what we would expect as we are bypassing any physical network connections. To confirm the validity of the connection, we can use netstat to show that we have not had any packet errors or network collisions:

```
hydrogen# netstat -i -I lo0
Name  Mtu  Net/Dest  Address  Ipkts Ierrs Opkts Oerrs Collis Queue
lo0   8232 loopback  localhost 524 0     524   0     0      0
hydrogen#
```

Configuring the Interface

Now that we have all the information we need, we can go ahead and configure the connection. We will do this two ways: dynamically and statically. Dynamically allows us to configure an interface while the machine is still running and is a task that is often carried out, but it will lose the settings at the next reboot. The static configuration requires a reboot before the changes will be activated, but ensures that the system retains the information across reboots.

Dynamic Configuration

Our systems have "hme" interfaces installed (these are 100 Mb per second Fast Ethernet network cards). It is the first, and only, instance on our system, and up to now hasn't been configured. We know this because `ifconfig` only reports the loopback interface:

```
hydrogen# ifconfig -a
lo0: flags=849<UP,LOOPBACK,RUNNING,MULTICAST> mtu 8232
        inet 127.0.0.1 netmask ff000000
hydrogen#
```

The next task is to create all the necessary connections for the "hme" device itself; this includes loading any streams drivers, opening the device itself, and informing the kernel that the network card is physically available:

```
hydrogen# ifconfig hme0 plumb
hydrogen# ifconfig -a
lo0: flags=849<UP,LOOPBACK,RUNNING,MULTICAST> mtu 8232
        inet 127.0.0.1 netmask ff000000
hme0: flags=842<BROADCAST,RUNNING,MULTICAST> mtu 1500
        inet 0.0.0.0 netmask 0
        ether 8:0:20:aa:bb:cc
hydrogen#
```

We now have an instance of "hme0" available, but by comparing its settings with that of the loopback interface, we can see that we are missing some values such as a valid IP address and netmask setting. The flags value also shows the interface is currently disabled (not "UP").

Adding the missing values and activating it can all be performed in the same step if we wish, as shown here:

```
hydrogen# ifconfig hme0 inet 192.168.22.1 netmask
255.255.255.128 up
hydrogen# ifconfig -a
lo0: flags=849<UP,LOOPBACK,RUNNING,MULTICAST> mtu 8232
        inet 127.0.0.1 netmask ff000000
hme0: flags=863<UP,BROADCAST,RUNNING,MULTICAST> mtu 1500
        inet 192.168.22.1 netmask ffffff80 broadcast
192.168.22.127
        ether 8:0:20:aa:bb:cc
hydrogen#
```

`Ifconfig` shows we have correctly started our interface. Since this is still the only machine we have connected on the network (assuming it is plugged in correctly!), the only thing we can do is to check it in a similar way to the loopback interface:

```
hydrogen# ping hydrogen
hydrogen is alive
hydrogen#
```

Success! We can see our own network connection. Again, netstat will confirm that packets are being sent and received:

```
hydrogen# netstat -in
Name  Mtu   Net/Dest     Address      Ipkts Ierrs Opkts Oerrs Collis Queue
lo0   8232  127.0.0.0    127.0.0.1    524   0     524   0     0      0
hme0  1500  192.168.22.0 192.168.22.1 4     0     4     0     0      0
hydrogen#
```

Permanent Changes

Now that the interface is up and running, we need to make sure it stays that way whenever the system reboots. This is actually quite a simple task, as all we need to do is to create or update two files: one that informs the system of which address to set, and a second to inform it of the netmask to apply. The first file is named after the interface type and the instance number, which in our case is */etc/hostname.hme0*. It contains the following information:

```
hydrogen# cat /etc/hostname.hme0
hydrogen
hydrogen#
```

This example uses the hostname, but it can contain an IP address instead. If the hostname is used, there must be a valid address for it in whichever name service is being used—in our case the local *hosts* file—otherwise the system will not be able to determine the correct address to apply.

The second file is */etc/inet/netmasks*. Ours now contains the following information:

```
hydrogen# cat /etc/inet/netmasks
192.168.22.0    255.255.255.128
hydrogen#
```

To check that the settings are correct, update the files, reboot the system, and when it comes back see that ifconfig shows the interface correctly and we can ping ourselves again.

The Rest of the Subnet

At this point, we'll connect another system and check that the two can communicate. This should actually be carried out on all systems that need to communicate with each other, at the time they are connected.

We will configure and check helium next, but this time we'll skip the dynamic settings and simply create or update the necessary files then reboot. After modification, the files contain the following information:

```
helium# grep helium /etc/inet/hosts
192.168.22.2    helium    he
helium#
```

```
helium# cat /etc/hostname.hme0
helium
helium#

helium# cat /etc/inet/netmasks
192.168.22.0   255.255.255.128
helium#
```

Now reboot the system, and when it comes back up check that helium can be seen OK:

```
helium# ping helium
helium is alive
helium#
```

We can see we are alive, so let's try and see hydrogen across the network. We haven't got an entry for it in the *hosts* file yet, so we'll ping its IP address:

```
helium# ping 192.168.22.1
192.168.22.1 is alive
helium#
```

Great! We can see the whole of the network (or the two machines we have connected), so check that the *hosts* file contains all the systems we showed in "Host Names" on page 258. We now have details of every machine ready for when they are connected, and we won't have to update the file a number of times. Now we will add the remaining machines onto the 192.168.22.0 network, apart from the gateway machine, which we'll come to in a minute.

The list below shows the machines to add. The tasks to perform will be very similar to those required to connect hydrogen and helium:

- lithium (192.168.22.3)
- beryllium (192.168.22.4)
- boron (192.168.22.5)
- carbon (192.168.22.6)
- nitrogen (192.168.22.7)
- oxygen (192.168.22.8)
- fluorine (192.168.22.9)
- neon (192.168.22.10)

Taking a look at what we have achieved so far, we have physically connected all the systems that are part of the same subnet to the physical network, and each system can see each other (we hope!). This provides us with a series of connections as shown in Figure 11.2.

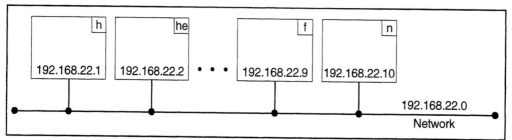

Figure 11.2 *The 192.168.22.0 network.*

Routing

We have managed to communicate between two machines connected on our network, but how did helium know where to send and receive information about hydrogen? The answer lies in a mechanism named "routing."

The kernel maintains a structure known as a "routing table." This contains information about where packets need to be sent, or routed, to get to their destination. We can view the routing table with `netstat`:

```
hydrogen# netstat -rn
Routing Table:
   Destination        Gateway          Flags   Ref    Use    Interface
-----------------  -----------------  -----  -----  ------  ---------
192.168.22.0       192.168.22.1       U        3      5     hme0
127.0.0.1          127.0.0.1          UH       0      2     lo0
hydrogen#
```

This shows us that any packets destined for the 192.168.22.0 network will be routed through a gateway with an IP address of 192.168.22.1 (i.e., the network interface that we defined earlier). It also shows that the loopback interface is routed, again through itself.

This is a fairly simple implementation of a routing table, but we will see how it can be expanded later.

Connecting the Second Subnet

The next stage is to connect the external facing servers that we chose to put onto a different subnet (192.168.44.0). We are assuming at this point that they only have a standard operating system installed; that is, they haven't been configured for the tasks they will perform. This will be carried out in later chapters.

After the systems have been added, we will have a network configuration that looks very similar to the 192.168.22.0 network. In fact, each system will be able to see everything else on this network, exactly as we saw after connecting the 192.168.22.0 systems.

We won't describe each machine's configuration files in detail; instead, in the best traditions of computer textbooks, we will leave that as an exercise for the reader! As a guide, we need to create or update the following files as we did previously:

- */etc/inet/hosts*
- */etc/hostname.hme0*
- */etc/inet/netmasks*

If we check the routing table on one of the systems, say antimony, we will see similar results to the systems on the internal network, in that they route via their own interface to send data to the network they are connected to:

```
antimony# netstat -rn
Routing Table:
   Destination       Gateway         Flags  Ref   Use   Interface
---------------- ---------------- ----- ----- ------ ---------
192.168.44.0     192.168.44.51    U       3     5   hme0
127.0.0.1        127.0.0.1        UH      0     2   lo0
antimony#
```

Adding the Gateway

We now have two networks: 192.168.22.0 and 192.168.44.0. Both contain a number of systems, each of which can communicate with every other system that is connected to their own network. However, they cannot see anything that is connected to the "other" network.

```
hydrogen# ping antimony
ICMP Net Unreachable from gateway hydrogen (192.168.22.1)
  for icmp unreachable from hydrogen (192.168.22.1) to
192.168.44.51
no answer from 192.168.44.51
hydrogen#
```

To enable this to work, we will use a gateway machine that is physically connected to both networks. This means it must have two network connections—one for each subnet. The machine we are using has two "hme" cards installed, so we'll go ahead and configure these next. After the tasks have been carried out, the network will be configured as shown in Figure 11.3.

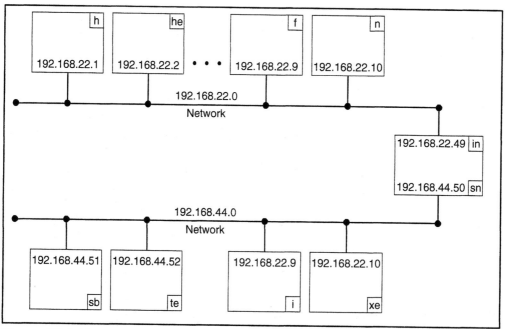

Figure 11.3 *The completed network, including the gateway.*

Each interface needs to be assigned an IP address. We have decided to connect the primary interface, "hme0," to the internal network (192.168.22.0), and the second interface, "hme1," to the external facing network (192.168.44.0). From the *hosts* file we built earlier, the following addresses were defined:

```
indium# more /etc/hosts
<lines removed for clarity>
#
# Gateway machine with two interfaces
# Supernet mask: 255.255.255.128
#
192.168.22.49    indium    in
192.168.44.50    tin       sn
<lines removed for clarity>
indium#
```

We have updated the files shown below to assign the correct IP address to the relevant interface:

```
indium# cat /etc/hostname.hme0
indium
indium#


indium# cat /etc/hostname.hme1
tin
indium#
```

```
indium# cat /etc/inet/netmasks
192.168.22.0    255.255.255.128
192.168.44.0    255.255.255.128
indium#
```

As an aside, we can see from the shell prompt that the machine is called "indium," rather than "tin." It gets this information from another file named /etc/nodename. If we check its contents we'll see it contains the information below. It doesn't matter which interface is the "primary" and which is the "secondary":

```
indium# cat /etc/nodename
indium
indium#
```

After rebooting the system, we will see both interfaces will be enabled, and the system will, by default, act as a router between the two subnets.

```
indium# ifconfig -a
lo0: flags=849<UP,LOOPBACK,RUNNING,MULTICAST> mtu 8232
        inet 127.0.0.1 netmask ff000000
hme0: flags=863<UP,BROADCAST,RUNNING,MULTICAST> mtu 1500
        inet 192.168.22.49 netmask ffffff80 broadcast
192.168.22.127
        ether 8:0:20:dd:56:32
hme1: flags=863<UP,BROADCAST,RUNNING,MULTICAST> mtu 1500
        inet 192.168.44.50 netmask ffffff80 broadcast
192.168.44.127
        ether 8:0:20:dd:56:32
indium#
```

We can see from the output below that packets to the subnets are sent through the interface that is connected to the particular network:

```
indium# netstat -rn
Routing Table:
  Destination       Gateway           Flags  Ref   Use   Interface
---------------   -----------------   -----  ----- -----  ---------
192.168.22.0      192.168.22.49       U      3     5      hme0
192.168.44.0      192.168.44.50       U      3     5      hme1
127.0.0.1         127.0.0.1           UH     0     2      lo0
indium#
```

For routing to work successfully, each machine needs a route to a host, and the host needs to have a route back. The gateway works fine because it has a network connection on each subnet, so each host it pings can acknowledge via its own subnet. This means that indium can now see every machine on both networks:

```
indium# ping hydrogen
hydrogen is alive
indium#
```

```
indium# ping antimony
antimony is alive
indium#
```

Routing—A Second Look

While we are talking about the gateway machine, it is an ideal time to take a further look at the intricacies of routing using Solaris.

Routes are added to the routing table either statically or dynamically. Static ones are added by the system administrator, using the `route` command, which we will do later. Dynamic ones rely on a process maintaining the routing table on our behalf.

The main protocols supported by Solaris are Router Information Protocol (RIP) and Router Discovery (RDISC).

Normally, when a multi-interface machine boots, RDISC and RIP will be started by the programs `/usr/sbin/in.rdisc` and `/usr/sbin/in.routed`, respectively. They discover all the available routes and advertise these around the network. At the same time, any single-interface systems will be listening for the advertised routes. From here, both systems will build the routing table automatically. Similarly, if any routes need to be altered (for example, if a router fails and a different route then becomes the valid one), the new routes would be re-advertised and the routing table will be rebuilt accordingly.

The second important part of this process is that IP forwarding is enabled by default on multi-interface systems. We'll see later in the section "Address Resolution" on page 271 how each interface contains the same Ethernet address, and that this is used to direct packets to a machine.

Enabling IP forwarding means that if an interface receives a packet with the correct Ethernet address, but an IP address that matches the other network, it will simply forward the packet onto the correct interface.

We can check that this is enabled using a command named `ndd`:

```
indium# ndd -get /dev/ip ip_forwarding
1
indium#
```

As with anything else, there are advantages and disadvantages to running RDISC/RIP. Some advantages are that the system administrator doesn't have to be concerned with ensuring that the routing table is up-to-date or whether a router fails since the routes will be maintained dynamically. Disadvantages are that `in.rdisc` is a potential security risk, and it can take a large amount of processing power from the server.

The decision as to whether to run it is again a site-specific choice. As a general rule of thumb, if your network is small, doesn't have a complex layout, and is unlikely to change often, there is no real need for dynamic routing. On the other hand, if you have a complex network where routers are often changing (or failing!), it will probably be worthwhile running it.

Our network is the former—small and unlikely to change often—so we will disable RDISC/RIP and add any routes we require manually.

Disabling Router Discovery

So, we know we don't want to enable router discovery, but how do we disable it? There are a number of different ways to do this. Let's look at some alternatives below.

Creating a Default Router File

The routing tables can contain an entry known as a "default route." As this suggests, it is the route taken by any packet that isn't destined for any other routes in the table. This is often used to connect to the outside world; in fact, we will use this ourselves in Chapter 13, "Connecting to the Internet." For this to work, the hostname or the IP address of the host is placed in a file named */etc/defaultrouter*. When the system boots, it will set up the default route and stop both RDISC/RIP from been activated.

Telling the System It Isn't a Router

There are many reasons why a multi-interface machine should not forward packets across its network interfaces, often security related. To stop this from occurring, an empty file named */etc/notrouter* is created. After the machine has been booted, `ndd` will show that IP forwarding has been disabled. Although we need this for our setup, the steps to carry this out would be as follows. After this task, the machine will be classed as a multihomed system; that is, a machine with multiple interfaces that doesn't forward packets between any networks it has configured.

```
indium# touch /etc/notrouter
<reboot the system>
indium# ndd -get /dev/ip ip_forwarding
0
indium#
```

Stopping the Binaries from Running

If the system doesn't have a *defaultrouter* file set, but the system administrator still wants to use static routes, the best method for disabling RDISC/RIP is to rename the binaries as shown below so that they won't be started by any of the start-up scripts:

```
indium# mv /usr/sbin/in.rdisc /usr/sbin/in.rdisc.disabled
indium# mv /usr/sbin/in.routed /usr/sbin/in.routed.disabled
indium#
```

Which Method Should We Use?

We'll use the last method—renaming the binaries—to stop RDISC/RIP from running. The reason for this is that we aren't ready to create the *defaultrouter* file at this point in the system build, since we will use this when we connect to the Internet later in the book.

We said earlier that we will disable RDISC/RIP on the whole network. So, we'll run these commands on all the systems to ensure that we have a consistent setup, and add the change to our list of customization scripts that we'll build later.

Manually Adding Static Routes

First we'll add the routes manually until we are happy that they are correct, then we'll update the system files to ensure that this route is added every time the system boots. To achieve the correct results, we need to add a route from one network to the other on all the machines. Each network will connect to the other through the interface on indium.

This means that all the systems connected to the 192.168.22.0 network will need the following route added:

```
hydrogen# route add net 192.168.44.0 indium 0
hydrogen#
```

While on all the systems connected to the 192.168.44.0 network, we'll add the following route:

```
antimony# route add net 192.168.22.0 tin 0
antimony#
```

After the route has been added, checking the routing table on (in this case) hydrogen should show something similar to that shown below:

```
hydrogen# netstat -rn
Routing Table:
  Destination       Gateway          Flags  Ref   Use    Interface
---------------- ---------------- ----- ----- ------ ---------
192.168.22.0      192.168.22.1     U      3     5   hme0
192.168.44.0      192.168.44.49    U      3     5   hme0
127.0.0.1         127.0.0.1        UH     0     2   lo0
hydrogen#
```

While on antimony, the routing table would be as follows:

```
antimony# netstat -rn
Routing Table:
  Destination       Gateway          Flags  Ref   Use    Interface
---------------- ---------------- ----- ----- ------ ---------
192.168.22.0      192.168.22.50    U      3     5   hme0
192.168.44.0      192.168.44.51    U      3     5   hme0
127.0.0.1         127.0.0.1        UH     0     2   lo0
antimony#
```

Now we can check that each subnet is visible from the other. We should be able to see, for example, hydrogen from antimony:

```
hydrogen# ping antimony
antimony is alive
hydrogen#
```

Again, we need to make the routes permanent across reboots. We could incorporate our changes into one of the standard networking start-up files, but we want to make sure the changes remain if we upgrade the operating system. The best way to do this is to create a specific start file in */etc/init.d*, and then a link to this from */etc/rc2.d*. The file below shows the one we have created for the 192.168.22.0 network:

```
hydrogen# cat /etc/init.d/routes
#!/bin/sh
#
# Create the required route to access 192.168.22.0 net
#
route add net 192.168.22.0 192.168.22.50 0
hydrogen# ln /etc/init.d/routes /etc/rc2.d/S99routes
hydrogen#
```

The files for the 192.168.44.0-networked systems will also be very similar, but instead will contain the route information that we added above. Again, these start-up scripts will become part of our standard customization build.

Address Resolution

Up to now, we've assumed that once we know the IP address of a machine, we can pass data to it. Unfortunately, that's not quite true. To explain why, let's look at the hardware in a little more detail.

Every machine in the world capable of being connected to a network is assigned a unique number, which is normally burnt onto a chip when the machine is built. Sometimes, as in the case of a Sun, it may be on the main machine motherboard, while at other times it may be built into a third-party network card. This number is known by a variety of names—the Ethernet address, the hardware address, or the Media Access Control (MAC) address.

An address is a 48-bit number usually written as six colon-separated hex bytes. Each manufacturer is assigned a particular range of numbers and left to assign the remainder as required. For example, Sun has been assigned "8:0:20." An example MAC address on a Sun system would be as follows:

```
8:0:20:aa:bb:cc
```

It is this address that actually receives the packets, which means we need some way of mapping a system's IP address to its MAC address. To do this, we use a mechanism known as the Address Resolution Protocol (ARP).

Determining the MAC Address

It's very useful to know the MAC address of a system, as it often helps when trying to troubleshoot network connectivity. For example, a common error is duplicating the IP address of a machine. When they are both connected to the network, an error message along the lines of "Duplicate IP address from 8:0:20:1:2:3" would be seen. Knowing the MAC addresses of the systems would allow us to pinpoint the offending machine.

There are various ways to find this out. One is to check the `banner` message when the system is powered on, which may look similar to that shown below:

```
Sun Ultra 5/10 UPA/PCI (UltraSPARC 440MHz), Keyboard Present
OpenBoot 3.25, 1024 MB memory installed, Serial #1234567
Ethernet address 8:0:20:aa:bb:cc, Host ID: 807014ac.
```

Another is to run `ifconfig`, as shown below:

```
hydrogen# ifconfig hme0
hme0: flags=863<UP,BROADCAST,RUNNING,MULTICAST> mtu 1500
        inet 192.168.22.1 netmask ffffff80 broadcast
192.168.22.127
        ether 8:0:20:aa:bb:cc
hydrogen#
```

A third method is to check the ARP table—this is the cache used by ARP to maintain its IP address to MAC address mappings:

```
hydrogen# arp -a
Net to Media Table
Device   IP Address              Mask         Flags  Phys Addr
------  --------------------  -------------  -----  ----------------
hme0    hydrogen 255.255.255.255      8:0:20:aa:bb:cc
hme0    indium   255.255.255.255      8:0:20:dd:56:32
hme1    indium   255.255.255.255      8:0:20:dd:56:32
<lines removed for clarity>
hydrogen#
```

Multiple Network Cards

We can see from the `arp` output, and also the earlier output from `ifconfig`, that both network cards configured for indium report the same MAC address. This is because it is burnt into the main system, rather than onto the card itself.

Sometimes this can cause problems, such as dropped packets, when communicating with other devices. Even if everything is working OK, some administrators prefer to have a different MAC address for every network interface. This is quite easy to do; we can simply reset it using `ifconfig`, as shown below:

```
indium# ifconfig hme1 ether 1:2:3:dd:56:32
indium# ifconfig -a
lo0: flags=849<UP,LOOPBACK,RUNNING,MULTICAST> mtu 8232
        inet 127.0.0.1 netmask ff000000
hme0: flags=863<UP,BROADCAST,RUNNING,MULTICAST> mtu 1500
        inet 192.168.22.49 netmask ffffff80 broadcast
192.168.22.127
        ether 8:0:20:dd:56:32
hme1: flags=863<UP,BROADCAST,RUNNING,MULTICAST> mtu 1500
        inet 192.168.44.50 netmask ffffff80 broadcast
192.168.44.127
        ether 1:2:3:dd:56:32
indium#
```

Choosing the correct value to use is the biggest problem here. If you only use Sun equipment, then the choice is easier since all your MAC addresses should begin with "8:0:20." Some sites even choose the address of a company whose kit they know they will never use!

Deleting Table Entries

The entries in the ARP cache are deleted after a period of time, but sometimes this may not be soon enough. For example, if a faulty system is swapped for another, but the original IP address is assigned to the new system, then the ARP cache will still contain the original MAC address. This means that data will be trying to locate the original MAC address instead of the new one. In this case, the best procedure would be to delete the entry from the cache and let ARP relocate the new machine. We could do this as shown below:

```
hydrogen# arp hydrogen
hme0    hydrogen 255.255.255.255        8:0:20:aa:bb:cc
hydrogen# arp -d hydrogen
hydrogen (192.168.22.1) deleted
hydrogen# ping hydrogen
hydrogen is alive
hydrogen# arp hydrogen
hme0    hydrogen 255.255.255.255        8:0:20:dd:ee:ff
hydrogen#
```

Reverse Address Resolution

Another protocol very similar to ARP is the Reverse Address Resolution Protocol (RARP). The main difference is that RARP works in the opposite direction—when it receives a MAC address it determines the correct IP address.

This mechanism is commonly used by machines configured to boot across the network (diskless clients, for example). One of their first tasks is to send broadcast RARP requests out to the network, which say something like "My Ethernet address is 8:0:20:aa:bb:cc; can someone tell me what my IP address is?" A machine configured as a RARP server would respond with the correct IP address, and the machine uses that to continue its boot process.

Whereas ARP will determine the mappings itself, RARP has to be provided with the correct information. We do this by creating a file named /etc/ ethers, which could look similar to the one below:

```
hydrogen# cat /etc/ethers
8:0:20:aa:bb:cc hydrogen
8:0:20:dd:56:32 indium     # for info - hme0
1:2:3:dd:56:32  tin        # for info - hme1
hydrogen#
```

The RARP server, in.rarpd, will start automatically at boot-time once it detects a valid *ethers* file.

IPV6—The Next Generation

While IP Version 6 (IPV6) is really beyond the scope of this book, this section will provide a very brief glimpse into what it is and one of the main driving forces behind its creation—the pending lack of available IP addresses.

All the IP addresses we have used up to now have been based on a 32-bit value, separated into four eight-bit fields. These are known as IP Version 4 (IPV4) addresses. One of the limitations we have with this protocol is that we only have around four billion addresses available (even less when we take network and broadcast addresses into account).

Nowadays, many more computers are being connected to the Internet than were first expected, each of them requiring an IP address. Coupled with this, many other types of hardware, such as microwaves, toasters and cars, are being assigned addresses and connected to networks in a way that the designers of IP could not have imagined.

It became obvious a few years ago that soon we would run out of IP addresses. To get around this problem, the next generation of the IP protocol was designed. This is known as IPV6 and is based on 128 bits, which allows a theoretical maximum of 340,282,366,920,938,463,463,374,607,431,768,211,456 addresses to be defined. Obviously this is quite a lot, which hopefully means we shouldn't run out in the near future!

IPV6 Addresses

An IPV6 address will generally be shown as a group of hexadecimal values, rather than the numbers we are familiar with. The separator between the groups has also altered, and is now shown as a colon (:) rather than the familiar dot (.). For example, our current 32-bit address for hydrogen (192.168.1.2) may become something like the following:

```
192.168.1.123.54.68.168.98.234.12.54.29.12.56.113.1
```

—whereas a typical IPV6 address may look like the following:

```
A00E:0023:0000:0000:0000:0083:125C:ABCD
```

Fortunately, the designers have recognized that this is still a bit of a mouthful, so there are a few shortcuts that we can use. First, we can drop any preceding zeros, and secondly, we can replace a 16-bit zero value number with a double colon. This means that the above address may now be written as follows:

```
A00E:23::83:125C:ABCD
```

Solaris uses a file named *|etc|hostname6.<interface name>* to provide address details for the interface. IPV6 includes autodiscovery within its standards, which means that an interface can determine its own IP address simply by querying its local router. This is the norm. Assuming the interface card is an "hme" type, this means that all that's required to set the simplest (default) address is to create an empty *|etc|hostname6.hme0* file.

Once set, `ifconfig` will report the interface and show something similar to the following:

```
hydrogen# ifconfig -a
<lines removed for clarity>
hfe0: flags=2000841<UP,RUNNING,MULTICAST,IPv6> mtu 1500 index 2
        ether 8:0:20:aa:bb:cc
        inet6 fe80::203:baff:fe08:ad6f/10
hydrogen#
```

Using `ping` to test the interface would produce something similar to the following:

```
hydrogen# ping -A inet6 fe80::203:baff:fe08:ad6f
fe80::203:baff:fe08:ad6f is alive
hydrogen#
```

Traceroute

From Solaris 2.7 onwards, `traceroute` is included with the operating system. This allows us to look at the routes that packets have followed, which is a very useful tool for detecting network problems. Running `traceroute` on hydrogen to check the route to antimony would show the following results:

```
hydrogen# traceroute antimony
traceroute to antimony (192.168.44.51), 30 hops max, 40 byte
packets
    1  indium (192.168.22.49)  1.516 ms  1.283 ms  1.362 ms
    2  antimony (192.168.44.51)  2.277 ms  1.773 ms  2.186 ms
hydrogen#
```

This correctly shows that we are going through the gateway machine to get to the "other" network. Since we have a pretty simple network configuration, running `traceroute` at this point really only provides a good source of timing information. It will be more useful as we progress through the chapters and create a more complex network.

Conclusion

We have now connected two subnets and managed to configure the gateway machine that will provide communication between the two networks. We have set up the necessary files and checked the network to ensure that the packets are being routed correctly.

12

NAMING SERVICES AND NIS

Objectives

In this chapter, we'll look at what naming services are, and work through configuring one in particular—Network Information Service (NIS). To do this we'll build both servers and clients for the machines that are connected to our network.

Naming Services

Before we start to look at what NIS is and how to configure it, we need to take a minute to explain what naming services are and how the two are related.

Certain administrative information is frequently used by Solaris machines, such as user names and passwords, hostnames and IP addresses, printer names, and so forth. This information can be held locally by each node in its own local files. It may ease adminstration, and save disk space, if all this commonly used information could be held centrally, on one machine, rather than duplicating it on many. A naming service gives us the ability to do precisely this.

There are a number of different naming services available on Solaris, with each having their own advantages and disadvantages. The more commonly used ones are NIS, NIS+, Domain Name System (DNS), Lightweight Directory Access Protocol (LDAP), and "local files." All these are briefly described below.

Local Files

The important point we need to make about the "local files" naming service is that, while it is commonly referred to as a naming service (we'll also follow that convention here), it doesn't possess the benefits of one; that is, a centralized "database" of easy-to-access information. It's really a fallback mechanism used whenever a naming service is *not* required.

"Local files" were the original method of storing configuration information before naming services were available, each machine holding its own administrative files in its own */etc* directory. However, "local files" are the simplest type of service to set up and understand and, because of this, they are still commonly used.

NIS

NIS provides a way of centralizing administration by keeping one central copy of every machine's administrative data on a master server. Slave servers can be configured to prevent the master from handling all the traffic, but essentially it is a flat single domain with one master. It can, however, be configured to hold almost any administrative data needed, as we'll see later in the chapter.

DNS

DNS is used to provide a mapping between hostnames and their IP addresses (it can also store some closely related information). Whereas NIS only uses a single domain, DNS allows multiple hierarchical domains.

NIS+

NIS+ attempts to bring the advantages of DNS and NIS together. Doing this allows the information stored within NIS to be more easily managed by replicating the hierarchical structure of an organization. The downside of this, however, is that it is proprietary software that has limited support outside of Solaris.

LDAP

LDAP uses a tree-like structure, known as the Directory Information Tree (DIT), to store its data. It is similar to NIS+, but is available on both UNIX and non-UNIX machines and is not proprietary.

Why Use Them?

We've already mentioned that "local files" can be used instead of a naming service if you prefer—they are easy to set up, so why have all the problems of configuring something else?

"Local files" can work fine when a small number of machines are involved. But as the number connected to the network increases, it becomes harder to be certain that they all have the correct revisions of the important administration files, and that they are all synchronized with each other. Up to this point, we have managed to work around these sorts of problems by manually copying any updated files around the system. For us, this isn't a problem since we only have a few machines on the network and so it isn't a very time-consuming task—we could even write a small script to do it for us if we wished. Eventually, however, the system will reach the point where it is impossible to manage, and using a name service becomes a necessity rather than an option.

With this in mind, over the next few chapters we will look at a few common naming services: NIS and DNS. We'll configure both these on our machines, using NIS for the local network, covered in this chapter, and DNS for connections to the Internet, which is covered in Chapter 16, "Configuring DNS."

Name Service Switch File

This is called */etc/nsswitch.conf,* and is used to control which name service will be used to access a particular type of data. We've briefly come across it in some other chapters, but we'll take a closer look at it here.

If we look at the file we're using for our currently configured name service—"local files"—we would see something similar to that shown below:

```
tin# cat /etc/nsswitch.conf
#
# An example file that could be copied over to
# /etc/nsswitch.conf; it does not use any naming service.
#
passwd:          files
group:           files
hosts:           files
ipnodes:         files
networks:        files
protocols:       files
rpc:             files
ethers:          files
netmasks:        files
bootparams:      files
publickey:       files
netgroup:        files
automount:       files
aliases:         files
services:        files
sendmailvars:    files
printers:        user files

auth_attr:       files
prof_attr:       files
project:         files
tin#
```

This shows that each entry consists of the name of an administration file along with a list of sources that should be used to locate the required data. The sources are essentially the name service entries, but also include additional methods. Table 12.1 provides us with the list of the available keywords that can be used.

Table 12.1 *Nsswitch.conf Sources*

Name Service	Description
Files	Use the machine's local */etc* files as the data source
NIS	Use NIS as the data source
NIS+	Use NIS+ as the data source

Table 12.1 *Nsswitch.conf Sources (Continued)*

Name Service	Description
LDAP	Use LDAP as the data source
DNS	Use DNS as the data source for the host details
Compat	Support the BSD "+" and "-" syntax in */etc/passwd*, */etc/shadow*, and */etc/group*
User, XFN	Introduced in Solaris 8 and valid only for printers; "user" allows a *${HOME}/.printers* file while "XFN" uses the Federated Naming Service (FNS)

For example, our "passwd" entry will use the "local files" source, the */etc/passwd* and */etc/shadow* files, for its data lookups.

Status Codes and Actions

Multiple source entries can be defined, as shown by the "printers" entry in our earlier example. These are simply searched in the order they are listed. However, we can also add some control to them using a series of status and action codes.

Each source will return a code that indicates the status of the search; that is, whether it was successful or not. The available codes are shown in Table 12.2 along with a description showing the conditions that would cause each of the codes to be returned.

Table 12.2 *Source Status Codes*

Status/Action	Meaning
SUCCESS	Entry was found in the name service
UNAVAIL	Service is not responding
NOTFOUND	No entry in the name service
TRYAGAIN	Service is busy; try again

Next we need to decide what action the system should take for each name service. A number of action codes are available to do this, and are shown in Table 12.3.

Table 12.3 *Source Action Codes*

Status/Action	Meaning
continue	Move to the next service listed
return	Return back
forever	Introduced in Solaris 8. When used with "TRYAGAIN," this will loop forever

Now we can tie the two together. For example, if we always want to end a search after correctly finding some data, we could use something similar to the directive below. This states that if NIS is successful and locates the data, it should return, rather than moving on and searching the next name service ("files" in this case).

```
passwd: nis [SUCCESS=return] files
```

Each name service needs to know what actions to perform for every one of the status codes, but fortunately a set of default values has been created to ease typing! These values are as follows:

- SUCCESS = return
- NOTFOUND = continue
- UNAVAIL = continue
- TRYAGAIN = continue

This means that the following two entries are identical:

```
passwd: nis [ SUCCESS=return NOTFOUND=continue \
             UNAVAIL=continue TRYAGAIN=continue ]files

passwd: nis files
```

We can see from this that the only time we need to add a status/action directive is when it differs from the default, as in the case of the standard NIS switch shown below:

```
hosts: nis [NOTFOUND=return] files
```

Template Switch Files

There are presently six files supplied with Solaris that relate to the switch file; these are listed below:

```
tin# ls /etc/nsswitch*
/etc/nsswitch.conf          /etc/nsswitch.dns
/etc/nsswitch.files         /etc/nsswitch.ldap
/etc/nsswitch.nis           /etc/nsswitch.nisplus
tin#
```

Five of these are template files, each one relating to a name service (files, DNS, LDAP, NIS, and NIS+), while the sixth (*nsswitch.conf*) is the master configuration file itself. The correct template to use is normally set by the installation mechanism when users select the type of service they are running, but are often copied later by the system administrator to alter the service type quickly. For example, throughout this chapter we'll alter between using files and NIS by copying the relevant file into place, as shown below:

```
tin# cp /etc/nsswitch.nis /etc/nsswitch.conf
tin# cp /etc/nsswitch.files /etc/nsswitch.conf
tin#
```

How NIS Works

NIS is a commonly used naming service that was originally known as Yellow Pages (YP), but had to be renamed to avoid conflict with the UK telephone company British Telecommunications. In fact, we can see from the manual page listing that many of the commands still refer to the older naming convention (ypbind, ypcat, etc.).

NIS uses a client-server concept similar to many other naming services. This approach ensures that we don't get data replication problems because the "real" data resides only on one main server. Through the use of slaves, NIS provides server redundancy to ensure that the data is still available if the master server fails.

So, how does NIS work? First, we define something known as a NIS domain. This is really just a token name to group a number of machines together that require access to the same set of data files.

One of the machines within the domain will be nominated as the master server—this is the one that controls the data files. (It's probably worthwhile pointing out now that a machine can be a server for multiple domains with a little configuration.) Next, although it's not a requirement, we normally create some slave servers that can be used to provide the data even if the master fails, thus achieving a level of server redundancy.

Finally, all the machines, including the master and slave servers, are added as clients of the domain. This may sound odd at first that a server also has to become a client, but hopefully it will make sense soon.

We can see from this general description that three different types of machines are used within NIS: master server, slave server, and client. We'll look at all of these in more detail shortly.

NIS Domain Names

NIS uses a domain name setting, as does DNS. Where they pick up their domain name from can become confusing, so let's clarify that now.

The DNS domain name is the one normally thought of as the "Internet domain name," while the NIS domain name is a token used to define the NIS boundaries. The two domains are treated as separate entities, and so they could both be set to the same value without any conflict.

The way each name service determines its domain name is shown in Table 12.4.

Table 12.4 *Domain Name Ordering*

Name Service	Meaning
NIS	Uses the value returned by domainname
DNS	Tries to use the variable LOCALDOMAIN Followed by the entry from */etc/resolv.conf* Followed by the value returned by domainname Lastly, tries to determine the domain from the *hosts* entry

The way that many administrators split the two is to use the file */etc/defaultdomain* to store the NIS domain entry and the file */etc/resolv.conf* to store the DNS domain settings (we actually do this in Chapter 16, "Configuring DNS"), so we'll follow those conventions here too.

The NIS domain name will be set to "nis.solarisbootcamp.com" using the following steps. This will ensure it remains set for both the current session and any subsequent reboots:

```
tin# domainname nis.solarisbootcamp.com
tin# domainname > /etc/defaultdomain
tin# domainname
nis.solarisbootcamp.com
tin#
```

NIS Maps

The following list shows the "important" administration files that will be brought under the control of NIS so we know which ones we need to be concerned with:

- */etc/aliases*
- */etc/auto_home*
- */etc/auto_master*

- */etc/bootparams*
- */etc/ethers*
- */etc/group*
- */etc/hosts*
- */etc/netgroup*
- */etc/netmasks*
- */etc/networks*
- */etc/passwd*
- */etc/protocols*
- */etc/rpc*
- */etc/services*
- */etc/timezone*

To do this, they are imported into NIS and stored as a series of database files under the NIS data directory, */var/yp*. These database files are known as the "NIS maps" and are based on a simple database format known as "dbm," which stores and indexes its data in files using the following naming convention:

- *<filename>.pag* (this contains the data)
- *<filename>.dir* (this is an index to the *.pag* file)

For example, the */etc/inet/hosts* file would be read and from it a NIS hosts database consisting of the following two files would be produced:

hosts.pag
hosts.dir

The "dbm" format works on a "key-value" pair. This means that each entry comprises a single key field that can be searched and a value that is associated with the key. Since the database can only have one key field, this means that if we need to search using a different key, we have to create another file that uses the new key.

For example, sometimes we may want to determine the hostname of a machine using its IP address as the key, while at other times we might want to determine the IP address using the hostname as the key. To do this, a *hosts.byname* and a *hosts.byaddr* file is generated. The *hosts.byname* is used when we know the name and want to find the IP address (the key is the name) and the *hosts.byaddr* map is used when we know the IP address but need the name (the key is the IP address).

Another example is the password database; the NIS password maps are *passwd.byuid* and *passwd.byname*, which use a key of the UID and the login name, respectively.

To automate the maps' creation we use two additional utilities—make and makedbm, which we'll take a look at now.

Makedbm

Makedbm takes an input file (or standard input) and generates the "dbm" formatted files (both the index and the data file). Let's run it on a portion of the password file to illustrate how it works:

```
tin# head -3 /etc/passwd | makedbm - /tmp/passwd
tin# ls -l /tmp/passwd*
-rw-------   1 root      other       0 Jun  6 12:11 /tmp/passwd.dir
-rw-------   1 root      other    1024 Jun  6 12:11 /tmp/passwd.pag
tin#
```

Once we have generated the database file, we can also use makedbm to display its contents, as shown below:

```
tin# makedbm -u /tmp/passwd
root:x:0:1:Super-User:/:/sbin/sh
bin:x:2:2::/usr/bin:
daemon:x:1:1::/:
YP_LAST_MODIFIED 1016794876
YP_MASTER_NAME tin
tin#
```

We can see that the output also contains additional lines. These are some of the keys that can be added along with the data. They are used by NIS and, because makedbm is primarily used for NIS, some of these keys are added by default.

The list of available keys and what they represent are shown in Table 12.5.

Table 12.5 *Makedbm "Special" Keys*

Makedbm Keys	**Meaning**
YP_MASTER_NAME	Name of the master for this map
YP_INTERDOMAIN	Forward failed NIS lookups onto DNS
YP_DOMAIN_NAME	NIS domain name
YP_LAST_MODIFIED	Modification date of the input file
YP_INPUT_FILE	Name of the input file
YP_OUTPUT_NAME	Name of the output file
YP_SECURE	Use reserved ports for clients
YP_MULTI_HOSTNAME	IP addresses of the interfaces

The following comparison shows how the key is stored in one of the NIS maps, along with how it is used by one of the NIS commands:

```
tin# cd /var/yp/nis.solarisbootcamp.com
tin# makedbm -u passwd.byuid | grep YP
YP_LAST_MODIFIED 0997357987
YP_MASTER_NAME tin
tin#

tin# yppoll passwd.byuid
Domain nis.solarisbootcamp.com is supported
Map passwd.byuid has order number 0997357987
The master server is tin
tin#
```

Make and Makefiles

Imagine how often the files might change due to, for example, users altering their passwords or machines being moved around the network. It's a very time-consuming process for us to have to run the makedbm commands manually—in fact, it has already taken us quite a few pages to get this far! To automate the procedure we use make, which is a tool often used by programmers to build files rapidly by defining dependencies between them.

Briefly, make allows us to define a series of targets (the files that need building) and a set of dependencies for them. It then checks the time stamps of the targets and their dependents to see if they are different. If the target is up-to-date, then fine, nothing happens. If it isn't, it will be rebuilt.

The rules, target, and dependencies are supplied to make through a file known as a *makefile*, which by default is called either *Makefile* or *makefile*.

NIS distributes a *makefile* that defines a whole series of rules that allows us to build the entire "standard" NIS maps. This automates the entire process for us, so we only need to enter the sequence of commands shown below to build the whole set.

If this sounds a little complicated, don't be too concerned; we'll take another look at it later in the section "Customizing NIS" on page 300.

One thing that we do have to be aware of is that make is installed in */usr/ ccs/bin*, which in most cases is not in the user's path (see Chapter 5, "Shells"). Just to be sure we'll use the full path here, but later in the chapter we'll assume the path has been set correctly and just refer to make, so everything looks clearer:

```
tin# cd /var/yp
tin# /usr/ccs/bin/make
tin#
```

Alternatively, we can build a specific map by passing it as a parameter to make:

```
tin# cd /var/yp
tin# /usr/ccs/bin/make passwd
tin#
```

DNS Forwarding

If the machine is configured for DNS, then any host lookups that cannot be determined can be passed onto the DNS server. This is termed "DNS forwarding" and is configured as follows.

First, we need to inform NIS that it should forward any failed queries onto DNS, which we do by updating */var/yp/Makefile*. After the changes, it will look like the one shown below:

```
hydrogen# cat /var/yp/Makefile
<lines removed for clarity>
#
# Set the following variable to "-b" to have NIS servers use the
# domain name resolver for hosts not in the current domain.
B=-b
#B=
<lines removed for clarity>
hydrogen#
```

When the maps are next rebuilt, `makedbm` will insert the YP_INTERDOMAIN key into them, which forces `ypserv` to pass its failed query onto DNS.

This also means that we don't need to specify both "dns" and "nis" as name service options when we add support for NIS to the system. For example, if the machine is already configured for DNS and "local files," we would probably have something similar to the following for the "hosts" entry:

```
hosts: files dns
```

After adding support for NIS, we should remove the "dns" service from the switch file and only use "nis," as shown in the entry below:

```
hosts: nis [NOTFOUND=return] files
```

Machine Types and Daemons

Earlier in the chapter we mentioned the different NIS machine configurations that are available. Let's look at them in more detail now and also see the processes that run on each type.

Master Server

There is one master server per NIS domain, and it's always the first machine to be configured whenever the domain is created. The master's local */etc* files are the ones used to generate the NIS maps, which are all built and stored on the master. (The NIS master doesn't have to use the */etc* directory on the master, but suffice it to say the master houses the text files which are used to generate the NIS maps.)

Slave Server

Slave servers are used to provide redundancy should the main server fail. They will also add a degree of load balancing, as clients can connect to these as they would the master server. We've already said that slaves are not necessarily required, but there are usually a number configured on the network.

Each slave contains backup copies of the NIS maps, which are automatically "pushed" out and downloaded from the master server whenever any changes are made.

Client

Clients are the machines that access the NIS servers whenever they require information, as clients don't store any NIS maps themselves. The type of task that would request this information would be a user logging on to a machine (the system needs to check that it is a valid user).

Booting and Binding

A number of processes that are part of the NIS service are normally started at boot-time using a command called ypstart. Table 12.6 shows which these are, and which one is started on each type of system.

Table 12.6 *NIS Processes*

Process	Machine Type
ypxfrd	Master
rpc.yppasswdd	Master
rpc.ypudated	Master
ypserv	Master, Slave
ypbind	Master, Slave, Client

Let's briefly work through these to show how the client-server communication works for each type of machine.

Ypserv

This daemon runs on both masters and slaves. It is responsible for reading information from its local version of the NIS maps and passing this data back to the client daemon (ypbind).

Ypbind

This is the client process and runs on all machines, including servers. It connects to a `ypserv` daemon (normally the first one that responds) to request data. For master or slave servers, this normally means that `ypbind` will often receive a response back from its own `ypserv` daemon first.

This is known as "binding." Once this has been performed, `ypbind` will create a file in the *binding* directory that contains the name of the server it has successfully bound to. In our case, the binding file would be */var/yp/binding/nis.solarisbootcamp.com/ypservers*.

On subsequent reboots, `ypbind` will try to rebind to the same server and only try another should the server fail or it is told to bind elsewhere.

Ypxfrd

This daemon runs on the master server. Its job is to perform high-speed map transfers to the slave servers.

Rpc.ypupdated

This daemon runs on the master server, where it is used to update the public-key map and any others that are referred to in the file */var/yp/updaters*.

Rpc.yppasswd

This daemon runs on the master server. It allows users to alter their passwords on any machine and remake the password map.

Our Machines

Now we're at the point where we can start to build our machines, so let's decide how they will be configured.

We will put *all* the machines on the network (in both subnets) under the control of NIS. We want to have at least one slave server for redundancy, so rather than just having the master server on the multihomed host, we've decided to add a slave to each subnet too. Earlier versions of NIS dictated that there had to be a server on each subnet that contained clients. Although this limitation no longer applies, it's still a common configuration to use. Following this convention, we've decided to use the machines listed in Table 12.7 as our servers.

Table 12.7 *NIS Server Host Details*

IP Address	Host	Function
192.168.44.50	tin	NIS master server on multihomed host
192.168.22.9	fluorine	NIS slave server on '22 subnet
192.168.44.53	iodine	NIS slave server on '44 subnet

The Packages

As usual, we'll check that the correct packages are installed before we start. We're using Solaris 9, but let's assume Solaris 2.6 is the oldest revision we refer to, as prior to this we also had to load a package known as the "NIS kit." This provided us with the means of running a NIS server on a Solaris 2 system. This package has since been removed and is now part of the standard Solaris release.

In theory, the required packages will also alter depending on whether we are building a master, slave, or client. But for consistency between the machines, we will install all of them on every one. The added advantage is that if we need to alter the function of a machine, say from client to server, it can be easily carried out (also the additional packages are quite small so it doesn't place any great overhead on disk space requirements).

```
tin# pkginfo SUNWypr SUNWypu SUNWnisr SUNWnisu
system      SUNWypr      NIS Server for Solaris (root)
system      SUNWypu      NIS Server for Solaris (usr)
system      SUNWnisr     Network Information System, (Root)
system      SUNWnisu     Network Information System, (Usr)
tin#
```

A *makefile* is included as part of the NIS distribution. This is used by the master to perform the build and distribution of the NIS maps, as we explained earlier. We also mentioned that make was part of another package, so let's make sure this is installed too:

```
tin# pkginfo SUNWsprot
system      SUNWsprot    Solaris Bundled tools
tin#
```

Build the Master Server

Now we'll configure the machines that are part of the NIS domain. The first step is to get the master (tin, in this case) up and running.

Let's first set the domain name and also make sure it's retained across reboots by adding it to the */etc/defaultdomain* file:

```
tin# domainname nis.solarisbootcamp.com
tin# domainname > /etc/defaultdomain
tin# domainname
nis.solarisbootcamp.com
tin#
```

Now let's run ypinit to initialize the master. This will prompt us to enter the list of servers we will use, so we'll add them all at this point. This information is stored in a map named *ypservers*, which is known as the server map. For now we'll add the servers to this map by passing them onto ypinit, but later we'll see how to update the map manually:

```
tin# ypinit -m
In order for NIS to operate sucessfully, we have to construct a
list of the NIS servers. Please continue to add the names for YP
servers in order of preference, one per line. When you are done
with the list, type a <control D>
or a return on a line by itself.
        next host to add:  tin
        next host to add:  fluorine
        next host to add:  iodine
        next host to add:

The current list of yp servers looks like this:

tin
fluorine
iodine

Is this correct?  [y/n: y]

Installing the YP database will require that you answer a few
questions.
Questions will all be asked at the beginning of the procedure.

Do you want this procedure to quit on non-fatal errors? [y/n: n]
OK, please remember to go back and redo manually whatever fails.
If you don't, some part of the system (perhaps the yp itself)
won't work.
The yp domain directory is /var/yp/nis.solarisbootcamp.com
There will be no further questions. The remainder of the
procedure should take 5 to 10 minutes.
Building /var/yp/nis.solarisbootcamp.com/ypservers...
Running /var/yp /Makefile...
updated passwd
updated group
updated hosts
make: Warning: Don't know how to make target `/etc/ethers'
Current working directory /var/yp
<lines removed for clarity>
updated auto.home
make: Warning: Target `all' not remade because of errors
Current working directory /var/yp

tin has been set up as a yp master server without any errors.

If there are running slave yp servers, run yppush now for any
data bases which have been changed. If there are no running
slaves, run ypinit on those hosts which are to be slave servers.
tin#
```

The output from ypinit shows that make reported an error while trying to access some of the files, including */etc/ethers*. It's not a problem in this case, as it simply indicates that the files couldn't be found (they don't exist by default). If we wish, we could create an empty file to get rid of these types of errors, as shown below:

```
tin# touch /etc/ethers
tin# cd /var/yp
tin# make ethers
updated ethers
pushed ethers
tin#
```

Now that we have initialized the master server, we can start the main processes. We'll do this manually now, but it will normally be carried out automatically at boot time:

```
tin# /usr/lib/netsvc/yp/ypstart
starting NIS (YP server) services: ypserv ypbind ypxfrd
rpc.yppasswdd rpc.ypupdated done
tin#
```

This shows that all the servers have been correctly started. As a secondary check, we can look in the messages file to make sure we don't have any NIS errors.

If everything appears to be OK, we'll check which server we are bound to. Hopefully, it will be tin, since it's the only server at the moment!

```
tin# ypwhich
tin
tin#
```

Good. This shows that ypbind is successfully communicating with ypserv. So let's query the server for its list of available maps:

```
tin# ypwhich -m
auto.home tin
hosts.byaddr tin
hosts.byname tin
<lines removed for clarity>
ypservers tin
tin#
```

So what have we actually done by creating the master? If we look in the NIS directory, */var/yp*, we can see that a directory has been created with the name of the domain it's serving—"nis.solarisbootcamp.com."

```
tin# cd /var/yp
tin# ls -ld nis.Solarisbootcamp.com
drwxr-xr-x  2 root      other       1536 Aug  1 12:02
nis.solarisbootcamp.com
tin#
```

If we look in this directory we can see that it contains all the relevant NIS files for the domain, including any variations that are required to allow us to perform lookups using different keys such as *hosts.byaddr* and *hosts.byname*:

```
tin# cd nis.solarisbootcamp.com
tin# ls
auto.home.dir                 networks.byname.dir
auto.home.pag                 networks.byname.pag
group.bygid.dir               passwd.byname.dir
group.bygid.pag               passwd.byname.pag
group.byname.dir              passwd.byuid.dir
group.byname.pag              passwd.byuid.pag
hosts.byaddr.dir              protocols.byname.dir
hosts.byaddr.pag              protocols.byname.pag
hosts.byname.dir              protocols.bynumber.dir
hosts.byname.pag              protocols.bynumber.pag
mail.aliases.db               publickey.byname.dir
mail.aliases.dir              publickey.byname.pag
mail.aliases.pag              rpc.bynumber.dir
mail.byaddr.dir               rpc.bynumber.pag
mail.byaddr.pag               services.byname.dir
netid.byname.dir              services.byname.pag
netid.byname.pag              services.byservicename.dir
netmasks.byaddr.dir           services.byservicename.pag
netmasks.byaddr.pag           ypservers.dir
networks.byaddr.dir           ypservers.pag
networks.byaddr.pag
tin#
```

Looking back in */var/yp*, we see the *binding* directory. If we follow this tree we'll find the file *ypservers*. We explained earlier that this contains the name of the server that the client was last bound to, and that it will try to bind to for subsequent reboots. If we look at it we can see it contains our own hostname—again, we are the only configured server so it couldn't contain anything else at this point. Later we should see that different clients bind to different servers:

```
tin# cat /var/yp/binding/nis.solarisbootcamp.com/ypservers
tin
tin#
```

Everything seems to be working OK as far as NIS is concerned, so let's alter the switch file to make it our default naming service. We'll use the NIS template file as explained earlier in the section "Name Service Switch File" on page 280:

```
tin# cp /etc/nsswitch.nis /etc/nsswitch.conf
tin#
```

Good. The master is now configured for NIS, so we can move on to the next machines.

Build the Clients

Next we'll configure the clients. The reason for doing these now is that the slaves need to be built as clients before they can become slave servers. We'll look at the reasons for this later on in the section "Build the Slave Servers" on page 296.

Building the client follows similar steps to building the master. First we need to set the domainname so that ypbind knows which domain the machine is a client of, and therefore which domain to search for a server in. After that we can run ypinit again to initialize the client—we'll use carbon for our example here:

```
carbon# domainname nis.solarisbootcamp.com
carbon# domainname > /etc/defaultdomain
carbon# domainname
nis.solarisbootcamp.com
carbon#
```

Now start the actual client installation by running ypinit, specifying the "client" option:

```
carbon# ypinit -c
In order for NIS to operate successfully, we have to construct a
list of the NIS servers. Please continue to add the names for YP
servers in order of preference, one per line.
When you are done with the list, type a <control D>
or a return on a line by itself.
        next host to add:  tin
        next host to add:  fluorine
        next host to add:  iodine
        next host to add:  ^D
The current list of yp servers looks like this:

tin
fluorine
iodine

Is this correct?  [y/n: y]
carbon#
```

Simple—ypinit doesn't actually need to do very much for the client, so let's try to start the NIS daemons and make sure everything runs OK:

```
carbon# /usr/lib/netsvc/yp/ypstart
starting NIS (YP server) services: ypbind done
carbon#
```

This time we can see that the only daemon started is the client side (ypbind). The other big difference is that we cannot bind to ourselves, so we must be bound to tin since it's the only available server:

```
carbon# ypwhich
tin
carbon#
```

Lastly, we'll update the switch file to use NIS as we did for the master:

```
carbon# cp /etc/nsswitch.nis /etc/nsswitch.conf
carbon#
```

Good. That appears to be working OK, so we can carry out these steps on all the remaining machines that will be configured as clients.

Build the Slave Servers

We stated earlier that the slaves should be built as clients first. The reason for this is that during the slave configuration process, ypinit needs to copy the NIS maps from the master back to the slave, which it does using NIS itself. This means that before we can run ypinit, the client side of NIS should already be running—in other words, ypbind should be running.

For our slave builds, we'll assume that they are already configured correctly following the steps just described in the section "Build the Clients" on page 295. This means that the domainname is set, the NIS services have started, and the server map contains the complete list of servers (including the slaves).

Let's use fluorine for this example and start by checking that the domainname is correct:

```
fluorine# domainname
nis.solarisbootcamp.com
flourine#
```

Just to make sure everything is correct, we'll stop and restart NIS to make sure ypbind is running:

```
fluorine# /usr/lib/netsvc/yp/ypstop
fluorine# /usr/lib/netsvc/yp/ypstart
starting NIS (YP server) services: ypbind done
flourine#
```

Good. Now the machine is acting as a NIS client, so we can start to initialize it as a slave:

```
fluorine# ypinit -s tin
Installing the YP database will require that you answer a few
questions.
Questions will all be asked at the beginning of the procedure.

Do you want this procedure to quit on non-fatal errors? [y/n: n]
```

```
OK, please remember to go back and redo manually whatever fails.
If you don't, some part of the system (perhaps the yp itself)
won't work.
The yp domain directory is /var/yp/nis.solarisbootcamp.com
There will be no further questions. The remainder of the
procedure should take a few minutes, to copy the data bases from
tin.
Transferring auto.home...
Transferring auto.master...
Transferring netmasks.byaddr...
Transferring netid.byname...
Transferring publickey.byname...
Transferring mail.byaddr...
Transferring mail.aliases...
Transferring protocols.byname...
Transferring services.byservicename...
Transferring services.byname...
Transferring rpc.bynumber...
Transferring networks.byaddr...
Transferring networks.byname...
Transferring hosts.byaddr...
Transferring hosts.byname...
Transferring group.bygid...
Transferring group.byname...
Transferring passwd.byuid...
Transferring protocols.bynumber...
Transferring ypservers...
Transferring passwd.byname...

fluorine's nis data base has been set up without any errors.
flourine#
```

This output shows that the maps have been transferred from tin. If we check the slave we can see that the directory */var/yp/nis.solarisboot-camp.com* has been created and that it contains copies of the NIS maps, just as we saw on the master.

NIS is only running in client mode on the server at present, so now we need to stop and restart it again to bring up both the client and server processes:

```
fluorine# /usr/lib/netsvc/yp/ypstop
fluorine# /usr/lib/netsvc/yp/ypstart
starting NIS (YP server) services: ypserv ypbind done
flourine#
```

Again, we can see the daemons that have been started, and this time both ypserv (the server side) and ypbind (the client side) are running.

Running some NIS commands will show that it appears to be working OK, and that we have bound to ourselves, rather than the master:

```
fluorine# ypwhich
fluorine
flourine#
```

```
fluorine# ypwhich -m
auto.home tin
hosts.byaddr tin
hosts.byname tin
<lines removed for clarity>
ypservers tin
flourine#
```

Good. We're happy that the machine is working as a slave, so let's alter the switch file and make NIS our default naming service as we did for the master and clients:

```
fluorine# cp /etc/nsswitch.nis /etc/nsswitch.conf
flourine#
```

The Server Map

When we initialized a master server or client, we were prompted to enter our list of servers. This information is used to generate another NIS map, named *ypservers*, which we can view using ypcat or makedbm, just as we would with any other map.

It's actually quite common updating this map. For example, many sites prefer to order the list of servers by their location and so they need to edit the map on a regular basis as servers are relocated.

Unfortunately, there are only two ways to do this. The first is using ypinit when a machine is initialized as we saw earlier. The second is to perform the updates manually.

Here, we'll look at the steps that need to be followed should you decide to do the latter. First we'll take a look at the entries that may be already in there:

```
tin# ypcat -k ypservers
tin
fluorine
iodine
tin#
```

To edit the map we first need to convert it to a temporary ASCII file:

```
tin# cd /var/yp/nis.solarisbootcamp.com
tin# makedbm -u ./ypservers > /tmp/newServers
tin#
```

Now we can edit the file to add or remove any servers as required:

```
tin# cat /tmp/newServers
YP_LAST_MODIFIED 0996667575
YP_MASTER_NAME tin
tin
fluorine
iodine
new_server_to_add
tin#
```

We've added a new server (called "new_server_to_add") to the end of the file. When everything is correct we can rebuild the map:

```
tin# makedbm /tmp/newServers ypservers
tin#
```

Lastly, we can check the file to make sure everything is OK:

```
tin# ypcat -k ypservers
tin
fluorine
iodine
new_server_to_add
tin#
```

Map Propagation

When any changes occur to the maps, the master needs to distribute the new copies to the slaves. It actually transfers the files using the NIS transport itself, as we saw earlier when we built the slaves (these were the "Transferring <map name>" messages).

There are two commands used to propagate the maps around the servers: ypxfr and yppush.

Ypxfr

This runs on the slave and communicates with the ypxfrd running on the master to request the download of an individual map. For example, to update the *hosts* file from the master we could run the following command:

```
fluorine# /usr/lib/netsvc/yp/ypxfr hosts.byname
flourine#
```

It's possible that sometimes the slave maps may not get updated for some reason; maybe the slave server was down at the time, or the transfer simply failed to complete. To ensure they remain up-to-date, ypxfr can be called on a regular basis using cron. In fact, a few scripts are provided with NIS for just this reason. They are located in */usr/lib/netsvc/yp* and are listed below:

```
fluorine# cd /usr/lib/netsvc/yp
fluorine# ls ypxfr_*
ypxfr_1perday    ypxfr_1perhour    ypxfr_2perday
flourine#
```

These can be edited to suit each site, but they should give you a start for the type of things you can place in each file. The scripts are named according to their recommended update times (i.e. "once per day," "once per hour," and "twice per day"), but obviously these can also be altered to suit depending on the update frequencies found at your site. For now, we'll stick to using these and add the following entries to *roots crontab* across all the slaves:

```
fluorine# crontab -1
<lines removed for clarity>
#
# entries to populate the NIS maps
#
00 23 * * * /usr/lib/netsvc/yp/ypxfr_1perday
00 12,23 * * * /usr/lib/netsvc/yp/ypxfr_2perday
15 * * * * /usr/lib/netsvc/yp/ypxfr_1perhour
flourine#
```

Yppush

This is called from the *makefile* and so is run every time we rebuild the maps using make. It is the program that issues the transfer request command to the slaves, which then run ypxfr to download the updated maps.

Customizing NIS

At times it may be useful to use the features of NIS ourselves. Doing this means we don't have to be concerned about ensuring that the same files are up-to-date on every machine or about distributing them. The problem is that we have to customize the *makefile* to add this support, which can be quite tricky.

To show how this can be done, we will add a hypothetical map to our setup. The one we'll use will be responsible for controlling which users have access to applications on which machines.

The "userAccessList" File

This is the input file that will be used to build the map. It contains a list of UIDs, the machine each UID can use, and a list of the applications the UIDs are allowed access to:

```
tin# cat /etc/userAccess
#
# UID    hostname    application list
#
1234     hydrogen    ls cat who
5678     hydrogen    ls rcp
825      helium      tar ufsdump
22       xenon       ifconfig
tin#
```

To make things easier to explain and understand, we will use just one key for the map—the UID field. The map that we'll build will be called *user-Access.byuid*.

The main task is to edit the *makefile* so that the map is automatically rebuilt and distributed whenever we do a make. Let's look at the changes we've made before we start to work through them (the changes are in bold):

```
tin# cat Makefile
<lines removed for clarity>
all: passwd group hosts ethers networks rpc services protocols \
    netgroup bootparams aliases publickey netid netmasks \
    c2secure timezone auto.master auto.home userAccess
<lines removed for clarity>
c2secure:
    -@if [ -f $(PWDIR)/security/passwd.adjunct ]; then \
        if [ ! $(NOPUSH) ]; then $(MAKE)  $(MFLAGS) -k \
            passwd.adjunct.time group.adjunct.time; \
        else $(MAKE) $(MFLAGS) -k NOPUSH=$(NOPUSH) \
            passwd.adjunct.time group.adjunct.time; \
        fi; \
    fi

userAccess.time: $(DIR)/userAccess
    @(awk 'BEGIN { OFS="\t"; } $$1 !~ /^#/ { print $$1, $$0 }' \
        $(DIR)/userAccess $(CHKPIPE)) | \
        $(MAKEDBM) - $(YPDBDIR)/$(DOM)/userAccess.byuid;
    @touch userAccess.time;
    @echo "updated userAccess";
    @if [ ! $(NOPUSH) ]; then $(YPPUSH) -d $(DOM)
userAccess.byuid; fi
    @if [ ! $(NOPUSH) ]; then echo "pushed userAccess"; fi

passwd.time: $(PWDIR)/passwd $(PWDIR)/shadow
    -@if [ -f $(PWDIR)/security/passwd.adjunct ]; then \
<lines removed for clarity>
netmasks: netmasks.time
timezone: timezone.time
auto.master: auto.master.time
auto.home: auto.home.time
userAccess: userAccess.time
$(DIR)/netid:
<lines removed for clarity>
tin#
```

We need to get an idea of what the *makefile* does and how it works, so let's look at that now. Generally we define a target that we wish to build; with NIS the targets are the maps. Next, we define a series of dependencies that the targets have. Finally we create some rules that dictate how each target will be built.

Let's see how all this relates to our new map by examining each stage in turn as we generate the *makefile* entries.

The target will be the map named *userAccess.byuid*. The dependency for the target is the original file, */etc/userAccess*. In other words, if the original source file has altered, we need to regenerate the map because it is out-of-date relative to the source file.

The rules show how to build the target—in our case we use makedbm. A simple example would look similar to that shown below:

```
userAccess.byuid: /etc/userAccess
        makedbm userAccess.byuid /etc/userAccess
```

This basically says, "If */etc/userAccess* has altered, then use the makedbm command to rebuild the corresponding map."

The NIS *makefile* makes the dependency checking a little different by using an intermediate file. When the maps are built a time stamp file is created. This is an empty file named, in this case, *userAccess.time*. The dependencies are altered slightly to check if the time stamp file is older than the */etc/userAccess* file; if so, we rebuild the maps. This gives us the following syntax for our target, which says that the *userAccess* map depends on the *userAccess.time* time stamp file:

```
userAccess: userAccess.time
```

Next we add the following dependency and rules:

```
userAccess.time: $(DIR)/userAccess
    @(awk 'BEGIN { OFS="\t"; } $$1 !~ /^#/ { print $$1, $$0 }' \
        $(DIR)/userAccess $(CHKPIPE)) | \
        $(MAKEDBM) - $(YPDBDIR)/$(DOM)/userAccess.byuid;
    @touch userAccess.time;
    @echo "updated userAccess";
    @if [ ! $(NOPUSH) ]; then $(YPPUSH) -d $(DOM)
userAccess.byuid; fi
    @if [ ! $(NOPUSH) ]; then echo "pushed userAccess"; fi
```

This uses the same targets, but also uses awk to parse the file and feed its output into makedbm, which builds the actual map. The time stamp of the *userAccess.time* file is updated using touch. Lastly, the modified maps are transferred out to any slaves with yppush.

The final change made to the *makefile* is to update the target known as "all." This builds the full set of maps whenever we run make without passing any map names as arguments. In this case, we simply need to add our custom map name to the end to make sure it is built whenever the target is used. This entry will look like the one shown below:

```
all: passwd group hosts ethers networks rpc netid services
    protocols netgroup bootparams aliases publickey netmasks
    c2secure timezone auto.master auto.home userAccess
```

Now that the *makefile* is in place, let's try to build the files:

```
tin# cd /var/yp
tin# make userAccess
updated userAccess
pushed userAccess
tin#
```

The maps appear to have been built correctly, so now we can check that the files have been created as expected. First we'll look in the domain directory to see if the files are there:

```
tin# cd nis.solarisbootcamp.com
tin# ls userAccess*
userAccess.byuid.dir   userAccess.byuid.pag
tin#
```

And now we can try to read them. At this point, we need to use the full map name:

```
tin# ypcat -k userAccess.byuid
5678 5678    hydrogen    ls rcp
1234 1234    hydrogen    ls cat who
825  825     helium      tar ufsdump
22   22      xenon       ifconfig
tin#
```

Good. We can read the maps themselves, so next we'll create an alias for them by updating the *nicknames* file. This will allow us to use the "standard" userAccess name without having to include the suffix every time:

```
tin# cat /var/yp/nicknames
passwd passwd.byname
group group.byname
networks networks.byaddr
hosts hosts.byname
protocols protocols.bynumber
services services.byname
aliases mail.aliases
ethers ethers.byname
userAccess userAccess.byuid
tin#
```

Once the nickname has been added, we can try and use the alias itself:

```
tin# ypcat userAccess
5678     hydrogen    ls rcp
1234     hydrogen    ls cat who
825      helium      tar ufsdump
22       xenon       ifconfig
tin#
```

Custom Map Propagation

The map is now usable and works fine on the master, but we have to propagate it to the slave. The first time this is performed we need to do it manually, since the slave won't update the map until it has a copy itself (this process is carried out as part of the slave initialization for the standard maps).

To get it onto the slave we'll do a map transfer from each one back to the master. For example, on fluorine we would run the following command:

```
fluorine# /usr/lib/netsvc/yp/ypxfr userAccess.byuid
flourine#
```

Now, because the slave has a copy of the map, whenever we run `make` on the master, `yppush` will send an update request to the slave, which will pull the updated map back from the master.

At this point we have a valid map that can be used on all the configured NIS machines. The only thing we have to do now is document the changes made so that we remember to update the *makefile* whenever we perform an operating system upgrade.

NIS Passwords

Before we go ahead and build the servers, now is a good time to make sure all the entries in the input files are correct and tidy them up if we need to. In particular, this means that we need to be careful about the password information. It's always recommended not to include *root* in the NIS *passwd* file for security reason, thus forcing each system to use the *root passwd* entry from their own */etc* files.

There are also a number of caveats we need to be aware of when implementing NIS; the main ones we'll look at are listed here:

- Password aging is not available; it is only supported in "local files," NIS+, and LDAP.

- The *shadow passwd* is not directly converted to a map. The passwords are pulled out and incorporated into the *passwd* map, which means that encrypted passwords can be seen by anyone using `ypcat`.

We'll look at password security in two parts, generating a "first level" of security that is easy to implement before creating a "second level" that will work around some of the security issues. For the first level we will carry out the following tasks:

- Each system's */etc/passwd* and */etc/shadow* will be left as standard, and so will only contain the "system" users, such as *root*, *uucp*, and so forth.

- Any additional users will be added on the master server and stored in a special password file.

The special password file that we'll use will be stored in the NIS data directory, */var/yp*, which means that the files */var/yp/passwd* and */var/yp/shadow* will become the master password files used to generate the NIS *passwd* map.

Update the User Creation Script

Earlier, in Chapter 3, "User Administration," we created a script named `createUser` that we'll run whenever new users are added to the system. This now needs to be modified to make sure that users are instead added to our special password file and that the NIS *passwd* map is rebuilt every time a user is added. The changes we'll make to the script are shown in bold below:

```
tin# cat /usr/local/utils/bin/createUsers
#!/bin/ksh
#
# A script to create users in a "company format."
# This uses a default, encrypted password that has been
# obtained by pulling a known password from the shadow
# file. Users are forced to alter it as first login.
# It assumes the group already exists and is valid.
#

#
# set our company defaults
#
home=/export/home
shell=/bin/ksh
skel=/etc/skel
password=hViVZtexneY8Y  # default encrypted password (changeme)
warnDays=5
validDays=60
ypPasswdFile=/var/yp/passwd
ypShadowFile=/var/yp/shadow
tmpShadow=/tmp/shadow.$$
tmpPasswd=/tmp/passwd.$$
<lines removed for clarity>
#
# set the password timeouts
#
passwd -f -w ${warnDays} -x ${validDays} ${user}
#
# Now move the acount into the yp location
#
tail -1 /etc/passwd >> ${ypPasswdFile}
tail -1 /etc/shadow >> ${ypShadowFile}
#
# Strip them from the "main" password/shadow files
#
sed -e "/^${user}:/d" /etc/passwd > ${tmpPasswd}
if [ -s ${tmpPasswd} ]; then
    mv ${tmpPasswd} /etc/passwd
    if [ $? -ne 0 ]; then
      echo "Error: Cannot copy new password file"
      exit 1
    fi
fi
sed -e "/^${user}:/d" /etc/passwd > ${tmpShadow}
if [ -s ${tmpShadow} ]; then
    mv ${tmpShadow} /etc/shadow
```

```
        if [ $? -ne 0 ]; then
          echo "Error: Cannot copy new shadow file"
          exit 1
        fi
fi
#
# Update the account with any "standard" settings
#
cd /var/yp
make passwd
edquota -p ${quotaAccount} ${user}
exit 0
tin#
```

So, what have we changed and why? We've altered the two variables, PASSWD_FILE and SHADOW_FILE, to point to our new location in /var/yp. The egrep statements have been altered to make sure we check the information in /etc as well as the ones in /var/yp when looking for existing users. Lastly, we make sure that the NIS maps are rebuilt and propagated. (We have to do this before checking the quotas, otherwise we would see nonexistent user errors, which is also why we use the UID rather than the user's name with the chown command.)

Update the Makefile

Whenever the NIS maps are built, /etc is used as the location for any source files by default and is specified in the makefile. We need to alter this so that it now uses the two new files we have just created: /var/yp/passwd and /var/yp/shadow. Fortunately, this is a common task, so a variable named PWDIR has been defined within it to indicate the password location. The default entry is shown below:

```
tin# grep "^PWDIR" Makefile
PWDIR =/etc
tin#
```

Let's alter this to the location of our new files, which in our case is /var/yp; we'll use sed to quickly perform the substitution:

```
tin# cd /var/yp
tin# cp Makefile Makefile.orig
tin# sed -e 's/^PWDIR.*$/PWDIR = \/var\/yp/' < Makefile.orig > Makefile
tin# grep "^PWDIR" Makefile
PWDIR =/var/yp
tin#
```

User Password Changes

The next thing we have to do is make sure that when users want to change their passwords, they can do so easily.

We've already said that `rpc.yppasswdd` runs on the master server and it allows remote password changes to take place, but we need to check that everything is in place to do so. A number of options can be passed to `rpc.yppasswdd`, including the location of the password file and the option to automatically rebuild the maps. NIS actually tries to detect the correct options at startup by performing a few checks. Interestingly, one of them is to check the PWDIR variable in the *makefile*, as we can see below in the code snippet from `ypstart`:

```
tin# cat /usr/lib/netsvc/yp/ypstart
<lines removed for clarity>
#
# The rpc.yppasswdd daemon can be started with a "-D" option
# to point it at the passwd/shadow/passwd.adjunct file(s).
# The /var/yp/Makefile uses a PWDIR macro assignment to
# define this directory. In the rpc.yppasswdd invocation,
# we attempt to grab this info and startup accordingly.
#
<lines removed for clarity>
   if [ -x $YPDIR/rpc.yppasswdd ]; then
       PWDIR=`grep "^PWDIR" /var/yp/Makefile 2> /dev/null` \
       && PWDIR=`expr "$PWDIR" : '.*=[   ]*\([^    ]*\)'`
       if [ "$PWDIR" ]; then
           if [ "$PWDIR" = "/etc" ]; then
               unset PWDIR
           else
               PWDIR="-D $PWDIR"
           fi
       fi
       $YPDIR/rpc.yppasswdd $PWDIR -m \
       && echo ' rpc.yppasswdd\c'
   fi
<lines removed for clarity>
tin#
```

This means that as long as we have updated the NIS *makefile* correctly, our new maps will also work with `rpc.yppasswdd`.

The other half of the NIS password daemon is the `passwd` command. Until recently a few other commands were provided for when some other naming services were in use, such as `yppasswd` and `nispasswd`. This has now altered and `passwd` can be used to change the password for all (or, in our case, both) naming services. For example, to change the password of a "normal" user whose entry is in the NIS *passwd* map, we would see something similar to that shown below:

```
fluorine# passwd msmith
New password: <enter the new password>
Re-enter new password: <enter the new password>
NIS passwd/attributes changed on tin
flourine#
```

For someone who is in the default password file, say *root*, we would see something similar to the following:

```
fluorine# passwd root
New password: <enter the new password>
Re-enter new password: <enter the new password>
Passwd (SYSTEM): passwd successfully changed for root
flourine#
```

It's also useful to note that we can explicitly specify which name service to use. For example, to change the NIS password we could use the following.

```
fluorine# passwd -r nis msmith
New password: <enter the new password>
Re-enter new password: <enter the new password>
NIS passwd/attributes changed on tin
flourine#
```

Passwd.adjunct *File*

We have now managed to split normal users from system users and put them into two separate password files, but unfortunately we now have the problem of users being able to see the encrypted passwords. For example, if we compare the password information for one of our users against the *passwd* map, everything will become clear:

```
tin# grep msmith /var/yp/passwd
msmith:x:1001:10:Mike Smith:/export/home/msmith:/bin/ksh
tin#
```

```
tin# grep msmith /var/yp/shadow
msmith:EwkdU786nskOz:11556:0:60:5:::
tin#
```

```
tin# su - msmith
tin$ ypmatch msmith passwd
msmith:EwkdU786nskOz:1001:10:Mike Smith:/export/home/msmith:/
bin/ksh
tin#
```

Just as expected, ypcat allows a normal user to view the encrypted password for anyone. We can also see that there isn't any aging information included anywhere.

Solaris supports a file named *passwd.adjunct* to be used within NIS. The *makefile* uses this file to build a map named *passwd.adjunct.byname*, which is used to define security data to the system. One of its other functions is to hide encrypted passwords, which is why we are interested in using it. The file format, very similar to */etc/shadow*, is shown below:

- Name
- Password

- Minimum security level for the user
- Maximum security level for the user
- Default security level for the user
- Flag defining the events that will always be audited
- Flag defining the events that will never be audited

When this file is available, NIS replaces the password entry in the NIS map with the string "##<user name>." For example, for our *msmith* user, we would see "##msmith" in the password field.

Many sites simply create the *passwd.adjunct* file using the contents of the *shadow* file. This works OK because the only field we are concerned with is the first one—the user name. The only problem is that when users change their passwords the *shadow* file is updated, leaving a copy of the original password in the *passwd.adjunct* file. This can become very confusing, so for that reason we'll create ours with only the first field and ignore the rest of the entries. This will give us a file that contains something similar to that shown below for *msmith*:

```
msmith::::::
```

First, we need to make sure that the *passwd.adjunct* map is built correctly. The *makefile* specifies the path to the file as *$PWDIR/security/ passwd.adjunct*. If we look back we'll see that we altered the location of PWDIR to suit our split password files, so this is now set to */var/yp*. This means the full pathname to our file is */var/yp/security/passwd.adjunct*. The security directory doesn't exist by default so we'll create it (and make sure no one can read its contents):

```
tin# cd /var/yp
tin# mkdir security
tin# chmod 700 security
tin#
```

Now we need to create the file. It will be based on the list of users we have in the "new" password file only—none of the users in */etc/passwd* will be in there as they will not be part of the NIS maps:

```
tin# awk -F: '{ print $1"::::::" }' ./shadow > ./security/
passwd.adjunct
tin# cat ./security/passwd.adjunct
testuser::::::
sysadmin::::::
msmith::::::
jgreen::::::
tin#
```

Now let's build everything again and take another look at the *passwd* map. This time we shouldn't see the encrypted password:

```
tin# make
tin# ypcat passwd
testuser:##testuser:500:100:Test User:/export/home/testuser:/
    bin/ksh
sysadmin:##sysadmin:1000:14:System Administrator:/export/home/
    sysadmin:/bin/ksh
msmith:##msmith:1001:10:Mike Smith:/export/home/msmith:/bin/ksh
jgreen:##jgreen:1002:10:John Green:/export/home/jgreen:/bin/ksh
tin#
```

If we also check the *passwd.adjunct* map, it should show that we have the encrypted passwords stored there:

```
tin# ypcat passwd.adjunct.byname
testuser:*LK*:::::::
sysadmin:*LK*:::::::
msmith: EwkdU786nskOz:::::::
jgreen:8CjcvwT4K.dxc:11556:::::::
tin#
```

Update the User Creation Script—Again

We have to make one more update to our standard creation script to support these changes. We need to make sure that when users are added, they are also placed in the *passwd.adjunct* file. This is quite a simple entry since we already have all the information we need to add, so we'll do it at the same time that we update the new *shadow* file, as shown below:

```
tin# cat /usr/local/utils/bin/createUsers
<lines removed for clarity>
tmpShadow=/tmp/shadow.$$
tmpPasswd=/tmp/passwd.$$
adjunctFile=/var/yp/security/passwd.adjunct
<lines removed for clarity>
#
# now move the acount into the yp location
#
tail -1 /etc/passwd >> ${ypPasswdFile}
tail -1 /etc/shadow >> ${ypShadowFile}
echo "${user}:::::::" >> ${adjunctFile}
#
# and strip them from the "main" password/shadow files
#
sed -e "/^${user}:/d" /etc/passwd > ${tmpPasswd}
<lines removed for clarity>
tin#
```

Disabling NIS

Before we finish this chapter, we'll look at the steps needed to disable NIS. This is actually quite easy to do, since there are only a few tasks that need to be completed. These will differ depending on whether we want to disable it completely, or, for example, demote a server to a client and so forth.

We also need to remember that we've been relying on NIS to supply most of our administration files, so we may need to copy them over to their correct locations before we disable NIS. Otherwise, we may have login failures, non-existent user problems, and so on.

Let's look at some of the options we have and what we would need to do in each case.

Disabling a Slave Server

We've already explained that servers run both `ypserv` and `ypbind`, so all we need to do here is disable the server functionality of the machine and continue to let `ypbind` run.

The first thing to do is to alter the server's map on the master server so it won't try to propagate any changes to the slave and will also stop any other clients from trying to bind to it. We showed how to do this earlier in the section "The Server Map" on page 298, but we'll run through the steps again for fluorine (we'll use `sed` to quickly edit the ASCII file):

```
tin# cd /var/yp/nis.solarisbootcamp.com
tin# makedbm -u /ypservers > /tmp/oldServs
tin# sed -e '/fluorine/d' < /tmp/oldServs > /tmp/newServs
tin# makedbm /tmp/newServs ypservers
tin#
```

Checking the *ypserver*'s map should show that fluorine is no longer on the server list, so then we can stop all the NIS processes running on it:

```
fluorine# ypcat -k ypservers
tin
iodine
fluorine# /usr/lib/netsvc/yp/ypstop
flourine#
```

Now we need to remove the map directory for the domain on the slave, which in our case is named */var/yp/nis.solarisbootcamp.com*. This will stop `ypserv` from running when we restart the NIS services:

```
fluorine# cd /var/yp
fluorine# rm -r nis.solarisbootcamp.com
flourine#
```

Next, we can run `ypstart`. This time, we should see that only `ypbind` has been started:

```
fluorine# /usr/lib/netsvc/yp/ypstart
starting NIS (YP server) services: ypbind done
flourine#
```

Finally, we should see that the machine has correctly bound to a server other than itself:

```
fluorine# ypwhich
tin
flourine#
```

Disabling a Client

We are assuming here that disabling the client means that we will completely remove it from NIS. This means that if it was running any server process, then this has already been disabled following a procedure similar to that described above. First, we'll stop the NIS processes:

```
carbon# /usr/lib/netsvc/yp/ypstop
carbon#
```

Now we'll update the naming service so it doesn't try to use NIS. We do this by either manually removing the "nis" entries from */etc/nsswitch.conf* or by resorting back to the "local files" version of the switch files as shown below:

```
carbon# cp /etc/nsswitch.files /etc/nsswitch.conf
carbon#
```

Next we can remove the */etc/defaultdomain* file so that the domain name won't be set at boot-time:

```
carbon# rm /etc/defaultdomain
carbon#
```

NIS is now disabled and won't be restarted the next time the machine is rebooted.

13

CONNECTING TO THE INTERNET

Manual Pages

defaultrouter (4)
hme (7D)
hosts (4)
ifconfig (1M)
ip (7P)
le (7D)
ndd (1M)
netstat (1M)
nslookup (1M)
ping (1M)
route (1M)
spray (1M)
tcp (7P)
traceroute (1M)

Files Affected

/etc/defaultrouter
/etc/inet/hosts
/etc/hostname.<interface>.<instance>
/etc/nsswitch.conf
/etc/resolv.conf

Objectives

In this chapter, we will look at how to connect our systems to an "external" network—in this case, the Internet. We'll see how to add routes to the systems to make sure they can all connect to the external machines.

We saw earlier in Chapter 11, "Connecting to the Local Area Network," how to configure systems for a local network. The next task is to extend this and connect them to another, wider, network.

Many companies now have a permanent connection to an external network; that is, something other than the LAN. This may be, for example, a remote part of the company network, or a connection to an Internet Service Provider (ISP), which in turn allows them to connect to the Internet. In simple terms these are all "internets" (i.e., networks of computers connected together by routers), and it is the method of connection we will describe here.

Although we are using a permanent network connection here, the basic theory and settings will also apply if you are using a modem—we'll discuss this method of connectivity in Chapter 15, "Dialing in with PPP." In general, the main tasks that we need to carry out here are very similar to a local connection, and are as follows:

- Assign a name and IP address to an additional network interface.
- Add any required routes.
- Configure resolving.
- Check that the interface is working correctly.

The Design

Let's look at how we will achieve this. Previously, we showed how to configure routing to allow data to flow between the two subnets by using a gateway (we defined the two interfaces "indium" and "tin" to accomplish this). Figure 13.1 shows the network at the stage where we had successfully connected all the systems together and had implemented any required routes and gateways.

We will now use "xenon" to perform a similar function, but this time to the external network. Once this has been set up, all the other machines will be able to access the external network using this route. This is normally implemented by using a default router, which is a piece of hardware such as a specialist device or another Sun workstation (as we used before). When a packet is sent from a system to a route where the destination address is not defined in the routing table, then the data will be passed to the system defined as the default router, which will then forward it to the correct machine, or perhaps to another router that has access to the destination system. We can see from this that each machine doesn't necessarily need to know where every system is—it only needs to know the whereabouts of the next router. In other words, the default router is a catchall for any addresses we do not know about—we expect it to know what to do with them.

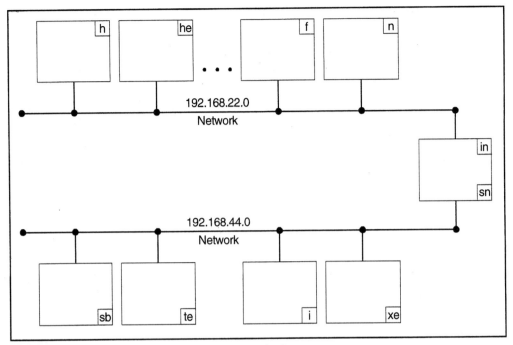

Figure 13.1 *The existing network—a reminder.*

Another obvious advantage of doing this is that we don't have to add a route to every machine we want to communicate with, which would be practically impossible for an Internet connection.

Allocating an IP Address

The first thing we need to do is install an additional Network Interface Card (NIC) and allocate an IP address for it. We have already seen that each interface connected to the network requires an IP address, and we also know that these addresses need to be unique. This rule extends to any TCP/IP connection—it must not clash with any machine already out there.

So, how do we choose what address to assign it? Either an ISP or one of the naming authorities responsible for maintaining sanity among Internet users will probably allocate at least part of it. For example, we may be allocated a range of addresses from which we assign each one as we see fit, or we may be given an individual address.

Domain Names and Addresses

Groups of numbers such as IP addresses are hard for people to remember, whereas names are much easier. To help overcome this problem, the Domain Name System (DNS) was introduced. We don't want to complicate things by introducing another topic that we cover in more detail later (see Chapter 16, "Configuring DNS"), so we'll just describe it briefly here.

DNS is used to perform host name resolving. This is a process in which we pass a fully qualified domain name to DNS (such as *www.sun.com*), and, in return, it will tell us what the corresponding IP address is. DNS does this by querying a machine known as a "nameserver," which if *it* doesn't know, will query *its* nameserver, and so forth.

Apart from the reserved and private network addresses that we discussed in Chapter 11, "Connecting to the Local Area Network," every address range that is allocated by the naming authorities needs to have an associated domain name. We would like our system to use a domain named "solarisboot-camp.com."

Registering a Domain Name

So, how do we get a domain name? A number of governing bodies administer domains; which one you turn to depends on whether you require a ".com" or a ".co.uk," for example. Each country has its own governing body that is responsible for handing out domains and their associated addresses.

For the purpose of this chapter, we will assume that our IP addresses have been allocated by either an ISP or our network administrator. The reason for this is that we don't want to complicate things too much by introducing another topic at this point (we'll cover this in more detail in Chapter 16, "Configuring DNS").

Our Values

After speaking to our friendly network administrator, we have been told that two routes are available for us to use, as listed in Table 13.1.

Table 13.1 *Available Routes to External Networks*

Route	Network Interface Address	Gateway/ Router Address	DNS Resolver Address	Netmask
1	175.35.63.50	172.35.63.1	172.35.63.2	255.255.255.0
2	195.10.132.50	195.10.132.1	195.10.132.2	255.255.255.0

Initially, we'll use route "1." Later, we'll show how to add route "2" to create a second default route to make use of both available routes.

Configuring the Interface

After the interface has been physically connected, we can assign an address to it in exactly the same way that we did for the internal gateway. The card we have installed is a secondary "hme" interface, so we have used the following values:

- hostname.hme1 value: xenon-gw
- netmask value: 255.255.255.0
- hosts entry: 172.35.63.50 xenon-gw

After the settings have been applied, we see the following with `ifconfig`:

```
xenon# ifconfig -a
lo0: flags=849<UP,LOOPBACK,RUNNING,MULTICAST> mtu 8232
        inet 127.0.0.1 netmask ff000000
hme0: flags=863<UP,BROADCAST,RUNNING,MULTICAST> mtu 1500
        inet 192.168.22.51 netmask ffffff80 broadcast 192.168.22.127
        ether 8:0:20:aa:bb:cc
hme1: flags=863<UP,BROADCAST,RUNNING,MULTICAST> mtu 1500
        inet 175.35.63.50 netmask ffffff00 broadcast 175.35.63.255
        ether 8:0:20:aa:bb:cc
xenon#
```

Now that the interface is up and running, let's `ping` the default router's address so that we can confirm the connection is OK. This is important because if we fail to get past this point we won't be able to see anything else!

```
xenon# ping 172.35.63.1
172.35.63.1 is alive
xenon#
```

Good. That works fine and proves that the physical connection is working. So let's move on to the next stage.

Adding a Default Route

Now we need to create the route itself. To do this dynamically, we can use the `route` command, just as we did for adding the routes between our subnets. But this time we use the "default" keyword to signify that this is the default route:

```
xenon# route add default 172.35.63.1 1
xenon#
```

Checking with `netstat` will show that the routes have now been created: the first to the network that the default route is connected to, and the second to the default router itself. It's always worth remembering that we must have a route to and from the default router!

```
xenon# netstat -rn
Routing Table:
    Destination        Gateway           Flags   Ref   Use   Interface
--------------- ----------------- ----- ----- ------ ---------
192.168.22.0    192.168.22.50     U       3       5   hme0
192.168.44.0    192.168.44.51     U       3       5   hme0
172.35.63.0     172.35.63.51      U       2       1   hme1
default         172.35.63.1       UG      3       5
127.0.0.1       127.0.0.1         UH      0       2   lo0
xenon#
```

To ensure that this is added whenever we boot the machine, we could add the above `route` command to the script named `/etc/init.d/routes` that we created in Chapter 11, "Connecting to the Local Area Network." The easier and most widely used method, though, is to create a file named */etc/ defaultrouter* and add the IP address of the router to it:

```
xenon# cat /etc/defaultrouter
172.35.63.1
xenon#
```

At boot-time, the system will check for the existence of this file and automatically create the route for us.

Host Names or Addresses

The *defaultrouter* file can contain either a host name or an IP address; we have decided to use IP addresses. The reason for this is that if host names are used, the system must be able to resolve them (i.e., determine their IP address), and communicate with them early in the boot process—normally before any additional routes have been configured, which means they must be in the local *hosts* file. By using addresses, we are sure we won't forget to update the *hosts* file and cause ourselves any problems.

Enabling Host Name Resolving

Now that we have the correct routes set up, we need to enable host name resolving. The reason for this is that we will almost certainly be connecting to machines that we don't know the IP address for—be it to send mail or view Web pages, for example.

We explained earlier that host name resolving is a function of DNS, so we now need to enable this. There are only two tasks we need to do at this point: The first is to instruct the system to use DNS for host name resolving, and the second is to inform it which nameserver it should use for the lookups.

To do the first, we update the nameservice switch file. Ours was previously set to use "local files" only, so we can now alter it to also use DNS. Since DNS is only used for host name entries, the change is very simple, resulting in only one line being altered:

```
xenon# grep hosts /etc/nsswitch.conf
hosts: files dns
xenon#
```

To inform DNS which nameserver to use, we create a file named */etc/ resolv.conf* (since it's not on the system by default) and add the relevant entries—the most important being the address of the nameserver. Again, we were provided with the IP address of the nameserver (which will normally be the case):

```
xenon# cat /etc/resolv.conf
search solarisbootcamp.com
nameserver 172.35.63.2
xenon#
```

We can have up to three nameserver entries in the *resolv.conf* file if we wish; as long as we have a route to them, everything will function correctly. For example, using the entry shown below would mean that the first nameserver listed would be used; the second entry is a "backup" in that it is only used should the first one become unreachable:

```
xenon# cat /etc/resolv.conf
search solarisbootcamp.com
nameserver 195.10.132.2
nameserver 172.35.63.2
xenon#
```

Checking the Connection

At the moment, we have DNS enabled for xenon only, so let's check that this works correctly before starting to reconfigure the remaining machines. We already know that the connection to the router is OK, but since we used an IP address rather than a host name, DNS wasn't required—we already knew the IP address, so didn't need to look it up. Now we will bring DNS into play to complete the test:

```
xenon# ping www.sun.com
www.sun.com is alive
xenon#
```

Good. DNS has managed to resolve the host name *www.sun.com* into the correct IP address and has successfully managed to ping it.

Nslookup

It's always nice when we can dig a little deeper into the details we are checking. For example, we don't really know that the nameserver was contacted—we certainly didn't see any communication with it. To see this sort of information we can use a program named nslookup. This is a utility that is able to carry out many DNS-related tasks, as we'll see later, but for now let's use it to confirm that DNS is working as we expect. The output below shows that our nameserver is able to determine the correct address of the system being queried:

```
xenon# nslookup www.sun.com
Server:  our.nameserver.com
Address:  172.35.63.2

Name:    www.sun.com
Address:  192.18.97.241
xenon#
```

Traceroute

We introduced traceroute earlier, but it is on this type of connection that this command really shines. Traceroute will detect the network routes that a machine takes to get to its destination, and also indicate if the machine is having problems along with the network that the problem lies with. For example, if we look at the route we took to get to the system above, we can see it is quite complex!

```
xenon# traceroute www.sun.com
traceroute to www.sun.com (192.18.97.241), 30 hops max, 40 byte
packets
  1   192.18.95.200 (192.18.95.200)  1.133 ms  1.099 ms  0.924 ms
  2   gateway.sun.com (193.18.96.1)  1.519 ms  1.130 ms  0.981 ms
www.sun.com (192.18.97.241)  1.147 ms  *  1.065 ms
xenon#
```

Traceroute also shows the time taken to reach the system. This helps us to spot any bottlenecks there may be along the way.

Ping

This is a useful, quick command to determine poor-performing networks. Running it with the "spray" option (or even running the spray command), we can see if packet loss is occurring, as well as approximate response times:

```
xenon# ping -s www.sun.com 64 5
PING www.sun.com: 64 data bytes
72 bytes from www.sun.com (192.18.97.241): icmp_seq=0. time=194. ms
72 bytes from www.sun.com (192.18.97.241): icmp_seq=1. time=193. ms
72 bytes from www.sun.com (192.18.97.241): icmp_seq=2. time=194. ms
72 bytes from www.sun.com (192.18.97.241): icmp_seq=3. time=193. ms
72 bytes from www.sun.com (192.18.97.241): icmp_seq=4. time=195. ms

----www.sun.com PING Statistics----
5 packets transmitted, 5 packets received, 0% packet loss
round-trip (ms)  min/avg/max = 193/193/195
xenon#
```

Configuring the Remaining Systems

At this point, we have one system that is able to send out data onto the external network. The remaining machines only have routes to the internal network defined on them, which means that while they can talk to each other quite happily, they don't know how to send out data onto the Internet. To allow them to do this, we'll create a default route on each system as before, but this time it will point to xenon. We will also need to update their *nsswitch.conf* as we did previously to use DNS for *hosts* lookup. Once this is complete, if any systems need to send or receive data from a machine they don't know about, they will pass it to xenon, which in turn will send it externally (see Figure 13.2).

Since we are using DNS, we'll also need to create a *resolv.conf* as before. The entries will be the same for the clients as they were for xenon, so we'll simply copy the entries over.

On these systems, the *defaultrouter* file will look like the one shown below:

```
hydrogen# cat /etc/defaultrouter
192.168.44.54
hydrogen#
```

As before, we have used IP addresses rather than host names to try and lighten any administration tasks. We also need to reboot the systems for the *defaultrouter* file to be used. After that, we can check that we can see an external system exactly as we did with xenon:

```
hydrogen# ping www.sun.com
www.sun.com is alive
hydrogen#
```

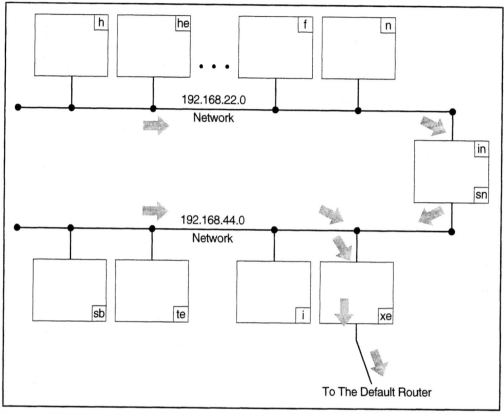

Figure 13.2 *External packet flow using the default route.*

Multiple Default Routes

We can also define multiple default routes on the system if we wish. To do this on our system (xenon), we could provide multiple connections to our external facing network interface. While this won't achieve load balancing, the system will "round-robin" between the interfaces (i.e., use one then the other, go back to the first, and so on).

We have already used 172.35.63.50 as the interface to 172.35.63.1. Now let's add the second route as another default route.

The first thing we need to do is add another physical interface—we will see this as "hme2." After that, we need to create */etc/hostname.hme2*, add the *hosts* entry to the *hosts* file, and activate the interface. These tasks are exactly the same as those we carried out earlier.

Now we can update */etc/defaultrouter* with the new entry:

```
xenon# cat /etc/defaultrouter
172.35.63.1
195.10.132.1
xenon#
```

If we also look at the routing table, we'll see that it now contains both default routes:

```
xenon# netstat -rn
Routing Table:
   Destination          Gateway             Flags  Ref   Use    Interface
-------------------  -------------------  -----  -----  ------  ---------
192.168.22.0         192.168.22.50        U        3      5     hme0
192.168.44.0         192.168.44.51        U        3      5     hme0
172.35.63.0          172.35.63.51         U        2      1     hme1
195.10.132.0         195.10.132.51        U        2      1     hme2
default              172.35.63.1          UG       3      5
default              195.10.132.1         UG       3      5
127.0.0.1            127.0.0.1            UH       0      2     lo0
xenon#
```

This mechanism is advantageous in that should one of the routes fail or become invalid, we still have a route that can be used, as shown in Figure 13.3.

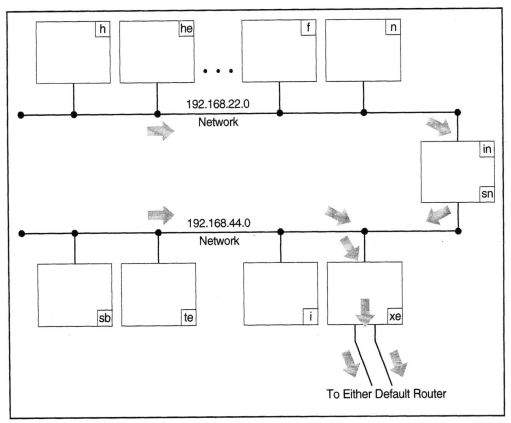

Figure 13.3 *The multiple default routes on xenon.*

We have now generated two main sets of files: one for the gateway and another for the remaining systems. Let's store these files under our standard distribution area, then they can be easily installed as required.

14

CONNECTING
SERIAL DEVICES

Files Affected

/dev/cua/*
/dev/term/*
/etc/remote
/etc/saf/*
/etc/ttydefs
/var/saf/*

Objectives

In this chapter, we will look at communicating with hardware devices (namely terminals and modems) using the serial interface. We'll also discuss the components that make up a serial interface, discuss the differences between Data Terminal Equipment (DTE) and Data Communication Equipment (DCE) devices, and see how to configure the Service Access Facility (SAF) to enable this communication.

Serial Communication

Nowadays, servers are often located in data centers, where they can be remotely accessed by both end-users and system administrators. The servers themselves are usually supplied "headless," which means that instead of having a graphics console (and associated keyboard), they are configured with a dumb terminal that connects via the serial port.

A modem may also be connected to provide access to the machine in the event of a network failure. Again, this will probably be via a serial port.

Although we'll only look at terminals and modems here, serial connectivity is used to control many other types of devices, including printers and digital cameras. The devices we'll describe use the RS-232 specification (officially known as TIA/EIA-232), which has been around for some time now. Sun serial ports support both this and its counterpart, RS-423, although you will need to check the hardware manual for any required jumper configurations.

Serial devices communicate by sending data one bit after another. At first glance, this seems a relatively easy task—just connect a few wires between the machines and start sending and receiving data. In practice, though, things are more complicated. For example, we need to be sure that the data is transmitted correctly, without any errors. The RS-232 specification achieves this by defining additional wires that are used for control and timing signals.

Table 14.1 shows the general RS-232 definition, although not all the signals are needed for every case, as we'll see later.

Table 14.1 *RS-232 Signals*

Pin	Signal	Common Symbol
1	Frame Ground	FG
2	Transmitted Data	TD
3	Received Data	RD
4	Request to Send	RTS
5	Clear to Send	CTS
6	Data Set Ready	DSR
7	Signal Ground	GND
8	Carrier Detect	DCD
9	Reserved for Testing	
10	Reserved for Testing	
11	Unassigned	
12	Secondary Carrier Detect	SDCD
13	Secondary Clear to Send	SCTS
14	Secondary Transmit	STD
15	Transmitter Signal Timing (DCE)	TC
16	Secondary Receive	SRD
17	Receiver Signal Timing	RC
18	Local Loopback	
19	Secondary Request to Send	SRTS
20	Data Terminal Ready	DTR
21	Signal Quality Detect	SQ
22	Ring Indicator	RI
23	Data Signal Rate Selector	DRS
24	Transmitter Signal Timing (DTE)	SCTE
25	Test Mode	BUSY

Synchronous versus Asynchronous

The two methods of serial data transmission are synchronous and asynchronous. The most common devices are asynchronous, which is the type we will look at here.

Synchronous transmissions use an accurate clock signal synchronized between the two ends. Data is sent or expected on every clock pulse, with errors being raised if either no data is received on a pulse or data is received between the pulses (Figure 14.1). The important feature about this method is that the clock signal must be accurate and synchronized between the two ends.

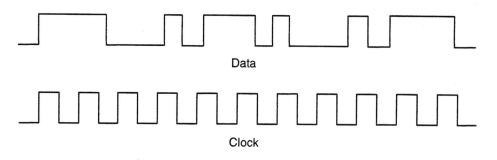

Data

Clock

Figure 14.1 *Synchronous serial transmission.*

Asynchronous transmissions, on the other hand, use a local timer at each end, which only needs to be approximately correct. This is because the timer is reset whenever a piece of data is received, which means that it will not be subject to large time-slew errors. This is achieved by following the steps below:

1. Both ends agree to transmit data at a specific rate.

2. A start bit is sent to mark the beginning of the data.

3. The timer is reset and the receiving end starts to sample the data.

4. The data (7 or 8 bits) is sent.

5. Optional parity data is sent.

6. One or two stop bits are sent.

We can see from this that for one 7-bit character, we could actually be transmitting 11 bits of data (1 start, 7 data, 1 parity, 2 stop). This is quite an overhead compared to synchronous transmission. A typical asynchronous data frame is shown in Figure 14.2.

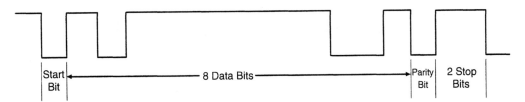

Figure 14.2 *Asynchronous serial transmission.*

We can see the additional data bits that are sent, so let's now look at what tasks they perform.

Start Bit

This is used to mark the start of the data frame. It is 1 bit in length and will always be transmitted.

Data Bit

This is the actual data itself. It can be either 7-bits or 8-bits long. The difference is that 7 bits allow the standard ASCII character set to be sent, whereas 8 bits allow binary characters to be used in addition to ASCII. Programs such as Point-to-Point Protocol (PPP) should always use 8-bit data, and, in fact, many people configure all their modem connections to use this value.

Parity

Parity data is a form of error detection. When a character is transmitted, a parity bit can be added to make the total number of ones in the character odd or even. Parity checking can also be disabled, in which case the parity bit is not sent at all, which removes 1 bit of the transmission overhead.

Parity may also be disabled when more efficient methods of error checking, such as X-modem and Automatic Request to Repeat (ARQ), are being used.

Each end of the line must agree on the data format that will be used—for example, 8 data bits, 1 stop bit, and no parity. This is often expressed in several ways, such as 8N1 or 8,n,1. So 7E2 would represent 7 data bits, even parity, and 2 stop bits.

Speed

We already mentioned that both ends of the link agree on the rate at which they will transmit data. This is measured by something known as the "baud rate," which, although not strictly correct, is commonly classed as "bits per second" (bps).

Baud and BPS

The baud rate is a measure of how many times per second a signal changes; for example, the signal on a 300-baud modem would change 300 times per second.

The number of bits transmitted per second is dependent on both the baud rate of the modem and the number of bits that it can transmit per baud. For example, if a 300-baud modem is able to transmit 1 bit per baud, it can transmit 300 bps. However, if the same modem can transmit 4 bits per baud, then the same 300-baud modem can transmit four times as many bits, or 1,200 bps.

Characters per Second

The number of characters transmitted per second (cps) depends upon the number of bits per character (bpc). For example, if the link is configured for 1 start bit, 8 data bits, no parity, and 1 stop bit, a total of 10 bits will be sent for every character, which means we can transmit 960 cps (9,600 bps/10 bpc).

Serial Devices

Two types of serial devices are available: Data Terminal Equipment and Data Communication Equipment. DTE devices are normally the source or destination devices, while DCE devices normally connect the source and destination together. Common examples of DTE equipment are terminals and printers, while the most common example of a DCE device is a modem.

The main difference between the two, as far as we are concerned, is that they transmit and receive data on different pins, as shown in Table 14.2.

Table 14.2 *DTE/DCE Transmit and Receive Details*

Hardware Type	Transmit	Receive
DTE	2	3
DCE	3	2

The RS-232 specification is titled "Interface Between Data Terminal Equipment and Data Circuit-Terminating Equipment Employing Serial Binary Data Interchange," which shows it was originally designed to connect DTEs together by adding a DCE between them. It is, however, common practice to connect DTEs without the intermediate DCE—we just need to reconfigure the cable connections.

DTE–DCE Connection

This is used to connect a computer to a modem. It is the designated type of connection and, as such, allows a "straight-through" cable to be easily used by connecting pin 2 (transmit) of the DTE device to pin 2 (receive) of the DCE device. A similar connection is made for transmit and receive connections on pin 3.

Figure 14.3 shows the typical cable pin-outs we would use for this type of connection.

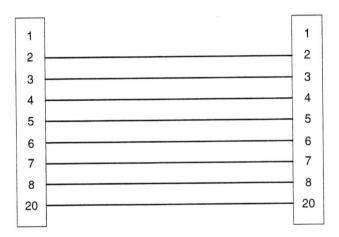

Figure 14.3 *DTE–DCE (modem) cable.*

DTE–DTE Connection

This type of connection is used to connect a terminal or printer to a computer. For this to work, we alter some of the connections to account for the fact that both devices transmit on the same pin, and both receive on the same pin. We need to connect the transmit pin (2) on one device to the receive pin (3) on the other, and vice versa—in other words, cross pins 2 and 3.

This is commonly known as a "null-modem cable." Although there are a number of different "recommended" ways to make these cables, we've shown two of the more-common ones in Figure 14.4. One is often used to connect terminals, while the second is used for other DTE devices that have full modem control support.

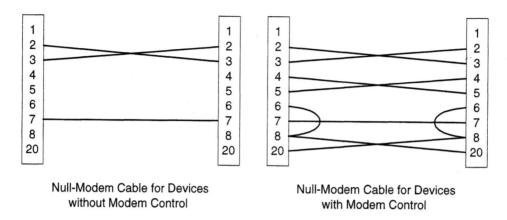

Null-Modem Cable for Devices
without Modem Control

Null-Modem Cable for Devices
with Modem Control

Figure 14.4 *DTE–DTE (null-modem) cables.*

Serial Ports

Sun computers normally come with two onboard serial ports, although some have one physical port that is internally wired to provide two ports when a special "splitter cable" is used.

Each port has two devices associated with it. They are defined in a way that follows a similar convention to the SCSI devices mentioned in Chapter 17, "Adding SCSI Devices." This means that they have an instance number, a physical device name, and a logical device name. Here, we'll only concern ourselves with the logical device names, which will be found in the *term* and *cua* subdirectories of /*dev*:

```
hydrogen# cd /dev
hydrogen# ls -lL cua
total 0
crw-------    1 uucp        uucp        29,131072 Sep  4  1997 a
crw-------    1 uucp        uucp        29,131073 Feb 11  1996 b
hydrogen# ls -lL term
total 0
crw--w----    1 root        tty         29,   0 Nov 12 08:03 a
crw-rw-rw-    1 root        .sys        29,   1 Mar 17  1997 b
hydrogen#
```

We can see that all the devices share the same major number (29), as we would expect, but the minor numbers are quite different. Let's quickly look at the physical names for one of the ports:

```
hydrogen# ls -l cua/a
lrwxrwxrwx    1 root        other          35 Oct 25  1998 cua/a ->
../../devices/obio/zs@0,100000:a,cu
hydrogen# ls -l term/a
```

```
lrwxrwxrwx   1 root      other      32 Oct 25  1998 term/a ->
../../devices/obio/zs@0,100000:a
hydrogen#
```

This shows that *⁄dev⁄term⁄a* and *⁄dev⁄cua⁄a* are the same physical device. The reason that two logical entries are provided has to do with the ways the serial ports are used for incoming and outgoing connections.

Normally, the serial port cannot be opened until the Carrier Detect (DCD) signal is high. If a modem is connected to the port, it will enable DCD when it answers an incoming call. This will allow the port to be opened and used, allowing a `getty` process to offer the incoming user a login prompt.

While this works fine for incoming connections, it means that any outgoing ones will hang waiting for DCD to be enabled before they can open the port. Obviously this won't happen because the modem is being used to dial out, rather than detecting an incoming call. To get around this, the *cua* devices have "software carrier" enabled, allowing them to be opened without DCD being enabled.

In summary, the devices and their functions are listed here:

- *⁄dev⁄term⁄* * (used for incoming connections)
- *⁄dev⁄cua⁄* * (used for outgoing connections)

Now that we've seen the types of devices that are available, and the settings we can apply to them, let's find out how to configure them.

Service Access Facility

The Service Access Facility (SAF) is used to control access to specific services on the machine. The main SAF program is the Service Access Controller (`/usr/lib/saf/sac`), which is responsible for managing the overall process, including spawning the individual daemons known as "port monitors."

Port Monitors

These, as their name suggests, are programs that monitor a port for incoming connection requests. Currently, two of these are supplied as standard, although the SAF can be extended to allow it to support custom monitors that have been written for specific applications. The supplied ones are listed here:

- `ttymon` (this monitors the serial ports)
- `listen` (this monitors the network ports)

Each port monitor needs to be "added" to the SAF and, after that, needs further configuration to be able to support any services. Since this chapter deals with serial devices, we will only configure the serial port monitor here (`ttymon`). After adding it to the SAF, we'll configure it to support two services: one for a terminal and one for a modem.

When a port monitor is added it has a name associated with it. This is known as the port monitor "tag" and is used to reference it later. The default tag used for the serial ports is "zsmon" (because the serial ports use the "zs" driver).

SAF Hierarchy

Before we go any further, let's look at how the SAF processes are started along with the hierarchy they use. This will show how sac determines which port monitors are available, and how each of these discovers the settings it should apply.

The examples below contain typical configuration data. We don't need to be too concerned about their contents just now, as we'll look at this in more detail as we progress through the chapter.

First, the main daemon, sac, is started automatically at boot-time using the */etc/inittab* entry shown below:

```
hydrogen# grep sac /etc/inittab
sc:234:respawn:/usr/lib/saf/sac -t 300
hydrogen#
```

Once started, it determines its configuration by checking the hierarchy generated beneath */etc/saf*, an example of which is shown here:

```
hydrogen# cd /etc/saf
hydrogen# ls -l
total 6
prw-------   1 root     root          0 Nov 19 13:41 _cmdpipe
prw-------   1 root     root          0 Nov 19 15:26 _sacpipe
-r--r--r--   1 root     other        52 Nov 19 15:11 _sactab
-rw-r--r--   1 root     sys          45 Aug 27  2000 _sysconfig
drwxr-xr-x   2 root     other       512 Nov 19 15:11 zsmon
hydrogen#
```

Next sac reads the file named *_sysconfig*. Often this is empty, as in our case, but it can be edited to set any system-wide configuration details if we wish:

```
hydrogen# cat _sysconfig
# This is the per-system configuration file

hydrogen#
```

After that, it reads its main configuration file, */etc/saf/_sactab*. This contains the current SAF version number along with an entry for each port monitor that has been added to the system:

```
hydrogen# cat /etc/saf/_sactab
# VERSION=1

zsmon:ttymon::0:/usr/lib/saf/ttymon #
hydrogen#
```

This example defines a port monitor tag named "zsmon" and specifies that the port monitor type used for this tag will be ttymon. As shown in the /etc/saf listing earlier, a directory is created for each port monitor tag defined in /etc/saf/_sactab. This means a directory named *zsmon* has been created. If we take a look in there we'll see the following contents:

```
hydrogen# cd /etc/saf/zsmon
hydrogen# ls -l
total 4
-rw-r--r--   1 root      other       4 Mar  9 14:06 _pid
prw-------   1 root      other       0 Mar  9 14:12 _pmpipe
-r--r--r--   1 root      other     248 Mar  9 14:20 _pmtab
hydrogen#
```

The _pmtab file contains all the settings that need to be applied by the port monitor—ttymon, in this case. It contains colon-separated strings, which can be quite hard work to decipher. The following example has two services configured, one named "ttya" and the other named "ttyb":

```
hydrogen# cat _pmtab
# VERSION=1
ttya:u:root:reserved:reserved:reserved:/dev/term/a:I::/usr/bin/
login::9600:ldterm,ttcompat:ttya login\: ::tvi925:y:#
ttyb:u:root:reserved:reserved:reserved:/dev/term/b:I::/usr/bin/
login::9600:ldterm,ttcompat:ttyb login\: ::tvi925:y:#
hydrogen#
```

Now that we've seen the files that define the SAF hierarchy, let's look at how the SAF processes tie together by showing which daemons are spawned along with their related configuration files (Figure 14.5).

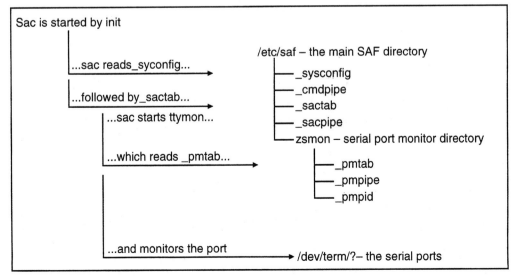

Figure 14.5 *The SAF process, using "zsmon" as an example.*

SAF Log Location

If we take a quick look in */var*, we'll see a similar hierarchy to */etc/saf* has been generated there, but this time for the log files:

```
hydrogen# cd /var/saf
hydrogen# ls -l
total 74
-rw-rw-rw-   1 root      root       36335 Nov 19 15:13 _log
drwxr-xr-x   2 root      other        512 Nov 19 15:11 zsmon
hydrogen#

helium# cd zsmon
helium# ls -l
total 4
-r--r--r--   1 root      root        1785 Nov 19 15:14 log
hydrogen#
```

Administration Programs

A number of programs are provided to administer the SAF, which are as follows:

- sacadm (used to control sac and its related port monitors)
- pmadm (used to control a port monitor's services)

For each type of port monitor there is also a "helper" program. This is used to provide port monitor specific information that has been formatted so that it can be easily passed onto both sacadm and pmadm. The helper program for ttymon is named ttyadm, while the one for listen is named nlsadmin. We'll look at ttyadm in more detail when we use it later to create our services.

Remove Existing Port Monitors

Now that we've seen the hierarchy and the type of data that is stored there, we can add the devices we require. The first task to perform is to clear out any existing configuration details and start with a clean sheet, so let's do that now.

When the system is installed, at least one port monitor will usually be created, and will probably be a service on the "zsmon" tag. Completely removing this tag will allow us to reuse it later and will hopefully make things clearer when we create the services on the system:

```
hydrogen# sacadm -r -p zsmon
hydrogen# sacadm -l
No port monitors defined
hydrogen#
```

Good. Everything has gone. Running pmadm to list the current port monitor details will also confirm that they've been removed:

```
hydrogen# pmadm -l
No services defined
hydrogen#
```

We could actually leave it at this point and start to reconfigure the ports as we require, but for this chapter we'll also remove the existing *zsmon* hierarchy. This will allow us to see how it is rebuilt automatically:

```
hydrogen# rm -r /etc/saf/zsmon
hydrogen# ls -l
total 4
prw-------   1 root     root         0 Mar  9 13:03 _cmdpipe
prw-------   1 root     root         0 Mar  9 14:12 _sacpipe
-r--r--r--   1 root     other       13 Mar  9 14:25 _sactab
-rw-r--r--   1 root     sys         45 Aug 27  2000 _sysconfig
hydrogen#
```

Looking at the contents of */etc/saf*, we can see that we are now left with the top-level configuration files only. We've already looked at the *_sysconfig* file, but let's look at *_sactab* to see what it contains now:

```
hydrogen# cat _sactab
# VERSION=1

hydrogen#
```

Just as we thought—apart from the version number the file is empty, confirming that all the services have been removed.

Adding a Terminal

Now we're ready to add the terminal. Table 14.3 shows the parameters we'll use to do this. Also, as we are going to connect it to port "A," we need to be aware of how this port functions when the machine is headless. For now we'll assume it has a graphics console and revisit the headless case later in the section "Consoles and Serial Ports" on page 343.

Table 14.3 *Terminal Configuration Details*

Setting	Value
Port Connection	A
Speed	9600
Data Format	7, e, 2 (7 data, even parity, 2 stop)
Terminal Emulation	VT100

The first thing we need is the terminal and the serial cable. Our cable will be a null-modem cable—it has pins 2 and 3 crossed, and 7 straight through. Once it is connected and powered on, you will probably be able to make sure it's working by sending data to the port that the terminal is connected to:

```
hydrogen# cat /etc/motd > /dev/term/a
hydrogen#
```

At this point, data should hopefully appear on the screen, which confirms that the cable is the correct type and that the terminal is configured correctly.

Add a Port Monitor

Now we're ready to add our first port monitor. We've already said that we'll use the standard "zsmon" tag, and that because we are dealing with a serial device, the port monitor used will be /usr/lib/saf/ttymon. Let's add the port monitor now:

```
hydrogen# sacadm -a -p zsmon -t ttymon -c
/usr/lib/saf/ttymon    -v `ttyadm -V`
hydrogen#
```

We can see that besides the port monitor and tag information, we've also specified the port monitor version number using the ttymon helper program, ttyadm. We'll see how useful ttyadm is when we visit it again later. For now, let's run sacadm again to confirm that the system has a valid port monitor defined:

```
hydrogen# sacadm -l
PMTAG     PMTYPE     FLGS RCNT STATUS    COMMAND
zsmon     ttymon      -    0   ENABLED   /usr/lib/saf/ttymon
hydrogen#
```

So, what tasks has sacadm performed for us? The main one, as far as we are concerned, is that it has updated the hierarchy beneath */etc/saf*. Let's look at this now to see what's been changed:

```
hydrogen# ls -l
total 6
prw-------   1 root      root       0 Mar  9 13:03 _cmdpipe
prw-------   1 root      root       0 Mar  9 14:12 _sacpipe
-r--r--r--   1 root      other     13 Mar  9 14:25 _sactab
-rw-r--r--   1 root      sys       45 Aug 27  2000 _sysconfig
drwxr-xr-x   2 root      other    512 Mar  9 14:06 zsmon
hydrogen#
```

We can see that the *zsmon* directory that we removed earlier has been recreated, and that the *_sactab* file has also been updated. If we look at its contents, we'll see that it now contains an entry for the new port monitor:

```
hydrogen# cat _sactab
# VERSION=1

zsmon:ttymon::0:/usr/lib/saf/ttymon      #
hydrogen#
```

We've already seen that the first line of this file relates to the SAF version information and is specified using the `ttyadm -V` command. The remaining entries describe any port monitors that have been added, with each line formatted as a colon-separated string. Table 14.4 uses the example port monitor definition shown above to describe each of the field details.

Table 14.4 Sactab *File Details*

Setting	Value
zsmon	Port monitor name
ttymon	Port monitor type
(blank)	Flags field (none in this case) If "d," do not enable port monitor. If "x," do not start it.
0	0 means don't restart the port monitor if it fails
/usr/lib/saf/ttymon	Port monitor path name
#	Comment field

If we look in the newly created *zsmon* directory, we can see the files listed below. We haven't defined any services yet, so the *_pmtab* file should be empty (apart from the version number).

```
hydrogen# ls -l zsmon
total 4
-rw-r--r--   1 root     other      4 Mar  9 14:06 _pid
prw-------   1 root     other      0 Mar  9 14:06 _pmpipe
-rw-r--r--   1 root     other     12 Mar  9 14:06 _pmtab
hydrogen#

hydrogen# cat zsmon/_pmtab
# VERSION=1
hydrogen#
```

Obviously we don't want to have to trawl through all these files to determine whether any services have been defined or not! Instead we can use `pmadm` in a way similar to how we used `sacadm` earlier, as shown in the following example:

```
hydrogen# pmadm -l
No services defined
hydrogen#
```

Configure the Port Monitor

Now that we have successfully added a port monitor, we need to configure it for a service. This is where the commands start to become a little more complicated, so to understand them better, let's run the command first and then break it down into each of its components:

```
hydrogen# pmadm -a -p zsmon -s ttya -i root -fu \
-v `ttyadm -V` -y "Terminal" -m "`ttyadm -l contty5H \
-d /dev/term/a -T vt100 -s /usr/bin/login -S y`"
hydrogen#
```

Table 14.5 shows most of the options used and what they refer to, although we'll deal with the individual options passed to `ttyadm` in a moment.

Table 14.5 *Port Monitor Parameters*

Option	Meaning
-p zsmon	Name of the port monitor that we are configuring
-s ttya	Defines a tag for the service
-i root	Run the service as root
-fu	Create a *utmpx* entry when the user logs in
-v `ttyadm –V`	Get the version number of *ttyadm* and pass it to *pmadm*
-y "Terminal"	Add a comment to the port details file
-m "<ttyadm command>"	Generate the *ttymon*-specific details

`Pmadm` has performed a set of tasks similar to those of `sacadm`; it has updated part of the SAF hierarchy and configured the port monitor for the correct service. We'll see how it has done this if we take a look at the *_pmtab* file:

```
hydrogen# cat zsmon/_pmtab
# VERSION=1
ttya:u:root:reserved:reserved:reserved:/dev/term/a:::/usr/bin/
login::contty5H::login\: ::vt100:y:#Terminal
hydrogen#
```

We'll look at most of these values in the next section, "Ttyadm," but for now let's run pmadm again to make sure that it knows the port has been successfully configured:

```
hydrogen# pmadm -l
PMTAG  PMTYPE  SVCTAG  FLGS  ID     <PMSPECIFIC>
zsmon  ttymon  ttya    u     root   /dev/term/a - - /usr/bin/login
   - contty5H - login: - vt100 y #Terminal
hydrogen#
```

Good. Everything looks OK. The port should now be accessible so that when we power the terminal on, we'll see the login prompt. Now that everything is working, let's have a look at some of the additional commands we've used above in a little more detail, before we move on and create the second service.

Ttyadm

We've already mentioned that ttyadm is the helper program for ttymon and is used to generate the colon-separated string for the _pmtab file that we saw in the earlier example. We did this by embedding the ttyadm output into the pmadm command, but in this section we'll run ttyadm as a standalone program. This will enable us to see its output and let us examine the values supplied to it at the same time.

First, let's run the command we used in the earlier example:

```
hydrogen# ttyadm -l contty5H -d /dev/term/a -T vt100 -s
   /usr/bin/login -S y
/dev/term/a:::/usr/bin/login::contty5H::login\: ::vt100:y:
hydrogen#
```

This confirms that ttyadm simply returns a correctly formatted string to suit the parameters passed onto it. This string is passed onto pmadm, where it is inserted into the _pmtab file. In fact, if we compare the earlier _pmtab entry to the output above we should see that they both match. Table 14.6 shows what each of the parameters in the earlier example refers to.

Table 14.6 Terminal Ttyadm Parameters

Option	Meaning
-l contty5H	Specify the line settings (see below)
-d /dev/term/a	Device used for the (incoming) line
-T vt100	Sets the TERM environment variable to vt100
-s /usr/bin/login	Name of the service that runs on connection
-S y	Enable software carrier

Line Settings

When we use the `ttyadm` command, one of the parameters we need to specify is the line settings that we would like to apply to the port. In our example, we've used "contty5H," so let's find out what this means.

A file named */etc/ttydefs* contains the list of all the line settings known to the system. Each one of these has a corresponding label that is matched against the option passed to `ttyadm`. Let's have a look at the one we have used:

```
hydrogen# grep contty5H /etc/ttydefs
contty5H:19200 opost onclr:19200 hupcl sane::conttyH
hydrogen#
```

So what does this mean? First, we can see that the file is colon-separated and split into fields. The first field contains the label that will be matched to find the correct entry. The next contains the initial line settings to apply. Following this we have the line settings that will be applied just before the service runs. Both of these can be any of the valid `termio` settings (see the manual pages for `termio(7I)` and `stty(1)`). Next we have the "autobaud" field. If this contains an "A," `ttymon` will determine the line speed by analyzing the carriage returns. Finally, the last field contains the name of the next entry to use if this one is unsuitable. This is often used to create a "hunt group" that cycles through each speed. The "hunt group" that relates to our settings (contty5H) is shown below:

```
conttyH:9600 opost onclr:9600 hupcl sane::contty1H
contty1H:1200 opost onclr:1200 hupcl sane::contty2H
contty2H:300 opost onclr:300 hupcl sane::contty3H
contty3H:2400 opost onclr:2400 hupcl sane::contty4H
contty4H:4800 opost onclr:4800 hupcl sane::contty5H
contty5H:19200 opost onclr:19200 hupcl sane::conttyH
```

The only differences between each of these entries are the line speeds and the labels. This means that if contty5H (19200) is unsuitable, conttyH (9600) will be tried, and if that is unsuitable, contty1H (1200) will be tried, and so on. The remaining line settings are all the same; by checking the `stty` man page, we can see they perform the following functions:

- opost—Post-process output
- onclr—Map newline to carriage return-newline on output
- hupcl—Hang up the connection on the last close
- sane—Reset all modes to reasonable values

The */etc/ttydefs* file has an associated administration command named `sttydefs`. This can be used to maintain the entries in the file, although many people simply edit it to make the necessary changes. It also provides options to list entries, so instead of running the `grep` command as we showed earlier, we could also run the following:

```
hydrogen# sttydefs -l contty5H
------------------------------------------------------------
contty5H:19200 opost onlcr:19200 hupcl sane::conttyH
------------------------------------------------------------

ttylabel:        contty5H
initial flags:   19200 opost onlcr
final flags:     19200 hupcl sane
autobaud:        no
nextlabel:       conttyH
hydrogen#
```

Consoles and Serial Ports

We mentioned earlier that there are some special cases of machine configuration that we need to be aware of when configuring serial ports. For example, we have just configured port "A" for a terminal connection, but this assumed the system already had a graphics console connected; the reason for this is as follows.

If a machine is headless (if it doesn't have a graphics console or, more correctly, a keyboard plugged into the keyboard port) then, by default, serial port "A" will become the main interface and will receive any console output. This includes EEPROM, bootup, and system output.

Because this port is effectively acting as the main console, it will also receive a login prompt, even though it hasn't been configured using pmadm—it is all carried out automatically by the following entry in /etc/inittab:

```
co:234:respawn:/usr/lib/ttymon -g -h -p "`uname -n` \
console login: " -T sun -d /dev/console -l console
```

It's also worth noting that this entry will also set the TERM environment to "sun," which will need overriding in the user's .profile (or by editing the previous entry if you prefer).

Therefore, having an attached graphics console will ensure that the console receives the main login prompt, allowing us to configure our terminal on serial port "A."

Adding a Modem

Now we're ready to add a modem to the system. This will use the same port monitor that we used for port "A" (ttymon), only it will be configured slightly different to suit our modem.

To configure this we'll follow similar steps to the earlier configuration for port "A," although we don't need to update the _sactab file as we already have a valid ttymon configured and running. We simply need to add a secondary service and let the existing ttymon manage both of them. This time we'll use a different set of values for the port, because it will be configured for a modem rather than a terminal. The ones we'll use are shown in Table 14.7.

Table 14.7 *Modem Configuration Details*

Setting	Value
Port Connection	B
Speed	38400
Data Format	8, n, 1 (8 data, no parity, 1 stop)
Mode	Bidirectional

Looking at this table, we can see that the data format is different. We mentioned earlier that many people like to use 8 data bits, no parity, and 1 stop bit for their modem lines, and often create an entry in */etc/ttydefs* specifically for this. To accomplish this, we'll add the following entry, named "DIAL_8," to */etc/ttydefs*:

```
hydrogen# grep DIAL_8 /etc/ttydefs
DIAL_8:19200 -parenb cs8 opost onlcr:19200 sane -parenb cs8
crtscts hupcl::DIAL_8
hydrogen#
```

We can see that in addition to the flags set previously, this sets the following values:

- -parenb—Disable parity
- cs8—Set the character size to 8 bits
- crtscts—Enable hardware flow control

Now we can configure the SAF to support the service. We've already added the port monitor (ttymon) when we configured the terminal earlier, so all we need to do here is add another service to it. Again, we'll run the command first and then break it down into its components:

```
hydrogen# pmadm -a -p zsmon -s ttyb -i root -fu \
-v `ttyadm-V` -y "Bi-directional modem" \
-m "`ttyadm -b -l DIAL_8 -m ldterm,ttcompat \
-d /dev/term/b -s /usr/bin/login` -S n"
hydrogen#
```

This shows that the pmadm generic parameters are very similar to the previous settings, and that most of the changes are within the ttyadm parameters. We'll look at these in a moment, but first let's check the *_pmtab* file again to see what changes have been made:

```
hydrogen# cat /etc/saf/zsmon/_pmtab
# VERSION=1
ttya:u:root:reserved:reserved:reserved:/dev/term/a:::/usr/bin/
login::contty5H::login\: ::vt100:y:#Terminal
ttyb:u:root:reserved:reserved:reserved:/dev/term/b:b::/usr/bin/
login::DIAL_8:ldterm,ttcompat:login\: :::: -S n#Bi-directional
modem
hydrogen#
```

Table 14.8 shows what the different parameters refer to.

Table 14.8 Modem *Ttyadm* **Parameters**

Option	Meaning
-b	Configure a bidirectional port
-l DIAL_8	Use the 8-bit line setting (see above)
-m ldterm,ttcompat	Use the STREAMS modules *ldterm* and *ttcompat*
-d /dev/term/b	Device used for the (incoming) line
-s /usr/bin/login	Name of the service that runs on connection
-S n	Disable software carrier

Hopefully, pmadm is aware of the changes that we've made, so let's make sure it knows the service is available:

```
hydrogen# pmadm -l -s ttyb
PMTAG  PMTYPE  SVCTAG  FLGS  ID    <PMSPECIFIC>
zsmon ttymon ttyb    u     root /dev/term/b b - /usr/bin/login
- DIAL_8 ldterm,ttcompat login: - - n #Bi-directional modem
hydrogen#
```

Again, the port appears to be configured correctly, so let's move on and test that the modem works.

Test the Modem

At this point the hardware has been configured correctly and we have the correct cable in place, so we should be able to confirm the modem is at least connected (although not necessarily configured) correctly by connecting onto it. We need to use the outgoing *cua* port for this:

```
hydrogen# tip -9600 /dev/cua/b
connected
at
OK
```

```
ati4
U.S. Robotics 56K FAX EXT Settings...
<lines removed for clarity>
OK
~.
hydrogen#
```

Good. We've managed to talk to the modem, which is a good start!

Configure /Etc/remote

Now we'll create an entry for the modem in */etc/remote*. This is an ASCII file that contains information about all the remote systems we need to connect to, including phone numbers and all the connection details. By default, an entry named "hardwire" is also included; it is normally only used to connect to the modem. We need to make sure it contains the correct settings, which means it will look similar to the following entry:

```
hydrogen# cat /etc/remote
<lines removed for clarity>
hardwire:\
        :dv=/dev/cua/b:br#9600:
<lines removed for clarity>
hydrogen#
```

Now we'll be able to `tip` directly to the modem using the newly created "hardwire" entry:

```
hydrogen# tip hardwire
connected
at
OK
~.
hydrogen#
```

Test Incoming Connections

All that remains for this service is for us to test the incoming connection to make sure that the modem answers the call (set the modem to "auto answer"). Then we need to make sure that `ttymon` detects our presence. Once it had done this, it will enable the port and ensure that the correct settings are applied to it. After that, we'll receive a login prompt.

Conclusion

We have now managed to add a device of each type (DTE and DCE) to the system, and successfully configured them with the SAF to accept incoming connections.

15

DIALING IN WITH PPP

Manual Pages

aspppd (1M)
cu (1C)
nscd (1M)
ppp (7M)
stty (1)
termio (4)
termio (7I)
tip (1)
uucp (1C)

Files Affected

/etc/asppp.cf
/etc/gateways
/etc/inet/hosts
/etc/nscd.conf
/etc/nsswitch.conf
/etc/resolv.conf
/etc/uucp/Devices
/etc/uucp/Dialers
/etc/uucp/Systems
/var/adm/log/asppp.log

Objectives

Many systems can only communicate with a remote network by using a serial connection (a modem). In this chapter we will configure a Point-to-Point (PPP) client to connect into a remote server and provide network connectivity. We'll also see how to configure the Services Access Facility (SAF) and UNIX-to-UNIX Copy Protocol (UUCP), which are used by PPP to make the connection.

Point-to-Point Protocol

In Chapter 13, "Connecting to the Internet," we demonstrated how to configure the system to allow us to connect into a remote network. This connection was based on a permanent link, such as a leased line. Here, we will describe how to connect remotely, assuming we don't have access to that line; instead we'll use a dialup connection in conjunction with a software component named PPP. PPP allows a virtual network to be created over a serial connection, which in turn allows TCP/IP to run across it.

Why Use PPP?

PPP provides many advantages over simply connecting to the remote machine with a modem—the obvious one being that it emulates a network. All the standard features of network connectivity are available, such as the ability to `ftp` files to and from the machine and allowing numerous `telnet` connections to it.

This is a much cheaper way of providing access to a remote system and may actually be the only way a connection can be obtained, such as in the case of a mobile user not at a fixed location. It is also a mechanism often used by home users to gain temporary or intermittent access to a network.

In our hypothetical network, we will use a separate system to provide a link to the outside world in case the main network itself fails. This link will be much slower than the original network as it relies on a modem to provide connectivity, but other than that it will be a fully functioning network.

PPP also brings automatic connection and disconnection with it, as we'll see in the section "Link Manager" on page 357.

The Components

PPP works in conjunction with software components from various packages that are supplied with the operating system. In this chapter, we'll break them down into their different layers and describe how to build the connection from the ground up.

Some packages are described in more detail in other chapters, in which case we'll point you to the relevant one, but still show the commands we are running. The main components we'll be dealing with are as follows:

- **Service Access Facility**—Allows us to configure the port used by the modem with the correct properties such as speed, data bits, stop bits, and so on.

- **UUCP**—Provides the "database" files used for the connection, along with utilities that are used to automate and test the dial-in procedure.

- **PPP**—Configures the serial line to provide a virtual network, which runs TCP/IP over it.

The System

We will use a system that is connected to the internal network, but doesn't have any external routing capabilities. We will also assume that it has been built to our standard configuration described in Chapter 11, "Connecting to the Local Area Network." Among other things, this means that both Router Discovery (RDISC) and Routing Information Protocol (RIP) have been disabled. The reason for disabling all the external routes is that this machine will only be used as a fallback system in case the main network fails, so we don't need to add them to start with (besides which, it makes everything much clearer to describe and document!).

Let's create the *hosts* entry for the machine and couple it to the LAN:

```
cesium# cat /etc/inet/hosts
<lines removed for clarity>
#
# PPP Dialout client
#
192.168.44.55   cesium   cs
<lines removed for clarity>
cesium#
```

Now that we have a rough idea of the hardware and software components that are involved, let's look at each one in more detail and show the settings for them.

Building the Connection

Various bits of information need to be gathered to make this connection possible. We probably need to rely on a number of different people to supply this information, such as the system administrator and the ISP. (Note that when we refer to the ISP, this may actually be an internal department that is responsible for the network. Bear in mind that your ISP may be different; for example, some ISPs will provide you with a user name while others may allow you to specify your own, or they may allocate a static IP address, while others may provide dynamic ones.) It doesn't really matter how the settings are supplied, as long as you are aware of who should be supplying them.

Table 15.1 shows the values we are using and, in our case, who has supplied them.

Table 15.1 *PPP Connection Settings*

Setting	Value	Supplied By
Serial Port	*/dev/term/b*	System Administrator
Serial Port Settings	56k, 8 data bits, 1 stop bit, no parity	System Administrator
Modem Type	Bidirectional	System Administrator
PPP Login	guest	ISP
PPP Password	guestPassword	ISP
Our IP Address	Dynamic	ISP
ISP IP Address	Dynamic	ISP
Name Server	136.89.22.4	ISP
Dial-in Phone Number	1234 567890	ISP
Protocol	PPP	ISP

The Serial Port

To create the connectivity between the local and remote machine, we'll use a modem connected to each machine—the phone line providing the link between the two. This is the most common way of using PPP, although it's also worth noting that the link could simply be a serial cable connected between the two machines if we wish (a method sometimes used for testing a configuration).

We need to set the port up as a "bidirectional" modem to allow data to flow in both directions. Luckily, we showed how to add modems and configure SAF in Chapter 14, "Connecting Serial Devices," so all that's needed here is to run through the commands required to configure the port to use the parameters shown in Table 15.1.

First, we'll make sure the port is deconfigured by simply removing any existing port monitors on it. Once they have been removed, we'll go ahead and recreate them:

```
cesium# pmadm -r -p zsmon -s ttyb
cesium# pmadm -a -p zsmon -s ttyb -i root -v `ttyadm -V` \
-fu -m "`ttyadm -d /dev/term/b -s /usr/bin/login -l \
contty5H -b -S n -m ldterm,ttcompat`" -y "Bidirectional Modem"
cesium#
```

The terminal definition we are using is "contty5H," which is set to 7 bits, even parity by default, although we actually modify the line at connection time to run at 8 bits, no parity, and hardware flow control.

Checking the port after running the command should show something similar to that shown here:

```
cesium# pmadm -l -s ttyb
PMTAG     PMTYPE    SVCTAG    FLGS ID      <PMSPECIFIC>
zsmon     ttymon    ttyb      u    root    /dev/term/b
                                           b - /usr/bin/login - contty5H
                                           ldterm,ttcompat login:  - - n
                                           #Bidirectional Modem
cesium#
```

Good. The port should now be enabled for the correct form of modem, so let's see if we can talk to it. We should be able to `tip` to the port and see the OK prompt if everything is working correctly:

```
cesium# tip /dev/cua/b
connected
AT
OK
~.
cesium#
```

We now have a modem that we know we can communicate with. This is a good start, so let's move on to the next stage and look at UUCP.

UUCP

UUCP was originally designed to allow systems to exchange files between, and run programs on, remote machines.

To enable this, all that was needed was to create logins on both systems for the "UUCP user," which provided both a degree of security and a mechanism for authentication. Next, the UUCP "database" files (which are actually text files, as we'll see later) are edited to allow everything to function correctly. Once everything was set up, users could connect in and run their tasks.

Nowadays, UUCP isn't used as much, although some of the files have been utilized by PPP. These are the ones we will be dealing with, and are listed below. The remaining ones are unused, so we'll ignore them to avoid any confusion:

- */etc/uucp/Devices*
- */etc/uucp/Dialers*
- */etc/uucp/Systems*

The first thing we need to do before we can start any configuration work is to check that the packages are installed on the system. Running `pkginfo` should show us that they are:

```
cesium# pkginfo | grep -i uucp
system        SUNWbnur          Networking UUCP Utilities, (Root)
system        SUNWbnuu          Networking UUCP Utilities, (Usr)
cesium#
```

Chat Scripts

Chat scripts are used to allow a computer to provide automated responses to a series of "questions" from another machine. For example, UUCP uses them to pass the login information to the remote system when the user is trying to login to it.

Chat scripts consist of sequences of words or characters separated by white space and are grouped together as "expect-send" pairs. The first sequence is read as "expect this," the next as "send this," then "expect," then "send," and so on. Note that we always start with an expect string. For example, take the following sequence below:

Hello   hiThere   whoAreYou   theSystemDialingIn   Connected

In this example, we would expect the remote system to send "Hello," reply back with "hiThere," expect it to respond with "whoAreYou," then return "the-SystemDialingIn," at which time the remote system would respond with "Connected."

The expect-send sequence may also be further broken down into "expect-send-expect" if required. For example, a common portion of a login sequence is as follows:

```
ogin:--ogin:
```

This translates to: "Expect the remote system to send the login prompt, and if it doesn't, we'll send a 'break,' and again expect the login prompt." We have not included the "l" in "login" as we aren't sure how the remote machine displays its prompts. For example, it may use any of the following, or perhaps even something completely different!

- login:
- Login:
- Remote Login:
- Fri Jan 01 Login:

The only "rule" we can apply, and that normally everyone follows, is that the login prompt ends with "ogin:", which the chat script would match. A similar rule applies to the password prompt, which is why we try to match "assword" (as we'll see later).

This convention of matching the last few characters is commonly used to get around these types of issues. The example above shows that it can be very difficult to know exactly what the script should consist of. There is really only one way to confirm this and that is to manually connect to the machine and note down exactly what key sequences you need to enter to successfully gain access. We'll see how to do this a little later when we create ours.

Devices *File*

This file contains entries for the hardware devices we are using to establish the link. ACU refers to "Auto Call Unit," which we can think of as our modem. The last field is simply a token name for our configuration, and will be referred to in some other files:

```
cesium# cat /etc/uucp/Devices
ACU      cua/b   -   Any     dialupModem
cesium#
```

We are using a modem connected to */dev/term/b* that will be used for all the connections we define—regardless of the connection speed we require. This is why we only need one modem entry defined.

OK, that seems easy enough, so let's move on to the *dialers* file.

Dialers *File*

The *dialers* file allows us to store the settings that will be applied to the modem whenever it is used. Modems can be very awkward pieces of hardware to configure correctly, so once the required settings are obtained they are best stored in this file. In this way, should the modem fail, we won't need to remember what the settings were. We simply swap the hardware (assuming it's the same type!) and let UUCP do the rest. This file also allows us to define numerous modem definitions, connect them all up, and know that, whichever we use, its settings will be correctly applied by UUCP.

In the following output, "dialupModem" is the token name that we used earlier in the *devices* file. It refers to the modem connected on */dev/cua/b*. The next field specifies a translation string, which in our case simply indicates we want to alter any "=" and "-" characters to be pauses, which are shown as ",". This is used to allow us to use standard characters ("=" and "-") in the system's file, which will be translated into the correct characters for this particular modem. The remaining fields contain the input for a chat script that will be used to initiate the modem:

```
cesium# grep dialupModem /etc/uucp/Dialers
dialupModem =,-, "" P_ZERO "" \dATZ\pE1V1\r\c OK\r ATDT\T\r\c
   CONNECT STTY=crtscts
cesium#
```

Let's break this down into its expect-send sequences and take another look at it. Doing this shows we have the following:

- ""—expect nothing (we always start with an expect string)
- P_ZERO—set the line to be no parity
- ""—expect nothing
- \d—send a delay
- ATZ—perform a reset of the modem to bring it back to a consistent state
- \p—send a pause
- E1—enable "echo"
- V1—set verbose return codes
- \r\c—send a return without a new line
- OK\r—expect to receive an "OK" followed by a return
- ATDT—dial the following number, using tone dialing
- \T—pass the telephone number
- \r\c—send a return without a new line
- CONNECT—expect to see the connection string to indicate the remote modem has connected
- STTY=crtscts—set hardware flow control

How do we know what values to set? Most modems nowadays use a common command set (Hayes AT command set), so there are some common settings that apply to most modems. For example, ATE1 nearly always enables "echo." Unfortunately, the settings to apply may also depend on the modem you are communicating with; the only real way to know exactly which settings to use is to read the manual and test them!

That said, there are a few settings that we always apply, regardless of the modem. These are the port settings (P_ZERO and STTY=crtscts). These values can be placed in the */etc/uucp/Systems* file if you wish, but we have put them here so that they will be applied to every connection that uses this modem.

We've already mentioned above that P_ZERO disables parity. A very common problem is for modems to connect, then suddenly disconnect—very often, the cause is incorrect parity settings. Placing an empty expect string and the correct parity setting in the chat script will force UUCP to apply the correct settings and overcome the problem. The available options that can be used are as follows:

- P_ZERO—sets parity bit to 0
- P_ONE—sets parity bit to 1
- P_EVEN—sets even parity
- P_ODD—sets odd parity

We also use STTY=crtscts to force hardware flow control, but any options available to `stty` or `termio` can actually be used.

Systems *File*

This file contains the dialup and login parameters for the system we will be connecting into. Let's take a look at ours and see what it contains:

```
cesium# cat /etc/uucp/Systems
theISP Any ACU 115200 1234567890 ogin:--ogin: guest word:
guestPassword\n\n otocol: ppp\n\n HELLO
cesium#
```

The first field is another token name, which will be used later to refer to this connection. Next, we specify that the remote system can be called at "Any" time. Then we look for an "ACU"-type device capable of a line speed of 115,200. (In our case, this will be the modem connected to port "B.") Next, we have the phone number of the ISP, followed by the script that contains the login information.

To create this entry, we dialed into the machine, using `tip`, and manually logged on to the system. This allows us to take note of the prompts and keystrokes that we need to enter to be able to login successfully. The actual login session is shown below:

```
cesium# tip -9600 /dev/cua/b
Connected
AT
OK
ATDT1234567890


Welcome to the ISP's System

login: <break>
login: guest<return>
password: guestPassword<return>
<return>
protocol: ppp<return>
<return>
HELLO
```

Working through this, we can see that we first expect the login prompt. We will send a break to kick the machine into life in case we don't see it. This gives the first expect string:

```
ogin:--ogin:
```

Now we send the login name, which becomes the send string:

```
Guest
```

Next we expect to see the password prompt, and we reply with our password. We also need to hit return twice before we see the next prompt, to produce the next expect-send sequence:

```
assword: guestPassword\n\n
```

After this, we see the protocol prompt. Our ISP has told us that we have to specify "ppp" at this point, followed by two returns. This forms the next expect-send sequence:

```
otocol: ppp\n\n
```

Finally, we expect to receive the word "HELLO." Again, this is specified by our ISP and appears when PPP has successfully started on the ISP's side. At this point we have connected and the login procedure is complete so the remaining tasks are ready to complete (PPP, in our case).

Checking UUCP

Once all the files have being correctly edited, we can start to check the UUCP configuration to make sure it will work when we use it for PPP. We can do this a number of ways, but probably the easiest it to run cu. We've run it with the following debug option below as this will show the sequences that cu is going through:

```
cesium# cu -d theISP
conn(theISP)
Trying entry from '/etc/uucp/Systems' - device type ACU.
Device Type ACU wanted
Trying device entry 'cua/b' from '/etc/uucp/Devices'.
<lines removed for clarity>
cesium#
```

We won't show the whole log file as that would take too much space, but you will see lots of entries saying things like "expect," "got it," and "sendthem," which indicates that cu is working through the UUCP files correctly. Eventually you should see the "Connected" string, which shows that the dialup parameters are correct. At this point we are happy that the UUCP configuration is OK (or at least accurate enough to start testing PPP with it).

PPP

The final layer is PPP. This is the part that runs IP over the serial line, establishing the network connection across it. When this has been created it will have all the standard network parameters, such as an IP address at each end, a netmask, and so on. Once it is up and running we can view its statistics using ifconfig and netmask just as we would any other network.

Again, we need to check that we have the correct packages installed before we can do anything. Running pkginfo should show us something similar to that shown below:

```
cesium# pkginfo | grep -i ppp
system   SUNWapppr   PPP/IP Asynchronous PPP daemon configuration files
system   SUNWapppu   PPP/IP Asynchronous PPP daemon and PPP login service
system   SUNWpppk    PPP/IP and IPdialup Device Drivers
cesium#
```

Which Configuration?

PPP can be set up in a number of different configurations, depending on the type of connection that is required. These connections are known as "point-to-point" and "multipoint" and will use one of two device drivers to establish links. For point-to-point links the driver is *ipdptp*, whereas for multipoint links it is the *ipd* driver.

Point-to-point links have a machine at either end of the connection (for example, a dial-out system connecting into an ISP), whereas multipoint links use one machine that acts as an end point for a number of different systems (for example, as a dial-in system that provides users with a method of accessing the machines).

Here, we will use PPP to dial out of our system and into the ISP, so it will be configured in dial-out mode and therefore use the *ipdptp* driver.

Link Manager

A powerful feature that PPP provides is automatic connection and disconnection of the link. When you need to connect to the remote system, a program known as the "link manager" will detect whether traffic is being directed there and will establish the connection. After the link has been inactive for a predetermined amount of time, the connection will be dropped. This is very useful and ensures that both costly communications links and possible security breaches are kept to a minimum—although some users prefer to be able to control when the link is made or torn down. We'll show how this can be accomplished a little later when we have everything working correctly.

The link manager is named */usr/sbin/aspppd* and is started at boot-time by the */etc/init.d/asppp* start-up script. When aspppd starts, it reads a configuration file named */etc/asppp.cf*. Let's have a look at ours now to see what it contains before we start everything:

```
cesium# cat /etc/asppp.cf
ifconfig ipdptp0 plumb local-ppp remote-ppp up
path
     interface ipdptp0
     peer_system_name theISP
     negotiate_address on
     inactivity_timeout 300
     default_route
     debug_level 9
cesium#
```

Again, we'll take each line one at a time and determine what each one does.

We've already seen in Chapter 11, "Connecting to the Local Area Network," how to use `ifconfig` to plumb the interface in. This command performs a similar task using the PPP point-to-point driver, which is *ipdptp0* in this case.

On a point-to-point link, we would expect to provide two addresses to PPP: one for the local end and another for the remote end. Often they may not be known in advance, such as when the ISP uses dynamic addressing for its customers (most do, nowadays!). To get around this, we can add the keyword "negotiate_address" to the configuration file and also provide dummy addresses to the `ifconfig` command—we've used the host names local-ppp and remote-ppp for this in our configuration file above. When the connection is made, PPP will negotiate with the remote system to obtain the correct addresses, which will be exchanged for the dummy ones previously specified (we'll see this when we check the connection later).

We could just use IP addresses rather than host names in *etc/asppp.cf*, if we prefer. However, we've used this standard across the rest of the machines, and it allows us to quickly scan the *hosts* file and see what has been allocated, rather than have IP addresses hidden away in files. Let's update the *hosts* file now to add the dummy addresses to it. The entries we'll use are shown below:

```
cesium# cat /etc/inet/hosts
<lines removed for clarity>
#
# Dialout PPP system - dummy addresses
# Uses dynamic local address
#
1.1.1.1          local-ppp
9.9.9.9          remote-ppp
<lines removed for clarity>
cesium#
```

The "path" keyword simply marks the start of a definition, which continues to the next "path" or "defaults" statement. Multiple path entries can be used to define multiple PPP connections (for example, to different ISPs).

As we explained earlier, "negotiate_address" indicates that we are using dynamic addresses, which PPP needs to exchange when the network is configured.

The keyword "peer_system_name" is where PPP ties into UUCP. It will pass the system name onto UUCP and let it establish the dialup link for us. The name should exactly match the entry we defined earlier in the *Systems* file.

The default timeout for PPP is set to 120 seconds. We will increase this to 300 seconds using the keyword "inactivity_timeout."

When the connection is made, we need to use this route as our default; "default_route" will add this entry into the routing table for us.

Lastly, "debug_level" allows us to control the amount of debug information that will be logged—we've set the highest value for now so we can check that everything works. We can also do this from the aspppd command line if we wish, but we've included it here so we don't have to alter the standard start-up script.

Log Files

PPP writes to a log file named */var/adm/log/asppp.log*. It's worth noting that this file can grow quite rapidly, especially at the higher levels of debug. It isn't automatically cleaned out by the system, either. How often you use PPP and the level of debug you have set will determine how fast this file grows and how often you will need to preen it.

While we're looking at the log file, let's run PPP and check to confirm that it starts OK:

```
cesium# /etc/init.d/aspppd start
cesium# tail -f /var/adm/log/asppp.log
16:51:01 Link manager (264) started 03/25/01
16:51:01 parse_config_file: Successful configuration
cesium#
```

At this point, the link manager has started, read the configuration file, and checked the syntax, and is now ready to establish the connection should we need it. If we take a look at ifconfig, we can see that aspppd has already plumbed the interface in, although it still has the dummy addresses in place since we have not yet connected in to get our dynamic ones:

```
cesium# ifconfig ipdptp0
ipdptp0: flags=8d1<UP,POINTOPOINT,RUNNING,NOARP,MULTICAST> mtu 1500
    inet 1.1.1.1 --> 9.9.9.9 netmask ff000000
    ether 0:0:0:0:0:0
cesium#
```

Testing the Link

Now we are ready to test the link to make sure everything is working. As we said earlier, the link manager is monitoring the connection, so we only need to direct traffic to the remote system—something simple like a ping will do this for us. The link manager "knows" that it needs to connect to "theISP" using the modem connected on */dev/cua/b*.

OK, let's `ping` the remote system and see what happens. We've already increased the debug level, so we can determine what is happening by `tailing` the log file while we're testing everything. We'll use a high time-out for `ping` so that it doesn't exit before the connection has had time to establish:

```
cesium# ping remote-ppp 300
<lines removed for clarity>
```

While the `ping` is working, we can monitor PPP's progress by checking the log file. We won't reproduce the whole of it here, but you will see the various stages that are being passed through, as we saw before when we checked the connection with `cu`. For example, we'll see UUCP opening the relevant files and executing the chat script. When the login is successful, we'll then see PPP starting to run over both ends of the link:

```
cesium# tail -f /var/adm/log/asppp.log
16:51:44 process_ipd_msg: ipdptp0 needs connection
conn(theISP)
Trying entry from '/etc/uucp/Systems' - device type ACU.
Device Type ACU wanted
Trying device entry 'cua/b' from '/etc/uucp/Devices'.
processdev: calling setdevcfg(ppp, ACU)
cesium#
```

Now the connection has been made, so we should have a network between the two systems, which `ifconfig` will confirm. The dummy IP addresses have also been replaced with the correct ones:

```
cesium# ifconfig ipdptp0
ipdptp0: flags=8d1<UP,POINTOPOINT,RUNNING,NOARP,MULTICAST> mtu 1500
    inet 195.2.137.61 --> 194.88.88.72 netmask ff000000
    ether 0:0:0:0:0:0
cesium#
```

Checking `netstat` will also show that the default route has being correctly added because we included the "default_route" keyword in the configuration file:

```
cesium# netstat -rn
Routing Table:
   Destination        Gateway           Flags   Ref   Use    Interface
-------------    ---------------   -----  ----- ------  ----------
194.88.88.72     195.2.137.61       UH      4     1    ipdptp0
224.0.0.0        127.0.0.1          U       0     0    lo0
default          194.88.88.72       UG      0     1
127.0.0.1        127.0.0.1          UH      0    67    lo0
cesium#
```

The only odd thing is that `ping` will timeout after 300 seconds and return an error that shows it cannot see the system "remote-ppp." The reason for this is that we initiate the connection by pinging the dummy IP address. This is enough to direct traffic to the dialup interface and start the whole process off, but when the connection is actually made the IP addresses are replaced, which means the dummy machine will never be seen. This isn't a problem since we're only using ping to initiate the process and we aren't really interested in it after that.

Host Name Resolving

When the connection is established, most network tasks are performed for us by PPP. The only one remaining is to enable host name resolving, which we do by running DNS. We have already performed this task in Chapter 13, "Connecting to the Internet," so it should be a relatively easy task.

To do this we have to create a */etc/resolv.conf* file and update */etc/nsswitch.conf* to support DNS. We were supplied the address of the nameserver by the ISP, so here are our entries after we have updated the relevant files:

```
cesium# grep hosts /etc/nsswitch.conf
hosts: files dns
cesium#

cesium# cat /etc/resolv.conf
search solarisbootcamp.com
nameserver 136.89.22.4
cesium#
```

Name Service Caching

When the connection has been torn down, you may find that the PPP link is often reactivated. The reason for this is that the name service cache daemon, /usr/sbin/nscd, will cache the *hosts* file and force the connection up to rebuild its data at certain intervals. We only really want the connection to be opened at our request, so we'll disable *hosts* caching. We do this by altering the *hosts* entry, then restarting the daemon. The file is shown below after modification, along with the tasks required to restart it:

```
cesium# grep enable-cache /etc/nscd.conf
        enable-cache            hosts           no
cesium# /etc/init.d/nscd stop
cesium# /etc/init.d/nscd start
cesium#
```

Routing

We don't need to add any additional routes, as these were built when the link was created, but we do need to control what traffic can run across them. By default, RIP is enabled on the system and will run over all the network interfaces that it finds. What this means for us is that packets will be directed toward the PPP interfaces and will force the connection to be made. Again, this isn't the behavior that we would like, so we have two choices. These are to either disable RIP, or to stop it from querying the dialup connection.

We are going to disable RIP; in fact, at the beginning of this chapter we said that the systems would be built to our standard build, which includes disabling both RDISC and RIP. If we had wanted to let these processes carry on running, we would have edited the *gateways* file instead and disabled RIP over the dialup interface, as shown here:

```
cesium# cat /etc/gateways
norip ipdptp0
cesium#
```

The Completed Network

Let's have a look at how the system is configured when the link has been established. Figure 15.1 shows the connection after it has been enabled; the dummy addresses at both ends of the serial connection have been replaced with their "genuine" ones.

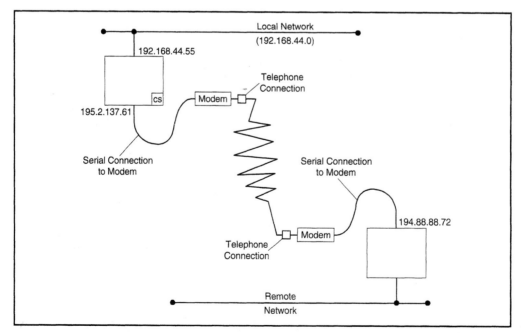

Figure 15.1 *The PPP network, after the connection has been made.*

Custom Scripts

We now have an interface that will connect into the ISP automatically and hang up after a predefined time period. This is great, although some users prefer to control the dialup and timeout processes themselves. To do this, we'll create a few short scripts: startPPP to initialize the connection and keep it open, and stopPPP to terminate the link.

Let's first look at how we start it:

```ksh
cesium# cat startPPP
#!/bin/ksh
#
# script to initiate the PPP link
#
remoteMachine="remote-ppp"    # the remote entry in hosts
sleepTimer=250                # must be less than ppp timeout
pidFile=/tmp/startPPP.pid


#
# check PPP is not already running
#
if [ -f ${pidFile} ]; then
   thePid=$(cat ${pidFile})
   pidStat=$(ps -p ${thePid} | grep -v PID | wc -l | awk '{ print $1 }')
   if [ ${pidStat} -gt 0 ]; then
        echo "Error: startPid is  already running"
     exit 1
   else
     rm ${pidFile}
   fi
fi
#
# start the ppp daemon
#
/etc/init.d/asppp start
#
# initiate the connection
#
ping ${remoteMachine} > /dev/null
pingableMachine=$(grep nameserver /etc/resolv.conf | head -1 |
   cut -d' ' -f 2)
ping ${pingableMachine} 300 > /dev/null
if [ $? -ne 0 ]; then
   echo "Error: Cannot connect to ${pingableMachine}"
   exit 1
fi
echo "$$" > ${pidFile}
#
# now keep it open by looping around indefinitely
#
while true; do
   ping ${pingableMachine} 60 > /dev/null
   sleep ${sleepTimer}
done
exit 0
cesium#
```

To open the connection, startPPP first checks to see if PPP is already established. If not, it will ping the remote machine to establish the connection, then will loop around pinging another accessible machine every so often to ensure the PPP inactivity time-out is never met. It also writes its process ID to a file to easily allow us to find the process later to stop it.

We can see that we use two different addresses for ping to check. This is because of the dummy address problem, where we need to ping the dummy address to initiate the connection, but once it is made the dummy address is exchanged for the real address. We need to use an address we know is external to keep the connection alive. We have done this in the script by picking the first nameserver entry out of */etc/resolv.conf.*

Now, let's look at how the connection is closed:

```
cesium# cat stopPPP
#!/bin/ksh
#
# script to stop the PPP connection
#
pidFile=/tmp/startPPP.pid

if [ -f ${pidFile} ]; then
  /etc/init.d/asppp stop
  kill $(cat ${pidFile})
  if [ $? -eq 0 ]; then
    echo "PPP connection terminated"
    rm ${pidFile}
  else
    echo "Error: Cannot terminate the connection"
    exit 1
  fi
else
  echo "PPP is not connected"
  exit 2
fi
exit 0
cesium#
```

To stop the process, the script checks for the existence of the file that contains the Process Identifier (PID) and, if there, stops the link manager. Next it kills off the ping process to the remote machine, and finally cleans up by removing the PID file.

Conclusion

We now have a setup that provides connectivity to external systems in the event of a major internal network failure, as well as providing a method of connection for our mobile users. Along with this, we have created scripts that allow users to choose whether they control the connection and disconnection, or whether PPP does this automatically.

16

CONFIGURING
DNS

Manual Pages

domainname (1M)
named (1M)
named-xfer (1M)
nslookup (1M)
resolv.conf (4)

Files Affected

/etc/named.boot
/etc/named.conf
/etc/named.pid
/etc/nsswitch.conf
/etc/resolve.conf
/var/named

Objectives

The Internet is a part of daily life now. Countless machines are connected to it, all of them trying to communicate with other machines that are also connected. The Domain Name System (DNS) plays a major role in allowing this to work, so here we'll look at how DNS relates to the Internet and show how it is configured.

What Is the Domain Name System?

DNS is a mechanism designed to simplify the administration and usability of host names/IP addresses for systems that are connected to a network. While the network may be a local area one, DNS is more commonly used for connections to the Internet. It achieves its goals through two main functions (and many smaller ones!):

- It allows us to use names rather than addresses when referring to machines. This is much better for us, since people tend to find it difficult to remember groups of numbers, but relatively easy to remember the corresponding names. For example, *www.sun.com* is much more memorable than 192.18.97.241.

- It acts as a global database to provide the name-to-address mappings by effectively splitting the network data into manageable chunks and allowing them to be administered locally.

Why Do We Need It?

Before we go into the details of how DNS works, let's take a quick look at what we are trying to achieve and what alternative ways there may be of doing this. Let's assume we are trying to access a machine somewhere in the world that contains a software package that we need to download. To connect to it, we need to first determine its IP address, which we may be able to do by carrying out one of the tasks listed here:

- Phone the administrator and ask what the address is. Obviously this is not very practical; we probably wouldn't even be able to find out who the administrator is at most companies. Even if we got the IP address, we would have to store it (probably in our local *hosts* file) and then check that it hadn't altered the next time we wanted to connect to it.

- Let someone maintain a global *hosts* file. Not as funny as it first sounds—this is the way things used to work before DNS came around. The file was maintained by the Network Information Center (NIC) and distributed as it changed. This soon became impractical simply because of the number of hosts connected to the Internet.

So, let's see how DNS works and helps us to get around these issues. To do this, we'll break it down into some of its component parts and explain what they do, before finally bringing them all together for our system.

DNS Hierarchy

The hierarchy and naming conventions operate in a similar way to the UNIX filesystem. Because of this, it's often easier to explain it by comparing the two, which is exactly what we'll do here.

Domain Name Space

Let's start with the Domain Name Space, which we can think of as being all the machines (yes, even PCs!) that are connected to the Internet. It's represented as a hierarchy, much like the inverted tree layout of the UNIX filesystem. The branches of the tree represent domains and subdomains instead of the directories and subdirectories of the UNIX tree. The leaves of the tree represent actual machines rather than the files of the UNIX tree. There is also a *root* entry, represented by a dot (.) in DNS, which is the parent of all domains in the Domain Name Space.

There are a few more differences from the UNIX tree: The first is that the dot (.) is used as the path separator, and the second is that the domain name is built up from right to left (root on the right), rather than from left to right (root on the left) as it is in the UNIX tree.

The domain name itself is built up by concatenating the absolute path from the root of the tree, again similar to the absolute path of a UNIX file. For example, comparing the two trees in Figure 16.1 we see that we have a UNIX path name of */usr/local/bin/somefile*, whereas the domain name is "machine.somedomain.com." (Note the trailing dot used to indicate "root.")

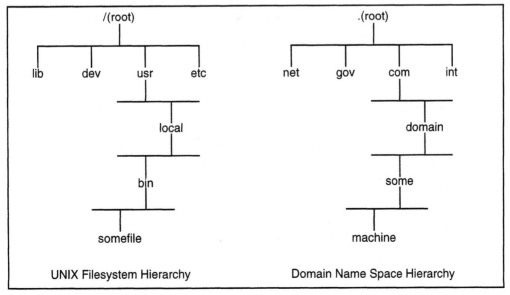

Figure 16.1 *Comparison between the UNIX filesystem hierarchy and the Domain Name Space hierarchy.*

What's a Domain?

We stated earlier that one reason DNS works is because of its ability to be locally managed. So somehow we need to be able to split up all the machines in the Domain Name Space into "local" areas to be able to achieve this. In this case, "local" does not necessarily mean geographically local. For example, a large multinational company could also administer its domain "locally."

The hierarchy we've already described allows us to do this by allocating a domain to "someone" (an individual, company, group of people, etc.), who then takes responsibility for it and any subdomains (or machines) it contains. So, we can think of domains as containers for sub-domains and machines. For example, if we look at the portion of the Domain Name Space shown in Figure 16.2, we can see that whoever is responsible for the domain "SolarisBoot-Camp.com" is also responsible for everything below it.

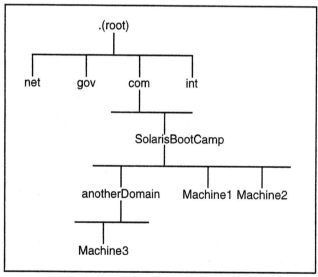

Figure 16.2 *Domains and subdomains.*

Each machine has a Fully Qualified Domain Name, often known as the FQDN, which is the absolute path from root. For example, a machine known as "somemachine" may have an FQDN of "somemachine.somedomain.com." (remember the trailing dot).

The FQDN can be set to virtually anything that doesn't already exist with the same absolute name in the Domain Name Space. To compare this again to the UNIX tree, we know that we can traverse down the tree until we get to, say, */export/home*. Here we can create a directory with whatever name we wish, say, *demoDummyDirectory*. It doesn't even matter if the same directory exists, except in */etc*; the main thing is that the absolute path names are different. We can do the same thing with domain names, which means that all the domains listed below are legal domain names:

- "somemachine.somedomain.com."
- "somemachine.somedomain.net."
- "somemachine.somedomain.anotherDomain.com."

Domain names are not case-sensitive, so although we've used "somedomain.com" as the domain name above, we could also have used any of the following (among others!):

- "SomeDomain.com"
- "SOMEdomain.COM"
- "SomeDOMAIN.com"
- "SoMeDoMaIn.com"

Top-Level Domains

At the top of the Domain Name Space, just below root, are a number of pre-defined domains known as the Top-Level Domains (TLDs). They are administered and assigned by the Internet Corporation for Assigned Names and Numbers (ICANN—see *www.icann.org*). Even as we write, ICANN is introducing new TLDs, such as biz (Business) and info (General); but currently, TLDs are split into generic TLDs (gTLDs) and country code TLDs (ccTLDs).

Generic Top-Level Domains

The names of these TLDs are primarily U.S.-based—the reason being that they have evolved from the "original" Internet (ARPAnet, which was the U.S. defense network):

- biz (Business organizations)
- com (Commercial)
- edu (Education)
- gov (U.S. government)
- info (General)
- int (International)
- mil (U.S. military)
- name (Personal)
- net (Network)
- org (Organization, usually nonprofit)

Country Code Top-Level Domains

There is also a set of two-letter domains, one for every country in the world. These domains are based on an International Organization for Standardization (ISO) specification (Country Codes–ISO 3166). Examples of these are "uk" (United Kingdom), "au" (Australia), and "fi" (Finland).

Each country then splits the domains further, following its own conventions. For example, the UK uses ".co.uk" as the commercial equivalent and ".gov.uk" as the government equivalent.

Registering Domains

Someone has to be responsible for making sure that the same domain isn't used more than once, and that when someone has registered a domain and taken responsibility for it, that the information being added is available to anyone else in the world.

To do this, each domain must be registered with some authority, which will differ depending on where and what you are registering. If you require a ".com" address, you would register this with NIC, while a ".co.uk" one would be registered with Nominet.

The actual registration is a very easy process usually taken care of by someone who is authorized to register domains, such as an ISP. An ISP will register the domain on your behalf and may supply you with the two IP addresses that you need to ensure you have a master and slave DNS entry.

Servers and Resolving

Now that we've defined the hierarchy, let's look at how we determine the information we're searching for. For example, let's assume we need to locate the IP address of our earlier example, *www.sun.com*. Figure 16.3 provides an overview of the steps that we'll follow to do this.

Now let's look at the different machine types that the figure refers to.

Name Servers

Name servers are the server portions of DNS. They are responsible for storing the domain information and handing it out to any clients who request it. For example, in our earlier explanation about DNS, we talked about determining the IP address of the machine we wanted to connect into. This would have been provided by one of the name servers for the domain. They are an important part of DNS because if a server for a particular domain fails, then after a certain amount of time everyone's queries to that domain will fail.

For this reason, at least two name servers must be used to store the domain's data; in fact, the IP addresses of the two name servers acting for you need to be provided when a domain is registered. These are referred to as the "master" and "slave" server, although many people still tend to use their old names of "primary" and "secondary."

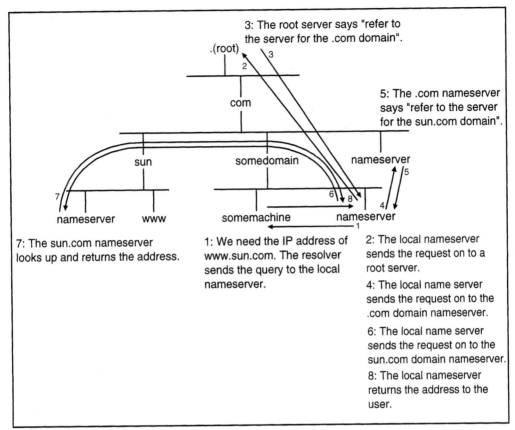

Figure 16.3 *Determining an IP address.*

Master and Slave Servers

Master servers hold the configuration files for the domains (or more correctly, the "zones," as we'll see later). Whenever changes are made to the files they are made on this system.

Slave servers contain copies of the files, which are automatically downloaded from the master on a regular basis, depending on the settings contained in the master configuration files.

It's also interesting to note that while one is a master and the other a slave, external connections cannot tell the difference. They simply know that they have received an answer to their query.

Caching Servers

All name servers cache data to a certain degree, but caching name servers *only* cache data (they don't hold any configuration files for the domain). These types of servers are often used to provide additional resources if the main name servers become heavily loaded.

Root Servers

These are "special" name servers and are very important to DNS. They are used to tie all the name servers in the locally managed domains together to form the Internet. Let's see how.

Suppose we want to look up "somemachine.somedomain.com." We query our name server, but it doesn't know the answer so it passes the query to one of the root servers (we've just seen this happen in Figure 16.3). From there, the query passes to a name server responsible for the top-level domain that the query relates to, in this case ".com." If this server cannot provide the answer, the query is passed to the one responsible for the domain ("somedomain.com"). This process continues until a response is returned.

To be able to do this, each name server must know how to contact one of the root servers. This information is freely available and is supplied as part of the configuration files when the system is built, as we'll see later.

We can see from this that the root name servers are even more important than the "standard" domain name servers, in that if the root servers fail, eventually all DNS would stop working. To overcome this potential problem, a number of these servers are scattered around the world.

Resolvers

These are the client portions of DNS—the parts responsible for making the queries to the name servers (commonly known as "host name resolving" or "host name lookups"). They are built into the operating system and so are transparent to the users. The only real options related to resolvers are whether to enable or disable them. We do this by editing the name service switch file, */etc/nsswitch.conf*, which we'll cover later when the systems are configured (it's also explained in more detail in Chapter 12, "Naming Services and NIS").

letc/resolv.conf

When the resolver starts up, it tries to determine the domain name of the system from a number of different places, which are listed below (again, these are explained further in Chapter 12, "Naming Services and NIS":

- The system variable LOCALDOMAIN (if set)
- The "domain" entry in */etc/resolv.conf*
- The domain setting used for NIS/NIS+ if they are enabled (the value of "domainname")
- The local *hosts* file if it contains a fully qualified domain name

The most common way of doing this is to create the configuration file named */etc/resolv.conf*. This file contains the configuration settings for the resolver, such as the default domain name and the IP addresses of the name servers it will use. We have created this in previous chapters and we'll use it here with every machine configured for DNS. This makes it easy to see what values we've set without searching in different places to find them and also means we can simply copy the file from machine to machine as required.

Forward and Reverse Lookups

We saw in Figure 16.3 the steps involved in resolving the host name *www.sun.com* (that is, finding its IP address). These steps are known as "forward lookups" and are the most common type of lookup carried out. They are generally used when a user wants to connect to a machine (for example, by entering a URL into a Web browser).

Reverse lookups go the other way—we know the IP address but need to determine the domain name. These types of requests are usually carried out by the system itself. For example, Web and ftp servers often use them to try and obtain the name of the connecting system, to output the information to a human-readable log file. In fact, many systems will terminate the connection if they cannot perform a valid reverse lookup and determine the host name of the machine connecting in.

A gTLD named ".arpa" is actually used for reverse lookups. The domain itself was part of the "original" Internet. It builds up a tree exactly in the same way as the other gTLDs, but this one is ordered by IP address, rather than domain name, as shown in Figure 16.4.

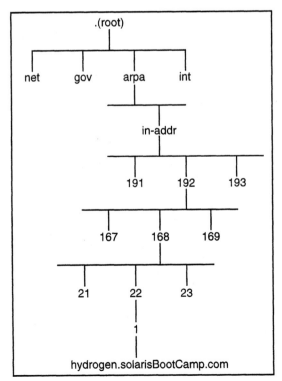

Figure 16.4 *The in-addr.arpa reverse domain.*

When we create our DNS server later we'll see how to define entries that will allow both forward and reverse lookups to be performed on our systems.

Zones

We have already said that if you "own" a domain, then, as such, you have the responsibility of ensuring that the data it contains is correct. You are the authority on that domain for the rest of us!

All this data is passed to the name servers through a series of files known as the "zone" files. This is the authoritative data for the domain.

So what is a zone? When a domain is small and doesn't contain any subdomains, it appears that the zone is simply another name for the domain—the zone files contain data about the domain. Unfortunately, it's not quite that simple, so let's look at an example to make it a little clearer.

Let's assume that we currently manage a domain named "bigcompany.com" and the company is growing from a small business into a large multinational. At the moment, it consists of a single domain/zone and the name servers managing the domain will have a zone file containing all the machines for "bigcompany.com." This existing DNS configuration is shown in Figure 16.5, with the name servers shown as ns0 and ns1.

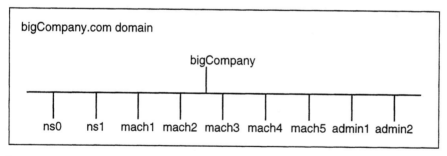

Figure 16.5 *The current domain of "bigCompany."*

Now we decide that we can't manage it all ourselves. There are too many machines being added and removed for us to keep track of, so we'll split them into smaller, more manageable chunks. We've decided to divide the domain into five subdomains: north, south, east, west, and administrative. To do this, we need to create the following subdomains:

- north.bigcompany.com.
- south.bigcompany.com.
- east.bigcompany.com.
- west.bigcompany.com.

OK, we have defined the domains, but who will manage them? There's no point leaving them under the control of the original name servers as that gives us the same problem that we originally had. So, we'll allocate a pair of name servers to each subdomain and keep the original name server for managing the administrative machines, as shown in Figure 16.6. The task of allocating responsibility is known as "delegation." Once the subdomain has been delegated, the name servers responsible become authoritative over their zones. The completed "bigcompany.com" domain will look like the one in the figure.

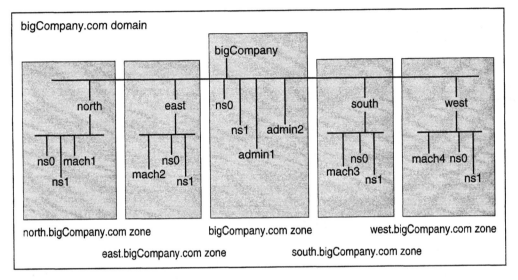

Figure 16.6 *The subdomains of "bigCompany."*

Zone Transfers

Slaves obtain their data from the masters through a mechanism known as a "zone transfer." The slave carries this out automatically, using a program called `named.xfer`.

This is made possible because part of the set-up process when configuring the slave involves defining the master of a particular zone so that the slave knows where to retrieve its data.

Is It DNS, BIND, or `Named`?

There is always some confusion about how DNS, BIND, and `named` relate to each other, so let's try and explain it.

We know that DNS refers to the Domain Name System, and that it comprises both a client and a server portion within its specification. BIND is an acronym for Berkeley Internet Name Daemon and is a popular free software implementation of DNS. It includes a binary called named, which is its server portion, and supplies a set of libraries that are the client portion and perform the resolving.

Solaris bases its implementation of DNS on BIND, and, as with BIND, a server portion is included, which in this case is a binary called in.named. Again, the resolver client is a set of libraries included with the operating system.

Named Versions

As with any program, there have been quite a few changes to BIND over the years and these are also reflected in Sun's version of in.named. We don't want to complicate matters by describing details about each revision, but one we will show later is the difference between the top-level configuration files of BIND Version 4 and BIND Version 8 (known as /etc/named.boot and /etc/named.conf, respectively).

Table 16.1 shows the relationship between the Solaris Release and the version of BIND that in.named is based on.

Table 16.1 *OS Release and BIND Version Comparison*

Solaris Release	BIND Version
2.6	4.9.4
7	8.1.2
8	8.1.2
9	8.2.4

This can easily be confirmed by checking the binary itself. For example, a system running Solaris 9 would show something similar to the following:

```
antimony# strings /usr/sbin/in.named |grep "(#)in.named"
@(#)in.named BIND 8.2.4 Tue Dec 11 22:09:49 PST 2001 s81_53-5.9-May 2002
antimony#
```

The Boot File

Now let's compare the two configuration file formats. We've created an example configuration that contains the equivalent entries within the two files so it's easy to see what is common between them. However, we'll also place the files in subdirectories to organize them better and ease future administration of them.

Version 4 File Format

```
antimony# cat /etc/named.boot
;
; boot file for the name server
;
directory   /var/named
cache       .                          named.root
primary     solarisbootcamp.com        hosts.primary
secondary   anotherDomain.com  137.84.63.1 hosts.secondary
primary     44.168.192.in-addr.arpa    hosts.reverse
primary     0.0.127.in-addr.arpa       hosts.local
antimony#
```

Version 8 File Format

```
antimony# cat /etc/named.conf
//
// named.conf file
//
options {
        directory  "/var/named";
};
zone "." in {
        type hint;
        file "named.root";
};
zone "solarisbootcamp.com" in {
        type master;
        file "hosts.primary";
};
zone " anotherDomain.com " in {
        type slave;
        file "hosts.secondary";
        masters { 137.84.63.1; };
};
zone "44.168.192.in-addr.arpa" in {
        type master;
        file "hosts.reverse";
};
zone "0.0.127.in-addr.arpa" in {
        type master;
        file "hosts.local";
};
antimony#
```

OK, so what does all this mean and how do the two files compare? Let's use Table 16.2 to show the different entries and how they relate to each other.

Table 16.2 *Boot File Syntax*

Version 4	Version 8	Meaning
;	# /*......*/ //	Used to specify a comment line. A common problem is forgetting to use the new comment syntax when upgrading from version 4 to version 8.

directory /var/named	options {
	    directory "/var/named";
	};
		Specifies the location of the zone files for this name server.

cache . named.root	zone . "in" {
	    type hint;
	    file "named.root";
	};
		Informs the name server which file contains information about the root servers (i.e., */var/named/ named.root*).

primary solarisbootcamp.com hosts.primary	zone solarisbootcamp.com in {
	    type master;
	    file "hosts.primary";
	};
		Specifies that the name server is acting as the master for the domain "solarisbootcamp.com" and that the zone file is called *hosts.primary*.

secondary anotherDomain.com 137.84.63.1 hosts.secondary	zone "anotherDomain.com" in {
	    type slave;
	    file "hosts.secondary";
	    masters { 137.84.63.1; };
	};
		Specifies that the name server is acting as a slave for the domain "anotherDomain.com," and the data can be obtained from 137.84.63.1 then stored in the zone file *hosts.secondary*.

primary 44.168.192.in-addr.arpa hosts.reverse	zone "44.168.192.in-addr.arpa" in {
	    type master;
	    file "hosts.reverse";
	};
		Specifies that the name server is acting as the master for the special domain used to provide reverse lookups. The zone file is called *hosts.reverse*.

primary 0.0.127.in-addr.arpa hosts.local	zone "0.0.127.in-addr.arpa" in {
	    type master;
	    file "hosts.local";
	};
		Specifies that the name server is acting as the master for the loopback interface. This is needed to translate "local host" reverse lookups.

Our Configuration

Now we're finally ready to start building the servers. As we do this, we'll look at each boot file entry in more detail. It's worth noting a few points now that we have seen the example files:

- They refer to both primary/master and secondary/slave entries. The Version 4 file names them primary/secondary, while the newer Version 8 format refers to master/slave entries. We'll refer to them as master/slave.

- A master server for one domain may also be a slave for another, and vice versa. In other words, when we refer to the master and slave servers later, that is only for the domain we are configuring here.

Our Domain

We currently have two subnets configured: one used by the internal facing machines, and a second used by the external facing machines. We will configure DNS so that only the 192.168.44.0 network is defined. This is for two reasons:

- We don't want to advertise our internal machines to the outside world.

- It makes it easier to describe the setup without confusing it all with multiple networks.

To do this, we'll use the following machines as our name servers. Bear in mind that we have used a range of addresses reserved for private networks here (see Chapter 11, "Connecting to the Local Area Network") and that when you register a domain you will actually be assigned a range of IP addresses of your own to use (see Table 16.3).

Table 16.3 *Our DNS Settings*

Setting	Value	Host Name
Domain Name	Solarisbootcamp.com	
Master Name Server	192.168.44.51	antimony
Slave Name Server	192.168.44.52	tellurium

If we check the *hosts* file, we'll see that we have two machines defined there, both built to our standard build in the same way as the rest of the systems as described in Chapter 11, "Connecting to the Local Area Network":

```
antimony# grep DNS /etc/inet/hosts
192.168.44.51    antimony    sb    # master DNS server
192.168.44.52    tellurium   te    # slave DNS server
antimony#
```

Zone Files

In this section we'll create the zone files that will be used on both the master and slave servers that control our domain. First, let's look at the format that the zone files are based on, which is known as the Standard Resource Record Format (RR, for short).

Several RRs have been defined, but we'll only use a few more common ones here, some of which are shown in Table 16.4. As with everything in computing, this list is expanding. For example, there are now resources that allow you to embed geographic positioning data for each host and others that let you embed digital signatures in the zone files.

Table 16.4 *Common Resource Records*

Resource Record	Record Name	Resource Record	Record Name
SOA	Start of Authority	HINFO	Host Info
NS	Name Server	AAAA	IPV6 address
A	IPV4 Address	MX	Mail Exchange
CNAME	Canonical Name	TXT	Text
PTR	Pointer to an address	RP	Responsible Person

The reason for only using a few of the records is that many companies don't like providing unnecessary information about their systems, so often they only specify the minimal amount of records. Some records appear in every file, such as Start of Authority (SOA) records, while others only appear in one or two files. For example, we have A records in the forward files to define an IP address and CNAME records to define an alias for the host name, with PTR records in the reverse files to define a host name.

SOA Records

We showed earlier how the domain is broken down into smaller, manageable portions known as zones. The Start of Authority record is where we define which zone this name server is authoritative over.

We'll create an SOA record that we can use as a template for all the zone files. This makes it as easy as possible to administer our DNS configuration and means that over time the only entry that will differ between them all will be the serial number, as the files increment independently. The record we'll use is shown below, so let's also see how we derive it:

```
@ IN SOA solarisbootcamp.com. root.solarisbootcamp.com. (
          2001043001 ; Serial num - <yyyymmddxx>
          86400      ; Refresh every 24 hours
          7200       ; Retry every 2 hours
          3600000    ; Expire in 1000 hours
          172800)    ; TTL is 2 days
```

The "@" symbol is an abbreviation for the "origin," which is passed in from the boot file as the entry after the "zone" keyword. For example, if we look at the entry for the master reverse zone in the configuration file, we have the entry listed below. In this case, the origin is set to "44.168.192.in-addr.arpa":

```
zone "44.168.192.in-addr.arpa" in {
        type master;
        file "master/192.168.44";
};
```

Because each entry in the boot file specifies its own origin in the zone file, this means we can use the "@" symbol in the SOA record of each file.

Serial Number

Whenever we make changes to any of the zone files we need to inform all the name servers that these changes are taking place. The way to do this is by updating the serial number field. It doesn't matter what number format you use, as long as the number increases; you could update it in increments of 1,000, for example, but then you may need to be careful you don't run out of numbers!

To get around these sorts of problems, the recommended way is to base the serial number on a date format and add some additional digits to allow us to update the number several times per day.

This translates to "YYYYMMDDxx," so if the date were October 22, 2001, then the first time we alter the file we would use the serial number 2001102201. The next update that day would be 2001102202 and so on. Updates the next day would revert back to 01 for the additional digits (i.e., 2001102301). This allows us to alter the file 99 times per day (which should be more than enough for anyone!).

Once the serial number has been updated, we can inform named by either restarting it or by sending it an HUP signal as follows:

```
antimony# kill -HUP `cat /etc/named.pid`
antimony#
```

Named will then reread its configuration files and, importantly, the slave servers will automatically pick up the changes.

Refresh, Retry, Expire, and Time-to-Live Values

These fields govern how long the data will be valid for and how often the secondary servers will try to reload this information.

"Refresh" is the time interval before the secondary server checks with the primary to see if the data is still valid. "Retry" is the amount of time that the secondary server will try to check with the primary server if it has failed to refresh itself. "Expire" is the amount of time the data is valid if it fails to refresh its data. "TTL" is the time-to-live field. This is the amount of time that the data is valid before it is reloaded from the server.

The times we have used are taken from the document "Ripe-203: Recommendations for DNS SOA Values" and should be adequate for "general" use. You may wish to adjust these to suit your site, but be careful about the values you use. Table 16.5 shows the range of values commonly seen and can be used as a guideline of the values to set.

Table 16.5 *Common SOA Values*

SOA Field	Range
Refresh	3–24 hours
Retry	1–2 hours
Expire	7–30 days
TTL	1–7 days

NS Records

In a similar way to the SOA record, we'll define the records that will be used for the name server (NS) records in every zone file. The entries we'll use are shown below:

```
;
; name server definitions
;
IN   NS   antimony.solarisbootcamp.com.
IN   NS   tellurium.solarisbootcamp.com.
```

This defines both machines as name servers (notice the trailing dot included with the domain name).

Now that we've got some standard records we can use within our zone files, let's move on and create all the files that will be needed for both the master and slave servers. This can become a little awkward to keep track of because quite a few files need to be created, all of which look quite similar. To help things along, Figure 16.7 indicates which files are used where.

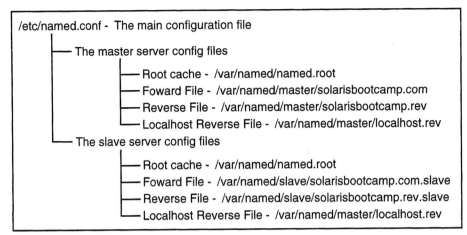

Figure 16.7 *The zone files.*

Master Server

Now we're ready to create the files for the master server. There are many recommendations about how these should be named and stored. Our domain has a simple layout, as it isn't large enough to be split into numerous zones, which means that the files will consist of one zone and so will be easier to work through. For this reason, the layout we'll use here is to store all the master files in a directory named *master*, all the slave files in a directory named *slave*, and the root server information in the top-level directory. Let's now create the *master* directory then move on to the configuration file:

```
antimony# cd /var/named
antimony# mkdir master
antimony#
```

Boot File

Since most systems by now will be using at least Solaris 7, their version of DNS will be based on BIND Version 8 and so will use the newer *named.conf* file format. Therefore, we'll also use the same file format, so let's first define it and then work through the values to see what we've done.

The main changes we have made to the example files shown previously are to isolate each particular type of file by creating a hierarchy under the main named area where we can store the relevant files. The boot file we've defined for the master doesn't contain any secondary server information, as we don't act as a slave for any other domain yet:

```
antimony# cat /etc/named.conf
//
// named.conf file
//
options {
        directory  "/var/named";
};

// root servers
zone "." in {
        type hint;
        file "named.root";
};

// master forward file for the main domain
zone "solarisbootcamp.com" in {
        type master;
        file "master/solarisbootcamp.com";
};

// master reverse file for the arpa domain
zone "44.168.192.in-addr.arpa" in {
        type master;
        file "master/solarisbootcamp.rev";
};

// reverse file for the loopback interface
zone "0.0.127.in-addr.arpa" in {
        type master;
        file "master/local.rev";
};
antimony#
```

Root Cache

This file contains the list of servers that are authoritative for the root domain and is a standard file that is available from *ftp.rs.internic.net*, where it is named *domain/named.root* (to download this, we can use a browser and connect to *ftp://ftp.rs.internic.net/domain/named.root*). Although this doesn't change very often, it ought to be checked/upgraded regularly; once a month should be adequate and easy enough to carry out.

The example below shows our downloaded file (we have removed any comments to conserve space). Looking at it, we can see it contains two entries for each machine: one that specifies the machine is a name server (the NS record), and a second that specifies its IP address (the A record):

```
antimony# cat named.root
.      3600000  IN  NS     A.ROOT-SERVERS.NET.
A.ROOT-SERVERS.NET.        3600000     A     198.41.0.4
.      3600000      NS     B.ROOT-SERVERS.NET.
B.ROOT-SERVERS.NET.        3600000     A     128.9.0.107
.      3600000      NS     C.ROOT-SERVERS.NET.
C.ROOT-SERVERS.NET.        3600000     A     192.33.4.12
.      3600000      NS     D.ROOT-SERVERS.NET.
```

```
D.ROOT-SERVERS.NET.          3600000      A      128.8.10.90
.       3600000      NS      E.ROOT-SERVERS.NET.
E.ROOT-SERVERS.NET.          3600000      A      192.203.230.10
.       3600000      NS      F.ROOT-SERVERS.NET.
F.ROOT-SERVERS.NET.          3600000      A      192.5.5.241
.       3600000      NS      G.ROOT-SERVERS.NET.
G.ROOT-SERVERS.NET.          3600000      A      192.112.36.4
.       3600000      NS      H.ROOT-SERVERS.NET.
H.ROOT-SERVERS.NET.          3600000      A      128.63.2.53
.       3600000      NS      I.ROOT-SERVERS.NET.
I.ROOT-SERVERS.NET.          3600000      A      192.36.148.17
.       3600000      NS      J.ROOT-SERVERS.NET.
J.ROOT-SERVERS.NET.          3600000      A      198.41.0.10
.       3600000      NS      K.ROOT-SERVERS.NET.
K.ROOT-SERVERS.NET.          3600000      A      193.0.14.129
.       3600000      NS      L.ROOT-SERVERS.NET.
L.ROOT-SERVERS.NET.          3600000      A      198.32.64.12
.       3600000      NS      M.ROOT-SERVERS.NET.
M.ROOT-SERVERS.NET.          3600000      A      202.12.27.33
antimony#
```

"Localhost" Reverse File

Next we'll create the reverse file for the loopback interface, as it's probably
the easiest one to do. This is used so that the server can translate the address
127.0.0.1 back to "localhost." The forward address for translating "localhost"
to 127.0.0.1 will be in the primary forward file for the domain:

```
antimony# cat master/local.rev
;
; local reverse file
;
@ IN       SOA    solarisbootcamp.com.  root.solarisbootcamp.com.  (
                        2001043001 ; Serial num - <yyyymmddxx>
                        86400      ; Refresh every 24 hours
                        7200       ; Retry every 2 hours
                        3600000    ; Expire in 1000 hours
                        172800)     ; TTL is 2 days
;
; name server definitions
;
    IN       NS     antimony.solarisbootcamp.com.
    IN       NS     tellurium.solarisbootcamp.com.


;
; localhost
;
1 IN       PTR    localhost.
antimony#
```

Looking at the file, we can see that after we have added the standard SOA
and NS records that we defined earlier, the only other entry we have is a PTR
record for "localhost."

Master Forward File

This is the forward file for the primary domain, which, as explained earlier, is used when performing standard (forward) lookups where we query a name and the IP address is returned:

```
antimony# cat master/solarisbootcamp.com
;
; named forward file for 192.168.44
;
@ IN       SOA    solarisbootcamp.com.  root.solarisbootcamp.com.  (
                   2001043001 ; Serial num - <yyyymmddxx>
                   86400      ; Refresh every 24 hours
                   7200       ; Retry every 2 hours
                   3600000    ; Expire in 1000 hours
                   172800)     ; TTL is 2 days
;
; name server definitions
;
   IN      NS     antimony.solarisbootcamp.com.
   IN      NS     tellurium.solarisbootcamp.com.


;
; definition for localhost
;
localhost IN A   127.0.0.1


;
; definitions for the remaining hosts
;
tin        IN A  192.168.44.50
antimony   IN A  192.168.44.51
tellurium  IN A  192.168.44.52
iodine     IN A  192.168.44.53
xenon      IN A  192.168.44.54
cesium     IN A  192.168.44.55


;
; host aliases
;
sn         IN CNAME tin
sb         IN CNAME antimony
te         IN CNAME tellurium
i          IN CNAME iodine
xe         IN CNAME xenon
cs         IN CNAME cesium
antimony#
```

Again, we first define the SOA and NS records for the zone. Next we have the IP addresses of all the systems (the A records), including one for "localhost," that we want to be seen under DNS. Following these we have the alias definitions (the CNAME records) for the machines, which, for this purpose, we can think of as providing a similar functionality to the alias entry in */etc/ hosts.*

Master Reverse File

Finally, here's the file that provides the reverse lookups for the domain. Once again, we use the same SOA and NS records, followed by a series of pointers to the hosts themselves (the PTR records). Note the trailing dots again on the records:

```
antimony# cat master/solarisbootcamp.rev
;
; named reverse file for 192.168.44
;
@ IN        SOA   solarisbootcamp.com.  root.solarisbootcamp.com.  (
                    2001043001 ; Serial num - <yyyymmddxx>
                    86400      ; Refresh every 24 hours
                    7200       ; Retry every 2 hours
                    3600000    ; Expire in 1000 hours
                    172800)     ; TTL is 2 days
;
; name server definitions
;
    IN      NS    antimony.solarisbootcamp.com.
    IN      NS    tellurium.solarisbootcamp.com.


;
; individual hosts
;
50 IN       PTR   tin.solarisbootcamp.com.
51 IN       PTR   antimony.solarisbootcamp.com.
52 IN       PTR   tellurium.solarisbootcamp.com.
53 IN       PTR   iodine.solarisbootcamp.com.
54 IN       PTR   xenon.solarisbootcamp.com.
55 IN       PTR   cesium.solarisbootcamp.com.
antimony#
```

resolv.conf File

Good. The zone files are installed on the master server. Now we need to add the /etc/resolv.conf file; ours is shown below:

```
antimony# cat /etc/resolv.conf
;
; resolv.conf that queries the
; master name server first, followed
; by the slave name server
;
search solarisbootcamp.com
nameserver 192.168.44.51
nameserver 192.168.44.52
antimony#
```

This file has a number of options that can be included, but again, we'll only use the most common entries. The "search" value contains the list of domains to be searched, and essentially will be appended to any host name that doesn't include a trailing dot.

We are allowed up to three name server entries in the file. They are queried in the order listed, so we've added our master and slave entries to it. ISPs often provide a name server that can also be used, in which case we can add that one as the third entry if required.

Once the file has been generated, it can be copied across all the machines that will be using DNS (both servers and clients).

Starting Named

The only thing we need to do now on the master is to start the servers. It will normally be started at boot-time via the file /etc/init.d/inetsvc, but we can also start it manually using the following command:

```
antimony# /usr/sbin/in.named &
antimony#
```

This will create a file called /etc/named.pid that contains the process ID of the running in.named, which can be used to force it to reread its zone files or to kill the process (as we showed earlier).

At this point, the master is configured, so let's move on and build the slave before testing the system.

Slave Server

Here we'll follow the original recommendations suggested when we set up the master, which means we also need a slave directory for the zone files. Let's create the hierarchy then move on to create the configuration files:

```
tellurium# cd /var/named
tellurium# mkdir master slave
tellurium#
```

Boot File

This file is very similar to the boot file on the master. The main difference between them is that this one also contains a "masters" entry for the slaves. This is used by the slaves to contact the master whenever they need to perform a zone transfer:

```
tellurium# cat /etc/named.conf
//
// named.conf file
//
```

```
options {
        directory   "/var/named";
};

// root servers
zone "." in {
        type hint;
        file "named.root";
};

// slave forward file for the main domain
zone "solarisbootcamp.com" in {
        type slave;
        file "slave/solarisbootcamp.com.slave";
        masters { 192.168.44.51; };
};

// slave reverse file for the arpa domain
zone "44.168.192.in-addr.arpa" in {
        type slave;
        file "slave/solarisbootcamp.com.rev.slave";
        masters { 192.168.44.51; };
};

// reverse file for the loopback interface
zone "0.0.127.in-addr.arpa" in {
        type master;
        file "master/local.rev";
};
tellurium#
```

Creating files for the slave is quite easy. Both the root cache (*named.root*) and the loopback reverse file (*local.rev*) can be copied directly from the master. The slave files will be automatically copied from the master when the next zone transfer is carried out, which we'll be able to check when everything is running OK. To complete the setup, the resolver configuration file, */etc/resolv.conf*, can also be copied from the master.

Finally, we can start named exactly as we did on the master:

```
tellurium# /usr/sbin/in.named &
tellurium#
```

Testing the Servers

Now that we've completed configuring the master and slave, let's check that they are working OK. The main tools we'll use for doing this are ping and nslookup. Nslookup ignores the settings defined in the name service switch file (*/etc/nsswitch.conf*) and uses DNS to perform any lookups. This will be fine for checking that the underlying files are set up correctly.

We need to make sure that we can resolve external names (assuming we are connected to the Internet at this point), hosts connected to the local network, the "localhost" entry, and all the above using reverse lookups. Once we are happy this is working, we'll use `ping` to do some "general" checks. This will use the switch file and therefore confirm that it's also set up correctly and actually using DNS.

First, we'll try to look up a host on the local network. One thing to point out is that we may see some responses that don't quite seem right. These are the "nonauthoritative answer" type responses. This means that the first time we made the request we received an "authoritative" answer back from the remote name server, which was then cached by our local one. Any subsequent requests will be answered by our local server, which, as the error suggests, is only authoritative for our own domain:

```
helium# nslookup
Default Server:  antimony.solarisbootcamp.com
Address:  192.168.44.51

> xenon
Server:  antimony.solarisbootcamp.com
Address:  192.168.44.51

Name:    xenon.solarisbootcamp.com
Address:  192.168.44.54

> cesium
Server:  antimony.solarisbootcamp.com
Address:  192.168.44.51
Name:    cesium.solarisbootcamp.com
Address:  192.168.44.55
```

Good. That worked OK, so let's try an external host name:

```
> www.sun.com
Server:  antimony.solarisbootcamp.com
Address:  158.43.128.72

Non-authoritative answer:
Name:    www.sun.com
Address:  192.18.97.241
```

Now, let's look for something that will test the reverse files—in other words, an IP address:

```
> 192.168.44.53
Server:  antimony.solarisbootcamp.com
Address:  192.168.44.51

Name:    iodine.solarisbootcamp.com
Address:  192.168.44.53
```

Lastly, we'll check that we can see the "localhost" entry using both the forward and reverse files:

```
> localhost
Server:   antimony.solarisbootcamp.com
Address:  192.168.44.51

Name:     localhost.solarisbootcamp.com
Address:  127.0.0.1
> 127.0.0.1
Server:   antimony.solarisbootcamp.com
Address:  192.168.44.51

Name:     localhost.solarisbootcamp.com
Address:  127.0.0.1
```

Next, we can switch to the slave server using the command below and try a set of similar tests to prove that it is working OK:

```
> server 192.168.44.52
Default Server:  tellurium.solarisbootcamp.com
Address:  192.168.44.52

> <run the above tests again>
```

Good. Both forward and reverse lookups are working OK. We've only run through a few sample checks here; in practice you may want to check the system a little more thoroughly. For example, you could retrieve all the records about a machine using the set type=any command.

Enabling Resolving

Everything appears to be working OK with DNS, apart from one thing. We still have to tell the system to use it! This is very easy to do, and we have already carried this out a number of times. Chapter 12, "Naming Services and NIS," contains more details about this.

In short, we enable DNS by updating the name service switch file, /etc/ nsswitch.conf. We do this by adding the "dns" token to the "hosts" entry as shown here:

```
antimony# grep hosts /etc/nsswitch.conf
hosts: files dns
antimony#
```

Simple—we've added "dns" as the final service so any host name lookups will first try to resolve the host name by looking in the local /etc files before trying DNS. Once we've done this, we should be able to check that it's working using any commands that will force a lookup to occur, such as ping, telnet, ftp, and so forth.

```
antimony# ping www.sun.com
www.sun.com is alive
antimony#
```

Note that the above switch file entry assumes the machine is not using any other name service. For example, if the machine was also configured for NIS, the entry would be something similar to that shown below:

```
hosts: nis [NOTFOUND=return] files
```

This is because NIS includes "DNS forwarding," which means it will automatically forward the request onto DNS if required. This is explained more in Chapter 12, "Naming Services and NIS." Finally, `ping` appears to be responding OK too, so let's move on and configure all the clients to use DNS.

Configuring the Clients

Now that we have the master and slave servers functioning correctly, we can configure the remaining clients to perform host name lookups. These are very easy to set up; in fact, we have already done this in Chapter 13, "Connecting to the Internet." The only difference is that the name servers we'll be using are the local ones we've just configured. Let's use xenon as an example machine to see the changes we've made.

First we'll create the resolver configuration file, which contains the addresses of the name servers we wish to use—this will be copied from the master as we said earlier:

```
iodine# cat /etc/resolv.conf
;
; resolv.conf that queries the
; master name server first, followed
; by the slave name server
;
search solarisbootcamp.com
nameserver 192.168.44.51
nameserver 192.168.44.52
iodine#
```

Now, we can run through a few `nslookup` checks to make sure the servers are responding with a valid answer. We don't need to carry out all the tests—we just need to make sure we get the answers in a reasonable amount of time:

```
iodine# nslookup www.sun.com
Server:   antimony.solarisbootcamp.com
Address:  158.43.128.72

Non-authoritative answer:
Name:    www.sun.com
Address:  192.18.97.241
iodine#
```

Next we can update the switch file to start performing host name lookups:

```
iodine# grep hosts /etc/nsswitch.conf
hosts: files dns
iodine#
```

As a final test, we'll run another `ping` check so we're happy everything is set up correctly:

```
iodine# ping www.sun.com
www.sun.com is alive
iodine#
```

Conclusion

We've now created a DNS server that contains all the hosts connected to the "public" side of the network.

17

ADDING SCSI DEVICES

Manual Pages

devfsadm (1M)
devlinks (1M)
disks (1M)
dmesg (1M)
drvconfig (1M)
fas (7D)
fmthard (1M)
format (1M)
format.dat (4)
mkfs (1M)
mount (1M)
newfs (1M)
path_to_inst (4)
prtconf (1M)
prtvtoc (1M)
sd (7D)
st (7D)
tapes (1M)

Files Affected

/dev/*
/devices/*
/etc/format.dat
/etc/minor_perm
/etc/name_to_major
/etc/path_to_inst

Objectives

SCSI (pronounced "scuzzy") devices are one of the most common device interfaces used with UNIX systems. Here we'll talk about the interface and determine how SCSI devices are configured. After that, we'll move on and add a
couple of the more "common" types of hardware to the system.

Introduction

Adding additional disks to machines is a common task, especially since they
are forever getting cheaper and users can easily find reasons to store larger
amounts of data! It's less common to add additional tape drives; once one has
been configured, it is usually kept until either it breaks or it just cannot back
up enough data in the allowed timeframe. Nevertheless, it is a task that still
needs performing and is carried out often enough to be useful to document
the steps involved.

In this chapter, we'll add a disk drive and a tape drive, but we'll do them as
two separate tasks. First, to add the disk, we'll bring the machine down to the
PROM level (the OK prompt) and start the tasks from there. After that, we'll
add the tape, but this will be carried out while the system is up and running.
This will allow us to show two methods of adding devices, but we need to
remember that in the real world the second method will depend upon the
hardware being used and may not be possible on all machines.

This chapter ties in very closely with Chapter 6, "The Filesystem and Its
Contents"; many of the commands described there have been used here.

Both devices will be SCSI-based, chosen because it is the interface most
commonly used in production-type environments. Before we start to add the
devices, let's take a brief look at SCSI itself.

What Is SCSI?

SCSI, or "Small Computer Systems Interface," is a standard used to connect
many different types of hardware devices to the system, including disks,
tapes, scanners, and CD-ROMs. The original SCSI specification has been
reworked a number of times so that now various flavors are available.

A SCSI controller, known as a "host adaptor," is used to connect the devices to the machine. Each host adaptor can support a number of devices over a set distance, which depends on the flavor of SCSI it supports. The devices are "daisy-chained" together, so that the host adaptor connects to the first device, the first connects to the second, the second to the third, and so on. Finally, both ends of the link, known as the "SCSI-bus," are terminated.

Table 17.1 on the following page shows the important details for the different flavors, along with the constraints that apply to each one.

Single-Ended versus Differential

Single-ended SCSI is the "normal" version of SCSI that we are used to. The term "single-ended" is often dropped so that most people just refer to either SCSI or differential SCSI. The difference between the two is that single-ended SCSI uses one wire to transmit its data, whereas differential SCSI uses two wires with the signal inverted between the two, as shown in Figure 17.1.

The single-ended signal is taken as the voltage difference between its one data wire and "ground," whereas the differential signal is taken as the voltage differential (hence the name) between its two data wires (see Figure 17.1). This provides a better data signal, which is less susceptible to noise and therefore allows longer cable lengths to be used.

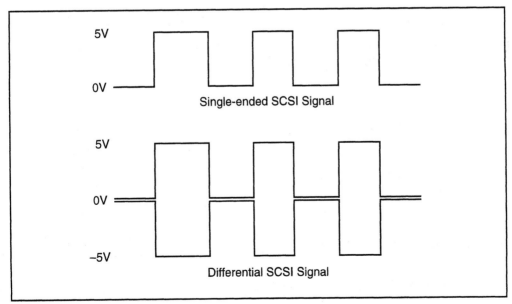

Figure 17.1 *Comparison between single-ended and differential SCSI signals.*

Table 17.1 *SCSI Implementation Details*

Type	Bandwidth (MB/sec)	Bus Width (bits)	Single-Ended Cable Length (meters)	LVD Cable Length (meters)	HVD Cable Length (meters)	Number of Supported Devices
SCSI-1	5	8	6	*	25	8
Fast SCSI	10	8	3	*	25	8
Fast Wide SCSI	20	16	3	*	25	16
Ultra SCSI-3	20	8	1.5	*	25	8
Ultra SCSI-3	20	8	3	n/a	n/a	4
Wide Ultra SCSI-3	40	16	n/a	*	25	16
Wide Ultra SCSI-3	40	16	1.5	n/a	n/a	8
Wide Ultra SCSI-3	40	16	3	n/a	n/a	4
Ultra2 SCSI-3	40	8	n/a	12	25	8
Wide Ultra2 SCSI-3	80	16	n/a	12	25	16
Ultra160 SCSI-3	160	16	n/a	12	n/a	16
Ultra320 SCSI-3	320	16	n/a	12	n/a	16

* See "Multimode LVD" on page 399.

High versus Low Voltage Differential

In the original SCSI implementation, only single-ended or differential versions were available. Recently, however, Low Voltage Differential (LVD) was introduced and the "original" differential was renamed High Voltage Differential (HVD).

LVD works on exactly the same principle as HVD (or as far as we're concerned here it does!). As we can guess, the difference between them is the voltage levels, which for HVD is 5 volts and for LVD is 3 volts. This lower voltage affects LVD's maximum allowable cable length, which at 12 meters is longer than single-ended, but shorter than HVD.

Multimode LVD

Also known as LVD/SE, multimode LVD allows either single-ended or LVD devices to be connected to the SCSI bus. If all the connected devices are LVDs, then the bus will operate as an LVD bus, and therefore allow cable lengths up to 12 meters. However, if any single-ended devices are connected, the whole of the bus will operate as a single-ended one, limiting the cable lengths to those listed in Table 17.1.

Narrow and Wide

This describes the width of the data bus; that is, how many data bits are transferred in parallel. "Narrow" is used to describe a 1-byte-wide bus and is the "normal" type of SCSI. "Wide" is used to describe a 2-byte-wide bus. Again, the word "narrow" is dropped most of the time.

Termination

We've mentioned that the bus must be terminated at both ends. This is done to stop the electrical signals from reflecting back along the bus and causing confusion. One of the ends of the bus will always be the host adaptor, which is automatically terminated so it doesn't cause us a problem.

The rest of the bus, however, will depend on the devices connected to it. Originally, SCSI devices came with terminators that had to be physically removed. Nowadays the devices usually detect whether they are the last device on the bus and, therefore, whether to apply termination.

SCSI IDs

Each device on the bus is allocated an identifying number, known as the SCSI ID, which must be unique and not clash with the ID of any other devices on the bus. It is used by the kernel to direct data to the correct device.

The host adaptor is known as the "initiator," with the remaining devices known as "targets." Table 17.1 shows how many devices each flavor of SCSI is allowed—this number includes both targets and initiators.

The SCSI ID also has a priority associated with it. ID priorities (ranging from highest to lowest) are listed below:

- 7, 6, 5, 4, 3, 2, 1, 0 (for narrow SCSI buses)

- 7, 6, 5, 4, 3, 2, 1, 0, 15, 14, 13, 12, 11, 10, 9, 8 (for wide SCSI buses)

This shows that ID 7 has the highest priority. Because of this, ID 7 is normally assigned to the host adaptor itself.

Altering the IDs

It needs to be easy to alter SCSI IDs on targets to avoid any conflicts. As such, each device will usually have a switch, electronic keypad, or even a series of jumpers that need to be set.

Normally, the only reason for changing the initiator ID would be to avoid ID conflicts when we have two systems connected to the same bus (for example, high availability or cluster configurations). If *all* the SCSI host adaptors are to be configured with a different initiator ID, then this can be carried out using the eeprom command (or the corresponding PROM command), as shown below and explained in Chapter 2, "Booting and Halting the System."

```
helium# eeprom scsi-initiator-id=6
helium#
```

For cluster-type configurations, it is normally recommended to keep all the local SCSI buses set to ID 7, and so only reset any connected SCSI buses. This can become quite a complex process, involving modifications to the NVRAM settings. As such, it is beyond the scope of this book.

Logical Units

Each SCSI target is also a SCSI controller itself, and as such can support a number of "logical units," known as LUNs. The actual number, again, depends on the type of bus in use, but can be any number up to its maximum supported devices. For example, a narrow bus can support up to 8 LUNs per SCSI target, while a wide bus can support up to 16 LUNs per target.

LUNs were often used when SCSI controllers were separate from the disk itself. This meant that more than one disk could be attached to a single controller and each disk would be seen as a LUN. Nowadays most disks use embedded controllers, which means that one controller connects to one disk only. However, they are still seen in more complex devices such as hardware Redundant Array of Inexpensive Disks (RAID) solutions where a SCSI target is allocated to the hardware device, and LUNs are used to define individual volumes or filesystems within it.

By default, LUNs are not configured (it also makes the boot process slower while the system checks to see if there are any available). However, they are easy to configure—we'll see how to do this later.

Solaris Devices

Now that we know a bit more about SCSI, let's see how the system refers to the devices once they are connected and how they are made available for us to use.

Solaris devices are located in two main directories—/*dev* and /*devices*—and appear in these as files in the filesystem, just as any other file or directory would. The difference between the two directories is that /*devices* contains "physical" device entries, while /*dev* contains "logical" device entries. Let's look at what these are in more detail.

Physical Devices

When devices are connected to the system they are added to its device tree. This is a list, generated by the OpenBoot PROM at boot-time, of all the connected hardware. The list is stored in memory as a tree hierarchy, much like the structure of the UNIX filesystem. The tree is built by equating the "root" entry to the main system board then using the directories of the tree to describe individual pieces of hardware or controllers connected to hardware. Let's look at an example of this to explain it better.

Let's assume that two disks are connected to the system, each via their own host adaptor (which have their own SCSI controller onboard). We know that the host adaptor connects to the system board, and the disk (via its onboard controller) is connected to the host adaptor. The tree that represents the series of connections would look like the one shown in Figure 17.2.

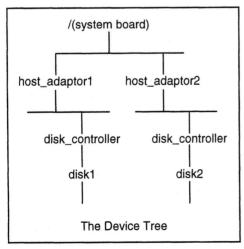

Figure 17.2 *The device tree.*

By following the tree through each hardware node, we can define a path to the device, which for the two disks in the tree above would be as follows:

```
/host_adaptor1/disk_controller/disk1
/host_adaptor2/disk_controller/disk2
```

These are known as the "physical device names" and are the type of entries that are stored in the *devices* directory. We don't need to be too concerned about the entries here because */devices* is maintained and used by the kernel.

Logical Devices

Physical device names aren't very user-friendly, so a logical device is available for every physical one. These are placed in the */dev* directory and linked back to the physical device entry in */devices*. The naming convention used for each one depends on the type of device itself; for example, the disk entries are quite different from the tape ones.

Instance Names

An instance name is also allocated to each device by the kernel. It does this so that instead of having to deal with awkward physical names, such as "/host_adaptor1/disk_controller/disk1," it can use an abbreviation, for example "sd0." We'll see lots of examples of this in the output from `prtconf` and the system bootup messages.

Naming Conventions

Disks

Solaris disks have two entries in the */dev* directory. The reason for this is that each disk can be accessed in two ways: either as a "block" device or a "character" device. The block device retrieves buffered data, in chunks of the block size, and is used by programs such as `df` and `mount`. The character device, also known as the "raw device," is used for retrieving unbuffered data, generally a character at a time, and is used by programs such as `dd` and `fsck`.

The entries for the block devices are created in */dev/dsk*, while the raw devices are created in */dev/rdsk*. The name given to each disk is based on the controller number (host adaptor instance), SCSI ID of the target, and the LUN number. For example, later we'll connect a disk, set to SCSI ID 2, to controller 1. It doesn't contain any LUNs, so this is in effect LUN 0. Therefore the disk itself is named c1t2d0. But, as we saw in Chapter 6, "The Filesystem and Its Contents," each disk can be partitioned into up to seven slices, so files are also created under */dev* to allow each individual disk slice to be referenced. Therefore, for each disk the following files will exist in the directories */dev/dsk* and */dev/rdsk*:

- c1t2d0
- c1t2d0s0
- c1t2d0s1
- c1t2d0s2
- c1t2d0s3
- c1t2d0s4
- c1t2d0s5
- c1t2d0s6
- c1t2d0s7

The name c1t2d0 refers to the whole disk and so does c1t2d0s2 because slice two always represents the whole disk. Each of the other names simply refers to the section of the disk that is defined as that slice in the disk VTOC (Volume Table Of Contents).

Tapes

The logical names for tape drives are much easier to understand. First, since the tape drive is a raw device only, the filenames are all placed in one subdirectory named *rmt*. Next, they are simply numbered sequentially—0 is the first tape, 1 the next, and so on.

Each tape drive allows data to be written slightly differently, including various compression ratios, rewind or no-rewind options, and so forth. To allow these different options, a number of devices are provided. For example, for the first tape drive, we see the following logical devices in */dev/rmt*:

```
helium# cd /dev/rmt
helium# ls
0      0c     0cn    0hbn   01b    0m     0mn    0ub
0b     0cb    0h     0hn    01bn   0mb    0n     0ubn
0bn    0cbn   0hb    01     01n    0mbn   0u     0un
helium#
```

Each of these relate to the various options. For example, "0c" is a high-compression device, whereas "0cn" is the same device but doesn't rewind automatically.

Autoconfiguration and /etc/path_to_inst

During the boot process, after the device tree has been built, the system will allocate an instance number to every device and create the physical and logical device entries. This is great when a new device has just been added, but we also need to make sure that the same device retains the same instance number and logical device name across any subsequent reboots. We can't have a disk being seen as the first disk one time, and the second disk another time!

To do this, the kernel uses a file named *etc/path_to_inst* to provide a mapping between the instance number allocated to a device and its physical name. This is consulted at boot-time to see which instance numbers should be allocated to which devices.

Adding the Disk

Now we're just about ready to connect the disk. We have decided to use a 4 GB drive that we have lying around and split it into the slices defined in Table 17.2.

Table 17.2 *Disk Details*

Slice	Size	Mount Point	Logical Device
0	2 GB	*/data*	*/dev/[r]dsk/c1t2d0s0*
0	2 GB	*/spare*	*/dev/[r]dsk/c1t2d0s1*
2	4 GB	- (backup slice)	*/dev/[r]dsk/c1t2d0s2*

Before we do, we need to take the machine down to the OK prompt (making sure no one is still using the machine!). After that we can make all the physical connections. We'll add a new SCSI controller to the system and connect the disk to that, which will be allocated SCSI ID 2.

Now we can use some of the OpenBoot PROM commands to check that the device is physically plugged in and functioning correctly. We'll do this by querying the devices connected to the SCSI bus and reading their PROM details. There are two commands to do this: `probe-scsi`, which only probes the default bus, and `probe-scsi-all`, which probes all the connected SCSI buses. Because we have connected our device to an auxiliary SCSI controller (in other words, not the main onboard one), we'll need to use the latter:

```
helium# init 0
<lines removed for clarity>
ok> probe-scsi-all
/iommu@f,e0000000/sbus@f,e0001000/espdma@f,400000/esp@f,800000

Target 3
  Unit 0    Disk     SEAGATE ST15230W SUN4.2G 0738

Target 6
  Unit 0    Removable Read Only device SONY    CD-ROM

/iommu@f,e0000000/sbus@f,e0001000/dma@3,81000/esp@3,80000

Target 2
  Unit 0    Disk     SEAGATE ST15230W SUN4.2G 0738
ok>
```

This shows that we have a disk and a CD-ROM connected to the internal SCSI bus, and our new disk, set to SCSI ID 2, connected to a separate SCSI bus. It's responding, which means the cable connections should be OK. We can also see that we don't have any conflicting IDs, so we can safely boot the machine.

We need to use the "reconfiguration" boot here so that the device nodes will be built and the system files will be updated correctly. We can do this in a few different ways: one is to use the `boot -r` command at the OK prompt; another is to create a file named */reconfigure* while the machine is still up. The next time the system is booted it will see this file and perform the reconfiguration boot itself. A third way is to reboot with `reboot -- -r`. Whichever way you use, when the system boots we should start to see messages informing us that the device has been seen. The output below shows details of the internal disk (sd0), the internal CD-ROM (sd1), and the newly installed drive (sd2):

```
ok> boot -r
<lines removed for clarity>
sd0 at esp0: target 3 lun 0
sd0 is /iommu@f,e0000000/sbus@f,e0001000/espdma@f,400000/
esp@f,800000/sd@0,0
        <SUN4.2G cyl 3880 alt 2 hd 16 sec 135>
sd1 at esp0: target 6 lun 0
sd1 is /iommu@f,e0000000/sbus@f,e0001000/espdma@f,400000/
esp@f,800000/sd@6,0
        <Sony CD-ROM>
sd2 at esp1: target 2 lun 0
sd2 is /iommu@f,e0000000/sbus@f,e0001000/dma@3,81000/
esp@3,80000/sd@2,0
        <SUN4.2G cyl 3880 alt 2 hd 16 sec 135>
<lines removed for clarity>
```

Device Tree

Good. The machine has now started booting, so let's take another look at the output above to see what we can determine about the new disk:

- The kernel has allocated it an instance name, which is "sd2."

- The physical device name has being generated and is set to */iommu@f,e0000000/sbus@f,e0001000/dma@3,81000/esp@3,80000/ sd@2,0*.

- The logical device name can be determined from the string "esp1: target 2 lun 0" information, which in this case is c1t2d0.

We should be able to look at */etc/path_to_inst* and tie all this information together. Let's look at the entries for both the original and the new disk:

```
helium# grep sd /etc/path_to_inst
"/iommu@f,e0000000/sbus@f,e0001000/espdma@f,400000/
esp@f,800000/sd@3,0" 0 "sd"
```

```
"/iommu@f,e0000000/sbus@f,e0001000/espdma@f,400000/
esp@f,800000/sd@6,0" 1 "sd"
"/iommu@f,e0000000/sbus@f,e0001000/espdma@f,400000/
esp@f,800000/sd@2,0" 2 "sd"
helium#
```

First, we can see that the file has been updated and now contains details of the new disk. The first column is the physical device name, the second is the instance number allocated to it, and the last is the name of the device driver used.

We should also find that a number of logical device entries have been created under /dev. This will include entries for both the raw (rdsk) and the block (dsk) devices. Let's check these now:

```
helium# cd /dev/dsk
helium# ls
<lines removed for clarity>
c1t2d0s0     c1t2d0s2     c1t2d0s4     c1t2d0s6
c1t2d0s1     c1t2d0s3     c1t2d0s5     c1t2d0s7
helium# cd /dev/rdsk
helium# ls
<lines removed for clarity>
c1t2d0s0     c1t2d0s2     c1t2d0s4     c1t2d0s6
c1t2d0s1     c1t2d0s3     c1t2d0s5     c1t2d0s7
helium#
```

We can see that a device has been created for every partition, even though we have only defined sizes for a few of them. If we also take one of the entries at random, say /dev/dsk/c1t2d0s0, and run an ls -l on it, we should see that it is in fact linked back to the corresponding physical name.

```
helium# cd /dev/dsk
helium# ls -l c1t2d0s0
lrwxrwxrwx   1 root      root         79 Oct 25  2000 c1t2d0s0 ->
../../devices/iommu@f,e0000000/sbus@f,e0001000/dma@3,81000/
esp@3,80000/sd@2,0:a
helium#
```

Lastly, let's run another listing, but this time follow the link and check its settings:

```
helium# ls -lL c1t2d0s0
ls -lL c1t2d0s0
brw-r-----   1 root      sys       32,16 Nov 19  2000 c1t2d0s0
helium#
```

First, we can see that the device is a block device, because the first character is a "b." The file's permissions and credentials have been applied to the file. These are obtained from a file named /etc/minor_perm. If we look at the entry for our driver, we see the following:

```
helium# grep sd /etc/minor_perm
sd:* 0640 root sys
helium#
```

Next, we have two numbers: the major device number and the minor device number. The major one is used to define the "general" type of device, and thus which driver is used for it. This is found in the file */etc/ name_to_major*. If we search for our major number (32), we can see it specifies the following driver:

```
helium# grep sd /etc/minor_perm
sd 32
helium#
```

Following the major number is the minor number, 16 in this case. This is used to specify exactly which instance of the major device we are dealing with. This number again ties into the */etc/path_to_inst* file. The minor devices are allocated sequentially, so the first disk (sd0) has the minor numbers 0 to 7, one for each partition. The next disk (sd1) has the next eight minor numbers, which means our disk sd2 has the next range, which is 16 through 23.

In other words, if we divide the minor device number by eight and drop any remainder, this will give us the instance number of the disk.

Format

At this point, we have successfully added the disk to our system and updated all the relevant files. Now we can go ahead and start to work with it. The first thing we need to do is define the partition map. We'll use the format program to do this. We'll use it interactively here, although it can also run noninteractively if you wish.

So, let's run format and work through creating the slices we require:

```
helium# format
Searching for disks...done

AVAILABLE DISK SELECTIONS:
0) c0t0d0 <SUN4.2G cyl 3880 alt 2 hd 16 sec 135>
/iommu@f,e0000000/sbus@f,e0001000/espdma@f,400000/esp@f,800000/sd@0,0
0) c1t2d0 <SUN4.2G cyl 3880 alt 2 hd 16 sec 135>
/iommu@f,e0000000/sbus@f,e0001000/dma@3,81000/esp@3,80000/sd@2,0
helium#
```

First, we need to make sure we select the correct disk. We don't want to start altering slices on the wrong one!

```
Specify disk (enter its number): 1
[disk formatted]

FORMAT MENU:
        disk       - select a disk
        type       - select (define) a disk type
        partition  - select (define) a partition table
        current    - describe the current disk
        format     - format and analyze the disk
```

```
repair    - repair a defective sector
label     - write label to the disk
analyze   - surface analysis
defect    - defect list management
backup    - search for backup labels
verify    - read and display labels
save      - save new disk/partition definitions
inquiry   - show vendor, product and revision
volname   - set 8-character volume name
!<cmd>    - execute <cmd>, then return
quit
```

Now we need to edit the partition map, which we can do using the Partition Menu:

```
format> partition
```

```
PARTITION MENU:
       0      - change `0' partition
       1      - change `1' partition
       2      - change `2' partition
       3      - change `3' partition
       4      - change `4' partition
       5      - change `5' partition
       6      - change `6' partition
       7      - change `7' partition
       select - select a predefined table
       modify - modify a predefined partition table
       name   - name the current table
       print  - display the current table
       label  - write partition map and label to the disk
       !<cmd> - execute <cmd>, then return
       quit
```

Before we start to make any changes, let's print the current map to see what has already been defined:

```
partition> print
Current partition table (original):
Total disk cylinders available: 3880 + 2 (reserved cylinders)

Part      Tag   Flag   Cylinders      Size           Blocks
  0      root   wm     0 -   71    75.94MB    (72/0/0)     155520
  1      swap   wu    72 -  557   512.58MB    (486/0/0)   1049760
  2    backup   wu     0 - 3879     4.00GB    (3880/0/0)  8380800
  3 unassigned  wm     0               0      (0/0/0)           0
  4 unassigned  wm     0               0      (0/0/0)           0
  5 unassigned  wm     0               0      (0/0/0)           0
  6 alternates  wm   558 - 3879     3.42GB    (3322/0/0)  7175520
  7 unassigned  wm     0               0      (0/0/0)           0
```

We can see there are already some partitions defined. They are not the size we need (and there is also one too many), so we'll recreate them using the sizes we want. It doesn't really matter which slice we use, so we'll use the first two—0 and 1. Let's make the changes to them both now:

```
partition> 0
Part    Tag  Flag   Cylinders      Size            Blocks
 0     root  wm     0 -   71     75.94MB  (72/0/0)    155520

Enter partition id tag[root]: alt
Enter partition permission flags[wm]:
Enter new starting cyl[0]:
Enter partition size[155520b, 72c, 75.94mb, 0.07gb]: 1940c
```

Why use "1940c"? This means we would like to use 1,940 cylinders. We can specify the size of the partition in a number of ways including blocks (b), cylinders (c), MB (m), GB (g), or to the end of the disk ($). We have used this value because we know the full disk (slice 2) consists of 3,880 cylinders and we simply want to split the disk in half.

```
partition> 1
Part    Tag  Flag   Cylinders      Size            Blocks
 1     swap  wu     72 -  557    512.58MB (486/0/0)  1049760

Enter partition id tag[swap]: alt
Enter partition permission flags[wu]: wm
Enter new starting cyl[72]: 1940
Enter partition size[1049760b, 486c, 512.58mb, 0.50gb]:$
```

This time, we've also had to make the partition writeable and mountable (wm). It was previously unmountable as it was defined as a swap partition. We also know that this partition runs to the end of the disk, so when it prompts us for the size we can simply enter "$." If we print the map again, we can see that we now have the sizes we require, but we still have the remaining extra slice:

```
partition> print
Current partition table (original):
Total disk cylinders available: 3880 + 2 (reserved cylinders)

Part    Tag    Flag  Cylinders      Size             Blocks

 0 alternates  wm     0 - 1939    2.00GB (1940/0/0)   4190400
 1 alternates  wm  1940 - 3879    2.00GB (1940/0/0)   4190400
 2     backup  wu     0 - 3879    4.00GB (3880/0/0)   8380800
 3 unassigned  wm     0           0      (0/0/0)            0
 4 unassigned  wm     0           0      (0/0/0)            0
 5 unassigned  wm     0           0      (0/0/0)            0
 6 alternates  wm   558 - 3879    3.42GB (3322/0/0)   7175520
 7 unassigned  wm     0           0      (0/0/0)            0
```

For neatness, we'll quickly run through setting it to zero. This is also useful because when we run commands such as `prtvtoc` later it won't confuse us. Don't forget that we leave partition 2 as the whole disk, so we just need to alter slice 6:

```
partition> 6
Part      Tag  Flag   Cylinders    Size          Blocks
  6 alternates wm     558 - 3879  3.42GB (3322/0/0) 7175520

Enter partition id tag[alternates]:
Enter partition permission flags[wm]:
Enter new starting cyl[558]: 0
Enter partition size[7175520b, 3322c, 3503.67mb, 3.42gb]: 0
```

The map should now be up-to-date and only contain a definition for slice 2 (as we mentioned earlier), and the slices we are interested in. We'll print the map one final time to make sure we are happy with the new layout. It also gives us a chance to make sure we don't have any incorrect values or overlapping partitions:

```
partition> print
Current partition table (original):
Total disk cylinders available: 2105 + 3 (reserved cylinders)

Part      Tag  Flag   Cylinders    Size          Blocks
  0 alternates wm      0 - 1939   2.00GB (1940/0/0)  4190400
  1 alternates wm   1940 - 3879   2.00GB (1940/0/0)  4190400
  2     backup wu      0 - 3879   4.00GB (3880/0/0)  8380800
  3 unassigned wm      0           0     (0/0/0)          0
  4 unassigned wm      0           0     (0/0/0)          0
  5 unassigned wm      0           0     (0/0/0)          0
  6 unassigned wm      0           0     (0/0/0)          0
  7 unassigned wm      0           0     (0/0/0)          0
```

That's better! Now we can safely exit from `format` and the original partition map will be kept. To use the new map, we need to tell the disk to store the information, which we do by writing it to the disk using the `label` command. When we do this, the new partition map will become the current one. This means that the filesystem layout won't match the partition boundaries and will cause `fsck` and `mount` to fail if we tried to work with the original partitions:

```
partition> label
Ready to label disk, continue? Y
```

All complete. We now have a disk that has our slices defined, so we can quit from the `format` program and continue working on the disk setup:

```
partition> quit
<lines removed for clarity>
format> quit
```

Format.dat

Prior to Solaris 2.3, the disk information needed to be specified with a data file, named */etc/format.dat* by default. When format started it would search for any disks that were connected and try to match them to one of the entries in */etc/format.dat*. This file is no longer required, as format will detect this information from the drive itself. It is, however, still a useful place to store any custom partition maps you would like to apply to any disks.

For example, we could generate the entry below for the partition map we have just created. This can be assigned to any other disk by using the "select" option within the Partition Menu:

```
partition = "DAD_SUN4.2G" \
    : disk = "SUN2.9G" : ctlr = SCSI \
    : 0 = 0, 4190400: 1 = 1940, 4190400 : 2 = 0, 8380800
```

Prtvtoc

We can display the volume table of contents (i.e., the partition map) from outside of format by using the prtvtoc command, as shown below:

```
helium# prtvtoc /dev/rdsk/c1t2d0s2
* /dev/rdsk/c1t2d0s2 partition map
*
* Dimensions:
*     512 bytes/sector
*     135 sectors/track
*      16 tracks/cylinder
*    2160 sectors/cylinder
*    4392 cylinders
*    3880 accessible cylinders
*
* Flags:
*   1: unmountable
*  10: read-only
*
*                         First  Sector   Last
* Partition Tag Flags Sector Count    Sector Mount Directory
        0   9   00        0 4190400 4190399
        1   9   00  4190400 4190400 8380799
        2   5   01        0 8380800 8380799
helium#
```

This shows that we have our two slices and the backup slice on the disk. If we do a quick calculation, we can check that the sizes are correct too:

- 1 sector = 512 bytes
- 4,190,400 × 512 = 2145484800 bytes
- 2,145,484,800 / 1,024 / 1,024 / 1,024 = 1.99 GB

Formatting Multiple Disks

Both format and prtvtoc are extremely useful and are often used for setting up multiple disks. For example, let's assume we have two disks that have the same geometry (number of heads, cylinders, and so forth). To copy the partition map of one (c0t0d0) to the other (c2t2d0), we could use the following command:

```
helium# prtvtoc /dev/dsk/c0t0d0s2 | fmthard -s - /dev/rdsk/c2t2d0s2
```

This will only update an existing map though, which means the disk must have previously been labeled. If we wanted to apply a known map to a group of new (unlabeled) disks we could do this with format, following the steps below.

First we need to create a file that contains the responses that format would expect, one per line (but don't include any "yes" or "no" confirmations). The example below simply selects the Partition Menu, then selects slice 7 and sets it to 0 size by entering the correct responses to the following questions:

```
Enter partition id tag[alternates]: <just hit return>
Enter partition permission flags[wm]: <just hit return>
Enter new starting cyl[100]: <0>
Enter partition size[206010b, 126c, 100.59mb, 0.10gb]: <0>
```

The file containing these responses is shown below:

```
helium# cat /tmp/part_map
partition
7


0
0
label
quit
quit
helium#
```

Once we have the data file, we can apply it to the group of disks as required. To apply it to all the disks connected to controller two (c2), we could use the following commands:

```
helium# sh
helium# cd /dev/dsk
helium# for disk in $(ls c2*s2); do
format -f /tmp/part_map -s $disk
done
helium#
```

Add a Filesystem

Now that we have defined the two slices and labeled the disk, we need to lay a filesystem on each of them. Again, we've explained this before in Chapter 6, "The Filesystem and Its Contents," so we'll quickly run through the commands here. We're using newfs to do the job here and letting it run mkfs for us, which means the default options to mkfs will be used:

```
helium# newfs /dev/rdsk/c1t2d0s0
/dev/rdsk/c1t2d0s0:      4190400 sectors in 1940 cylinders of 16
tracks, 135 sectors
    2046.0MB in 80 cyl groups (46 c/g, 48.52MB/g, 6080 i/g)
super-block backups (for fsck -F ufs -o b=#) at:
 32, 99536, 199040, 298544, 398048, 497552,
<lines removed for clarity>
4132567, 4160862
helium#
```

We can see that the locations of the superblock backups are given. Often it's useful to have a log of these for times when fsck fails and needs us to specify an alternative superblock. We can often retrieve this information using the "-N" option to newfs, although we have to be aware of some caveats when doing this. First, the "-N" option simply runs newfs nondestructively. This means that if called with the same options, as when the original filesystem was created, it will output the same superblock locations. However, if newfs (or mkfs) was called with any nonstandard flags, then the output will be different. Obviously, this means the best time to get a copy of the superblock list is immediately after creating the filesystem, while we can remember which options were used!

With this in mind, let's create a log file now so that we have a copy of the information within our hierarchy:

```
helium# newfs -N /dev/rdsk/c1t2d0s0 > /usr/local/utils/data/
vtoc/c1t2d0s0
helium#
```

We also need to perform the same task for the second slice:

```
helium# newfs /dev/rdsk/c1t2d0s1
<lines removed for clarity>
helium# newfs -N /dev/rdsk/c1t2d0s1 > /usr/local/utils/data/
vtoc/c1t2d0s1
helium#
```

Mount the Filesystem

Now the slices contain a valid filesystem and are ready to be mounted. First, we'll create the mount point for the device, then we'll run the filesystem checker (fsck) to make sure the filesystems are clean. They should be clean now, but you should always fsck the device before mounting it, unless you are using some type of journal/logging filesystem:

```
helium# mkdir /data /spare
helium# fsck /dev/rdsk/c1t2d0s0
** /dev/rdsk/c1t2d0s0
** Last Mounted On
** Phase 1 - Check Blocks and Sizes
** Phase 2 - Check Pathnames
** Phase 3 - Check Connectivity
** Phase 4 - Check Reference Counts
** Phase 5 - Check Cyl Groups
2 files, 9 used, 2956350 free (12 frags, 115171 blocks,  0.1%
    fragmentation)
helium#

helium# fsck /dev/rdsk/c1t2d1s1
** /dev/rdsk/c1t2d0s1
** Last Mounted On
** Phase 1 - Check Blocks and Sizes
** Phase 2 - Check Pathnames
** Phase 3 - Check Connectivity
** Phase 4 - Check Reference Counts
** Phase 5 - Check Cyl Groups
2 files, 9 used, 2956350 free (12 frags, 115171 blocks,  0.1%
    fragmentation)
helium#

helium# mount /dev/dsk/c1t2d0s0 /data
helium# mount /dev/dsk/c1t2d0s1 /spare
helium#
```

Good. The partitions have mounted without any errors, so let's make sure we can see them:

```
helium# df -k
Filesystem            kbytes   used   avail capacity  Mounted on
/proc                      0      0       0    0%     /proc
/dev/dsk/c0t2d0s0      48349  16889   26626   39%     /
/dev/dsk/c0t2d0s6     770543 522712  193893   73%     /usr
fd                         0      0       0    0%     /dev/fd
/dev/dsk/c0t2d0s1      61463   5592   49725   11%     /var
/dev/dsk/c0t2d0s7     519718  82791  384956   18%     /export/home
/dev/dsk/c0t2d0s5      38539   5928   28758   18%     /opt
swap                  130064     28  130036    1%     /tmp
/dev/dsk/c1t2d0s0    1798534    100 1536260    1%     /data
/dev/dsk/c1t2d0s1    1798534    100 1536260    1%     /spare
helium#
```

Lastly, we need to update */etc/vfstab* to make sure the device is checked and mounted at boot-time. The new entries are shown below:

```
helium# cat /etc/vfstab
#
#device     device    mount   FS    fsck   mount    mount
#to mount   to fsck   point   type  pass   at boot  options
#
```

```
<lines remove for clarity>
/dev/dsk/c1t2d0s0 /dev/rdsk/c1t2d0s0 /data  ufs 2 yes -
/dev/dsk/c1t2d0s1 /dev/rdsk/c1t2d0s1 /spare ufs 2 yes -
helium#
```

Configuring LUNs

We mentioned earlier that sometimes LUNs need to be configured (although this is normally only for special cases and should include all the instructions required). The change itself is very simple since the only thing we need to do is edit the kernel configuration file for the SCSI disk driver—*/kernel/drv/ sd.conf.*

An example of this type of requirement would be for some hardware RAID units. Often, a single SCSI ID is allocated to the disk cabinet as a whole—for example, target 4, which means the cabinet itself would be seen as t4. This can then be configured as a number of logical disks (LUNs), which would be seen as t4d0, t4d1, t4d2, and so forth.

If we assume that the device supports up to eight logical disks, we could include the following settings in the relevant configuration file. Don't forget that, as with most kernel changes, we'll need to reboot the machine for the changes to take effect:

```
helium# cat /kernel/drv/sd.conf
#
# SCSI disk configuration file
#
name="sd" class="scsi" target=0 lun=0;
name="sd" class="scsi" target=1 lun=0;
name="sd" class="scsi" target=2 lun=0;
name="sd" class="scsi" target=3 lun=0;
name="sd" class="scsi" target=4 lun=0;
#
# configure the additional target 4 luns
#
name="sd" class="scsi" target=4 lun=1;
name="sd" class="scsi" target=4 lun=2;
name="sd" class="scsi" target=4 lun=3;
name="sd" class="scsi" target=4 lun=4;
name="sd" class="scsi" target=4 lun=5;
name="sd" class="scsi" target=4 lun=6;
name="sd" class="scsi" target=4 lun=7;
#
# end of additional luns
#
name="sd" class="scsi" target=5 lun=0;
name="sd" class="scsi" target=6 lun=0;
name="sd" class="scsi" target=7 lun=0;
name="sd" class="scsi" target=8 lun=0;
name="sd" class="scsi" target=9 lun=0;
<lines removed for clarity>
helium#
```

After connecting the devices and rebooting, we'll find that we now have a set of logical devices for target 4 in the */dev* directory. We've only shown the *dsk* subdirectory, but we would find the same in the *rdsk* subdirectory and also the corresponding physical devices:

```
helium# cd /dev/dsk
helium# ls *t4d0*
c1t4d0s0    c1t4d0s2    c1t4d0s4    c1t4d0s6
c1t4d0s1    c1t4d0s3    c1t4d0s5    c1t4d0s7

helium# ls *t4d1*
c1t4d1s0    c1t4d1s2    c1t4d1s4    c1t4d1s6
c1t4d1s1    c1t4d1s3    c1t4d1s5    c1t4d1s7

helium# ls *t4d2*
c1t4d2s0    c1t4d2s2    c1t4d2s4    c1t4d2s6
c1t4d2s1    c1t4d2s3    c1t4d2s5    c1t4d2s7
<and so forth>
```

Adding the Tape Drive

Now that we've successfully added the disk, we can start to add the tape drive. We'll do this while the system is alive, but we need to bear a few things in mind:

- Whether we can add devices to a live system depends upon the hardware supporting this functionality.
- It's always better to add devices by taking the machine down when possible. If it isn't down, we need to be extra careful about allocating the correct SCSI ID and trying to ensure that the SCSI bus is as quiet as possible.

First, we need to assign a SCSI ID to it, making sure that it doesn't conflict with anything else on the bus. By convention, these are normally target 4 for the first tape and target 5 for the second, so we'll use 4 for this one, since it's our first tape drive to be connected.

Drvconfig and Devfsadm

Once the tape drive is physically connected, we need to notify the system that it is accessible. Two commands are available to do this. Prior to Solaris 7, drvconfig and its associated commands were used; since Solaris 8, another command, devfsadm, has been used.

To add the tape using the original commands, we would issue the following:

```
helium# drvconfig
helium# tapes
helium# devlinks
helium#
```

To perform the same operation with devfsadm, we would use the following command:

```
helium# devfsadm -c tape
helium#
```

Instead of having to call drvconfig (to configure the /*devices* tree), tapes (to create the /*dev* entries for the tape), and lastly devlinks (to create the /*dev* links), we can simply call devfsadm with the correct class (tape, in this case). It will then go ahead and create everything as required. We can use the same procedure for all class types it supports, which are as follows:

- Disk
- Tape
- Port
- Audio

The main difference between the two command sets is that devfsadm is much more reliable and allows the devices to be configured with fewer problems—it even works well when the bus is busy. For this reason, if devfsadm is available the system will always use it; in fact, after Solaris 8, drvconfig, tapes, and so forth are simply links back to devfsadm.

That was easy! The physical devices have been created under /*devices*, the instance mapping file /*etc*/*path_to_inst* has been updated, and lastly the correct logical entries have been created in /*dev*.

Checking the Tape

Now we should be able to check that the tape is working correctly. We'll use the mt command to do this. We need to make sure there is a tape in the drive first; otherwise, we'll see errors reported saying that the drive is "offline":

```
helium# mt -f /dev/rmt/0 stat
HP DDS-4 DAT (Sun) tape drive:
    sense key(0x6)= Unit Attention   residual= 0   retries= 0
    file no= 0    block no= 0
helium#
```

Nonstandard Tape Drives

That was easy enough, but how do we add a tape drive that is unsupported by Solaris or even alter some of the parameters of one of the standard tapes? Let's show this by assuming that we have a new tape device. We'll update the kernel files so that the tape is supported, which will also show how a standard supported tape can be altered.

The tape we will add is a "New Everlasting Tape," which has the characteristics shown in Table 17.3. This data should be easily available from each tape manufacturer.

Table 17.3 *Tape Drive Hardware Specification*

Setting	Value
Name	"Everlasting Tape"
Density Switches	0x14, 0x15
Fast Wide SCSI	20
Ultra SCSI	20
Ultra SCSI	20

Configuring St.conf

The file */kernel/drv/st.conf* is very similar to *sd.conf* that we saw earlier in that it is used to set configuration parameters for the SCSI tape drive. It also allows us to create additional tape drive entries if we wish.

The first step in the process is to get the vendor identification string for the device. If we don't know what this is already, we'll have to go to the PROM level to obtain it by running a `probe-scsi`, which we'll do here:

```
helium# init 0
ok>
ok> probe-scsi

Target 3
  Unit 0    Disk SEAGATE ST15230W SUN4.2G 0738

Target 5
  Unit 0    Removable Tape EVER_LASTING 1000
ok>
```

We can see that we have allocated SCSI ID 5 to the tape and plugged it onto the internal bus. The `probe-scsi` has queried the PROM on the device to see what it is, and the device has responded by returning its vendor and revision strings. We need to make a note of these, as they are needed for the */kernel/drv/sd.conf* entry. The additions to the file are shown below:

```
helium# cat /kernel/drv/st.conf
Tape-config-list=
    "EVER_LASTING", "Everlasting 8mm", "Ever_Last",
<lines removed for clarity>
#
# CONFIGURATION STRINGS SECTION -
#
Ever_Last = 1,0x36,0,0xCE39,4,0x14,0x1B,0x8C,0x8C,1;
<lines removed for clarity>
helium#
```

So what does all this mean? The device details consist of two entries. The first, which is "tape-config-list," consists of three parts, which are described in Table 17.4.

Table 17.4 *Tape-config-list Details*

Value	Description
EVER_LASTING	This is the SCSI inquiry string, which we obtained from the output of the `probe-scsi`.
Everlasting 8mm	Often known as the "pretty print string," this is used for any output relating to the device, such as messages in */var/adm/messages*.
Ever_Last	This is a token that identifies the entry containing the properties for the drive.

We can see from this that the SCSI inquiry string is the only one that is fixed; the other two can be altered as we wish. Table 17.5 shows what is in the device property string.

Table 17.5 *Device Property Details*

Value	Description
1	The version number. Currently, this should always be set to 1.
0x36	The type of device. The full list is specified in */usr/include/sys/mtio.h*. We've stated that ours is a "MT_ISOTHER," which is used for a "generic other type of tape drive."
0	The preferred block size of the device. Zero is used to specify that it's a variable block-size device.
0xCE39	A bit pattern specifying the device capability. These are defined in */usr/include/sys/scsi/targets/stdef.h*. We have specified the following capabilities; ST_VARIABLE, ST_BSF, ST_BSR, ST_LONG_ERASE, ST_KNOWS_EOD, ST_UNLOADABLE, ST_SOFT_ERROR_REPORTING, ST_BUFFERED_WRITES, and ST_NO_RECSIZE_LIMIT.
4	The number of densities that the device supports.
0x14, 0x1B, 0x8C, 0x8C	The density switches from the hardware manual. This drive uses 0x14 for no compression, 0x1B for medium compression, and 0x8C for maximum compression.
1	The default density (starting at 0).

Now that we have specified the correct details, let's reboot the system for the changes to take effect and see how the values chosen are used. We'll see the device being reported in the bootup messages as expected, but this time we'll see our "pretty print string":

```
helium# init 6
<lines removed for clarity>
st1 at esp0: target 5 lun 0
st1 is /iommu@f,e0000000/sbus@f,e0001000/espdma@f,400000/
esp@f,800000/st@5,0
        <Everlasting 8mm>
<lines removed for clarity>
```

This shows that the tape has been recognized and its entry correctly picked up from *st.conf*. From there, the same steps as adding any "normal" device have been followed—a physical device, an instance number (st1), and a logical device have been created.

The first thing would be to see how mt reports it:

```
helium# mt -f /dev/rmt/1 stat
Everlasting 8mm tape drive:
    sense key(0x6)= Unit Attention   residual= 0   retries= 0
    file no= 0   block no= 0
helium#
```

The entry in *sd.conf* also specified that the device has four density switches. The devices will again be created in the same way as the "normal" tape devices. Table 17.6 shows how the density switch relates to the tape device.

Table 17.6 *Density Switches*

Tape Device	Compression Level	Density Switch Used
/dev/rmt/1l	Low	0x14
/dev/rmt/1m	Medium	0x1B
/dev/rmt/1h	High	0x8C
/dev/rmt/1c	Compressed	0x8C
/dev/rmt/1 (default)	Medium	0x1B

SCSI Options

Sometimes we may need to force a device to operate in a specific mode. For example, a fast SCSI may be set to work as a "normal" SCSI—although we need to remember that the device must support the capability that we are trying to enable or disable. For example, we cannot enable fast SCSI on a "normal" SCSI device.

A number of different SCSI options are available and are shown in Table 17.7. These can be set to affect the device functions:

Table 17.7 *SCSI Options*

Type	Meaning
0x1	Debug (target driver)
0x2	Debug (library)
0x4	Debug (host adaptor)
0x8	Disconnect/reconnect
0x10	Linked commands
0x20	Synchronous transfer capability
0x40	Parity support
0x80	Tagged command support
0x100	Fast SCSI support
0x200	Wide SCSI support

For example, to support fast SCSI, tagged commands, global parity, synchronous transfer, linked commands, and global disconnect/reconnect (i.e., everything except wide SCSI and the debug options), we would apply the following values:

```
scsi_options=0x1f8
```

If we wanted this to affect every device on the machine, we would add the entry to the */etc/system* file as follows:

```
helium# grep scsi_options /etc/system
set scsi_options=0x1f8
helium#
```

If, on the other hand, we only had a single type of bus that this should affect, we would add the value to the card's configuration file. For example, if the SCSI card used the FAS driver named */kernel/drv/fas*, then we would add the following entry to *fas.conf*:

```
helium# grep scsi_options /kernel/drv/fas.conf
scsi_options=0x1f8;
helium#
```

We could also isolate a particular device on that bus by applying further constraints if we wish. Creating the correct constraints can become quite complicated, but the various ways of applying them can be found in the manual pages for the relevant driver.

18

NFS, DFS, AND AUTOFS

Manual Pages

automount (1M)
automountd (1M)
dfmounts (1M)
dfshares (1M)
dfstab (4)
fstypes (4)
lockd (1M)
mnttab (4)
mountd (1M)
mount_nfs (1M)
nfsd (1M)
nfssec (5)
rmtab (4)
rpc (3N)
rpc (4)
rpcbind (1M)
rpcgen (1)
rpcinfo (1M)
share (1M)
shareall (1M)
share_nfs (1M)
sharetab (4)

Manual Pages *(Continued)*

showmount (1M)
statd (1M)
unshare (1M)
unshareall (1M)
vfstab (4)
xdr (3N)

Files Affected

/etc/auto_master
/etc/auto_home
/etc/dfs/*
/etc/mnttab
/etc/netconfig
/etc/nsswitch.conf
/etc/rmtab
/etc/rpc
/etc/vfstab

Objectives

Up to now, we have created a small group of machines that are networked together. Each one has its own disk, which is used for local storage. This means that if a machine needs to access data residing on any of the other servers, the data will have to be copied manually.

Although time-consuming, this may not be a common task and so won't cause problems in many companies; in fact, the data may actually need to be segregated for some other reason. If, on the other hand, the data needs to be accessed often, this setup can prove very problematic.

In this chapter, we'll look at three related pieces of software that can be used to get around these issues and accomplish the task. These are NFS, DFS, and Autofs.

Network Filesystem

The Network Filesystem (NFS) is a type of distributed filesystem. It is a technology originally created by Sun and now licensed by many other companies. As such, it is supplied as core software with many UNIX operating systems, including Solaris, and is also available on many other non-UNIX computing environments.

NFS is a client-server product that allows data to be transparently accessed by machines across the network. To do this, a server allows access to some of its data. Clients then mount the data on their local filesystem in a way similar to mounting a local disk. Once the data is mounted locally, clients can read and write into the NFS-mounted areas.

NFS is based on Remote Procedure Calls (RPCs), which carry out the underlying reads and writes on behalf of the user.

Distributed Filesystem

A Distributed Filesystem (DFS) allows data on one or more servers to be shared throughout the network, using a mechanism that is normally transparent to the user. In this way, users do not need to be aware that the data they are using does not physically reside on their local machine.

Many types of DFSs are available, each one working slightly differently. The one we are interested in here is NFS.

Several programs are supplied with Solaris for the purpose of administering a DFS, and while they default to controlling NFS, they are not limited to it.

Autofs

Solaris can use the standard mounting mechanism (mount and */etc/vfstab*) for NFS-based filesystems to provide a static connection between the client and the remote file system. This means that when a machine boots, it will mount the device just as it would a local disk and it will remain connected while the machine is available.

When many machines act as NFS servers, it can become cumbersome and awkward to manage all the mount points, so Autofs is supplied to alleviate these problems. It is an "automatic-mounting filesystem," and is commonly known as the "automouter."

Autofs can also be incorporated into a naming service, allowing them to be centrally administered.

The Build Order

To show how these individual pieces of software work together, we'll first configure NFS/DFS to provide us with a series of static mounts for the clients. After that, we'll configure Autofs to make the static mounts dynamic and more manageable.

Remote Procedure Call

Many programs are designed to work in a client-server mode. These are applications that have been written as two components: a server and a client. Each component has the ability to run on separate machines across the network if required. Often, the server contains the main "guts" of the program, maybe controlling a centralized database, while the client might be a relatively small program that takes user requests and passes them on to the server.

There are many ways that client-server programs can be written; a common way is to use socket-based libraries. Another is to base them on RPC, as in the case of NFS.

Let's look at some of the features of RPC that make this possible.

Rpcbind

This program is the "RPC server." It is started on every machine at boot-time by the start-up script /etc/init.d/rpc. It is commonly known as the "portmapper" and is essentially a program that controls mapping between an RPC program and a network port number.

To understand the reason why we need to perform this mapping, let's quickly look at how "normal" socket-based client-server programs communicate with each other.

Let's assume that we start the telnet daemon on a server. It will determine the port number it should listen on by querying the /etc/services file, which will be port 23. Telnet is a "well-known" service, so every machine that runs the telnet daemon will start it on that port.

When a client machine starts a telnet session, it will also query the services file and determine that it should connect to port 23 on the server, where the telnet daemon is listening for incoming connections. Once the client has successfully bound to the server, the two can communicate.

When RPC was introduced, it was decided to make the port allocation dynamic. One of the reasons for this was to try and avoid the port conflicts that may arise as more people use RPC to create client-server applications.

The way that dynamic allocation works is that RPC-based programs contain a "program number" and a "version number." The program number is different for every program (although the client and server portions of the same program will have the same number).

When an RPC-based server's process starts, it contacts rpcbind and requests a port that it can use for communication. Rpcbind obtains the program and version number from the server and registers them, along with the port that it has assigned to the process.

Now, when a client starts, it will send a request to rpcbind, also including its program and version number, asking for the port that it can contact its server on. Rpcbind will check which server it has registered with those details and inform the client of the correct port.

Rpcbind itself is classed as a "well-known" service and as such is defined in */etc/services* to run on port 111, as shown below. This enables clients on remote machines to easily access it:

```
hydrogen# grep rpcbind /etc/services
sunrpc     111/udp     rpcbind
sunrpc     111/tcp     rpcbind
hydrogen#
```

As an example, we may see the following conversation taking place between the client, server, and rpcbind:

- server -> rpcbind (port 111): Hello, my program number is 200001230, my version number is 1, what port can I use?

- rpcbind -> server: Hi, you can use port number 12345.

- client -> rpcbind (port 111): Hello, my program number is 200001230, my version number is 1, where can I find my server?

- rpcbind -> client: Hi, your server is at port number 12345.

- client -> server (port 12345): Ah, there you are!

Program and Version Numbers

So, how do we know which program number to use? To avoid confusion between RPC-based programs, the program number should be selected from a specific range. Table 18.1 shows the values, along with who is responsible for administering numbers from each range.

Table 18.1 *The RPC Program Number Range*

Number Range (Hex)	Allocated By	Used For
0–1FFFFFFF	Sun	"Well-known" products, such as NFS
20000000–3FFFFFFF	Developers	Third-party/in-house software
40000000–5FFFFFFF	Transient programs	Temporary numbers for new programs, or ones being debugged
60000000–6FFFFFFF	Reserved	
80000000–7FFFFFFF	Reserved	
A0000000–9FFFFFFF	Reserved	
C0000000–BFFFFFFF	Reserved	
E0000000–FFFFFFFF	Reserved	

The version number is much easier to select. It is simply the version number of the program and is incremented with every release.

For example, we saw from the earlier "conversation" between the machines that we have assigned a program number of "200001230," and, as it's the first version, it has a version number of "1."

Transport and Machine Independency

"Transport independent" means that RPC isn't concerned about what it is running on—it just uses whatever is requested by the application. This also means that RPC isn't concerned about any errors; either the application or the underlying transport will need to cater for them, and react to any errors as it sees fit.

For example, if the application uses a reliable transport such as TCP/IP, the error checking will be handled there. If, on the other hand, an unreliable transport such as User Datagram Protocol (UDP) is being used, the application will have to handle its own errors.

External Data Representation

If an application is written to work on many types of platform/operating systems, it must be able to work around problems such as different byte ordering schemes. To do this, the server encodes data in a format known as External Data Representation (XDR). This includes the specifics of any data structures that need to be passed to the client. When the client receives the data, the client decodes it and uses it accordingly.

RPC Database

When we query rpcbind, we can either use the program number or the program name. This is possible because certain "well-known" RPC-based services are included in the RPC database file named /etc/rpc. This file simply provides a name, and any aliases, for a program number, in a way similar to the hosts and services files. For example, the NFS mountd process that we will use later has the following entry:

```
helium# grep mountd /etc/rpc
mountd          100005 mount showmount
helium#
```

This allows the name (mountd), the number (100005), or any of the aliases (mount, showmount) to be used as arguments to commands such as rpcinfo (which we'll come across later).

NFS Daemons

Now that we know how RPC works in general, let's look at the part of NFS that uses it. Listed in Table 18.2 are the NFS daemons, along with the type of machine they run on.

Table 18.2 *NFS Daemons*

Daemon	Runs On	Started By
mountd	Servers	/etc/init.d/nfs.server
nfsd	Servers	/etc/init.d/nfs.server
statd	Servers and clients	/etc/init.d/nfs.client
lockd	Servers and clients	/etc/init.d/nfs.client

The main ones we are interested in here are mountd and nfsd. These run on the NFS servers and are responsible for answering client requests, providing the NFS mounts, and passing the data back to the clients.

We won't deal with the client processes (statd and lockd) in any detail, as there isn't anything we can really do with them other than check that they are responding. All we really need to know here is that they are used for the NFS file-locking services.

Resources and Filehandles

Although it is called the "Network Filesystem," NFS doesn't really think of filesystems in the way we think of them. The reason for this is that NFS is written to work with machines on different platforms, which have different ideas of what a filesystem is! Instead, NFS deals with "resources," which are actually the systems files and directories.

The next problem we have is that the server needs to be able to provide a consistent way of referring to a given file at any time—even when it is communicating with different platforms.

For example, a PC might mount */extra_disk/some_dir* as its G drive. When it wants to read something, say *G:\demo_file*, the Solaris server must know that the file it is referring to is actually */extra_disk/some_dir/demo_file*. It also needs to be able to cope with any other differences such as physical drive details, path name separators, illegal characters, and so forth.

To achieve this, the server allocates each resource something known as a "filehandle." This is a string of characters built up from details such as the filesystem the file resides on and the inode number of the file. It acts in a way similar to a file descriptor for local files, in that all NFS transactions use the filehandle rather than the actual file name. By doing this, the problems we mentioned earlier can be overcome because the server is the only one that needs to know the low-level details of the file and to be able to decode the file-handle.

In NFS Version 2, the filehandle was a fixed array of 32 bytes, while in Version 3 it's a variable-length array of up to 64 bytes. They may look something similar to that shown below:

- 73a 1 a0000 f105 50b037ce a0000 2 5a8ad1ed

Decoding Filehandles

A command named showfh used to be supplied with SunOS (Solaris 1.x) to determine the file details for any given filehandle. This was useful when any NFS errors were seen because, as the example below shows, the filename is not shown:

```
NFS write error on host helium: Permission denied
(filehandle: 800025 2 a0000 ce620 95b3f69b a0000 2 5987f29a)
```

This command is no longer supplied, but its functionality has been reproduced as a script that dissects the filehandle passed in to determine the file details. The script is widely available as fhfind, but we have included it below, removing nonfunctional lines to save space:

```
#!/bin/sh
#
if [ $# -ne 8 ]; then
   echo "Usage: fhfind <filehandle> e.g."
   echo "fhfind 1540002 2 a0000 4df07 48df4455 a0000 2 25d1121d"
   exit 1
fi
fileSystemID=$1
fileID=`echo $4 | tr [a-z] [A-Z]`

#
# Use the device id to find the /etc/mnttab
# entry and thus the mountpoint for the filesystem.
#
E=`grep $fileSystemID /etc/mnttab`
if [ "$E" = "" ]; then
   echo "Cannot find filesystem for devid $fileSystemID"
   exit 0
fi
set - $E
mountPoint=$2

#
# alter the inode number from hex to decimal
#
inodeNum=`echo "ibase=16 $fileID" | bc`
echo "Now searching $mountPoint for inode number $inodeNum"
echo
find $mountPoint -mount -inum $inodeNum -print 2>/dev/null
```

Client-Server Communication

Once a server has been defined and its resources selected, they need to be advertised as being available. To do this, the server "shares" (or "exports," as it was originally known) the resources using DFS administration files and commands.

The client is then able to access the remote data. For this, it needs to talk to the NFS-related server processes, mountd and nfsd. As these are RPC-based programs, we'll see the same steps being followed that we outlined in the section on RPC, which will be as follows:

1. The client issues a mount request for the resources it requires.
2. The client's mount will first contact rpcbind on the server to find out which port its mountd can be found on.
3. The client's mount will contact mountd on the server and request the filehandle for the mount point it is trying to access.
4. The resource is mounted on the client and /etc/mnttab is updated. This contains the list of currently mounted devices.
5. When the device has successfully mounted, the server's mountd will update its own /etc/rmtab. This contains a list of resources that have been remotely mounted, along with the name of the machine that has the resources mounted.
6. The client can now try to access this data. To do this, it will contact rpcbind again to determine the nfsd port.
7. The client will contact nfsd, passing it the filehandle of any data it needs.
8. The server's nfsd will work with the data, either writing it to disk or passing data back to the client for any reads.

NFS Versions

We mentioned earlier that RPC uses whatever transports the application requests. Originally NFS was written to only use UDP, but it has since been modified to support both TCP and UDP. Table 18.3 highlights this and other changes between the releases, along with the release of Solaris that the NFS version was available in.

Table 18.3 *NFS Versions*

NFS Version	Solaris Release	Notes
1	Never released	
2	Pre Solaris 2.5	UDP support only

Table 18.3 *NFS Versions (Continued)*

NFS Version	Solaris Release	Notes
3	Solaris 2.5	TCP and UDP support Files < 2 GB
3	Solaris 2.6+	TCP and UDP support Files > 2 GB Caching improved

DFS Files

We stated earlier that the DFS package is used to administer the NFS configuration. A number of commands are available for controlling which resources are available. We'll look at these in a moment, but first let's look at how DFS determines which resources it should control. If we take a look in */etc/dfs*, we'll see the following files listed:

```
helium# ls /etc/dfs
dfstab      dfstypes     sharetab
helium#
```

Dfstypes contains the list of available distributed filesystem types; in other words, the types of filesystems that can be controlled with DFS. By default, it only contains an entry for NFS, as shown below:

```
helium# cat /etc/dfs/dfstypes
nfs NFS UTILITIES
helium#
```

The *dfstab* file contains entries for each resource that can be shared, along with the DFS type and any constraints that may apply. For example, to share a file named */file/to/share* using NFS, we could use the following entry in *dfstab*:

```
helium# cat /etc/dfs/dfstab
share -F nfs /file/to/share
helium#
```

The *dfstab* file is needed to cause the NFS server daemons to launch. For example, to share the file above (once the daemons are running), we could run the following command (assuming the path was a valid path; otherwise, we would see an error indicating that the file doesn't exist):

```
helium# share -F nfs /file/to/share
```

This would update the final file in this directory, *sharetab*. This lists any resources that are currently shared, and in this case would contain the following entry:

```
helium# cat /etc/dfs/sharetab
/file/to/share    -    nfs    rw
helium#
```

Similarly, we can use unshare to prevent the resource from being shared out, as shown below:

```
helium# unshare -F nfs /file/to/share
helium#
```

It's also possible to share or unshare a whole set of resources at once, which is achieved by running the commands shareall and unshareall. By default, these commands will use the first entry in */etc/dfs/dfstypes* as the filesystem type to work on. This is normally NFS so it shouldn't cause you any problems, but if you have a number of other DFS types available you may need to run the following for NFS:

```
helium# shareall -F nfs
helium# unshareall -F nfs
helium#
```

Configuring the Server

Up to now, we have been looking at how the components tie together, but now we will start to configure our actual systems. For this example, we'll use helium as the server, and assume we have a large disk connected to it that contains some important data. We're not worried about the type of data here; for all we know, it may be the company database or the internal telephone list! For now, we just know that we need access to it from every machine around the network.

The disk we are interested in is mounted on */data*, which is shown in the output below:

```
helium# df -k
Filesystem          kbytes   used  avail capacity  Mounted on
/proc                    0      0      0     0%    /proc
/dev/dsk/c0t2d0s0    48349  16889  26626    39%    /
/dev/dsk/c0t2d0s6   770543 522712 193893    73%    /usr
fd                       0      0      0     0%    /dev/fd
/dev/dsk/c0t2d0s1    61463   5592  49725    11%    /var
/dev/dsk/c0t2d0s7   519718  82791 384956    18%    /export/home
/dev/dsk/c0t2d0s5    38539   5928  28758    18%    /opt
swap                130064     28 130036     1%    /tmp
/dev/dsk/c0t1d0s0   504305 443210  53626    93%    /data
helium#
```

The information we would like to access is actually located in subdirectories of the */data* filesystem. We've already said that NFS works on a file/directory level rather than a filesystem level, which means that we don't have to share a complete filesystem from the machine—we can specify individual directories if we wish. In fact, if we list */data*, we can see it contains two directories: *local_files* and *remote_files*. The *local_files* directory contains helium's local files, so we don't want that shared, but everyone else can safely mount *remote_files*:

```
helium# ls /data
local_files     remote_files
helium#
```

We'll update */etc/dfs/dfstab* with any share settings that we wish to apply. This means they will be automatically shared whenever the system is rebooted. (If we only require temporary access, we could simply use the `share` command line instead if we wished.)

```
helium# cat /etc/dfs/dfstab
<lines removed for clarity>
share -F nfs /data/remote_files
helium#
```

Now we can start the NFS server. This will normally be carried out automatically at boot-time when the system detects that we have some filesystems to be shared. But since we have just created our *dfstab* file, we'll need to start it manually here:

```
helium# /etc/init.d/nfs.server start
helium#
```

This will also perform a `shareall` for us, so let's check that we have a valid entry in the */etc/dfs/sharetab* file:

```
helium# cat /etc/dfs/sharetab
/data/remote_files      -           nfs     rw
helium#
```

The *sharetab* file is up-to-date, which means that everything should have been shared from the system correctly:

```
helium# dfshares
RESOURCE                SERVER      ACCESS      TRANSPORT
helium:/data            helium      -           -
helium#
```

Good. Everything appears to be shared, but we haven't checked that `mountd` and `nfsd` are actually working correctly, so we'll do that next. We know that both of these are RPC-based processes, so let's check that they are responding using some of the RPC commands.

Checking RPC

The first task is to make sure that `rpcbind` has started OK; otherwise, any RPC-based servers won't be able to register with it. This also causes the client side to fail, as it cannot determine its server port:

```
helium# ps -ef | grep rpcbind
    root   98   1  0 08:50:33 ?    0:00 /usr/sbin/rpcbind
helium# netstat -a
<lines removed for clarity>
TCP
   Local Address  Remote Address   Swind Send-Q Rwind Recv-Q State
   *.sunrpc        *.*               0    0     0     0 LISTEN
<lines removed for clarity>
helium#
```

The process is running and listening on its port, so now let's use `rpcinfo` to query it. First we'll get a list of the processes that are currently registered with `rpcbind`:

```
helium# rpcinfo helium
<lines removed for clarity>
program version netid      address        service    owner
100005    1      udp     0.0.0.0.128.13   mountd     superuser
100005    2      udp     0.0.0.0.128.13   mountd     superuser
100005    3      udp     0.0.0.0.128.13   mountd     superuser
100005    1      tcp     0.0.0.0.128.8    mountd     superuser
100005    2      tcp     0.0.0.0.128.8    mountd     superuser
100005    3      tcp     0.0.0.0.128.8    mountd     superuser
100003    2      udp     0.0.0.0.8.1      nfs        superuser
100003    3      udp     0.0.0.0.8.1      nfs        superuser
100227    2      udp     0.0.0.0.8.1      nfs_acl    superuser
100227    3      udp     0.0.0.0.8.1      nfs_acl    superuser
100003    2      tcp     0.0.0.0.8.1      nfs        superuser
100003    3      tcp     0.0.0.0.8.1      nfs        superuser
100227    2      tcp     0.0.0.0.8.1      nfs_acl    superuser
100227    3      tcp     0.0.0.0.8.1      nfs_acl    superuser
<lines removed for clarity>
helium#
```

We can also get a more compact listing of this if we wish, which can sometimes be easier to read:

```
helium# rpcinfo -s
program  version(s)  netid(s)                         service   owner
<lines removed for clarity>
100005   3,2,1       ticots,ticotsord,tcp,ticlts,udp  mountd    superuser
100003   3,2         tcp,udp                          nfs       superuser
100227   3,2         tcp,udp                          nfs_acl   superuser
<lines removed for clarity>
helium#
```

From this, we can see that `rpcbind` currently supports three versions of the `mountd` process (Versions 1, 2, and 3), and that it can use a number of different transport mechanisms, including TCP and UDP. Let's interrogate it a little more and check that the program is responding. To do this we'll use rpcinfo to run the equivalent of a ping on the process:

```
helium# rpcinfo -T tcp -u localhost mountd
program 100005 version 1 ready and waiting
program 100005 version 2 ready and waiting
program 100005 version 3 ready and waiting
helium#
```

The NFS programs should also respond with a similar message, in which case all the RPC servers appear to be working OK. So let's move on to one of the clients and configure it to use the new resource.

Setting Up the Clients

Now that we have a set of resources that the server has shared out, how do we make use of them on the client? Fortunately, this is relatively easy to do because the standard mount command is used to provide access to them. We don't even need to start any daemons ourselves since the ones we need (statd and lockd) are started as part of the normal boot process.

Let's run through the commands "manually" the first time, using lithium as our example client. Once we are happy with everything, we'll make the necessary changes to mount the filesystem automatically at every reboot. First let's check that lithium can see the server:

```
lithium# ping helium
helium is alive
lithium#
```

Good. Helium is responding, so we'll do a quick check to see what resources are available on it. We can use the DFS commands again to do this:

```
lithium# dfshares helium
RESOURCE                        SERVER     ACCESS     TRANSPORT
helium:/data/remote_files       helium     -          -
lithium#
```

Now we'll create a directory on the client to mount the server's resources on:

```
lithium# mkdir -p /data/remote_files
lithium#
```

Finally we can mount the resource. We mentioned above that the standard mount command is used; only the syntax is slightly different—we commonly refer to the device as "hostname:resource," as shown below:

```
lithium# mount -F nfs helium:/data/remote_files /data/remote_files
lithium#
```

Lots of other options can be used at mount time to control the way NFS functions. We'll cover some of these later in the chapter.

The process we described in "Client-Server Communication" on page 431 has now started. This means that the filehandle has been returned to the client's mount process and the relevant files on the client and server have been updated to show that the mount has taken place. Let's look at them to see the changes. Here's the client's */etc/mnttab* first:

```
lithium# cat /etc/mnttab
helium:/data/remote_files  /data/remote_files  nfs
rw,dev=2d40002  1003587797
lithium#
```

Meanwhile, the server's */etc/rmtab* now contains the following entry to show that lithium has the device mounted:

```
helium# cat /etc/rmtab
lithium:/data/remote_files
helium#
```

Again, we can use one of the DFS commands, dfmounts, to confirm that helium is aware we have its resource:

```
lithium# dfmounts helium
RESOURCE     SERVER    PATHNAME              CLIENTS
-            helium    /data/remote_files    lithium
lithium#
```

All of this means that we should be able to see that the device has been mounted:

```
lithium# df -k
Filesystem                 kbytes   used   avail  capacity  Mounted on
<lines removed for clarity>
helium:/data/remote_files  504305  443210 53626   93%      /data/remote_files
lithium#
```

Lastly, we can add the entry to */etc/vfstab* to force the mount to occur automatically at boot-time. For now, we'll just use a basic entry without any options (we'll add these later in the chapter). After we have added this line, the file will look like the one shown below:

```
lithium# cat /etc/vfstab
#
#device    device    mount   FS    fsck  mount    mount
#to mount  to fsck   point   type  pass  at boot  options
#
<lines remove for clarity>
helium - /data/remote_files /data/remote_files nfs - yes bg
lithium#
```

This states that we wish to mount helium's resource, */data/remote_files*, and that it's an NFS-based filesystem. We don't need to fsck it, as this will be carried out on its local machine. We do want it mounted at boot-time, but we don't need to mount it with any special options. We use the mount option "bg," which will cause the mount to take place in the background so that if, for any reason, helium were not available when lithium rebooted, no part of the boot would be blocked. The default option is to mount the filesystem in the foreground and if the remote server is not available the boot of the local server would hang until the request timed out (around three hours later).

It's interesting to see the options the resource has actually been mounted with. We can use a variation of the `mount` command to do this:

```
lithium# mount -p
<lines removed for clarity>
helium:/data/remote_files - /data/remote_files nfs - yes rw
lithium#
```

The output shows the resource has been mounted in read-write mode. We can also see that it is formatted in the same way as the entries in */etc/vfstab*, so as well as providing us with information about the mounted devices, it also allows us to easily add the correct contents to the file if we wish.

Server Share Options

The settings above have worked fine; the clients can see the data and access it OK. The only problem is that we have allowed every machine on the network to have read-write access to the whole of */data/remote_files*, and everything below it. There may be a valid reason for this and it may be what we actually need, but let's look at how we can restrict machines and tighten security a little by specifying some share options for each resource.

We'll alter the settings so that only the machines that actually need access to a resource can get it. We'll also force the type of access they are allowed, where possible. For example, there is no point providing write access to read-only data, such as NFS-mounted manual pages.

Looking in */data/remote_files*, we find there are a number of subdirectories, each of which is used by different machines on the network. Table 18.4 summarizes which clients will be allowed access to which directories, along with the level of access they are allowed. Again, we don't need to be concerned about the information that the subdirectories contain.

Table 18.4 *Allowed Client Access*

Directory	Clients	Access Required
/data/remote_files/log	All machines	Read-only
/data/remote_files/general	Lithium, boron	Read-write
/data/remote_files/admin	Nitrogen	Read-only

To do this, we need to update the settings in /etc/dfs/dfstab. We'll remove the line that allowed access to everything and replace it with entries for each of the subdirectories instead. Each of these will also contain the correct options needed to achieve the access control. After making the changes to the configuration file, it will look like the one shown below:

```
helium# cat /etc/dfs/dfstab
<lines removed for clarity>
share -F nfs -o ro             /data/remote_files/log
share -F nfs -o rw=lithium:boron /data/remote_files/general
share -F nfs -o ro=nitrogen    /data/remote_files/admin
helium#
```

We can see from the file above that we've passed all the options in a comma-separated list to the "-o" argument. Let's look at the entries we have used:

- ro (the resource is available to everyone, but with read-only access)
- ro=nitrogen (the resource is available only to nitrogen, with read-only access)
- rw=lithium:boron (the resource is available only to the named machines, but with read-write access)

Finally, we'll remove access to the top-level directory by unsharing everything and allow access to the subdirectories instead by rerunning the share command for the new information:

```
helium# unshareall
helium# shareall
helium#
```

Access Lists

Access lists allow us to group machines together when specifying share options. In fact, we've just shown the most common method of using them: a list of individual host names, similar to that shown below:

```
server# share -F nfs -o ro=helium:lithium /file/to/share
server#
```

An access list can be formatted in a number of other ways. These are shown in the table below. Any of the types in Table 18.5 can be used, so long as the list is colon-separated.

Table 18.5 *Access List Types*

Type	Used For	Example
Host name	List of individual hosts	lithium
Netgroup	Name of an NIS netgroup map	some_machines
Network	Network name or IP address, identified by an "@"	@192.168.22
DNS	Machines in a specific domain, identified by a "."	.sun.com
(Deny access)	Deny access to this type, identified by a "-"	-hydrogen

Using this allows us to create quite a complicated access list. For example, to deny read-write access to lithium, allow all machines on the 192.168.22.0 network, allow any that are in the "some_machines" netgroup, and lastly include hydrogen, we could use something similar to the following syntax:

```
server# share -F nfs -o rw=-lith-
ium:@192.168.22:some_machines:hydrogen /file/to/share
server#
```

Using Netgroups

Netgroups are a special case—they only work with NIS or NIS+, not "local files." For example, if NIS is configured on the network, the netgroup's map can be used to provide a series of machine or user names that can be used when sharing resources. It may prove easier to maintain an NIS map and plug the netgroup into the *dfstab* file, rather than adding every machine.

Each entry in the configuration file, */etc/netgroup*, is defined as a set of triples consisting of the host name, user name, and the domain name. We're only concerned about machine-level access here, so we can ignore the other two entries in each triple. To configure netgroups we would create the input file, */etc/netgroup*, on the NIS server. This is only used as an intermediate file, to populate the NIS map. Next, we would build the maps following the steps explained in Chapter 12, "Naming Services and NIS."

For example, if we wanted to create two netgroups to suit the machines on our two subnets, say, machines_22_net and machines_44_net, the */etc/netgroup* file could be similar to that shown below:

```
nis server# cat /etc/netgroup
machines_22_net (hydrogen,,), (helium,,), (lithium,,) ? (n,,)
machines_44_net (tin,,), (iodine,,), (xenon,,) ? (n,,)
nis server# cd /var/yp
nis server# make
nis server#
```

Once the map has been built, it can be used within the share options, as shown below, as long as the NFS server was also configured for NIS:

```
helium# cat /etc/dfs/dfstab
share -F nfs -o rw=machines_22_net /data
share -F nfs -o ro=machines_44_net /data
helium#
```

Client Mount Options

Now that we have tightened up the server side, we need to make similar changes to the client, otherwise we'll start to see errors when we try to mount the resources. For example, we can't mount them with read-write access if they have been shared with read-only access.

Again, this is very easy to do. We simply supply the NFS-specific options to the mount command and it will take care of it for us.

First let's look at the commands we would need to run for the share options we've defined above. First we'll mount the log area with read-only access onto /data/remote_files/log on any client:

```
<any client># mount -F nfs -o ro helium:/data/remote_files/log
/data/remote_files/log
<any client>#
```

Now we'll mount the general area onto boron, with read-write access:

```
boron# mount -F nfs helium:/data/remote_files/general/data/
remote_files/general
boron#
```

And finally we'll mount the *admin* files onto hydrogen, again with read-only access:

```
nitrogen# mount -F nfs -r helium:/data/remote_files/admin/data/
remote_files/admin
nitrogen#
```

This time we've used slightly different syntax for mounting the resource read-only. We've used the generic "-r" option rather than the NFS-specific "-o ro" just to show that there are different ways of using the options.

There are many other NFS options available (these can be found in the mount and mount_nfs manual pages), but Table 18.6 shows some of the more commonly used ones.

Table 18.6 *Common NFS-Related Mount Options*

Option	Access Required
rw, ro	Mount the device with read-write access (the default) or with read-only access.
fg, bg	If the mount attempt fails, retry it in the foreground (which will cause the local machine boot process to hang if the hard option is also used) or in the background.
hard, soft	"Hard" (the default) will send an error if the server does not respond; "soft" will continue retrying.
intr, nointr	"Intr" (the default) allows the client to interrupt a hung, hard-mounted resource; "nointr" does not.
suid, nosuid	"Suid" (the default) allows setuid programs to be executed; "nosuid" doesn't.

Authentication

We have now successfully mounted the resources on the clients, and all the users can access their data correctly. The only odd thing is that if we try to create a file as *root*, it doesn't get created with the correct ownership. In fact, depending on where we try to write it, we may not have permission to create the file at all!

For example, if we run the following commands, we can see that we end up with a file owned by someone known as *nobody*:

```
server# share -F /temp_dir
server#

client# mount -F nfs server:/temp_dir /temp_dir
client# touch /temp_dir/testfile
client# ls -l /temp_dir/testfile
-rwxr-xr-x  1 nobody   nobody 0 Oct 22 2001 /temp_dir/testfile
client#
```

We haven't created the user, so where has it come from? If we look in the password file, we can see the following entries for *nobody*:

```
helium# grep "^nobody" /etc/passwd
nobody:x:60001:60001:Nobody:/:
nobody4:x:65534:65534:SunOS 4.x Nobody:/:
helium#
```

The reason the *nobody* users are defined has to do with the way that users are authenticated within NFS (actually by the underlying RPC mechanism); let's see why.

"Authentication" is the term used to define a process that is used to prove you are who you say you are! For example, on a local machine you would authenticate by following the normal login process, listed below:

1. The system offers you the login prompt and asks you to login.

2. You say you are "Mike Smith" and enter the correct user ID for him, "msmith" in this case.

3. The system asks you to prove this by entering the correct password.

4. You do—the system is happy with this and logs you on.

A similar process is followed when using an RPC-based application, but the steps taken will alter depending upon how the application has been written. RPC supports several different authentication levels, which are shown in Table 18.7. Any RPC-based application can use these facilities to create a more secure product, if you wish.

Table 18.7 *RPC Authentication Levels*

Level	Access Required
AUTH_NONE	No authentication. Supported for `share_nfs` only (not `mount_nfs` or `automount`). Maps clients to the *nobody* user.
AUTH_SYS	The user's UID and GID are authenticated by the NFS server.
AUTH_DH	Also known as AUTH_DES. Uses the "Diffie-Hellman" public key system.
AUTH_KERB4	Also known as AUTH_KERB. Uses the Kerberos Version 4 authentication system.

NFS uses the level of security known as AUTH_SYS by default. For this, the user's ID and group ID are passed to the server for authentication. This means that all the user's IDs should be the same across the network (it's a common problem for a user to have different IDs on different machines; this will cause files to appear to be owned by the wrong user).

To improve security at this level, the *root* user's special privileges are revoked on NFS-mounted filesystems. To do this, the user ID is remapped to the user *nobody*, leaving the *root* user with normal user privileges. This means *root* must be granted read-write permissions for anything *root* requires, just as a normal (nonprivileged) user would be.

If, however, we do want to allow *root* access, we only need to alter the share option on the server to include the "root=access_list" option for the relevant resource. For example, to allow the machines named "client1" and "client2" to have *root* access to a directory named */temp_dir*, we would use the following entry in */etc/dfs/dfstab*:

```
server# share -F nfs -o root=client1:client2 /temp_dir
server#
```

Secure NFS

NFS can be configured to use one of the stronger authentication mechanisms (AUTH_DH or AUTH_KERB4). This is known as "Secure NFS." While it is beyond the scope of this book, we'll briefly note the steps that need to be taken to configure it. The example here is based on AUTH_DH authentication:

1. Establish public and secret keys with `newkeys`.
2. Login with `keylogin`.
3. Configure the server resource (for example, "share -F nfs -o sec=dh / temp_dir").
4. Mount the resource on the client with the correct options (for example, "mount -F nfs -o sec=dh server:/temp_dir /temp_dir").

Client Failover

NFS supports something known as "client failover." This is a concept similar to that available with Autofs, as we'll see later. The idea is that if there are a number of machines that can provide the same resource, we can list them all as redundant servers in */etc/vfstab*.

A few caveats go with this type of configuration: The filesystems must all be mounted read-only (ro) on the client and the file layout should be exactly the same within the hierarchy. The data will be read from the first host until it fails, then the next will be used, and so on.

One of the best examples to show this is the standard manual page hierarchy (it should be the same across all the servers, and can easily be mounted read-only). The entry used to mount them would be something similar to this:

```
lithium# cat /etc/vfstab
#
#device     device    mount  FS    fsck  mount    mount
#to mount   to fsck   point  type  pass  at boot  options
#
<lines removed for clarity>
hydrogen,helium,lithium:/usr/share/man - /usr/share/man nfs - yes ro
lithium#
```

NFS URL

Throughout the chapter, we have used the most common method of referring to a resource: "hostname:pathname." As an alternative, NFS allows an Internet style of reference to be used also, known as an "NFS URL," and written as "nfs://hostname/pathname."

As an example, the following syntax shows the two ways of mounting the same resource:

```
mount helium:/export/home/users/msmith /home/msmith
mount nfs://helium/export/home/users/msmith /home/msmith
```

The Autofs

By using NFS we have managed to create a series of static NFS mounts on the machines around the system, with the only ongoing task being to maintain */etc/dfstab* on the servers and */etc/vfstab* on the clients.

This works fine, but after a while we may start to notice a few things, such as:

- Some mounts are hardly used for most of the time. For example, users may have their home directories NFS-mounted onto a machine they never actually log on to.

- As the number of servers increases, we can start to see "cross-mounting" problems.

To explain cross-mounts, let's look at the present setup. Helium is the NFS server and so must be available before all the other machines boot up; otherwise, any hard mounts will force the clients to hang when they boot. As long as we are aware of this we can work around this issue.

Now let's alter the server configuration so that, say, helium becomes the NFS application server and carbon the server for the user's home directories. Each machine needs to mount the other's resources, so we now have cross-mounts between them. This means that if they were both rebooted at the same time, helium would hang waiting for carbon, and vice versa.

We could actually work around this by mounting the resources with the background option, but Autofs provides another solution and also allows us to free up the redundant user mounts we mentioned earlier.

Autofs works by allowing us to define a series of mount points, along with the devices that will be automatically mounted when they are required. When a user needs to access any data within an Autofs mounted area, the request will be intercepted and the device will be mounted, transparently to the users. After a predefined inactivity period, the mounted device will be unmounted, again by Autofs.

The Autofs service is started at boot-time by a script named /etc/init.d/ autofs, which runs two programs—automount and its daemon automountd.

The `automount` process is responsible for determining all the mount points that it needs to control, which are defined in a series of plain-text files known as "maps." The `automountd` daemon carries out the actual mounting or unmounting of any devices as required.

Three types of maps can be used: the master map, direct maps, and indirect maps.

Master Map

This is named */etc/auto_master* and is the first map read by the `automount` process. Each line consists of the path name of a directory controlled by Autofs, followed by the name of the submap that contains the actual mount details, and finally any options for `automount` to use. These options are only used if the submap itself doesn't contain any options. Each directory is known as a "trigger node." This is used by Autofs to detect when its resource needs mounting.

An example master map is shown below:

```
helium# cat /etc/auto_master
#
# Master map for automounter
#
/net       -hosts                -nosuid,nobrowse
/xfn       -xfn
/home      auto_indirect_map
/-         auto_direct_map
helium#
```

Predefined Maps

The first two entries in the master map above, "/net" and "/xfn," refer to two predefined maps: *-hosts* and *-xfn*, respectively. There are actually three predefined maps available. These are shown in Table 18.8.

Table 18.8 *Predefined Autofs Maps*

Map Name	Description
-hosts	Locates all the shared resources for the machines around the network and makes them available through Autofs.
-xfn	Mounts the initial context of the FNS (Federated Naming Service).
-null	Cancels the previous map that was linked to the directory mount point.

Taking the *hosts* map as an example, we know that helium has */data/ remote_files/general* shared, so we would be able to list its contents using the commands below:

```
<client># cd /net/helium/data/remote_files/general
<client># ls
<output from the ls>
<client>#
```

We'll see an example of the *null* map later in the section "Included Maps" on page 453.

Direct and Indirect Maps

These maps are used within the master map and contain the actual mount information. The main difference between direct and indirect maps is that direct maps define the mount point as an absolute path name, whereas indirect maps use a relative path instead. Let's look at a few examples to explain this a little more.

A common example of a direct map is one used to control the manual pages—*/usr/share/man*. The syntax for the direct map would be as follows:

```
helium# cat /etc/auto_man
/usr/share/man -ro oxygen:/usr/share/man
helium#
```

Here we have specified that */usr/share/man* on oxygen will be mounted, read-only, on the directory */usr/share/man*. Because we have used an absolute directory as our mount point, we don't need to put that information in the master map. Instead a special key of "/-" is used in the directory field to signify that the map is a direct map. So, in this case, the corresponding master map entry would be as follows:

```
/-      auto_man
```

An indirect map, on the other hand, only uses a relative path for its directory specification and so *does* need the remainder of its mount point specified in the master map. An often-used example of this would be *user* directories. The map below contains the directories of each of the users:

```
helium# cat /etc/auto_home
msmith    helium:/data/users
jgreen    helium:/data/users
helium#
```

The corresponding master map entry for this would be as follows.

```
/home     auto_home
```

The relative path of the user would be appended to the directory listed in the master map, which means that the home directory "msmith" would appear as /home/msmith.

Map Naming Conventions

All maps within Autofs can be put under the control of a naming service. This means that the normal /etc/nsswitch.conf changes will need to be made. It also means that when we refer to a map name, we normally use the filename only, rather than including the directory name as well. This is why in the master maps above we refer to auto_indirect_map and auto_direct_map, rather than /etc/auto_indirect_map and /etc/auto_direct_map.

Our Configuration

Now that we know how to do it, let's move on and build some maps. We also talked about removing the redundant user mounts, so we'll take this opportunity to move them all onto one machine, still in /export/home, but now under the control of Autofs. We'll use neon for this task.

While we are moving things around, we'll also NFS-mount the manual pages onto every machine from oxygen. This allows us to free up some space on all the local disks if we wish.

Table 18.9 shows the original location, along with the name of the map we will create and its type.

Table 18.9 *Our Maps*

Original Location	Map Name	Map Type
/usr/share/man	auto_man	Direct
/export/home	auto_home	Indirect
/data/remote_files/log	auto_data	Indirect
/data/remote_files/general	auto_data	Indirect
/data/remote_files/admin	auto_data	Indirect

We'll create them all on one machine first, using lithium again. This will allow us to test most of the functionality of Autofs, although we'll also need to copy the maps to other machines to test the access control settings.

We need to make sure that home directories are shared correctly from neon now, and that the NFS daemons have all been started. We don't need to make any changes to helium, though, because everything is already correctly shared from it.

The Master Map

After using the information provided in the table above and incorporating the predefined *hosts* map, we've created the following master map:

```
lithium# cat /etc/auto_master
#
# Master map for automounter
#
/net     -hosts          -nosuid,nobrowse
/data    auto_data
/home    auto_home
/-       auto_man
lithium#
```

We've added the "nosuid" and "nobrowse" options to */net*, to add a little more security. We've also included options within some of the maps themselves, as we'll see below. Let's now work through the remaining maps, creating each one in turn.

The Direct Map

The first one we'll look at is *auto_man*, which is shown below:

```
lithium# cat /etc/auto_man
/usr/share/man -ro,soft oxygen:/usr/share/man
lithium#
```

This allows access to the online manual pages and is very similar to the examples we have already seen. We've included options for it, too. The access will be read-only, and the "soft" option will allow the request to continue without an error. This is generally OK for read-only filesystems, but it's always recommended to use the "hard" mount option for read-write filesystems.

The Indirect Maps

Next we have the *auto_home* and *auto_data* maps, both of which are indirect-type maps:

```
lithium# cat /etc/auto_home
testuser neon:/export/home/testuser
sysadmin neon:/export/home/sysadmin
msmith   neon:/export/home/msmith
jgreen   neon:/export/home/jgreen
lithium#
```

This again is quite simple and similar to the previous example. It takes each of the *user* directories from */export/home* on neon and mounts them onto */home* on the client.

Now let's look at the *auto_data* file. Here we have added options that reflect the access control we would like applied. We can see that entries for *general* and *admin* only refer to three machines, so there is an argument for leaving them as standard NFS mounts, rather than pass the details onto every machine; we've simply done it this way for completeness:

```
lithium# cat /etc/auto_data
log       -ro                 helium:/data/remote_files/log
general -rw=lithium:boron helium:/data/remote_files/general
admin   -ro=nitrogen       helium:/data/remote_files/admin
lithium#
```

Metacharacters

Autofs provides a facility to allow metacharacters to be included within the maps—in the same way that the shell allows them within its syntax. Table 18.10 shows the ones that are available, along with an example of how they may be used.

Table 18.10 *Metacharacters*

Metacharacter	Function	Example
&	Substitute the key	msmith neon:/export/home/&
*	Matches any key	* neon:/export/home/&
"	Escapes special characters	msmith neon:/"some location"

For example, we can see that most lines in the *auto_home* map are the same, apart from the user name. Using metacharacters, we could shorten the *auto_home* file to the following:

```
testuser neon:/export/home/&
sysadmin neon:/export/home/&
msmith   neon:/export/home/&
jgreen   neon:/export/home/&
```

Or to match every home directory, we could use the following:

```
* neon:/export/home/&
```

Client Failover

We saw earlier that NFS supports server redundancy by providing a failover feature, and mentioned that it is also supported with Autofs. All we need to do to add this support is to list the alternative servers in the map.

We'll do this for the manual pages. The map is shown below after we have made the modifications:

```
lithium# cat /etc/auto_man
/usr/share/man -ro neon,carbon,nitrogen:/usr/share/man
lithium#
```

In this case, we now have three servers that are able to supply the data we require. The order in which each server will be used depends on a number of factors, such as network location, response time, and the level of the NFS protocol that is supported. The fact that response time is considered helps with load balancing, to some extent, as the most heavily loaded server will respond later and so is less likely to be chosen.

Preferred Servers and Weighting

If we want to define which server becomes our preferred one, we can add some weighting to it, although this will only be considered after the above factors have been taken into account. Our preferred order is neon, followed by carbon, followed by nitrogen. Adding some weighting, we get the following map:

```
lithium# cat /etc/auto_man
/usr/share/man -ro neon,carbon(1),nitrogen(2):/usr/share/man
lithium#
```

This shows that, the higher the weighting, the less chance the server will be selected.

Testing

The most obvious way of checking that everything is working correctly is to change into the relevant directories and check that the data is available. We should also find that logging in as any of the users produces the correct results, since the users' home directories are now under Autofs control.

Another test we need to carry out is to make sure that clients cannot see any data they shouldn't, as in the case of the *general* and *admin* directories in the *auto_data* map.

We can check that the files have been mounted in a number of ways. One is by running a df to see the device; another is by checking the */etc/mnttab* file on the client. For example, if we force a resource to be mounted, by changing into, say, *jgreen*'s *home* directory, */home/jgreen*, we should see the following information:

```
lithium# df -k
Filesystem                kbytes   used   avail capacity  Mounted on
<lines removed for clarity>
neon:/export/home/jgreen 519718   82791 384956   18%  /home/jgreen
lithium#
```

The above shows that the device has been mounted as expected. The following shows two entries, one for the map itself, and the other for the mounted device:

```
lithium# cat /etc/mnttab
auto_home /home autofs ignore,indirect,dev=2b80001 1004515802
neon:/export/home/jgreen /home/jgreen nfs dev=1980000 1004546700
lithium#
```

Naming Services and Autofs

We've already mentioned that Autofs can be incorporated into a naming service. This allows a whole series of maps to be administered centrally. This can save system administrators a lot of time, since they will not have to have maps copied around the network to the correct machines. There are, however, a number of things we need to be aware of first.

We need to make the usual changes to */etc/nsswitch.conf*. The following entry will tell automount to use NIS, followed by the local */etc* files:

```
lithium# grep automount /etc/nsswitch.conf
automount: nis files
lithium#
```

NIS supports two existing maps: *auto_master* and *auto_home*. This means that we'll need to create entries in the NIS *Makefile* for any custom maps we have created (*auto_man* and *auto_data*). This is easy to do, as we can copy the existing entry for *auto_home*. We won't explain how this is done, since we've created custom maps before in Chapter 12, "Naming Services and NIS."

Direct Maps

We need to be especially careful if the system is being moved from "local files" to NIS or NIS+, because while a local master map can have multiple direct map entries, an NIS or NIS+ map file can only have one entry.

The reason for this is that the key (the directory entry) for multiple direct maps would be the same "/-" and so would conflict with each other. The way we can get around this problem is to amalgamate all the direct map entries into one large direct map file.

Included Maps

Autofs also allows maps to be included in a variety of ways. Using NIS, we can specify "+mapname" to include the map named *mapname*. This allows us to further control how the map information is used. For example, if we are using "local files," and the local master map contains the following entries:

```
lithium# cat /etc/auto_master
+auto_master
/net       -hosts         -nosuid,nobrowse
/data      auto_data
/home      auto_home
/-         auto_man
lithium#
```

then the "+automaster" directive forces the NIS map named *auto_master* to be read in first, before the remaining entries. This type of configuration is often where the *null* predefined map is used. To show how this may be used, let's assume that the NIS *auto_master* added the following entry, but it wasn't required for any production system:

```
/test_area development_map
```

We could use the following */etc/master_map* definition to remove the entry. Note that the *null* map should be inserted before the included map:

```
lithium# cat /etc/auto_master
/test_area -null
+auto_master
/net       -hosts         -nosuid,nobrowse
/data      auto_data
/home      auto_home
/-         auto_man
lithium#
```

Conclusion

We have managed to mount resources using NFS for simple static mounts. Then, by coupling them with Autofs, we have altered them to become automated mounts. With both these configurations, we have been able to add support to allow for server failure by configuring them with client failover.

Finally, we have shown that incorporating Autofs into a naming service can make the system easy to administer, although there are a few things to think about and plan along the way.

More features are available within Autofs, but the ones shown here should be enough to provide an overview of how it works and to configure an initial system.

19

TIME, DATE, AND NTP

Manual Pages

date (1)
ntptrace (1M)
ntpq (1M)
rdate (1M)
TIMEZONE (4)
timezone (4)
zic (1M)
zdump (1M)

Files Affected

/etc/default/init
/etc/services
/etc/TIMEZONE
/etc/inet/ntp.conf
/usr/lib/inet/xntpd
/usr/share/lib/zoneinfo/*

Objectives

In this chapter we'll look at how time is controlled and displayed on the system. We'll look at the different ways it can be set, and discuss ways we can control time on a network of systems.

Introduction

All computer systems have a clock that is used to maintain the time, and it is the system administrator's responsibility to ensure that it is set correctly. Most of them are inaccurate to some degree, be it a second per hour, or a second per year. The system administrator needs to decide what level of inaccuracy is considered acceptable.

This problem highlights further issues that we need to be aware of. The first is trying to maintain the "correct" time across a network of machines, and the second is trying to keep the clocks synchronized with each other, regardless of how accurate they are.

Here, we'll look at how the system determines the correct time and look at the various ways this can be administered, along with advantages and disadvantages of each method. After that we'll move on to the next (and possibly more important) issue, which is how we can ensure that all the machines around the network are set to the same time.

System Time

On most UNIX systems, time begins at 00:00:00 January 1, 1970, Greenwich Mean Time (GMT), which is often known as the "epoch." The kernel maintains a count of the number of seconds that have passed since the epoch and uses this count for everything that is time-related, such as file creation, time stamps, user logging, and how long processes have been running.

GMT or UTC

Historically, time standards have always used GMT as the reference for all other time zones. In 1986, UTC (Universal Time Coordinated) was introduced as the replacement for the international standard for time. UTC is based on atomic measurements, whereas GMT is based on the Earth's rotation. For this reason, UTC is a more accurate value. However, as far as we are concerned, UTC can be thought of as equivalent to GMT; the differences are unimportant at the levels of accuracy we are dealing with here.

Displaying Time

Whenever any commands are run, if they need to display a date, the internal value for the time will first be converted into UTC and from there into a displayable format using a series of rules that defines how to convert the time to suit the geographical location of the system. These rules are known as "timezones." Various commands exist to set and query the system time and to define the time zone rules to the system. These commands are described in the sections below.

The value for time is stored as a 32-bit value on many UNIX systems. For these, time will "end" at 03:14:07 January 19, 2038, GMT. However, Solaris now uses a 64-bit value for time, which is good news for us as time will "continue" for the next 10 billion years or so!

We can view the system date before it is converted using the time zone rules by displaying it as UTC. A comparison between the local time and UTC is shown below:

```
hydrogen# date -u; date
Thursday April  4 08:18:57 GMT 2002
Thursday April  4 09:18:57 BST 2002
hydrogen#
```

Date

Setting the correct time and date on the system is a fundamental requirement. If it is not correct, we cannot be sure that the reported times for user logins are correct, or that log entries in a file are in the correct order. At its most basic, setting the date is a manual and therefore relatively inaccurate task (well, maybe to the nearest second or so). To do this, we would use the date command as shown below:

```
hydrogen# date 102217302002
Sun October 22 17:30:00 GMT 2002
hydrogen#
```

Setting the time this way is fine for a few machines. But it rapidly becomes a headache to administer as more machines are added, and also becomes more complex if you are trying to maintain a close accuracy between the systems.

Since the system clock is not 100 percent accurate, we should run date on a regular basis to ensure that the time is set correctly, probably by setting the date to a reference time such as a Web page, a speaking clock, or some other system that is known to be accurate. Before we see how to do this, let's look at how the time zones we mentioned are involved.

Time Zones

In the output from date, we can see that the time zone setting is also displayed. The output below shows this is currently set to GMT on our system:

```
hydrogen# date
Sun October 22 17:30:00 GMT 2002
hydrogen#
```

Time zones are controlled by an environmental variable named TZ:

```
hydrogen# echo $TZ
GB
hydrogen#
```

Setting the Time Zone

All systems should be configured for a particular time zone; this allows the system to set the clock to the rules that each time zone describes. There are various ways of setting this, although most users will perform this task once, when the operating system is installed by answering a question about where the system is located. This will place an entry for TZ into a file named */etc/default/init*:

```
hydrogen# grep TZ /etc/default/init
TZ=GB
hydrogen#
```

Other UNIX systems and older versions of Sun OS used to place the time zone information in a file named */etc/TIMEZONE*. To ensure compatibility with these systems, this file is still used in Solaris, but is now linked to */etc/default/init*:

```
hydrogen# ls -ld /etc/TIMEZONE
lrwxrwxrwx  1 rootroot14 Oct 22 1999 /etc/TIMEZONE -> ./
default/init
hydrogen#
```

What Do the Time Zone Settings Do?

The time zone settings provide us with an indication of the system's geographical location, or probable intended location. Secondly, and most importantly, the settings allow the system to apply a series of rules that govern how the time is displayed for that particular time zone. For example, we know that in the UK the time zone is GMT and that we switch to BST (British Summer Time) in March, then back again to GMT in October. Whereas in China, for example, the switch occurs between mid-April and mid-September. By knowing which time zone it is set up for, the system is able to apply these changes automatically.

It is important to note again that the time zone settings do not alter the system clock in any way, simply the way the time is displayed. This can always be confirmed by comparing the output of the local date and the date in UTC, as we showed earlier.

Once we have set the systems correctly, it may be useful on occasions to check the time zone rules (for example, to confirm exactly when BST occurs for a particular year). All the time zone files are located in */usr/share/lib/zoneinfo* and contain the time conversion information in a compiled form. To view these rules, we use zdump as shown below:

```
# zdump -vc 2004 GB
GB  Thu Apr  4 07:36:47 2002 GMT = Thu Apr  4 08:36:47 2002 BST isdst=1
GB  Fri Dec 13 20:45:52 1901 GMT = Fri Dec 13 21:45:52 1901 BST isdst=0
GB  Sat Dec 14 20:45:52 1901 GMT = Sat Dec 14 21:45:52 1901 BST isdst=0
GB  Sun May 21 01:59:59 1916 GMT = Sun May 21 02:59:59 1916 BST isdst=0
GB  Sun May 21 02:00:00 1916 GMT = Sun May 21 03:00:00 1916 BST isdst=1
GB  Sun Oct  1 01:59:59 1916 GMT = Sun Oct  1 02:59:59 1916 BST isdst=1
GB  Sun Oct  1 02:00:00 1916 GMT = Sun Oct  1 02:00:00 1916 GMT isdst=0
```

```
...<output removed for clarity>
GB   Sun Mar 30 00:59:59 2003 GMT = Sun Mar 30 00:59:59 2003 GMT isdst=0
GB   Sun Mar 30 01:00:00 2003 GMT = Sun Mar 30 02:00:00 2003 BST isdst=1
GB   Sun Oct 26 00:59:59 2003 GMT = Sun Oct 26 01:59:59 2003 BST isdst=1
GB   Sun Oct 26 01:00:00 2003 GMT = Sun Oct 26 01:00:00 2003 GMT isdst=0
GB   Tue Jan 19 03:14:07 2038 GMT = Tue Jan 19 03:14:07 2038 GMT isdst=0
GB   Mon Jan 18 03:14:07 2038 GMT = Mon Jan 18 03:14:07 2038 GMT isdst=0
hydrogen#
```

This shows the time one second before the rule is applied, the time when the rule is applied, and the time one second after the rule has been applied. It's interesting to note that the "final" 32-bit UNIX time is also displayed. The "isdst" value indicates whether we are in Daylight Savings Time or not, where "isdst=1" means we are.

We can see from the above that we switch between GMT and BST depending on whether Daylight Savings Time is in force or not. This results in the system displaying the following output when run at the relevant times:

```
hydrogen# date
Fri December  1 09:00:00 GMT 2001
hydrogen#
```

```
hydrogen# date
Thu July  1 09:00:00 BST 2002
hydrogen#
```

Zdump can also be used to display the time for a particular time zone. For example, to check the date for EST (Eastern Standard Time), we could run either of the commands below. Comparing the times relative to UTC (GMT) will confirm that the offsets are correct:

```
hydrogen# date -u; TZ="US/Eastern"; date
Thursday April  4 08:27:45 GMT 2002
Thursday April  4 03:27:45 EST 2002
hydrogen#
```

```
hydrogen# date -u; zdump US/Eastern
Thursday April  4 08:32:55 GMT 2002
US/Eastern  Thu Apr  4 03:32:55 2002 EST
hydrogen#
```

Since the time zone setting does not affect the system time, only the displayed value, we could take this a stage further and display a clock for any time zones we were interested in, as shown below, without affecting the rest of the system:

```
hydrogen# TZ=GB; xclock &
hydrogen# TZ="US/Eastern"; xclock &
hydrogen# TZ=CST; xclock &
hydrogen#
```

Creating Time Zone Files

A time zone information file needs to be created and passed onto `zic`, the time zone compiler. This file needs to contain a series of entries consisting of rules, zones, or links.

For example, let's say that we need to create a new time zone named "Mars," and that the required time zone obeys the following rules:

- The time zone will be valid from 1995 onward.
- It is 12 hours ahead of GMT.
- It changes to Daylight Savings Time every year, on April 1 at 17:30 GMT, by moving backward two hours.
- It shifts out of Daylight Savings Time every year on the Sunday after October 22 at 15:00 GMT.
- The time periods are known as MMT and MST, these being "Mars Mean Time" and "Mars Summer Time," respectively.

Now, we'll create the file that contains the time zone rules; in this case, we have called it *mars*. We'll store the input file in our data area in case we need it later:

```
hydrogen# cd /usr/local/utils/data
hydrogen# cat mars
Rule MARS 1995 max - Apr 1       17:30 -2:00 MST
Rule MARS 1995 max - Oct Sun>=22 15:00 0     MMT
Zone planetMars 12:00 MARS MMT/MST
hydrogen#
```

Next, we can compile the rules using the time zone compiler. This will place a file in */usr/share/lib/zoneinfo* named after the zone itself, in this case *planetMars*:

```
hydrogen# zic mars
hydrogen#
```

To ensure that this is correct, let's first check that we have the correct time offset from GMT, by comparing it with the current UTC time:

```
hydrogen# date -u; TZ=planetMars; date
Thursday April  4 09:00:21 GMT 2002
Thursday April  4 19:00:21 MST 2002
hydrogen#
```

Next, if we take a look at the rules, we can see when the switches between MST and MMT occur and check that these are correct:

```
hydrogen# zdump -vc 2004 planetMars
planetMars  Thu Apr  4 09:30:20 2002 GMT = Thu Apr  4 19:30:20 2002 MST isdst=1
planetMars  Fri Dec 13 20:45:52 1901 GMT = Sat Dec 14 06:45:52 1901 MST isdst=0
planetMars  Sat Dec 14 20:45:52 1901 GMT = Sun Dec 15 06:45:52 1901 MST isdst=0
planetMars  Sat Apr  1 05:29:59 1995 GMT = Sat Apr  1 15:29:59 1995 MST isdst=0
planetMars  Sat Apr  1 05:30:00 1995 GMT = Sat Apr  1 15:30:00 1995 MST isdst=1
```

```
planetMars  Sun Oct 22 04:59:59 1995 GMT = Sun Oct 22 14:59:59 1995 MST isdst=1
planetMars  Sun Oct 22 05:00:00 1995 GMT = Sun Oct 22 17:00:00 1995 MMT isdst=0
<lines removed for clarity>
planetMars  Tue Apr  1 05:29:59 2003 GMT = Tue Apr  1 17:29:59 2003 MMT isdst=0
planetMars  Tue Apr  1 05:30:00 2003 GMT = Tue Apr  1 15:30:00 2003 MST isdst=1
planetMars  Sun Oct 26 04:59:59 2003 GMT = Sun Oct 26 14:59:59 2003 MST isdst=1
planetMars  Sun Oct 26 05:00:00 2003 GMT = Sun Oct 26 17:00:00 2003 MMT isdst=0
planetMars  Tue Jan 19 03:14:07 2038 GMT = Tue Jan 19 15:14:07 2038 MMT isdst=0
planetMars  Mon Jan 18 03:14:07 2038 GMT = Mon Jan 18 15:14:07 2038 MMT isdst=0
hydrogen#
```

At this point, we could implement the new time zone by altering */etc/ default/init* and inserting the correct (new) time zone:

```
hydrogen# grep TZ /etc/default/init
TZ=planetMars
hydrogen#
```

Now that we have established what the rules for this particular system are, we usually need to apply the same rules across all the systems on the local network. Each one will need to have the time zone set individually, but this is not usually a problem because, as noted earlier, it will be performed once, at install time.

This leaves us with the problem of synchronizing the clocks across all the systems. We'll take a look at ways this can be performed.

Host Names

In Chapter 11, "Connecting to the Local Area Network," we described how it is easier to manage a system by creating an alias for a particular service. This allows us to move the service from one host to another easily without reconfiguring all the clients should the need arise. We are following that advice here and creating all host entries using this convention. Even if you haven't implemented a centralized naming service, it's worth doing this, since you will only need to alter the *hosts* file should a machine alter and not lots of different configuration files scattered around the system. The entries from the *hosts* file, complete with the new aliases, are shown below:

```
hydrogen# grep timeserver /etc/hosts
192.168.22.1 hydrogen  h  timeserver
hydrogen#
```

Rdate

To get around the problems of manually setting the date on every system, a utility named rdate can be used. This will set the local system time to that of a specified remote machine. For example, to set helium to the same date as hydrogen we would run:

```
helium# rdate hydrogen
Sun October 22 17:30:00 GMT 2002
hydrogen#
```

To automate this procedure, we could nominate a machine to be our "time server." As explained above, we have chosen hydrogen for this task. First, we set the correct time on hydrogen. Next, we run rdate on a regular basis, by adding an entry to the *root crontab*. The redirection will ensure that we don't receive the output as mail every time cron runs:

```
helium# crontab -l | grep rdate
0 4,12,20 * * * rdate timeserver > /dev/null 2>&1
helium#
```

Then, we create a start-up script that performs exactly the same job at boot-time. These two methods ensure that the system will only be out of synchronization for a relatively short period:

```
helium# cat /etc/rc2.d/S99rdate
#!/bin/sh
#
# Set the system date to that of the "time server"
#
rdate timeserver > /dev/null 2>&1
if [ $? -ne 0 ]; then
    echo "Error: Check the date - cannot set it to the time server"
fi
helium#
```

These two files would be copied around all the systems on the network to set them to the same time as hydrogen, our nominated time server.

Setting the system time using rdate is a common method of synchronization, but may not be reliable enough in certain cases. For example, there could be problems if the system being used as the reference was down, or there could be problems with applications that required the time to be consistent within a small time window.

The command can also have a detrimental effect on log files or time stamps, since it is easy for the reference system to be "older" than the local system and rdate would simply set the local clock back, rather than slowing it until the remote system caught up. This means we could end up with files created in the future; entries in log files would be out of order and so forth.

Network Time Protocol

The Network Time Protocol (NTP) was designed to ensure that time could be accurately set and maintained over a wide area network, such as the Internet. It achieves this with much better accuracy than utilities such as rdate, by providing clients with a way to synchronize their clocks against a reference time signal. This may be either a piece of hardware, such as a radio clock, or perhaps another server that has access to an accurate signal.

NTP can also be used to regulate the systems on a network that doesn't have access to a reference signal. In this case, we are trying to make sure that the times on each system are correct relative to each other; we are not really concerned with how accurate the times are to a reference source (well, maybe to a few minutes). The point is that we end up with a master system that we know we can control the time on, and clients can simply refer to this master and set themselves from there. The advantages of this method are that we don't need any additional hardware or network connections to the outside world. This allows us to use this method on an internal network and add any additional configuration requirements afterward, if required.

Only a few configuration files are needed to set up NTP, and the system itself is easy to maintain. But before we show how to do this, let's look at how NTP works and the components it uses.

How NTP Works

Let's assume that there was only one clock in the world that gave the correct time, and that this clock is 100 percent accurate, 100 percent of the time. We'll call this our "reference clock."

Obviously, if we only had the one reference clock it would soon become overloaded as everyone tries to determine the correct time from it. We would need some way of balancing this load across more clocks.

Now let's say that we only allow 10 clocks to query our reference clock, and that everyone else has to get the correct time from one of these. The overloading would be vastly reduced because we have increased the number of clocks that can be queried. These new clocks would probably not be quite as accurate, but would be good enough for most purposes.

If these 10 clocks also get overloaded, we can apply the same rule again: 10 new clocks per existing one, which would provide us with 100 "time access points."

We can see that we have created a hierarchy of clocks here, each level providing more access points, although this is at the cost of some accuracy—the further we move away from the main "reference" source, the less accurate the new clock becomes.

This example is the basis of NTP (although the numbers involved are very different). The levels that we've described are known within NTP as "stratum levels." It uses stratums to assign a value to a clock that represents its distance away from the top-level source—in other words, its accuracy.

Stratum Levels

The available stratums are 0 for the best available source (such as a radio clock), followed by 1 through to 15, with 16 being used as an unknown source (this is often seen for a server that has been set up on a broadcast network, or one that has not yet synchronized). Stratums are assigned to a server automatically by the NTP software (although this can be altered, as we'll see later).

Stratum-0 servers are the NTP equivalent of the 100 percent accurate clock we described above. They must be connected to a machine, since they cannot be interrogated directly by the NTP software.

A machine will always be one level lower than its server. The reason for this is that it is "further" away from the server it is getting its time from. In other words, a stratum-0 hardware device feeds a machine that becomes a stratum-1 server, which feeds another machine that becomes a stratum-2 server, and so on. The outcome of this is that, as far as NTP is concerned, the best available source is a stratum-1 server—that is, the machine running NTP that is connected to a stratum-0 hardware device.

The idea is that there are a few level-1 servers, feeding more level-2 servers, feeding lots of level-3 servers, and so forth. Most systems should try to connect to stratum-2 servers; this leaves the stratum-1 servers free to feed the stratum-2s. The difference in accuracy between the two will be negligible for most users, especially after any network delays have been taken into account.

One thing we need to be aware of when dealing with stratum levels is that it's possible to assign a different stratum level to a particular server by using the "fudge" keyword in the NTP configuration file. This is useful in certain situations—in fact, we use it in our internal system described later. The downside of this is that it's possible to connect to something advertising itself as a stratum-1 server, when in fact it has a highly inaccurate clock and its stratum has been altered manually.

Delays, Offsets, and Dispersion

So now that we have a highly accurate server that we can connect to, the next thing we need to be concerned about are network issues. For example, let's assume it takes 10 seconds for the server to respond to our query—by the time we've received the reply, it will be incorrect.

However, if we take this a step further and calculate that the network delay to this server is *always* 10 seconds, we can work out what the correct time will be when we receive the server response—this should be 5 seconds out (half the roundtrip across the network). Adding this calculated delay to the returned time will give us the correct value.

Let's look at an example of this. Figure 19.1 shows an example of an NTP data packet being sent by a client to a server.

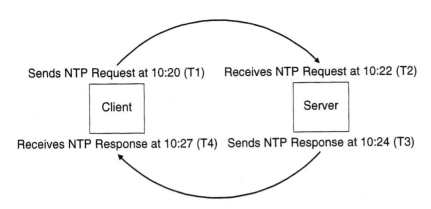

Figure 19.1 *Client-server network delays.*

We can see here that it takes 7 seconds from sending the client request to receiving a response back from the server (this is grossly exaggerated, but makes things easier to see!). We can also see the times at which the packet was either sent or received by both machines. NTP places time stamps into the NTP packets at these points, which are as follows:

- When the client sends the request
- When the server receives the request
- When the server sends the response
- When the client receives the response

Once we have the time stamps, we can make a few calculations; two of the important ones are known as "delay" and "offset." "Delay" refers to the time taken to send the packet to the server and get a response, ignoring any machine processing times (in other words, the network portion only). We can calculate this as follows:

```
(T4 - T1) - (T3 - T2)
```

"Offset" is the estimated time difference between this system and the server, and is calculated as follows:

```
0.5 [(T2 - T1) + (T3 - T4)]
```

Calculating these values for the times shown in Figure 19.1 gives us the following:

```
delay = (10:27 - 10:20) - (10:24 - 10:22) = 5 secs
offset = 0.5 [(10:22 - 10:20) + (10:24 - 10:27)] = 2.5 secs
```

Now when the NTP client receives the time back from the server, it knows the offset that it needs to add to determine the "correct" time. However, if the local clock is wildly inaccurate, it could produce a highly incorrect value. The problem we may see here is that after adding the offset to it, it is even further out. To overcome this, we use a value known as "dispersion." This is an estimate of the maximum error seen between the local clock and the server. By adding the dispersion value to the local time we can place limits around its inaccuracy.

Servers

The earlier example assumes that one server has been used, whereas in reality NTP prefers to work with a number of servers—at least three are recommended. The reason for this is that the software will compare each of the servers against the others to see which is providing the best results. This method of calculation gives preference to lower stratum clocks that have the smallest roundtrip time.

We've referred to servers as "hardware devices" in earlier examples and explanations. In reality there are various types of servers available; let's look at them in more depth now.

An NTP server is something that responds to requests from a client, and can be either a system or a hardware reference device. If it is another system, its IP address will be used, while a reference device would be allocated a loopback address. This is described in more detail below.

Reference Devices

Table 19.1 is generated from the sample NTP configuration file supplied with Solaris, */etc/inet/ntp.server*. It shows the device numbers that have been allocated to some standard reference devices by the NTP software. Each device is allocated an address and treated as if it was simply another machine. The address is generated by combining the loopback network with the Xtype reference number from Table 19.1 and the instance number of the device, to give an address of 127.127.<Xtype device number>.<instance number>.

For example, if you wanted to use the IRIG Audio Decoder device (Type 6 in the table below), and it was the first instance of the device connected to this system, it would be allocated an IP address of 127.127.6.0.

Using this method of treating hardware devices as IP addresses makes it very simple to alter a device for a higher-level server at a later date.

Table 19.1 *NTP Reference Devices*

XType	Device	Name	Description
1	(none)	LOCAL	Undisciplined Local Clock
2	trak	GPS_TRAK	TRAK 8820 GPS Receiver
3	pst	WWV_PST	PSTI/Traconex WWV/WWVH Receiver

Table 19.1 *NTP Reference Devices (Continued)*

XType	Device	Name	Description
4	wwvb	WWVB_SPEC	Spectracom WWVB Receiver
5	goes	GPS_GOES_TRUE	TrueTime GPS/GOES Receivers
6	irig	IRIG_AUDIO	IRIG Audio Decoder
7	chu	CHU	Scratchbuilt CHU Receiver
8	refclock-	GENERIC	Generic Reference Clock Driver
9	gps	GPS_MX4200	Magnavox MX4200 GPS Receiver
10	gps	GPS_AS2201	Austron 2201A GPS Receiver
11	omega	OMEGA_TRUE	TrueTime OM-DC OMEGA Receiver
12	tpro	IRIG_TPRO	KSI/Odetics TPRO/S IRIG Interface
13	leitch	ATOM_LEITCH	Leitch CSD 5300 Master Clock Controller
14	ees	MSF_EES	EES M201 MSF Receiver
15	gpstm	GPS_TRUE	TrueTime GPS/TM-TMD Receiver
17	datum	GPS_DATUM	Datum Precision Time System
18	acts	NIST_ACTS	NIST Automated Computer Time Service
19	heath	WWV_HEATH	Heath WWV/WWVH Receiver
20	nmea	GPS_NMEA	Generic NMEA GPS Receiver
22	pps	ATOM_PPS	PPS Clock Discipline
23	ptbacts	PTB_ACTS	PTB Automated Computer Time Service

Public Time Servers

These are servers that provide an accurate time signal for general use. A number of these are available and their details can be found by searching for "public time servers" on most search engines. Anyone who advertises a time server will normally provide information similar to the following:

ntp2a.mcc.ac.uk (130.88.202.49)

Location: University of Manchester, Manchester, England

Synchronization: NTP secondary (S2), Sun/SunOS

Service Area: UK

Access Policy: Open Access

Contact(s): timelords@mcc.ac.uk

Note: Please use DNS for address, subject to change

We can see that this particular system advertises itself as a stratum-2 server and has an open access policy, meaning we can simply connect to it as required. Other systems may ask you to mail them your contact details so they are aware of who is using their service.

Bear in mind that we don't really know how accurate any public time server is because it may have been assigned a higher value than it should have by using the "fudge" keyword we mentioned earlier. This means that if you are going to use a public time server, it is always worth checking the accuracy of its clock beforehand. And, if you are setting one up, always make sure you are advertising the correct stratum level.

Our Configuration

Now we'll start to configure our machines. We'll do this by connecting to a public time server on the Internet first, then follow this by building our own NTP server, which the remaining clients can synchronize with. Doing it in this order will enable us to quickly get all the machines working as NTP clients, while allowing us to build a local master server in our own time.

We'll use hydrogen as the client example here, although each system will require the same configuration details to be installed. First, let's check that the NTP packages have been installed. Running `pkginfo` should show us something similar to that shown below:

```
hydrogen# pkginfo | grep -i ntp
system      SUNWntpr      NTP, (Root)
system      SUNWntpu      NTP, (Usr)
hydrogen#
```

We'll also check that we have a port defined for NTP in the *services* file—this will normally be set to 123:

```
hydrogen# grep ntp /etc/services
ntp         123/tcp        # Network Time Protocol
ntp         123/udp        # Network Time Protocol
hydrogen#
```

Kernel System Variables

Versions of Solaris prior to 2.6 will require a system variable named "dosynctodr" to be set to 0 to avoid conflicts between the hardware and software clocks. This is carried out by adding an entry into the *system* file:

```
hydrogen# grep dosynctodr /etc/system
set dosynctodr=0
hydrogen#
```

However, if the machine is using Solaris 2.6 or above, the default is to ensure that the two clocks are synchronized, so this value must not be set.

Build the Clients

We've already mentioned that NTP actually prefers to be configured with a number of servers. Since we have quite a lot of public time servers available, we'll select three of them. We have chosen the two listed below, for no other reason than they are reasonably close (at least to us!), along with ntp2a.mcc.ac.uk, which we listed earlier in the section "Public Time Servers" on page 467.

salmon.maths.tcd.ie (134.226.81.11)

Location: Trinity College, Dublin, Ireland

Synchronization: NTP secondary (stratum 2), MIPS Magnum

Service Area: Ireland, UK

Access Policy: open access

Contact: *time@maths.tcd.ie*

Note: salmon.maths.tcd.ie (134.226.81.11), ashe.cs.tcd.ie (134.226.32.17), and lib1.tcd.ie (134.226.1.24) peer together over local area net, and one or more usually run at stratum 2. It is normally sufficient just to pick one machine to peer with.

ntp.cs.strath.ac.uk (130.159.196.123, 130.159.196.125)

Location: Dept. Computer Science, Strathclyde University, Glasgow, Scotland

Geographic Coordinates: 04:14W, 55:52N

Synchronization: NTP V3 secondary Sun/UNIX

Service Area: UK/Europe/any

Access Policy: open access

Contact: Ian Gordon (*ntp@cs.strath.ac.uk*)

Note: IP addresses are subject to change; please use DNS.

All three systems specify that they are "open access," which means we can simply use them when we're ready. Before we do that, it's a good idea to test that we are happy with the accuracy they will provide—we do this by querying them. For example, we can use ntpq to check the Strathclyde University Server (ntp.cs.strath.ac.uk), and see which peers it knows about and what their current status is. This may show results similar to the following:

```
hydrogen# ntpq -p ntp.cs.strath.ac.uk
     remote           refid      st t when poll reach   delay   offset   disp
==============================================================================
+fleming.cs.stra harris.cc.strat  3 u   19  128  363    0.82    0.536  251.30
-canon.inria.fr  .GPS.            1 u   43 1024  377   52.51    5.567    0.76
-faui45.informat .DCFp.           1 u  442 1024  377   75.65   11.674    2.21
-Time1.Stupi.SE  .PPS.            1 u  245  512  377   65.95    5.646    1.85
+ntp0.cs.strath. harris.cc.strat  3 u   43  128  352    0.92    0.506    0.46
+rockall.cc.stra ntp0.ja.net      2 u    9  128  377    2.76   -0.805    0.05
*harris.cc.strat ntp1.ja.net      2 u  121  128  377    2.01    0.541    0.08
 ntp1.belbone.be 0.0.0.0         16 u   36 1024    0    0.00    0.000 16000.0
 ntp2.belbone.be 0.0.0.0         16 -    - 1024    0    0.00    0.000 16000.0
+130.159.62.11   ntp1.ja.net      2 u   79  128  377    4.04    1.399    0.66
hydrogen#
```

Ntpq uses the first character to display the synchronization status—the current server is indicated with a "*." This example shows it is currently using the server named harris.cc.strat, which is a stratum-2 server.

The delay, offset, and dispersion values are all very small, so we can be quite confident in synchronizing to this system. If we wished, we could also carry out similar tests on the other machines. To save space here, we'll assume that they are OK.

Now that we know which servers we would like to use, we need to configure NTP accordingly. This is quite easy as there is only one configuration file for both servers and clients, which is named */etc/inet/ntp.conf*. The one we have created for hydrogen is shown below:

```
hydrogen# cat /etc/inet/ntp.conf
#
# Server config for Internet NTP clients
#
server ntp2a.mcc.ac.uk
server ntp.cs.strath.ac.uk
server salmon.maths.tcd.ie
driftfile /var/ntp/ntp.drift
hydrogen#
```

Let's work through the entries to see what they all refer to. First, we specified the servers, which in our case are the three public time servers mentioned earlier. Next, we specified the path name of a file known as the "drift file." This allows NTP to store the frequency error it has calculated for the clock. If this file exists, NTP will read the value when it starts and adjust the clock accordingly. This means the time will be accurate immediately, and we won't have to wait for it to smooth out over a number of hours. NTP will create the file if it doesn't exist and update it every hour—we just need to make sure it can write into the directory.

Once */etc/inet/ntp.conf* has been created, we can either start the NTP daemon manually by running the start-up script provided by the system, or wait for the next reboot and let the system start it automatically. We'll do it manually here:

```
hydrogen# /etc/init.d/xntpd start
hydrogen#
```

That's the entire configuration! We just need to check that NTP is working correctly before we move on and copy the configuration file around the remaining clients.

Checking the Clients

As the first check, let's run ntpq to display a list of all the servers that this system can see ("-n" simply returns the server names as IP addresses rather than the names of the hosts/clocks). This shows that we are currently synchronized with 130.88.202.49, which is set to stratum 2:

```
hydrogen# ntpq -np
     remote           refid      st t when poll reach  delay  offset  disp
==============================================================================
*130.88.202.49   194.81.227.227  2 u   57   64   77   16.94   2.481  3.22
+130.159.196.118 130.159.248.11  3 u   57   64   77   23.65   3.875  2.73
+134.226.81.11   134.226.81.3    2 u   57   64   77  122.02 -42.051  6.58
hydrogen#
```

The "poll" column indicates how often the server will be queried, with "when" showing the countdown to the next poll. Whenever a poll is successful, a "reachability" register is updated and its value displayed in the "reach" column as an octal value. NTP uses the last eight polls in its calculations and displays the results as follows:

When the NTP daemon is started, the register is cleared out and set to 0; since it is only interested in the last eight polls, this will effectively be 00000000. At the next poll, if the server returns OK, a "1" will be entered from the right-hand side to give us 00000001. If we follow this pattern and, for example, see the next four polls, lose the one after, and see the remaining two, we would end up with a value of 11111011 in binary, or 373 in octal. The correct value for the full eight polls will be 377 (binary 11111111).

We can see that in our output we have "reach" set to octal 77, which is equivalent to 00111111 in binary. This indicates that we have seen the last six polls and, in our case, since we have recently started the daemon, probably means it hasn't yet completed its eight polls.

Now we'll use ntptrace to show the chain of servers back to the primary time source:

```
hydrogen# ntptrace
localhost: stratum 3, offset 0.000026, synch distance 0.12448
maverick.mcc.ac.uk: stratum 2, offset 0.017359, synch distance 0.05569
ntp1.ja.net: stratum 1, offset 0.017014, synch distance 0.00258,
    refid 'GPS'
hydrogen#
```

From the output we can confirm that we are synchronized correctly, running one stratum lower than the server (stratum 3), as expected. This also shows that the root of our servers is a stratum-1 hardware device. At this point, we are happy that NTP is configured and working on the server, which means we can copy the configuration around the remaining machines.

Build the Local NTP Server

Now that all the clients are synchronized to a public server, we'll "upgrade" hydrogen so that *it* now becomes our "master" server instead. We don't have any specialized hardware available to connect to, so instead we'll use its own clock as the reference device. In reality, all this means is that NTP will query the system clock and use whatever value it returns.

Although we have chosen hydrogen to be our NTP server, it isn't really critical which one is used—obviously, all the other systems must be able to see it on the network. It also makes sense to run it on a server, rather than one of the desktops, even though NTP doesn't generate too much overhead.

The NTP daemons are already running on this machine, so the first task is to stop them:

```
hydrogen# /etc/init.d/xntpd stop
hydrogen#
```

As we are using the local clock as the reference source, we ought to make sure it's adjusted correctly. This is a manual task and should be done before we start to configure NTP, although in our case, since we've only just stopped it, the clock should already be correct:

```
hydrogen# date <correct time>
hydrogen#
```

Next we need to alter *ntp.conf* and replace the public time server's entries with the one for our local clock. After the changes have been made, our file looks like the one shown below:

```
hydrogen# cat /etc/inet/ntp.conf
#
# Server config for host hydrogen
# (expected to operate via local clock at stratum 10)
#
server 127.127.1.0
fudge 127.127.1.0 stratum 10
driftfile /var/ntp/ntp.drift
hydrogen#
```

Let's look at the entries we've used. First we've specified the server, which is the onboard clock. We only have one of them so it is instance 0. Looking at Table 19.1, we can see that the local clock is device type 1. All this gives us a server address of 127.127.1.0.

By default, the clock will advertise itself at stratum 3, but we want to set it to a lower stratum (using the "fudge" keyword). This is because we don't want to advertise it as a relatively high-stratum server. Also, we may at some point connect a better time source, for example, a public time server. If we forget to update the clock entry it could confuse NTP into thinking it was a better server than the new time source.

NTP uses the highest stratum server it has access to, regardless of whether it is stratum 3, 10, or whatever, so we are OK to have the clock set low even if it is the only device. (The internal code is actually written to force every other device to be used before querying this one, as it is known to be relatively inaccurate on many systems.)

Lastly, we've included a drift file, which is the same one as the previous configuration.

Now that everything has been configured, we can restart the NTP daemon by running its start-up script:

```
hydrogen# /etc/init.d/xntpd start
hydrogen#
```

Checking NTP on the Server

Once the daemon has started, let's run ntpq again to display the server list. This time the output should be similar to that shown below:

```
hydrogen# ntpq -np
remote          refid          st  t  when poll reach delay offset disp
==============================================================
127.127.1.0  127.127.1.0 10  1  8    64   1     0.00  0.000  15885.0
hydrogen#
```

This shows that the server is the local clock and is operating at stratum 10. We haven't yet synchronized with it, which we know because there isn't a "*" character in the first column.

We can see that "reach" is set to octal 1 (binary 00000001), which indicates we have only seen the first poll—the reason for this is that it has just started running.

"Delay" and "offset" are both set to 0, which is really what we should expect as we are connected to the local machine and, therefore, shouldn't have any network-related delays.

Interestingly, "dispersion" is very high at the moment. Again, this is because the daemon has just started running and has not synchronized yet—it should settle down to a correct level when it has.

If we run ntpq again some time later, we'll see something similar to the following. Here we can see we've synchronized with the server, "reach" indicates we've seen the last six polls, and "dispersion" has fallen to a realistic level:

```
hydrogen# ntpq -np
remote          refid          st  t when poll reach delay offset disp
==============================================================
*127.127.1.0  127.127.1.0 10  1  8    64   77    0.00  0.000  10.01
hydrogen#
```

Let's also run ntptrace to follow the chain of servers back to the primary time source:

```
hydrogen# ntptrace
localhost: stratum 11, offset 0.000072, synch distance 0.0022
127.127.1.0:     *Timeout*
hydrogen#
```

This confirms that we are synchronized with the local clock and we are running at stratum 11, one level lower than the clock as expected. At this point we are happy that NTP is configured and working on hydrogen. (The time-out simply occurs because the clock cannot be queried in the same way as a "genuine" time device would.)

Configuring the Clients

Now we can move on to the remaining machines on the network and synchronize them to the new server. To do this, we need to alter each machine's existing configuration file and restart the NTP daemon, just as we did for hydrogen—we'll use helium for this example. The configuration file, *ntp.conf*, after we've made the changes is shown here:

```
helium# cat /etc/inet/ntp.conf
#
# Client config file.
#
server timeserver
driftfile /var/ntp/ntp.drift
hydrogen#
```

This uses the time server entry that we defined for hydrogen earlier in the section "Host Names" on page 461. We've also used the same drift file as the previous setup.

If the local clock is out of synchronization with the server by more than 1,000 seconds (around 16 minutes), NTP will not start. To ensure that this is not a problem, we'll set it to approximately the correct time on the server before we start. We can do this using either rdate or ntpdate. Ntpdate will use the same service as the NTP daemon, so it's also a good check that everything is communicating, but ensure that the daemon isn't already running or they will conflict (we'll stop it first to make sure):

```
helium# /etc/init.d/xntpd stop
helium# ntpdate hydrogen
24 Jun 12:31:32 ntpdate[13362]: adjust time server 192.168.22.1
   offset 0.000432 sec
helium#
```

Now we can start the NTP daemon by running the start-up script provided:

```
helium# /etc/init.d/xntpd start
helium#
```

Checking the Clients

First, we'll let NTP "settle" down. This should take around 10 minutes (8 passes, multiplied by the poll time of 64 seconds) before we acknowledge synchronization (although it will take much longer, perhaps a day, before the frequency error starts to stabilize). When we check ntpq, we can see that "reach" is set to 377, indicating that all the polls have worked. The delay and offset values are low, as we would expect running over the local network, and we have successfully synchronized with the server named "timeserver," which is advertising itself as a stratum-11 server:

```
helium# ntpq -p
remote       refid       st  t  when poll reach delay offset disp
==============================================================
*timeserver LOCAL(0)    11  u  33   64   377  0.37  -0.165 0.05
helium#
```

An association number identifies every connection to a server. If we wished to check further and monitor the individual poll times for a particular server, we could query its association ID. First we need to obtain the correct ID, which we can do with ntpq:

```
helium# ntpq -c as
ind assID status  conf reach auth condition  last_event cnt
==========================================================
  1 51316  9614   yes   yes  none sys.peer   reachable  1
helium#
```

Now we can query the association:

```
helium# ntpq -c "rv 51316"
status=9614 reach, conf, sel_sys.peer, 1 event, event_reach
srcadr=timeserver, srcport=123,
dstadr=192.168.22.1, dstport=123, keyid=0, stratum=11, precision=-18,
rootdelay=0.00, rootdispersion=10.25, refid=LOCAL(0),
reftime=bd1d9e73.31595000  Mon, Jul 17 2000 16:02:11.192,
delay=0.38, offset=-0.26, dispersion=0.02, reach=377, valid=8,
hmode=3, pmode=4, hpoll=6, ppoll=6, leap=00, flash=0x0<OK>,
org=bd1d9e87.c4ca2000  Mon, Jul 17 2000 16:02:31.768,
rec=bd1d9e87.c4e7c000  Mon, Jul 17 2000 16:02:31.769,
xmt=bd1d9e87.c4c60000  Mon, Jul 17 2000 16:02:31.768,
filtdelay=    0.38    0.38    0.37    0.37    0.35    0.37    0.35    0.27,
filtoffset=  -0.26   -0.26   -0.26   -0.23   -0.21   -0.17   -0.14   -0.17,
filterror=    0.02    0.99    1.97    2.94    3.92    4.90    5.87    6.85
helium#
```

Most of the output here refers to values for some of the internal values used by NTP, but the last three lines show the last eight poll times for delay, offset, and dispersion, which can be useful to check.

Running ntptrace will again trace the hierarchy back to the root server, and confirm we are communicating with "timeserver" (hydrogen) and that the stratum levels have been adjusted as we saw earlier running ntpq:

```
helium# ntptrace
localhost: stratum 12, offset 0.000023, synch distance 0.01082
timeserver: stratum 11, offset -0.000185, synch distance 0.01041
127.127.1.0:    *Timeout*
helium#
```

Checking the date on any system is a quick way of confirming that we have achieved clock synchronization:

```
helium# rsh hydrogen date; date
Mon Jun 26 15:22:19 BST 2000
Mon Jun 26 15:22:19 BST 2000
helium#
```

The only task left to do now is to check hydrogen's system clock on a regular basis and, depending on the required accuracy, make any changes to it. NTP will propagate the changes around the system from there.

The Final Configuration

As the last step, we could amalgamate both these configurations; in other words, use a local server that synchronizes with a number of public time servers, while providing the ability to fall back to its local clock if the connection to the public servers failed. To do this, we could use the following configuration file on the server:

```
hydrogen# cat /etc/inet/ntp.conf
#
# Server config for host hydrogen
#
server ntp2a.mcc.ac.uk
server ntp.cs.strath.ac.uk
server salmon.maths.tcd.ie
server 127.127.1.0
fudge 127.127.1.0 stratum 10
driftfile /var/ntp/ntp.drift
hydrogen#
```

The clients, on the other hand, would use their existing configuration file as this already synchronizes with hydrogen. This means they will be using the following configuration file:

```
helium# cat /etc/inet/ntp.conf
#
# Client config file.
#
server timeserver
driftfile /var/ntp/ntp.drift
helium#
```

Check the Final Configuration

To check that everything is working correctly, we'll run both ntpq and ntp-trace from "timeserver" and one of the clients, say helium.

On hydrogen, we can see that we are once more synchronized with 130.88.202.49 at stratum 2, while ntptrace shows that we are correctly running at stratum 3 and also that we can traced back to the level-1 server:

```
hydrogen# ntpq -p
remote           refid           st t when poll reach  delay offset  disp
==========================================================================
 127.127.1.0     127.127.1.0     10 1 27   64   377    0.00   0.000 10.01
*130.88.202.49   194.81.227.227   2 u 57   64   377   16.94   2.481  3.22
+130.159.196.118 130.159.248.11   3 u 57   64   377   23.65   3.875  2.73
+134.226.81.11   134.226.81.3     2 u 57   64   337  122.02 -42.051  6.58
hydrogen#

hydrogen# ntptrace
localhost: stratum 3, offset 0.000026, synch distance 0.12448
maverick.mcc.ac.uk: stratum 2, offset 0.017359, synch distance 0.05569
ntp1.ja.net: stratum 1, offset 0.017014, synch distance 0.00258, refid 'GPS'
hydrogen#
```

Running the same commands on helium confirms that hydrogen is advertising at stratum 3 and that helium itself is set to 4:

```
helium# ntpq -p
remote        refid       st t when poll reach  delay  offset  disp
====================================================================
*timeserver maverick.mcc.ac  3  u 18   64   377   0.35  -3.583  0.64
helium#

helium# ntptrace
localhost: stratum 4, offset 0.000041, synch distance 0.11223
timeserver: stratum 3, offset -0.002903, synch distance 0.10863
maverick.mcc.ac.uk: stratum 2, offset 0.012206, synch distance 0.05421
ntp1.ja.net: stratum 1, offset 0.012867, synch distance 0.00275, refid 'GPS'
helium#
```

Which Is Best?

Rdate is easy to understand and implement and, once the clocks are synchronized, should be accurate enough for most situations. The clock adjustment is harsh in that if the client's clock is incorrect, rdate will simply reset it. This can produce problems if the date needs to be set backwards, since log entries can become mismatched, which can cause problems with some applications.

NTP is more complex to understand, but once configured requires virtually no maintenance and each client will be very accurate relative to each other. The advantages are that a number of servers can be configured and if the main server is later upgraded from a local clock to a more accurate device, the clients will benefit without any alteration. Its clock adjustment is very sophisticated, ensuring that the clock is slowed down rather than shifted back in time. This means that things such as log file entries will always be in the correct order (i.e., chronological).

As an approximate guide, `rdate` should be accurate to within a second, whereas NTP should be accurate to within milliseconds. There are lots of factors that will vary these values, but it provides a good indication of the order of magnitude in accuracy between the two.

In our case, we will implement NTP, so we'll add the client configuration files to our "client directory" and use hydrogen as the main NTP server.

20

SETTING UP THE MAIL SYSTEM

Manual Pages

aliases (4)
biff (1B)
m4 (1)
mail (1)
mail.local (1M)
mailq (1)
mailx (1)
newaliases (1M)
sendmail (1M)
vacation (1)

Files Affected

/etc/mail/*
/usr/lib/mail/*
/var/mail/*
/var/spool/mqueue

Objectives

Electronic mail, commonly known as "email," is *the* application that everyone knows about; as such, many people use it on a daily basis. While we cannot hope to provide all the information needed to configure a complex mail system in one chapter, here we'll examine how the mail system works and how the underlying protocols are used. After that we'll look at some of the tasks that need to be performed to get a simple mail system working.

What Is Mail?

We can think of mail as being the electronic version of the normal postal service—in fact, let's use this comparison to see how it works in more detail. If we look at the following steps, we'll see they are the tasks that are carried out whenever we send a "manual" letter to someone:

1. Write the letter and sign it.
2. Address it to the correct person.
3. Put it in an envelope.
4. Post it.
5. Send it to the post office in the correct area.
6. Deliver it to the correct recipient.

All these tasks are also performed when sending email, although we aren't always aware of this because the task may be carried out automatically by the system. To find out how it achieves this, let's work through the above steps, using the "manual" letter shown in Figure 20.1 as an example.

Harry King
some-corp.com

Jim Davies
destination.com

    Re: Design timetable

Hi Jim,
Thanks for the letter earlier -- I'll work on the
design timetable and get it to you asap.

Regards, Harry

Figure 20.1 *The "manual" letter.*

The electronic version of this letter will actually be split into a number of different components by the mail system. We'll use the labels shown in Figure 20.2 to describe each of these.

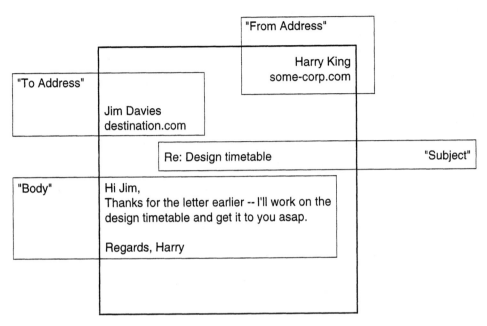

Figure 20.2 *The different components of the letter.*

1. Write the Letter

The first task is to create the "Body" of the message. This can be done in a variety of ways: Text may be entered into a GUI application such as `mailtool` or `dtmail`, typed into one of the command line variants such as `mail` or `mailx`, or perhaps fed in from an input file. Whichever one of these is used, they are all examples of a Mail User Agent (MUA). This forms the interface between the user and the mail system.

For our examples here, we'll continue with our practice of using non-GUI commands; therefore, we'll use `mail` to enter any details. Let's now start to create the message by passing the "To Address" and the "Subject" fields on the `mail` command line:

```
hydrogen# mail -s "Re: Design Timetable" jim.davies@destination.com
```

`Mail` is now waiting for us to enter the message. It will read our text from standard input until either a single dot (on a line by itself) or an EOF (End-of-file) marker is seen.

```
Hi Jim,
Thanks for the letter earlier--I'll work on the design timetable
and get it to you asap.

Regards, Harry
.
hydrogen#
```

Here we've entered the text and the correct end-of-message marker, then received our prompt back. This means that the message has been sent, as far as we're concerned. What that means in reality is that the mail system will carry on with the rest of its processing and will only need to contact us if it has any delivery problems with the message.

2. Address It

We can see that in step 1 we included the address of the recipient in the `mail` command. This looks suspiciously similar to the syntax that we used to describe domain names earlier in Chapter 16, "Configuring DNS." There, we referred to machines such as "somemachine.somedomain.com." Domain names and mail addresses are tightly related. In fact, the mail address is simply an extension of the domain name and allows us to specify the name of a user along with the name of the machine (or domain) that the user belongs to (the two being separated by an "@" character). This is known as their "absolute mail address."

For example, the address of our recipient is *jim.davies@destination.com*. This means that the letter will be sent to the machine that handles mail for the domain "destination.com." Once it arrives there, the local mail system will deliver it locally to the user known as "jim.davies." (Note that, in this example, the mail is sent to the domain rather than to a specific machine.)

3/4. Put It in an Envelope/Post It

Now that we know where to send the message, we can "post it" by passing it on to a piece of software known as a Mail Transfer Agent (MTA). This obtains the addresses of both the sender and any recipients from the MUA. From there the MTA generates the envelope for the message—ours will look like the one shown here:

```
Mail From: harry.king@some-corp.com
Rcpt To: jim.davies@destination.com
```

The envelope now contains the address information, which is formatted exactly as the MTA needs it (or, more correctly, as the mail protocol specifies). It will only contain one "Mail From" field, but may have a number of "Rcpt To" ones, depending on whether we were sending the message to multiple people or not. When it's been created, the envelope is used by the MTA to correctly route the mail to the specified recipients and also to send any errors back to the sender if any delivery problems occur.

The Header

Besides creating the envelope, the MTA also generates a header that is prepended to the body of the message. This is formatted as a series of "keyword: value" entries, and is the "readable" version of the envelope. The header also includes other information, such as time stamps, message IDs, reply addresses, and so forth. It will be updated by each MTA that it passes between. By the time the message arrives at its intended user, the header may contain a whole series of information that shows all the stages and timings taken to get to its destination. A simple example of a header is shown below:

```
Reply-To: harry.king@some-corp.com
Date: Mon, 22 Oct 2001 11:07:59 GMT
To: jim.davies@destination.com
From: harry.king@some-corp.com
Subject: Re Design Timetable
```

Delivery Checks

The MTA takes responsibility for any mail passed to it, which means that messages should either be delivered or returned back to the sender with an error message—no mail should ever be lost. Many MTAs are configured to perform a variety of different checks before they accept the message. Examples of these are listed below:

- Check that the domain of the sender and the recipient are valid
- Check the number of recipients for the mail (to guard against junk mail)
- Check that the user sending the mail is a local user

If all the delivery checks are successful, the MTA will take ownership of the mail, allocate a message ID number for it, and place it on the mail queue ready for sending.

5. Send It to the Correct Area

If the message is not for a local user, the MTA must forward it to the machine that acts as the MTA's mail server. To do this, the MTA needs to determine which machine to forward to by performing a DNS lookup (we'll look at this in more detail in the section "DNS and Mail" on page 491). When it has obtained this information, the local MTA will open a connection to the remote one and try to pass the mail on to it. The remote MTA will also probably perform some delivery checks, similar to those mentioned earlier, before deciding whether to accept the mail or reject it.

6. Local Delivery

Finally, the mail has arrived on the correct system and has been accepted by the receiving MTA. From here, it is passed on to a program known as the

Mail Delivery Agent (MDA). On Solaris, this is a program named /usr/lib/ mail.local. It is responsible for delivering the mail to the user's mailbox. It does this by simply taking the new message and appending it onto the user's existing mail file. Once the user's mailbox has been updated, the user will be able to access and read mail.

Mail Files

So where is all the mail stored? On Solaris, each user is allocated a mailbox. This is actually one big ASCII text file. If we take a look in *var/mail*, we should see a number of files already there. There will normally be one for each user. However, there isn't any cause for concern if any are missing—it simply means the user hasn't received any mail yet. When the user does receive mail, a mailbox will automatically be created.

For example, let's assume that John Green has received some test mail. It has been received by the MTA and delivered into his mailbox:

```
hydrogen# cd /var/mail
hydrogen# ls -l jgreen
-rw-rw----   1 jgreen    mail      660 Dec 19 19:54 jgreen
hydrogen#
```

We can see that each file takes the name of the user's login, and that all users have ownership of their own mail files. Let's take a look to see what it contains:

```
hydrogen# cat jgreen
From root Wed Dec 26 19:58:57 2001
Received: (from root@localhost)
    by xenon.solarisbootcamp.com (8.9.1b+Sun/8.9.1) id TAA00564
    for jgreen; Wed, 26 Dec 2001 19:58:56 GMT
Date: Wed, 26 Dec 2001 19:58:56 GMT
From: Super-User <root>
Message-Id: <200112261958.TAA00564@xenon.solarisbootcamp.com>
Content-Type: text
Content-Length: 17

First test mail

From root Wed Dec 26 19:59:57 2001
Received: (from root@localhost)
    by xenon.solarisbootcamp.com (8.9.1b+Sun/8.9.1) id TAA00565
    for jgreen; Wed, 26 Dec 2001 19:59:56 GMT
Date: Wed, 26 Dec 2001 19:59:56 GMT
From: Super-User <root>
Message-Id: <200112261958.TAA00565@xenon.solarisbootcamp.com>
Content-Type: text
Content-Length: 18

Second test mail

hydrogen#
```

This shows that each message begins with the header that we described earlier. The header is separated from the body of the message by a single blank line. After that we can see the body of the message, and lastly another blank line that is used to separate each message. This example shows that *jgreen* currently has two mail messages waiting for him.

Mail Protocols

Now that we've seen how the mail process works, let's look at some of the protocols that are used to tie everything together. First we need to be aware that while there are a number of different mail protocols, we are primarily referring here to what's commonly known as "Internet mail"—that is, TCP-based Simple Mail Transfer Protocol (SMTP) mail.

We'll also briefly describe some of the "surrounding" protocols that help to make mail retrieval possible on non-SMTP servers. While these aren't bundled with the operating system, they are used often enough to make it worthwhile documenting them here.

Simple Mail Transfer Protocol

Let's start with the SMTP. The program that uses this protocol is named `/usr/lib/sendmail` and is the main component used by the MTA to send mail. Its task is to listen on port 25 for any incoming connections. These could be from an MUA or another MTA that is trying to forward mail. When a connection is established, the client should supply enough information to "address" the mail and deliver it to either a local user (via an MDA) or a remote one (via the remote MTA).

SMTP is a relatively simple protocol that expects to receive a command and issue a three-digit code in return. This is used to indicate the status of the command.

We can emulate an SMTP session by using `telnet` to connect to the correct port (25). The following example shows how to introduce ourselves to the server, enter the envelope details, and follow this with the data. We can see the server accept the mail and generate a message ID for it:

```
hydrogen# telnet smtp_server.some-corp.com 25
<lines removed for clarity>
220 smtp_server.some-corp.com ESMTP Sendmail 8.9.3+Sun/8.9.3;
Wed, 19 Dec 2001 09:04:30 GMT
HELO harrysmachine.some-corp.com
250 some-corp.com
mail from:harry.king@some-corp.com
250 Sender <harry.king@some-corp.com> Ok
rcpt to: jim.davies@destination.com
250 Recipient <jim.davies@destination.com> Ok
data
354 Enter mail, end with "." on a line by itself
Subject: Re Design Timetable
```

```
Hi Jim,
Thanks for the letter earlier--I'll work on the design timetable
and get it to you asap.

Regards, Harry
.
250 TAA17372 Message accepted for delivery
quit
hydrogen#
```

This example uses the "standard" SMTP protocol. We know this because the user (or MUA) introduced itself using the "HELO" keyword. We can also see that `sendmail` indicates that it supports ESMTP, which is an "enhanced" version of SMTP (it displays ESMTP in the welcome banner). We can use this instead by simply introducing ourselves with the correct keyword ("EHLO"), as shown here:

```
hydrogen# telnet smtp_server.some-corp.com 25
220 smtp_server.some-corp.com ESMTP Sendmail 8.9.3+Sun/8.9.3;
Wed, 19 Dec 2001 09:04:30 GMT
EHLO harrysmachine.some-corp.com
<lines removed for clarity>
hydrogen#
```

Relaying

When an MTA sends mail to another MTA, it is said to be acting as a mail relay. This is a normal, valid function of the MTA and is perfectly valid in some situations. For example, many administrators will allow mail to be relayed as long as it involves a local user. In other words, they will allow either of the following tasks:

- Local users sending mail externally
- External users sending mail to a local user

However, if you are accepting mail from a remote user and forwarding it to another remote user, you are acting as a third-party relay. This is usually a very bad idea (although there are machines that may have a perfectly valid reason for acting as a third-party relay). Machines configured this way are sought by people wanting to send junk mail (known as "spam"), since it allows them to use your machine to process and send out bulk mail on their behalf. Apart from the fact that someone else is using your machine, you will quickly be recognized as an "open relay" and blacklisted so that any remote MTAs will simply reject any mail coming from you.

If the mail server is allowed to relay, make sure you are controlling it correctly. For example, the file */etc/mail/relay-domains* can be configured to list the domains that are allowed to relay. It's worth checking that your MTA is working correctly after you've finished configuring it—a number of Internet sites offer a service to check whether your machine is acting as an open relay.

Other Issues

Several other issues are based around catching spam mail. For example, many MTAs allow further checking of the messages in an attempt to deny junk mail. A few examples of what they look for are listed here:

- Receipt harvesting—programs that interrogate the MTA, trying to obtain a list of valid recipients
- User logins—programs that interrogate the MTA, trying to find valid local user names
- Numerous connections—programs that make lots of connections to an MTA, trying to bring the service down

Post Office Protocol

Good. Now we know how to send mail, so let's move on and look at ways it can be read (besides using *mail.local*).

Sometimes it may not be possible to run an SMTP server on a machine—maybe it doesn't have enough resources, or perhaps the operating system does not include the required software. Whatever the reason, this could prove to be a problem if we need access to a mailbox. The Post Office Protocol (POP) was designed to get around this by allowing machines such as these to access a mailbox on an SMTP server.

Let's look at a practical example of this. We'll assume that Jim Davies (to whom we sent the example letter earlier) works on a laptop most of the time. While it doesn't contain an SMTP server, it does have a mail client (MUA) that allows him to manipulate his mailbox—if he can download it. This leaves him with the problem that his machine cannot accept mail directly, because of its lack of an SMTP server. Instead, it must be sent to the main mail server at "destination.com," where he has a mailbox allocated to him.

If the mail server also supports POP, however, he can use this to download his mailbox. He simply needs to configure his mail client with the correct POP settings that he's been provided with, which could be similar to those shown in Table 20.1.

Table 20.1 *POP Connection Details*

Setting	Value
POP Server Host Name	pop_server.destination.com
POP User Name	jim
POP Password	jims_passwd

His mail client will connect to the POP server on port 110, where it will be listening for any connections. Once it has authenticated correctly, it will be able to download the mail to his local system.

POP is very simplistic, with a limited set of commands. The real choices for the user is to list, retrieve, or delete mail—the user cannot create folders or organize it. The example below uses `telnet` to connect to the correct port (110) and emulate the types of commands that may be used by Jim's mail client to access his mail. We can see that after each command is entered, the POP server replies with either "+OK" or "-ERR," followed by information text:

```
hydrogen# telnet pop_server.destination.com 110
<lines removed for clarity>
+OK Pop server is ready.
user jim
+OK please enter your password
pass jims_passwd
+OK jim has 1 mail messages
stat
+OK 1 1117
list
+OK 1 message (1117 octets)
retr 1
+OK 1117 octets
Received from: smtp_server.some-corp.com by pop_server.destina-
tion.com
Reply-To: harry.king@some-corp.com
Date: Mon, 22 Oct 2001 11:07:59 GMT
To: jim.davies@destination.com
From: harry.king@some-corp.com
Subject: Re Design Timetable
Status: U
<lines removed for clarity>

Hi Jim,
Thanks for the letter earlier—I'll work on the design timetable
and get it to you asap.

Regards, Harry
dele 1
+OK message 1 deleted
stat
+OK 0 0
dele 1
-ERR message 1 already deleted
quit
+OK bye
hydrogen#
```

Notice that POP wasn't concerned about the machine that Jim was using to connect in with—it's only concerned with authenticating him.

An analogy between POP and "normal" mail would be that your messages are delivered to a central location and sit there until you phoned up to see if there was anything for you. At that point, it would be delivered to wherever you were currently located. Using this method, you would receive all of your mail OK, but it could be scattered around different locations around the world if you weren't careful!

Internet Message Access Protocol

The Internet Message Access Protocol (IMAP) uses port 143 to provide similar functionality to POP, but takes it a step further by allowing messages to be accessed and manipulated as if they were located on the client machine. Mail administration is included, which means folders can be created and removed, and messages can be moved between them. This can be carried out by the IMAP client either while it's connected or disconnected to the server; in the latter case, the IMAP server will simply synchronize the two at a later date.

Again, using a `telnet` session to connect to the correct port (143), we can emulate an IMAP session from a mail client. This example assumes the user's name and password are the same as the ones used for the POP connection.

IMAP supports a large subset of commands, which means that sessions can become quite complex. The one below highlights some of the available commands and the syntax involved. It also shows that a short identifier tag precedes each command; we've used "a01" for this example:

```
hydrogen# telnet imap_server.destination.com 143
<lines removed for clarity>
* OK IMAP4 server ready Thu, 11 Jan 2001 00:08:59 (GMT)
a01 login jim jims_passwd
a01 OK LOGIN completed
a01 select inbox
* 257 EXISTS
* OK [UIDVALIDITY 979153065] UIDs valid
* FLAGS (\Answered \Flagged \Deleted \Draft \Seen)
* OK [PERMANENTFLAGS (\* \Answered \Flagged \Deleted \Draft
\Seen)] Permanent flags
* 257 RECENT
a01 OK [READ-WRITE] SELECT completed
a01 fetch 1 rfc822
* 1 FETCH (RFC822 {546}
<message removed for clarity>
 FLAGS (\Recent \Seen))
a01 OK FETCH completed
a01 list "" ""
* LIST (\Noselect) "/" ""
a01 OK LIST completed
a01 list "" "*"
* LIST () "/" "Inbox"
* LIST () "/" "SentMail"
* LIST () "/" "Trash"
a01 OK LIST completed
a01 logout
hydrogen#
```

The analogy here would be that all your mail is stored at the central post office. They've allocated a filing cabinet for you and you can add or delete folders from it as you wish. You don't need to allocate space for it at your own office, but it's a little slower to work with your mail because it's not local.

Web Mail

While Web mail isn't really a protocol, lots of people use this form of interface to manage their mailbox. Users connect to a URL supplied by their ISP, where they can carry out any tasks they require, such as sending or receiving mail, and even managing their folders and mail options.

The mail messages are entered into the Web interface and dispatched using the Hypertext Transfer Protocol (HTTP) (port 80), where they are transparently passed on to the correct mail protocol, such as SMTP or POP.

The analogy here would be that you are located somewhere in the world, along with a phone number to contact someone on (you may not even be sure where the person is!). You contact the person to see if any mail has been received for you, and if so, the person reads it out to you. If you wish to send any mail, this person will do it on your behalf.

Secure Communication

Secure versions of the above protocols are available. These communicate on the ports listed below:

- SSL-enabled SMTP uses 465.
- SSL-enabled POP uses 995.
- SSL-enabled IMAP uses 993.

These are beyond the scope of this book. Consequently, we won't discuss these in any more detail.

Which Is Best?

Which method you use will depend upon a number of factors, such as the capabilities of the machine, how you wish to access mail, and where you would prefer it to be stored. Table 20.2 summarizes the advantages and disadvantages of each of the different retrieval protocols.

Table 20.2 *Mail Protocol Details*

Protocol	Advantages	Disadvantages
POP	Machine does not need to run SMTP.	Cannot selectively read messages.
	Downloaded to client.	Not designed for access from multiple machines.
	Easier than IMAP for "offline" reading.	
IMAP	Allows folder and mail manipulation.	High reliance on mail server as mail is often stored remotely.
	Individual messages can be downloaded.	More complex than POP, and so not as available.
	Mail is easily accessed from multiple locations.	Not supported in all mail clients.
Web Mail	Mail stays on server.	Needs a browser and an ISP connection.
	Easy to read selective messages.	Mail server is out of your control.
	Mail can also be sent.	Security of the mail is an issue.

DNS and Mail

In our earlier example, in the section on SMTP, we managed to `telnet` to port 25 on the MTA and send some mail. This was easily accomplished, as we knew the name of the machine that we wanted to connect to.

However, if we are sending mail to a different domain, we need to locate the name of the machine that handles mail for the domain; that is, the MTA. Once we know this, we can connect to it and perform the same task. To do this we use a DNS lookup, which will search for the domain's Mail Exchange (MX) records. These records are used to indicate the mail server. For example, if we search for the MX records for Sun's domain, we may see something similar to the following:

```
hydrogen# nslookup
Server:  antimony.solarisbootcamp.com
Address:  158.43.128.72

set type=mx
> sun.com
<lines removed for clarity>
sun.com preference = 40, mail exchanger = mx6.sun.com
sun.com preference = 40, mail exchanger = mx7.sun.com
sun.com preference = 5, mail exchanger = mx4.sun.com
sun.com preference = 5, mail exchanger = mx1.sun.com
```

```
sun.com preference = 5, mail exchanger = mx3.sun.com
sun.com preference = 5, mail exchanger = mx2.sun.com
sun.com preference = 15, mail exchanger = mx5.sun.com
<lines removed for clarity>
hydrogen#
```

This shows that there are a number of machines acting as mail servers. We can also see that each of them has a "preference" value associated with it. This is used to indicate the priority of the server. When a mailer daemon tries to send mail to the domain, it will try to communicate with a machine that has the lowest priority, moving on to the next if that fails, and so on. The values used do not mean anything other than the relative order of machines. This means that instead of assigning priorities of say 0, 10, and 20 to a series of machines, we could quite easily use 0, 1, 2, or even 5,061, 11,389, or 43,765, if we prefer.

Sendmail

In this section we'll look at how we can configure sendmail to enable it to be used for mail delivery on our system. This has traditionally been a very awkward task to perform. The main reason for this concerns the configuration file itself, *letc/mail/sendmail.cf*—it contains everything required to get the mail system functioning, but is notoriously difficult to set up.

Originally, there was only one way to create the correct *sendmail.cf*. This was by copying an existing (functioning) or template file, working through it, and editing it as required. Two template files (*main.cf* and *subsidiary.cf*) were, and still are, included to help with this should you still want to follow that procedure—you'll find them in *letc/mail*. When the operating system is installed, the *letc/mail/sendmail.cf* file is actually a copy of the *subsidiary.cf* template. The choice of which template file to use depends on the required operating mode of the machine. Table 20.3 shows the different modes along with the name of the correct file that the working *sendmail.cf* should be based on.

From this table we can see that if we are setting up a mail client or mail server, we don't have to make any changes to the system to get it working. The only machine we would need to configure would be the mail host.

Thankfully, starting from Version 8 of sendmail, this manual method has been replaced by a mechanism based on a program named m4. This is a macroprocessor that has long been associated with C and other programming languages. In fact, because of this association, it's also located in the same directory as the programming-type tools—*/usr/ccs/bin*. This directory isn't defined in the normal profile by default, but for our examples here, we'll assume we have updated the path to suit.

In this chapter, we'll concentrate on this newer method of configuration. So let's move on and see how it works.

Table 20.3 *Mail Configuration Modes*

Operating Mode	Explanation	Configuration File
Mail Host	The main mail machine on the network	*main.cf*
Mail Server	A system that stores mail in its mailbox directory, */var/mail*	*subsidiary.cf*
Mail Client	A machine that uses the mail capabilities (including the mailbox area) of the mail server	*subsidiary.cf*
Mail Gateway	A machine that handles connections between different networks or protocols	*main.cf*

M 4

Before we look at how it's used with sendmail, let's have a brief look at m4 itself. We've just mentioned that it is a macroprocessor, but what exactly does that mean, and what does it do?

Given a text file as input, m4 will scan the file looking for predefined tokens it has been told about. If it finds any, it will perform a transformation on them, which will differ depending on what tasks we would like it to perform. Let's look at an example to show how this works in practice:

```
hydrogen# m4
define('eg', 'this is the first example')

eg
this is the first example
hydrogen#
```

First we can see that m4 reads standard input and writes to standard output. After starting the program, we've defined a macro that will substitute the string "eg" for the longer string "this is the first example." Once the macro has been defined, we've entered the text to be scanned—"eg," in this case. M4 realizes that this is a token it should work on and it has transformed it and generated the correct output.

The define command that we used is built into m4, along with many others such as ifdef, eval, ifelse, and len.

The following example expands on this by passing a file on to m4 that contains both the definitions and the input to be processed. We've also used the common convention of using a ".m4" extension for the file.

```
hydrogen# cat /tmp/test.m4
define('eg', 'this is example number ')

eg 1
eg 2
hydrogen# m4 /tmp/test.m4
this is example number 1
this is example number 2
hydrogen#
```

As a final example, let's create two files: one that contains the m4 defini-tions (we'll call this *defs.m4*), and a second that is the input file (we'll call this *inputfile*):

```
hydrogen# cat defs.m4
define('eg', 'this is example number ')
hydrogen#

hydrogen# cat inputfile
eg 1
eg 2
hydrogen#
```

We stated earlier that m4 writes to standard output, so let's run the pro-gram, passing the two files on the command line, and redirecting the stan-dard output to a file at the same time—this will be our output file:

```
hydrogen# m4 defs.m4 inputfile > outputfile
hydrogen# cat outputfile
this is example number 1
this is example number 2
hydrogen#
```

This shows that *outputfile* now contains the correct processed text. Using this method has given us two main advantages over creating the file manu-ally. It has allowed us to cut down the amount of text we need to enter in the input file, and it has automated the output file build procedure, which makes it less error-prone. Obviously these are very simple examples and so the advantages don't appear to be that great. But if we move on and examine m4's relationship with sendmail, the advantages should become clearer.

Sendmail and M4

We know that m4 is only used within sendmail for generating the configura-tion file, *sendmail.cf*—although as we've said before, this is the main task involved in getting mail working! The process to do this follows the same steps we used for our last example, only on a much greater scale. In other words, we pass a definition file and a small input file on to m4 and it creates the correct output file. All the definition files are supplied with sendmail in a directory named */usr/lib/mail*. There are also a number of other files in here that help make all this work. Let's look at what's in there by default:

```
hydrogen# cd /usr/lib/mail
hydrogen# ls -l
total 176
drwxrwxr-x  2 root        mail         512 Aug 27 2000 cf
drwxrwxr-x  2 root        mail         512 Aug 27 2000 domain
drwxr-xr-x  2 root        mail        1536 Aug 27 2000 feature
drwxr-xr-x  2 root        mail         512 Aug 27 2000 m4
drwxr-xr-x  2 root        mail         512 Aug 27 2000 mailer
drwxr-xr-x  2 root        mail         512 Aug 27 2000 ostype
-r--r--r--  1 root        mail       81509 Sep  1 1998 README
drwxr-xr-x  2 root        mail         512 Aug 27 2000 sh
hydrogen#
```

The *README* file is probably the most important file to look at first. It describes the hierarchy, how to run the program, and, importantly, the macros that are available and the functionality of each one. The remaining directories are organized as follows:

- cf: Contains the template configuration file and stores the output produced
- domain: Domain definitions
- feature: Special features that may be included
- m4: General m4 definitions
- mailer: Definitions for different types of mailers
- ostype: Operating system definitions
- sh: Utility "check" programs

So, how do we use all this? Let's start by looking at one of the configuration files and work back from there to decipher what's happening. These are all located in the *cf* directory, which by default looks like the following:

```
hydrogen# cd cf
hydrogen# ls -l
total 132
-r--r--r--  1 root        mail       27781 Sep  1 1998 main-v7sun.cf
-r--r--r--  1 root        mail        2309 Sep  1 1998 main-v7sun.mc
-r--r--r--  1 root        mail        2489 Sep  1 1998 Makefile
-r--r--r--  1 root        mail       28407 Sep  1 1998 subsidiary-v7sun.cf
-r--r--r--  1 root        mail        3255 Sep  1 1998 subsidiary-v7sun.mc
hydrogen#
```

All the files with a *mc* suffix are the templates (input files) that can be fed into m4. We can see that there is one named *main-v7sun.mc* and another named *subsidiary-v7sun.mc*. These are the template versions of the standard *main.cf* and *subsidiary.cf* files that are supplied by default in */etc/mail*.

All the files with a *cf* suffix are the output files that have been generated as a result of running m4 on the templates. Again, the *main-v7sun.cf* and *subsidiary-v7sun.cf* should be exactly the same as *main.cf* and *subsidiary.cf* in */etc/mail*.

The *Makefile* is supplied to help automate the build procedure if we wish, which means we don't have to remember the correct m4 commands that we should run (we discussed make and *Makefiles* in Chapter 12, "Naming Services and NIS"). We'll see how this is used later.

Let's look at one of the input files now—we'll use *main-v7sun.mc* as an example. We've removed the comments from it to make it smaller:

```
hydrogen# cat main-v7sun.mc
divert(-1)
divert(0)dnl
VERSIONID(`@(#)main-v7sun.mc      1.2 (Sun) 01/27/98')
OSTYPE(solaris2.ml)dnl
DOMAIN(solaris-generic)dnl
MAILER(local)dnl
MAILER(smtp)dnl
hydrogen#
```

That's it! When we run this through m4, it will generate a configuration file that is more than 1,000 lines long. All the commands we can see here are m4 directives, some of which are necessary, and others that are optional. Let's take one of these lines and follow it back to the m4 macros—we'll use the following line:

```
OSTYPE(solaris2.ml)dnl
```

This entry is used to set values for things such as help file path names and must be included in any configuration file. OSTYPE is a macro defined in the *ostype* directory. We've called it with an argument of *solaris2.ml.m4*, which means it will use the following file:

```
hydrogen# cat /usr/lib/mail/ostype/solaris.ml.m4
divert(0)
VERSIONID(`@(#)solaris2.ml.m48.8+1.2 (Berkeley+Sun) 05/19/98')
divert(-1)

define(`ALIAS_FILE', dbm:/etc/mail/aliases)
ifdef(`HELP_FILE',, `define(`HELP_FILE', /etc/mail/
   sendmail.hf)')
ifdef(`STATUS_FILE',, `define(`STATUS_FILE', /etc/mail/
   sendmail.st)')
ifdef(`LOCAL_MAILER_PATH',, `define(`LOCAL_MAILER_PATH',
   `/usr/lib/mail.local')')
ifdef(`LOCAL_MAILER_FLAGS',, `define(`LOCAL_MAILER_FLAGS',
   `fSmn9')')
ifdef(`LOCAL_MAILER_ARGS',, `define(`LOCAL_MAILER_ARGS',
   `mail.local -d $u')')
ifdef(`UUCP_MAILER_ARGS',, `define(`UUCP_MAILER_ARGS',
   `uux - -r -a$g $h!rmail ($u)')')
define(`confCW_FILE', /etc/mail/sendmail.cw)
define(`confEBINDIR', `/usr/lib')dnl
hydrogen#
```

We can see that this looks remarkably similar to our earlier example, *defs.m4*, which was used when we introduced m4—only this one is a lot more complicated! We also notice a few common commands keep appearing in the input files—we've already used `define`, and mentioned `ifdef`, but we can see that `divert` and `dnl` are also used often. Again, these are standard commands built into m4—`divert` allows output redirection to be controlled, while `dnl` means "delete to new line" and is used to get rid of excess white space in the output.

If we dig a little further and look at one of these definitions, we'll see where it has been used in the output file. For example, let's take the following entry from *solaris2.ml.m4*:

```
ifdef(`LOCAL_MAILER_PATH',, `define(`LOCAL_MAILER_PATH',
  `/usr/lib/mail.local')')
```

This essentially set the variable LOCAL_MAILER_PATH to the value of */usr/lib/mail.local*, and will create the following entry in the relevant file:

```
Mlocal,   P=/usr/lib/mail.local, F=lsDFMAw5:/|@qfSmn9, S=10/30,
   R=20/40, T=DNS/RFC822/X-Unix, A=mail.local -d $u
```

Gosh! Now we can see why the macro is much easier to use. This also helps to highlight the second advantage of using m4—automation; working through *sendmail.cf* checking for mistakes is nearly an impossible task.

Generating the Configuration File

Now we're ready to generate an output file. We haven't actually made any changes to anything yet; we'll do that in the next section. For now, we'll just see how to recreate the default template for a "main" machine.

We know that we'll use m4 to do this, but we need to remember that a whole set of definitions must be included with it—otherwise it won't know what to do!

There are really two ways to perform the build. The first is by using the supplied *Makefile*. It includes everything required and so simply running `make` will generate the file. The second way is to build the file manually. It's not a complex task so we'll do that now; that way, we'll see how the main definitions are specified. First we need to be in the correct directory:

```
hydrogen# cd /usr/lib/mail/cf
hydrogen# m4 ../m4/cf.m4 main-v7sun.mc > main-v7sun.cf
hydrogen#
```

This shows that we've passed two files into m4; the first is the top-level definition file, *cf.m4*. This automatically pulls in all the other subfiles as necessary. The second file is our input, *main-v7sun.mc*.

So, what would have happened if we had used the *Makefile* instead? Let's do that now and find out!

```
hydrogen# make main-v7sun.cf
/usr/bin/mv main-v7sun.cf main-v7sun.cf.prev
/usr/ccs/bin/m4 ../m4/cf.m4 main-v7sun.mc > main-v7sun.cf
hydrogen#
```

There are two differences we can spot. The first is that if the output file already exists, it will rename it and save it. The second is that m4 is called using its full path name, which helps get around the problem with the "PATH" that we mentioned earlier.

Once the correct file has been generated, we simply need to replace the current configuration file, */etc/mail/sendmail.cf*, with the new copy, and restart the daemons for the changes to take effect. The following commands would do this for us:

```
hydrogen# cp /etc/mail/sendmail.cf /etc/mail/sendmail.cf.orig
hydrogen# cp ./main-v7sun.cf /etc/mail/sendmail.cf
hydrogen# /etc/init.d/sendmail stop
hydrogen# /etc/init.d/sendmail start
hydrogen#
```

Adding Functionality

Now that we've seen that we can easily recreate the *main.cf* and *subsidiary.cf* configuration files, let's look at what we would need to do if we require anything else. For example, we may want to add virus-checking software or perhaps alter some of the "rules" that sendmail uses.

Additional functionality is commonly added through the use of a macro known as the "FEATURE" macro. This allows us to easily enable or customize some of the sendmail facilities. There are lots of "features" available, but the downside of this is that the only real way to find out which you need is by reading through the *README* file we mentioned before. This information is also replicated on the sendmail Web site (www.sendmail.org).

For example, if we wanted to include the local host domain, even on internal mail, we could do this with the following code:

```
FEATURE(always_add_domain)
```

Similarly, the following entry means, "don't do anything special with UUCP addresses":

```
FEATURE(nouucp)
```

If we also look in the subsidiary template file, we'll see that it contains the following:

```
hydrogen# cat subsidiary-v7sun.mc
divert(0)dnl
VERSIONID(`@(#)subsidiary-v7sun.mc       1.7 (Sun) 05/27/00')
OSTYPE(solaris2)dnl
DOMAIN(solaris-generic)dnl
FEATURE(`remote_mode')dnl
```

```
define(`SMART_HOST', `mailhost.$m')
MAILER(local)dnl
MAILER(smtp)dnl
hydrogen#
```

This shows that the feature "remote_mode" has been enabled and the variable SMART_HOST has been defined. These are both features that are used to control mail flow. For example, SMART_HOST sets the name of the relay that all outgoing mail will be sent to.

Once these features have been added to the file, we need to follow exactly the same steps we did to build and use the "main" file.

Now let's move on and build the actual systems.

Our Configuration

Our mail system will be based on a common design: one machine that acts as both a central mail server and the mail relay to the outside world. We'll use xenon for this task. All the remaining machines will act as mail clients and NFS-mount their mail directory *(/var/mail)* from the server. Figure 20.3 shows this configuration.

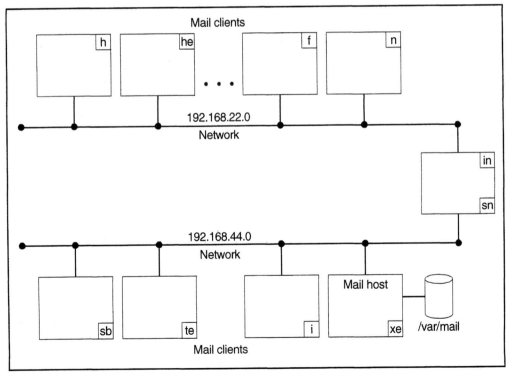

Figure 20.3 *The mail system design.*

Update DNS

The first thing we'll do is update our DNS entries so that xenon is recognized as the mail server for our domain. This will allow external machines to perform a DNS lookup and search for our MX records. We won't add any redundant servers or allocate any priorities either, all of which means the setup will be easier to implement.

We described DNS in Chapter 16, "Configuring DNS," so we'll quickly run through the commands here. All the changes will be made on the master machine, which is antimony. The only thing we need to do is to add an MX record into the forward file and update the serial number so that the changes are picked up, as shown here:

```
antimony# cd /var/named
antimony# cat master/solarisbootcamp.com
;
; named forward file for 192.168.44
;
@ IN       SOA    solarisbootcamp.com. root.solarisbootcamp.com.   (
                  2001123001 ; Serial num - <yyyymmddxx>
                  86400      ; Refresh every 24 hours
                  7200       ; Retry every 2 hours
                  3600000    ; Expire in 1000 hours
                  172800)     ; TTL is 2 days
<lines removed for clarity>


;
; mail server
;
solarisbootcamp.com. IN  MX  0  xenon.solarisbootcamp.com.
<lines removed for clarity>
antimony#
```

Now that we've made the changes, we can inform named about them. After that, the data will be available to all DNS servers that query our domain:

```
antimony# kill -HUP `cat /var/named/named.pid`
antimony#
```

Some servers may have already cached our details in the past, so we should allow at least two to three days before we can consider this information "available everywhere."

The Mail Host

Now let's configure the main mail host, xenon. A requirement with sendmail is that it knows the fully qualified name of the system it is running on. We can use one of the utility scripts located in */usr/lib/mail/sh* to check this is correct, as shown below:

```
xenon# /usr/lib/mail/sh/check-hostname
Hostname xenon OK: fully qualified as xenon.solarisbootcamp.com
Xenon#
```

Next, we'll add a "mailhost" alias to the *hosts* file. We'll see later that the client uses this to forward mail on to the server. To do this, we'll simply update the *hosts* map on the NIS server as follows:

```
tin# cat /etc/inet/hosts
<lines removed for clarity>
192.168.44.54    xenon    xe    mailhost
tin# cd /var/yp
tin# make
updated hosts
pushed hosts
tin#
```

Generate *Sendmail.cf*

Now we're ready to install the correct *sendmail.cf* file. We know that xenon is the main mail host, which means we need to use something similar to the *main.cf* template.

We're not using any special features on this machine either, so all that remains is to copy the correct file into place and restart the sendmail daemons. Let's do that now:

```
xenon# cd /etc/mail
xenon# cp /etc/mail/sendmail.cf /etc/mail/sendmail.cf.orig
xenon# cp main.cf sendmail.cf
xenon# /etc/init.d/sendmail stop
xenon# /etc/init.d/sendmail start
xenon#
```

Good. Everything is in place, so let's move on and check that it all works OK.

Send and Receive Test Mail

To check that mail is working, we'll send a few test messages to one of the users. After that we'll login as that user and check that the user has received everything correctly.

```
xenon# mail jgreen
First test mail
.
xenon# mail jgreen
Second test mail
.
xenon#
```

This should have been sent via the MTA and delivered to the user's mailbox by *mail.local*. As before, we'll use the mail command to check that the user can read it correctly:

```
xenon# su - jgreen
xenon$ mail
From root Wed Dec 26 19:59:57 2001
Date: Wed, 26 Dec 2001 19:59:56 GMT
From: Super-User <root>
Message-Id: <200112261958.TAA00565@xenon.solarisbootcamp.com>
Content-Length: 18

Second test mail

?
d
From root Wed Dec 26 19:58:57 2001
Date: Wed, 26 Dec 2001 19:58:56 GMT
From: Super-User <root>
Message-Id: <200112261958.TAA00564@xenon.solarisbootcamp.com>
Content-Length: 17

First test mail

?
d
xenon#
```

Good. We've managed to read both messages.

Share the Mail Directory

The mail directory, */var/mail*, needs to be shared from the mail server to allow it to be mounted by clients. This means that we will be more dependent upon xenon being up and running, otherwise we cannot read our existing mail, but it will be easier for us to administer.

We explained how to share files in Chapter 18, "NFS, DFS, and Autofs," since we're using the standard mount options, we'll simply run through the commands here. First let's share the files:

```
xenon# cat /etc/dfs/dfstab
share -F nfs /var/mail
xenon# shareall -F nfs
```

The filesystem is now shared from xenon, so let's move on and configure the clients.

Configure the Clients

We'll use carbon as an example client for now. The first thing we'll do is to NFS-mount the mailbox directory from xenon. We can do this by updating either */etc/vfstab*, so that the mount takes place at boot-time, or by updating the Autofs files to allow it to be mounted on demand. We'll do the latter because we're using Autofs to control the mounts on our system. We've already described this in Chapter 18, "NFS, DFS, and Autofs," so we'll quickly run through the commands here.

Our entry will be placed in the direct file on the NIS master (the automounter maps are under the control of NIS). The following examples show the NFS mount options. These are that the device is "hard" mounted, with the minimum and maximum time-outs ("actimeo" variable) set to 0 (we need to do this to make sure the mailbox locking and access mechanisms work correctly):

```
tin# cat /etc/auto_direct
<lines removed for clarity>
/var/mail -rw,hard,actimeo=0 xenon:/var/mail
tin# cd /var/yp
tin# make
updated auto_direct
pushed auto_direct
```

If we didn't want to use Autofs, the corresponding entry for */etc/vfstab* would be as follows:

```
lithium# cat /etc/vfstab
#
#device    device   mount  FS    fsck  mount    mount
#to mount  to fsck  point  type  pass  at boot  options
#
<lines removed for clarity>
xenon - /var/mail /var/mail nfs - yes rw,hard,actimeo=0
```

Generate *Sendmail.cf*

This step is very similar to the one performed for the master. We've already seen that the subsidiary file contains the definitions needed for a mail client and we've already updated our *hosts* file to include the mailhost entry so that the SMART_HOST setting will work. This means that we can simply copy the subsidiary template file into place and restart the daemons, which we'll do now:

```
carbon# cd /etc/mail
carbon# cp /etc/mail/sendmail.cf /etc/mail/sendmail.cf.orig
carbon# cp subsidiary.cf sendmail.cf
carbon# /etc/init.d/sendmail stop
carbon# /etc/init.d/sendmail start
carbon#
```

Send and Receive Mail

Again, we need to check that we can send and receive mail to the users correctly. This means running the same sort of tests that we did for the main server. For that reason, we won't repeat them again here.

At this point, we have a simple mail system up and running. However, external mail still needs to be addressed to the login names of the users for them to receive it (i.e., *jgreen*, and *msmith*). It would be nice to tidy this up, so let's look at how we can do this with aliases.

Aliases

Mail aliases allow us to define alternative names for users or groups of users. Each alias consists of a name and an associated array of one or more user names. They are stored in a file named */etc/mail/aliases*. Historically, this was named */etc/aliases*, and in fact a link still exists to allow */etc/aliases* to be used.

It's useful to create aliases for many reasons, some of which are listed below:

- Aliases allow us to provide a consistent look to our external email addresses, regardless of the login name assigned to each user. We'll use them to provide an external address for all users to allow them to receive email using a "firstname.lastname" address.

- We can make allowances for names that may be easily confused or shortened. For example, we'll add aliases for "msmith," so that he'll receive mail sent to "Mike," "Michael," or even "Micheal" (as his name is commonly misspelled).

- They allow us to send mail easily to a group of people. By assigning a number of addresses to an alias, we can direct mail by department (sales, marketing, etc.) and make sure that important mail isn't missed if someone is away. We'll do this for any backup-related mail.

- We can "hide" internal user names from the outside world. Common examples of these are the "postmaster" and "webmaster" accounts.

After we've made the changes, our file is as follows:

```
xenon# cat /etc/mail/aliases
#
# std alias for returned messages
#
MAILER-DAEMON: postmaster
#
# aliases for the users
#
Mike.smith: msmith
Michael.smith: msmith
Micheal.smith: msmith
John.green: jgreen
#
# add an alias for any backup messages
#
backup: sysadmin,msmith
#
# create the common accounts
#
postmaster: sysadmin,root
webmaster: sysadmin,root
xenon#
```

Although the aliases file is an ASCII text file, `sendmail` actually requires a DBM-based database. The aliases database is stored in two binary files named *letc/mail/aliases.dir* and *letc/mail/aliases.pag*, which are generated using the `newaliases` command as shown below:

```
xenon# newaliases
/etc/mail/aliases: 8 aliases, longest 15 bytes, 148 bytes total
xenon#
```

If the system is configured with a naming service, the aliases database can be incorporated into it. We discussed how to do this in Chapter 12, "Naming Services and NIS," but we'll quickly run through the process using our NIS server tin as an example:

```
tin# cd /var/yp
tin# make
updated aliases
pushed aliases
tin#
```

Next we'll update *letc/nsswitch.conf* so that it contains the following entry, which checks the local aliases first, followed by the NIS map:

```
tin# grep aliases /etc/nsswitch.conf
aliases:           files nis
tin#
```

Now that we have an aliases map, we need to check that it works by sending a number of mails once more. They should be addressed to some of the alias names, such as *backup* or *John.Green*, for example.

Conclusion

By breaking down the mail process into individual tasks, we've seen how it functions and how the mail protocols interact with each other. We've also seen how we can use a combination of protocols to allow mail to be delivered and received in different ways.

We've also managed to build a very simple mail system, which (although it's not what we would call a production system) has allowed us to learn the steps needed to get things working.

21

KERNELS AND ALL ABOUT THEM

Manual Pages

arch (1)
dmesg (1)
exec (1)
modinfo (1M)
modload (1M)
modunload (1M)
pargs (1)
prex (1)
sar (1)
showrev (1M)
sysdef (1M)
uname(1)

Files Affected

/etc/system
/kernel/*
/var/adm/messages

Objectives

If you have been using UNIX systems for a while, you have probably come across the term "kernel" before, but you may not know exactly what it is because it is not something you will interact with on a daily basis. In fact, you won't actually ever interact with it directly.

In this chapter we will look at what the Solaris kernel is and how it fits into the operating system as a whole. Following this we will look at some of the tools available to help troubleshoot operating system problems. We will also look at kernel modules, kernel parameters, and kernel messages.

What Is the Kernel?

The kernel forms the core of a UNIX system and acts as the interface between the hardware and the programs that run on it. It manages specific system-related functions, like opening files and deleting files; any program that wants to make use of one of these functions does so by means of a system call.

The kernel also manages the allocation of space to many system features, such as the process table; the size of these can be altered by the system administrator by setting kernel parameters. The setting of kernel parameters is often referred to as "tuning the kernel."

How Does It All Fit Together?

The interface between the user and the computer processor can be thought of as a series of layers. At the bottom is the computer processor, memory, disk, and all other hardware devices. The next layer is the kernel—one of its jobs is to manage these items and manage all communication with them. The layer following the kernel is the program (or application) layer. This layer includes all the programs on the server, apart from the kernel itself. The kernel includes the processes sched, pageout, and fsflush, as we saw in Chapter 2, "Booting and Halting the System." There will only ever be one kernel layer, but there can be as many application layers on top of the kernel as the system can cope with. The final layer is the end-user. This layer is optional as not all programs interface with a user. The following example shows a layer diagram of the typical configuration of a user logged in and running a shell.

user
shell
kernel
hardware

The user is interacting with the shell process and will interact with commands that are executed during the login session. If the user chose to edit a file using the `vi` editor, a new layer would appear in the diagram as shown here.

user
`vi`
shell
kernel
hardware

The user is now interacting with the editor. When the file is saved and the user quits, the `vi` layer will disappear again. As mentioned earlier, the user can never talk directly with the kernel because it has no user interface. Its only interfaces are with the computer hardware and other programs (some of which do have user interfaces).

Every time a running program (including the shell) needs to perform an action that is controlled by the kernel, it will call a function within the kernel that will perform the required task on behalf of the calling program. This is called "making a system call" and is required because there are actions that only the kernel is able to perform. These actions are too numerous to list in their entirety here, but they include:

- Opening a file
- Reading data from a file
- Writing data to a file
- Closing a file
- Deleting a file
- Spawning a subprocess
- Sending a signal to another process

Because UNIX systems treat everything like a file, the actions concerning files also refer to directories and devices (e.g., disks, terminals, printers, etc.). Whenever the processor is running a nonkernel program, it is said to be in user mode, but when the program makes a system call it changes into system mode as the kernel is now running.

We can see evidence of these modes by running the `sar` command (sar stands for "system activity report," and it is used for monitoring the performance of the system).

The following command takes 10 samples of system activity at 5-second intervals and displays the results:

```
hydrogen# sar 5 10

SunOS hydrogen 5.7 Generic_106541-08 sun4m    12/22/01

16:32:59    %usr    %sys    %wio    %idle
16:33:04     1       2       0       97
16:33:09     0       1       0       99
16:33:14     0       1       0       99
16:33:19     5      10       0       85
16:33:24     4      11       0       85
16:33:29     0       2       0       98
16:33:34     0       1       0       99
16:33:39     0       1       0       99
16:33:44     0       1       0       99
16:33:49     1       2       0       97

Average      1       3       0       96
hydrogen#
```

For each line displayed, we see the percentages of the sample time the CPU was running in user mode, running in system mode, waiting for I/O and idle. The system mode column represents when the kernel was running in the CPU; this could be from the kernel running in its own right (e.g., the sched process) or from the kernel running due to system calls from other processes.

When the above command was run, the system wasn't doing very much and there were no other users logged in. But another user logged in during the time sar was running; it can be seen by an increase in the user and system percentages and a corresponding decrease in idle time in the fourth and fifth entries of the above output.

Troubleshooting

Occasionally, problems or unusual behavior can arise in processes. Solaris provides a number of tools to help us troubleshoot problems.

Truss

Solaris provides a tool called truss that can be used to actually see the system calls that a program makes during its execution. If we were to look at a simple example of a program that makes a system call, we could choose the rm command, which simply deletes a file. We know that whenever a program wants to delete a file it must make a system call to the kernel to actually perform the action. The system call to delete a file is actually called "unlink"; the name is appropriate because if a file has many links and we remove one of them, the file won't actually go. It is only when the last link is removed that the file no longer exists (see Chapter 6, "The Filesystem and Its Contents"). The following command will run the rm command and display all the system calls that were made while it ran:

```
hydrogen# ls -l testfile
-rw-r--r--   1 root     other        583 Dec 22 17:46 testfile
hydrogen# truss rm testfile
execve("/usr/bin/rm", 0xEFFFFD0C, 0xEFFFFD18)  argc = 2
open("/dev/zero", O_RDONLY)                   = 3
mmap(0x00000000, 4096, PROT_READ|PROT_WRITE|PROT_EXEC, MAP_PRIVATE, 3, 0) =
    0xEF7C0000
stat("/usr/bin/rm", 0xEFFFFA00)               = 0
open("/usr/lib/libc.so.1", O_RDONLY)          = 4
fstat(4, 0xEFFFF7BC)                           = 0
mmap(0x00000000, 4096, PROT_READ|PROT_EXEC, MAP_PRIVATE, 4, 0) = 0xEF7B0000
mmap(0x00000000, 770048, PROT_READ|PROT_EXEC, MAP_PRIVATE, 4, 0) =
    0xEF6C0000
munmap(0xEF764000, 61440)                      = 0
mmap(0xEF773000, 27668, PROT_READ|PROT_WRITE|PROT_EXEC,
    MAP_PRIVATE|MAP_FIXED, 4, 667648) = 0xEF773000
mmap(0xEF77A000, 5480, PROT_READ|PROT_WRITE|PROT_EXEC,
    MAP_PRIVATE|MAP_FIXED, 3, 0) = 0xEF77A000
close(4)                                       = 0
open("/usr/lib/libdl.so.1", O_RDONLY)          = 4
fstat(4, 0xEFFFF7BC)                           = 0
mmap(0xEF7B0000, 4096, PROT_READ|PROT_EXEC, MAP_PRIVATE|MAP_FIXED, 4, 0) =
    0xEF7B0000
close(4)                                       = 0
open("/usr/platform/SUNW,SPARCstation-LX/lib/libc_psr.so.1", O_RDONLY)
    Err#2 ENOENT
close(3)                                       = 0
brk(0x00022C20)                                = 0
brk(0x00024C20)                                = 0
open("/usr/lib/locale/en_GB/en_GB.so.2", O_RDONLY) = 3
fstat(3, 0xEFFFF19C)                           = 0
mmap(0x00000000, 4096, PROT_READ|PROT_EXEC, MAP_PRIVATE, 3, 0) = 0xEF7A0000
mmap(0x00000000, 86016, PROT_READ|PROT_EXEC, MAP_PRIVATE, 3, 0) = 0xEF6A0000
munmap(0xEF6A4000, 61440)                      = 0
mmap(0xEF6B3000, 5934, PROT_READ|PROT_WRITE|PROT_EXEC,
    MAP_PRIVATE|MAP_FIXED, 3, 12288) = 0xEF6B3000
close(3)                                       = 0
open("/dev/zero", O_RDONLY)                    = 3
mmap(0x00000000, 4096, PROT_READ|PROT_WRITE|PROT_EXEC, MAP_PRIVATE, 3, 0) =
    0xEF790000
close(3)                                       = 0
munmap(0xEF7A0000, 4096)                        = 0
getrlimit64(RLIMIT_NOFILE, 0xEFFFFC98)          = 0
lstat64("testfile", 0xEFFFFBA0)                 = 0
access("testfile", 2)                           = 0
unlink("testfile")                              = 0
llseek(0, 0, SEEK_CUR)                          = 2660
_exit(0)
hydrogen#
```

Each line of output displays a system call, along with any parameters being passed to it. The return code from the system call is shown after the equals sign. Generally, a return code of zero means the system call was successful and any other return code demonstrates that an error occurred, but this is not always the case. The system call open() tells the kernel that you wish to open a file. As we saw in Chapter 6, "The Filesystem and Its Contents," each time a file is opened a file descriptor is assigned to it, so this system call will return the value of the file descriptor that has been assigned to it. When a program wants to close a file it calls the close() system call and passes the file descriptor as the parameter.

It can be seen that even a relatively simple program can still make many system calls. The first system call comes from the truss process as it executes the rm process by calling the execve() system call (system calls are usually written with the empty brackets following their name).

There are many other system calls until the one that actually does what we want, which is the call to unlink(). The command finishes with the exit() call, passing a zero as the command succeeded in deleting the file.

The truss command can be very useful for troubleshooting processes that are not doing what they should. If the program you are trying to run ends without doing anything, then you can use truss as in the above example. You may find that a program is terminating prematurely because a system call is failing, in which case you should see the offending system call near the end of the truss output. Possible problems you would pick up here include failure to create a file (maybe due to a lack of permissions) or failure to open a file (maybe it is not there or has incorrect permissions). Alternatively, you may find that a program you are running appears to be hanging for no apparent reason. In this case, you can use truss to examine an already running program by using the "-p" option:

```
hydrogen# ps -ef | tail -5
   jsmith   537   535   0 15:38:34 pts/0      0:01 -sh
   jsmith   643   537   1 15:53:11 pts/0      0:00 pg
     root   579   577   0 15:44:39 pts/1      0:00 -sh
     root   644   579   2 15:53:17 pts/1      0:00 ps -ef
     root   577   173   0 15:44:38 ?          0:00 in.telnetd
hydrogen#
```

If, for example, we were worried that process ID 643 (shown above) had hung, we could examine it using truss to see what it was doing:

```
hydrogen# # truss -p 643
read(0, 0xEF73B150, 1024)         (sleeping...)
hydrogen#
```

Here we see that the process is currently in the read() system call, but it is sleeping rather than actually reading any data. This means that the process (in this case pg) is trying to read data from a file but there is no data for it to read, but there is also no end of file, so it just sits there waiting for data. In this case, we can see what must have happened. The user *jsmith* has run the pg command without supplying a filename so it is reading the standard input instead. The standard input is attached to the keyboard so it will read whatever is typed until it receives the EOF character (which is usually <control-d>). The user that ran the command is not typing anything, so the process goes into a sleeping state while it waits to receive data. This is a very simple example, but it demonstrates the type of troubleshooting that can be performed using truss to examine the system calls that a process is making.

Pargs

This command was only introduced with Solaris 9, but provides a number of useful features that would make a system administrator wonder how (s)he got on without it.

The default action of pargs is to display all the arguments that were supplied to a running process. This is very useful, but can't we get this information from a ps listing? We can for most processes, but there is a fixed length limit to the amount of information displayed by ps so we may not see all the arguments and parameters that a certain process was started with.

The following example shows the console login process. If we were a bit unsure of the arguments it was called with we could simply look using ps:

```
hydrogen# ps -ft console
     UID   PID  PPID  C    STIME TTY      TIME CMD
    root   244     1  0 13:22:56 console  0:00 /usr/lib/saf/
ttymon -g -h -p hydrogen console login:  -T sun -d /dev/console
hydrogen#
```

However, if we look using pargs we see that some information was missing from the ps listing:

```
hydrogen# pargs 244
244:    /usr/lib/saf/ttymon -g -h -p hydrogen console login:
   -T sun -d /dev/console
argv[0]: /usr/lib/saf/ttymon
argv[1]: -g
argv[2]: -h
argv[3]: -p
argv[4]: junibacken console login:
argv[5]: -T
argv[6]: sun
argv[7]: -d
argv[8]: /dev/console
argv[9]: -l
argv[10]: console
argv[11]: -m
argv[12]: ldterm,ttcompat
hydrogen#
```

There are other options to pargs. Possibly the most useful is the "-e" option, which will display the environment variables of a process:

```
hydrogen# pargs -e 244
244:    /usr/lib/saf/ttymon -g -h -p hydrogen console login:
   -T sun -d /dev/console
envp[0]: PATH=/usr/sbin:/usr/bin
envp[1]: TZ=Europe/Stockholm
hydrogen#
```

If you look at the man page you will see that there are a few other options to pargs, but these are the most useful.

Prex

This command will get a mention here, but that is about all. It has existed in Solaris for a while, but the man page only appeared at Solaris 8. `prex` is a very powerful tool that is much more informative than `truss`, but it does take some time to get used to. It enables you to control tracing and set probes points in running processes or even the kernel itself. If you are familiar with debugging tools, such as `sdb`, then you may want to have a play with `prex` to see what it can offer.

Kernel Modules

We saw at the beginning of the chapter that the kernel deals with all hardware communication and it does this by the means of system calls. But how does the kernel know how to talk to so many different hardware devices, and what happens when a new device that it doesn't know about is added?

The answer is found in the heading of this section. Kernel modules provide the kernel with all the information it needs to be able to talk to a specific type of device. This information includes how to open and close the device, how to read from and write to it, and how to configure and control it. Because there are so many different devices available and only a fraction of them would ever be connected to any given Sun computer, the information is provided in the form of individual modules that can be loaded into the kernel (usually at boot-time, but not exclusively) or unloaded as required. Originally, the kernel had to be recompiled to add a new module, but now (and for some time) it was possible to load and unload modules while the system is actually running, although it would normally be done at boot-time.

The kernel modules are located in the directory */kernel/drv*. Each module usually consists of two files: a binary file (which is the actual driver for the hardware) and a configuration file (which allows the device to be easily configured). For example, if we purchased a Quad Fast Ethernet (qfe) Card we would need to load the qfe module into the kernel to be able to use it. The module would include a driver called *qfe* and a configuration file called *qfe.conf*. Editing the *qfe.conf* file allows us to set such attributes as the transmission speed and whether the card should run in full- or half-duplex mode.

We can see the modules we have loaded by using the `modinfo` command:

```
hydrogen# modinfo
<lines removed for clarity>
 95 f5aee750    e53  24   1  pts (Slave Stream Pseudo Terminal dr)
 96 f5b11eb0   163b  14   1  ptem (pty hardware emulator)
 97 f5a0f994   1972  15   1  telmod (telnet module)
 98 f5ab8294   1ad8   4   1  logindmux ( LOGIND MUX Driver)
 99 f5aef2dc    858  72   1  ksyms (kernel symbols driver)
100 f6101000   29de  88   1  devinfo (DEVINFO Driver 1.24)
hydrogen#
```

Modules can be loaded into the kernel using `modload` and unloaded using `unloadmod` while the system is running (see the man pages), but this is not usually required as modules are automatically loaded as soon as any program tries to access any device that is controlled by one. It is also possible to force the system to load a kernel module at boot-time; this is done by updating the file *⁄etc⁄system*.

The */Etc/system* File

When Solaris is first installed, the *⁄etc⁄system* file contains only comments, but it can be updated in various ways to configure the kernel at boot-time. Each comment section describes a certain type of modification that can be made, along with some examples. These include the following:

- Set the search path for kernel modules.
- Set a filesystem type for the *root* filesystem.
- Define kernel modules that should not be loaded.
- Define kernel modules that must be loaded at boot-time.
- Set kernel parameters.

Kernel Parameters

A number of aspects that are controlled by the kernel can be changed by altering the values assigned to various kernel parameters. "Tuning the kernel" is often thought of as some arcane ritual similar to alchemy that can only be performed by seventh-level UNIX Wizards and above. In reality, it is a fairly straightforward task that is considered to be slightly mystical probably because it used to be much more complicated; also, it is a task that some system administrators will never actually have to do.

Listing Kernel Parameters

The names of the kernel parameters and their current values can be displayed using the `sysdef` command as follows:

```
hydrogen# sysdef
<lines removed for clarity>
*
* Tunable Parameters
*
 1970176     maximum memory allowed in buffer cache (bufhwm)
    1514     maximum number of processes (v.v_proc)
      99     maximum global priority in sys class (MAXCLSYSPRI)
    1509     maximum processes per user id (v.v_maxup)
      30     auto update time limit in seconds (NAUTOUP)
```

```
      25    page stealing low water mark (GPGSLO)
       5    fsflush run rate (FSFLUSHR)
      25    minimum resident memory for avoiding deadlock (MINARMEM)
      25    minimum swapable memory for avoiding deadlock (MINASMEM)
*
* Utsname Tunables
*
     5.7    release (REL)
hydrogen    node name (NODE)
   SunOS    system name (SYS)
Generic_106541-08  version (VER)
*
* Process Resource Limit Tunables (Current:Maximum)
*
0xffffffff:0xfffffffd    cpu time
0xffffffff:0xfffffffd    file size
0xffffffff:0xfffffffd    heap size
0xffffffff:0xfffffffd    stack size
0xffffffff:0xfffffffd    core file size
0xffffffff:0xfffffffd    file descriptors
0x00000000:0x00800000    mapped memory
*
* Streams Tunables
*
       9    maximum number of pushes allowed (NSTRPUSH)
   65536    maximum stream message size (STRMSGSZ)
    1024    max size of ctl part of message (STRCTLSZ)
*
* IPC Messages
*
       0    entries in msg map (MSGMAP)
       0    max message size (MSGMAX)
       0    max bytes on queue (MSGMNB)
       0    message queue identifiers (MSGMNI)
       0    message segment size (MSGSSZ)
       0    system message headers (MSGTQL)
       0    message segments (MSGSEG)
*
* IPC Semaphores
*
      10    entries in semaphore map (SEMMAP)
      10    semaphore identifiers (SEMMNI)
      60    semaphores in system (SEMMNS)
      30    undo structures in system (SEMMNU)
      25    max semaphores per id (SEMMSL)
      10    max operations per semop call (SEMOPM)
      10    max undo entries per process (SEMUME)
   32767    semaphore maximum value (SEMVMX)
   16384    adjust on exit max value (SEMAEM)
*
* IPC Shared Memory
*
 1048576       max shared memory segment size (SHMMAX)
       1    min shared memory segment size (SHMMIN)
     100    shared memory identifiers (SHMMNI)
       6    max attached shm segments per process (SHMSEG)
```

```
*
* Time Sharing Scheduler Tunables
*
60        maximum time sharing user priority (TSMAXUPRI)
SYS       system class name (SYS_NAME)
hydrogen#
```

The `sysdef` command produces many pages of output, most of which have been removed from the above example to display only tuneable parameters. Viewed as a whole, the output would also list all hardware devices, pseudo devices, system devices, and loadable kernel modules.

Modifying Kernel Parameters

If you wish to change the current value of any kernel parameter, you need to add an entry to the /etc/systems file. When the kernel sets up all its parameters at boot-time, it will use the default value for each one unless it sees a `set` command for that parameter in the systems file.

The parameter "max_nprocs" defines the maximum number of processes that can run on the system at any one time. In the above example, we can see that it is currently set to 1,514 (though unfortunately the output from sysdef doesn't tell us that "max_nprocs" is the name of the parameter). This controls the number of allowed processes by setting the size of the process table, as each process takes up one slot in the table. If we found that this was not enough for the needs of our system, we could add an entry to /etc/system to increase the value of "max_nprocs" and so increase the size of the process table.

You can tell that your process table is full if you get messages such as "cannot fork" when trying to run commands. If you do get such messages, it does not necessarily mean that you should immediately increase the "max_nprocs" parameter; the process table could be full because an out-of-control process has filled it by continuously spawning subprocesses. At first thought, this might be a problem because if the process table is full, how can the system administrator kill the rogue process, as there is no room in the process table to run the `kill` command? Fortunately, this situation is prevented by the fact that the last slot in the process table may only be taken by a process run by the *root* user. Therefore, providing the rogue process is not running as *root*, the problem can be resolved without resorting to a reboot.

Assuming that we are sure we do need to increase the size of the process table (and we have decided it should be set at 2,000), we would add the following entry to the /etc/system file:

```
set max_nprocs = 2000
```

Once we have rebooted the system we can check that the new value has been assigned:

```
hydrogen# sysdef | grep process
   2000              maximum number of processes (v.v_proc)
   1995              maximum processes per user id (v.v_maxup)
   10  max undo entries per process (SEMUME)
    6  max attached shm segments per process (SHMSEG)
hydrogen#
```

By far the most likely reason for needing to alter the values of system parameters is to meet the requirements of an application or database, in which case the installation guide will explain which parameters need altering and how you should calculate the values to set.

The */etc/system* file is very important as it can greatly affect the way the kernel is configured and setting something incorrectly could cause the system to become unusable. Therefore, it is important that we always make a backup copy before changing the file. That way, if the system fails to boot successfully, we can boot the system with boot -a, which will cause us to be prompted for the location of the system file. At that time, we can specify the backup copy, which we know works (see Chapter 2, "Booting and Halting the System"). If we don't have a backup copy, we could always specify the file */dev/null* as the system file, which should act as an empty file and cause the system to set all kernel parameters to their default values.

Kernel Messages

One of the log files we mentioned in the section "Log Files" on page 165 of Chapter 6 ("The Filesystem and Its Contents") was */var/adm/messages*. This file contains messages from the kernel and is therefore one of the most important log files. The messages contained in this file are not neceserily error messages; in fact, you should find that most are simply informational messages. But if your server does suffer a major error, chances are there will be messages from the kernel in this file that can help you (or the Sun Support Team) diagnose the fault. Since Solaris 8 was introduced, every message has a specific ID number associated with it, which makes the job of interpreting the messages much simpler.

As well as examining the *messages* file manually, you can use the command dmesg to display the most recent messages from this file:

```
hydrogen# dmesg | tail -4
Apr 13 13:22:44 hydrogen obio: [ID 349649 kern.info] obio0 at obio0:
   obio 0x400000, sparc ipl 11
Apr 13 13:22:44 hydrogen genunix: [ID 936769 kern.info] fd0 is
   /obio/SUNW,fdtwo@0,400000
Apr 13 13:23:12 hydrogen pseudo: [ID 129642 kern.info] pseudo-
   device: pm0
Apr 13 13:23:12 hydrogen genunix: [ID 936769 kern.info] pm0 is
   /pseudo/pm@0
hydrogen#
```

This shows the four most recent messages written to the *messages* file. They are all information-type messages and were actually written as the machine was last booted. The format of the new-style messages is as follows:

- Date and time stamp
- Host name
- Kernel module (if the message was from the kernel)
- Message ID number and class of message
- The message itself

22

BACKING UP AND RESTORING THE SYSTEM

Objectives

This chapter starts with a brief discussion on the importance of a backup strategy then looks at how a backup can be taken on a Solaris system. As well as looking at the commands that are available, we will discuss the merits of each and look at the different types of backups (e.g., compressed, incremental, etc).

The chapter ends with a look at the backup script we have written to back up our servers.

Why Do We Need a Backup Strategy?

Computers perform an ever-more useful role within businesses. They are entrusted with increasingly complex jobs and are usually expected to be 100 percent reliable.

Unfortunately, there is always something that can fail, usually at the wrong moment, which makes it imperative that regular backups are taken to ensure that you are able to deal with all types of problems. A backup is a copy of the data that is stored on the computers hard disk(s) that can be used to recreate that data should it become lost or corrupt. Problems requiring restoration from backup range from a user inadvertently removing the wrong file to a major hardware failure causing loss or corruption of whole disks worth of data.

Backing up a system is not simply a matter of copying all the files to tape. There are a great many factors to take into account, which means each server is likely to require its own backup strategy.

Once a backup strategy is defined, it should be fully tested, which should include the recovery of data from the backup, as well as the actual backup process. It is all very well to take a full system backup every night, but if you haven't tested how you will use it to rebuild the system, you will find that the hours following an emergency are not the best time to do it.

What Is a Backup Strategy?

Defining a backup strategy is one of the key tasks to be performed during the implementation of a new computer system. This task is often left until just before the system goes live and, in most cases, this is already too late. If the system has a 10 GB database, but only has a 2 GB tape drive installed, it is probably not going to be sufficient for the task. Likewise, if a system is going to be used for 20 hours a day, but takes 6 hours to perform a backup, a certain amount of ingenuity will be required to identify a workable solution. It is likely that a solution will be obtainable, but the earlier in the project this is done, the least likely it will impact the "go live" date.

A backup strategy needs to answer the following questions:

- When will the backup be taken?
- What mechanism will be used to take the backup?
- How many tapes will be required?
- How will they be labelled?
- Who will be swapping tapes over?
- Where will the tapes be stored?
- How will we deal with requests, from users, to restore specific files?
- How will we recover from an application/data failure?
- How will we recover from an operating system failure?
- How will we recover from a major disaster (such as an earthquake)?

The latter point is often not included in the backup strategy but is instead the subject of a disaster recovery strategy, as a true disaster will require more than just the recovery of the computer and its data. It is also likely to involve input from many other people in addition to the system administrator.

Unfortunately, there is no standard backup strategy so you will have to define your own. What we will do, however, is show different commands, provided by Solaris, that can be used to perform the backups defined in your strategy and recover lost files or data. It is also worth noting that, as well as the commands provided by Solaris, there are also many third-party backup products available. These can provide many useful features (such as the control of external tape libraries) and may provide the best solution if you have very specific backup requirements.

How Do We Back Up the System?

Solaris provides us with many different commands for backing up and restoring data. Which one we choose will depend on a number of factors; it might simply be that it is the method that we are already most familiar with. We will look at the main commands and utilities in this section.

Just be aware that they are not compatible or interchangeable with each other, so the command we use to back up the data will determine the command needed to restore data from the backup.

Dd

The most basic of the backup and restore commands is probably dd (which stands for "direct dump"; it was originally to be called "copy and convert," but cc was already taken). It will copy data from one file to another and you can specify the block size, which can affect the speed of the copy.

In the following example, we use dd to back up the data stored in a file called *fred* (i.e., the contents of *fred*) into another file called *fred.bak*:

```
hydrogen$ dd if=fred of=fred.bak
1125+1 records in
1125+1 records out
hydrogen$ ls -l fred*
-rw-rw-r--   1 jgreen     staff       576415 Nov 29 10:02 fred
-rw-rw-r--   1 jgreen     staff       576415 Nov 29 10:34 fred.bak
hydrogen$
```

Here, we literally set the input file (*if*) to point to the file *fred* and the output file (*of*) to *fred.bak* and let dd get on with making the copy. It will read from the input file one block at a time and write the data to the output file one block at a time. The default block size is 512 bytes. When it has finished, dd reports the number of complete and incomplete blocks that were copied. In this example, dd copied 1,125 complete blocks and one partial block.

To restore the data back from *fred.bak* we would just reverse the above so that the input file was *fred.bak* and the output file *fred*:

```
hydrogen$ rm fred
hydrogen$ dd if=fred.bak of=fred
1125+1 records in
1125+1 records out
hydrogen$ ls -l fred*
-rw-rw-r--   1 jgreen     staff       576415 Nov 29 10:48 fred
-rw-rw-r--   1 jgreen     staff       576415 Nov 29 10:34 fred.bak
hydrogen$
```

This is very straightforward but only useful if your system only has one file to back up, otherwise you would need to run an instance of dd for each file to be backed up. You may also have noted that the backup of *fred* will be created in the same directory as *fred*, which is not the usual way to secure your valuable data. In fact, while we are on the subject of the suitability of dd as a backup tool, surely the cp command would do exactly the same job with less typing.

It is true that if we wanted to copy *fred* to *fred.bak*, dd is probably not the obvious tool to use. However, if we wanted to copy *fred* to tape, that is another matter.

Let's assume that we only have one important file on the system (*fred*) and we will use dd to back it up. However, we don't want the backup copy to be located elsewhere on the hard disk—we want to back it up to tape instead. Fortunately, this is just as easy to do as the above example, but this time we just need to specify that the output file is the tape device (or rather the file associated with the tape device—see Chapter 17, "Adding SCSI Devices").

```
hydrogen# dd if=fred of=/dev/rmt/0
1125+1 records in
1125+1 records out
hydrogen#
```

Here the data in the file *fred* is copied to the tape in the tape drive associated with rmt/0 (and now, at last, we have done something that we couldn't with the `cp` command). The reason we say that the data in *fred* is copied to tape rather than just saying *fred* is copied to tape is that the name associated with the data is not copied (nor are the permissions or anything else stored in the inode—see Chapter 6, "The Filesystem and Its Contents"). This command literally copies the data contained within the file *fred* on to the tape. In fact, not even the name of the file is stored on the tape with the data. To restore the data we would type:

```
hydrogen# dd if=/dev/rmt/0 of=sebastobold
hydrogen# ls -l fred sebastobold
-rw-rw-r--   1 jgreen    staff      576415 Nov 29 10:48 fred
-rw-rw-r--   1 root      other      576415 Nov 29 11:14 sebastobold
hydrogen#
```

A file called *sebastobold* is created, which contains an exact copy of the data that was originally stored in the file *fred*. The ownership and group of the new file are determined by the user that ran the command and the permissions are based on that user's umask. So, even though the original file was owned by the user *jgreen*, because we restored the data as *root* the restored file is also owned by *root*.

You have probably already come to the conclusion that dd is not the most useful command for backing up a server as it will only back up one file and it doesn't store any of the file's ownership and permissions details. But, we saw in Chapter 6, "The Filesystem and Its Contents," each disk slice, and also each disk, has a file associated with it under the */dev* directory. If we used this file as the input file to dd, then we could make a backup copy of a whole filesystem or disk with one simple command:

```
hydrogen# dd if=/dev/rdsk/c0t0d0s2 of=/dev/rmt/0 bs=2028k
201751+1 records in
201751+1 records out
hydrogen#
```

Here we are backing up the whole of disk c0t0d0 to tape (remember that sector 2 is equal to the whole disk). We have also increased the block size to 2,028 KB to speed things up a bit. This specifies the amount of data that is transferred with each read and write operation. If you set a small block size, the process will take longer as it is wasting time constantly switching from reading to writing. If you choose to copy from the block device rather than the raw device, you will find that the last block copied is padded with nulls to make it end on a block boundary, so setting a large block size could cause a large amount of wasted space.

It doesn't matter that we aren't saving the owner and permissions of the file */dev/c0t0d0s2* because we are storing this information for each of the files that are stored on that disk. If we want to restore the data, we set the input file to be the tape device and the output file to be the disk. We do not need to restore to the disk we actually backed up from; it could be any disk as long as it is big enough to hold all the data. However, if it is bigger than the original disk, we will not be able to access the whole of the new disk, as it will now appear to be the same size as the original. This is because it will now have the disk label from the original disk. Also, we should be aware that if the geometry of the disk we are restoring to is different from the one we backed up from, although it should still work, the performance may not be optimized, so trying to stick with the same type of disk is recommended. Recovery this way is quick and simple, but we can't recover individual files from this backup, just a whole disk at a time.

We can also use dd to copy directly from one disk to another, as shown below:

```
hydrogen# dd if=/dev/rdsk/c0t0d0s2 of=/dev/rdsk/c1t0d0s2 bs=2048k
201751+1 records in
201751+1 records out
hydrogen#
```

This will build the disk c1t0d0 as a complete replica of disk c0t0d0. This could be used to duplicate a large number of system disks, which can then be placed in other servers to provide a standard build. Alternatively if we have a small backup window but lots of room for removable disks, we could back each disk up to an identical one during our backup window, start the services back up again, then remove the duplicates to a safe location. If we need to recover the system, we can simply remove all the live disks and replace them with the backup disks (they were properly labelled, weren't they?). We can then boot up the system and carry on from the point of time at which the backup was taken.

If you look in the man page for dd, you will see that it has many uses other than simply copying data from one file (or device) to another. This includes activities such as converting data from one format to another. In conclusion, dd could not really be described as a general-purpose backup utility, but it is a useful tool to know about and can be used for a number of specific tasks.

Tar

We will now look at the utilities tar and cpio. Both these commands perform similar tasks. System Administrators tend to favor one or the other and may often be heard arguing over which is the better of the two. I suspect system administrators will prefer the one they learned first, as this is probably the one they also know most about.

The manual pages for tar provide full information on all its available options, of which there are many, so we will get straight on with an example showing how to back up the contents of a directory to tape:

```
hydrogen# tar cvf /dev/rmt/0 ./*
a ./dir1/file1 1K
a ./dir1/file2 1K
a ./dir2/file1 2K
a ./dir2/file1 3K
<lines removed for clarity>
hydrogen#
```

This command says that we are going to create ("c" for create) a backup (or archive) to the file */dev/rmt/0* ("f" for file), which, in this case, is the tape device. We want to see the names of the files as they are backed up ("v" for verbose) and the files we want to back up are all those in the current directory ("*" matches all files). You will notice that the above example also backs up all subdirectories and their contents. If we want to use tar to back up a whole filesystem, we simply need to specify the *root* directory of the filesystem on the command line.

As an aside, the fact that we used "./*" in the above example may have an unwanted side effect because "./*" will not match files beginning with a dot in the current directory (often referred to as "hidden files"). This is fine if there are no such files. But if you know the directory does contain hidden files and you wish to include them, "." should be used instead of "./*".

If we want to check what is on the tape we can run the following command:

```
hydrogen# tar tvf /dev/rmt/0
-rw-rw-r-- 1001/10     781 Oct  7 07:51 1999 ./dir1/file1
-rw-rw-r-- 1001/10     653 Nov 25 11:40 1999 ./dir1/file2
-rw-rw-r-- 1001/10    1391 Jun 18 15:00 2001 ./dir2/file1
-rw-rw-r-- 1001/10    2371 Jun 18 15:00 2001 ./dir2/file2
<lines removed for clarity>
hydrogen#
```

The "t" stands for table—we are asking to see the table of contents of the tape. You will notice that the output is similar to an ls -l listing, but instead of seeing the name of the owner and group, we see the UID and GID instead.

If we want to recover all the files on the tape, we would type:

```
hydrogen# tar xvf /dev/rmt0
x ./dir1/file1, 781 bytes, 2 tape blocks
x ./dir1/file2, 653 bytes, 2 tape blocks
x ./dir2/file1, 1391 bytes, 3 tape blocks
x ./dir2/file2, 2371 bytes, 5 tape blocks
<lines removed for clarity>
hydrogen#
```

This would extract ("x" option) all the files on the tape and put them in the current directory. If we only want to recover a few files, we can do so as follows:

```
hydrogen# tar xvf /dev/rmt0 ./dir1/file1 ./dir2/file2
x ./dir1/file1, 781 bytes, 2 tape blocks
x ./dir2/file2, 2371 bytes, 5 tape blocks
hydrogen#
```

The files are restored relative to the directory you are in when you run the command, unless they are stored on the tape with full path names, in which case they will be restored to their original location. When we supply the names of the files we wish to restore, we have to specify each name exactly as it appears when we list the contents of the tape.

If any files backed up by `tar` have ACLs set, the file will be backed up but not the ACL. So if you make use of ACLs you need to have a way of reapplying these following a recovery.

When `tar` backs up files that are linked, it will simply back up one full copy of the file and the names it was linked to. This ensures that space is not wasted in the archive and the files will remain linked when they are restored. `Tar` is also able to handle symbolic links in the same way.

Cpio

The `cpio` command does a similar job to `tar` (it collects the files whose names it is supplied with into an archive) but it is used in a slightly different way. It is often recommended, over `tar`, as being more compatible between different versions of UNIX (although in practice I have never had any compatibility problems with either `tar` or `cpio`).

The `cpio` command expects the names of the files we require to be backed up, to be passed as a list on its standard input. This means we need a way of producing the list of files we want to back up. This is usually achieved using the `find` command:

```
hydrogen# find /home -print | cpio -ovc -O /dev/rmt0
/home
/home/lost+found
<lines removed for clarity>
6142 blocks
hydrogen#
```

This command will find all files and directories below the */home* directory and pass their names to the `cpio` command, which will back them up to the tape device. We can restore all the files with the following command:

```
hydrogen# cpio -ivcud -I /dev/rmt0
/home
/home/lost+found
<lines removed for clarity>
6142 blocks
hydrogen#
```

This is a perfectly good way of backing up a directory tree, a filesystem, or even a whole system. But you need to be aware that because the `find` command presented each file or directory to `cpio` as a full path name, this is how they were backed up and it is the only practical way of restoring them. In other words, there is no easy way of restoring the files to a location other than their original location. (There is a way of doing it—look up the "-r" option in the cpio man page—but unless you want to recover one or two files you won't want to go to all that trouble.) If you want the flexibility of restoring files to an alternative location, you should pass relative file and directory names to cpio:

```
hydrogen# cd /home
hydrogen# find . -print | cpio -ovc -O /dev/rmt0
.
./lost+found
<lines removed for clarity>
6142 blocks
hydrogen#
```

To list the contents of a cpio archive, we would use the "-t" option (as with tar), but we use it in addition to the "-i" option rather than instead of it:

```
hydrogen# cpio -ivct -I /dev/rmt/0
drwxr-xr-x   10 root      root             0 Nov 23 10:45 2001,  .
drwxr-xr-x    2 root      root             0 Jun 28 13:48 2001,
lost+found
<lines removed for clarity>
hydrogen#
```

If we wanted to restore a number of files from a cpio archive, we would specify them on the command line just as we did with the tar command:

```
hydrogen# cpio -ivcdmu ./dir1/file1 ./dir2/file2 -I /dev/rmt/0
./dir1/file1
./dir2/file2
hydrogen#
```

The options we have used in this example are listed in Table 22.1.

Table 22.1 *Cpio Options*

Option	Description
i	We are reading data in from the archive, rather than writing out to the archive ("-o" option).
v	This is verbose mode. The name of each file processed is displayed on the standard output. If we used a capital V, cpio would display a dot for each filename instead.
c	We are using an ASCII header (which is always recommended for portability of the archive between platforms).
d	Directories will be created automatically if needed.
m	Retain the original modification time of the file.

Table 22.1 *Cpio Options (Continued)*

Option	Description
u	If the file being restored already exists, unconditionally over-write it.
I	We use "-I" before the input filename (or "-O" before the output filename). If "-I" is omitted cpio will read from standard input (likewise, if "-O" is omitted, cpio will write to standard output).

The commands tar and cpio are not only used for backing up data—they are also very useful for transferring files from one location on the directory tree to another. For example, if we had a group of files that we wanted to copy to other servers on the network, we could ftp each file individually, but this would be time-consuming and may not preserve the ownership and permissions of each file. Instead, we could place the files into a single archive file (using either tar or cpio), ftp that file to each server, and then extract the files at the other end.

Links and ACLs are handled by cpio in exactly the same way as tar handles them.

The cpio command can also be used to copy a directory along with all its subdirectories and files using the "-p" option:

```
hydrogen# find . -print | cpio -pvdmu /new_location
/new_location/.
/new_location/file1
/new_location/dir1
/new_location/dir1/file2
<lines removed for clarity>
hydrogen#
```

As well as copying all the files and directories, the above command will also preserve all ownerships and permissions.

The same action can be undertaken with both tar and ufsdump/ufsrestore, but the commands used are more cumbersome. Examples of both are shown here, although we haven't yet looked at ufsdump and ufsrestore:

```
hydrogen# tar cvf - . | (cd /new_directory; tar xvf -)
a ./dir1/file1 1K
a ./dir2/file1 1K
x ./dir1/file1, 802 bytes, 2 tape blocks
x ./dir2/file2, 649 bytes, 2 tape blocks
<lines removed for clarity>
hydrogen# ufsdump 0f - . | (cd /new_directory; ufsrestore rf - )
  DUMP: Writing 32 Kilobyte records
  DUMP: Date of this level 0 dump: Sat 29 Dec 2001 17:00:28 GMT
  DUMP: Date of last level 0 dump: the epoch
  DUMP: Dumping /dev/rdsk/c0t2d0s1 (hydrogen:/var) to standard output.
  DUMP: Mapping (Pass I) [regular files]
  DUMP: Mapping (Pass II) [directories]
```

```
DUMP: Estimated 2844 blocks (1.39MB).
DUMP: Dumping (Pass III) [directories]
DUMP: Dumping (Pass IV) [regular files]
DUMP: 2814 blocks (1.37MB) on 1 volume at 363 KB/sec
DUMP: DUMP IS DONE
<lines removed for clarity>
hydrogen#
```

Both these examples work in a similar way. They have a backup process writing to one end of a pipe and a restore process reading from the other end. The example using ufsdump/ufsrestore is recommended as being the quickest of the three methods mentioned for copying large quantities of data between two directories. However, because ufsdump likes to work with entire filesystems, if we are not copying a whole filesystem we will get a number of messages complaining that certain directories were not found on the volume. However, these can be ignored since the command will copy what we expected it to.

How Do We Fit More Data on the Tape?

Before we move on and look at the commands ufsdump and ufsrestore in more detail, we'll have a quick diversion and look at data compression. Compression is a way of reducing the amount of storage space required for a given chunk of data by converting it into a form which represents the data more efficiently.

Software Compression

If we wanted to compress the data in a file so it used up less space, we would run a compression program on the file. The program would look through the data and work out how to reduce the space taken up based on a compression algorithm. The compressed version of the file is usually given a specific extension to make it is easier to distinguish compressed files from standard files.

Unfortunately, once a file has been compressed it cannot be used in the same way as it was before, because the data contained in the file is now different. If you want to use the data in the file you must uncompress it first, which will make it exactly the same as it was before (which of course means it now takes up the original amount of disk space).

The following example shows how we can compress a file to reduce the amount of space it uses on the disk:

```
hydrogen# ls -l
total 1304
-rw-r--r--   1 root     other      665205 Dec  9 16:54 fred
hydrogen# compress fred
hydrogen# ls -l
total 216
-rw-r--r--   1 root     other      110247 Dec  9 16:54 fred.Z
hydrogen#
```

There are a number of different commands available that can compress and uncompress files. They are not interchangeable and come in pairs (e.g., `compress` goes with `uncompress` and `pack` goes with `unpack`). The extension given to the compressed file will help you to see which command was used to perform the compression. The `compress` command will produce a compressed file ending in ".Z" and `pack` will produce a file ending with ".z."

We can see that we have managed to save a fair bit of space by compressing this file, but now that it is compressed we cannot use it unless we uncompress it. The original file was a standard ASCII text file, but if we look at what type of file the compressed version is, using the `file` command, we see that it is no longer a text file. Consequently, it is no good trying to look at its contents with any of the usual Solaris commands (e.g., `cat`, `vi`, `pg`, or `more`):

```
hydrogen# file fred.Z
fred.Z:            compressed data block compressed 16 bits
hydrogen# uncompress fred
hydrogen# file fred
fred:              ascii text
hydrogen# ls -l fred
-rw-r--r--   1 root      other        665205 Dec  9 16:54 fred
hydrogen#
```

The `file` command looks in the file supplied as an argument and tries to work out what type of file it is. It isn't actually clever enough to know what all the possible file types are; it knows some common file types, but will also make use of the information contained in */etc/magic* to help it out. This file contains a list of byte positions along with byte sequences and descriptive text. If a file contains one of the byte sequences at the byte position specified, the text is displayed.

Since the `file` command doesn't actually know how to tell if a file is compressed, it does a bit of cheating. If we search for the string "compressed" in the *magic* file, we can see exactly how the `file` command knows that the file *fred.Z* is actually compressed:

```
hydrogen# grep "compressed data" /etc/magic
0        string          \037\235          compressed data
hydrogen#
```

Here we see that if a file contains a string of the character sequence represented by \037\235 at byte position 0, the `file` command will print the text "compressed data." The remainder of the output from the `file` command (shown above) was displayed because other sequences matched other lines in the */etc/magic* file.

If we do need to uncompress a file, we may not have enough space on the disk to perform this operation (after all, it is probably lack of disk space that caused us to compress the file in the first place). To save us having to juggle files between filesystems to free up enough space, there is a command provided that will let us look at a compressed file without uncompressing it first. This command is `zcat`, which is just like the standard `cat` command, but it will uncompress the data it reads from the file, in memory, writing the uncompressed version to its *stdout*:

```
hydrogen# file archive.Z
archive.Z:          compressed data block compressed 16 bits
hydrogen# zcat archive | pg
first line of the archived file
<lines removed for clarity>
last line of the archived file
hydrogen#
```

When you use the commands uncompress or zcat, they expect the file to have a ".Z" extension, so you do not need to supply it. The command zcat has a number of useful applications; for example, if you wish to search for a string in a compressed file (in the same way you would use grep), then you could simply pipe the output from zcat into the grep command:

```
hydrogen# zcat compressed_file.Z | grep "string"
<lines removed for clarity>
hydrogen#
```

So, how does all this help us to fit more data on the tapes? Well, we could compress each file before we backed it up, but a better way would be to compress the data as it was backed up leaving the version on disk in its original form.

To do this using cpio but compressing the data as it is being backed up we could use the following command:

```
hydrogen# find . -print | cpio -ovc | compress >/tmp/backup.cpio
<lines removed for clarity>
hydrogen# ls -l /tmp/backup.cpio
-rw-r--r--   1 root     other     168649 Dec 19 17:13 /tmp/backup.cpio
hydrogen# file /tmp/backup.cpio
/tmp/backup.cpio:          compressed data block compressed 16 bits
hydrogen#
```

When compress is used without any arguments, it will expect to receive its input as a stream of data on its standard input (*stdin*). It will compress any data it reads and write the compressed version to its standard output (*stdout*). The result of the above example is that the file */tmp/backup* contains a compressed version of the cpio archive. If we were backing up to tape, we would simply replace the output file with the name of the tape device (e.g., */dev/rmt/0*).

To view the contents of the archive or recover data from the archive we simply need to use the uncompress command at the beginning of the command:

```
hydrogen# uncompress </tmp/backup.cpio | cpio -ivct
drwxrwxr-x   6 root     sys            0 Apr 29 16:04 2001, .
drwxrwxr-x   2 adm      adm            0 Oct 18 22:55 2000, log
drwxrwxr-x   2 adm      adm            0 Oct 18 22:55 2000,
passwd
```

```
-rw-r--r--    1 root      bin            360 Dec 19 17:08 2001, utmp
<lines removed for clarity>
hydrogen# uncompress </tmp/backup.cpio | cpio -ivc "utmp"
-rw-r--r--    1 root      bin            360 Dec 19 17:08 2001, utmp
2755 blocks
hydrogen#
```

The first example shows how we can view the contents of the compressed cpio archive, and the second shows how we can extract a file from it.

The following examples show how we can do the same using the tar command (this time we will also show that zcat can be used when reading from the compressed backup file, though zcat expects the file to end in ".Z" and so we will need to rename it):

```
hydrogen# tar cvf - . | compress >/tmp/backup.tar\
<lines removed for clarity>
hydrogen# ls -l /tmp/backup.tar
-rw-r--r--  1 root      other       169286 Dec 19 17:28 /tmp/backup.tar
hydrogen# file /tmp/backup.tar
/tmp/backup.tar:          compressed data block compressed 16 bits
hydrogen# uncompress </tmp/backup.tar | tar tvf -
drwxrwxr-x   0/3        0 Apr 29 16:04 2001 ./
drwxrwxr-x   4/4        0 Oct 18 22:55 2000 ./log/
drwxrwxr-x   4/4        0 Oct 18 22:55 2000 ./passwd/
-rw-r--r--   0/2      360 Dec 19 17:08 2001 ./utmp
<lines removed for clarity>
hydrogen# mv /tmp/backup.tar /tmp/backup.tar.Z
hydrogen# zcat /tmp/backup.tar.Z | tar xvf - "utmp"
x ./utmp, 360 bytes, 1 tape blocks
hydrogen#
```

If we are running short of tape space we can compress the data as shown, which will enable us to get more data on the tape. However, this will increase the overall time taken to perform the backup.

Hardware Compression

Some tape drives have the ability to perform compression themselves by making use of the actual hardware on the tape device. If we can perform the compression this way, we can relieve some of the workload of the server CPU. The other benefit is that we won't need to remember where to put the compress or uncompress commands in our backup and restore scripts.

To make use of hardware compression, we just need to alter the name of the device we use, so if our tape device was /dev/rmt/0 we would use the device /dev/rmt/0c to either write to or read from the tape in compressed mode. Depending on the facilities available on the tape drive, there will be a number of different device names that can be used. Most tape drives will provide as a minimum a rewind device (which is the name we would normally use) and a nonrewind device (which will cause the tape to remain at its current position after use). The nonrewind device will end in the letter "n"—for example, /dev/rmt/0n (see Chapter 17, "Adding SCSI Devices").

Ufsdump and Ufsrestore

The commands we have looked at so far have been concerned with backing up or archiving files. With these commands, simply supply the command with a filename and it will be backed up. However, there are also commands that are designed for backing up and restoring a whole filesystem. The commands that we will look at are probably the ones most commonly used for backing up live systems (where a third-party backup tool is not being used). These are ufsdump (which will back up a filesystem or individual files) and ufsrestore (which will recover either a whole filesystem or individual files). They are based on two older commands, dump and restore, but are designed for use with UFS filesystems.

Full Backup

We will start by looking at how to perform a full backup of a single filesystem, then look at incremental backups, and end up with a single backup script that we can use on all our systems:

```
hydrogen# ufsdump 0uf /tmp/var.backup /var
DUMP: Writing 32 Kilobyte records
DUMP: Date of this level 0 dump: Sat 08 Dec 10:05:15 2001
DUMP: Date of last level 0 dump: the epoch
DUMP: Dumping /dev/rdsk/c0d0s4 (hydrogen:/var) to /tmp/var.backup.
DUMP: Mapping (Pass I) [regular files]
DUMP: Mapping (Pass II) [directories]
DUMP: Estimated 2235926 blocks (1091.76MB).
DUMP: Dumping (Pass III) [directories]
DUMP: Dumping (Pass IV) [regular files]
DUMP: 2235774 blocks (1091.69MB) on 1 volume at 11100 KB/sec
DUMP: DUMP IS DONE
DUMP: Level 0 dump on Sat Dec 08 10:05:15 2001
hydrogen# ls -l /tmp/var.backup
-rw-rw-r--   1 root     other    1144717312 Dec  8 10:08 /tmp/var.backup
hydrogen# file /tmp/var.backup
/tmp/var.backup:  ufsdump archive file
hydrogen#
```

This command backs up the whole of the filesystem */var* to the file */tmp/var.backup*. If we had wanted to write the dump to tape, we would just replace the filename we specified with the filename associated with the tape device (e.g., */dev/rmt/0*). We have specified that we have used a dump level of 0, which will always result in a full rather than an incremental backup (we will look at dump levels in more detail when we look at incremental backups.

Backing up a filesystem using ufsdump is generally much faster than using either tar or cpio, but we still have the control to either restore the whole filesystem or just the files we wish:

```
hydrogen# ufsrestore rf /dev/rmt/0
hydrogen#
```

We use the "r" option to specify that we want to restore the entire contents of the tape without any prompting for input from the user. The backup will be restored relative to the current directory and there will be no output (apart from errors and warnings) unless the "v" flag is also specified. We can also restore individual files; ufsrestore actually provides a nice interactive interface for doing so:

```
hydrogen# ufsrestore if /dev/rmt/0
ufsrestore > ls
.:
 adm/          dt/          news/        sadm/        tmp/
 audit/        log/         nis/         saf/         yp/
 crash/        lost+found/  ntp/         snmp/
 cron/         lp/          opt/         spool/
 dmi/          mail/        preserve/    statmon/
ufsrestore > cd adm
ufsrestore > ls
./adm:
 acct/         log/         sa/          utmp         wtmp
 aculog        messages     spellhist    utmpx        wtmp.old
 lastlog       passwd/      sulog        vold.log     wtmpx
ufsrestore > add utmp
ufsrestore > extract
You have not read any volumes yet.
Unless you know which volume your file(s) are on you should start
with the last volume and work towards the first.
Specify next volume #: 1
set owner/mode for '.'? [yn] n
ufsrestore > quit
hydrogen#
```

We can add as many files as we wish before typing "extract," which will then cause ufsrestore to begin recovering those files. When we are asked to "specify next volume," we should enter "1" since we know the file we want is on this tape. If we were recovering from an incremental backup, we might not know which volume contained the file we wanted so we might need to look through more than one.

Backing Up Many Filesystems to One Tape

We can see that ufsdump and ufsrestore have some useful features, but we may have one slight problem. If we use ufsdump to back up the first filesystem onto tape, how do we back up the second of the filesystems without overwriting the first, and so on? The answer to this is to use the nonrewind device. When you access a tape using the standard device (e.g., /dev/rmt/0), as soon as the command that is accessing the device completes, the tape is automatically rewound. But if you use the nonrewind device (e.g., /dev/rmt/0n), then when the command completes the tape will remain at its current position. You can then back up another filesystem; as long as you keep using the nonrewind device, the tape will not be rewound and you can go on adding more filesystems.

When you have finished, the tape will need rewinding before you can access any of the data you have placed on it. The tape can be rewound using the mt command as follows:

```
hydrogen# mt -f /dev/rmt/0 rewind
hydrogen#
```

This command is specifically instructing the tape device to rewind the tape. However, we have just seen that any command that opens the tape device using the standard device name will cause the tape to automatically rewind when it closes the device file on completion. Therefore, all we need to actually do is open and close the device. This can be achieved simply by typing the following:

```
hydrogen# </dev/rmt/0
hydrogen#
```

In this example, we haven't actually typed a command in, just an instruction for the shell to open the tape device for reading. As we saw in Chapter 5, "Shells," when we type "return" at the end of a line the shell scans our line looking to see what we want it to do. It sees the less-than symbol and knows that this means we are redirecting the standard input. Then it closes the standard input and opens the file we have specified (in this case, */dev/rmt/0*) so it will get the file descriptor that standard input had. The shell then removes this part of the line and looks to see if there is anything else for it to do before actually running the command. At this point, there is actually nothing left on the command line so the shell simply closes the file it opened and gets ready for its next instruction. By the time the close operation is complete, the tape has rewound and the shell can then display the prompt for the next command. This means that you will notice a delay before the shell displays the next prompt, but you know that when it is displayed the tape is now back at the beginning.

Restoring Files from a Tape with Multifile Sets

Backing up many filesystems to a single tape is easy enough. But when it comes to trying to restore the data, things get slightly more complicated. If we try reading from a tape containing many file sets, we will see that the ufsrestore command actually only reads the first one then acts as though it has reached the end of the tape. This is because each file set acts as though it was a complete tape archive in its own right.

The problem we have then is how to get the tape to go past the end of the first file set and stop at the beginning of the one we want. One way to do this would be to use ufsrestore to display a table of contents of the tape using the nonrewind device. When the command had finished, the tape position would be at the start of the second file set. If we issued the same command again, the tape would be at the beginning of the third file set, and so on.

We now have a way of getting to the position we want the tape to be at, but it is a bit tedious. What we need is a command that takes us straight to the point in the tape that we want to be, without us needing to display the list of files stored on each file set. Fortunately, the command mt allows us to do exactly this:

```
hydrogen# mt -f /dev/rmt/0n fsf 3
hydrogen#
```

This command will cause mt to wind the tape forward and skip three end-of-file markers, leaving the tape positioned at the beginning of the fourth file set, which will be the fourth filesystem backed up. It is important to remember to use the nonrewind device, otherwise mt will find the correct place but the tape will then be automatically rewound back to the beginning.

Incremental Backups

We have seen that the amount of tape space required for a backup can be reduced using data compression. But another way of doing this, that also helps reduce the amount of time taken to perform the backup, is to perform an incremental backup. This will only back up files that have changed since a specific time or event in the past. This would usually be when the last backup was taken. An incremental backup is not something you would normally do only once, but would be part of your overall backup strategy.

The process would usually be that a full backup is taken, followed by an incremental backup each night. The first incremental backup would just contain the files that had changed since the full backup was taken. The second incremental could contain all the files that had changed since the full backup, or only those that have changed since they were last backed up.

The former method will result in each incremental backup containing progressively more data, while the latter would ensure that the backup was as small as possible but would increase the work when it came to restoring data. If we wanted to restore the entire contents from an incremental backup (which could be an entire filesystem or an entire system), we would first need to restore the entire contents of the initial full backup then restore the latest version of the files that have changed since the full backup.

If the incremental backup backed up all files that had changed since the full backup every night, then we would only need to restore the entire contents of the latest incremental backup to be sure we had recovered the latest version of everything. However, if our incremental backups only contained the files that had changed since they were previously backed up, we would need to restore all files from every tape used since the initial full backup, starting with the oldest, to be sure that we had recovered everything correctly.

Thus, the trade-off is between having an incremental backup that gets progressively larger each night, but makes it simple to restore from, or an incremental backup that remains small, but will take more effort and a longer time to restore from. A similar problem exists even if you only want to restore a single file. With the former type of incremental backup, we know that the latest version of the file is on either the full backup tape or the latest incremental tape. However, with the latter method, we do not know which tape holds the latest version of the file without trying to restore from each tape in turn (again, starting with the oldest). We could make it easier, however, if we made a list of what files had been backed up each night. We could then search through the lists to see which tape held the latest version of the file in question.

Which form of incremental backup we choose to implement depends on the local requirements. It may well be preferable to keep the backup as small as possible and not worry too much about the extra time taken to restore, since we hope that this is not something we will need to do often.

If we wanted to perform incremental backups using cpio, we would have to manage which files were to be backed up ourselves, since cpio does not know anything about incremental backups. It will simply back up the files that are supplied to it on its standard input. This isn't such a problem though, since we can make use of the "-newer" option of the find command. Assuming that the file named /backup_marker was created at the time of the last full backup, the following command would back up all files that had changed since then:

```
hydrogen# find . -newer /backup_marker -print | cpio -ovc /dev/rmt/0
<lines removed for clarity>
hydrogen#
```

The same is also true for the tar command. The following example shows how we can use the same method to take an incremental backup using tar:

```
hydrogen# tar cvf /dev/rmt/0 $(find . -newer /backup_marker -print)
<lines removed for clarity>
hydrogen#
```

As mentioned earlier, ufsdump is aware of the concept of an incremental backup, so we don't need to worry about how we will work out which files to back up. Whether an incremental backup is being performed depends upon the dump level that is selected when the ufsdump command is issued. If the dump level is 0, ufsdump will always do a full backup. If the dump level is in the range 1 to 9, ufsdump will back up all files that have changed since the last backup at a lower dump level was taken.

For example, we might perform a level-0 backup on the first night followed by a level-2 backup the next night. If we perform a level-4 backup the following night it will only back up files that have changed since the level-2 backup; if we perform a level-1 backup the following night, we will get all the files that changed since the level-0 backup. The concept of dump levels gives us more flexibility in balancing the amount of data backed up against the ease of restoration. As always, with incremental backups, the procedure for recovering files will be much simpler if you have a list of the files included on each tape.

Remote Backups

If you don't have a tape device installed in all your Sun servers, you may think you will be a bit stuck when it comes to taking backups of the ones without the drives, but it is still possible. If you have an external tape device, you could connect it to each server in turn and take the backup. This may be acceptable in some environments, but for most production environments, something that doesn't have to rely on this kind of manual intervention is usually preferable. Ideally, you will have a tape device on each server, but if you don't, provided your server is on a network along with another that does have a tape drive it will be possible to use that tape drive.

The facility to back up to a remote tape drive is provided by ufsdump/ufs-restore but not by any of the other backup commands we have looked at so far. However, we can still perform a remote backup using the other commands by making use of the remote shell facility with whichever of the above commands you prefer to use.

To make use of the remote shell facility, we must first create a configuration file to enable it. This file is called .rhosts and should be created in the root directory of the machine on which the tape drive is connected. In this file we simply add the names of all the hosts that we want to allow to back up to this tape drive. It should be noted that setting up this file does have security implications. By adding a host to the file, you are allowing the root user of that host to run anything it wants (locally as root). As long as you are aware of this and its implications, then this can be an acceptable solution.

If the drive is connected to the host hydrogen and we want to allow lithium and iodine to back up to the drive, we would create the following .rhosts file in the root directory on hydrogen. (Note that the permissions of this file should be restrictive otherwise somebody could add additional hosts to it and use this to gain access to a root shell.)

```
hydrogen# cat /.rhosts
lithium root
iodine root
hydrogen# ls -l /.rhosts
-r--------   1 root       other          48 Oct 23 17:46 /.rhosts
hydrogen#
```

We can test that we have set this up correctly by attempting to run a command on hydrogen from either lithium or iodine:

```
lithium# rsh hydrogen tail -1 /etc/shadow
msmith:H2hEPH7vDggKX:11649:7:35:14:::
lithium#
```

We know that everything has worked because only *root* would have permission to read from the *shadow* file.

Now we can try to write something to the remote tape drive:

```
lithium# tar cvfb - 1024 .  | rsh hydrogen dd of=/dev/rmt/0 obs=1024b
<lines removed for clarity>
lithium#
```

Here we are using tar to produce a backup from the current directory and write it to the standard output, rather than a file, and use a block size of 1,024 bytes. The other end of the pipe has a remote shell command, which will be run on the host hydrogen. This runs a dd command, which will read its input from its standard input and write its output to the tape device on hydrogen. The block size is also set to 1,024 bytes.

To restore files we would use the following command:

```
lithium# rsh hydrogen dd if=/dev/rmt/0 bs=1024b | tar xvBfb - 1024 .
<lines removed for clarity>
lithium#
```

Here we do the exact opposite. We use rsh to run a dd command on hydrogen that will read its data from the tape device and write it to its standard output (which is a pipe). A local tar command is running at the other end of the pipe, which restores the data into the current directory. The "-B" option tells tar to read its input from a pipe. Again, we specifically set the block size to 1,024 bytes, which ensures that the dd and tar commands are in step with each other.

If you prefer to use cpio, the following example shows how the same thing can be achieved:

```
lithium# find . print | cpio -ovcC 2048 | rsh hydrogen dd of=/dev/rmt/0
    obs=2048b
<lines removed for clarity>
lithium#
```

To restore from the backup taken using the command above, we would use:

```
lithium# rsh hydrogen dd if=/dev/rmt/0 bs=2048b | cpio -ivcdmuC 2048
<lines removed for clarity>
lithium#
```

The command to perform the backup with cpio is slightly more complex than the tar version, in that it has three pipes, but cpio does not require any special option to read from or write to a pipe. Here we have set the block size to 2,048 bytes.

The following examples show how we can perform a remote backup and recovery using ufsdump and ufsrestore:

```
lithium# ufsdump 0f hydrogen:/dev/rmt/0 .
<lines removed for clarity>
lithium# ufsrestore ivf hydrogen:/dev/rmt/0
<lines removed for clarity>
lithium#
```

Backup Consistency

Whichever command we choose to perform our backups, it is important to remember that the backup will not be consistent if the files being backed up are being worked on while the backup is taking place. Therefore, we need some way of ensuring that the system is in a state that allows us to back it up consistently. The files could be changed if people are using the system while the backup is taking place, but if an application, such as a database, is running it too may be changing files as the backup is running.

The safest way of ensuring that a filesystem is not changing would be to unmount it. But it is not always practical to manage to include this in an automated backup procedure, and we can't just go unmounting the *root* filesystem whenever we want to. The next best thing is to ensure that all applications are shut down and all users are logged off before the backup starts. We can also prevent users from logging on while the backup is taking place by creating a file called */etc/nologin* just before the backup starts.

Any text we put in this file will be displayed on the terminal of any user attempting to login, prior to the user being logged out again. Once the backup has been completed the applications can be started up again and the *nologin* file removed.

The Implementation

The backup implementation for our systems will consist of two parts. During the day we will take copies of key system files into an archive area and during the evening we will perform a full system backup. You may think we are cheating a bit because none of our systems have 80-GB databases with 2-hour backup windows. But we can't account for all situations, and systems that fall into this category tend to be prime candidates for third-party products that enable online backups to be taken. The purpose of this book, though, is to show how to use Solaris and the tools that come with it.

System File Backup

The script archiveFiles is called four times a day from the *root crontab* file (see below). It takes a backup of key system files into a cpio file in the directory */archive*. We have chosen to store the backups on the *root* filesystem to ensure we can get to them in the event that we have a problem mounting any other filesystem. The files to be backed up are stored in the configuration file */usr/local/utils/filesToBackup*, one file per line:

```
#!/bin/ksh
arch=$(date +%d%m%y).cpio
conf=/usr/local/utils/filesToBackup
while read sys_file
do
  if [[ -f ${sys_file} ]]
  then
    echo ".${sys_file}" >>/tmp/file_collection
  fi
done <${conf}
cd /
cat /tmp/file_collection | cpio -ovc >/archive/${arch}
if [[ "$?" -ne 0 ]]
then
  echo "System file backup failed" | mail root
fi
rm -f /tmp/file_collection
```

We now have a script that provides an easy way to recover key system files and allows us to revert easily to previous versions of any files should their contents become lost or corrupt. We just need to make sure that we decide how many of the archive files we want to keep and update the housekeeping configuration file to ensure we don't end up filling the filesystem.

As mentioned, we will run the above script four times each day, using the following *crontab* entry:

```
0 9,12,15,18 * * * /usr/local/utils/bin/archiveFiles >/dev/null 2>&1
```

If we don't redirect the output from any command or script that is executed by `cron`, the owner of the *crontab* file will receive any output from that command in his or her mail.

Our Backup Strategy

The next stage is to implement the actual backup itself. Each of our systems has a local tape drive (*/dev/rmt/0*) and we know that one tape will hold the entire contents of each server so we don't need to bother with incremental backups. From this information, we can form a basic backup strategy that will meet our requirements, which are, admittedly, fairly simple.

We know that we can fit all the data on a single tape, but unless somebody changes the tape everyday, we will keep overwriting the data that was backed up on the previous night. Our office is not open on Saturdays and Sundays, so we will only be able to change tapes Monday through Friday. So, if we start off with five tapes, we can perform a backup each night from Monday through Friday. If we label the tapes "Monday," "Tuesday," "Wednesday," "Thursday," and "Friday," then we just need somebody to put the correct tape in the drive on each weekday. We will then be able to recover any file that was lost over the last week.

This isn't quite good enough for our needs since we would like to be able to recover data older than one week, so we will simply multiply the number of tapes by four and add a week number to the tape label. This is almost good enough for our strategy, but not quite. So, we will also remove one tape from the cycle every four weeks and keep that in the safe. In this way, we can recover any file that was backed up within the previous four weeks, and we have access to data going back to when the backup first ran.

For our backup strategy to work effectively, it is very important that it is fully documented and that we label the tapes clearly with the server name, the week number, and the day of the week. Every four weeks we will be removing a tape (which should have the date it was removed clearly marked on it) so we will need a new tape to replace it with. If we remove the same tape every four weeks, we will build up a collection of tapes that have only been used once, while all the other tapes slowly wear out, so we should ensure that we also cycle the tapes that we remove. We will get around this issue by stating in our strategy that we always remove the tape used on the first weekday of each month.

From this we can calculate that for each server we have, we will need to buy 32 tapes to provide a full year's backup capability. We should also buy a number of cleaning tapes and include the regular cleaning of each tape drive within our backup strategy.

The Backup Script

To make our backup script as flexible as possible, we won't hard code the names of the filesystems to back up within the script. Instead, we will take them from the output of the df command. This means that if a filesystem is not mounted, it won't get backed up; this also means that we will need to filter out the filesystems that are not UFS types.

```ksh
#!/bin/ksh
# Simple backup script to back up each UFS filesystem to tape.
dt=$(date +%y%m%d)
log=/logs/backup
for fs in $(df -l | awk '{print $1}')
do
  # Get filesystem type from /etc/vfstab file.
  fs_type=$(grep "       ${fs}       " /etc/vfstab | awk '{print $4}')
  if [[ "$fs_type" != "ufs" ]]
  then
    # This filesystem is not type UFS so skip it.
    continue
  fi
  # For / replace the / with root for log filename.
  if [[ "$fs" = "/" ]]
  then
    fn="root"
  else
    # Replace any / in fs name with _ for use in log filename.
    fn=$(echo $fs | sed 's:/::g')
  fi
  if ufsdump 0uf /dev/rmt/0cn ${fs} >${log}.${fn}.${dt} 2>&1
  then
    echo "Backup of ${fs} completed successfully" >>/logs/summary
  else
    echo "ERROR: Backup of ${fs} failed" >>/logs/summary
    echo "ERROR: Backup of ${fs} failed" | mail root
  fi
done
echo "Rewinding tape" >>/logs/summary
</dev/rmt/0
```

The script is called from the following entry in the *root crontab* file:

```
0 2 * * 1-5 /usr/local/utils/bin/fullBackup >/dev/null 2>&1
```

Our backup script is simple, but does the trick. Each night it will back up each of the UFS filesystems to the tape in the drive, one after the other. In order that the backup of a filesystem does not overwrite the previous one, the no rewind device is used. We also want to take advantage of the compression built into the tape device, so we also specify that in the device name also.

We produce a log file for each filesystem in the directory */logs* and also write a message to a summary log file stating whether each individual filesystem backup was successful. We keep the backup logs on the *root* directory so that if we ever get into a situation where we have lost one of the other filesystems, we will still have access to the logs to check when the most recent successful backup was taken. If a backup fails, we also send an email to the *root* user to alert the *root* user of that fact.

For the backup to be consistent, we need to be sure that the system is not being used (by users or applications) during the backup. Our backup will run at 02:00 in the morning so we are pretty sure no one will be logged in, but we could modify our script to put out a message using the `wall` command to ask any logged-in users to log out. If we wanted to take that a step further, we could even kill any user processes before starting the backup.

If we have any databases or other applications that could be running throughout the night, it is a good idea to write a script that will stop them running (which can be called from `cron` just before calling the backup script) and another to start them again (which can be called when the backup completes).

Each company's requirements will be different, so that will impact the best way to implement a backup. But however you end up doing it, remember it is a backup strategy that needs to be implemented—not just a backup script.

A

SETTINGS USED THROUGHOUT THE BOOK

Overview

This appendix contains the settings that are used within each chapter. It provides a quick way of locating the major settings.

Chapter 1: User Details

Table A.1 *User Details*

Real Name	Login Name	UID	Group	GID
Test User	*testuser*	500	*test*	100
System Administrator	*sysadmin*	1000	*sysadmin*	14
Mike Smith	*msmith*	1001	*staff*	10
John Green	*jgreen*	1002	*staff*	10

Chapter 6: Standard Disk Layout

Table A.2 *Standard Disk Layout*

Filesystem Name	Mountpoint	Device
root	/	c0t2d0s0
usr	/usr	c0t2d0s6
var	/var	c0t2d0s1
opt	/opt	c0t2d0s5
home	/export/home	c0t2d0s7
tmp	/tmp	swap (c0t2d0s3)
system_tools	/usr/local/utils	c0t2d0s4

Chapter 11: System Details

Table A.3 *System Details*

Machine Name	IP Address	Netmask	Aliases	Primary Tasks
hydrogen	192.168.22.1	255.255.255.128	h, timeserver	NTP server
helium	192.168.22.2	255.255.255.128	he	NFS server of /data
lithium	192.168.22.3	255.255.255.128	li	
beryllium	192.168.22.4	255.255.255.128	be	
boron	192.168.22.5	255.255.255.128	b	
carbon	192.168.22.6	255.255.255.128	c	NFS server of /usr/share/man
nitrogen	192.168.22.7	255.255.255.128	n	NFS server of /usr/share/man
oxygen	192.168.22.8	255.255.255.128	o	NFS server of /usr/share/man
flourine	192.168.22.9	255.255.255.128	f	NIS slave server on 22 subnet
neon	192.168.22.10	255.255.255.128	ne	NFS server of /export/home
indium	192.168.22.49	255.255.255.128	in	Gateway between subnets
tin	192.168.44.50	255.255.255.128	sn	Gateway between subnets NIS master server on multihomed host

Table A.3 *System Details (Continued)*

Machine Name	IP Address	Netmask	Aliases	Primary Tasks
antimony	192.168.44.51	255.255.255.128	sb	DNS master server
tellurium	192.168.44.52	255.255.255.128	te	DNS slave server
iodine	192.168.44.53	255.255.255.128	i	NIS slave server on 44 subnet
xenon	192.168.44.54	255.255.255.128	xe	Gateway to Internet Mail hosts/mail server
cesium	192.168.44.55	255.255.255.128	cs	Dialup PPP server

Chapter 14: Serial Device Details

Table A.4 *Terminal Configuration Details*

Setting	Value
Port Connection	A
Speed	9,600
Data Format	7, e, 2 (7 data, even parity, 2 stop)
Terminal Emulation	VT100

Table A.5 *Modem Configuration Details*

Setting	Value
Port Connection	B
Speed	38,400
Data Format	8, n, 1 (8 data, no parity, 1 stop)
Mode	Bidirectional

Chapter 15: PPP Connection Details

Table A.6 *PPP Connection Settings*

Setting	Value	Supplied By
Serial Port	*/dev/term/b*	System Administrator
Serial Port Settings	56k, 8 data bits, 1 stop bit, no parity	System Administrator
Modem Type	Bidirectional	System Administrator
PPP Login	guest	ISP
PPP Password	guestPassword	ISP
Our IP Address	Dynamic	ISP
ISP IP Address	Dynamic	ISP
Name Server	136.89.22.4	ISP
Dial-in Phone Number	1234 567890	ISP
Protocol	PPP	ISP

Root Crontab Entry

This shows the standard *root crontab* entry:

```
hydrogen# crontab -1
#
# Perform a full system backup.
#
0 2 * * 1-5 /usr/local/utils/bin/fullBackup > /dev/null 2>&1
#
# Copy the key system files.
#
0 9,12,15,18 * * * /usr/local/utils/bin/archiveFiles > /dev/null 2>&1
#
# Check the su log for failed logins.
#
15 02 * * 1-5 /usr/local/utils/bin/checkSuLog
#
# Tidy up the log files.
#
15 7 1 * * /usr/local/utils/bin/tidyLogs >/dev/null 2>&1
#
# Check filesystem usage.
#
0,15,30,45 * * * * /usr/local/utils/bin/fswarn >/dev/null 2>&1
#
# Check user disk quotas.
#
35 01 * * 1-5 /usr/local/utils/bin/checkQuotas
hydrogen#
```

B

SECURITY CHECKLIST

Manual Pages

chmod (1)
inetd.conf (4)
nologin (4)

Files Affected

/etc/default/login
/etc/default/passwd
/etc/group
/etc/inetd.conf
/etc/nologin
/etc/notrouter
/etc/passwd
/etc/shadow
.rhosts

Objectives

This appendix provides a quick checklist of recommended security practices.

Description

Security is becoming an increasingly important topic, particularly now that more and more computers are connected to the Internet. This is a very complex subject, and one that deserves a book unto itself. Here we will provide an overview, but to fully understand all the issues involved, we strongly recommend you read *Solaris Security* by Peter Gregory.

The issues surrounding security will always be a compromise. The most secure server is in a locked, guarded room with no network connection, but then it may not be much use to anyone. Therefore, some of the points given below will be applicable to your circumstances, but not all. Bear this in mind when reading them.

User Security

- Ensure that all users are allocated a password.
- Users should never share their passwords.
- You can set passwords to expire after a predefined time to improve password security.
- It is good practice to check regularly */etc/passwd* for users with their UID set to 0.
- Regularly check for invalid users.
- It is good practice to disable direct *root* logins by configuring the */etc/default/login* file. This will force users with access to *root* to use the su command, thus leaving an audit trail.
- Check the */var/adm/sulog* regularly for users attempting to gain access to the *root* account.
- Provide users with a nonwriteable *.profile* if you want to try and enforce a default environment.
- For users that only use a specific application, specify this instead of the shell in their password entries.
- Ensure that user accounts are closed (if not deleted) when somebody leaves the company or changes job.
- If you wish to temporarily prevent users from logging in, create the file */etc/nologin*.

File Security

- Ensure that file and directory permissions are the minimum needed to allow users to do their jobs.

- Use groups and group permissions, where possible, to control access to files.
- Use ACLs where appropriate, but make sure you keep track of the files that use them.
- Regularly search for *setuid* and *setgid* programs and investigate any that look suspicious.
- Setting the sticky bit on all publicly writeable directories used for temporary files will prevent users from deleting other people's files.

Network Security

- If you use *.rhosts* files, ensure that they have the strictest possible permissions.
- Create the empty file */etc/notrouter* if you don't want your server to act as a gateway.
- Disable all the network services you don't actually need by editing */etc/inetd.conf* to decrease the risk of unauthorized access.
- Tighten network security by enabling secure RPC within products such as NIS.
- Avoid the use of NFS to prevent remote machines from having access to your filesystems, unless necessary.
- Make use of firewalls to control remote access to your servers.

General Security

- It is good practice to disable the *rc* files of applications or daemons that aren't required.
- If you have a modem attached, be aware of the modem settings; only have "autoanswer" set if you really need to.
- Keep all backup tapes, and any other media containing confidential data, in a secure location.

INDEX

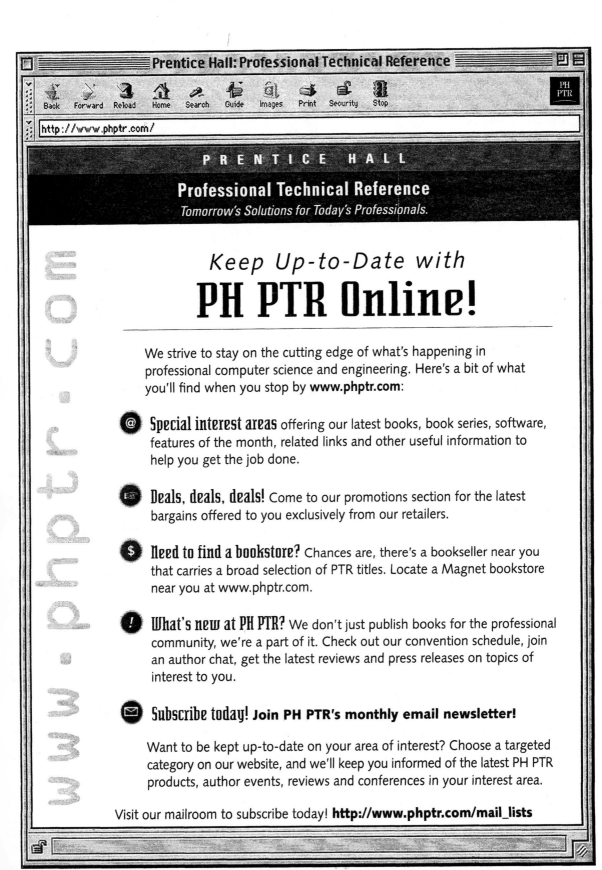

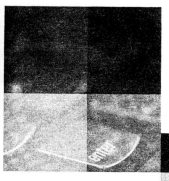

inform**IT**

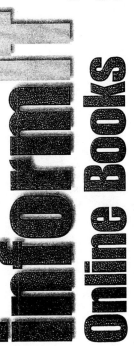

GET READY!

Congratulations on taking control of your career! With Sun certification, you can enjoy the benefits of increased job opportunities, greater career advancement potential, and more professional respect.

The first step in preparing for exams is discovering what you need to know. The next step is discovering what you don't. To help you measure your skills and understand any gaps, Sun offers online skills assessments. They'll help you focus your energies on learning the skills that can lead to certification. Online skills assessments are available at: http://suned.sun.com/USA/solutions/assessments.html.

GET SET!

Preparation is the key to success, and this study guide is a good first step. However, our years of experience have taught us that few people learn in exactly the same way. So we've created innovative learning solutions that can augment this guide, including:

Learning Solutions: Delivered via the Sun Web Learning Center, Sun's innovative eLearning solutions include Web-based training, online mentoring, ePractice exams, and the benefits of a community of like-minded people. Available by subscription, eLearning solutions from Sun give you anywhere, anytime learning—providing the flexibility you need to prepare according to your schedule, at your pace. You can visit the Sun Web Learning Center at http://suned.sun.com/WLC.

Practice Exams: Also available through the Sun Web Learning Center, ePractice exams are practice tools that can help you prepare for Sun's Java platform certifications. The questions in the ePractice exams are written in the same format as the certification tests, helping acquaint you with the style of the actual certification exams. You get immediate results and recommendations for further study, helping you prepare and take your certification tests with more confidence. You can register for ePractice exams at http://suned.sun.com/US/wlc/.

Instructor-Led Training: Sun's expert instructors provide unparalleled learning experiences designed to get you up to speed quickly. Available at over 200 Sun locations worldwide or at your facility, instructor-led courses provide learning experiences that will last a lifetime.

Self-Paced CD-ROM-based Training: Using JavaTutor, our CD-ROM-based learning solutions help you prepare for exams on your own terms, at your own pace, in a dynamic environment. After you're certified, they'll serve as perfect reference tools.

GO!

After you take your exams and become certified, go ahead and celebrate. For more information, visit: http://suned.sun.com.

Your road is wide open. Enjoy the journey.

Take the Lead

Check out Sun Microsystems Press special offers:

Take advantage of Sun product, technology, training, and service discounts today!

To see the latest Sun customer promotions, go to sun.com/sunusers_bookpromo.

Check back often as new offers will be updated frequently.

*Offers available to qualified customers in the USA and Canada only